W9-CEY-968

Variety in
Religion and Science

Variety in Religion and Science

Daily Reflections

Varadaraja V. Raman

iUniverse, Inc.

New York Lincoln Shanghai

Variety in Religion and Science
Daily Reflections

Copyright © 2005 by Varadaraja V. Raman

All rights reserved. No part of this book may be used or reproduced by any means, graphic, electronic, or mechanical, including photocopying, recording, taping or by any information storage retrieval system without the written permission of the publisher except in the case of brief quotations embodied in critical articles and reviews.

iUniverse books may be ordered through booksellers or by contacting:

iUniverse
2021 Pine Lake Road, Suite 100
Lincoln, NE 68512
www.iuniverse.com
1-800-Authors (1-800-288-4677)

ISBN-13: 978-0-595-35840-3 (pbk)
ISBN-13: 978-0-595-67281-3 (cloth)
ISBN-13: 978-0-595-80303-3 (ebk)
ISBN-10: 0-595-35840-3 (pbk)
ISBN-10: 0-595-67281-7 (cloth)
ISBN-10: 0-595-80303-2 (ebk)

Printed in the United States of America

I dedicate this book to my close friend and dear companion of forty-five plus years:
The one and only Dr. MLR

yAdum UrE yAvarum kELIr
tIdum nanDRum piRartara vArA

It is all my town, where I'm in.
Whoever they are, the're also my kin.

—*Tamil poet KaNian*

Homo sum,
humani nil a me alienum puto:
I am a man,
And nothing of the human condition can be foreign to me.

—*Latin writer Terence*

At the Metanexus Institute, we are honored to count Dr. Raman as an active board member, a Senior Fellow, and our most published author in our Online Journal. Our website contains some 8000 essays penned and processed by hundreds of different authors and receives upward to 140,000 page views per month. Raman alone accounts for over 400 contributions—book reviews, commentaries, and most significantly his series "Today in Religion and Science."

In this collection, you receive a selection from Raman's "Today" series. The entire collection of essays span almost everyday of the year with a pithy insight into historical figures from both science and religion or important holidays and discoveries. The juxtaposition of these nuggets of information from the separate universes of religion and science is sometimes jarring. What does Socrates have to do with Galileo (2.15)? What does Parinirvana Day and Daniel Bernoulli have to do with each other (2.8)? The Kitchen of God and Ham the Chimp (1.31)? Mahasivaratri and Urbain Le Verrier (3.11)? Tellus Mater Festival and Leonhard Euler (4.15)?

Sometimes the connections which Raman draws are happenstance, sometimes circumstance, and sometimes also instances of profound and neglected insights. The juxtapositions are always interesting and as a whole create a beautiful *bricollage* of human history and a mosaic of human aspirations from the ancients to the moderns across all traditions and disciplines.

What does it all mean? Raman does not say, but his generous spirit and open mind given indication of a greater Spirit and Mind that permeates human history and the very universe itself. Our poet and philosopher friend, V.V. Raman, has woven a magical Indian carpet which will fly us to new heights and vistas and inspire us to learn more about different places and times and bring us safely home to a better future. Enjoy.

—William Grassie, Ph.D., Executive Director, Metanexus Institute

Contents

Foreword xxxi
Acknowledgments xxxiii

January

January 1
    JANUARY 1
    GIUSEPPE PIAZZI 2
January 2
    SAINT BASIL 3
    RUDOLF CLAUSIUS 5
January 3
    SAINT GENEVIÈVE 6
    BHASKARA 8
January 4
    THE ÂZHVÂRS 9
    WILHELM BEER 10
January 5
    GURU GOBIND 12
    X-RAYS 13
January 6
    EPIPHANY 15
    SAMUEL MORSE 16
January 7
    SEKHMET 18
    SATELLITES OF JUPITER 19

January 8

    FREYJA AND ST. GUDULA 21

    ALFRED RUSSELL WALLACE 22

January 9

    SAINT RAMANANDA 24

    THE GOLDEN GATE BRIDGE 25

January 10

    MUHAMMED IBN 'ALI IBN 'ARABI 27

    GEORGE WASHINGTON CARVER 28

January 11

    KAGAMI-BIRAKI 30

    LAO TZU 31

January 12

    SWAMI VIVEKANANDA 33

    LAZARRO SPALLANZANI 34

January 13

    SAINT CANUTE 36

    OSCAR MINKOWSKI 37

January 14

    PONGAL FESTIVAL 39

    MATTHEW F. MAURY 40

January 15

    ZOROASTRIAN BEHMAN 41

    LEWIS M. TERMAN 43

January 16

    KING JAMES' BIBLE 44

    DIAN FOSSEY 46

January 17

    SAINT ANTHONY 47

    BENJAMIN FRANKLIN 48

January 18
A HORRIFIC RELIGIOUS PERSECUTION 50
CASPAR FRIEDRICH WOLFF 51
January 19
DOGEN KIGEN 53
JAMES WATT 54
January 20
WORLD RELIGION DAY 56
BÉGUYER DE CHANCOURTOIS 57
January 21
SAINT AGNES 58
SOPHIA LOUISA JEX-BLAKE 60
January 22
TIMOTHY 61
ANDRÉ MARIE AMPÈRE 63
January 23
CONFUCIUS 64
HIDEKI YUKAWA 66
January 24
SAINT SAMBANDHAR 67
FERDINAND J. COHN 69
January 25
AJINATH DAY 70
ROBERT BOYLE 71
January 26
XENOPHON 73
THE CYCLOTRON 74
January 27
WOLFGANG AMADEUS MOZART 76
JOHN C. ECCLES 77

January 28
    TU B'SHEVAT 79
    AUGUSTE PICCARD 80
January 29
    EMANUEL SWEDENBORG 82
    ABDUS SALAM 83
January 30
    ASSASSINATION OF MAHATMA GANDHI 85
    MAX THEILER 86
January 31
    ZAOWANG 88
    HAM'S SUBORBITAL FLIGHT 89

February

February 1
    EVE OF CANDLEMAS 91
    EMILIO SEGRÈ 92
February 2
    GROUNDHOG DAY 94
    JEAN BAPTISTE BOUSSINGAULT 95
February 3
    MEERA BAI 96
    ELIZABETH BLACKWELL 98
February 4
    ISIDORE OF PELUSIUM 99
    CLYDE TAMBAUGH 101
February 5
    JAPANESE MARTYR'S DAY 102
    PLANETARY CONJUNCTION IN 1962 104
February 6
    INTELLECTUAL FERMENT IN ISLAMIC WORLD 105

MARY DOUGLAS NICOL 107

February 7

FREDERICK DOUGLASS 108

WILLIAM HUGGINS 110

February 8

PARINIRVANA DAY 111

DANIEL BERNOULLI 113

February 9

FEAST DAY OF APOLLO 114

JACQUES MONOD 115

February 10

SAINT PAUL IN MALTA 117

SUNYATA AND ZERO 118

February 11

KENKOKU KINEN NO HI 120

BERNARD DE FONTENELLE 121

February 12

CHINESE NEW YEAR 123

CHARLES DARWIN 124

February 13

ASH WEDNESDAY 126

WILLIASM SCHOCKLY 127

February 14

ST. VALENTILE'S DAY 129

FRITZ ZWICKY 130

February 15

SOCRATES 132

GALILEO GALILEI 133

February 16

TITUBA 135

DISCOVERY OF TUTANKHAMEN 136

February 17
>   BURNING OF BRUNO 138
>   HORACE BENEDICT SAUSSURE 139

February 18
>   BERNADITA SOUBIROUS 141
>   ALESSANDRO VOLTA 142

February 19
>   AANDAAL 144
>   NICOLAUS COPERNICUS 145

February 20
>   MR. NOYES' REVELATION 147
>   LUDWIG BOLTZMANN 148

February 21
>   CHANDIDAS 150
>   AUGUST VON WASSERMANN 151

February 22
>   ARTHUR SCHOPENHAUER 152
>   HEINRICH HERZ 154

February 23
>   KARL JASPERS 155
>   CASIMIR FUNK 157

February 24
>   THE GREGORIAN CALENDAR. 158
>   JACQUES DE VAUCANSON 160

February 25
>   FEAST OF ESTHER (2002) 161
>   IDA NODDACK 163

February 26
>   THE COMMUNIST MANIFESTO 164
>   JOHN HARVEY KELLOGG 165

February 27
> JALALUDDIN RUMI 167
> DAVID SARNOFF 168

February 28
> SAINT VILLANA 170
> LINUS PAULING 171

February 29
> THE LEAP YEAR 172
> HERMAN HOLERITH 174

March

March 1
> ON MARCH 176
> FIRST HYDROGEN BOMB 177

March 2
> ST. AGNES OF BOHEMIA 179
> PIONEER 10 181

March 3
> HINA MATSURI 183
> GEORG CANTOR 185

March 4
> ROYAL DEBT OF WILLIAM PENN 187
> GEORGE GAMOW 189

March 5
> KYONCHIP 191
> GERHARD KREMER 192

March 6
> MICHEALANGELO BUONARROTI 194
> THE ROYAL SOCIETY OF LONDON 196

March 7
> VIBIA PERPETUA 198

STANLEY MILLER 200

March 8

INTERNATIONAL WOMEN'S DAY 201

HYPATIA 203

March 9

PYTHAGORAS 204

MESON CREATION 205

March 10

TRANSLATION OF "LA DIVINA COMMEDIA" 207

MARCELLO MALPIGHI 208

March 11

MAHASHIVARATHI 209

URBAIN LE VERRIER 211

March 12

GEORGE BERKELEY 212

GUSTAV ROBERT KIRCHHOFF 214

March 13

GREGORIAN CHANTS 215

JOSEPH PRIESTLEY 217

March 14

NISAN AND ROSH CHODESH 218

ALBERT EINSTEIN 219

March 15

ISLAMIC NEW YEAR 221

GEORGE P. MARSH 222

March 16

ST. UHRO'S DAY 224

GEORG SIMON OHM 225

March 17

ST. PATRICK 227

VANGUARD I 228

March 18

    EDGAR CAYCE 230

    CHRISTIAN GOLDBACH 231

March 19

    ST. JOSEPH'S DAY 233

    FREDERICK JOLIOT 234

March 20

    ODUN 236

    BURRHUS K. SKINNER 237

March 21

    VERNAL EQUINOX 239

    JEAN BAPTISTE FOURIER 240

March 22

    WORLD DAY FOR WATER 242

    MUHAMMAD TARAGAY 243

March 23

    TURIBIUS DAY 245

    EMMY AMALIE NOETHER 246

March 24

    HILARIA AND MATRIS DEUM 248

    ADOLF BUTENANDT 249

March 25

    KUAN YIN 250

    RAYMOND FIRTH 252

March 26

    JOSEPH CAMPBELL 253

    PAUL ERDÖS 255

March 27

    DATE OF RESURRECTION? 256

    KARL PEARSON 258

March 28
    FESTIVAL OF HOLI 259
    THREE MILE ISLAND 261
March 29
    CRUCIFIXION 262
    EDWIN LAURENTINE DRAKE 264
March 30
    MAIMONEDES 265
    MARY WHITON CALKINS 266
March 31
    JEWISH PASSOVER 268
    RENÉ DESCARTES 269

April

April 1
    APRIL FIRST 272
    SOPHIE GERMAINE 273
April 2
    THE LAST CRUSADE 275
    FRANCESCO MARIA GRIMALDI 276
April 3
    GEORGE HERBERT 278
    KATHETINE ESAU 279
April 4
    DOROTHEA DIX 280
    JOHN HUGHLINGS 282
April 5
    THOMAS HOBBES 283
    HATTIE ELIZABETH ALEXANDER 285
April 6
    THAI FESTIVAL 286

PHILIP HENRY GOSSE 288

April 7

WORLD HEALTH DAY 289

JACQUES LOEB 291

April 8

HANA-MATSURI 292

THE GREAT SUN SPOTS 293

APRIL 9

SAINT WALDERTRUDIS 295

HIPPOCRATES 296

April 10

HUGO GROTIUS 298

SAMUEL HAHNEMANN 299

April 11

BHAKTA KABIR 301

JAMES PARKINSON 302

April 12

CERELIA 304

CARL LOUIS LINDEMANN 305

April 13

MAHA SONGRAN 307

BRUNO BENEDETTO ROSSI 308

April 14

INDIC NEW YEAR 310

CHRISTIAAN HUYGENS 311

April 15

TELLUS MATER FESTIVAL 313

LEONHARD EULER 314

April 16

BENEDICT JOSEPH 316

JOSEPH BLACK 317

April 17

    LUTHER BEFORE THE DIET 319

    GIAMBATTISTA RICCIOLI 320

April 18

    EARTHQUAKE IN SAN FRANCISCO 322

    CLARENCE DARROW 323

April 19

    DALAI LAMA'S REFUGE 325

    LYSERGIC ACID DIETHYLAMIDE 326

April 20

    HANGING OF ELIZABETH BARTON 328

    GERALD STANLEY HAWKINS 329

April 21

    BIRTHDAY OF SRI RAMA 331

    PERCY WILLIAM BRIDGMAN 332

April 22

    EDWARD DE VERE 334

    EARTH DAY 335

April 23

    SAINT GEORGE 337

    MAX PLANCK 338

April 24

    HAPPENSTANCE AND COINCIDENCE DAY 340

    HERACLITUS OF EPHEOS 341

April 25

    MAHAVIRA DAY 343

    WOLFGANG PAULI 344

April 26

    MARCUS AURELEUS ANTONIUS 346

    CHARLES RICHTER 347

April 27

    HANUMAN JAYANTI 349

    HERBERT SPENCER 350

April 28

    ORTHODOX EASTER 352

    NEWTON'S PRINCIPIA 353

April 29

    SAINT CATHERINE 355

    HENRI POINCARÉ 356

April 30

    NIGHT OF THE WITCHES 358

    CARL FRIEDRICH GAUSS 359

May

May 1

    MONTH OF MAY 361

    SANTIAGO RAMÓN Y CAJAL 362

May 2

    THEODOR HERZL 364

    D'ARCY WENTWORTH THOMPSON 365

May 3

    NICCOLÒ MACHIAVELLI 367

    STEVEN WEINBERG 368

May 4

    SPAIN, PORTUGAL, SOUTH AMERICA 370

    THOMAS HENRY HUXLEY 371

May 5

    SØREN KIEREGAARD 373

    FERDINAND Von RICHTHOFEN 374

May 6

    RABINDRANATH TAGORE 376

SIGMUND FREUD 377
May 7
CHORAL FINALE OF BEETHOVEN'S NINTH 379
ALEXIS CLAIRAULT 380
May 8
HENRI DUNANT & THE RED CROSS DAY 382
EMIL CHRISTIAN HANSEN 383
May 9
CHRIST'S ASCENSION TO HEAVEN 385
GASPARD MONGE 386
May 10
KARL BARTH 388
AUGUSTIN JEAN FRESNEL 389
May 11
JIDDU KRISHNAMURTHI 391
RICHARD FEYNMAN 392
May 12
MOTHER'S DAY 394
JUSTUS Von LIEBIG 395
May 13
FATIMA 397
RONALD ROSS 398
May 14
WINFRID, THE DO-GOODER 400
DANIEL GABRIEL FAHRENHEIT 401
May 15
PARASURAMA RISHI 403
PIERRE CURIE 404
May 16
JOAN OF ARC 405
MARIA GAETENA AGNESI 407

May 17

SHANKARACHARYA JAYANTI 408

EDWARD JENNER 410

May 18

UMAR AL-KHAYYAMI 411

BERTRAND RUSSELL 413

May 19

MALLEUS MALEFICARUM 414

TITUS LUCRETIUS 416

May 20

NICENE COUNCIL 417

BUREAU INTERNATIONAL DES POIDS ET DES MÉSURES 419

May 21

ELIZABETH FRY 420

ANDREI SAKHAROV 422

May 22

DANIEL DEFOE'S ARREST 423

WILLEM EINTHOVEN 425

May 23

HERMAN GUNKEL 426

FRANZ ANTON MESMER 427

May 24

ABRAHAM GEIGER 429

WILLIAM WHEWELL 430

May 25

RALPH WALDO EMERSON 432

PIETER ZEEMAN 433

May 26

VAISHAKH 435

ABRAHAM DE MOIVRE 436

May 27

MEMORIAL DAY 438

RACHEL CARSON 439

May 28

RELIGION AND SCIENCE 441

JEAN LOUIS AGASSIZ 442

May 29

PASSING AWAY OF BAHA'ULLAH 444

PAUL EHRLICH 445

May 30

MIKHAIL BUKANIN 447

HANNES OLOF ALFVEN 448

May 31

FIRST CATACOMB 450

DISCOVERY OF KRYPTON 451

June

June 1

MONTH OF JUNE AND MARY DYER 453

NICOLAS SADI CARNOT 454

June 2

HARRIET TUBMAN 456

DONATI'S COMET 457

June 3

UGANDAN MARTYRS 459

JAMES HUTTON 460

June 4

NELSON GLUECK 462

JEAN ANTOINE CHAPRAL 463

June 5

RUTH BENEDICT 465

JOHN COUCH ADAMS 466

June 6

YMCA 468

REGIOMONTANUS 469

June 7

VESTALIA 471

JAMES SIMPSON 472

June 8

ANGLICAN CHURCH 474

GIAN DOMENICO CASSINI 475

June 9

EPHRAIM SYRUS 477

GEORGE STEPHENSON 478

June 10

IMMANUEL VELIKOVSKY 479

E. O. WILSON 481

June 11

JOHN BALL 482

CHARLES FABRY 484

June 12

BUDDHA'S ASCENSION IN BHUTAN 485

OLIVER JOSEPH LODGE 487

June 13

SAINT ANTHONY 488

THOMAS YOUNG 489

June 14

INDEX AUCTORUM ET LIBRORUM PROHIBITORUM 491

ALOIS ALZEIMER 492

June 15

MAGNA CARTA 494

LEONARDO FIBONACCI 495

June 16

    FATHER'S DAY 497

    BARBARA McCLINTOCK 498

June 17

    JOHN WESLEY 500

    WILLIAM CROOKES 501

June 18

    IBN SINA 503

    WILLIAM LASSEL 504

June 19

    BLAISE PASCAL 506

    FRIEDRICH SERTUERNER 507

June 20

    DAY OF CARRIDWEN 509

    ROGER BACON 510

June 21

    REINHOLD NIEBUR 511

    SIMÉON-DENIS POISSON 513

June 22

    COUNCIL OF EPHESUS 514

    HERMANN MINKOWSKI 516

June 23

    SAINT RAMANUJA 517

    ALAN TURING 519

June 24

    ENCYCLICAL OF POPE PAUL IV 520

    FRED HOYLE 521

June 25

    FORMILARIO CONCORDIAE 523

    WALTHER NERNST 524

June 26
    UNITED NATIONS CHARTER 526
    CHARLES MESSIER 527
June 27
    DAY 17 OF TAMMUZ 529
    EUCLID 530
June 28
    JEAN JACQUES ROUSSEAU 532
    ALEXIS CARREL 533
June 29
    SAINT PETER 535
    GEORGE ELLERY HALE 536
June 30
    THE TUNGUSKA EVENT 538
    ADOLF FURTWÄNGLER 539

Index of Topics 541

Foreword

Religion strives to discover the roots of the intangible human spirit which reflects, rejoices, creates, loves, cries, laughs, and does myriad other things that even the most complex configurations of mute matter seem unable to do. Religions are born of an irrepressible longing to experience the Universal Grandeur. They aid us in our efforts to commune with the Cosmic Whole through bonds that defy easy description.

Science tries to explore, explain, and exploit the phenomenal world of matter and energy. It unveils the root cause of everything from the core of matter to the vast galaxies at inconceivable distances. It brings before the minds's eye the variety and complexity pervading perceived reality. Science is a mode of understanding and experiencing the world that affects, alters and amplifies human experience.

Science and religion are two of the most lofty expressions of the human spirit. Both have found countless expressions in culture and civilization. The sheer variety of modes and symbols through which humanity has concretized its religious quest is staggering. Many of these are interesting, meaningful, and enriching. Most people are familiar with at least one religious tradition. Things far from one's own affiliation seem strange. Yet, even while being connected and loyal to one's own tradition, it can be spiritually enlightening to remember the words of Samuel Longfellow in his hymn:

Light of ages and of nations, every race and every time
Has received thine inspirations, glimpses of thy truth sublime.

As to variety in science, this too is limitless. The mere contemplation of names and discoveries in science, technology, and mathematics can be enriching and inspiring.

The essays in this book are from a daily internet-column I wrote in the year 2002 for the Metanexus Institute on Science and Religion. The collection contains entries from January 1 to June 30. I have included some poets and philosophers in the sections on religion. I have not always been strict about dates. All the reflections are personal. I might have erred in some interpretations. Yet, I trust the reader will find these interesting and informative, and also get a flavor of the richness of our scientific and religious heritage. My goal has been to show the wealth and scope of human culture and science, not to argue for science or for religion, much less for any particular belief-system.

V. V. Raman: April 2005

Acknowledgments

I am indebted to countless biographies and books, as well as to the vast internet library for informing me in my reflections. I am also grateful to the many daily readers who used to write to me their own thoughts on some of my notes. Most were very gracious and a few were somewhat critical of my choices. I take responsibility for the errors, whether factual or in perspective, that some might detect in this book. I gave up striving for perfection years ago. In particular, I would like to thank Dr. S. Swaminathan of the Mathematics Department, Delhousie University, Halifax, Nova Scotia, for scrupulously reading through every page, and suggesting improvements. I am also indebted to the thoughtful comments of Dr. M. L. Raman.

From the World of Religion: JANUARY

Like days and weeks and months, years also come and go, except that these make us aware we are growing in age. That is why it is not traumatic for some to peel a page from the calendar or to replace a calendar with one with a larger number on top.

We may picture the passage of time in spatial terms: a room which holds the past within, and the space beyond as where the future lies, the entry door separating the two. In this metaphor, we fling open the door to another new year in our calendrical reckoning of years. As a door has two faces, one looking inside and the other outside, so too this new month has two faces, one looking back into the accumulated past-years, and the other facing the future yet to be born. That is the significance of Janus: the two-faced God of the Romans, who is invoked as January in this, the first month of the year. Indeed Janus was the beginning of everything in the Roman world. He was the god of all exits and entrances. Hence all gates and doors were regarded as holy. In this, there is more than mythology: We see here a deep insight into the nature of Time, for between the has-been and the yet-to-come is the winking present that alone is perceived reality. The Hindu world pictures this as Shiva's third eye which transforms all to naught, as does every fleeting instant in the incessant stream of time. Christ is sometimes described as *pater futuri seculi*: Father of Ages unborn.

In most traditions, as at one time among the ancient Romans too, the year began with the onset of spring. It was March, the month of sowing, which was the first of the months, making—as their names still remind us—the months from September to December seventh (*septem*: seven) to the tenth (*decem*: ten) months. Though this is the time of the year when the earth is at its perihelion (closest to the sun in its elliptical orbit), 1 January has no observed astronomical significance such as a solstice.

The little Temple for Janus that Claudius Duilus is said to have erected in 260 BCE in the Forum Olitorium is buried in antiquity, alive only in the obscure pages of history, but his name is here to stay on the calendars of many peoples.

Who can tell what is in store for humanity for the year 2002? As always, possibilities are immense and unpredictable, for good and for bad: The discovery of a new and limitless non-polluting energy source could bring about a golden age of prosperity for all of humanity. The rise to power of a mindless maniac with nuclear capabilities could unleash irrevocable devastation. Education and science could free more humans from ignorance and superstition, but scarce resources could deepen the chasm between the haves and the have-nots. Religious and racial bigotry could fire simmering suspicions into horrendous conflagrations, or perhaps the emergence of an enlightened religious outlook could foster under-standing and harmony among differing faiths and convictions. Or again, the long and checkered course of human history could be snuffed into a mere glitch in the planet's saga by the rude intrusion of a stray asteroid lured by earth's gravity.

Rarely has a year ended on such a dismal note as the last one (2001), and rarely has one begun with so much fear and such little promise of betterment. But we must not give up. The flame of hope must be kept alive, whether with prayer or with silent wishes, but above all with every individual effort we can muster to snub inclinations to feel bitter or belligerent, to extend hands and hearts of friendship to those who come our way, and to right the wrongs the best we can.

From the World of Science: GIUSEPPE PIAZZI

In the memorable year of 1789 when the French Revolution exploded, Giuseppe Piazzi furnished his observatory in Palermo, Sicily, with new equipment. His was the southern-most observatory in Europe. From here, exactly two centuries ago: on 1 January 1801, while painstakingly cataloging the stars, Piazzi stumbled upon an object unrecognized by any human eye until then. He described it in Italian as *la nuova stella scoperta il 1 gennaio 1801 nell'Osservatorio di Palermo*: the new star discovered on 1 January 1801 in the Observatory of Palermo. It turned out to be the first asteroid to be observed by any human being. Piazzi named it Ceres, the patron goddess of Sicily.

The astronomer William Herschel called it an *asteroid* (star-like object). More exactly, it is a *planetoid*, for like the planets of our system it is orbiting the sun. The current technical term for it is *small* or *minor planet*. But the original etymo-logically inappropriate name persists in popular books and in the media.

More than a hundred thousand asteroids are whirling around the sun; the vast majority of them are in the region between Mars and Jupiter. About seven thou-sand of them have been individually spotted, named, and cataloged. The thou-sandth asteroid that was discovered (in 1923) was named Piazzia in honor of Piazzi. Other asteroids bear such names as Gaussia, Washingtonia, and Rockefellia.

Asteroids are mostly amorphous chunks of rock, from a fraction to a few miles across. It was once speculated that they are perhaps splinters from what may have once been a wholesome planet which, for some reason, was blown to smithereens. All this stony junk is now cluttering the calm void of interplanetary space, like smoke in clean air from the exhaust of a truck, yet trapped by the gravitational pull of the sun. These bits of planetary debris constitute what is picturesquely described as the *asteroid belt*. If they are countless in number, they are also meager in mass: it is estimated that the combined mass of all asteroids will barely equal five percent of the moon.

As petty planetoids way out there, they are astronomical oddities, like a bunch of minute insects buzzing in the white zones of the Antarctic. Like fleas and flies, these cosmic chips are okay as long as they are far, very far away. But should they happen to come into our vicinity, we better watch out. And astronomers calmly inform us that there are about eleven asteroids whose paths lie within our earth's orbit. These *Aten* asteroids (as they are called) are potential threats to our survival. Minuscule as they are in mass and size (in astronomical terms); they carry stupendous kinetic energy because of their horrendous speeds. Any encounter with them would be deadly.

There was an age in which, viewing the world from a different framework, our ancestors feared distant stars, planets and comets because they believed that celestial bodies control our fates and fortunes, and forebode disasters. A Latin poet put it very simply: *Astra regnunt homines* (The stars rule men). Recall Kent's words in Shakespeare's King Lear: "The stars above us govern our conditions." The word *disaster* simply means *bad star*.

Soon after the rise of modern science, one used to laugh at such fears. Ironically, now, enriched by scientific knowledge, we have reason to be frightened once again, not by mammoth and majestic stars, but by tiny pebbles in the cosmic sea. Little did Giuseppe Piazzi realize to what fears his innocent discovery would lead us some day. We generally hear about knowledge being power. This is an instance where knowledge can be frightening.

January 2

From the World of Religion: SAINT BASIL

All cultures have their elders: men and women of wisdom and experience who guide the newer generations. Any society with a religious tradition also has its initiated leaders who lead a life of discipline with more than average commitment to spiritual life. In the Christian world many of them live in monasteries and nunneries. A spiritual aspirant may move away from society and become a recluse: a solitary seeker living on sparse food, spending the waking hours in meditation and contemplation. Or, such a one may become part of a group of like-inspired individuals.

Saint Basil of the 4th century was a spiritually inspired soul. His Feast Day is 2 January. The saint rejoiced in the name of Christ, felt divinity deep in his heart, traveled afar to places like Syria to learn from ascetics there. Though he was much impressed by fasting and penitence, he felt that religious life must involve more than austerities and emaciation, however commendable spiritually motivated self-denial might be. So, upon his return, he set about establishing monasteries close to towns and villages rather than in distant places, so that monks could also work for, and serve, the community. He articulated his own ascetic inclinations by writing on moral codes for general practitioners and for those in monasteries.

Arius of Alexandria had propounded a doctrine to the effect that Christ was not of the same substance as God and the Holy ghost. This metaphysical thesis was an interpretation of an earlier theologian by the name of Lucian who had spoken of Christ as the embodiment of Logos (God's power and wisdom). Arius's elaboration was so contrary to accepted view that it was declared a heresy by the Catholic Church.

However, it was appealing to many people, including the Roman emperor Valens who used to persecute orthodox Christians now and again. Basil was also an erudite defender of Church doctrines. When he was Archbishop of Caesarea, he used his considerable debating skills to persuade many that Arianism was a mistaken understanding of the true nature of Christ. It is interesting to recall that in other religious traditions also, keen theological minds have arisen to prevent the further spread of new and disturbing doctrines and/or defeat and replace heretical movements which had grown within the system. In eras when religions dominated the minds of people, strict adherence to doctrine and dogma carried more weight than today. Indeed, this was the origin of sectarian divisions within various religious traditions.

When Basil was warned they would confiscate his properties, he said he owned only his clothing, and so did not fear any confiscation. When told he would be exiled, he replied that the whole world was his, and so no matter where he went he would feel at home. Finally, when he was threatened with death, he replied that death would only bring him closer to God, and so he would welcome it.

Bishop Basil was not just a preacher. He tended to the sick, he worked with the poor, he was kind to his opponents, and he labored to bring about reconciliation among divergent views. His long-range impact was mainly among the Greek and Slavonic peoples. In Greece they make a cake on New Year's Eve that has his name. One of St. Basil's prayers were the following: "There is still time for endurance, time for patience, time for healing, time for change. Have you slipped? Rise up. Have you sinned? Cease. Do not stand among sinners, but leap aside. For when you turn away and weep, then you will be saved."

From the World of Science: RUDOLF CLAUSIUS

We have all noticed how, after lots of house cleaning or arranging the furniture, things get messy again. We also know that all it takes are a few shuffles to mix up a well-ordered deck of cards whereas the reverse process of bringing a well shuffled set of cards back to an ordered pattern cannot be accomplished that easily. We grow only older, never any younger, a flower withers away, never blooms back to brightness after it has wrinkled and dropped. Salt is quickly mixed into the soup, but it is difficult to extract it back from the soup. Digested food cannot be brought back to original form, any more than that we can retrieve a moment that has just elapsed, for the arrow of time never reverses direction. As if all this is not enough, we can never make an engine that is a hundred percent efficient.

It turns out that all these and many more observed facts follow from the same basic principle: There is something in the physical world that causes disorder out of order rather than the other way around. Left to itself, Nature's spontaneous behavior is to increase chaos, and reduce organization.

This understanding is incomplete until it is quantified. So we introduce a measure for disorder: *entropy*. Any spontaneous occurrence in nature tends to increase the total entropy of the system. Physicists call this the SLT: *second law of thermodynamics*. The word *total* is crucial here because in one portion of a system there may be a decrease in entropy, provided that in another part there is much more of an increase in this.

The term *entropy* was introduced by Rudolf Clausius (born: 2 January 1822) in 1865. It has become one of the key concepts in our understanding and interpretation of natural phenomena. Living organisms display an impressive *decrease* in entropy: After all, it is quite a leap in order and organization when basic molecules combine to form complex biochemical units. However, this is accomplished by a substantial increase in the entropy of the environment, somewhat like buying too many things while the corresponding debtedness to the bank increases by more than the price of what we buy. The entropy loss in an organism is more than that gained by the environment.

Clausius argued, much to the consternation of many, that since the entropy of the whole world is gradually increasing, as the universe breathes its rhythms in time, there will come a moment, sooner or later, when the whole darn thing will be degraded into chaos of the highest order. This omega state was described by Clausius with the ominous German word *Warmetod*: heat-death. This was probably the first scientific declaration of a finality for the physical world: No God or Resurrection or Judgment Day in this view, no roasting in boiling oil in hell or houris in heaven, just one all-consuming cosmic conflagration to clear up all the mess that has been building up for eons and eons and more eons. Such frightful annihilation, none had imagined before.

This may be poetry to the scientific mind, but it is of the most depressing and dismal kind for most normal mortals who shudder at the thought of that the whole world will be annihilated some day. So there have been all sorts of twisting and turning of physical theories to rescue humanity from this conceptual calamity of hot nothingness at the end of the cosmic day. "Good dreaming!" say die-heard materialists who have given up their capacity to be poetic and to fill the human heart with hope while the going is good.

Who is to say Clausius didn't miss some other feature of the world? Maybe, at some distant moment, the SLT will cease to operate. Then things could be different.

January 3

From the World of Religion: SAINT GENEVIÈVE

Geneviève, the patron saint of Paris, was born in the year 422, at Nanterre, not far from the City of Lights. During that time there was a theologian by the name of Pelagius whose ideas on Christ and grace, sin and heaven, differed considerably from those of St. Augustine. He went so far as to deny the doctrine of original sin (so central to Christianity), and to say that even pagans can enter the portals of heaven if only they behave well. Such views were condemned by the Council of Ephesus. Now the Bishop of Auxerre, on his way to Britain to preach against this *Pelagian heresy*, happened to stop at Nanterre. There, in the crowd that came to pay homage to Bishop Germanus, stood a seven year old lass whom the holy man spotted. He beckoned her to accompany him to the church, blessed her, gave her a brass medal bearing the cross, and told her parents that little Geneviève was ordained for something truly great.

In the years that followed Geneviève became part of the religious order, sub-sisted on meager food, traveled to many regions in France, impressed people by her words and miracles, and also enraged a few others also. In 450, Atilla the Hun went on a rampage into many parts of Europe, like a roaring tornado, and was about to descend on Paris. Parisians were scared, but Geneviève asked them not to lose courage for, she assured them, God was going to protect them. She urged them to pray and fast, and have full faith in God. It has been recorded that for some strange reason, the Hun, like an unpredictable hurricane, changed course, leaving Parisians alone.

Years later, the Franks came down on Paris like another disease, and the much older Geneviève now arranged to bring food and other things to her famished compatriots. These extraordinary services, combined with reports of other medieval miracles like giving sight to the blind, earned sainthood for Geneviève. As the proverb says, "The saint who works no miracles, has no pilgrims."

Today the Panthéon in Paris stands majestically atop the highest hill on the left bank of the Seine. Here is where Geneviève's body used to lie buried for a long time. Until the French Revolution turned many ancient traditions topsy-turvy, there used to be regular appeals to Geneviève through fasting and processions whenever there was trouble in sight. Appeals to gods and saints to resolve the pressing problems of a community are common to all religions. A religion that provides no comfort to the disheartened is of little relevance to people.

The imposing Parisian Panthéon was built in the 18th century, erected by a grateful Louis XV when he recovered from a life-threatening illness, as homage to the patron saint of Paris. During the free-for-all of the French Revolution, fired by what was called the spirit of the Enlightenment, unruly mobs broke into the church of Saint Geneviève like brutish descendants of Atilla himself, and set fire to the relics of the patron saint of Paris, and flung her ashes into the silent Seine. How the madness of masses can erase the vestiges of history in a mindless moment.

Whether the saints and sages of times past, and of whatever religion, did all the physical miracles they are credited with, no one can say with certainty. But of their impact and influence, of the charisma of their person and the courage they infused in countless human hearts, of their humility and compassion and sincer-ity and other virtues, there can be little doubt.

This was certainly so with St. Geneviève, whose Feast Day is January 3.

From the World of Science: BHASKARA

We have precise knowledge about the places and dates of more recent scientists and mathematicians. But there have been many in the ancient world, working fruitfully in different regions and cultures, the fruits of whose labors are known but to a handful of scholars probing into ancient sciences. They are certainly deserving of recognition from everyone. It is good to remember that original thinkers and keen minds, discoverers and inventors have been there in all cultures, some more successful in propagating their results and ideas than others. Though ancient science has had to give way to newer ones, it would be unfortunate if we were to erase them from our collective memory. That's why I have decided to recall some of them on arbitrarily chosen dates.

Bhaskara was an eminent mathematician of India who lived in the 12th century. Since there had been another astronomer of that name earlier, this one is referred to, in a royal sort of way, as Bhaskara II. What is often regarded as the first book on modern arithmetic was authored by the twelfth century Hindu mathematician Bhaskara. This work, named after Bhaskara's young daughter Lilavati, has a romantic, and probably legendary, story behind it. It is said that astrologers had predicted that there would be no moment in Lilavati's life auspicious enough for her marriage.

Being an astrologer Bhaskara. made computations and recognized, on the basis of her horoscope, a precise congenial moment at which Lilavati could be betrothed without fear of an ill-starred married life. He now constructed a device consisting of a cup with a hole, which was left floating in a bucket of water. Water gradually began to enter the cup. The instant when enough water seeped through to sink the cup would be the auspicious moment when the formal step for Lilavati's wedding was to be taken. Fair Lilavati was so fascinated by the device that she bent over to gaze at the gradual trickling of the water into the cup. While she was in that state of wonderment, a little gem broke loose from her garment and fell into the cup. This blocked the hole and obstructed further entry of water. The carefully computed instant of good omen could no longer be caught. Lilavati was not to marry!

Bhaskara was as dejected as his daughter. To cheer her up, he decided to dedicate a work on mathematics to her. He told her that marital thrills would pass away, but she would be remembered for ever by that work. Lilavati's name has indeed lasted a thousand years, since it is associated with a classic in the history of mathematics.

We do not know how far this legend is true. But we do know that Bhaskara wrote a mathematical masterpiece called *Sidhhantasiromani* which has three parts, of which the first one bears the title of *Lilavati*. The book has a dozen chapters, dealing with various aspects of ancient mathematics, from arithmetic to calculations of simple interest. It is one of the earliest works to introduce the decimal system of numeration. It prescribes rules for multiplication and division by zero: rather sophisticated concepts in mathematics. Bhaskara II also wrote on astronomy: on planetary conjunctions with stars, on solar orbits and lunar phases, and even on the radius of the sun's path. He gave formulas for plane and spherical geometry. On all counts, he was among the great scientific thinkers of his time.

Though the details of his world are recalled by only a few, his name brings pride and joy to many people in India to this day. For the name and glory of the great personages in one's history is always a source of much fulfillment to most people.

January 4

From the World of Religion: THE ÂZHVÂRS

A unique feature of the spiritual quest in the Tamil world is the variety and richness in poetry and music through which the aspirant attempts to experience transcendence. One happy consequence of this is that whether one is religiously inclined or not in the traditional sense, anyone familiar with and sensitive to Tamil and its euphonies can be transported to aesthetic ecstasies, if and when the poetry is recited by well-trained voices.

The practitioner is fortunate if he or she resides near a Tamil temple, for on days clearly marked on the almanac these poems, regarded as sacred *mantras*, are recited with profound piety in the temples.

The poems are generally sectarian in content: propounding one school of theology or another, venerating one deity or another. Their themes range from abstract metaphysics to lauding a formless, nameless Divine Principle or one of the deities mentioned in the mythologies. Of the countless poet-saints who have thus graced the Tamil language and enriched its religious poetry, there are twelve who are held in the highest esteem by those who see the Divine through the names and attributes of Vishnu, the Sustaining Principle. They are known as the *Âzhvârs* (mystics immersed in the divine). Their works exude deep devotion and intense love for the Supreme. They sing hymns to the Transcendent in its aspects of Rama or Krishna, sing of their glories in exuberant verses. They are inspired by events and episodes in the epics and mythic lore of classical Hinduism.

The spiritual verses of the Âzhvârs add up to 4000, and they date back to several centuries. They were put together as an anthology by sage Nâdamuni. The work is entitled *Nâlâyira Divya Prabandham* (Four Thousand Divinely interlinked Poems). This work has become the scripture of Tamil Vashnavites (worshippers of Vishnu).

The foremost Âzhvaars is Nammâzhvaar (8th–9th century). He contributed 1296 psalms. Like many Tamil sages, he came from a lower caste. Legend has it that he was in a deep trance for sixteen years. The poet Mathurakavi, upon seeing him, forced open his mouth. Lo and behold! He saw the Divine inside, and mystical hymns gushed forth. Mathurakavi memorized them all and presented them to the world. It is believed that these embody the wisdom of all the sacred Vedas. Of these, *Tirumozhi* (Mystic Language) contains the essence of the Upanishads. The hymns also yearn for union with the divine, reminding one of some the canticles of St. Francis of Assisi.

The hymns of the Âzhvârs are kept alive and vibrant to this day, for they are sung all over the Tamil world, in one temple or another. They continue to bring a kind of spiritual joy that sermons and prosaic readings seldom bring about. What we see here, as elsewhere in the world of the spirit, is cultural continuity, the sacredness of traditions, and the power of words and music. These are dimensions of the religious quest to which one seldom pays much attention. Yet, through verses and songs, through the rhythm of words and the melody of music, heart and soul can be elevated to lofty heights, and the mind of the seeker can be turned around one way or another.

Poetry is an important element in religion. Through its metaphors and meanings it gives us deep insights. Through its rhyme and rhythm it evokes our capacity for trans-material enjoyment. And through devotional melodies it brings the aspirant that much closer to the Divine. That is what the psalms of the Divyaprabandham do.

From the World of Science: WILHELM BEER

Everyone knows that the sun rises in the morning and that it is one blindingly bright patch of light. But what about the moon? Practically all of us have seen the moon, but how many have really observed it? Look at the full moon some clear night and notice its slightly darker regions. We know that these are shadows cast by tall mountains and huge craters on the lunar surface. But, even with a telescope of modest size, how many such mountains can you count from here, and how many craters in all? With a powerful telescope and sustained study, one can chart the regions of the moon.

It is fun to see forms, whether of a human face or a rabbit, on the silvery moon. There is even some thrill in imagining the moon to be made of Gouda or Roquefort. But one can also get serious and calculate its distance, compute its mass and predict its phases, and do things with numbers and telescopes. The knowledge and understanding thus acquired need not diminish our experiential appreciation of the moon.

It is hard to imagine our earth without its continents and countries, its oceans and mountains. Every patch on earth has been assigned a name, and a globe without name-bearing regions is only an abstraction. But what about the Moon and the planets? Do we envisage them with regional subdivisions?

There once was a banker in Berlin by the name of Wilhelm Beer (born: 4 January 1797) who developed a fascination for astronomy. He had a special fondness for the Moon, and could well have exclaimed like the poet Keats:

What is there in thee, Moon!

That thou shoulds't move my heart so potently?

After spending hours keeping accounts and counting money in the bank, he would go to a little observatory, which he had made for himself. Here, he and Johann Maedler carefully observed the moon night after night through their telescope with a 9.4 cm free aperture for eight full years during which they noted down every shade and feature of every nook and spot of the whole visible face of the Moon. Little by little, they jotted down with meticulous care so much data that they published in 1836 the most detailed map of the Moon the world had every seen. It had measurements of the diameters of 148 craters and the heights of 830 mountains. Careful observations can reveal the existence of several thousand craters and mountains on the Moon. Whether as Selene of the Greeks or as Shashi of the Hindus, every spot and wrinkle on the face of the Moon-Goddess has been pictured and photographed by the probing power of the telescope, and Wilhelm Beer's work was pioneering in this regard.

All the ups and downs and plains and peaks on our side of the Moon have thus been named, generally after great thinkers and scientists on earth. Somewhat as in Dante's heaven a great many worthy personages who have lived on earth have now a place on the *mappa selenographica* (lunar map), not just Aristarchus and Archimedes, Pythagoras and Plato, but also Tycho and Herschel, and many more.

The progress of science is effected by a great many people whose various efforts complement and reinforce the overall structure that emerges. And, as with the focused persistence of a painter or a pianist, the participating scientist will have to spend countless hours immersed in the subject of the study. Again and again, that is what we see in the lives and outputs of specialists in science. In former centuries such concentration could be done on a part-time basis, as with Wilhelm Beer. In our own times, one can't *do* science with such part-time commitment.

January 5

From the World of Religion: GURU GOBIND

Sikhism is one of the four major Indic religions. Its 15th century founder Nanak became the first *Guru* (master), and its followers are known as Sikhs (disciples). Guru Nanak proclaimed that "There is but one God, the Creator, whose name is Truth. He is devoid of fear and enmity, immortal, unborn and self-existent, great and bountiful."

Sikhism was a protestant religion in that it rejected certain doctrines and practices of the Hindu world in which its founder was born, but it is also a synthesized religion in that it was formed by the incorporation of some of the finest principles of both Hinduism and Islam. It developed during the next couple of centuries under the leadership of a series of ten successive Gurus.

The tenth and last of these was Guru Gobind (1666–1708) who assumed leadership after his father (the ninth Guru) was assassinated. He was the chief of the Sikhs from 1675 to 1708. Those were the dark days when much of India was under the dictatorial rule of a Mogul potentate by the name of Aurangzeb who had little respect for Hindus or Sikhs. Guru Gobind inspired his people with a sense of we-won't-take-this-nonsense-anymore, and transformed them into a fiercely militant group with a sense of ardent nationalism. He gave the title of Singh (lion) to all Sikhs, and infused his followers with a religious zeal which was not unlike that of his Islamic opponents. He abolished the lingering casteism among the Sikhs. This attracted many lower caste Hindus to the new faith. He proclaimed all Sikhs to be *Khalsa* (the pure ones).

Guru Gobind introduced a ritual ceremony, like the baptismal or the bar mitzvah, by which youths are formally initiated into the fold. He invested Sikhs with (what came to be called) the five K's: *kes* (full-grown and never-cut hair), *kachch* (shorts made of simple cloth), *kara* (a bracelet made of iron), *khanda* (a little dagger), and *khanga* (a comb). Though the founder Guru Nanak preached against externalities in religion, and undervalued the appearance of piety and devotion, Sikhism became the only religion whose (male) followers can be identified by their appearance alone. [In the year 2001, in reaction to the September 11 tragedy, some uncontrollably outraged, but appallingly ignorant individuals in the United States, mistook some bearded and turbaned Sikhs for bearded Muslims, and murdered them.]

Most important of all, Guru Gobind Singh established the *Guru Granth Sahib* as the Sikh Scripture and as the Eternal Guru. It is an anthology of the religious poetry of the period, including spiritual utterances from other traditions. Guru Arjan Dev says, "All the sources of creation, and all languages meditate on Him, forever and ever." Pious repetition of the Lord's name is stressed in Sikhism. The spiritual energy in this *Adi Granth* is what is revered in Sikh places of worship: gurudwaras.

Excerpts from it are read in the places of worship (*gurudwaras*) all over the world to this day. Guru Gobind also instructed all Sikhs to proclaim: *sri wa guruji ka khalsa, sri wa guruji ka fatah* (Purity of God, Victory to God). In Sikh worship services the congregation repeats this somewhat like the Lord's prayer in the Christian tradition.

This year (2002) the Sikhs celebrate Guru Gobind's day on January 5. If you know of a Gurudwara in your vicinity I urge you to pay a visit. You will be received warmly there. One needs to take off one's foot-wear and put on a symbolic covering for the head. At the end of the service you can taste the *kara parshad* which is an offering that is sweet, delicious, and rich.

From the World of Science: X-RAYS

In the year 1896, the *Daily Chronicle* of London wrote that "the noise of the war's alarm should not distract attention from the marvelous triumph of science, which is reported in Vienna." The war was the Boer War, and the triumph was Konrad Roentgen's discovery which the *Wiener Presse* had reported on 5 January 1896.

Roentgen himself was so puzzled by his discovery that he called it X-rays, meaning unknown radiations. Using them, he promptly took a picture of his wife's hand, revealing the bony structure underneath the soft and cushiony skin. She was frightened.

The news spread fast through journals, newspapers, and magazines. Not everyone understood its scientific import. Some thought it was a fad that would fade away, while others imagined its mischievous potentials. One legislator, nervous that some naughty inventor would come up with a device (using X-rays) enabling peeping Toms in a theater to get a glimpse of things beneath the garments of actresses, introduced a bill to ban X-ray opera glasses. Some clothiers advertised X ray proof dresses.

Within a year, almost a thousand scientific papers were published on X-rays. One writer found all this to be a trifle excessive, and he exclaimed in rhyme:

The Roentgen Rays, the Roentgen Rays,

What's this craze: The town's ablaze

With the new phase of x-rays' ways....

The earliest medical application of X-rays was in wars: The Italian army in Ethiopia (1896), the British army in the Nile Expedition (1896), and the U.S. army in the Spanish American War (1898) used X-rays to reveal broken bones. Today they are used to detect infected lungs, dental decay, diseased tissues, etc. X rays were once used for curing arthritic pain, fungus ailments, pimples, herpes, and even tumors.

Less than a year after their discovery, X ray photographs were used as evidence in a case in Denver, CO, to prove that a man suing his employer had broken a leg during work. There were heated debates as to the admissibility of such "ghost pictures."

X-rays have served in detecting art-fraud: one can find the percentage of lead in paint and know if a painting is from an old master or a modern copy-cat whose paints have less lead. The forgery by Hans van Meegeren who had sold several "old Masters" to Nazis was exposed when the paintings were subjected to X ray analysis.

When Roentgen generated X rays in his lab, little did he know that the entire universe is bathed in X-rays emanating from a myriad spots. In the 1960s astronomers detected a powerful X-ray source in the constellation of Cygnus: this suggested that there is a black hole in the region. Intense X ray sources have been detected near the center of our galaxy.

Laboratories have generated incredibly intense X ray beams enabling scientists to probe directly into the heart of matter, exposing molecules and atoms. Thus, X-rays tell us about the most minute entities as well as the most distant cosmic concentrations.

X-rays have opened up vast vistas of knowledge and application, revealed new facts relating to matter and energy, and engendered new insights into the nature of the physical universe. A scientific discovery is like the first sentence of a new novel that is being written down. Not even the author can predict how the story will evolve. The discovery, exploration, and applications of X rays are among the marvelous triumphs of the intellect and of the scientific quest, as significant as the countless acts of kindness and selflessness that punctuate every hour and day of human history.

January 6

From the World of Religion: EPIPHANY

Baptism is the formal sacrament by which one becomes part of the Christian Church. The rite of sprinkling water for purification is ancient. As per Christian sacred history, when Christ, coming from Nazareth to Galilee, was baptized in the River Jordan, the heavens opened, and the Spirit in the form of a dove descended upon him, and there was a voice from above which said: "Thou art my beloved son, in whom I am well pleased." [Mark:1: 9-11] So, through baptism, a person is infused with the spiritual dimension that is otherwise absent in him or her. Since the Trinity was revealed through the baptism of Christ, those who don't accept the Christian Trinity don't go through the baptismal rite.

The Baptism of Christ was an event in which the Divine became manifest. Hence it was called *Epiphany* (*showing* or *displaying*). It has been reckoned to have occurred on a day corresponding to our January 6. It was during the 4th century that the Feast of Epiphany was declared by the Eastern Church to be "the most honored festival." Its main feature is the Solemn Blessing of Water in accordance with prescribed rules. Traditionally, the priest also blesses the homes of the Church members on this day.

We have the story of the Three Wise Men: Gaspar, Melchior, and Balthazar, who, guided by a moving star, came to Bethlehem with gold, frankincense, and myrrh as gifts for New-born Jesus. The Greeks called them *magoi* (*magi* in Latin), derived from the Persian word for priest (*magu*) in Zoroastrianism, leading to our *magic*. Legends sometimes acquire flesh and blood, as in this case: For it is stated that their bodies were taken to Constantinople, then to Milan, and finally ended up in the two-spire Gothic Cathedral in Cologne, or so we are told. Relics tend to reinforce religious beliefs.

In some traditions, the wise men are said to have been kings: In Spanish countries Epiphany is celebrated as *el día de los tres reyes* (the day of the three kings).

Then again, as we read in the Gospel according to John (2: 1-11) Jesus performed his first miracle at a wedding in a place called Canaa. When there wasn't enough wine left for the guests, Jesus ordered pots to be filled with water to the brim, and transformed it all into good wine. This too is remembered on the day of Epiphany.

The chronological coincidence of Christ's baptism, the arrival of the Magi, and the miracle in Canaa has no relevance to Epiphany. When the roots of traditions are examined with a scholar's microscope, it has little impact on religious beliefs. Like the parent who loves the child even when the latter becomes rebellious, commitment to traditions is seldom affected by lack of sufficient proof, historical inconsistencies, or even logical loopholes. The poetry of religion transcends scientific nitpicking.

In the collective memory of cultures and traditions, sacred history is no less important than monuments to kings and soldiers. Aside from the recall of events they carry inner meaning and inspiration. The baptism of Christ is an affirmation of his spiritual glory, the three wise men represent the rejoicing and gratitude of humanity, and the miracle is to remind us of the extraordinary powers of the divine.

Verrochio's *The Baptism of Christ* and Botticelli's *Adoration of the Magi*, both at the Uffizi Gallery in Florence, Italy, are among the magnificent masterpieces that have commemorated two of the Epiphany episodes. It is said that Epiphany was celebrated with great fanfare in Shakespeare's time. That's why Shakespeare renamed his play *What you Will*, which was to be performed on that occasion, as *The Twelfth Night*.

From the World of Science: SAMUEL MORSE

The electric current is an invisible silent flow of minuscule electric charges, caused by the flip of a switch. It serves many of our needs and adds much to our experience and enjoyment. Normally we think of it in the context of lighting and heating and whirling our motors for the countless gadgets that clutter our homes. But it also plays a most important role in our communications technology. Much of this has come about because of our understanding of the relationship between electricity and magnetism.

There was a time when messages were hand-delivered. In ancient Persia they trained pigeons to fly to destinations and back: the first airmail letters. The technique spread to other countries, and lasted well into the 19th century. During the Franco-German war of the 1870s, Germans trained hawks and falcons to attack messenger pigeons to thwart enemy communications. Those seem distant and impossible times.

In our age of instant communication, telephones and e-mails are all around us. However, for well over a century, miles and miles of copper wires crisscrossed many nations, linking post offices to transmit messages. This was the telegraph, the first major long distance communication using electricity.

In 1832, on his way back from England, while talking about electromagnetism Samuel Morse said: "If the presence of electricity can be made visible in any part of the circuit, I see no reason why intelligence (information) may not be transmitted by electricity." In other words, by varying the amount or duration of currents through a wire, one could send signals. This sounds like a simple idea today, but it was revolutionary and it did not receive much support from government or organizations initially. It was in this context that he developed the code that is named after him.

In 1833 Karl Gauss and Wilhelm Weber connected the rooftops of an observatory and a laboratory in Goettingen with a double copper wire 3000 meters long, and sent a mild electric current through it. Devices at either end responded, indicating the current intensity. Morse developed this idea with Alfred Vail in New Jersey. The first public demonstration of the electric telegraph was given on 6 January 1838. A local newspaper reported "Time and distance are annihilated, and the most distant points of the country are by its means brought into the nearest neighborhood." It took six more years before the first electric telegraph line was inaugurated in the United States. During the following decade some 23,000 miles of telegraph wires linked many parts of the country. It has been estimated that by the first quarter of the 20th century, there were more than 600,000 miles of telegraph wires all over the world.

Puck in Shakespeare's Midsummer Night's Dream says: "I'll put a girdle about the earth in forty minutes." The cables under the oceans and overhead and buried underground are literally girdles about the earth. Like arteries and veins in the body, they are conduits, not just long stretches of wire. Even as the corpuscles in the blood nourish and sustain the organs, the mute electrons whizzing through the wires are messengers of information, nourishing and sustaining society and civilization.

By accelerating message-flow, telegraphy served the governments and railroads, and also assisted greatly in the establishment of settlements in distant places. In a journal entry in 1851 Henry Thoreau wrote: "As I went under the new telegraph-wire, I heard it vibrating like a harp high overhead." Science transformed the music of the heavenly spheres of ancient philosophers into music of lines of copper wires: decidedly a leap from the mystical to the material.

January 7

From the World of Religion: SEKHMET

There is but one God, as all religions declare, but that One has been described in different ways, worshipped in different modes, and called by different names. Some of the ancient visions have been erased from humanity's cultural heritage, and some have remained dormant for long and risen up again.

Consider, for example, Sekhmet, a goddess of ancient Egypt. It has been said that Sekhmet was all opposites heaped into a single whole. Darkness and light, genesis and disappearance, disease and cure: everything was part of this ancient goddess. She means nothing today, but she touched the fancy of the people of Egypt millennia ago. Egyptians of yore believed, as others have always accepted of their respective gods, that she existed before earth and man came to be.

She was a personage in grand Egyptians mythologies. The great God Ra was once enraged by the human race, because it had conspired to kill its maker. Whereupon sparks flew from his eyes which became the goddess Sekhmet with a leonine face. Sekhmet was now instructed to rid the world of humanity. But Ra changed his mind and to avert the ordered destruction he created a pool of red libation which looked very much like human blood. Sekhmet drank this to the full, and fell into a deep slumber. She was carried by Thoth, the god of Wisdom, all the way to a river in Egypt, and dunked into it. Sekhmet now woke up as the cat-faced Bastet, and thus was transformed into the loving Mother Goddess Hethor.

We may not fully comprehend the meaning behind this story which has its parallels in other traditions as well. Like all mythologies it could have arisen from pure fantasy, or from a profound experience, or as an encrypted message of something profound, or as an esoteric truth that only the initiated can decipher. Whatever it be, there is a magical power in such ancient tales that touches many people deeply as embodying some inscrutable magical mystery.

Grand mythologies have a power of persistence, not just by their poetry, but also from their being amenable to multiple interpretations. Even many centuries later, different people have seen in Sekhmet different meanings and lessons. I take this story as painting the human predicament. Man's destruction of Ra could be taken to signify our exploitation of Nature. Sekhmet from Ra could mean the response of Nature to Man's irresponsible behavior. Ra's change of heart could mean that Nature is giving us a second chance to behave better. Sekhmet's drinking of the pseudo-blood could well be the environmental disasters that have come so close to us. Hethor stands for the compassion that Nature has shown us, giving us the knowledge and the wisdom to change.

Sekhmet is but one instance of many in various cultures where the relationship between the human and the animal species has found expression. Lamb and fish, monkey and pig, elephant and lion, boar and more have entered the pantheon of religions. In some cases, as with Sekhmet, the ancients conceived of anthropo-therio divinities also. Today, sitting erect in the Metropolitan Museum of Art in New York City, is a slim Sekhmet in stone unearthed from Karnak, with human hands and bare feet with long toes, with hair like the wig of a British judge. So many gods and goddesses of ancient religions have found homes in museums all over the world.

Sekhmet is not forgotten. There are groups which consecrate January 7 to this Egyptian goddess.

From the World of Science:
SATELLITES OF JUPITER

We often hear it said that we live an information age or in an age of science. Not many people on earth have ever seen the planet Jupiter, let alone know if it has any satellites. Some of us know that Jupiter has several moons, and you may guess how many, and check the answer when you come to the end of this posting. It certainly has more than four.

One may wonder when and how we came to know about Jupiter's satellites. Well, it happened on the night of 7 January 1610 when Galileo Galilei was still playing with his new toy: the first telescope that was turned to the skies just a few days earlier. He found what he imagined to be three new stars near the planet Jupiter. As he observed them night after night, their positions were changing, and a fourth came in his field of vision

Galileo had seen the granular structure of the Milky Way and the rugged surface of the Moon, but these companions of Jupiter were the very first new celestial bodies to be discovered with this new and potentially very powerful tool of astronomy. In honor of his patron Cosmo of Medici, he called them Medicean planets: Kepler's suggestion to call them satellites was adopted only later on.

Galileo was quick to announce his celestial discoveries to the world. As early as in March of the same year he published his *Sidereus nuncius* (Starry Messenger) in Latin so that all of Europe might know. Sure enough, he became famous very soon thereafter, and he could move from Padua to Florence with a bigger job.

The 1572 Nova of Tycho was a naked-eye discovery. It was large enough and bright enough to be visible without a telescope. But Galileo's Medicean planets were faint little things, invisible without the lens-equipped tube. When people heard about it, some thought it a hoax, or perhaps that it resulted from spots on the eye-piece. There were also theological objections to the existence of more than seven planets in the sky. According to the old view the human body was a minia-ture universe: the seven planets (ancient science and astrology) were the Sun, Mercury, Venus, the Moon, Mars, Jupiter, and Saturn. They corresponded to the seven apertures on the human face. So, some thinkers wondered how there could be more than seven planets up there. Then again with more planets in the sky, we might have to add four more days to the week. The transition from one paradigm to another does not occur easily.

Today the four satellites of Jupiter that Galileo discovered are called Io, which is terribly volcanic; Europa, on which ice has been detected; Ganymede, which is larger than the planet Mercury; and Callisto, which has lots more craters than our own moon. A fifth satellite of Jupiter was discovered a hundred years ago, in 1892. Four more were discovered between 1914 and 1951; four more still, bring-ing the total to sixteen. The Voyager missions which sent us detailed pictures of Jupiter & Co., including information on live volcanoes on Io, also caught three satellites which had escaped detection from terrestrial telescopes. Thus we know of sixteen satellites for Juptier: all perhaps stray asteroids which had been cap-tured by the largest planet's compelling gravitation. And the gradual discoveries of Jovian satellites began with Galileo on 7 January 1610.

Astronomers have discovered water on one of Jupiter's satellites, leading to the suspicion that perhaps life of one kind or another may have evolved there. If this is ever established, it would be one of the greatest discoveries of all times, for so far as we have observed, the one thing that is unique about our own planet is that life has evolved on it. From the larger universal perspective of science, there is no reason for this uniqueness.

January 8

From the World of Religion:
FREYJA AND ST. GUDULA

The ancient Scandinavians had their own Norse religion. The Norse Gods were collectively known as Aesir. The group included Odin (Wodan/Wotan), Thor, and Frigga. The religion which worshipped Aesir was called Asatru. There was a time when the Gods of the Norse dominated the minds of many people. There was also another group of Norse gods, known as the Vanir. Freyja was one of these. Though there has been a revival of interest in this ancient tradition, today those gods linger mainly in the names of some days in a few languages. For example, the English Friday used to be in honor of Freyja. The German word Frau (for Lady) is derived from her name.

In ancient Norse culture, Freyja was a major goddess. She was connected to the seasonal cycles. She brings abundance to the harvests, and riches to people. She was a fertility goddess too. She was pictured as a provocative woman, blue-eyed, blond and beautiful whom gods and men both desired. Like Venus of the Romans, she was the goddess of Love, but also of lust. She was strong willed and would brook no nonsense. The elder tree is associated with her, as is the rose flower. Many birds and beans are associated with her also. Her cart is pulled by two cats. In one of the representations of this goddess we see her on a winged horse in flight, her legs and thighs showing.

It is said that Freyja once strayed into a world where only dwarfs live. There she saw four dwarfs making a most marvelous gold necklace. She wanted to have it. They would give it to her on condition she would spend a night with each one of them. This she did and thus acquired the necklace which is called Brisingamen. That necklace became Freyja's talisman.

According to another legend her lover Odur once left her. She went everywhere in search of him, shedding tears all over. These are the tears that still come from trees as precious amber. Often mythology is also ancient science.

Freyja was a Vanir deity and queen of the Valkries. She reigned from a huge hall known as Folkvang. In ancient mythologies, gods and goddesses were often belligerent. Thus Freyja and friends used to fight with another group to which belonged Odin. When she defeated her enemies, she used to carry them away to a huge hall which was known as Sessrumnr. Freyja used unite former wives and husbands after their death. This is why, in ancient times, the women of that culture used to accompany their men to battle-fields, there to die with their brave husbands.

January 8 is also Feast Day for St. Gudula (7th century) who is the patron saint of Belgium. She is said to have come from a noble family, but she gave it all up in her quest for the Divine. She used to visit a church in Meerzeele and used to go to pray at pre-dawn hours. Once her lantern was extinguished by evil forces, but she was undeterred by that.

After she died, her body was removed from place to place, and was eventually placed in the famous Church of St. Michel in Brussels, in the middle of the 11th century. Later it was moved to a church which was dedicated to her name. Five hundred years later, a heretic mob pillaged the church and scattered her relics in hate and disrespect. Such behavior is not new in history.

The members of that fierece mob are long forgotten, but her church in Brussels is still there. It has undergone a magnificent renovation, and continues to be visited not only by the devout, but by hundreds of tourists also.

From the World of Science:
ALFRED RUSSELL WALLACE

If we are asked what name comes to mind when we hear the words *natural selection* and *evolution*, chances are we would say *Darwin*.

But there is another name that may be mentioned here: Alfred Russell Wallace (born: 8 January 1823).

He lived to the ripe old age of ninety, arguing for socialism and women's rights in his later years. When a youth of eighteen, he bought a book on botany to guide him in making a herbarium. The book stirred his mind and drew him to other books on nature. As a result, he wanted to explore plants and animals in distant lands, and set sail for the Amazon in Brazil with a friend named Henry Bates. He was overwhelmed by the plush richness of the forests; he followed remote rivers, encountered indigenous peoples, marveled at the variety and abundance of plants, trees and flowers, birds, reptiles and monkeys. He became more and more inclined to reject the idea that the species were fully formed when they first came to be. He was convinced that they arose as a result of physical laws, that they changed as a result of external influences. He jotted down the details of all that he saw and reflected upon, but he lost his notes in an accident on his way back home. In fact, he barely escaped when his ship caught fire. But he published a book on his travels nevertheless.

The calamity at sea did not deter him from undertaking another long voyage, this time to the Indonesian archipelago, thousands of miles away. He was away once again from his native England, for eight years this time, studying the land and the people, the rocks and the life forms of those regions. He amassed information on some hundred and twenty seven thousand specimens: enough material for many scientific papers. Most important of all, during this stay in the 1850s Wallace formulated his principle of natural selection. He wrote about a struggle for existence "in which the weakest and the least perfectly organized must always succumb."

In 1858, Wallace sent his essay *On the Tendency of Varieties to Depart Indefinitely from the Original Type* to Charles Darwin. It was received and read with great admiration and shock. "If Wallace had my manuscript sketch written out in 1842, he could not have made a better short abstract!" Darwin exclaimed to Lyell (see: November 14). This was undoubtedly one of the most remarkable instances of simultaneous discovery.

Already in the 1860s, Wallace was concerned about species extinction. He urged governments to do something for the preservation of various plants, trees and animals, warning that, if that were not done, "future ages will certainly look back upon us as a people so immersed in the pursuit of wealth as to be blind to higher considerations."

Though not strictly religious in a traditional sense, Wallace was attracted to spiritualism. He published a small book on the Scientific Aspect of the Supernatural. This shocked some of the naturalists like Charles Darwin and Darwin's ardent supporter Thomas Huxley. They didn't understand how this apostle of evolution could speak of the spirit. But then, so did Faraday and Maxwell, both deeply religious, and many other creative contributors to science. Non-believers are convinced that anyone with common sense and a scientific bent of mind should be immune to God-talk, spirituality, and such. But, generally speaking, believers are not perturbed by how they are appraised,

In any event, when we talk about biological evolution, it is important that we remember Alfred Wallace as well.

January 9

From the World of Religion: SAINT RAMANANDA

There was a saintly man in the Hindu world by the name of Ramananda, of whom, like many other medieval personages, we have little or no record as to place and date of birth, but whose name and fame and following have survived to this day.

Scholars tentatively suggest that he was born sometime in the 14th century. What is known is that he was inspired by the teachings of an earlier saint-scholar by the name of Ramanuja. There is a line of succession in the genealogy of some saints in India which consists of the principal gurus of the tradition during a given period of time. By this reckoning, Ramandanda fugures on the Ramanuja list.

It is said that Ramananda once belonged to a monastic tradition where, as elsewhere, there were strict rules and rituals on meal-taking. At one point Ramananda felt such rules made no sense. He left the group and began his independent spiritual quest. He went to a spot on the bank of the sacred river Ganga in Varanasi. His personality attracted a few others, and so began the sect known as Ramanandis (Raamaanandees).

A great devotee of Lord Rama (the divine hero of the Hindu epic), he used to proclaim: "All you need to do is to surrender yourself to Rama and Sita. Everything else is of little value." His own name means *one who derives bliss in Rama*. Ramananda was a loud critic of casteism. He stressed, like other enlightened souls, and perhaps with as much or as little success, the great truth that we are all equal in the eyes of the Almighty, and that distinctions of caste and color and creed really don't mean a thing. The multitude worshipped him for such wisdom, while continuing with their age-old prejudices.

Ramananda's *bhakti* (pure love of personal God) replaced the abstract metaphysics of earlier gurus. His movement is regarded as one of the forces which led to the worship of the icons of Rama and Krishna in Hindu temples. The power of preachers should never be underestimated. Some scholars have said that it was Ramananda's inspiration that led to the magnificent Hindu temples we find all over India and beyond today. To him is due the cult of Rama which is a powerful cultural-religious force all over the Hindu world.

Like Jesus Christ, he had twelve apostles. These included a barber, a goldsmith, a tanner, a peasant, a Muslim (the great mystic poet Kabir), a prince and also two women. It is said that when Pipa, a prince, came to become one of his disciples, Ramananda was engrossed in a spiritual exercise. When the prince persisted, it upset the guru who asked the intruder to go jump in the well. The prince promptly obeyed, for to act as a guru commands is the highest virtue. But he was quickly rescued. Upon hearing this, Ramananda regretted the incident, and accepted Pipa as the twelfth disciple. Ramanda descrbed his disciples as *avadhutas*: the liberated ones.

Time and reverence have churned many tales about this godly man who inspired people to intense godly devotion. According to one legend, Ramananda once fought and subdued a lion, and turned it into a vegetarian beast. It has been said that once his barber-disciple was intensely meditating on the Divine (Vishnu) while cutting the hair of the local king. There was the likelihood that this would result in an awkward coiffure for the royal head, or worse still, the absent-minded barber might snip a royal ear. To avert such unhappy occurrences, Lord Vishnu incarnated briefly as a hair-dresser and completed the hair-cutting job to perfection. Nowhere else, in mythology or religious fantasy, has God become a hair-dresser. The story is to remind us that the Divine can manifest itself in any form or person to help the truly devoted ones.

From the World of Science:
THE GOLDEN GATE BRIDGE

When we walk or drive and reach a stream or lake, how do we get to the other bank? We take a boat or cross a bridge. The bridge is a very ancient invention. Like the flint and the wheel, the idea must have occurred to more than one bright mind. Perhaps the first bridge was a sturdy log that was flung across a narrow stream. What a thrill it must have been for the people who first walked over this contraption just going from land to dry land over flowing water underneath!

Since then thousands of bridges have been built all over the world: of countless sizes, shapes and designs. Many ancient bridges have been replaced, many modern ones are crying out for attention and repair. Like the Pyramids and the Taj Mahal, bridges are also often landmarks in cities. The Tower Bridge of London and many of bridges on the Seine have induced songs and poems.

Today I have in mind a suspension bridge which took four and a half years to build: from 5 January 1933 to 27 May 1937, on which date the 2824 meter long Golden Gate Bridge was officially opened. Its cables are thicker than any in the world. Each cable, made up of 27,572 parallel wires, is about 2550 meters long.

The bridge, as many of you know, is in San Francisco, and spans the sides of the Golden Gate Strait. As for countless others, it was a thrill for me to drive across it, just as it was to walk over the little Pont Neuf in Paris. When the Pont Neuf was opened in the 1600s, Henri IV is said to have walked on it first, though he was warned of its questionable stability. When the Golden Gate Bridge was inaugurated in 1937, some 200,000 people are reported to have walked across first, most of them wearing a special hat for the occasion. There was great jubilation which culminated in a musical pageant appropriately called The Span of Gold.

I am recalling this bridge today because its chief architect was born on 9 January 1870. His name was Joseph Baerman Strauss. He was the first to have even thought of a bridge that would go over the Golden Gate. Many thought the idea to be too ambitious, even silly, but Strauss did not. He persisted and convinced the people and the powers that be that this was a worthwhile project to invest money in. Strauss also wrote poems in his spare time. When the Golden Gate Bridge was completed, he wrote one entitled, *The Mighty Task Is Done*:

At last the might task is done;
Resplendent in the western sun;
The Bridge looms mountain high
On its broad decks in rightful pride,
The world in swift parade shall ride
Throughout all time to be.

Launched midst a thousand hopes and fears,
Damned by a thousand hostile sneers.
Yet ne'er its course was stayed.
But ask of those who met the foe,
Who stood alone when faith was low,
Ask them the price they paid.
High overhead its lights shall gleam,
Far, far below life's restless stream,
Unceasingly shall flow....

January 10

From the world of religion: MUHAMMED IBN 'ALI IBN 'ARABI

Religion is more than community worship and the observance of fasting and feasting. It is more than hagiography and God-talk. It involves more than routine rites and rituals, sacraments and singing. Every religious tradition has a mystical dimension also. Indeed mystics often serve as media between the practitioner and the larger Whole, for it is their experiences and utterances that constitute the scripture and substance of religions. Mystics are in the realm of religion what practicing scientists are in the world of science.

In mystic tradition in Islam Islamic is called *tasawwuf* or Sufism. Some Muslims regard it as un-Islamic, perhaps because it had its origins after Islam's encounter with the Hindu world. But there are also Islamic scholars who have argued that Sufism is very much part of Islam. More importantly, there have been great souls in the Islamic world who have written profound poetry that can properly be called mystical. These are the Sufis.

Consider Muhammed Ibn 'Ali Ibn 'Arabi, born in Moorish Andalusia in 1165. He studied Aristotle and Plato which infused him with a spirit of inquiry. He was born a Muslim and he rubbed shoulders with Christians and Jews. He witnessed what ancient Hindus had proclaimed: that one may attain the Divine by following different paths.

Like other saints he felt there was a call for him from the Beyond. It is said that one evening while regaling with friends in a pleasure house in Seville, he heard a voice which said that he was meant for something grander. He had a vision of the three great prophets of the Abrahamic traditions: Moses, Jesus, and Mohammed. The experience was too profound to be ignored. Indeed, it transformed his life. He was convinced that all the prophets had the same divine experience.

Ibn 'Arabi continued to study and learn from various masters, including an elderly woman by the name of Fatimah who developed great affection for him. He traveled widely, including. He wrote scores of books, theological and philosophical reflections mostly. "Some works I wrote at the command of God, sent to me in sleep or through a mystical revelation," he said. He also has a collection of poems to his credit, called *Interpreter of Desires*. These are love poems, bordering on the erotic. But, like the works of Jayadeva in the Hindu world, they were symbolic of intense love for the Divine: a matter he had to explain to his shocked readers. He affirmed, like other mystics before and since, that God is pure Being, not amenable to logic and interpretations, but experience. He proclaimed, again like other mystics, that spiritual experience is different from philosophical analysis. The ground of all existence is the Divine. Commentators on Ibn Arabi, unfamiliar with more ancient Hindu visions, have sometimes said that this is a unique Semitic insight. Further, like the Buddha, Ibn Arabi said that every one of us, knowingly or unknowingly, is on a path of discovery, indeed that each must choose one's own path for realization. This, he contended, is the core of the spiritual quest. He wrote:

"O Marvel! a garden amidst the flames. My heart has become capable of every form: it is a pasture for gazelles and a convent for Christian monks, a temple for idols and the pilgrim's Kaa'ba, and the tables of the Torah and the book of the Qu'ran. I follow the religion of Love: whatever way Love's camels take, that is my religion and my faith."

This may have been a bit much for many of his co-religionists. So his works were banned in Islamic countries. Recognizing alien modes of worship is anathema in many circles: a corollary to the conviction that one's system alone has the key to the kingdom.

From the World of Science:
GEORGE WASHINGTON CARVER

Do you enjoy the pod of *Arachis hypogaea*, containing ovoid seeds in a thin reticulated shell? I am referring to the plant with a hairy stem and pinnate leaflets. I am sure you have tasted it in one dorm or another, for there was an agricultural scientist who made at least three hundred products out of this plant which is more commonly known as peanut, groundnut, monkey nut and so on.

The scientist who churned out products from peanuts in remarkably ingenious ways. We are not sure about the precise date of his birth, perhaps in the 1860s, but since some have declared 10 January to be Black Scientist Day, it is appropriate to recall this remarkable Black American today.

He was born in those dark days of American history when slavery was still in vogue. He too was a GW (George Washington), but owned by a master by the name of Moses Carver in Missouri. So he came to be called George Washington Carver. When he was a child, he was slave-napped along with his mother, and rescued after the Civil War, and brought back to the Carvers who adopted him as their son.

The lad was sickly, but he learned to cook and sew, and read and write. He enjoyed Nature, loved plants and trees, worked in a farm, went to a school in Kansas where he did exceptionally well. He was highly recommended by his teachers for admission in Highland University which gladly accepted him. When he showed up, they reneged upon discovering he was black!

GWC did not give up. In 1890 he secured admission at Simpson College in Iowa where he studied a variety of subjects, including music and art, but biology above all. From there he went on to Iowa State Agricultural College, where he studied plants and painted them too. He used to say that when he talked to flowers they revealed to him their secrets. He studied fungi and explored ways of protecting plants from fungal infections.

From here he moved on to the Tuskegee Normal and Industrial Institute which, with only meager resources, was training African Americans in many professional fields. Here he headed the department of agriculture and worked on ways to help the farmers. He taught the farmers rotation of crops and this helped the quantity and quality of the harvests. He demonstrated the value of plowing deeper into the soil before planting the seeds.

His most important contributions came when, as a result of some pests that affected cotton, farmers over produced peanuts in its place. This was to have disastrous affects on the price of peanuts. To avert this, GWC came up with hundreds of other uses for peanuts, making butter and oil and soap and cheese and dye and ink, all with peanuts. His innovations were not confined to peanuts. He made cardboard with corn stalks and paints from clay.

George Washington Carver was a prolific inventor, but also humble in his recognition of a higher power. "Nature is an unlimited broadcasting station," he wrote: "through which God speaks to us every hour, if we only will tune in." He was also a scientist who felt God in all of nature. He felt, "More and more, as we come closer and closer in touch with nature and its teachings, we are able to see the Divine and are therefore fitted to interpret correctly the various languages spoken by all forms of nature about us."

Washington Carver's life shows that the human spirit can overcome the most daunting obstacles, and it can serve as an inspiration for millions of disadvantaged people all over the world. His mind reveals that science is trans-cultural and trans-racial.

January 11

From the World of Religion: KAGAMI-BIRAKI

As Hinduism is associated with India, Judaism with Israel, and Islam with Saudi Arabia, one thinks of Shinto with respect to Japan. This is an ancient religion whose etymology has been traced to Chinese words meaning 'The Way of the Spirits'. By the 8th century CE, Shinto and Buddhism became the integrated religion of the Japanese people.

Shinto accepts the existence of many Kamis: invisible spirits (deities) which may manifest themselves in Nature or in the skies, sometimes even as human beings. This is why Shinto encourages the worship of rivers and mountains and all of Nature. There are several Shinto shrines all over Japan which the followers of Shinto are expected to visit a certain number of times during their life. The shrines are often adorned with origami (which means 'paper of the spirits').

The chief of the Kamis is Amaterasu Omikami, the Sun Goddess. The imperial family of Japan is said to be descended from her. [In the Hindu epic *Ramayana*, the emperors of his line are said to be of the solar dynasty also.] According to the Shinto sacred history, the first emperor of Japan was Jimu Tenno. Ametesaru gave a round mirror called *mochi* to Jimu Tenno who was her grandson, to be included in the royal treasures.

In modern Shinto calendar, 11 January is a celebratory day. It is known as *Kagami-biraki*. A rough translation of this would be the 'breaking of (the New Year) rice cake'.

When steamed rice is pounded hard, it becomes what they call mochi in Japanese. If this is made to set, it hardens. When this is warmed, it becomes like a kind of very hard glutin which cannot be easily broken. The word *kagami* means a mirror, and *bikari* refers to its breaking or opening. The rice cake is in the form of a small circular mirror.

This is also a festival for celebrating the martial arts, which are part of the Samurai tradition in Japan. Jujutsu is an ancient Japanese martial art. It is said that as early as in the third century BCE, there used to be combative competitions between unarmed participants. These were known as hikara-karube. Over the centuries various schools and systems of the marital art emerged. Indeed, it has a long and fascinating history.

In the 1880s jujutsu was revived, modified, and popularized by a certain Jigoro Kano as Judo. Kano had received training from different masters. He was a pacifist. Aside from developing physical fitness and agility, the goal of judo is also to inculcate self-confidence and mental concentration. Like Yoga from India, it has spread to many other countries of the world. In 1964, judo gained recognition as an Olympic game. The word judo is sometimes translated as the *gentle way*. Like the Christian precept of showing the other cheek, judo teaches one to overwhelm an enemy by simply giving in, rather than by force.

Coming back to Kagami-biraki, in the Shinto tradition of Japan, every family has a little altar at home. It is called Kami-dana. The altar is usually made up of wood that is not painted. The mochi is put in an unpainted box with symbolic objects in the shape of pine or lobster for strength, prosperity, etc. Then it is placed ritualistically on the Kami-dana over which a white rope called Yokozuna hangs. The mochi is now taken for breaking, not cutting, because cutting is considered inauspicious. Since it is fairly hard, one may use a hammer or other instruments for accomplishing this. This is called breaking open the mirror. It is said that once in a while people choke [GET CHOKED] by the mochi pieces.

On this day, there are community speeches, collective jubilations, and the inevitable gatherings for imbibing stimulating liquids.

From the World of Science: LAO TZU

The *do* in judo refers to *the way*. The concept was popularized by the eminent Chinese philosopher and (ancient) scientist Lao Tzu in the 4th century BCE. His name literally means the old master. Scholars have questioned if such an individual ever existed. But the principles associated with his teachings are among the sturdiest pillars of Chinese thought. Their reverberations continue to this day.

Some have even seen parallels between them and some world views of current physics. Ultimately physics is an attempt, through concepts, mathematics, instruments and experiments to discover the Way of Nature: how it functions and how it is sustained. When this is done with no reference to the human presence in the cosmos, we get post-Cartesian science. When it is done with humanity at the center of it all, we have ancient science. Post-Cartesian science is more fruitful. Ancient science is more fulfilling.

According to Chinese tradition, Lao Tzu spent a whole lifetime observing and reflecting, and then when he was past eighty, he wrote a book that was weighty. The book had two parts, *Tao* (the Way) and *Te* (Virtue). Tao is the Way in which Nature works, and the path that we as humans ought to take. The peaceful stream and the gentle breeze, the steady course of the stars and the unfailing periodicity of the seasons: these are reflections of *Tao*, the Order in Nature. If we wish to find inner peace and experience spiritual tranquility, then we must make every effort to become one with Nature, for when we are alienated from Nature, there can be only stress and strife.

Tao cannot be described in words. To expound this idea millions of words have been said and written. Recall the poem by Po Chü-yi on a famous saying of the Lao-tzu:

> The wordy ones, they know not aught
> The silent ones, they know a lot.
> The wisdom of Lao-tzu
> May be found in words so few.
>
> But if Lao-tzu said what was true,
> And he himself was one who knew,
> How could he have been right
> If a five-thousand-word-book he did write?

Ta [Tao] is spontaneous and is the mode of the heavens. Chang Tzu saw in *Tao* the never ending metamorphoses in the physical world. It is the very essence of all changes. One may be inclined to look upon Taoism as yet another philosophical system, but from a larger perspective, it may also be regarded as a scientific theory about the nature of the world. For ultimately, that's what unified theories are all about: to bring under a single simple formulation all the chaos and complexities that rule the world.

In our own times many piecemeal theories are constructed on the basis of astronomical data, physical principles, and mathematical formulation. But there is also the search for one underlying principle that links the multiplicity. However, that linkage is attempted through equations and abstractions, with no reference to the experiencing consciousness or the reflecting mind. In ancient science, no theory of nature was without relevance to life and living. The ancients never forgot the bonds between humans and the world around. Lao Tzu spoke of good and bad, of kindness, compassion, and sincerity.

Even as we remember the names and achievements relating to modern sciences, it is good to recall occasionally on the reflections of ancient thinkers also.

January 12

From the World of Religion:
SWAMI VIVEKANANDA

We live in a world of many faiths and religious traditions. How do we get to know about them? From travelers' tales and missionaries, from books and scholarly expositions, of course. And then there are itinerant preachers like Billie Graham and eloquent speakers like Vivekananda (born: 12 January 1862).

He was born as Narendra Nath Datta in India. He was a bright student, endowed with an inquiring and doubting mind. No clear-thinking scholar could tell him anything definite about God. But when, in his twenties, he chanced to meet Saint Ramakrishna Paramahamsa, he experienced a transformation. He had a spiritual awakening. He changed his name to Vivekananda (One who experiences the bliss of enlightenment).

Vivekananda was proud of his people's spiritual heritage, but was also acutely aware of the chasm between ideals and practice in some aspects of Hindu society. He was against casteism, and declared there was nothing in Hindu scriptures that proclaimed untouchability, nothing that banned lower castes from reading the Vedas (as used to be sadly the case in those days). He was pained by India's material weakness, and felt that India could benefit from the science and technology of the West.

Vivekananda spoke to many audiences in India: he tried to enlighten the orthodox and brought knowledge of Hindu world views to the educated classes in India which were moving away from their traditions. He felt there was much to be learned from the Hindu mode of religious tolerance. He recognized that India's greatest strength was its spiritual approach to life. "This is the same land," he declared in a speech, "where wisdom made its home before it went into any other country…"

He wanted very much to propagate Hindu thought to the rest of the world. He came to the first Parliament of World Religions, held in Chicago in 1893 where he expounded to a large audience the visions of the Hindu sages. The morning after his lecture one Chicago newspaper commented: "After hearing him, we feel how foolish it is to send missionaries to this learned nation." He was described as "an orator by divine right," and as the "greatest figure in the Parliament of Religions."

Upon returning to India, Vivekananda established the Ramakrishna Mission in 1897 in a place called Belur on the outskirts of Calcutta. Over the years, the

Mission opened branches in several parts of India. Today, the Ramakrishna Mission may be found in many countries of the world. One of its goals, especially abroad, is to propagate the message of Hindu philosophy and world views.

Monks in this movement have to undergo training in Hindu practice and philosophy. They have to do social service. Vivekananda insisted that service to the needy ought to be an important dimension of the RK Mission. "Your duty is to serve the poor and the distressed, without distinction of caste or creed," he declared.

Some criticized Vivekananda as not being a scholar, but only an inspired preacher who sometimes interpreted ancient world views to make them palatable to the modern mind. There, ay be nothing wrong in this criticism. Unless this is done, any religion or tradition would stagnate and wither away. For the healthy survival of religions its leaders must keep interpreting and re-interpreting ancient tenets so as to make them relevant and meaningful in a changing world, even while retaining the essence and spirit at the root of the tradition for many long centuries. This is what Swami Vivekananda tried to do for the Hindu tradition.

From the World of Science:
LAZARRO SPALLANZANI

He went to the university of Bologna to study law where his cousin Laura Bassi was professor of physics and mathematics. This was in 1749. She inspired him to turn to science and mathematics. But he finished with a degree in metaphysics and theology and became an ordained priest. He was well read in the classics, translated some ancient authors, and gained enough reputation to be invited to many universities, from Portugal to St. Petersburg. He traveled widely, spent a year in Turkey, and was received with great respect everywhere he went. For three decades he served as professor of Natural History at the University in Pavia. His name was Lazarro Spallanzani (born: 12 January 1729).

Spallanzani did countless experiments in a variety of fields: from blood circulation and digestion to the migration of swallows. He showed that in a number of creatures some organs are regenerated when cut off, as with the jaws of salamanders, tails of tadpoles and the legs of frogs. In the case of snails, even the heads grow back when severed, eyes, tongue and all! [This is possible because the snail's brain is not in its head.] His report created quite a controversy. His was one of the earliest works on the regeneration of organs. Voltaire is said to have been so impressed [WITH OR BY]Spallanzani's report that he repeated the experiments himself.

Spallanzani studied the Vesuvius, the volcano near Naples, and Stromboli in the Lipari islands off the northeastern coast of Sicily. He put forth a theory to the effect that volcanic eruptions result from interaction between atmospheric air and the interior of volcanoes: a now discarded notion in the light of more knowledge, but a scientific explanation nevertheless.

It was believed for a long time that maggots on spoiled meat, flies and even frogs just come out of nowhere: that they were spontaneously generated. This was a natural assumption for no one had seen the egg of a fly, and of worms that suddenly appear apparently out of nowhere. According to one 18th century theory, living organisms ultimately decomposed into organic molecules, from which animalcules (microorganisms) could emerge as "animals of an inferior species." This was brought about by a vegetative force which pervaded all organic matter. This explained how minute organisms arose spontaneously. Scientific hypotheses consist of statements about not directly perceived entities in order to explain what is observed.

Spallanzani's scientific work led to quite different conclusions. He experimented with containers of various sizes and openings. He studied infusions in them, and showed that animalcules did not arise when the flasks were made air tight and the infusions are heated. He published his results in 1776. But for almost a hundred more years the old views persisted even among scientists. Paradigm shifts don't occur easily in the world of science. Today we know of spores and invisible seeds in the air and of microscopic entities thriving everywhere. The principle on which modern food preservation is based is consistent with Spallanzani's discovery of eliminating microorganisms by heating. It was only after the work of Louis Pasteur that the spontaneous generation theory was buried once and for all times, and the role of microorganisms in diseases came to light.

Spallanzani also experimented with bats. He found that even when blinded, bats could fly without difficulty. He found insects in their stomachs. A line in a 15th century ballade says, "The blind eat many a fly." Spallanzani proved this to be true of bats, but he was puzzled. When their ears were plugged, the creatures were helpless. He wondered if bats could see with their ears. The world of science had not yet discovered ultrasonic sound.

January 13

FROM THE WORLD OF RELIGION: SAINT CANUTE

Not every saint has led a simple and peaceful life. The patron saint of Denmark, for instance, became king of the country in 1080. His mother wasn't married to his father who was King Sweyn III Estrithson. He had a brother called Harald the Slothful, after whose short reign he himself became king. This saint's name was King Canute (Knud) IV (born: 10 January 1040?). His son, who is known as Charles the Good, also became a saint. [The pages of European history speak of many Charleses: Charles the Bald and Charles the Bold, Charles the Good and Charles the Fat, and of course Charles the Great (Charlemagne), let alone so many king Charles numbered from from I and XVI.

Saint Canute was an extremely devout Christian. As in most religious frameworks, he subjected himself frequently to harsh penitence and fasting in his efforts to evolve spiritually. He subsidized missionaries to go to many lands, built churches for the people, and enforced Christianity with considerable zeal.

King Canute felt he had a claim to the English throne. After all, his predecessor Knud den Store (Canute the Great) had been Lord of Denmark, England, Norway and southern Sweden. That was the great Canute who is said to have commanded the sea to calm the waves. His underlings were probably more impressed by the royal boldness than by how the sea responded. But the great man quickly explained the tidal disobedience by declaring loudly and clearly: "Let all men know how empty and worthless is the power of kings. For there is none worthy of the name but God, whom heaven, earth and sea obey" It was thanks to him that Denmark was Christianized.

In an episode in Valmiki's epic the Ramayana, King Vishvamitra, unable to overpower a saint, exclaims: "Fie unto royal strength! Spiritual power alone is true power!"]

Canute IV understood that his goal of getting the English throne could be realized only by force of arms since the Normans had installed themselves firmly on English soil. Since war meant extra military expenses, Canute levied taxes for his army to boot the Norman barons out of the Anglo-Saxon realm. They say he sent a fleet of 200 ships to assist rebels against William the Conqueror, but he was not successful. Guillaume le Conquerant and his French-speaking entourage were there to stay.

Canute's subjects now became impatient and angry, even his own brother Olaf rebelled. Canute fled to the little island of Funen (where Hans Christian Andersen was to emerge centuries later). But his opponents wouldn't let him live there in peace. They hunted him all the way to the town of Odense where, according to tradition, he was mercilessly killed along with a handful of his followers while he was in a prayerful posture at Saint Alban's Church: perhaps the first Murder in the Cathedral, well before the awful event in Canterbury.

It is said that in medieval times they used to perform a Ludus de Sancto Kanuto Duce (Play of Saint King Canute) in public squares.

According to the English monk Ælnoth, after Canute the Holy died in 1086, some miracles occurred at his tomb. Because of such reports and his commitment to Christianity, he was declared a saint, and his Feast day was specified to be January 13.

This day is observed as Tyvendedagen in Norway, and as Tjugondedag In Sweden: twentieth day after Christmas. According to one custom, people eat all leftover goodies on this Little Christmas day. Ornaments are removed from Christmas trees which are not supposed to be in homes any longer for now the season is officially over.

From the World of Science: OSCAR MINKOWSKI

Humanity has known diseases from the most ancient times. Many cures for ailments were found by trial and error, and some with an understanding of the causes of the disease in question. The search for such causes is a complex detective work. In the modern world this is done in laboratories under controlled conditions. Sometimes exploring one line of research leads to discovery of something quite unexpected.

For example, as we all know, one of the killer-diseases in today's world is diabetes, and it is very much on the rise. According to one report, there are more than fifteen million people suffering from diabetes in our world today. Even the ancients were familiar with this once fatal disease. The so-called Ebers Papyrus, discovered in 1872 and dating back to more than 3500 years, mentions many diseases of that period, and it includes diabetes.

It has also been known for a long time that the disease has to do with the intake of sugar. But the source and actual cause of diabetes was not known until late in the 19th century.

Oscar Minkowski (born: 13 January 1858) was a physiologist of German extraction. He joined the faculty of the University of Strasburg in 1891. In those days this city was part of Germany. Minkowski and a colleague by the name of Von Mering were doing some work on how lipid (greasy substances) is absorbed in the body, and what the role of pancreas is in this.

Dogs served as guinea pigs in this research, which meant that their pancreas was removed for study. One of Minkowski's assistants noticed that a dog whose pancreas had been removed urinated more frequently than the others. Furthermore, he observed that flies were congregating in large numbers in the urine of that dog. He reported the matter to Minkowski. It was quite a feat in those days to keep a dog alive after pancreatectomy.

Minkowski analyzed the urine of the dog and discovered it contained large amounts of sugar. Frequent urination was known to be a feature of diabetes, and the disease was also associated with sugar intake. This prompted Minkowski to investigate the matter further from this perspective. Further research and reflection led him to the recognition that th pancreas plays an important role in urination, and that, in fact, it was involved in processing the sugar intake of the body. Thus Minkowski discovered that diabetes involved the malfunctioning of the pancreas.

More specifically, he established that the pancreas creates a substance which regulates the sugar content in the blood stream. From this he concluded that if this substance, whatever it was, was injected into the body's blood stream, that could control diabetes. Soon it became clear that there are clusters of specialized cells in the pancreas from which that substance arose. A physiologist dubbed that, as yet unknown, substance insulin (from the Latin word insula for island). When this substance was isolated by Frederick Banting and Charles Best of the University of Toronto in the early 1920s, it came to be called insulin.

When Minkowski received the first sample of insulin in Strasbourg, he is said to have remarked: "It has been sent to me by those who have discovered it. It was once my hope that I would be the father of insulin. Now I am happy to accept the designation as its grandfather, which the Toronto scientists have conferred on me so kindly."

Insulin was also the first protein to be fully sequenced and chemically synthesized, and the first protein to be manufactured by genetic engineering.

January 14

From the World of Religion: PONGAL FESTIVAL

Pongal is the Tamil version of a specifically South Indian mode of celebrating the winter solstice. Unlike other Hindus festivals which are generally devoted to one or another of divine manifestations, Pongal has an astronomical and seasonal significance: the arrivel of the sun to the vernal equinox in its northward journey.

The apparent passage of the sun from the southern to the northern hemisphere is called *uttarayana*: northern movement. The reverse passage from the north to the south is the *dakshinayana* or southern movement. *Makara samkranti* is the first day of the sun's northward journey with the sun on the Tropic of Capricorn. Hindu reckoning, based on a more ancient systems, takes this to be around the middle of January. That is why the festival is celebrated at this time of the year.

Unless the Sun turns back northwars, it will get colder in the northern hemisphere. So one is thankful when the Sun begins this journey. In Tamil, the literal meaning of *pongal* is to boil. Pongal is also the name of a delicacy made by boiling rice with milk and lentils. The third meaning is the festival because one makes pongal on this day. A standard greeting on this day is: "pongiyachchaa, (Did it boil?)." The reference is to the milk. This is taken as an auspicious sign. More precisely, the festival is known as *Thai Pongal*: Thai being the name of the month whose first day is the Pongal festival.

Many practices have evolved in the Tamil tradition for the celebration of the Pongal festival. Early in the morning, a ceremonial bath is taken, after which people put on new clothes. In classical times, one would gather in a porch and cook the lentil-rice dish, called pongal. It has two varieties: one sweetened and the other salty. This used to be done ceremoniously in a clay pot at a spot which was decorated with colored patterns, called kolams. The oldest member of the family was expected to start the cooking, usually assisted by others.

The ingredients for pongal include brown sugar, cardamom and cashew nuts. The cooking is usually done in sunlight because the festival honors the Sun God. The meal is served on banana leaves which are later given to the cows as food. With changing times, some of the traditional modes have been disappearing.

In olden times workers in the fields used to carry sugar cane and freshly harvested paddy with coconuts and plantains to their landlords. Nowadays such offerings are made only to the gods at home. Brothers give gifts to sisters. In the countryside where there are cow-sheds attached to homes, the horns of the cattle are adorned, cows are fed sugar cane and banana leaves, and escorted to the river or the local tank for a special drink. We must remember that harvest and agriculture have always gone hand in hand with cattle in ancient cultures. During the day there are visits to and from friends, and in the evening there are cultural programs.

On the day after pongal, in some parts of Tamil Nadu—in the regions of Kauveri and Vaigai—there were bull fights in the Tamil style, called Jallikootthu. Adorned bulls with bells around their necks are provoked and let loose in an open meadow where they are subdued by sturdy young men, to the applause of an admiring audience that includes young women. This event is described in a famous Tamil novel called *Kamalambal Caritram* by Rajam Iyer.

Like all festivals, Pongal is a joyous event. It welcomes the Spring which is also harvest time in that part of the world.

From the World of Science: MATTHEW F. MAURY

The solid stretches on which we tread are small compared to the waters and ice that form much of the earth's surface. It is a little recognized fact that the Pacific Ocean alone is more expansive than all the land areas put together: so vast are the oceans. If we consider the life forms that throb in the various waters of our world, all our terra firma shrinks to insignificance.

Science has brought us much knowledge about the oceans. Many investigators contributed. The initial push for the systematic study of ocean depths, exploring the floor of the seas, and for learning about the details of ocean currents came from Matthew F. Maury (born: 14 January 1806).

Maury sailed with the Navy and wrote a book on navigation. So when he was made head of the National Observatory, his interests centered more on the blue below than on the one above. He began to issue Wind and Current Charts to help sailors at sea, which proved to be very valuable since maritime commerce was then on the rise. His famous and memorable statement with regards to the Gulf Stream was: "There is a river in the ocean." Indeed, as we know today, such rivers affect the climate of many regions.

When they began to lay cables in the Atlantic for intercontinental telegraphy, Maury began fathoming the ocean. That the Atlantic was not quite as deep in mid-ocean as near the continents came as a complete surprise to the scientific world. This is how the mountains and valleys and plateaus deep underwater were discovered. Unlike in a swimming pool, the bottom of the ocean is rugged indeed. A systematic study of marine biology and the new field of micropaleontology had their origins from samples from the oceanic depths.

Maury recognized the importance of countries working together in the exploration of the seas and of weather patterns. He took a leading role in organizing the first international meeting on this which was held in Brussels in 1853. Though his intention was to make weather prediction more international, the focus of discussions was on the sea. He was thus one of the pioneers in international scientific cooperation which is now taken for granted by the scientific community. Today, it is almost impossible to do serious science in certain fields when one is confined to just one's own country.

Maury's career was colored by rivalry, jealousy, and political intrigues, and with some biases and prejudices that would be embarrassing in today's world, but which were not uncommon in his time. For example, he was unhappy with the outcome of the American Civil War. He was so disappointed that he moved to Mexico where he wanted to set up a colony for like-minded Virginians. It did not happen. If he had, there would have been Anglos south of the border as we have Latinos here.

In science, Maury's genius was in extensive explorations and the organization of meetings. These were not trivial talents and they served the cause of science. But he was not much of a theorist. His capacity for scientific theories seems to have been constrained by his anchors to sacred texts, committed as he was to natural theology. His religious inclinations served him well in his total dedication to science, but they did not serve him as well in explaining natural phenomena. As a result, when he let his imagination take off, he sometimes came up with strange ideas, such as his hypothesis that earth's magnetism affects air currents.

Matthew Maury's major contributions were in the data he collected and the incentive he gave to the science of oceanography, and for these we will always be remembered.

January 15

From the World of Religion: ZOROASTRIAN BEHMAN

More than three millennia ago, there emerged in the region we now call Iran a spiritual master by the name of Zarathushtra Spitama. He proclaimed there was but one God, who was the Fount of All Wisdom (Ahura Mazda). Ahura is the life-giving principle, and mazda is superior intellect. Zarathrushtra uttered his revelations in what are called Gathas. These have become parts of the Scripture of the religion practiced by the followers of this ancient prophet who call themselves Zoroastrians (or Zarathustis). The Zoroastrian scripture is known as the Zend Svesta (literally, commentary on the law).

The essence of Zoroastrianism is to engage in noble thoughts (humata), words (hukhta), and deeds (havarastra). All prayers in the Zoroastrian tradition start with the phrase: Kshnotra Ahurai Mazda: glory to Ahura Mazda.

Ahura Mazda is the Creator of the world and of all life in it. For this reason he is worshipped and thanked. He has no form or color, and is therefore never represented in pictorial or sculptural modes. He is regarded as pure light.

Ahura Mazda endowed human beings with Vohu Manoh: a mind that can think and discriminate between good and bad, between right and wrong.

In the Zoroastrian tradition, the word Jashan refers to the formal celebration of a commemorative or religious event. Its goal is to build the community and to express collectively humanity's gratitude to the Almighty for the gifts we have received.

As in most ancient religions, two primal forces struggle in the universe: the Good and the Evil. All that sustains and enriches Life constitutes the Good. All that is inimical to Life is Evil. Angra Mainyu created Evil.

Corresponding to the angels or deities of other religions, Zoroastrianism has Yazata. They too were created by Ahura Mazda. They are his servants, as it were, helping him maintain order in the universe. One could interpret Yazata as the benign laws of Nature that sustain the world. They also assist human beings in their spiritual betterment.

In Zoroastrian chronology, the universe has a life span of 12,000 years. It consists of four separate phases of 3000 years each. The separation of good from evil occurred in the first phase. Then bad ones reigned. In the third phase, the good ones dominated. Saviors emerge in the last phase, and every evil will be routed out.

The twelve months on the Zoroastrian calendar are devoted to twelve Yazata. The system was adopted by Shiite Islam which has twelve Imams. The Zoroastrian bifurcation of Good and Evil influenced Judaic and Christian thought in subtle ways.

The 11th month on the Zoroastrian calendar is called Behman: the name of the Yazata presiding over cattle. January 14 is the second day of Behman. Zoroastrians observe it as the festival of Bahamangen. The 12th, 14th and 21st days of this month are also important. On these days, out of respect for cattle, one abstains from food that has meat.

When the aspirant prays in this religion, he or she asks that the benefit of the prayer be for the well being of others.

Every religion has its history, each fascinating in its own way. As we probe into their framework, visions and values, we see profound differences at one level, but also elements in common. Whether we look upon religions as vestiges of proto-human recognitions of levels of Reality which elude us today, or as the inevitable emergence from the neuro-chemistry of the brains, the connecting commonalty cannot be denied. Indeed, in a sense, religions reflect the deepest recesses of the human psyche.

From the World of Science: LEWIS M. TERMAN

Lao Tze remarked centuries ago that "to perceive things is the germ of intelligence."

Psychologists, like medical practitioners, are generally concerned with problems that arise in the functioning of the mind. One of the first to be interested in the normally functioning mind was Alfred Binet. As quantitative elements enhance scientific analysis, he introduced (in 1905) a system to measure the mind's intrinsic capacity for reasoning and thinking. His work led to the notion of IQ (Intelligence Quotient) which compares (as a percentage) a person's mental age to the chronological. Thus if your IQ is 1, you are perfectly normal. If a 6 year old displays the mental capacity of a 9 year old, her IQ would be (9/6) or 1.5. These were later expressed as larger numbers by multiplying by 100. Unfortunately this system led to dangerous and questionable assertions regarded the intelligence of peoples and groups.

Lewis Terman (born: 15 January 1877) wrote a doctoral dissertation which had the very insensitive title of: *Genius and Stupidity: A Study of the Intellectual Processes of Seven 'Bright' and Seven 'Stupid' Boys.* In the course of this work he developed intelligence-testing methods which gauged a wide array of abilities that included creativity, logical process, mathematical ability, interpretation of stories, verbal skills, ability to learn chess, memory, and even motor skills.

Terman made extensive studies of the intelligence of children. Nevertheless, he came to some scientifically questionable generalizations, such as that gifted children were taller and healthier. He was interested in the question of what constitutes giftedness and genius in children.

It was during his more than three decades of tenure as Head of the Psychology Department at Stanford University that Terman developed his famous Stanford

Achievement Test (SAT) which has determined the academic fate and fortunes of millions of youngsters over the years. Its validity has sometimes been questioned by various experts.

As is well known, the notion of IQ, and especially the methods and contents of the associated tests have also come under much criticism. It has been argued that they are culture dependent, that even if IQ is a measure of capacity for words and numbers, it in no way reflects abilities for imagination, creativity, etc. which are no less important, and much less amenable to quantitative assessment. Then again, it is as important to measure emotional quotient (EQ) as IQ in the larger context of human culture and civilization, for a person without emotions can be more dangerous than one without too much intelligence.

One of the startling discoveries at the end of the Second World War was that most of the faithful lieutenants of Herr Hitler had very high IQs. If we adopted Emerson's standard by which "it is good-will that makes intelligence," then these would be considered as morons rather than men of intelligence.

Indeed it is important to recognize that whereas intelligence is an important and very powerful tool for human beings in many contexts, there are other capacities of the human person, perhaps not as powerful and aggressive as intelligence but which are certainly no less important, and far more fulfilling for a sane and useful life: for example, the capacity to care and be kind. Traditionally education has dealt only with the cultivation of matters which call for intelligence. Perhaps education needs to pay some attention to the fostering of other faculties as well.

January 16

From the World of Religion: KING JAMES' BIBLE

Back in the 17th century, Dr. John Reynolds of Corpus Christi College in Oxford came up with a proposal for a new English version of *Bishop's Bible*. King James I liked the idea. To achieve this, he convened a conference at Hampton Court on 16 January 1604. Scholars would do the translation and ecclesiastics would check for accuracy. There would be no commentaries. This was the starting point of what was published seven years later under the imposing title:

The Holy Bible, conteyning the Old Testament and the New: Newly translated out of the originall tongues & with the former translations diligently compared and reuised, by his Maiesties speciall comandement. Appointed to be read in Churches.

This is referred to more briefly as the *Authorised Version*. It was based on man-uscripts, at a time when there was not yet serious critical scholarship as to authen-ticity or accuracy of language. So as the years rolled by, it was subjected to scholarly criticisms. In the 17th and 18th centuries revisions and other transla-tions were attempted. By the 19th century, the need for a more careful edition had become considerable. So, with the collaboration of numerous scholars, a *Revised Version* appeared in 1895.

By this time, not only had the public gotten accustomed to the King James version, but there were also a great many more scholars and educated readers. With more alert readers there were more criticisms and objections. Therefore, it took much more time for the *Revised Version* to be accepted. Towards the close of the 20th century, yet another version of the Bible came out. Some traditionally inclined people have felt that removing the *ye* and the *thou* from the Bible takes away some of its ancientness which contributes to its dignity. Language is impor-tant in the collective experience of religion.

The goal in all these undertakings was to make the sacred work of the tradi-tion intelligible to the practitioners, and to be as faithful as possible to the origi-nal. Even slight changes and minor mistranslations could lead to misunderstanding and misinterpretation. This may not matter much to the devout and the faithful. But for scholars and students, for those who probe and analyze, every word and statement must be appropriately rendered and properly evaluated. For example, it has been pointed out that whether the Greek *metanoia* is to be translated as *going beyond* or *repent* could make a big difference in what Jesus was saying in Mark 1:14: "The time is fulfilled, and the Kingdom of God is at hand; repent and believe in the gospel."

Thus, it is no doubt true that the precise meanings of whatever is written in the scriptures of various religions are extremely important when it comes to ana-lyzing and accepting its doctrines and the statements of its prophets. However, once someone becomes affiliated to a tradition by virtue of birth or early upbringing, this might not be all that important for that person.

Perhaps that's why in some traditions, especially in those which are not as eager to proselytize, reverential repetitions of ancient verses, with appropriate intonations, are far more important for the religious experience than understand-ing the meanings of passages, at least for the practitioners. Generally speaking, in the context of religion meaning is important when one does theology; serene sounds and reverential moods are all that one needs at the experiential level. Ultimately, religion is for merging the core of our being with the Cosmic Whole, and if a sacred book assists us in this, its purpose is served.

From the World of Science: DIAN FOSSEY

Some have said that Hanno, the Carthaginian explorer of the fifth century BCE was the first to write about an unusually large animal. Then, an English sailor by the name of Andrew Battel who spent a year in West Africa in the late 16th century, wrote something about it. But it was only in the middle of the 19th century that, upon reading a report about a huge non-human skull which was found by a missionary in West Africa, the presumed animal was named *Gorilla savegei* by the English zoologist Richard Owen.

The so-called Mountain Gorilla was first observed only in 1902 in Rwanda. Because they were first spotted by Von Beringe they are known as Gorilla Beringe. They were pictured as wild beasts in the famous movie *King Kong*.

Gorillas are very large anthropoid apes. We can well picture them as our very distant cousins who have been happily thriving in the wilds of equatorial Africa for eons, and who probably emerged long before our own first ancestors.

Systematic and sympathetic studies of the nature and behavior of animals have dispelled many of our misconceptions. For example, in cages in zoos, gorillas may strike one as ferocious and unapproachable. Actually they are rather shy animals, very friendly in their own way. They have specific life-styles. Gorillas are nomadic, moving from place to place, looking for edibles: mostly plants and berries, and spending the night in groups. They communicate with grunts, alerting one another of intruders and potential dangers. We have come to know all this and much more about gorillas, thanks to Dian Fossey (born: 16 January 1932) who spent years studying gorillas, and actually lived with them for some time. After being trained as an occupational therapist, she happened to go to Central Africa where her interest in gorillas was aroused.

She began to study these animals in 1967, later established the Karisoke Research Center for gorillas, and spent nearly 18 years among a group of gorillas that gradually developed an affinity for her. However, it took a long time for her to gain the trust of the animals. "Their bright eyes darted nervously from under heavy brows as though trying to identify us as familiar friends or possible foes. Immediately I was struck by the physical magnificence of the huge jet-black bodies blended against the green palette wash of the thick forest foliage," she wrote in her famous book entitled *Gorillas in the Mist*. Gorillas attack humans out of fear, and not for sport, as humans sometimes do to them. When she befriended them, Dian gave her animals names like Uncle Bert and Digit, and soon developed personal bonds with some of them.

Fossey returned to the United States and wrote the book in which she narrated her experiences and insights deriving from her many years of studies. She went back to Africa to continue her research, and to work for the protection of this endangered species. But in 1985 she was killed, probably by a poacher, in her cabin.

Gorillas were, and still are killed by poachers. Dian did much for the protection of these endangered animals. Thanks to the awareness she brought, many governments have made poaching illegal. Yet, there continue to be some obsessive poachers who continue in this activity. In 1998 a man was arrested on Afi Mountain; he had been caught for the same crime many times before.

Dian Fossey's life reveals a commendable aspect of the human potential. The behavior of the poachers and their customers reveal another aspect. Human beings can nurture, and they can also extinguish life; we can create and we can also destroy. education and awareness, or lack thereof, fosters one kind of characteristic or another.

January 17

From the World of Religion: SAINT ANTHONY

When Western observers came to India in the 17th and 18th centuries, they were struck by the other-worldliness of Hindu ascetics, and they jumped to the conclusion that this was a peculiarity of Hinduism. What they did not realize, as many still don't, is that in Christian world too the spiritual path has been associated with ascetic life. The idea that one has to sacrifice life's common pleasures and undergo pain and penance to connect with the Divine is reflected in the hermitages and monasteries of Christianity as much as in the *ashramas* and *tapovanams* of the Hindu world.

The origins of Christian monasticism have been traced to an Egyptian spiritual seeker who was to become St. Anthony (3rd–4th century), whose Feast Day is 17 January. He is said to have been so inspired by Mark's statement: ""If thou wilt be perfect, go and sell all thou hast," that he gave away to charity the home and all the possessions which he inherited from his wealthy father.

From teenage to thirty-five he tried to be a recluse, staying in a graveyard in Egypt, but there, wild beasts came and made life awful for Anthony. He interpreted this as the work of demons, and withdrew to an abandoned fort. His persistent prayers were still thwarted by temptations. Many artists have depicted St. Anthony's plight. The 15th century Dutch artist Hieronymus Bosch, whom Carl Jung described as "the master of the monstrous and the discoverer of the unconscious," made a magnificent three-panel painting which depicts the mental and spiritual turmoil of St. Anthony most dramatically. One needs a magnifying glass to see all the details even in a large reproduction. It tellingly depicts the ancient world views of supernatural perturbations that stand in the way of ascetic discipline. The demonic creatures are poetic representations of distractions that pull us away from serious pursuits.

Anthony advised his disciples to be firm to the demons that come at night, and to tell them unequivocally that "We are angels." For, it is by affirming emphatically our innate goodness that we can resist our proclivity for doing harm. He spent many years in seclusion, Gautama Buddha-like on the sparse sustenance which people brought him from time to time.

In the Christian tradition, Saint Anthony is believed to have been one of the first to introduce monastic living in the spiritual quest. Hence he is regarded as the Father of Cenobites (monastery-dwellers). After establishing a couple of monasteries, he went to Alexandria to preach and to combat the doctrine of Arianism: the heretical teaching of Arius by which Christ was a demigod rather than the Son of God.

It was Saint Anthony who buried Saint Paul the Hermit, for which reason he is claimed as the patron saint of gravediggers.

There is also a famous depiction of a bearded St. Anthony with a halo round his head in which he is standing with a tall cross. There is a pig near him, as also a dog and a hen. According to one legend, he used to treat skin infections with pork fat. Hence the association of pigs with this saint.

Cardinal Newman who wrote on Church Fathers, had this to say about Saint Anthony: "His doctrine surely was pure and unimpeachable; and his temper high and heavenly, without cowardice, without gloom, without formality, without self-complacency. Superstition is abject and crouching, it is full of thoughts of guilt; it distrusts God, and dreads the powers of evil. Anthony at least had nothing of this."

From the World of Science:
BENJAMIN FRANKLIN

The father was a candle-maker, and the son became bright as a thousand candles: a source of extraordinary light to his fellow countrymen and to the world. He was clever and creative, inventive and insightful, wise and witty: this unusual personage whose life spanned much of the 18th century. His name was

Benjamin Franklin (born: 17 January 1706): One of the most illustrious of all Americans.

Franklin was among the enlightened thinkers of his age, and he also brought enlightenment to his generation. He had the distinction of signing the birth certificate for the world's longest lasting democracy. He was a prolific writer with printing devices at his disposal, one even in Paris. He was a scholar who could communicate with ease with his readers. He dished out wisdom and witticisms like people share candies with children, bringing out Poor Richard's Almanack which was filled with *bons mots*.

Ben Franklin was a diplomat, but an erudite one at that, representing his country in France. He was an American, but gained the respect and admiration of European, including French, thinkers for his knowledge, sophistication, and intelligence: an unusual accomplishment even in those days.

This versatile amateur scientist was good enough to be elected to the Royal Society and to be awarded the coveted Copley Medal. He probed into the nature of electricity: an emerging experimental field in the 18th century. Everyone has heard of his dangerous kite-experiment in which he flew a kite with silk threads attached to a thin wire atop and a metallic key below. Sparks flew from the key when there was a thunderstorm, revealing the electrical nature of lightning. [Two people, one in Russia and one in France, who repeated the experiment were electrocuted.] The experiment demolished the older view of lightning as fire in the sky, caused by friction in the air. From this recognition Franklin devised the lightning rod which has saved thousands of homes. He suggested that the two kinds of electricity might be two subtle fluids, and dubbed their dichotomy positive and negative: epithets that have survived to this day. When he was praised for his experiment on lightning and for his contributions to American independence, he wrote to a friend: "Notwithstanding my experiments with electricity the thunderbolt continues to fall under our noses and beards (referring to the French Revolution); and as for the tyrant, there are a million of us still engaged in snatching away his scepters (referring to George III of England)."

Franklin is credited with the invention of the bifocal lens, a more fuel-efficient heating stove, and the rocking chair: all three of which could come in handy for a retired person who likes to read in a cozy room in winter.

He wrote a prayer which invoked powerful Goodness, bountiful Father, and merciful Guide. He preferred reading to listening to sermon, reflecting to attending church. He had difficulty accepting Christ as God, but respected Christian ethics.

Benjamin Franklin wrote on an incredible range of topics including paper currencies, the gulf-stream, and population problems.

He wrote his own epitaph in which he said that his body had become food for worms, but that his work "shall not be lost" and that it would "appear once more in a new and more elegant edition, revised and corrected by the Author."

A fascinating aspect of human history is that now and again there appears a human being with extraordinary talent and genius. Benjamin Franklin was such a one.

January 18

From the World of Religion:
A HORRIFIC RELIGIOUS PERSECUTION

There are events in history that are hard to forget, indeed they shouldn't be forgotten. We need to remember them, not because they are worth remembering for their intrinsic value, but because they were so painful and shameful that the likes of them should never happen again in the saga of humanity. Nevertheless, they continue.

So we may recall 18 January 1945 when, in the thick of the Second World War, the Soviet Army came very close to Cracow and Oswiecim (Auschwitz), and this was the beginning of a redemption. Auschwitz was the site of the notorious Nazi camp where, from July 1940 to its closing on 27 January 1945, hundreds of thousands of human beings were registered and exterminated because of their ethnic affiliation. One of the many episodes that have brought unimaginable pain and the darkest shame to civilization.

The Nazis were holding some 5,800 prisoners there, Jews for the most part. They were dispatched on what has come to be known as death marches. Men, women and children were all forced to walk for miles in the bitter cold, and when some children slowed down they were taken away and done away with. Sickly prisoners were left to die. Others too, in due course, were to die in unimaginable ways. The ensuing atrocities were so horrible, so abominable, and such an affront to humanity, it is hard to imagine they were perpetrated.

This is not the place to recount the gory details of all that happened then because they are too excruciating and numbing even in their recall. Frequent reference to the atrocities that one group of people inflicted on another—on the basis or race or religion or minority status or whatever—is not always healthy, for in the process we evoke anger and outrage and group resentment; and we inspire a spirit of vengeance or a lingering hatred between groups.

Yet, it would be unwise to shove it all under the rug, as the expression goes. Indeed, recent history shows that there are forces to this day in several pockets of the world which are scheming or wishing for the revival of such hate-filled atrocities against this or that group. So we have coined the ugly term ethnic-cleansing: a monstrous mode by which large numbers of human beings, men and women, old and young, toddlers and babies, are brutally slaughtered on the basis of their tribal, religious, or racial affiliation.

We need to speak in general terms about the variety and virulence of Man's inhumanity to Man in such contexts, provoked often by political or economic urgencies, or by hurtful illusions of collective superiority or self-righteous religious disdain of others. We need to tell our children that such behavior deserves to be held in contempt, condemned and cursed, and must be severely punished.

Much as we trust the innate goodness of human beings, it would be naïve to imagine that the days of monstrous madness are gone. If history is any lesson, in every generation there arise charismatic individuals whose minds are warped and whose hearts are poisoned with hate. If and when they come to power, not one but a thousand innocents fall prey to madness. To avert disasters from future Genghis Khans and Hitlers, we need more than education in science and history. We must indoctrinate the young in humane and humanistic values and we need to condition growing minds in an enlightened ethical framework such as may be drawn from the noblest elements of our humanity's religious heritage. This is far more urgent that debates on whether the Scriptures and Science are compatible or diverging.

From the World of Science:
CASPAR FRIEDRICH WOLFF

There was a time when people spoke of *homunculi*: little human beings, microscospic in size which resulted from the fusion of sperm and egg, which grew and grew and became so big they were ejected from the mother's womb. The word *embryo* originally meant simply a young animal (in the womb). It was derived from a Greek word which means to swell or be full. This was the scientific equivalent of the idea that God created man: face, body, limbs and all, as a full-formed creature in His image. It was in this framework that Marcus Aurelius wrote: "Mark how fleeting and paltry is the estate of man: yesterday an embryo, tomorrow a mummy or ashes."

Equipped with the knowledge that derives from basic courses in biology, most people brush off the idea of a miniature man in the uterus, gradually expanding in size, growing like a photograph which is being enlarged to visible dimensions from a tiny film. We can't even imagine such a thing. In years long past this notion of completed minuscule creatures bulging to become babies used to be called the theory of *performation*. During much of the 18th century, the term *evolution* meant the gradual development of preexisting organs of the embryo: something very different from what it connotes today.

In 1759, a young medical student at the University of Halle by the name of Caspar Friedrich Wolff (born: 18 January 1734), published a dissertation entitled *Theoria Generationis*. In this, he rejected the theory of performation which was held by many eminent scientists, and thus incurred their displeasure. As a result, he wasn't allowed to lecture at the University of Berlin. Rather than be intimidated, Wolff went ahead and published a book in 1764, entitled Theorie von der Generation, expanding further on his original idea. His work gave scientific credibility to the notion of epigenesis: development from what seems to be a homogenous state to a very heterogeneous one. His work brought him some fame beyond his Germany, and he was invited to the newly established scientific academy in St. Petersburg. The Russian Empress Catherine II who founded this institution, used to import scientists from Western Europe during the 18th century, somewhat as the U.S. started doing in the 20th century from all over the world. Wolff felt so satisfied in St. Petersburg that he became a Russian citizen.

Wolff's view that there is a gradual development of the organism, plant or animal, from its initial formation, was based on careful studies of plants and unhatched chicks. His explanations on how this development occurs involve ideas no longer acceptable, and though it took several decades and translations before his insight came to be universally recognized, he is now considered to be the founder of modern scientific embryology. Students of anatomy have heard the term Wolffian body.

It was only after a few decades, and as a result of further work by a few others, that Wolff's ideas began to gain universal acceptance in the mainstream of science.

Such is the progress of science: not always smooth or easy for those who bring about major shifts in our views about how the world behaves. The word of authority, be it of individuals or of institutions, can be quite strong even in the march of science whose avowed goal is truth about how the world functions. But that quest is carried out in well defined frameworks, under clear cut parameters in different fields. Making breakthroughs and discoveries within the existing framework in terms of the generally accepted parameters is fine. But if and when one tries to change these, the task becomes horrendously difficult. Yet, and this is strength of science, sooner or later, as a Hindu maxim declares, *satyam eva jay-ate*: Truth alone will win.

January 19

From the world of Religion: DOGEN KIGEN

He lived in the 13th century, was from Japan, and went to China where he was initiated into Buddhism by a Chinese master. He returned to his native land and wrote a work called Shobogenzo which has been called a masterpiece of Zen Buddhism. His name was Dogen Kigen.

Buddhism trains its sages in monasteries. So Dogen Kigen decided to found one. It attracted many aspirants, both men and women.

The ultimate goal of spiritual exercises is to become aware of a Reality that is not apparent in the course of ordinary living. This awareness-acquisition is called awakening.

How is this to be achieved? Various processes have been prescribed. Different yoga and meditation techniques are meant for this. One of these is called *shikon taza*: sitting only. The idea is, rather than be engaged in all kinds of rituals and ceremonies, one must do nothing but meditate. There must be but one mode, as awakening involves the awareness of Oneness.

Another method in this system is known as *shinjin datsuraku*. It means, literally, the giving up of body-mind. This is to convey a physical and metaphysical emptiness whose experience will be the awakening. In this state there is no awareness of the self. Everything one does is integrated with happenings in the world at large.

All this is part of Zen Buddhism which is not a religion but a mode by which life is said to be experienced in its deeper fullness. Our everyday experiences are filled with dualities, with contradictions and complementarities, dichotomies and dilemmas. These can be philosophically intriguing, metaphysically confusing, and practically frustrating. Zazen is a technique by which one sees, recognizes, and experiences unity behind and beneath all the conflicts and diversity. In that state of understanding, one is freed of all anxieties and stresses that make life difficult to cope with. And when the awakening occurs, say the masters, there is perfect peace: this is the state of *samadhi*. It is indeed the ultimate goal of spiritual seekers.

To those unfamiliar with the framework of meditation and mysticism, all this may sound arcane, if not absurd. But it is good to remember that when one begins to reflect on the meaning and nature of this fleeting flicker called consciousness, all sorts of puzzles arise. There has always been a search for an understanding of who we really are in this vast and long lasting Cosmos, how and why we came to be, not just as complex molecules subject to biochemistry and neurophysiology, but as experiencing entities, cast on earth for a few fast-moving years, and then disappearing for eternity. This search has led many seekers to apprehend a level of Reality that is beyond the spatio-temporal and the material-energetic. Many cultures and civilizations have been built on such findings, and they still hold sway on the human psyche. The sacraments of religions to celebrate birth and before, and to commemorate death and beyond may not be mere fantasies of a less illumined world. They could well be echoes of a distant past of the human race when the sheer primitiveness of our ancestors enabled them to become aware of aspects of the experienced world that, to us, are as dim and opaque as our quantum field theory and double helix would have been to them.

So, as Dogen Kigen, the greatest Japanese master of Zen, told his disciples, "If you keep your fists closed, you will obtain only a few grains of sand. But if you open your hands, you will obtain all the sand in the desert."

From the World of Science: JAMES WATT

Technology is essentially the harnessing of the forces of nature to transform matter and energy from one (unwieldy) state to another (usable) one. This has been going on since ancient times, when the first spark of fire was lit, when flint was sharpened, and the wheel fashioned. But a major thrust to this occurred in the closing years of the 17th century when the first steam pumps were devised, and by the first quarter of the 18th century simple steam engines with cylinders and pistons were widely used in England.

It was only much later in that century that significantly more efficient steam engines were made with significant improvements. Undreamed of consequences flowed from these changes in the older steam engines; changes which were brought about by the Scottish inventor James Watt (born: 19 January, 1736).

As a youth, aside from studying Greek and Latin and some geometry, Watt learned quite a bit from what we call hands-on experience by applying himself to such practical fields as metalworking, smithy, and instrument making. He spent a year in London as an apprentice, getting more acquainted with scientific instruments. Upon returning to Glasgow he managed to get a position as an instrument maker at the university where he came in contact with the eminent physicist Joseph Black.

Watt's main mission in life was almost thrust into his hands in the mid 1760s when the demonstration model of what used to be called an atmospheric engine was given to him for some repair work. Watt quickly discovered how inefficient the contraption was, and he wanted to make modifications which would result in a much better engine. His efforts led him to the idea of a condenser. Little by little, Watt kept improving his models, and finally came up with several versions of steam engines that were sold to industries. But it took a few more years before this was applied to the steam locomotive.

Today, looking at the popping lid of a pan with boiling water, it should seem obvious to anyone that steam can cause something to move. Harnessing the power for locomotion without the benefit of muscular power of man or beast would have sounded fantastic, if not preposterous to most people in the eighteenth century. At one time, even Watt would not have believed that steam could be used to pull a train some day. It was only by the first decade of the 19th century that this was achieved.

Watt was more of an inventor than a scientist, but his invention spurred theoretical science. Indeed the rich field of thermodynamics began with a theoretical analysis of the efficiency of steam engines. During much of the 19th century pure science and technology developed more or less independently, only slightly helping or influencing each other.

Emerson said, not without a touch of humor that "It was Watt who told King George III that he dealt with an article of which kings were said to be fond— Power." The concept of *power* means something very different to a physicist from what it means to an administrator or a politician. We are familiar with expressions like "More power to him!" and "power-hungry politicians." But Watt defined power as a the technical term by introducing the notion of the horsepower. But much later, the international scientific community decided to call the unit of power (the rate at which energy is consumed or expended) the watt. Today he is remembered in every lamp and appliance because of that unit. The next time we get our electric bill let us pause and notice how much energy we have used in terms of kilowatt-hours, and let us remember James Watt of more than two hundred years ago.

January 20

From the World of Religion:
WORLD RELIGION DAY

The world of religion faces two major challenges: One is to reconcile its explana-tory dimensions with the findings of modern science. Theologians within various traditions attempt to resolve this in their different ways. The second arises from the existence of multiple religious traditions with different views, interpretations, and visions as to the role, relevance, and nature of Human life and the Divine.

One may envisage three possible solutions for the second problem: The first, is to silence those who hold on to different (mistaken) doctrines. In former cen-turies, this was carried out with partial success. Today this is still being practiced in some countries. The second is to argue that essentially all religions say the same noble truths, though with different metaphors and mythologies. Allowing for some exaggerations and well-meaning distortions of facts, one can maintain such a thesis for the sake of peace. But the real practitioners know deep in their hearts that this is not really true. The third and most realistic alternative is to grant everyone their choice of what constitutes true religion, while being faithful to one's own tradition.

It is in the spirit of this last approach that that the 20 January 2002 (the third Sunday of the Gregorian calendrical year) was declared by the Bahai community as World Religion Day. In this context, the I wrote the following at the Cape of Good Hope while attending the Third Parliament of World Religions in December 1999.

Universal Reflection

> In striving to recognize the primacy of Fire and Light,
> I feel kinship with my Zoroastrian brothers and sisters.
> In striving to obey the Ten Commandments,
> I feel kinship with my Jewish brothers and sisters.
> In striving to be kind to neighbor and the needy,
> I feel kinship with my Christian brothers and sisters.
> In striving to be compassionate to creatures great and small,
> I feel kinship with my Buddhist—Jaina brothers and sisters.
> In striving to surrender myself completely to God Almighty,
> I feel kinship with my Muslim brothers and sisters.
> In the recognition that wisdom flows from enlightened masters,

I feel kinship with my Sikh brothers and sisters.
In remembering that serving people should be the goal of religion,
I feel kinship with my Bahai brothers and sisters.
In my respect and reverence for Nature that sustains us,
I feel kinship with my Native American brothers and sisters.
In feeling that these and more are all paths to the same Divinity,
I feel kinship with my Hindu brothers and sisters.
In my love and laughter, joy and pain,
I feel kinship with all my fellow humans.
In my need for nourishment and instinct to live on,
I feel kinship with all beings on the planet.
In my spiritual ecstasy with this wondrous world,
I feel kinship with the Cosmic Whole.

From the World of Science:
BÉGUYER DE CHANCOURTOIS

Consider the endless variety of substances in the material world: water, iron, gold, milk, glass, air, and many more, each with its own specific properties. One can go on and on with the list. Scientists have enriched the list of naturally occurring substances by synthesizing new ones in the laboratory. They have studied and catalogued more than four million of them. And they continue to introduce new substances year after year.

The variety of substances may be divided into two broad categories: Those which can be analyzed chemically into simpler and different components; and those which cannot be SO ANALYSED. The former are called (chemical) compounds; and the latter, elements. Water, sand and salt are examples of compounds. Oxygen, carbon and mercury are examples of elements.

There are some 94 different elements in our part of the universe. Human ingenuity has concocted a dozen more. These elements are grouped into several families on the basis of their properties. Such a classification leads to what is known as the Periodic Table of Elements. In the Periodic Chart each element is represented by letter symbols. Thus, H stands for hydrogen, C for carbon, Zn for zinc, and Cl for chlorine. Some symbols, such as Na for sodium, Ag for silver, and Fe for iron, arise from their Latin names (*natrium*, *argentum* and *ferrum* respectively).

Combinations among different elements in well defined proportions result in countless different compounds that are found or made in the physical world. The processes by which compounds are formed from elements are called chemical reactions. Chemical reactions are taking place incessantly in nature. They are invariably associated with the absorption or release of energy.

Many have learned this in chemistry classes. The creation of the periodic table has a fascinating history. For instance, the notion of periodicity implies recurrences, which introduces the idea of a circle. But since elements grow increasingly heavy as we move from the lightest, hydrogen, to heavier ones like sodium and iron. It occurred to Béguyer de Chancourtois (born: 20 January 1820) that it would be a good idea to arrange the elements on a circle that is evolving in height, like a spiral on a cylinder.

In fact, he took a cylinder whose base was punctuated by sixteen equi-spaced points and drew a helical curve on the surface of the cylinder, specifying points on them in such a way that the 17th point was right above the 1st, the 18th above the second, etc. This was the very first explicit representation of the periodicities of elements. De Chancourtois was a professional geologist, and he presented his model of the telluric screw (as he called it) in 1862, but it did not attract the attention of chemists as much as the works of John Newlands, Lothar Meyer and Dmitri Mendeleev.

Incidentally, Chancourtois also tried to develop a universal alphabet: a more realistic ambition than that of inventing a universal language.

At least two features of the scientific enterprise stand out in the recall of Chancourtois's efforts. First, classification and ingenious arrangement of data play a very important role in the development of science. They are essential before one can develop theories to explain observed phenomena, but they are not sufficient. In fact, many ancient scientists were adepts at classification, but they did not go much farther. Secondly, as science was getting more and more specialized in the 19th century, it was very difficult for workers in one field to gain the respect or attention of experts in a different field. This situation has become even more severe in our own times.

January 21

From the World of Religion: SAINT AGNES

She is probably the youngest one ever to have been beatified. Her name was Agnes, a gentle lass who had been inspired by her devotion to Christ at a very tender age, even as another young woman by the name of Meera was drawn to Krishna in another period and in another land.

We don't know much about her, except that she must have lived before the 4th century, for writers from this time on make fond references to her.

When it was declared illegal to call oneself a Christian, she did precisely that. She received many threats, but she did not swerve from her devotion to Christ.

They wanted to parade her through the streets and throw her into fire. She did not mind. She wanted only to veil her face from the stare of the crowd for she felt her chastity would be soiled by the lustful look of some. On this she was very particular: She would have nothing of carnal pleasures, she wanted to be pure in the religious sense.

But she was a beautiful maiden, and many young men would have willingly taken her as a bride. She would refuse, insisting like the Hindu Meera insisted with respect to Krishna, Jesus alone was her Spouse.

Then there was the son of the Governor by the name of Procop. He became very enamored of her. He gave her gifts and promised more, and wanted to marry her. She rejected him too, saying she was promised to the Lord of the Universe who was brighter even than the sun and the stars. Procop became furious and told his father this was a Christian woman, which was a serious charge in those days.

The governor tried to persuade her with more gifts, but to no avail. He ordered her to be chained, but she did not relent. He sent her to a heartless judge, an evil one, who condemned her to stay in a brothel: those were terrible days. It is said that when Roman youths went to that sinful place while Agnes was there, they were transformed at once, and henceforth treated her with reverence. And when one of them approached her with evil intent, he was blinded and flung to the floor as if struck by a lightning. But by her blessing he got back his sight.

Now the people in power became furious, and they condemned her to die. Little Agnes simply smiled, and willingly accepted death. So it was that she became a martyr, when barely eleven or twelve. It is said that she was decapitated, as they used to slaughter animals as sacrifice for God. This was a common mode of execution in those days, giving rise to the term capital (of the head) punishment.

Her feast day is 21 January. There is a custom by which monks give two lambs to Benedictine nuns on this day, to be reared as pets. The lambs are brought in a basket adorned with red and white flowers to symbolize martyrdom and purity. During the festal Mass girls in white dress and veils carry lambs which are blessed and sent to the Pope.

The lamb was an animal used for slaughter in even in Biblical times, as we read in Jeremiah: "I was like a lamb or an ox that is brought to the slaughter." Yet, the lamb stands for gentleness, tenderness, and innocence. We read in John, "Behold the Lamb of God." Agnes, the youngest saint of all, as gentle and innocent too. *Agnes* means *lamb* in Latin.]

This is the story of Saint Agnes. Dissect it with the investigating microscope, and like other legends, it too will become hollow: history of questionable authenticity or tales of sheer imagination. But it carries the weight of centuries and the poetry of traditions, and for these alone they are worth preserving.

From the World of Science:
SOPHIA LOUISA JEX-BLAKE

Those who are fortunate to be part of an enlightened phase in society are sometimes shocked by the backwardness in the thinking of people in some other societies. Thus, the suppression and oppression of women in some regions of the world strike us as terrible. When asked about these, leaders and thinkers in non-Western societies quickly become defensive and they try to explain away the injustices and the absurdities as being really benignly motivated, not as terrible as ill-informed outsiders appraise them, and that in fact, their traditions and scriptures give a far higher position to women than in the so-called modernized societies. This, of course, is the best way of perpetuating ancient horrors. What such thinking fails to understand is that by defending wrongs one cannot bring about positive changes.

We also need to remember that enlightenment has not always been there in the West either. It has been a gradual and difficult struggle for women (and other oppressed minorities) to find their legitimate place in Western societies and nations.

Consider, for example, the plight of Sophia Louisa Jex-Blake (born: 21 January 1840) from England. When she wanted to enter college she encountered some resistance from her own father. As a devout Christian, father Jex-Blake, though a physician himself, honestly believed that women ought not to be going to college, though he could not have spotted where in the Scriptures it was so ordained. Somehow, Sophia managed to enter Queen's College for Women where she studied enough mathematics to become a tutor.

Later, she came to the United States where she met a woman physician. Conversations with her inspired Sophia to take up the medical profession: an idea which had never occurred to her before.

So, upon returning to her native England, Sophia tried to do the needful to join a medical college. She quickly discovered, much to her surprise, that as a woman she simply had no right to become a doctor. This was in the 1860s. So, she went on to Edinburgh University where she was allowed take courses in medicine. There, she experienced much unpleasantness: fellow male students were certainly not welcoming. some of them even protested her presence. When she finished the courses successfully, the university wouldn't grant her a degree because it was against the rules to give a woman a physician's license.

Much angered by this, Sophia Louisa Jex-Blake brought her case to public attention. Some politicians took up her cause, but it took a few years for the British Parliament to finally pass a bill in 1876 that would permit women to become physicians. Sophia went on to Switzerland and then to Ireland to work before she was accepted as a full-fledged doctor in England. The Irish College of Physicians was the first medical institution in Great Britain to open its doors to women students, and this was barely a hundred and twenty-five years ago.

Jex-Blake had other struggles in her career but she worked hard and doggedly for women's rights and for women's suffrage. She was involved in the establishment of the London School of Medicine for Women.

It is thanks to people like her and to a few enlightened men who were supportive of the cause, that the unconscionable hurdles and deep-set prejudices against women and other groups began to slowly attenuate, though they have not yet been completely eradicated. Enlightened thinking, like scientific knowledge, unfortunately does not spread as easily or as rapidly as technology and fast foods.

January 22

From the World of Religion: TIMOTHY

It is said that this "dear and faithful child of the Lord," as Saint Paul called him, was by nature shy and reserved. He is known in hagiography as the constant companion of Paul for well over a decade and a half. Paul had full trust in him when he sent him on missions, for he was known to be a selfless man whose sole interest was in the spread of Christianity. He is believed to have been in poor health, but this did not deter or soften his determination to work for Christ. His name was Timothy (Timotheus), meaning the Honor of God.

Much of what we know about Saint Timothy is from the Bible. It is said that when Paul came to Lystra, Timothy's native town, he was stoned and left bleeding on the street. Timothy came to tend to Paul, at grave risk to his own life. Little by little, Paul won over more and more people to the Christian faith, and became a leader among them.

When Paul went to preach in Ephesus, a great city of ancient times, where even Mary, mother of Christ, is said to have gone with Paul, Timothy was one of his principal assistants. It was through him that Paul sent his letters which have become immortal in the Christian framework. At one point, Timothy was sent to Ephesus as Paul's representative.

The people in Ephesus were practicing in those days the ancient cult of Artemis: the Greek goddess of fertility and nature. They had built a magnificent temple for her, a masterpiece in marble. It is said that the temple was begun sometime in the seventh century BCE. It used to be listed among the Wonders of the World. People who came to worship the goddess brought gifts of gold and ivory. They also rejoiced and regaled in her name. The story goes that in 356 BCE a demented man burned the temple down so that he might be remembered in history.

But the cult of Artemis did not die. It persisted and thrived with even greater vigor. This was a major problem for Paul: to uproot this time-honored tradition and replace it with the religion of Christ. Indeed, this is a most fascinating process in history: the gradual transformation of a people from one religion to another. The great-great grandparents of many Christians were pagans, the ancestors of many Muslims in the Indian subcontinent were Hindu. Such changes are occurring even in our own times.

Later, in his epistles to Timothy, Paul urged him to continue to preach and to convert, explaining all the obstacles, opposition and resistance he could expect. After Paul became a martyr, Timothy turned to John the Evangelist as his guru. When the latter was forced into exile from Ephesus, Timothy became bishop there. According to one version, the non-Christians attacked him without any provocation, and killed him. The fourth century bishop Eusebius, described it this way: On the 22 of January of the year 97, Ephesians were celebrating Katagogian, their festival to honor Artemis. Timothy, who had a tendency to be very strict about these matters, and had no sympathy for pagan gods, was very upset by what he saw. He simply could not stand such licentious ribaldry in the name of a heathen goddess. Driven by his religious zeal, and somewhat impetuously, he tried to stop the frenzied revelers. The mob did not appreciate this, and became furious. They stoned the godly man to death.

Timothy thus became a martyr also, like his master Paul. His relics were moved eventually to Constantinople where they were placed along side with those of St. Luke and St. Andrews.

From the World of Science:
ANDRÉ MARIE AMPÈRE

The flow of water may form a slender stream or a mighty river: it is water in motion, often from a higher to a lower level. So too, the flow of electric charges could be a slender stream or a mighty river of electricity. We call it an electric current. (*Current* comes from a word which means to run.)

We have all seen on a dial in the dashboard of the car the letters AMP, and we know that it is a measure of the electric current, and is to be read fully as ampères. Some of us, unfamiliar with physics, may wonder why it has this name.

The convention of naming physical quantities after scientists may strike some as the scientific equivalent of ancestor worship. Actually it is a mode of remembering and honoring those who have contributed to the advancement of scientific knowledge.

André Marie Ampère (born: 22 January 1775) was an exceptionally brilliant child who mastered mathematics as easily as Latin, and had an insatiable thirst for knowledge. Botany appealed to him as much as poetry and history, but mathematics attracted him most of all. Upon discovering that the great mathematician Euler had written most of his papers in Latin, Ampère began a thorough study of the language, mastered it well enough to read Euler (most of whose work is in Latin), but also to compose poems in Latin.

In September 1820 Ampère became aware of the observation of the Danish physicist Hans Christian Oersted, that a magnetic needle was affected when current flowed in a nearby wire. He started investigating this, and presented a paper to the French Academy of Sciences a week later, presenting a thorough analysis of the phenomenon. He showed that the needle deflections reversed if the current flowed in the opposite direction. With this, Ampère opened up the field of electromagnetism. He wrote more papers on the subject in the weeks that followed. Then, many more physicists pursued these ideas. Their combined efforts created one of the most revealing and fruitful fields of physics.

During the next several years, Ampère arrived at more results, such as: two wires carrying currents sometimes attract each other, sometimes repel each other. This led him to the notion of direction of current in a wire. He introduced the convention that current always flows from the positive to the negative pole of a battery. Ampère formulated the actions between electric currents and magnetic effects in terms of mathematical formulas. He quantified electric currents, which is one reason the unit of current has been named after him. But he also introduced new ideas, not all of which turned out to be appealing. His mathematical formulation wasn't very clear to the other scientific giant of the period, Michael Faraday, who was not as versed in abstract mathematics.

Ampère's work led to the precise relationships between currents in wires of various geometrical forms and the magnetic fields they produce. We know today that ultimately all magnetic fields arise from electric currents (moving electric charges). He also wrote a book on the game of chance which showed with mathematical reasoning what anyone with common sense ought to know: that a repeated gambler will lose in the long run.

In his earlier years Ampère had been very much affected by the death of his father who was guillotined for political reasons, and that of his wife who passed away prematurely. In his later years he turned to poetry and philosophy.

Ampère was a very sensitive and deeply religious person. He found convincing evidence for the existence of God in the harmony of the laws of nature. Gifted he certainly was, and creative and successful. Yet, the disappointments in his life made him an unhappy man.

January 23

From the World of Religion: CONFUCIUS

As per tradition, Confucius (6th century BCE) was born in the country of Lu. After traveling widely he returned to his native place where he became a very respected teacher. When his country got into a war and was defeated, Confucius followed the ruler, Duke Zhao, who had to flee. He also spent some years as an itinerant philosopher, taking his disciples along with him. He prized good conduct above money or things. He never held a high position, and died at the age of 72.

Though he began with only a few disciples, during his life Confucius gathered thousands under his fold. Tseng Tzu, a great humanist, has left behind some of the teachings of the Master. Confucius sought unity behind diversity, preached dispassionate inquiry, virtue and wisdom. He recommended careful investigation, furtherance of knowledge, regulation of family, and striving for peace among nations. As with Jesus and Buddha, the words of Confucius touched millions living beyond his place and time.

Confucianism is primarily concerned with ethics. Moral law should be the basis of behavior. It has the same inexorable power as physical law is to nature. Confucius said: "The moral law is a law from whose operation we cannot escape for one instant in the course of our existence. A law from which we may escape is not a moral law." The key-term Li in Confucian thought refers to a system governed by ethical principles.

In the re-writing of ancient wisdom many things change. So too it has been with Confucius. Neo-Confucian versions of his writings have parallels with Western metaphysics. They talk about dispassionate inquiry which does not seem to have been there in earlier Confucian writings. Neo-Confucianism shows a sensitivity to the wonders of the world. The sun and the stars as well as the trees and the mountains move one to philosophical reflection, if not to scientific analysis. Confucius is reported to have said: "Nature is vast, deep, high, intelligent, infinite, and eternal. The heaven appearing before us is only this bright, shining mass. But in its immeasurable extent, the sun, the moon, the stars and constellations are suspended, and all things are embraced under it. The earth, appearing before us, is but a handful of soil. But in its breadth and depth, it sustains mighty mountains without feeling their weight. Rivers and seas dash against it without causing it to leak. The mountain appearing before us is only a mass of rock. But in all the vastness of its size, grass and vegetation grow upon it, birds and beasts dwell on it, and treasures of precious minerals are found in it. The water appearing before us is but a spoonful of liquid. But in all its unfathomable depths the largest crustaceans, dragons, fish, and turtles are produced in them, and all useful products around them."

Meaningful reflections rather than logical explanations is what distinguishes philosophy from science. Explanation without reflection would be meaningless. Reflection without explanation would be fruitless. Hence the importance of both philosophy and science in the human quest.

During the ups and downs of dynastic upheavals, Confucianism was periodically eclipsed. Competing worldviews sometimes encroached upon his teachings. In the long run, like sturdy grass on plush lawn, Confucianism survived. Hundreds of commentators, lay and learned, have written on what the Master taught. Confucian philosophy is entirely human, it never dabbles in murky metaphysics. It expresses basic truths in simple terms. Eventually, Confucius met the fate of other thinkers who spoke insightfully on the human condition: He was deified by the devout, and even came to be worshipped in temples. As no specific day is known for him, we might as well remember him on January 23.

From the World of Science: HIDEKI YUKAWA

Matter, we all know, is made up of molecules, and molecules are made up of atoms. Atoms are made up of a central core and orbiting electrons. The central core of atoms is called the nucleus. The atomic nucleus is known to consist of positively charged entities called protons, and neutral ones called neutrons.

Careful experiments show that these constituents of the nucleus (generally called nucleons) are tightly bound together. What this means is that they cannot be easily separated from one another. They are, as it were, tightly glued together. Physicists describe this by saying that they are bound together by a very strong mutual force or interaction. The existence for such a strong nuclear force was discovered in the 1930s. Until then physicists had known of only two other universal forces: gravitation and electromagnetism, and there were clues of a third one called the weak force

In the conceptual framework of quantum mechanics (quantum field theory, to be more exact), the interaction between electric charges involves the exchange of electro-magnetic energy bundles: these are the so-called photons. We say that photons are the field particles of the electromagnetic field.

It occurred to a young theoretical physicist that strong interaction must also involve a similar exchange of particles between the nucleons. The physicist was Hideki Yukawa (born: 23 January 1907). As per convention, the name is from his mother's family.

Yukawa set out to explore the nature of such an exchange particle. He probed into this on the basis of all the known properties of the strong force, such as had been unraveled by experimental physicists. He could roughly compute, for example, what should be the bases of such particles, what kind of electric charges they would carry, what spin property they should have, etc. Since the estimated mass was somewhat between the mass of the electron and that of the proton, these Yukawa-particles (as they were once referred to) came to be called *mesons* (from the Greek for middle). Today, the word refers to a whole class of fundamental particles.

Such particles were experimentally discovered in 1936 in cosmic rays, which caused great excitement in the world of physics. However, those particles were found to have properties which are quite different from what Yukawa's theory had predicted. This puzzle was resolved when it was realized that the Yukawa particles, now called *pions* (or pi mesons) quickly decay into another type of particles (called *muons*) which were observed in cosmic rays.

In the current framework of physics, there are four fundamental interactions at our level: the gravitational, the electromagnetic, the weak, and the strong: each characterized by its one field particles. The field particle of the nuclear strong force, namely the pion of Yukawa, is itself made up of a quark and an anti-quark. Quarks are among the ultimate constituents of all matter.

In 1949 Yukawa received the Nobel Prize for Physics for this work which is at the basis of quantum field theory for strong interaction. He was the second Asian physicist to receive this honor: C. V. Raman was the first one in 1930. These were defining moments in the history of modern science which was fast crossing its Euro-defined borders.

Yukawa founded a prestigious international journal in Japan, called Progress of Theoretical Physics. He also became the first director of the Research Institute for Fundamental Physics in Kyoto.

January 24

From the World of Religion:
SAINT SAMBANDHAR

Saint Sambandhar is one of the most revered poets of the Tamils. He lived in the 7th century. His works turned the tide of Tamil religious trends from Jainism back to Shaivite Hinduism. He is known as the Sambandar of Holy Wisdom (*Thiru-gnyaana-sambandhar*).

According to tradition, when he was barely three, Sambandhar was left one day alone on the bank of the temple pond while his father was taking a dip. The child felt abandoned and cried, whereupon the deity Shiva responded, asking his consort Parvati to give the child some milk. Sambandhar imbibed this divine milk of spiritual wisdom, and became enlightened at once.

When the father came back and saw milk dripping from his child's mouth, he became furious and demanded to know who had given the milk. The little child is said to have answered in beautiful Tamil verse:

He with ear-rings Who rides on the Bull that's sacred,
He with the crescent on top, and with ash on his body spread,
The One Who blessed Brahma, has taken my heart away:
This Lord of Pirammapuram: the place where we stay.

This crude translation does little justice to the mystical grandeur of the original.

This is the first verse of the classic work known as Thevaaram, of which Panniru Thirumurai is the beginning. Each of the verses here has a superficial as well as a profound esoteric meaning. There are references in the verses to episodes from Hindu sacred history, such as the defeat of the demonic Raavana by Shiva. The poem refers to Jaina atheism. The poet describes Lord Shiva as a strict father and Parvati as a loving mother in the spiritual quest of the aspirant. In another poem Sambandhar says that it isn't necessary to renounce the world. Simply choosing the path of Shiva will liberate us.

People were amazed by the child's poetic outpouring. They bowed to the little one, asked him to visit their village. For many years, Sambandhar traveled from one place of pilgrimage to another, composing poems everywhere.

When he was invested with the sacred thread, Sambandhar chose to repeat the pentasyllable Namashivaaya (Prostrations to Lord Shiva) rather than the traditional gayatri mantra. Namashivaaya is the primary mantra in the Shaiva Sidhdhaanta tradition.

At one time the queen of Madurai invited Sambandhar to her kingdom to persuade her husband to give up Jainism and become a Hindu. Sambandhar is said to have succeeded in this with powerful poetry. Many other miracles are also attributed to him.

Sambandhar was a major poet of the Shaiva Sidhdhaanta tradition: a rich spiritual framework based on unconditional devotion to Shiva. Here God is called *pathi* (Lord), creatures are called *pasu*, and *paasam* is bondage to life. The bondage results from a sense of a separate Self or ego (aanavam), actions and consequences (kanamam), and the illusion of reality (maayai). Pasu is condemned to be with paasam, but when pathi comes to pasu, all the paasam melts away. This notion is expounded in many verses. This would be the equivalent of attaining grace and being freed of all sins, in the Christian tradition.

When Sambandhar was sixteen they chose a bride for him, daughter of a Brahmin in the town of Nellur. But he pleaded with God to shield him from carnal cravings. He recited a song he had composed earlier to thank the Lord for that blessing. Then, they say, Sambandhar, his bride, and all the people assembled, vanished in a fiery effulgence, never to be seen again.

From the World of Science:
FERDINAND J. COHN

Consider the stupendous richness of the vegetable kingdom with its endless variety of plants and trees. Some plants have seeds and flowers, some don't. These latter are known as cryptogamia: literally hidden marriage. They include fungi and algae. Anyone who has waded in the waters of the ocean or even a dirty pond has encountered algae. The word *alga* simply means seaweed in Latin. The University Herbarium of the University of California informs us that an index of them could contain some 200,000 algae names. Some algae are harmful to humans, some are useful as food, and many are threatened with extinction.

If it is awkward for people to think that we have something in common with the chimp, it must be even more shocking to be told that essentially there is not much difference between the cell of a noble human being and that of a lowly alga. This is not unlike the fact that the same ink may be used by a child to scribble a labyrinth of lines or by an artist to draw a magnificent scenery.

We have come to know this as a result of the careful observations of Ferdinand J. Cohn (born: 24 January 1828).

By the middle of the 19th century, it had been established that there is in every cell something called the protoplasm. This was regarded as the basis of all living organisms. [The notion and role of the protoplasm were better understood by the close of the 19th century.]

It was thought at the time that there was a fundamental difference between the protoplasm of a plant and that of an animal. When Cohn studied the one-celled alga called *protococcus pluvialis*, he discovered remarkable similarities between the cell of this plant and that of animals. It became clear that the unity of life IS included both plants and animals: an idea that was very much in the air already. Cohn's observations with the microscope showed that the contractile content in plant cells was very much like that in animal cells.

Aside from exploring the sexuality of algae, Cohn also studied bacteria. He made a classification of bacteria as a function of their forms [SHAPES?]: round, short cylindrical, thread-like, and spiral. [Edwin Hubble was to do this for galaxies some fifty years later.]

Cohn showed, contrary to the then current belief, that bacteria belong to the plant kingdom, rather than to the animal. His definition of bacteria became classic: "chlorophyll-free cells of (various) forms, which multiply exclusively by transverse division and occur either isolated or in cell families." He showed that bacteria derived nitrogen from compounds of ammonia and carbohydrates. He also discovered the reproductive bodies of organisms like algae and fungi: what are called spores today; this was a major step in clarifying the spontaneous generation controversy. His researches revealed the distinction between putrefying and pathogenic bacteria. His work on bacteria is so fundamental that he is regarded as the founder of microbiology. Cohn established the first research center for the study of plant physiology (in Breslau, Poland), and founded a journal for the biology of plants. (*Beitraege zur Biologie der Pflanzen*).

Though he was a precocious child and did outstanding work at the university, Cohn was not admitted into a doctoral program at the university in Breslau because he was Jewish. This turned out to be a blessing, because it prompted him to go to the University of Berlin in 1846 where he received his doctorate and came in contact with some outstanding scientists. Eventually he was declared an honorary citizen of Breslau.

January 25

From the World of Religion: AJINATH DAY

Jainism is one of the four major religious traditions of the Indian subcontinent. It dates back to the fifth century BCE, but its followers hold that aside from its historical founder, Vardhamana Mahavira, the system owes its existence to twenty four founders, known as Thirthankaras, and that Maha Vira was the last of these. The first Tirthankara was called Rishabha to whom the vision of Non-violence first arose The 23rd was Parsva, born two centuries before Mahavira. The Thirthankaras are also called Jainas: the Victorious Ones, for they had conquered the bondages of life. This is the origin of the name Jainism.

There is a vast corpus of Jaina literature, which includes forty-five sacred works called Agamas. Classical Jaina writings include philosophical and scientific speculations about the nature of matter and mind. Jaina thinkers propounded the thesis of *anekanta-vada*: doctrine of multiplicity, according to which any issue can be considered from a variety of perspectives, each leading to a different conclusion. The common example is the description of the elephant by six blind men, each thinking, on the basis of his own observation, that the elephant is like a rope, a wall, a pillar, etc. Related to this is *asti-nasti-vaada*: is-and-is-not-doctrine by which a statement and its opposite might both be correct, again depending on one's perspective. Thus, both the following two propositions may be true: (a) There is a God; (b) There is no God.

Perhaps the most important tenet of Jainism is ahimsa: non injury. By this is meant, not only the non-hurting of fellow humans, but also abstention from injury to, and respect for, all creatures great and small. Some have even suggested that ahimsa should include love for all creatures. Jains are meticulous vegetarians, often eating only fruits and vegetables that fall off from trees and plants. They refrain from lighting fires for fear that unwittingly insects will fall into it. Whether practicable or not, this is surely a very enlightened ethical principle: To care and be compassionate towards all beings, not just to family and friends, or only to fellow humans.

In principle, Jainism recommends simple life, bordering on asceticism. Yet, Jains are among the most industrious and wealthy communities within India and beyond. Their places of worship, often grand and colorful, with abundant marble and rich architecture, are a delight to visit, and they reflect considerable financial resources.

The second Thirthankara was called Ajinath. The sacred history of the Jains claims that he lived several billion years ago: As with other sacred histories this might sound fantastic to those attuned to modern methodologies of dating, but it accepted as literally true by countless practitioners who repeated it even in some modern Jain writings. Regarded as sacred history, this would be acceptable. In mythological terms, Ajinath is said to have dwelled in the realm of the gods before being born a prince to queen Vijaya Devi and king Jitshaturu. One day, after he was crowned king, he saw a lightning, and felt that life too was but a flash that would disappear in a jiffy. He gave his kingdom to his son, and became an ascetic. He practiced asceticism for well over twelve years before attaining ultimate enlightenment. It is said that the spiritual strength he acquired by his penitence brought to his vicinity all kinds of animals, tame and wild, small and large, and they stayed peacefully with him.

This year (2002) [IN 2002] Jains all over the world remember this great founding father of their tradition by observing Thirthankara Ajinath Day on January 25.

From the World of Science: ROBERT BOYLE

One of the reasons for the power and success of scientific knowledge above others is that science relies heavily on observation and experimentation. Many had engaged such efforts before, but it was not until the 17th century that careful experimental investigation became almost an obsession. Among the ardent practitioners of this rapidly developing methodology was the Irish man of science Robert Boyle (born: 25 January 1627) who settled down in Oxford, after inheriting a considerable fortune from his father.

Boyle was fascinated by news of a new invention: the air pump. He constructed one for his own studies. With this he could create vacuum in closed spaces. He used this to demonstrate that air was necessary for the propagation of sound: he placed a ticking clock in a closed flask, and as air was gradually removed, one could no longer hear the ticking. This seems all too simple today, but it was a major experimental revelation in the 17th century.

Boyle used the air pump to study the compressibility of air. By precisely measuring the volume and the corresponding pressure of a given amount of gas he discovered that these two were related in a specific manner: the greater the volume, the less the pressure; and vice versa. The fact that air is compressible suggested that there must be space into which matter could be pressed, and it gave credence to the idea of atoms and interatomic space. This elementary property of a gas thus led to an insight into the ultimate nature of matter. Boyle's quantitative finding is taught to school children in our own times as Boyle's Law. [It has a different name in France where a French scientist—Mariotte—had made this same discovery.]

Boyle authored one of the first treatises on chemistry as the term came to be understood in the modern scientific framework. In this book, entitled *The Sceptical Chymist*, he discussed what we call chemical reactions today. He introduced the notion of chemical elements and compounds, not as speculative constituents like the ancients had done, but as experimentally irreducible substances. He insisted on careful methods of analysis for purifying substances.

Boyle was a strong advocate of the emerging (mechanistic) philosophy which looked upon the whole universe as a giant machine with countless well-regulated parts. He also eloquently advocated the empirical method which gives observational evidence priority over logical consistency: a matter of much dispute in those days of infancy for modern science. The empirical framework of modern science has much to do with its successes in unraveling the nature of the phenomenal world.

Boyle contributed to the development of science by being one of the founders, and among the first fellows, of the Royal Society whose goal is to pursue science without accepting any source as supreme authority, and to internationalize the enterprise. It has been successfully living up to this goal for more than three centuries now.

Like other scientists of the time, Boyle was a deeply religious person. He served as governor of the Society for the Propagation of the Gospel in New England. In his view, God was much more than a Creator of the material universe: He created laws and rules by which the world functions. Boyle felt, unlike latter day romantics, that our appreciation of the Divine is enhanced, not diminished, by an understanding of the laws of Nature; and he was convinced, unlike latter day scientific atheists, that science reveals, rather than disproves, the existence of a Supreme Intelligence behind the phenomenal world.

Boyle left behind a large sum of money for bridging science and religion.

January 26

From the World of Religion: XENOPHON

Occasionally it happens that parent and offspring take to the same profession: be it business or science, writing or acting. But it is rare to find a whole family: father, mother, and two children, all assigned to the same category in history. This happened with the family to whom January 26 is dedicated in the tradition of the Eastern Church. It was the family of Xenophon of the sixth century.

The name Xenophon literally means: the voice/sound of a stranger. The family was from Constantinople, then vibrant in Christian faith. The father came from a well-to-do family, and he was very God-fearing by nature. He married a woman by the name of Mary, and she was very much like him also. In due course they had two sons whom they named Arkadios and John.

When the boys grew up they were sent to Lebanon, there to study Law at the institution in Beirut. But on the way they were shipwrecked. Apparently, the young men held on to logs from the unhappy vessel, and let the waves take them ashore. So John was hurled on land some place, not far from the ancient city of Tyre; and Arkadios landed a few miles away. The young men, separated and each imagining the other to be drowned in sea, prayed for the salvation of the brother.

John was taken in by monks in Jerusalem who took such care of him that he decided to become one of them also. After a lapse of a couple of years, Arkadios had a vision to the effect that his brother was alive somewhere. In the course of his search, he too arrived at a monastery, and became a monk.

Xenophon and Mary came to know about their sons' fate from some passing visitors to Constantinople. The parents set out to look for their children right away, and arrived in Jerusalem. It is said that when they reached the tomb of Christ, there to kneel and pray, they saw their sons who had come that very day and hour for praying too. This was an extraordinary coincidence, brought about, they felt, by God's grace. They heard the stories of the sons. There was great joy at the reunion. Xenophon felt such gratitude to God that he decided to relinquish his position as a senator in Constantinople and become a monk also. Mary joined a nearby nunnery. Thus all four members of the Xenophon family dedicated their lives to the service of the Lord.

News of their coincidental convergence to the same spot in the Holy Land, and their collective decision to enter religious life soon spread to Constantinople. The family gained enormous respect from the people who heard their incredible story, and soon they came to be regarded as worthy saints in the Eastern tradition. Xenophon is said to have declared: "To want nothing is God-like. The less we want, the closer we are to the Divine." Hindu saints have expressed similar thoughts.

The Xenophon family has received the highest esteem in the Eastern Church, not for any miracles they performed, nor for their preaching, but for their simple piety and devotion to the Divine. Such souls exist in all religious traditions, and they are the ones who keep the religious spirit alive and meaningful in the temples and churches, mosques and synagogues all over the world. It is not by insisting on doctrinal truths or by forcing others to one's own vision of God, but by humble prayer and service that God is best served in any religious tradition.

There is a monastery in Mount Athos, in Greek Macedonia, reverberating with the name of this ancient pious family.

From the World of Science: THE CYCLOTRON

As physics is the most fundamental of all sciences, high-energy physics is still, in the view of many, the most fundamental branch of physics. In recent years, there has been some controversy on this contention.

In any event, perhaps the most impressive, size-wise and complexity-wise, of all scientific laboratories are the centers where experimental High-Energy physics is conducted. Consider, for example, the Fermilab some fifty kilometers from Chicago, occupying almost 7,000 acres of land. Its Tevatron has a diameter of 2 km. Through its 10 cm wide steel pipes zoom protons which can attain as much as a thousand gigavolts of energy. Some 20 million-million protons are spurt out every minute. Instigated by 2000 electromagnets, these collide and disintegrate and generate pions and kaons and all the rest of it. There are similar centers in Switzerland, Japan, and Russia, and in other places as well.

On 26 January 1932, a device was patented by Ernest O. Lawrence which gave a huge boost to what has become the gigantic enterprise called Big Science.

In this enterprise, international teams consisting of thousands of workers, young and old, speaking broken English, probe into the heart and core of the material world, unraveling its ultimate mysteries, confirming esoteric theories, and trying to replicate the very processes of Cosmic Creation.

The goal is the following: To bombard the nuclei of atoms with heavy charged particles like protons and alpha particles (helium nuclei) so as to probe deeper into them. Since the nucleus is also positively charged, the target would repel the projectile. This meant that the bombarding particle should be hurled with great speed in order to overcome the repulsion. Such acceleration was first achieved by boosting the particles to high voltage. Lawrence and his group came up with another idea: to make electrically charged particles (ions, protons, etc.) go round and round in spirals, each time adding a small incremental potential so that they were flung with greater speed. The spiral paths were brought about by suitably configured electromagnets. When such fast-moving protons collide with matter, they generate new particles, as happens in the so-called cosmic rays.

The first instrument used simple wires, sealing wax and sundry materials: all of which are said to have cost some twenty five dollars in all. It was proposed that the device should be named magnetic resonance accelerator, but eventually it came to be called a cyclotron. The first cyclotron, built by Lawrence and his graduate student Stanley Livingston, accelerated ionized hydrogen molecules to energy of the order of 80,000 electron volts: modest compared to the thousand billion electron volts that is achieved these days in the Fermilab.

The cyclotron quickly became a basic tool in experimental nuclear physics. It not only revealed many properties of various nuclei, but also served to produce artificial isotopes which are of considerable practical value also.

Needless to say, Lawrence quickly gained fame, name and the Nobel Prize for this enormously fruitful invention. He earned the epithet: the atom-smasher. When he died in 1958, the University of California at Berkeley renamed the lab where he worked in his honor. It continues to be active in the pursuit of experimental physics, and is one of the many temples of science all over the world where bright and inquisitive minds continue to unravel the secrets of Nature.

January 27

From the World of Religion:
WOLFGANG AMADEUS MOZART

In the Hindu framework, there are several modes (mârga) of experiencing the Divine, and Music (*gâna*) is one of them. So one speaks of the *gâna mârga* as a spiritual path. Indeed, at its best, Music is spiritual experience of a superior order, and can provide us with an ecstasy that is as close to an inkling of the Divine as any. Even as the saints and the seers of the traditions guide us to religious insights and awakening, the great composers of the world raise us to lofty heights through their magnificent works.

One of the most universally known and loved of such composers was Wolfgang Amadeus Mozart (born: 27 January 1756): a most remarkable creative genius whose prolific works are cast in every form and format: lively minuets, heart warming symphonies, operas serene or comic, concertos and more.

Wolfgang inherited his talents, at least partially, from his father who was a composer-violinist himself.

Like Sambandhar of the Tamil tradition, Mozart began composing when he was but a child. And his father thought it was a great idea to make a spectacle of his son's extraordinary talents. The lad and his older sister Maria played the keyboard and violin traveling from town to town, performing even at the royal court in Vienna. Then they went to Paris, Milan, London and Munich, displaying Mozart and his music.

As years rolled by quickly Mozart created more symphonies, sonatas and operas. He also became a member of the then growing Freemasonry movement. [This was a society sworn to secrecy with symbols and inspiration drawn from ancient Babylon and Egypt, as well as stone masons of medieval cathedrals. Many leaders of the American Revolution, including Ben Franklin and George Washington, were Free Masons.]

Mozart lived at the Classical Period in Western musical history, and he enriched it immensely. This was the time when creative minds in art, poetry and music were influenced as much by the balance and stature of ancient Greece as by order and symmetry of the laws of physics. Thus inspired, some of the most lasting works emerged in both the arts and sciences. There is something as grand and sweeping in Mozart's or Hayden's composition as in a theorem of Euler, a poem by Schiller, or a law in a Newton's Law of Motion. They all have an ideal perfection about them. But in due course, there arose a rebellion against such detailed balance and order.

Even with all the romantic abandon, rhymeless verses and free-for-all creativity, those marvelous works have continued to live and be loved, like the religions of our distant ancestors. Since those decades of the second half of the 18th century, down to our own times, countless musicians have played Mozart's great many pieces, for these give unadulterated joy to all who have had the opportunity to perform or listen to his works.

There are so many jubilant movements in Mozart's symphonies, so many dancing fingers in his piano pieces, there is never a dull moment in a music by Mozart. Those who haven't listened to the *Eine Kleine Nachtmusik*, haven't hummed with Papageno, or chuckled at the rake Don Giovanni as he recounts his exploits in Spain and Italy, have surely missed some of the most tickling musical delights available to human ears.

The notes and melodies that enter the creative mind of the gifted composer are like the majestic lines that flow through the pen of the epic poet, or the theorems that light up the mathematician's mind. Even those who are skeptical about religious revelations, will have to admit there is something very mysterious in human creativity.

From the World of Science: JOHN C. ECCLES

Conscious experience is a marvelous state through which we all stay for a span of time, and then, who knows! It is filled with wonders or mysteries, depending on one's perspective. Nothing is more remarkable than human consciousness which is rooted in the brain. As far as one can tell, nothing more complex in structure or properties has evolved in this grand and glorious world we call the physical universe.

Australia-born John C. Eccles (born: 27 January 1903) was among those who have probed this puzzle. When he entered the field in the 1920s, it was known that nerve cells communicate through synapses. Eccles explored whether this communication occurred through release of chemicals from neuron to neuron or by electrical coupling between them, requiring only the flow of ions from one cell to another. The answer in most cases (and in the ones he studied) was that it was accomplished by release of chemicals, partly triggered by voltage changes in the first (communicating) cell.

Eccles, who had first been inclined to the electrical view, established from his own investigations that ultimately the process is fundamentally chemical. It is interesting that by moving away from his initial position and working from the opposite (chemical) perspective, he was led to results significant enough to be recognized with a Nobel Prize in 1963. Alan Hodgekins, a co-winner of the Nobel for Physiology, recalls that, upon seeing other laureates somewhat ill, Eccles exclaimed: "Looks like the Physiological contingent has the best health round here!"

Scientists, philosophers, and theologians converge on the question of the origin of human consciousness, and the associated mind-body problem. Most scientists hold that our mental states are essentially aspects of neurochemistry. As per materialist science, the brain is essentially a supercomplex supercomputer, fueled by oxygen-carrying blood. It manages to do something marvelous: It creates a sense of self. Like ancient Hindu thinkers, Dennet has argued that this sense of ego is no more than an illusion.

Eccles did not believe that sooner or later we can explain everything through physics and chemistry alone. In his book "Evolution of the Brain, Creation of the Self," he brushed off science's claims as "promissory materialism." In another book, "How the Self Controls Its Brain," he refers poetically to "the wonder and mystery of the human self with its spiritual values, with its creativity, and with its uniqueness for each of us."

It is known that the mind (concentration, meditation, auto-suggestion) bring about modifications in neurochemistry, that a mere decision to act can initiate the firing of neurons milliseconds before the action occurs. Yoga practitioners can even control involuntary physiological processes. For some hard-nosed neuroscientists, this is no big deal. After all, our brain chemistry is constantly at work even when we just smile, watch a violent movie, or whatever. There is nothing mystical in any of this.

Eccles maintained that there is a transcendental component to human beings. The experienced world results from interactions between this and the brain. He introduced notions like dendrons and psychons as bases for consciousness: concepts or terms generally used in neuroscience. His speculative ideas gave respectability to mysticism and such, and were not looked upon favorably by the scientific establishment.

It is not likely that the controversy among hard-core materialists, spiritualists, and midway theorists on the fundamental issue of Matter and Mind will ever be resolved to the full satisfaction of everyone. In his time, Sir John Eccles added a sizable quota of fuel to the fire.

January 28

From the World of Science: TU B'SHEVAT

People of the Jewish faith who follow the Beit Hillel (the Hillel tradition) remember January 28 (in 2002) as the 15th day of Shevat as a festival for celebrating trees. Rabbi Hillel is famous for his statement to someone who wanted to know all about the Torah in a very short time: "That which is hateful to you, do not do to your neighbor. That is the whole Torah; the rest is commentary."

The day is called Tu B'Shevat. Shevat is the 11th month in the 13-month Jewish calendar. In the Beit Shammai tradition, the first of this month is observed this way.

The Jewish calendar has a New Year Day for kings, a New Year's Day for giving away a tenth (tithe) of one's possessions, and one for the general calendar. In Chapter 19 of Leviticus it says that the Lord gave many instructions to Moses. Among them was the following (23): "And when ye shall come into the land, and have planted all manner of trees for food, then ye shall count the fruit thereof as uncircumcised: three years shall it be as uncircumcised unto you: it shall not be eaten of." This is the basis for Tu B'Shevat. The day is regarded as the conclusion and as the beginning of the Tree New Year.

Fruits which have attained a third of their full growth on this date are said to belong to the previous year. As per tradition, one eats a new fruit on this day. Since the almond fruit ripens the earliest in the land of Israel, there is a song for this day which goes somewhat like this:

Almonds in bloom, bright sunshine our way,

With birds on roofs, we welcome this day!

There are rules for which fruits may be used for tithes, and which not. It says in the Talmud: "If one picked fruit from an esrog tree on the eve of the 15th of Shevat before the sun went down, and he then picked more of its fruit after the sun went down, we may not separate the tithes from one batch for the other…either from the new crop for the old or from the old crop for the new one…"

Rabbi Dov Lipman reminded has us that Moses started delivering his speech on the first day of Shevat, and the speech lasted for fourteen days. So it was only on the fifteenth that the people fully assimilated its spiritual significance. Hence both the 1st and the 15th of this month become significant.

It is explained that trees are also taken as symbols of humans: growing, being useful, and then being felled. So this reverence is equally a reverence for humanity.

The Torah refers to the importance of trees. It speaks of Israel as "a land of wheat and barley and vines and fig trees and pomegranates, a land of olive trees and honey."

It is interesting to look into the origin of the name of this festival: As with Roman numerals, the Hebrew numerals are also expressed with letters. The rich field of Gematria or Jewish number mysticism is based on this. The number eleven would be yod-aleph (10 + 1). The number fifteen, when expressed this way, spells the name of G-d (as one would write God in the Jewish framework). Since this should not be uttered, it is expressed as Tet-Vav (which is 9 + 6). Therefore the 15th day of this month is called Tet-Vav Shevat, which (by euphonic liaison) becomes Tu B'Shevat.

Many cultures recognize the value of trees, and associate holiness with them. Here then is a beautiful tradition, celebrating Nature and its blessings of trees, ancient like the Hindu reverence for forest and Arbor day of our own times.

It is a day to wish one's Jewish friends, "Happy Tu B'Shevat!"

From the World of Science: AUGUSTE PICCARD

These days, thousands of people are transported through the upper layers of the earth's atmosphere in cozy comfort, being fed frequently in large pressurized vessels. The airplane has become commonplace.

Normal planes fly within the troposphere which extends to some 6 miles above ground. Beyond that, and extending up to some 25 miles high, is the stratosphere. Beyond that is the mesosphere spread over another 50 miles, and beyond that, extending to another 175 miles is the thermosphere. The exosphere stretches to 250 more miles. Thus, in all, the earth's slim mantle of dense and very rarefied atmosphere extends to about 500 miles in all.

Human beings have ventured there too, and even beyond, in satellites and rockets. One may wonder who was the first to reach stratospheric heights and when. This was accomplished by the Swiss explorer-physicist Auguste Piccard (born, along with his twin brother Jean, on 28 January 1884). After receiving his doctoral degree in engineering from the Swiss Institute of Technology, Auguste Piccard became fascinated with balloon flights. He devised a hot air balloon in 1913 in which he took, along with his brother, a sixteen hour ride over France and Germany. He was eager to go higher up, and soar beyond the heights where birds and even planes fly. He knew that air pressure and temperature fall as one climbs higher and higher. So he constructed an air-tight 500,000 cubic foot balloon, using rubberized cotton.

On 27 May 1931, the day the World's Fair opened in Chicago, Auguste Piccard took vertically off with Paul Kipfer, from Augsburg in Germany. Their balloon gently ascended to the impressive height of 51,775 feet (almost ten miles). No human being until then had ventured that far high for pleasure or for probing. The two were in the sealed aluminum gondola for 16 hours, before they landed somewhere in the Austrian Alps. They became celebrities.

Brother Jean had come to the United States where he met and married Jeannette Ridlon. While teaching at the University of Chicago, he also pursued his work with balloons. On 23 October 1934, Jean and Jeannette got into the "Century of Progress Balloon," which took them to almost 58,000 feet. They did some scientific experiments there into the effect of altitudes on liquid gases. Jean was also one of the first to make balloons with plastic materials. And Jeannette became the first woman in the rarefied regions of the earth's atmosphere. Their craft may now be seen at the Museum of Science and Industry in Chicago.

Auguste Piccard also set out to explore the under-sea world for which he built a device called the bathyscaphe (deep ship). The American naturalist William Beebe had done this in 1930 in his Bathysphere. Eventually, a number of these were built. Two Frenchmen used one of these in 1954, diving into the Mediterranean to more than 13,200 feet below the surface. In 1960, with another of Piccard's ships again, two men from the U. S. navy touched the bottom of the Pacific, some 33,600 feet under water.

In his book, "Earth, Sky and Sea," Auguste Piccard narrates his projects and adventures. He says that his first fascination while still at school was to go underwater rather than into the upper reaches of the atmosphere.

The pioneering attempts of the Piccard brothers were a prelude to humanity's extensive exploration of space above and aquatic depths below. Incredibly, only 36 years later human beings set foot on the Moon.

January 29

From the World of Religion:
EMANUEL SWEDENBORG

The major religions of the world recognize Zoroaster, Moses, the Buddha, Mahavira, Jesus, Mohammed, Guru Nanak, and the like as their prophets. But there have been a few others in history who have received and preached esoteric wisdom at various times, and within various cultures. Some, like Baha'ulla, have succeeded in initiating yet other religions; others, like Sri Ramakrishna, have attracted large followings within an established tradition; and a few others are somewhere in between. To this last category belongs Emanuel Swedenborg (born: 29 January 1688) who was both seer and scientist, who felt he had revelations, and attracted admirers. Some of them have established a near-religion in his name.

Swedenborg was a versatile man: thinker, inventor, discoverer, writer, and spiritually awakened. He traveled widely for his time, studied an impressive range of subjects (both theoretical and practical such as watch-making and bookbinding), and had uncanny intuitions in the sciences of his times. He wrote on the nervous system and spoke of connections between the cerebral cortex and respiration. Like Leonardo da Vinci, he fantasized about the possibilities of inventing submarines, airplanes and steam engines.

When he was 56, Swedenborg began having visions in which God was urging him to serve as a vehicle to communicate with humanity. He delved into studies of Hebrew and Greek and went back to the Bible. At this time he felt we was in touch with beings in the celestial and in the nether worlds. He began to see esoteric meanings in Biblical passages. He found the Book of Genesis to be glorification of God and an expression of the spiritual regeneration of Man. He was seeing deeper meanings in the Book of Revelation.

It is said that on one occasion when he was past 70, during dinner at a friend's home in Gothenborg, Swedenborg suddenly exclaimed there was a fire at his home in Stockholm some 300 miles away. In due course, he calmed down. Apparently there had in fact been a fire at that very moment, and fortunately, it had been put out.

Swedenborg's theological reflections and writings grew after this incident. He was convinced of a divine force undergirding the material world, he spoke of connections between the finite and the infinite, and he affirmed bonds between God and the human species. He felt there were two modes of revelation: one from within oneself when the mind and spirit have been properly prepared for it. The other consists of visions from the outside world, such as religious prophets have had.

Because of his scientific background, his interpretations were anchored to a logical framework. Like other enlightened spirits, he tried to bridge the gap between various Christian sects through newer interpretations of the basic Christian doctrines relating to the Trinity, the original sin, etc.

Swedenborg's *Arcana Coelestia* is like Madame Blavatsky' *Secret Doctrine* and Sri Aurobindo's *Life Divine*: esoteric, erudite, and intelligible only to fairly sophisticated readers.

At one time, Swedenborg's writings were not looked upon with favor by the Swedish Church establishment. His books were published in England and the Netherlands. Some of his sympathizers were tried for heresy. But today he is held in the highest esteem in his native country, and is regarded as a spiritual and intellectual jewel in its crown. The Church of New Jerusalem, inspired by Swedenborg's teachings, with its mission to "bring the world into a new era of religious understanding," is popular in many countries.

From the World of Science: ABDUS SALAM

Anyone who has read something about developments in 20th century theoretical physics has heard of unified field theories. What exactly are these?

When Newton discovered in the 17th century that what makes the apple fall is also what keeps the Moon and the planets in orbits, he formulated the first unified gravitational field theory in physics: the explanation of apparently diverse force-based phenomena in terms of a single unified force.

Electrical and magnetic phenomena had been observed since very ancient times, and studied more systematically in the 18th century. But in the 19th century it was discovered that these are not distinct in their roots: that there is an underlying electromagnetic field in terms of which all these phenomena may be cogently explained and understood. This was another unified field theory in physics.

In the course of the twentieth century, Einstein spent much intellectual effort and many years trying to unify the gravitational and electromagnetic fields. That is to say, he wanted to find a single source of which these two are different manifestations; but to no avail.

In the meanwhile, two other fundamental fields were discovered in the context of atomic nuclei: these are the so-called weak and strong fields.

Many physicists exerted their talents towards unifying these new fields with the other two. The task requires considerable expertise in sophisticated mathematics. Among those whose works bore impressive fruit three stand out: Steven Weinberg, Abdus Salam (born: 29 January 1926), and Sheldon Glashow. For their achievement, all three shared the Nobel Prize for Physics in 1979.

The W-S-G theory is known as the electroweak theory because it combines the electromagnetic and the weak interactions. This was a tremendous intellectual achievement in that it unraveled one of the most fundamental features of the physical universe. It is one further step in the direction of unveiling that ultimate single source of the entire physical universe: to be enshrined in a Theory Of Everything (TOE).

The electroweak theory shows that at extremely high energies, the electromagnetic and the weak fields are indistinguishable. What we observe as electromagnetic and weak interaction phenomena are only superficially different. There is a level at which they are really one and the same. The mathematical aspect of this theory implies that there must be certain fundamental (field) particles corresponding to the weak-part of this unified field. These are the so-called W+, W-, and Z-0 vector bosons. The existence of these particles was established at the high energy accelerator in CERN, Switzerland in 1983.

Salam was born in what became Pakistan. He was for long an outcaste in Pakistan because he belonged to the *Ahmadi* sect which is regarded as heretical in that country. In 1974 an Act of the Pakistani Parliament formally excommunicated him. So he spent much of his productive life in the West. But he always considered himself to be a devout Muslim. He once said: "The Holy Quran enjoins us to reflect on the verities of Allah's created laws of nature; however, that our generation has been privileged to glimpse a part of His design is a bounty and a grace for which I render thanks with a humble heart."

Pakistan claimed him after he won international recognition. and asked him to advise the government in scientific matters. In the 1960s he was instrumental in establishing the International Center for Theoretical Physics at Trieste, whose goal is to assist physicists from the Third-World. Thus, Abdus Salam served both physics and physicists.

January 30

From the World of Religion:
ASSASSINATION OF MAHATMA GANDHI

On 30 January 1948, when he was walking out of a worship center where he had participated in a prayer session in which Christ and Allah and Ishvar (a Hindu mode of addressing God) were all evoked, an angry young man approached him, saluted him, and fired shots at his chest, whereupon he slumped down and died. Thus ended the life of Mohandas Karamchand Gandhi, known with affection as Babuji, and with reverence as Mahatma Gandhi to India's people.

The nation mourned, as did millions more all across the world. Einstein once remarked the world wouldn't believe that such a man as this once trod the earth. Gandhi was regarded as saintly, steadfast in truth and in ahimsa: non-violence. He was generous to his adversaries, often stubborn in his insistence on what is right, and (in the view of some) went overboard in his kindness to undeserving and ungrateful foes.

He was admired for his piety and his principles, and recognized as Father of the (modern) Indian Nation. But there were also many Hindus, as there still are, who hated him from the core of their hearts. They felt that because of him India lost much to Muslims. It was this resentment which provoked his assassination.

Gandhi's principle of non-violence was not just a matter of not hurting people or animals. It was not just vegetarianism and avoiding leather shoes. Rather, it was the application of ahimsa in the context of confrontation. For the challenge is when we have to deal with someone who is clearly out to get us.

No doubt, in many cases "an eye for an eye and a tooth for a tooth" works. But returning good for bad, and love for hatred, is also an ancient experiment in civilization, and it too has worked in many instances. It has invariably produced more happiness, peace and harmony. There is greater glory in a victory achieved through nonviolence and handshakes than in all the battle cries and bombs of violent and hateful confrontations.

Gandhi felt that industrialization should take into account local conditions and needs. He insisted on cottage industries as expressions of national unity, a determination to work and serve, and as symbols of discipline for the peasants.

Gandhi was aware of the potential evils of technology in prescient ways, long before we began to recognize ecology and waste. In this matter he impressed many as backward and simplistic; they failed to see that in industrial-technological civilization a time bomb would soon begin to tick, spelling the extinction of the species itself if mankind did not take steps to avert the disaster.

Gandhi has lost much of his luster in his native India. The new generation, frustrated with Kashmir, blame it on Gandhi's goody-goodiness. There is, alas, some truth in this. Yet, in these times, when nations confront one another with mistrust, when we seem to be sliding to catastrophes of mutual destruction, the world is crying out for Gandhis: in Palestine and Israel, in India and Pakistan, in Northern Ireland, and elsewhere. The world needs not a Gandhi here or a Gandhi there, but Gandhis everywhere, by which I mean leaders in all nations, who are more sensitive to the needs and predicaments of the adversary, more willing to sacrifice and serve, more caring and compassionate.

Civilizations survive and evolve by tireless perseverance in adhering to ideals. Love is surely nobler than hatred, non-violence more civilized than violence, kindness better than cruelty. Those who cling on to such principles add glory to society and history, whether they win or lose. Such are martyrs and saints. Such was Mahatma Gandhi.

From the World of Science: MAX THEILER

According to some medical historians, the disease called yellow fever was already known to the ancients. They say that from the relics of ancient Egypt, it appears as if the pharaohs were aware of the disease. There have been many times when yellow fever reached epidemic proportions.

Between 1635 and 1670 there were several reports of this *nova pestis* (as it was called) from some islands of the West Indies. Spanish explorers to Central and South America fell ill quite often, and there was no question that ships sailing back and forth helped spread the disease. There was a great epidemic of the ailment between 1793 and 1805. In the course of the 19th century, it claimed many victims in Africa and in South America. The disease was more prevalent in tropical and subtropical regions, especially during the hot and humid seasons. Places close to the water were often more susceptible to the disease than inland locations.

In 1881, a certain Dr. Charles Finlay, who was then practicing in Havana, was the first to suggest that yellow fever was being transmitted by certain types of mosquitoes. Recognizing this, people would leave the U.S. Southern States in large numbers when summers came because of the abundance of these mosquitoes. When an epidemic of yellow fever broke out in 1888 in Jacksonville

(Florida) the government arranged to evacuate the people by train. Finlay's suspicion was confirmed by Dr. Walter Reed.

As with many other diseases, countless people suffered, and a great many died, in spite of the ad hoc remedies that were administered to alleviate the pain, the vomiting, the fever, and other attendant symptoms of the disease.

Many diseases result from unwelcome intruders into normally healthy bodies. By the second half of the 19th century it was becoming clear that a number of microorganisms were responsible for the havoc. What was not yet so clear was that there are any number of other creatures which serve as transmitters of the real pathogenic organisms.

In 1918, a young man by the name of Max Theiler (born: 30 January 1899) sailed all the way from his native South Africa to England to study medicine at the London School of Tropical Medicine. After getting his degree in three years, he went to work at the Harvard School of Medicine. It was while he was doing research here that in 1927—some 75 years ago—he came to understand that the deadly yellow fever was caused, not by a bacterium, as had been imagined until then, but by a filterable virus. Theiler also found that the disease could be given to mice, and then transferred back to monkeys. This made it easier and far less expensive to do research on yellow fever. Prior to this, monkeys were the experimental agents for such work.

The next step was to develop a vaccine. Theiler and his co-workers also succeeded in developing 17D, which is the generally used vaccine against yellow fever. This vaccine, and improved versions of it, have been used on countless people all over the world. In 1951, Theiler was awarded the Nobel Prize for his work.

In his later life Theiler worked on other diseases, such as Dengue and Japanese encephalitis. Then he got interested in the field of immunology. Most of all, he realized that mice can become infected with ailments that had been thought to be reserved only for primates. He also discovered a new condition in mice which has come to be called Theiler's disease.

Men and women who have contributed to the cure and alleviation of a disease are seldom as well remembered as emperors, politicians, and saints.

January 31

From the World of Religion: ZAOWANG

Practically every major religion has something to say about food: after all, there can be no life and health, culture or civilization, without food. We pray to the Lord for our daily bread, we express gratitude for the food we get, and seek blessings on what we eat.

Every religion has its place of worship, but do we praise God for food in Church? One may wonder about the place where food is sacred. It is fair to say that this must be the kitchen where it is prepared. Should we perhaps think of an aspect of the Divine that oversees what is happening in that sacred place where food comes to life every morning and evening for palatal pleasure and for the body's nourishment? The answer to this question is a resounding yes in the Chinese tradition. For there, from distant days, they have had a god assigned to the kitchen of the house.

We have all heard about Confucius and Lao Tzu, about yin and yang and I Ching. Many of us may have even dined in Chinese restaurants. But not many outside of the Chinese cultural matrix may know about Zaowang, (also known as Tsao Chung), who is a deity associated with the kitchen. This god is always present in the kitchen, during breakfast, lunch and dinner, while one is cooking or cleaning, and even when one is having a late night snack.

Chinese homes have a symbol of this *Deus culinae* as a gorgeous figure with his consort and a horse. Sometimes he is flanked by servants with jars which are supposed to contain little report cards about our deeds and misdeeds in the eating room. Sometimes they simply hang a paper banner in red which represents the Kitchen God. The symbol of Zaowang is placed not far from the stove or the hearth where cooking actually occurs.

Zaowang is not there to tell you if you have added the right amount of salt to egg-drop soup, or chopped the meat to the right size, but to oversee your conduct while you are in the kitchen. For he makes regular reports of your behavior in the sanctum of the cooking room, and, as I said, these are collected in the jars of his servants.

People burn incense and candles for this god and pay periodic homage to him, for he protects the home from fire and accident, and blesses the home with good fortune. It was Zaowang who created Fire: how much food of significance can there be without fire?

In the last week of the year, he takes off to heaven, there to present our records to the Jade Emperor. On the 24th day of the 12th lunar month there is a festival for Zaowang. To pamper him with sweets, they paint his lips with honey, they venerate him with special fondness, so that he may say only good things to the power that be about the members of the family. Some have seen this as bribing a heavenly official, but what's wrong in being good to someone who has power over us? Others view this simply as being nice to one who is about to embark on a long trip. Others, in a similar cynical vein, argue that the honey is to seal his mouth so he won't blurt out family misbehavior to the one above. In fact, they make a special sweet cake for this day, which is unusually sticky: to symbolically seal Zaowang's mouth. In any event, in this day and age, most people know that it is all for fun and tradition. So there is mirth, laughter, and only symbolic seriousness when honey is smeared on the Kitchen God's lips.

They also prepare a feast of rice and pork, or noodle and beef and offer it to the deity, and generally the Kitchen God likes what everyone else likes.

There is beauty in all traditions. Enlightened multiculturalism is in the appreciation of cultural beauty. The festival for the Kitchen God fell on 31 January in 2002.

From the World of Science:
HAM'S SUBORBITAL FLIGHT

There is much to be proud of in many of the intellectual, moral, and material achievements of the human family. Of course there is also much to be ashamed of. Unfortunately, as with successful individuals, we sometimes tend to forget our indebtedness to other species in many of the things that have brought us enrichment and fulfillment.

Thus, for example, in the field of space exploration, not many may recall that animals have served us in important ways.

Consider, for example, Ham the chimpanzee who was the first primate to be launched into a suborbital flight from Cape Canaveral on 31 January 1961. Few may remember him or the many other creatures that have been sent in space capsules to learn about the safety of such adventures for human beings. Ham was 4 years old and weighed 37 pounds. He was put in a Mercury spacecraft; we have no idea how he felt, and whether or what he thought of the experience. We do know that during that flight he experienced weightlessness for seven whole minutes.

His spacecraft attained a speed of 5857 miles per hour and reached an altitude of 157 statute miles: a significant reach in the upper atmosphere.

He had been well prepared and trained for the mission. He responded appropriately by pulling this lever or that when the right color of light was switched on or off, receiving enjoyable banana pellets or a mild but uncomfortable electric shock, depending on his performance. He was subjected to an acceleration of almost 15 G on his way down to the earth's surface.

Thanks to Ham's flight, when Alan Shepard entered the spacecraft as the first Mercury astronaut, he felt much more confident.

The report says that some things went wrong in the experiment, especially in the way the rocket performed during return. The craft crash-landed on the sea with more vehemence than had been expected. The titanium pressure bulkhead was perforated and some 800 pounds of water gushed in. Fortunately Ham was unhurt when he was recovered after the splashdown.

Ham was more fortunate than some other creatures that had been sent for such experimental purposes. Laika, the Husky dog, which had been sent on Sputnik 2 in November 1957, lived for a week and died in orbit because the oxygen supply ran out. Gordo, the Squirrel monkey, launched in a Jupiter booster, did well in the suborbital flight, but the flotation mechanism of the rocket's nose failed during re-entry, and the creature died.

Other chimps: Able, Baker, Sam, Enos, Lapik, Muktik, etc. have also been sent on such missions, and we may be grateful for the knowledge and confidence they brought to human astronauts, for they were made to risk their lives before we would venture our own. And there have also been countless unnamed members of other species: flies, worms and turtles which have been hurled into space to bring us useful information for our explorations.

It is not simply as sources of meat and protein that animals have been of use to us, nor just as beasts of burden, or as a source of milk and cheese, wool and gelatin. The next time we hear about a scientific achievement of the human species, especially in space exploration, fundamental biology, or medicine, let us remember those other creatures, great and small, that have also made contributions to science in their own ways.

From the World of Religion:
EVE OF CANDLEMAS

In the Christian tradition, the first evening of February is the Eve of Candlemas. Known in Latin as *Festum candelarum sive luminum* (Festival of candles or of light), the festival has had different interpretations. Christ is said to have been presented in the Temple on Candlemas day. Hence candles are blessed and given to the people as a symbol of the spiritual light they will receive from the Church. The day is also known as Feast of the Purification of the Blessed Virgin Mary. In the ancient worldview, there was the belief that a woman was impure for six weeks after childbirth. Therefore, Candlemas was observed forty days after Nativity, on 14 February. But as a result of the Gregorian calendar reform, it was moved to 2 February.

According to another interpretation, the observance was introduced in the fifth century to counteract the persisting pagan festivity of Lupercalia which used to be in the beginning of February. In ancient Roman event, fun and frolic and unrestrained frivolity were the order of the day, when Pagan priests ran around roads in Rome tapping young women to bestow fertility upon them.

Since ancient times, the Welsh have had a Nos Gwyl (meaning Night Festival) Fair by the beginning of February. On this night, the windows of homes are lit up with candles. One celebrates the prelude to the coming of spring, for by the first of February we are more or less at the midpoint of the cold season. In the Wiccan tradition, the day is also called Imbolic which refers to the womb of Mother earth, for the belief is that seeds planted in harvest season are beginning to stir at this time. Soon one will see buds on stems, suggesting that the blossoming of flowers is only a few weeks away.

At this time of the year when the sun has advanced from the lowest latitudes toward the northern hemisphere, the Irish used to honor Brighid: the goddess of fire and midwifery. In the mythopoesie of the Irish people, Brighid guides the Sun during these dark wintry days back to our regions to bring us more warmth. Her name became Anglicized to Brigit. [Incidentally, the English word bride is derived from her name.]

There was a strong feminism in the cult of Brigit at Kildare, for on the Eve of Candlemas, 19 women priests kept the flame at the temple. Men were not allowed in.

So, during this Pagan festival, people light candles in homes. There is something silent, serene and soft in the burning of candles which is perhaps why this is done in many cultures and on many occasions.

Modern Pagans and Wiccans consider Candlemas as a festival for remembering the ancient goddess Brighid. For them, this is the same as what became St. Valentine's Day which was shifted to mid-February because of the Gregorian calendar reform. They associate it with the Roman festival. White flowers and orange candles with the fragrance of musk and cinnamon are popular in the pagan mode.

According to one view, just as Sanskritic Hindus incorporated Dravidian gods and goddesses into their own pantheon, the Catholic Church transformed Brigit into a saint. This was an effective mode of assimilation, and it made Irish Catholics feel very comfortable. It was not unlike the British conferring knighthood on eminent citizens of in the countries they colonized, which made the common people feel they really belonged to the British Empire.

Cultural assimilations and transformations are slow and subtle, and they have been occurring all through history.

From the World of Science: EMILIO SEGRÈ

Many of us have read in our high school science texts that there are 92 naturally occurring elements, and that these have been meaningfully arranged in what is called the Periodic Table. This is not exactly true: not all the 92 elements are *naturally* occurring. In fact, elements 43 and 85 were missing up until the 1930s. In 1937, Italian-born Emilio Segrè (born: 1 February 1905) and a co-worker separated out the first artificial element in history. This was the missing element 43, and they called it technetium (Tc), from the Greek word *technetos* which refers to something artificial. They found this element from a careful chemical analysis of a sample of molybdenum which had been bombarded by deuterons (heavy hydrogen) in a cyclotron. Technetium has been used in rendering some alloys more resistant to corrosion, and also in nuclear medicine as a tracer element. Some stars seem to contain this element, perhaps because of the many nuclear reactions occurring there. But this is certainly the first human-made element on earth.

Three years later Segrè managed to synthesize another element which fitted into the empty space number 85 in the periodic table. He named it astatine (At), from the Greek word *astatos*, which means unstable. It is the heaviest element belonging to the halogen group. This is a highly radioactive element, with a half life of a little more than seven hours. It is made by bombarding the nuclei of bismuth with alpha particles (nuclei of helium). Astatine has been used in the paper industry in the so-called beta gauges to measure the density of paper.

Segrè also made another major contribution to fundamental physics. We all know that ordinary matter is made up of atoms, and that the atoms consist of a central nucleus which carries positive protons and neutral neutrons, surrounded by tinier orbiting electrons which carry negative charges.

It is legitimate to ask: Why don't we have positive electrons and negative protons? The answer is, of course there are positive electrons and negative protons. These are called positrons and anti-protons respectively. Their existence is a requirement in the framework of current physics.

But it is true that whichever hydrogen atom we pick, it will have only a negative electron and a proton in it, never the other way around. Indeed, all the atoms in our universe have only negative electrons and positive nuclei. If it were the other way around, we would call it anti-matter. Thus an atom of anti-hydrogen would have an anti-proton (positively charged proton) as nucleus and an orbiting positron.

All this is not mere speculation. This follows from the framework of 20th century physics. Positrons, whose existence was a natural consequence of an important theory formulated in the late 1920s, were actually detected in cosmic rays in 1932.

We had to wait for two more decades before the existence of the anti-proton was experimentally demonstrated. This was also done by Emilio Segrè and his co-workers in 1955. He shared the Nobel Prize for this achievement.

Forty years later, in 1995, atoms of anti-hydrogen were created. Such atoms simply cannot remain for long in our universe. Matter and anti-matter (like electrons and positrons) simply cannot coexist. At the first encounter they will annihilate each other and turn into pure (radiant) energy as per Einstein's famous equation of the century.

In his interesting autobiography (*A Mind Always in Motion*: 1993) Segrè speaks about his physics, his colleagues, and also his sensitivity to the beauty of flowers.

February 2

From the World of Religion: GROUNDHOG DAY

Whether from the flight of birds in ancient Rome or the sounds of lizards among the Tamils, the entrails of animals in ancient Babylonia or the behavior of cows elsewhere, human beings have often believed that animals can somehow portend things to come. This becomes even more reasonable when we imagine that the behavior of some animals, like mercury level in a barometer, is an indication of weather conditions, present or in the near future.

So, if you watch the weather channel on any TV station in North America on 2nd February, chances are they will make a reference to the groundhog, and say something half-seriously about how much longer we may see this year's winter linger. This is more tradition than science.

It won't be a surprise if animals that hibernate have developed instinctive capacities for behaving in their own best survival interests in the context of a given environment. It is therefore not inconceivable that the groundhog experiences a certain degree of thermal comfort which indicates to it how long winter might last. If the animal returns to its hole for a longer nap, this would suggest that it feels the winter will last a few more weeks than usual. There is the belief that it determines this course of events by looking at its own shadow. This is as much of a scientific standing as one can give to the Groundhog Day tradition. It would be unfair, not to say futile, to probe into how the groundhog knows that this is to be done exactly on 2 February every year.

The Ground Hog Day custom was introduced in American culture by mid-nineteenth century by German immigrants. Back home, the badger (Dachs) used to perform this weather-predicting service. It began in Pennsylvania in 1841 in the town of Punxsutawney which has modestly proclaimed itself to be the Weather Capital of the World. In that year, the groundhog was officially declared to be "Punxsutawney Phil, Seer of Seers, Sage of Sages, Prognosticator of Prognosticators, and Weather Prophet Extraordinary." With admirable modesty, *Marmota monax* (its scientific designation) hasn't displayed the slightest degree of vanity from the honorific.

Groundhog Day coincides with the Christian Candlemas. A groundhog-equivalent theory, carrying about as much scientific weight, is enshrined in the verse:

If Candlemas be fair and bright,
Winter has another flight.

If Candlemas brings clouds and rain,
Winter will not come again.

It may be recalled that even before Darwin's suggestion of humanity's simian ancestry, and before the arrival of German immigrants to Pennsylvania, Native Americans of the Delaware region had their own theory to the effect that ground-hogs were among their ancestors. As they imagined it, we were first creatures inside Mother Earth (like groundhogs in winter) before we came on land. They had a legend about a groundhog called Wojak: a name that gave rise to our word woodchuck whose official (technical name) is Marmota monax.

Some cultural historians have suggested that the Groundhog Day—which is a reckoning in midwinter, with its correspondence in Candlemas, St. Brigit, Lupercalia, and all that, is a relic of some even more ancient practice in humanity's very ancient history.

From the World of Science:
JEAN BAPTISTE BOUSSINGAULT

Back in the closing decades of the 18th century a Scottish chemist by the name of Daniel Rutherford kept a mouse in an airtight box until it died. He collected the air in the enclosure and found that it couldn't support another mouse. Nor would a candle burn in it. He tried to explain this in terms of the prevailing phlogiston theory, but actually he had discovered what we call nitrogen today.

Everybody knows how important oxygen is for life, but our atmosphere contains almost four times as much nitrogen. Why such abundance of what Lavoisier called a life-less (azote), in contrast to the life-giving oxygen, element one might wonder.

Whether through intelligent design or random chance, Nature is consistently extraordinarily generous in providing for the sustenance and long-range preservation of living organisms on earth. And nitrogen is immensely essential for this. It is at the heart of the life process: the central element in amino acids, proteins, and nucleic acids.

We get the needed nitrogen from the foods we consume, and Nature has devised, or in Nature there has emerged (whatever be your theological perspective: poetic or scientific) one gigantic complex system called the nitrogen cycle which synthesizes the appropriate nitrogen compounds which enable the bodies of living organisms to absorb and metabolize.

Some of our first understanding of the role and source of nitrogen in the bio-world came from the work of the French agricultural chemist Jean Baptiste Boussingault (born: 2 February 1802). Interestingly enough, Boussingault studied minerology to begin with, and a mining company sent him to South America. At that time, the Spanish colonies, under Simon de Bolivar, were fighting a war of independence. Boussingault served Bolivar in this context, before he returned to France. Here he became a professor of Chemistry at Lyons, and did some good work. But he was let go because of his politics, which infuriated the faculty who threatened to resign en masse. Boussingault was reinstated.

He did much of his research in his farm in Alsace, and obtained results of lasting significance. Thus, he discovered, among other things, that legumes (lentil, pea, etc.) can restore nitrogen to the soil if they are grown with cereals, and that they can get nitrogen directly from air. Actually, it is the nitrogen-fixing bacteria that do this. He also found that all plants, except legumes, derive their nitrogen from organic fertilizers. More exactly, it is through ammonium ions (NH_4^+) and Nitrate ions (NO_3^-) that plants derive their nitrogen. All this is useful knowledge for agricultural productivity.

But because of the tricks we have been playing with Nature, we have significantly increased the rate at which nitrogen has been kept in a balance in the grand nitrogen-eco-cycle. We have been increasing the amounts of nitrous and nitric oxides, diminishing the concentration of calcium and potassium in the soil, accelerating the transport of nitrogen in water streams, etc. None of these steps towards slow suicide are apparent on a day to day basis, but knowledgeable eco-scientists are warning us that there is a ticking time-bomb in all of these, at least as dangerous perhaps as an asteroid impact. The least we should start doing, they tell us, is to reduce our consumption of fossil fuels and our production of chemical fertilizers.

One wonders helplessly if all this technological progress, prospering economy, and ever-increasing creature comforts are all that healthy, even desirable.

February 3

From the World of Religion: MEERA BAI

The similarity between the lives of Hindu and Christian saints is sometimes quite striking. The devotion of the saintly Meera Bai to Krishna, for example, was as intense and passionate as that of many Christian saints to Christ.

Meera was a Rajput princess who is remembered in the Hindu world for her extraordinary love of Krishna which found ample expression is some of the most moving religious lyrics in any culture. Her songs have touched the hearts of millions during the past half a millennium since she lived.

When Meera was a little girl, an itinerant ascetic once handed her a little icon of Lord Krishna. She took an instant fascination for it, saw here Divinity in compact form, and kept it close to her heart for many years. Soon after she reached teenage she was married to a handsome prince, but she had little interest in worldly life.

She spent most of her hours worshiping Krishna, indeed she rejected the Goddess Kali: the deity of the Rajput Ranas, as the kings were called.

Barely five years into her married life, her husband died in a battle. Widowed Meera was drawn even more to Krishna. She spent her waking hours in song and hymn to the Lord. When her husband's brother, Ratan Singh, was crowned king of the realm, life became difficult for young Meera. News of her abnormal attachment to God spread, and she was becoming somewhat of an embarrassment to the royal family.

Many tales have been told about how the king tried to get rid of Meera. Once, he hid a venomous snake in a basket of flowers that she was to receive for her prayers. But, it is said, when musical Meera opened the basket, the secret serpent had been transformed into a Krishna icon. On another occasion, a lethal potion was dispatched to her, camouflaged as a refreshing drink. Gentle Meera is said to have imbibed it, with no fatal result. And she knew it, prompting her to compose a verse which said in effect:

It was poison that was sent by king.
 I knew it, though I wasn't told.
But I shine the brighter by that thing,
 Like fire-treated nugget of gold.

The persecutions continued. They tried to drown her, but to no avail. Meera could not handle it any more. [Recall the Christian martyrs under some Roman emperors.] She moved away to Brindavan, and then to Dwaraka: places which are rich in sacred history, for Lord Krishna is said to have lived.

But she was summoned to the palace from the temple in Dwaraka where she was staying. Unable to disobey a royal command she begged to stay one more night at the temple. When morning came she was not to be found there or anywhere else. The general belief was that Meera had merged with the figure of Krishna in the temple.

Meera is a supreme example of the bhakti mode in which one feels the pain and pleasure of one's attachment to the Divine, not unlike the bond that an infant has for mother, one for the beloved. Meera pleads for piety pure, for the banishing of evil thoughts. She wonders why the wise are often penniless while wealth accumulates with fools. Meera's songs reflect her deepest conviction of a Krishna with whom she is in love, one she seems to have known even in previous births. Meera is one of those saints of the Hindu world whose devotion to God created magnificent music and powerful poetry. This alone has secured for her a permanent place in the collective memory of the Hindu world.

From the World of Science:
ELIZABETH BLACKWELL

During his State of the Union address in 2002, President Bush introduced a woman from Afghanistan who had been emancipated from the chain that denied her the right to find professional fulfillment in a cultural-social-political framework that has now been replaced. It is important to realize, however, that the crime of societies and governments that stifle human freedom, practice discrimination, and persist in gender inequality, is not in what they do but in the unacceptability of what they do in this day and age. For, as the sad history of humanity reveals, in most of the nations and cultures of the world, some of the values that many of us consider shameful today were very much in vogue for much too long.

Thus, for example, today we have thousands of women physicians all over the world. But in 1848 there was not a single woman who had a doctor's title prefixed to her name, anywhere in the modern world. Sure there were nurses, female assistants and even some practitioners of folk medicine, but nobody—neither men nor women—imagined a woman could be called a "doctor". And it all seemed quite normal to most people.

Then came Elizabeth Blackwell (born 3 February 1821) who had moved as a child with her parents from England to the United States. When Elizabeth was in her twenties, a friend of hers died young. Before dying she said to Elizabeth she wished she had been attended to by a woman doctor. This inspired her to apply to more than two dozen medical schools. All she accomplished was to raise eyebrows. She was told that this was an exercise in futility, for letting her come in (like bringing Mary's little lamb to school) was against the rule. But one school, Geneva Medical School in Upstate New York (now transformed into Hobart and William Smith Colleges) did not reject her application summarily. The School brought it to the student body for a vote. This was considered to be no more than a joke. And in sheer fun, they voted her in. She reminisced later:

"I had not the slightest idea of the commotion created by my appearance as a medical student in the little town…I had so shocked Geneva propriety that the theory was fully established either that I was a bad woman, whose designs would gradually become evident, or that, being insane, an outbreak of insanity would soon be apparent."

Indeed, even the professors felt embarrassed discussing reproductive anatomy in class in her presence, and they asked her to skip the lecture. But she did not.

Elizabeth Blackwell studied diligently and in 1849 she became the first woman in the United States—perhaps in the whole world—to be awarded the degree of Medicinae Doctor. The ceremony took place at a Presbyterian Church in Geneva, N.Y. Even with her medical degree she could not find any opening. With sister Emily she started an infirmary for women and children in 1857. Later, she went back to England.

Blackwell also authored some books, including an inspiring autobiography (1895).

We must be grateful to the likes of Blackwell who declared: "If society will not admit of women's free development, then society must be remodeled." Thanks to the courage and determination of women like her, society is being remodeled, however slowly. "I do not wish to give [women] a first place, still less a second one," she once said, "…but the most complete freedom to take their true place whatever it may be,"

There are many things wrong in our world today, but it's simplistic to think that everything was better in former times. In matters of freedom, equality, justice and fairness we have improved considerably, though we still have long, long ways to go. Only a very naïve understanding of social history would want one to long for "the good old days".

February 4

From the World of Religion: ISIDORE OF PELUSIUM

Part of being faithful to one's religion is the careful observance of its rules and rites. Some of these include fasting and other austerities. If one is interested in the well being of the religious institution to which one belongs, then one is also concerned about the kind of people who gain recognition and power therein. And one gets involved with the defense of the doctrines of the religion against assaults on it, whether from within or from without. In all of these matters, a 4th century Chritstian from Alexandria distinguished himself. He was canonized. His name was Isidore of Pelusium. His Feast Day is 4 February.

It is difficult to get dependable information on someone who lived that long ago. But, thanks to the labors of scholars who go through ancient manuscripts and references to personages so far removed from us in time, we do have some idea of such people. There is a charm in knowing what specific thinkers did in ancient times.

Thus we do know that St. Isidore was a great scholar and that he wrote some books. St. Chrisostom was his guru. He was a monk in the monastery in Pelusium, a town in ancient Egypt. Scholars have retrieved a couple of thousand of his ten thousand letters. From a careful reading of these, we know about his views on Christian dogma, and about the strict discipline in the monasteries of the time. He was of the opinion that new members to monasteries should be allowed to gradually grow into ascetic life, rather than be required to follow all the abstinences right away. But he insisted that one should forget all links with the past, including interactions with pagans. He recommended that monks eat only the herbs such as was given by the chief in the monastery, and wear clothing made of animal skin. He was against the reading of non-Christian (pagan) authors and their beliefs, because he wisely realized the impact that such readings could have. He noted perceptively: "Just as fishermen hide the bait and covertly hook the fish, similarly, the crafty allies of the heresies cover their evil teachings and corrupt understanding with pietism and hook the more simple people, bringing them to spiritual death."

We also learn about his ethical framework from his letters. For example, in one of them he says it would be improper for soldiers to walk with swords among the people in a city during peace time. When some question was raised about the appropriateness of venerating religious relics, he argued that this was a perfectly right thing to do.

It is said by scholars who have looked into Isidore's letters say that they are written with much literary elegance, and that they are always gentle in tone, even when he refers to something he is not very happy about.

Isidore is remembered most of all for his opposition to Nestorianism which interpreted Christ as two distinct persons who were inseparably united rather than, as orthodoxy would have it; a single person with two distinct natures.

Today we have the city of Tell el-Farama in Egypt where the town of Pelusium once thrived. It is still remembered because of Saint Isidore. In the Bible (Ezekiel: 30-15) when the Lord says that He would pour His fury upon Sin, the reference was to Pelusium for that was another old Greek name for Pelusium. We are reminded of the silt of the region by that ancient the name Pelusium, for in Greek *pelos* means mud. Once pagans inhabited the place, then Christians, and now the inhabitants of the region are ardent Muslims, some of them probably descendants of Isidore's extended family. As history winds its way through time, loyalty and allegiance shift from age to age.

From the World of Science: CLYDE TAMBAUGH

Since very ancient times humanity has been aware of the five planets from Mercury to Saturn, and in the 16th century we recognized that the earth too is a planet. During each of the 18th, 19th, and 20th centuries: an additional planet was discovered. The last of these was Pluto.

The young astronomer who made the world aware of that farthermost planet known thus far was Clyde Tambaugh (born: 4 February 1906). In 1927 he built a 9 inch reflector telescope, using parts from farm machineries. His interest and enthusiasm for astronomy soon won him a position at Lowell observatory (named after the eminent astronomer Percival Lowell). At that time, the world of astronomy was aware of the existence of such a planet on the basis of our observations of the somewhat erratic behavior of Neptune. This behavior could be explained only in terms of the gravitational perturbation caused by another (as of then unknown) body in the neighborhood.

Tombaugh launched the search for the new planet. Night after night he took innumerable photographs of the sky, concentrating on a given sector during every two consecutive nights. Then he would study the thousands of stars in them with the utmost care. If there was but one small difference in the pictures of two consecutive nights, it would help locate the planet. The 24 year old astronomer's tireless search led him to spot a very faint object in the dark sky of 18 February 1930. He repeated his observations of the region near Gemini for more weeks, and made his discovery known to the world on 12 March 1930. This object indeed was the culprit disturbing Neptune's orbit.

The planet is in the deep darkness of the solar system. From where it is, the sun must look like a dim candle. Its distance from the sun ranges from thirty to fifty Astronomical Units. [An Astronomical Unit is the earth's average distance from the sun: about 150 million km.] Hence it was named after the Greek/Roman god who, as per mythology, was given the nether world after the Jovian gods defeated the Titans. [PL are also the initials of Percival Lowell.] Pluto is said to have carried away Persephone to his realm after he fell in love with her because of Cupid's arrow. Ancient tales also tell us that the souls of the dead are escorted to Pluto's world by a boatman called Charon. So, when a satellite of Pluto was discovered, it was dubbed Charon. Pluto was for long a much hated and feared deity in the Greek world, but his image improved later, and he came to be regarded as the provider of the earth' abundance, as a source of wealth: from where we get the word plutocracy, rule by the wealthy.

In its long trek, Pluto takes 248 earth-years to circumambulate the Sun once. Because its orbit intersects with that of Neptune, Pluto is not always the most most distant planet from the sun. From January 1979 to February 1999, it was closer to the Sun than Neptune. We will have to wait until the 23rd century before Pluto becomes the 8th planet again.

It is a relatively small planet, with a diameter of about 2300 km, spinning in a leisurely manner. Some have wondered if Pluto is really a planet or only an old satellite of Neptune that happened to break away from that planet's hold. Its single day lasts almost a week by our calendar. And at that distance it is awfully cold on Pluto: a perennial freeze at minus136 degrees on the Celsius scale.

Thus, for countless generations that speck of a planet has been whirling around like all the other planets of our solar system, but none before the 1930s knew of its existence. Pluto doesn't seem to have any significance to terrestrial life, unless one takes astrology seriously. Who knows how many more things are still hidden from human knowledge!

February 5

From the World of Religion:
JAPANESE MARTYR'S DAY

Religions spread from their geographical source by several means: by gentle persuasion, by propaganda, by force of arms, through evangelical fervor, through books and teachings, etc. In the process, those to whom the new religion is brought may be curious, resistant, sometimes eager to adopt, sometimes violent in response.

Recently, Christian evangelists were imprisoned in Afghanistan for trying to spread Christianity. That reaction to the spread of Christianity shocked those who have evolved into the 21st century, but it was mild compared to some others in earlier times, as illustrated in the lives of Christian martyrs. [Initially a martyr was anyone who bore witness to Christ's teachings, later it came to mean somebody who died for Christianity.]

Christianity began spreading in Japan by the mid-16th century, initiated by Francis Xavier. But in the province of Hirado (Japan) there started a protest against Christian influence, and a woman was beheaded for praying to the cross. Others were warned to give up the new faith which they had embraced. But then came a leader who was sympathetic to Christianity, and by the 1570s they began building more churches there. It has been estimated that within a decade there were some 200,000 Christians in Japan.

Now another fiercely religio-nationalistic monarch came. Under his direction a hundred and forty Christian places of worship are reported to have been decimated. The property of Christians was confiscated. One reason for this was that some missionaries were overstepping the rights they were given in the country. In the words of one commentator, "the zeal of certain religious Franciscans and Dominicans was wanting in prudence, and led to the persecution." Then again, in a Spanish vessel which landed on Japanese shores, allegedly because of a storm, lots of firearms were discovered, and the Japanese ruler suspected that there was a plot afloat for Japan to be taken over by expansionist Europeans. This began another series of persecution of Japanese Christians, since these were seen as witting or unwitting agents of the Western intruders.

An angry ruler by the name of Taikosama gave orders to the governor of Nagasaki to execute 26 Christians (6 Europeans and 20 Japanese) in the presence of a crowd. On 5 February 1597 (now called the Japanese Martyrs Day by many Christians) the condemned had to trek a long way barefoot, hands bound, and left ears cut, before they reached a wheat field. They were laid on crosses, tied with ropes and iron rings. The crosses were raised erect and let fall into a hole where all died.

But Christianity was not completely routed out of Japan. Little by little, like Buddhism, it too took deep roots in the hearts and minds of many people. When other episodes arose against Christian converts, more people were prepared to die for their religion. A Jesuit missionary reported with some pride and surprise that some of the people "have been confirmed in the faith and hope of eternal salvation; they have formally resolved to lay down their lives for the name of Christ."

It may not be appropriate to be judgmental about such incidents. Missionaries come with a sincere conviction that they are going to save the souls of the pagans from eternal damnation. People who have had other faiths for long centuries feel their ancient traditions are threatened by the new religion. It is a conflict between a commitment to save others and one to save one's own ancient past.

When Buddhism spread to China and Japan, or Islam to Persia and Indonesia, there does not seem to have been martyrs such as we find in the Christian world.

From the World of Science:
PLANETARY CONJUNCTION IN 1962

For casual on-lookers, the night sky is just a sprinkling of little twinkles, the same one night as any another. To star-gazers, there are patterns and periodicities up there, and they can tell one star or group from another. To astronomers, they all have names and histories, discernable motions and predictable configurations.

Of the many interesting episodes that come to pass in the firmament, one is called conjunction: when a couple or more planets are very close in our line of sight.

It is easy to picture how conjunctions occur: Consider the dial of a clock with its three hands, the second hand, the minute hand, and the hour hand, moving at different rates. But once every so often two or three hands are very close, as for example, at ten minutes and twelve seconds past two. Now imagine we have a clock with day hands, week hands, and month hands also. One may envision closeness of these too on the dial.

On 5 February 1962, a very unusual conjunction of five planets and the Moon occurred with a minimum seperation of 15.8 degrees, when there was also a solar eclipse. What this means is that there was a conjunction of all the seven astrological planets. We may expect another such minimum separation (of 8.3 degrees) of five planets and the Moon on 8 September 2040.

Dr. Donald Luttermoser of East Tennessee State University has computed when next such conjunctions arise. On 18 March 2002, one could see Venus soon after sunset, and then, by about 10 at night, Mars, Saturn, and Jupiter were all be visible, keeping company with a crescent Moon.

The rarity of seven-planet conjunction has had an impact on some people. For example, in the 12th century, an astrologer who signed himself as Juan de Toledo sent out a letter to the effect that terrible catastrophes were in store in 1186 because in that year all the five planets would be in the constellation Libra. This caused unbelievable panic, not just in Europe but in such distant places as Turkey and Persia. The terrified people dug protective shelters in Germany, the Archbishop of Canterbury instructed everyone to fast, the Emperor of Byzantium had the windows of his palace sealed, and thousands of people genuflected out of panic rather than for prayer.

Fear of conjunctions has not melted away with the rise of modern science. Prior to the 5 May 2000 conjunction soothsayers were terrorizing simple folk with predictions ranging from the melting of the Polar ice-caps to winds blowing as 2000 mph.

Conjunctions have also been interpreted in mystical ways. One preacher informed his flock that the conjunction of Venus and Saturn of 20 May 1999 was to inform us that the covenant of Jesus Christ to be married to the Church was being fulfilled. [Venus was Love and Saturn had the ring.]

Brian Monson calculated the probability of all planets aligning themselves completely with respect to the sun, and found out that there is one chance in 180 million years that this would happen. It should be noted that though, from an anthropocentric standpoint, the event is pretty rare, when one considers the 4.5 billion life thus far of the solar system, some 45 million such conjunctions would have occurred by now.

Stars and planets, sprinkled in the sky, change as if shaken at random in a kaleidoscope. But, in fact they rearrange themselves in accordance with predictable patterns. When we to get to know them, we not only experience the thrill of a celestial connection, but realize how through them we connect with our ancestors too, for all of them have witnessed and wondered about those same twinkling lights.

February 6

From the World of Religion: INTELLECTUAL FERMENT IN ISLAMIC WORLD

Philosophical questions have often arisen in the context of great religions. Thinkers and intellectuals are prone to interpret and analyze ideas, whether new or old.

So it was in the Islamic tradition also: Not long after the Prophet and because of his inspiration, intellectual awareness and rationalist inquiries rose to great heights in the Islamic world. Already in the 9th century, Caliph al-Mamun established *Bayt al Hikmah*: House of Wisdom in Baghdad. It was here that the early translations took place on a grand scale which led to the intellectual flowering in the Arab world.

Once the light of reason is lit, there is no telling where it will lead to. A school of philosophers, called the *Mutazilites* emerged to interpret and justify revealed religion and beliefs on rationalistic grounds. Al Kindi (9th century), the first philosopher in the tradition, who was also a scholar in physics and mathematics, sought to reconcile Aristotelian and Neo-Platonist thought with

Qur'anic revelations, insisting, like others at later times in the Christian tradition, that religion and philosophy (science) are not incompatible. Though for the faithful, the Qur'an is revealed and religious, it also embodies what an outsider might describe as ancient scientific theories. There are passages in the Qur'an which speak of creation, of the world from smoke, of seven heavens and seven earths, of life out of water, of Man from clay, even of successive stages of life. Al Kindi's major impact on Islamic thought was his insistence on, and efforts to, find concordance between Aristotelian science and Qura'nic verses, that is to say, his blending of Islamic doctrines (religion) with Greek philosophy (science).

However, there is always some danger in attempting logical proofs for religious faith, for an infidel with a sharper mind might outwit the believer. This is one reason why staunch orthodoxy, in all traditions, is not always sympathetic to such efforts.

A towering figure in Islamic philosophy was ibn Sînâ (11th century) who argued for the compatibility between science and religion as parallel visions of Truth. He stated that there were three factors at the root of the world: matter, form and existence. God, he argued, was pure existence, devoid of form and matter. God's existence was necessary for the emergence of the world. Ibn Sînâ saw religion as a dramatization of higher truths, a symbolic way of communicating the higher truths to the masses. But his system was perceived by some as dangerous, and he was vehemently attacked.

The wisdom that religious truths is attained by mysticism, not logic, was propounded by another eminent thinker of the glory days of Arab civilization, al-Ghazâlî (11th century). He felt that God had cured him of a serious illness, not through signs or sayings, but through a light which God placed in his heart. He had a mystic experience.

Al-Ghazâlî classified philosophers as materialists, naturalists, and theists. He went on to say that the first were atheists; the second, while recognizing God's glory in natural and biological phenomena, were nevertheless inclining towards irreligion; and the third group alone was faithful to Islam. In a work entitled Incoherence of philosophers, al-Ghazâli made scathing attacks on rationalist thinkers. He put his illustrious predecessors al Fârâbî and ibn Sînâ in the second group, because they were staunch admirers of Aristotle.

Al-Ghazâlî's writings and those of other Sûfi mystics sounded the death-knell for rationalistic philosophy in the Islamic world for quite some time. One scholar put it this way: "After him (al-Ghazali)…philosophy hit itself in the remote corners of the Moslem world; the pursuit of science waned…" It has also been suggested that if al Fârâbî and ibn Sînâ, rather than al Ghazâlî had won the day, modern science could well have emerged in the Arab world. Who can tell!

From the World of Science:
MARY DOUGLAS NICOL

Some of us may wonder sometimes about our great grandparents, but it is not often that one thinks of a distant progenitor a thousand or so years ago in the past. And perhaps rarely if ever does one even consider a great, great ancestor a couple of million years ago. If we do the thought experiment (*Gedankenexperiment*, as it is called in German) of retracing the branches of our genealogical tree, each of us may imagine a very distant anthropoid couple of whatever kind or constitution from whom we have descended. Darwin et al. did say we have come from apes or the like, but to locate the remains of one such is a different matter.

Mary Douglas Nicol (born: 6 February 1913) did something like that. She did not have a formal degree in archeology. She began her career as an assistant to professionals in the field, working in England, then became assistant and companion to the already well established archaeologist Louis Leaky (who became her husband). With her husband, Mary Leaky exercised her interest in archeology in many locations in East Africa. A great many of Mary Leaky's finds were in the archeological digs at the Olduvai Gorge in Tanzania. In the Olorgesaile site near Nairobi she and her husband unearthed hundreds of stone tools of the earliest humans, dating back to hundreds of thousands of years. It is said that they used the services of Italian war prisoners in some of their excavations. In 1948, the Leakys were working in Rusinga Island where Mary Leaky ran into several bone fragments near a cliff. She was able to reconstruct the skull and jaws of a creature that looked very much like that of an ape. Indeed, this provided the oldest body-part-evidence of a being who must have been a common ancestor to us humans and our primate cousins, the apes: *Proconcul Africanus*. The remains were dated to be at least 20 million years old.

In 1959 Mary Leaky discovered the remains of a Zinjanthropus. [Zinj, in Arabic, refers to East Africa.] This specimen has been dated to be 1.75 million years old. It was the first of this species which may belong to the human ancestral line.

Even after her husband died in 1972, Mary Leaky continued her search for traces of ancient human presence on our planet. In 1978, she found something even more eerie at Laetoli, not too far from Olduvai: footprints of a 3.5 million old hominid on volcanic ash, perhaps the oldest legacy of a very ancient ancestor of ours. This was not a manuscript, but a "pediscript" of ancient Man.

Leaky became quite famous and respected in her field. She received academic honors from the universities of Yale, Chicago and Oxford, and the Linnaeus Medal from the Royal Swedish Academy of Sciences. The Society of Women Geographers in Washington gave her a gold medal. The autobiographies of most people disclose their own past. But that of Mary Leaky, entitled, *Disclosing the Past*, published when she was 71, discloses humanity's past also.

We live in an age when people wish to discover their "roots." By this they mean their particular cultural heritage and ancestry. But there is a genealogical tree that embraces all cultures and peoples. That is the tree of the human family. Probing into its roots can be as exciting as going back to the village where a great-great grandparent once lived, and discovering our most ancient ancestors binds us all as humans.. That is the kind of work that Mary Leaky did. The findings of pre-historians and archeologists remind us that in a profound way, we are all connected. In an earlier era, religions did this through Adam and Eve, Manu and P'an Ku; but modern science, more modestly, unearths ancient teeth and jaw bones to make the point. Remembering our connectedness is very important.

February 7

From the World of Religion:
FREDERICK DOUGLASS

If one is asked to name an eloquent African-American orator, Martin Luther King and Jesse Jackson come to mind at once. But in the last century there was another great orator who had significant impact on America's moral conscience. His name was Frederick Douglass (born: 7 February 1818). He spoke against the scourge of slavery long before the American Civil War and served as advisor to President Abraham Lincoln during that war.

Born in a slave setting, Douglass lost his parents when still quite young. He stayed with his grandmother, and got the rudiments of reading from a lady who "owned" him. But he learned a good deal on his own. At the age of 12, a book called the "Columbian Orator" happened to come his way. It made him understand the power of public speaking and persuasive writing, and he determined to cultivate and use these skills in freeing himself and his people from the shackles to which they had been condemned in the country to whose growth they too were contributing in significant ways.

Frederick Douglass toiled hard and worked as a conductor in a locomotive, but managed to escape from the institutional chain that bound him in Maryland, sneaking into New York.

He impressed the abolitionists, and was solicited by the American Anti-Slavery Society to go on a lecture tour to inform, instruct, and enlighten the citizenry on a practice that should have no place in any society, least of all American. His great gift was the gift of speech, for his oratory was powerful like Shakespeare's Mark Anthony's. Consider the following start of a speech he gave, entitled: "What to the Slave is the Fourth of July?"

"Mr. President, Friends and Fellow Citizens:…I do not remember ever to have appeared as a speaker before any assembly more shrinkingly, nor with greater distrust of my ability, than I do this day. A feeling has crept over me, quite unfavorable to the exercise of my limited powers of speech. The task before me is one which requires much previous thought and study for its proper performance. I know that apologies of this sort are generally considered flat and unmeaning. I trust, however, that mine will not be so considered. Should I seem at ease, my appearance would much misrepresent me. The little experience I have had in addressing public meetings, in country school houses, avails me nothing on the present occasion."

Douglass became famous and marked after the publication of his autobiography in 1845. So as not to be abducted again, and to educate the British of the shameful system of slavery, he sailed to England. But the sailing wasn't smooth. A meeting to honor him, organized by some of the more enlightened folks on board the ship, infuriated some southern gentlemen who felt insulted by uncomplimentary references to their age-old custom. They threatened to dump Douglass into the deep. Credit is due to Captain Judkins who used authority and threat to return calm and enforce decent behavior.

Douglass's successful lecture tour lasted a year and a half. He won over many in England to the noble cause, secured sufficient support, financial and otherwise, with which he started a newspaper when he returned to the U.S.. He settled down for a time in Rochester, N.Y. where he initiated a paper called *North Star* with the motto: "Right is of no sex—Truth is of no color—God is the Father of us all, and we are all brethren."

The establishment did not appreciate this venture. *The New York Herald* asked Rochesterians to sink Douglass's press into Lake Ontario. Today the city speaks of Frederick Douglass with much pride. What a difference the passage of time can make!

From the World of Science: WILLIAM HUGGINS

One of the tenets of ancient science was that celestial bodies are made of a material that is of an altogether different category from the kinds of matter that we see and study here on earth. This seems fairly reasonable in the framework of a Earth-Heaven dichotomy. Indeed there was no way that this thesis could be proved or disproved.

But today we hear about stars containing calcium and interstellar space interspersed with hydrogen. One may wonder how on earth, I mean how from earth, we can determine the chemical composition of a chunk of the sun or a lump of empty space.

This knowledge is fairly recent in human history: it dates back to mid-19th century. The first scientist to put into evidence the uniformity of matter in all regions of the universe was the English astronomer William Huggins (born: 7 February 1824).

Like everything in science, his work rested on the discoveries of others. It had been known for a few years that by analyzing light from a hot source with a spectroscope (which measures the precise wavelengths of radiant light), one can identify the chemical composition of the source. This is because chemists had studied light from some burning substances, and discovered that each chemical element has its own characteristic spectrum: a sort of light-fingerprint from which it can be identified.

As Galileo had turned the telescope from spying on enemies to gazing at celestial bodies, Kirchhoff turned the spectroscope from candle flames to the Sun. To Huggins the news of Krichhoff's idea came, as he said later, "like the coming upon a spring water in a dry and thirsty land." He systematically studied the spectra of 24 elements here on earth, and began spectroscopic analysis of light from the stars. He established by this method that the stars are no different from our own sun, or rather that the sun is but another star, more bulged in appearance only because of far greater proximity.

Huggins systematized this line of research. He directed his attention to the so-called nebulas which had once been described as "shining fluids." The investigations of Huggins revealed that these were of two kinds: one made up of countless clusters of stars, and another a mere gaseous (largely hydrogen) spread. When he recorded an utterly unknown spectrum in a nebula, he thought he had discovered a new element, and even named it nebulium. Decades later it was shown that this was simply the spectrum of ionized oxygen and nitrogen.

Huggins was the first to apply the Doppler principle to stars. He discovered by this means that the brightest star Sirius is moving away at quite a speed. This implies that in principle, though not in practice (since this will take millions of years), some day Sirius won't hold the distinction of being the brightest first magnitude star.

All it takes is a spectroscope: a device with tubes, a calibrated scale, and prism or glass on which lines are etched. When it is used with a sound knowledge of the nature of light and of the elements, we can uncover the composition of matter trillions of miles way: matter which is for ever beyond our physical grasp. Through the same spectroscope, light also reveals to us if stars and galaxies are coming towards us or fleeing away.

Such is the power of science: not just in its capacity to bring about technological marvels, but more importantly, in its potential for unraveling, through ingenious devices and fruitful concepts, aspects of physical reality that are by no means obvious to the superficial observer. It is through science that, in the worlds of the poet William Blake, we can truly "see the world in a grain of sand and heaven in a wild flower, hold infinity in the palm of your hand, and eternity in an hour."

February 8

From the World of Religion: PARINIRVANA DAY

Feast and fast days in most traditions are based on the lunar calendar. Lunar calendars were adopted earlier in most cultures because the phases of the moon are more readily recognized than the 365 day solar cycle. Lunar phases and asterisms also tied up astrology and astronomy with religious observances. Matters become more complicated when some of the festival-assigners of traditional calendars are not schooled in basic astronomy. This results in incorrect attribution of full moon and new moon days.

Another consequence of this is that the dates of festivals become region-dependent. This is especially the case with the Buddhist calendar. In a way this is good, because the significance of a religious observance really has nothing to do with the phase of the moon or its date as per the Gregorian reform.

In some Buddhist traditions, 8 February is denoted in 2002 as Parinirvana Day. The term refers to the liberation of Buddha from his physical frame. The stories associated with the birth and passing away of prophets are generally awe-inspiring. Irrespective of their historical accuracy, such days are remembered on dates fixed by tradition.

It is said that, for some political reasons, Buddha's cousin Devadutta tried to kill him by instigating an elephant that had gone berserk to trample over him. But when Buddha gently raised his hand, the beast calmed down and knelt before the Master. Then, Devadutta arranged to roll a massive boulder towards Buddha, but it barely grazed his foot. Eventually he regretted his evil actions and joined the Buddhist order.

In 483 B.C.E., the 80 year old Buddha went to Vaisali, and then to Kusinagara where he gently laid down, turned to a side, let his head rest on his raised right hand, closed his eyes, and attained Nirvana (liberation from physical life) in a grove of Sala trees, There are Buddha statues in the *Parinirvana* pose. Like all Buddha statues this too is an embodiment of peace and serenity.

Buddha is said to have abhorred reports of miracles, but his disciples and later followers, as in other traditions, could not find enough greatness in his teachings without associating miraculous events with his name. Thus, an ancient text by Nagarjuna describes in majestic and mythological terms what happened on the day of Parinirvana: The earth shook, rivers rolled back, dark and fearsome clouds were formed in the skies, there was thunder and lightning, and a tremendous downpour. One could see meteor showers, and hear the roaring and the screaming and the howling of animals. Plants and trees split, mountains moved, and gigantic tides splashed over the land. Comets appeared in broad daylight. Even the Gods moaned. All this expresses the intense anguish that people must have felt when they heard that the Great Master had passed away.

It is said that Buddha was cremated, and his ashes were sprinkled in seven different places where *stupas* (dome-shaped shrines) were erected to remember him. Legend has it that Emperor Ashoka dug the ashes out and spread them in 84,000 spots on earth where Buddhist stupas were built. Gradually, they were replaced by temples where an icon of Buddha was placed at the altar. Among the earliest of such Buddha sculptures were the magnificent mountain carvings in Gandhara (present Afghanisthan) where mindless fanatics destroyed them in 2000.

According to tradition, after Parinirvana, a group of 500 worthy ones (*arahants*), led by a Mahakasyapa (Senior Theologian) met at Rajagrha, and compiled the original teachings of the Master. Thus emerged the Sutra Pitaka: canonical texts of Buddhism.

From the World of Science: DANIEL BERNOULLI

Like the Bachs in music history, the Bernoullis were prolific as mathematicians. The family had lived for many generations in Flanders before it emigrated to Switzerland. In the days of religious fervor of the 17th century, God-fearing Catholics were doing some terrible things to their (Huguenot) Protestant cousins in the name of Christ.

In due course, at least eight Bernoullis made names for themselves, and a couple of them left lasting results. As E. T. Bell, an eminent historian of mathematics noted, "The Bernoullis and (Leonard) Euler were in fact the leaders above all others who perfected the calculus to the point where quite ordinary men could use it for the discovery of results which the greatest of the Greek could never have found."

One of the most productive members of the Bernoulli clan was Daniel Bernoulli (born: 8 February 1700). After studying logic, philosophy, and medicine at various universities, he tried unsuccessfully to become a professor of botany and anatomy in Basel. In 1724 he published a paper on some aspects of mathematics which made him so famous that he received an offer from the prestigious St. Petersburg Academy where the great Leonard Euler (another Swiss) was also working at the time.

There is more to mathematics than numbers and addition. Mathematics is also a powerful tool in the formulation, elucidation, and analysis of natural phenomena.

Consider, for example, the flow of water through pipes. In practical applications, as also in natural flows, the width of the channel might change from one place to another. Bernoulli studied fluid flow and deduced a principle that bears his name. The Bernoulli principle is actually an early instance of what we call today the principle of conservation of energy. His studies of fluid flow led to his book on hydrodynamics.

From the tremor of hands to the vibration of strings in a musical instrument, there are many instances of small oscillations. Bernoulli was one of the first to investigate such phenomena mathematically. He is remembered especially for his analysis of the vibration of strings and in organ pipes.

Because of all this, Daniel Bernoulli is reckoned, along with Euler and D'Alembert, as one of the founders of what later became the field of mathematical physics.

He worked on the theory of probability, and derived some results in games of chance. He made calculations on the relative values of the moral and the material worth in a person's assets, and tried to apply this in the field of insurance.

In his work on the pressure-volume relationships of gases, Bernoulli suggested that a volume of gas could be looked upon as being made up of a very large number of small particles which are moving in it at random. He applied the theory of probability to study this. This is the germinal idea in the kinetic theory of gases and statistical mechanics which were to develop only in the second half of the 19th century.

Furthermore, Bernoulli wrote on human anatomy and physiology, on breathing and muscular contraction.

During his long life (he died at the ripe old age of 82), Daniel Bernoulli competed in and won ten prize-awarding competitions of the French Academy of Sciences, which was no mean achievement.

Bernoulli's scientific productivity was impressive. Yet, he is only one among many contributors to human knowledge and insights. People like him are rarely remembered in the annals of human history which recall more often the names of political leaders, military generals, and tyrannical monarchs.

February 9

From the World of Religion:
FEAST DAY OF APOLLO

Ancient Gods are like friends of our childhood days: we may remember them vaguely, but they are no longer as close or dear or worthy of attention to us, as the friends of our later years. So it is, for example, with Apollo of ancient Greece. There was a time when he was worshiped and venerated, not just in Greece, but also in Rome at one time. Today, however, he is largely only a name in archived mythology: no longer a life-giving force to a civilization, as he once was.

In a Homeric hymn Apollo is invoked as the son of Zeus and Leto, born under a palm tree in Delos where Helios, the sun-god, was the primary deity. Artemis was his sister. He imbibed the immortalizing ambrosia, and grew to manhood right away. He killed the awesome Python when still very young.

By ancient accounts, Apollo was born on the 7th day of the Greek month of Thargelion, but people of later eras fixed 9 February as the Feast of Apollo. We read in the Odyssey that when Odysseus was gone for a whole decade and thought to be dead, his queen Penelope was wooed by many suitors. Penelope, little interested in any of them, organized an archery contest on the Feast Day of

Apollo, for Apollo was a fine archer too. So the day has been observed since very ancient times.

He was a versatile god: he would strum the strings of the lyre as easily as he would wield the string of the bow. When the gods had a banquet he would play his lyre. Indeed, he was very jealous of his instrument. When Marsyas claimed to play the flute better, he was flayed by Apollo. Like Krishna in Hindu lore, Apollo protected the cattle. He was athletic, and the first winner of the first Olympic Games. He was a singer and poet as well, yet warlike no less. And he is also known to have sent plague and pestilence to the people.

Emperor Augustus of Rome, who regarded himself as a protégé of Apollo, had temples built for him. Games were instituted in his honor. I remember seeing a seven foot high statue of Apollo in a museum in Rome, and found it hard to believe this was the image of a god. But as sculpture, it was impressive, with flowing marble cloth gracefully draped around the neck and hanging over the part of the arm that still was there, and more modest in its exposure than the one in Greece. Later I read that this statue, known as Apollo Belvedere, was much admired by Goethe as a supreme example of Greek ideal of beauty. The poet Swinburne described Apollo as "with hair and harpstring of gold, a bitter God to follow, a beautiful God to behold."

We may not know exactly how the Feast of Apollo may have been observed in those distant days. Some have suggested it could not have been much different in essence from such days that are observed in our own times: visit to the temple of Apollo with little gifts, selling of memorabilia by merchants around the temple, special foods and drinks, singing, dancing and performing on the lyre, etc. For, in spite of all the differences with varying forms, names and legends, in matters of religion we are all very much alike. Of course we all have the same number of chromosomes and similar genes, but even culturally speaking, we are not all that different. Just as our physical hunger prompts us to make food, and that food is in form and taste and variety different from region to region and culture to culture, this is true in our religious expressions as well. For they too spring from another kind of hunger: the yearning to connect in some way with that which seems to be beyond and elusive, yet very near to our deepest core.

From the World of Science: JACQUES MONOD

Back in the mid-18th century La Mettrie wrote a book entitled: "L'homme machine" (Man-machine). The thesis of the book was that human beings are essentially machines: the brain secretes thought the same way as the liver secretes bile.

In the twentieth century, armed with considerably more scientific knowledge, and basing himself on his own ground-breaking research, another French scientist-thinker came to very much the same conclusion: "The cell is a machine. The animal is a machine. Man is a machine." His name was Jacques Monod (born: 9 February 1905).

It is well known that genes control pretty much everything that the human body does. Thus they also regulate the metabolism of cells. Monod's work revealed that this happens when genes direct the biosynthesis of enzymes. Monod and his colleague Jacob Loeb proposed that aside from the DNA there is, what they called, a messenger ribonucleic acid (mRNA). The base sequence of mRNA is complementary to the DNA's base sequence. The mRNA carries information encoded in the base sequence to ribosomes where protein synthesis occurs. There the base sequence of the mRNA gets translated into the amino acid of the protein-accelerating enzyme. Monod also put into evidence the feedback mechanism which regulates the production of proteins. He introduced the term operons to describe gene complexes.

Monod worked at the Pasteur Institute in Paris to which, like quite a few others before him, he brought glory with a Nobel Prize. He worked under rather strenuous conditions, for which he criticized his government. He declined lucrative offers from the United States, preferring to work in his own native France.

Like most people who work at the most fundamental levels of living organisms, Monod was convinced that an organism is nothing more than an extraordinarily complex biochemical lab where millions of chemical reactions are continuously taking place to keep the whole unit in working condition. In his framework, he simply couldn't take seriously traditional religious doctrines on life, afterlife, god or creation. In a very widely read book called *Le hasard et la necessité*(1970) [*Chance and Necessity*] he presented with great clarity and persuasiveness the philosophical view by which there is no purpose or meaning in life as a phenomenon. He simply could not subscribe to the notion that ethics and morality can be derived from our understanding of the world. While repudiating traditional religion, he also showed the futility of trying to connect science and religion. Indeed he had no respect for all the talk about God, Cosmos in the religious sense, mysticism, and the like. He forcefully expounded the thesis that, whether we like it or not, we are just chance occurrences in an otherwise lifeless universe which, by the way, ignores us as less than nothing. As he put it, "Chance alone is the source of all novelty, all creation in the biosphere." He referred to this doctrine of no intent or purpose as the "postulate of objectivity."

Declaring that "the ancient covenant is in pieces", he added: "Man at last knows that he is alone in the universe's unfeeling immensity, out of which he emerged only by chance."

It followed from this recognition, said Monod, that there simply is no such thing as human destiny, no heaven or hell. We have to act and behave as if heaven is here below and there is no hell.

He was aware, like most thoughtful people, that in many ways humankind has reached the brink, and that unless we act quickly, our species is doomed to perish very soon.

February 10

From the Word of Religion:
SAINT PAUL IN MALTA

Pure fiction may be interesting, and factual history could be informative. Sacred history combines religious world views, scriptural references, and historical tidbits, and is often associated with specific geographical locations. It can be deeply meaningful for the devout.

Consider the island of Malta not far from the coast of Italy. It has a small bay called St. Paul's Bay. The reason for this name is as follows: Paul, we recall, was born in the Judaic tradition: his father was a Roman citizen, therefore he too was one. But, after a profound personal experience, he converted to Christianity. He was so taken by the new Faith that he set out to bring more members into the fold. In this mission he traveled to Syria, Cyprus, Greece and many other places.

At one point, he was arrested and brought for trial in Judea. He demanded, as a Roman citizen, to be sent to Rome to be tried in Caesar's court. This was granted, and along with others, he was put on board a ship. During the voyage, a fierce storm broke out and the tides swelled perilously. When the passengers were in panic, Paul calmed them down by declaring that all would be safe, for an Angel had assured him of this.

Indeed the ship was tossed to the shores of Malta. This was in the year 60 C.E. When the shipwrecked passengers landed, they were greeted and received cordially by the people, led by their ruler, Publius.

They lit a bonfire for warmth, and someone spotted a venomous snake creeping on Paul's neck. It is said to have bit him, but there was no visible effect, and the people were astounded. Paul was escorted to the mansion where Publius lived, and there he saw the governor's father gravely ill. Paul is said to have cured him by simply placing his hand on the ailing old man. Other people started to bring their own sick family members, and Paul is said to have cured them all by the touch of his hand and with fervent prayer.

News of this extraordinary man spread all through the island. Paul went from place to place, spreading God's word as conveyed through Jesus, and narrated how Christ had been crucified, and how he had given his own life to save us all from the torments of Hell. In a matter of three months, practically everyone in Malta became Christian.

So, over the centuries, they built on the Maltese islands monuments to remember the unexpected arrival of him who has become their patron saint. There is a Church of San Pawl Milgi which stands at the very place, it says, where Publius received Paul. Another edifice, called Tal-Huggiega Church, has been erected at the very spot where the bonfire was lit. Then there is a grotto named after the saint, where Paul is said to have lived during those three months. There is also a St. Paul's Church in Valletta where, they say, a forearm of the saintly martyr is still preserved as a relic. We can also see a fountain, now across a restaurant, which is said to have been instigated miraculously by Paul, and from whose waters he baptized the first Christians of Malta.

Moving from sacred history to recorded history, the Church of St. Paul's Shipwreck, whatever may have been its more antique aspect, was rebuilt in the 17th century. The frescoes one sees on the ceiling were created in 1904. But many of the treasures in it have accumulated more ancient histories.

By one reckoning, the fateful ship with St. Paul arrived on the island on February 10. So the people of Malta have a joyous celebration on this date every year, for that day surely changed the course of their history.

From the World of Science: SUNYATA AND ZERO

In the hieroglyphic notation of ancient Egypt, arbitrary symbols were used for one, ten, and multiples thereof. The Greeks used the first ten capital letters of their alphabet to denote numbers from one to ten, and then used (the Greek equivalent of) K, M, L, N for 20, 30, 40, 50, etc., then R, S, T, U, F, etc. for 100, 200, 300, 400, 500, etc. The Roman numerals may still be seen on the face of some clocks. In this system, X, L, C, D, and M stand for 10, 50, 100, 500, and 1000 respectively. The Hebrews also use letters for numerals. You can imagine how cumbersome it can be to add or multiply say, CXIII and LVI, using only Roman numerals.

The people of India were the first to use the place value system which is common in most parts of the world today. In 1881, several folios of birch bark were discovered at a place called Bakshali. This Bakshali manuscript is filled with arithmetical problems. It has rules, problems, solutions, fractions, square roots and progressions, notes on incomes, expenses, profits, and losses, etc. Several problems relating mensuration and miscellaneous subjects are also dealt with here. Dated back to the 3rd or the 4th century CE, these are the oldest extant record of the use of the decimal notation for numbers.

By the 7th century, such notation had become quite common in India. But it wasn't until the 13th century that its was imported into Europe through the intermediary of Arab scholars. Our words zero and cipher come from the Arab word *sifr* for the Sanskrit word *sunya*.

The place value notation had its origin in the concept of the zero. This was a tremendous leap forward, as great a breakthrough as the invention of the wheel in locomotion.

Interestingly, the zero idea is related to an interpretation of Reality as Nothingness. The credit for this insight is attributed to the Buddhist philosopher Nagarjuna who argued that everything is unreal, including consciousness. Nothing, in his view, was real: neither soul nor transmigration, neither lived life nor nirvana (liberation from the birth-death cycle). If anything is real, it is nothing, emptiness, void. Nagarjuna called this *sunyata*.

Commentators have pounced on this idea and written volumes on the metaphysical nothingness. Contemplating on utter void became a mode of mystical experience. Some have argued that Nagarjuna was speaking, not of physical void, but of a transcendental contemplative emptiness.

All this speculation on the empty was not empty speculation. In its silent way it spoke loudly on aspects of the universe that are not readily apparent. After all, every number has a negative counterpart, and when the two are combined, what do we get but zero?

Unbridled speculation about the ultimate nature of the world led to one of the most powerful concepts in mathematical thought. The idealist extreme of regarding the world as no more than a passing illusion generated by our senses is not unique to Hindu culture, but in India they gave it a symbol. For, in their worldview, there is an inner Reality behind the illusory concreteness. They introduced a simple dot for this. So, from the contemplation on nothingness emerged one of the most profound elements in mathematics, namely the concept of and the symbol for what we have come to call zero.

An Arab poet by the name of al-Shabhadi noted in one of this books that the Hindus were proud of three things: the invention of fables in which animals talk; [The so-called Aesop's Fables have been traced back to India.] The invention of the game of chess, to which references occur in many ancient texts; and the invention of their number system. Perhaps they had reason to be.

February 11

From the World of Religion: KENKOKU KINEN NO HI

In most cultures, since the most ancient times, kings have claimed a divine right. In some instances they have even assumed a divine genealogy. Sometimes, the realm itself is imagined as having been founded by a god of the tradition. Unlike in eras past, modern commentators use the epithet "mythical" to describe this situation.

During the past 35 years, Japan has been celebrating a national holiday called Kenkoku Kinen No Hi. It is meant to remember the mythical founder of the Japanese nation, known as Jimmu, who is believed to have lived in the 7th century B.C.E. His more formal name of Hiko-hoho-demi appears in the most ancient extant Japanese book known as Kojiki. An epithet for him is Kamu-Yamato-Ihare-Biki: One who brought the divine rule of the Sun Goddess (Amaterasu) down to the earthly realm. Like Indra in the Vedic tradition, and episodes in the Book of Judges of the Old Testament, Jimmu was a conqueror par excellence, an imperial hero of whom the common people were proud, one whom they venerated. It is believed that the clan of Yamato which claims him most of all spread eastward and eventually dominated much of Japan.

Legend says that Jimmu's mother Tama-yori-hime was born to the Sea-God, and that he was her fourth child. He became king at the age of fifteen and married fair Ahira-tsu-hime who was from the province of Hiunga.

When he was forty five, Jimmu assembled his family and ministers and spoke to them about his divine ancestry, reminding them that it was 1,792,470 years since their Heavenly ancestor had descended on earth. During these millions of years heavenly beings had blessed the country. He spoke to them about beautiful places in the east of the country which would benefit by their presence.

Everyone agreed, saying it was meant to be so because very similar thoughts were crossed their minds too. Then, under the leadership of Jimmu, the great conquest began, and many regions came under the sway of this godly king. After six years of success, Jimmu addressed his people: "During the six years that our expedition against the East has lasted, owing to my reliance on the Majesty of Imperial Heaven, the wicked bands have met death. It is true that the frontier lands are still unpurified, and that a remnant of evil is still rebellious. But in the region of the Central Land there is no more wind and dust. Truly we should make a vast and spacious capital, and plan it great and strong."

Mythologies remind us of what inspired our ancestors; they also give a sense of cultural unity, making a people proud of their past, especially when they have suffered defeat in war or come under colonialist occupation. However, like all mythologies that speak of conquests, the Jimmu story brings pride only to those who belong to the conquering class. When ancient tales of conquest are presented as historical truths to inspire the masses, unhealthy nationalism and ludicrous chauvinism could emerge.

Therefore, there were protests from enlightened scholars in Japan when there was a move to re-write history to indoctrinate children with feelings of national superiority. Since the 1950s, the Japanese Association for History Studies, like its counterparts in some other countries, has been objecting to nationalistic undercurrents in new history texts which foster fascist tendencies.

In most traditional cultures, religion and history are intermingled, and when politics too becomes part of the mixture, the situation can become explosive, not exactly awe-inspiring to outsiders, and sometimes dangerous to weaker neighbors.

From the World of Science:
BERNARD DE FONTENELLE

Scientific knowledge lives at two levels: First, it is in the minds of those engaged in science. Then it is in the public mind, where it ranges from some understanding to total incomprehension. Most people can understand basic science, just as all can appreciate art and music. With science, it helps to have guides: people with a sound knowledge of what they are talking about, and who can express and explain it in terms that make sense to the intelligent, but unaware reader.

In this context we may recall Bernard de Fontenelle (born: 11 February 1657) who lived to be almost a hundred years. He was an erudite scholar, brilliant wit, and effective exponent of science. He fostered enlightened thinking using enjoyable language. He warned that people would reject science as useless if they didn't understand it. He was so impressed with the power of mathematics that he said "even a work of morality, politics, criticism will be more elegant, other things being equal, if it is shaped by the hand of geometry." He felt the joy that mathematics can give, saying: "Nothing proves more clearly that the mind seeks truth, and nothing reflects more glory upon it, than the delight it takes, sometimes in spite of itself, in the driest and thorniest researches of algebra."

In 1686 Fontenelle wrote a charming book on planets and stars. In the form of conversations with a marquise while taking walks in a garden, he expounded the Copernican system and speculated on the possibility of life on the Moon and elsewhere in the universe. This book saw many editions, and brought basic knowledge of the new astronomy to thousands of educated people. It was the first example of (what is called in French) *vulgarisation* (popularization) of scientific knowledge: a genre in which many authors were to write in the generations to come. This was as much a service to science as the discovery of a new satellite or organism.

Fontenelle reflected on history and subtly suggested that mythologies were fables of ancient peoples. He sowed the seeds for a critical study of religious texts and a historical approach to hagiography. He was so impressed by the Dutch author A. van Dale's Latin book on oracles that he rendered it into French. He was not inclined to believe in miracles, and had an aversion for superstitions. These were revolutionary and rebellious, even reprehensible attitudes in those times, so Fontenelle often published anonymously.

He was brought up as Catholic, but he argued for religious tolerance: in those days this meant not being too harsh on Protestants. [Jews, Muslims, Hindus and Buddhists, were nowhere near to be intolerant toward.] In 1697, when the French king revoked the Edict of Nantes which used to give equal rights and protection to French Protestants, Fontenelle wrote a piece against this in a disguised format: as a conflict between two people called Eegenu and Mreo in a distant island. Actually these were anagrams of Calvin's Geneva (u and v are same in Latin) and Catholicism's Rome. He could have been arrested for this attack on the king, but he promptly wrote a poem praising Louis XIV under whom religion had triumphed. Besides, he had good connections at the court.

Fontenelle foresaw that science would rise to great heights, but he also feared humanity was too weak to look at truth straight in the eye. Fontenelle served as Perpetual Secretary of the Academie Royale des Sciences for forty years. In this capacity he delivered several eulogies and wrote a systematic history of the institution. These writings are valuable to scholars to this day. Fontelle was one of the spirits that inspired the French Encyclopedie, and the associated Enlightenment which were to significantly affect the course of human history.

February 12

From the World of Religion: CHINESE NEW YEAR

We have all heard of the Yin-Yang principle in the Chinese framework: of the complementing dichotomies in the world. Just as 7 is sacred in the Middle-Eastern religious traditions, the number 5 is sacred in China. Thus Chinese music is pentatonic, there are five cardinal directions (including the center), five principal colors, five important tastes, five principal fruits, etc. and there are five elements in ancient Chinese science: Wood, Fire, Earth, Metal, and Water. These give rise to what are called the stems in the Chinese calendar. There are ten stems, two (Yin and Yang) for each of the elements.

The Chinese calendar also has twelve branches, named after 12 animals: six male and six female. These are (alternating male and female) Rat, Cow, Tiger, Rabbit, Dragon, Snake, Horse, Sheep, Monkey, Hen, Dog, and Pig (Hog). The 5 stems times the 12 branches give a sexagesimal (60) framework on which the calendar is built.

There are different modes of reckoning the New Year Day in China. As per one, 12 February 2002 is when a new year starts. This is the beginning of the 4699th year. The number is based on the traditional year (2697 B.C.E.) when the Yellow King began his reign. He is the one who is said to have begun the construction of the Great Wall.

If we divide 4699 by 60, we get a remainder of 19. Now if we go through the cycle from Rat to Pig as listed above, in the second round we will hit upon the Horse. Therefore this is called the year of the Black (Yang) Horse. The Yin-Yang table also assigns the element Water to this year. On the other hand, from the perspective of Chinese astrology, Fire and Red are associated with the Horse. This combination of Fire and Water in the same year is said to be unhappy. The logical (as per astrological thinking) conclusion is that this will not be a peaceful year. Indeed, a good deal of folk astrology is associated with these combinations of animals and elements, which not only predict bad and good things, but also recommend ways to avert or accelerate these. Some people are furious with such pseudo-science, some take it quite seriously, and yet others are silently indifferent to soothsayers, expending no more than a chuckle in the context.

On New Year's Day, families clean house, physically and symbolically, for they are also driving out all the accumulated evil forces. The Kitchen God (see January 31), after giving a (hopefully good) report to the Jade King, returns today to the kitchen. And of course there is the huge meal which must include a whole fish (signifying abundance) and aquatic creatures like shrimps, crabs, oysters, each having a significance which arises from the pronunciation of their names.

Red and gold, symbolizing happiness (for the mind) and wealth (for the body) are used in decorations on this day.

Thus it is New Year's Day for another great tradition of the human family. But even there, there are two schools of thought: the astrological (by which the day was on 4 February) and the astronomical: February 12. Perhaps this reflects unwittingly the tension or at least the difference in perspective between the two very different modes of reacting to the world of experience.

Whatever it be, and whether you have studied some Chinese or not, if you make an effort to say Jia-zhi-yu-kuai to a Chinese knowing friend, it may be appreciated because it means "Have a good holiday!"

From the World of Science: CHARLES DARWIN

Charles Darwin (born: 12 February 1809), by no means precocious, decided on a medical career, dropped the idea quickly, then toyed with the idea of becoming a minister, gave that up, and was fascinated by natural history. He volunteered to collect plants in an expedition to South America. During that trip, while thinking about the finches in the Galapagos Islands, the first embers of Darwin's revolutionary theory began to light up in his mind. The orninthologist John Gould's separation of the Group Finches from other finches was also an inspiration for Darwin. Darwin began to suspect that the birds in that island and those in mainland South America once had a common ancestor, and that the former had become a different species over the eons as a result of varying foods and other environmental factors. His book, *A Naturalist's Voyage on the Beagle* appeared when he was 30, and won great praise. But it was his *On the Origin of Species* (1859), with a much longer full title which began a controversy that persists to this day. His work, *The Descent of Man*, elaborated the shocking thesis that human beings have evolved from a subhuman species. Darwin often used the phrase "descent with modification", rather than evolution.

"Evolution," with which Darwin's name is often associated in the popular mind, has a much older history, both in usage and in concept. His contribution was (like Alfred Wallace's) the notion of natural selection as the cause of species transformations. It was Darwin's admirer and promoter Herbert Spencer who propagated the idea in the sense that all gradual changes are progressive. Like all scientific theories, Darwinian evolution not only had a past, but a future too, in that it has also evolved: undergone appropriate modifications in the context of new data.

Like Copernicus, Darwin shook the world of science by the bold formulation of a vision that was not altogether new in the history of ideas, but which emerged with firmness and greater clarity from his own observations and reflections. Quite unwittingly, again like Copernicus, Darwin's work provoked the wrath of some religious thinkers in Western Christianity. Neither Copernicus nor Darwin were irreligious atheists, indeed both were God-fearing Christians in their own ways, but they saw the world in grander ways than their ancient ancestors had imagined and sanctified in Holy Books.

Darwin saw Man as a byproduct of slow processes that chart life on earth. In the older picture, one imagined that creatures were put on earth fully made, like toys from a factory. Darwin suggested that they slowly emerged in myriad forms, fashioned and transformed with the passage of time. The emergence of life is governed by the immutable laws that keep the world functioning, and also unforeseeably directed by random factors, some helpful, some hurtful, for the continuance of characteristics. Given a sufficiently long stretch of time, such factors metamorphose some aquatic animals into amphibians, some amphibians into land creatures, even some monkeys into humans. And that's the rub: this last possibility which Darwin suggested. There is, in the view of some, something demeaning, degrading, indeed dehumanizing in the idea that some of our distant ancestors once swung from branch to branch, with no language or morals, let alone notion of God.

In our own times, even people who grant that biological evolution is there, have sometimes argued that this does not occur by pure chance alone. They feel that there is an intelligent design behind it all: Change in life forms is not like the mindless doodle of a monkey, but rather like the magnificent creativity of a master artist who delights in the variety and Himself is uncertain about what the next move in his creative process will be. As poetry I find this idea beautiful. As science it is debatable and debated.

February 13

From the World of Science: ASH WEDNESDAY

Ash Wednesday, which falls on February 13 in 2002, is sometimes defined as the 40th weekday before Easter Sunday. This is an important day of observance, marked in most Catholic traditions. Scholars have traced its roots in Chapter 27 of Deuteronomy where, like the series of "Blessed are the" we read in Matthew (5), there are a number of "Cursed be…" which spell out at least twelve different ways in which one can be cursed, ranging from making graven or molten image (an "abomination unto the Lord") to some highly objectionable kinds of incest and perversion. Traditionally, the threats from God used to be read out to the congregation in what is called a *commination* service. It is said that at one time, there used to be public penances. Those who felt they had sinned would come forward in a sackcloth which they are supposed to have worn for forty days, and they would be covered with ash. They were allowed to return only after forty days of penance, on Maundy Thursday. There is a reference to such a service in a 10th century work by the Anglo-Saxon writer Aelfric.

Like all ancient rituals, this one has also undergone modifications. In our own times, ashes are made by burning the palm which was used in the Palm Processional of the previous year. They are mixed with the anointed oil. The priest, using his thumb, makes with the ash a mark of the cross on the forehead of the kneeling penitent. And he utters the words:

Momento, homo, quia pulvis es et in pulverem reverteris

Remember, man, that thou art dust, and unto dust thou shalt return.

As I see it, the essence of Ash Wednesday is this: It is to make us recognize periodically that we hurt and harm in countless ways, which is what much of sinning really is. We must acknowledge this openly and with humility. When St. Francis says, "Lord, I'm a worm, and no man," it is a profoundly sincere expression of that humility. Furthermore, even in the midst of our happy life and paltry successes, we need to remember that ultimately we too will perish like others before us. And who can tell what awaits us in the Beyond!

So, like Buddhists on Parinirvana day, Catholics on dies cinerum (Day of the Ashes) reflect a little on the ephemeral nature of human existence. In the Hindu Shiva (Shaivite) tradition also one smears the forehead with ash which is a feature of Shiva who is the principle of dissolution for the whole universe.

As this is the beginning of Lent, one begins a period of self-discipline on this day, abstaining from excess, and living on less, as Jesus did for forty days. There is an ancient tradition which recommends the eating of pretzels during the Lent period. The pretzel is simple and made in the form of arms folded in prayer. It is sometimes called the Lenten bread.

All religious traditions recommend days of fasting. In our more enlightened age one chooses to fast from one's free will. There was a time when this was enforced. Anyone indulging in meat or eggs could be prosecuted and punished. There was also a custom by which whatever one saved by sacrificing meals was given to charity. It is recorded that in England there was a provision for those who couldn't fast. They could buy a license which would allow them to eat, and money went to the poor in St. Paul's Churchyard.

In 1930, T. S. Eliot wrote a beautiful poem entitled Ash Wednesday which breathes hope even in the recognition of the dust to which our bodies should eventually return.

From the World of Science:
WILLIASM SCHOCKLY

Not a day passes in our lives these days when we don't use a gadget that has no transistor in its entrails. Like the wheel and the vehicle, the transistor has become an intrinsic element in our civilization.

The credit for its invention goes to three physicists. One them was William Schockly (born 13 February 1910), who was born in England and who grew up in the United States. After studying advanced physics in prestigious institutions, he joined Bell Telephone Laboratories, and also worked in some military projects during the World War II years.

Electric current are of two kinds: direct (flowing in one direction only in a wire) or and alternating (periodically changing directions). A rectifier is a device which changes an alternating current into a direct current by preventing flow along one direction (somewhat like a valve). It had been known for quite some time that certain crystalline materials can be used as rectifiers. in circuits within radio receivers.

Normally, materials are either conductors (of electricity) or nonconductors. Some non-conducting substances become conductors under certain conditions. These are the so-called nonconductors. In the period following the War, while still in Bell Labs, Shockly and his colleagues began to study semiconductors. Shockly worked out a theory which, if true, it should be possible to get rectification and amplification when an external electric field is applied to a configuration with a semi-conducting film and a metal piece. This did not work. The theory was modified by John Bardeen, and by December 1947, the trio managed to achieve amplification with semiconductors. The transistor was formally announced to the world on 1 July 1948. After six years the first transistor radio was made. The IBM computer model 7090 consumed barely 5% of the power used by a a similar, much more bulky computer which used vacuum tubes. The microprocessor made was born quite early in the 1970s. The rest, as they say, is history.

Shockly's biographer Joel Shurkin (*Broken Genius: A Biography of William B. Shockly*) says that if he had been a better manager of finances, Shockley—"the father of Silicon Valley"—could have become a billionaire, like Bill Gates.

Instead, after he became a professor at Stanford University, he got entangled in social sciences, and became more interested in establishing the relationship between genes and intelligence. As if this was complex enough as a problem, he went on to hypothesize that certain races are genetically constrained in intelligence, and proposed to test it scientifically. But his very proposal was regarded by a great many people as not just inappropriate, but rude, crude, and deserving of contempt and ridicule. As a result Shockley was in his last years a persona non grata in many academic institutions. Indeed, he became, in the words of his biographer, "probably the most hated scientist in America." This man whose discovery revolutionized electronic technology, whose invention led to computers and e-mail, and all the rest of it, was driven out of the public domain because he entertained and articulated ideas that were not only value-laden, but reprehensible to most enlightened people.

Future historians may argue about Shockly's ideas and the reception to his proposal, but what seems clear is that as far as society is concerned, at any given time, there are issues and values which are not amenable to scientific analysis, nor to be decided on the basis of experimental data. The episode shows that one has to draw a line somewhere.

February 14

From the World of Religion:
ST. VALENTILE'S DAY

The mention of most saints conjures up images of somber asceticism, miracles and martyrdom. But say St Valentine: bouquets of roses and heart-shaped chocolates, lovely cards with sweet little notes, hugs and loving kisses come to mind.

According to some, there was a priest with this name who lived in Rome in the third century. He was thrown into jail because of his Christian inclinations. He became enamored of his warden's blind daughter to whom he once sent a *billet doux* (a sweet little loving note) and signed it as "From your Valentine": the first Valentine card ever.

According to another story, when the Roman Emperor Claudius II banned marriages for eligible soldiers to save them from the pangs of parting, a local priest by the name of Valentine continued to unite lovelorn couples in holy matrimony, in defiance of the imperial order. When this was discovered, Valentine was apprehended and put to death for legitimizing amorous entanglements against Caludius II's orders. He became a martyr for the cause of love. Another version says that there was a Valentine who adamantly held on to Christianity much against the establishment, and was therefore executed.

We don't know whose memory we are evoking every February 14. This is what prompted Charles Lamb to exclaim, "Mysterious personage! like unto thee, assuredly, there is no other mitred father in the calendar." Perhaps this is true of most saints of most religions: for what are they now but remembered names and associated legends, some of dubious existence and to most of whom one attributes deeds of questionable authenticity, but whose lives, as per received tradition, are inspirational and meaningful to millions?

Love is unconditional in parents, romantic in youths, stable in mature relationships, lofty and giving in a universal context, ecstatic in its spiritual mode. Of all these, it is the normal inter-gender love that is emphasized on Valentine Day.

In former times, Valentine Day was mainly for expressing man-woman love: of knights of chivalry, of Romeos and Juliets, of newly weds, of spinsters in search. There are references to it in medieval times. Chaucer mentions a "Seynt Valentyne's day when every foul cometh there to choose his mate," reflecting on the belief that birds select their mates on this day. Shakespeare's Ophelia sings about the day, reminding us of the belief that the first man a maid saw on St. Valentine's Day would become her spouse.

Valentine Day isn't for lust or carnality, yet some have misunderstood that this is so. For example, in 2001 in India, there were protests from Hindu traditionalists against (what they regarded as) this corrupt Christian practice. In the West too, some have objected to aspects of the custom, somehow imagining it to be demeaning to the female of our species, for, once Valentine expressions used to come more often from men to women.

In the U.S, we recall Esther Howland (1828–1904) who began making modest Valentine cards and lots of money in the name of the Love-Saint, inspiring future generations of Hall-Mark-artists.

In the context of religion and science, let us remember that love is elevating, meaningful, joyous and colorful, hope-giving and human: it is for the heart. And at the highest level, as Henry van Dyke said:

Love is not getting, but giving; not a wild dream
of pleasure, or a madness of desire—oh, no,
love is not that—it is goodness, and honor,
And peace and pure living.

From the World of Science: FRITZ ZWICKY

Today we read in the papers novas, supernovas, galaxies and pulsars. They have become part of everyday vocabulary. It is interesting to inquire about their origins in the worldview of science.

Already in the 16th century the term nova was introduced by Tycho Brahe. Novas refer to stars which appear all of sudden in the darkness of void. Never before was a star spotted where a nova is detected by an astronomer. Such novas gradually fade way.

During the 1920s, thanks to observations from the Hubble telescope, we became aware of the existence of galaxies: island universes way beyond the borders of our own Milky Way. Each of them is made up of billions of stars also. When novas were observed in distant galaxies, it became clear that those must be extraordinarily luminous entities. Among the astronomers and astrophysicists who were studying these phenomena was the Swiss Fritz Zwicky (born 14 February 1898) who was then working at Caltech.

During the 1930s, not long after the discovery of the neutron, Zwicky (and his colleague Walter Baade) came up with idea of neutron stars: stars in which matter would be compressed to inordinate densities. Almost three decades later, it turned out that the so-called pulsars are actually the neutron stars Zwicky had considered.

Zwicky also discovered the distinction between a nova and a much larger explosive stellar event which he called a supernova. The nova is now known to occur in a double star system, due to the explosive stage of one of the duo. A supernova, on the other hand, is the final stage of an enormously massive star. In its last collapsing implosion, the nuclear matter at its core get so squeezed that heavy elements get synthesized in its infernal furnace, and the whole thing explodes with cosmic fury, spewing out matter and radiation of enormous magnitude. Zwicky (and Chandrasekhar) were the astrophysicists who worked out the details of such stellar catastrophes.

Zwicky estimated that barely two or three supernovas occurr in a galaxy every millennium or so. He also revealed an uncanny similarity between stars within galaxies and molecules in an enclosed volume of gas: a new version of the ancient world view by which Man, the microcosm, is a miniature mirror of the macrocosm.

Zwicky developed techniques for provoking creativity in the face of complex problems. In a system which he called Morphology, one would tabulate all the parameters of the problem in rows and columns, and toy with combinations of them to see what sort of solutions could be found. This method sometimes took him to science fictional fantasies. Thus, for example, he spoke of making planets and asteroids habitable some day, and even fantasized affecting the motion of our sun within our galaxy with human technology so as to get much nearer another star.

Zwicky was a scientific genius all right, sometimes displaying unpleasant quirks. He was not embarrassed to speak about his own capacity for creativity. "I have a good idea every two years," he is said to have told the eminent physicist Millikan. Like some people of superior intelligence, he had little respect for mediocrity. He is said to have referred even to some of his colleagues as "spherical bastards," explaining that they were bastards from no matter which direction one looked. It has been said that such attitudes perhaps came from a feeling that that he wasn't given the credit that was his due. Some have also argued that this was as much due to his curtness as to the fact that even after working for four decades in the United States, he chose not to take up American citizenship. Whatever it be, he will be remembered as a good scientist who contributed to astronomy.

February 15

From the World of Religion: SOCRATES

Socrates is one of the most famous names in philosophy. His greatness, or at least his fame, derives from the fact that he linked philosophy to life and values, rather than treat it as just a game of the mind. He was like his counterparts in the Hindu tradition for whom philosophy was much more than an intellectual exercise: Its goal was self-realization.

As a young man Socrates was very much interested in science. In one of Plato's dialogues we hear Socrates saying:

"I was most amazingly interested in the lore which they call natural philosophy. For I thought it magnificent to know the cause of everything, why it comes into being and why it exists: I kept turning myself upside down to consider things like the following: Is it that living things are bred, as some have said, when hot and cold get some fermentation into them....?"

In his later years, however, Socrates was wont to say, "The only thing I know is that I know nothing," and though this sounds like commendable humility, he meant this to apply to all human beings. The Tamil poetess Auvaiyar expressed the same idea in a less extremist manner when she said, "What has been learned has the measure of a handful of dust; what is yet to be learned is vast as the world."

One consequence of his wisdom was that Socrates developed a rather negative attitude towards the pursuit of knowledge. Indeed, he regarded this as a dangerous delusion. It was dangerous because it tended to take people away from moral considerations. It was a delusion because true knowledge was forever beyond human grasp. This is a spirit that exploring scientists may not be very sympathetic to, but it is one that has never vanished from the history of human thought.

Like some other great thinkers, Socrates considered himself to be inspired by God. But he was also a very modest man, refusing to claim that he was wiser than others. He did not think it was his duty to reveal to the world what God had revealed to him. Rather, he felt that his responsibility was to elicit truth from people as they saw them. As he put it, "...God compels me to be a midwife, but forbids me to bring forth." To him, our goal in life should be: "To know how to live happily and honorably, and be a good citizen."

Socrates expressed an immortal injunction: *gnothi seauton*, know thyself. One gets the impression from Plato's *Republic* that in the Western tradition Socrates was the one who introduced the idea of an immortal soul associated with every individual. What a powerful and long-lasting idea this has been!

No reference to Socrates would be complete without mention of his famous death. Socrates was a member of the Committee of the Senate in Athens, and he once disagreed very strongly with certain decisions and actions of a questionable nature in which the committee engaged in 466 BCE. He persisted in his dissenting views for several years. Finally, in 399 BCE, he was brought to trial. He was charged with the offense of "not worshipping the gods whom the State worships, but introducing new and unfamiliar religious practices, and of corrupting the young."

Socrates was found guilty, and he was condemned to die by drinking poisonous hemlock. Socrates is said to have asked his disciples to be of good cheer, reminding them that they were burying only his body.

Though it is difficult to be precise about ancient dates, according to one convention, Socrates drank the poisonous hemlock potion on February 15 in the year 399 B.C.E.

From the World of Science: GALILEO GALILEI

He was not just one of the giants in the first phase of modern science: he is reckoned as its founder. But he also got into trouble with ecclesiastical authorities, as much for espousing views about the world then declared to be heretical, as by his intransigence and what struck some as arrogance. His full name was Galileo Galilei (born: February 15, 1564), and he is universally known as Galileo.

Galileo went to the university to become a physician. He heard a lecture on mathematics, and fell in love with the subject. He was stirred to explore the world by observing it, rather than by speculating on it.

His biographer says that Galileo measured the time of swing of a pendulum by observing swinging chandeliers in church and using his pulse to measure time. [Tourists are shown the pendulum in Pisa which Galileo is said to have observed, though this one was installed five years later.] He analyzed the motion of projectiles, studied bodies slide down inclined planes, initiated the quantitative study of motion, and revealed that the laws of nature are written in the language of mathematics. He was one of the first to formulate the law of inertia: we don't need a force to keep bodies in motion. He turned the telescope skyward, and brought to human knowledge aspects of the heavens which none before had seen or suspected such as craters on the Moon, the grainy structure of the Milky Way, and four satellites of Jupiter. He detected spots on the sun, and theorized that tides resulted from the orbital rush of the Earth around the Sun. He served the new astronomy by propagating the Sun-centered model through a popular book.

He was God-fearing and faithful, attended mass on Sundays, visited a place of pilgrimage to express thanks for recovery from an illness, and attributed to God the wonder of the phenomenal world. But he was stubborn in his conviction that truths about the physical world can be known only through observation and experiment, and he doubted that the Holy Book can be regarded as an authority in the mathematical sciences. Like al-Farâbi of the Islamic tradition, he argued that sacred books must not be taken literally, but only metaphorically. Fortunately for the West, its al-Ghazâlîs (6 February) lost the battle in curbing freedom of thought so essential for the progress of science.

Galileo befriended cardinals and popes, and they respected him. But he also made enemies among scholars and clerics who rejected the heliocentric world-view. They saw in Galileo a threat to long-cherished scriptural cosmography. He had but scant respect and much contempt also for the unscientific authorities who dictated world views.

When he was almost seventy, he was brought to trial: not for offense against God, but for propagating the idea that the earth was moving around the Sun. He conceded he had been arrogant in writing the book, and promised not to engage in heresies any more. Because he pronounced the *mea culpa*, and also because of his age and stature, he was spared the torture chamber, only sentenced to house arrest, and ordered to read regularly passages from the Bible. If it is difficult for us to imagine such a punishment, we may be happy that some societies have made progress in the matter of intellectual freedom and have been freed from the tyranny of those who presume to speak for the Almighty.

Galileo was close to his children: most of all to his older daughter Maria Celeste who wrote to him regularly from the nunnery to where she had retired at an early age.

His inquiring, insightful, and inventing mind enriched human knowledge and creativity in ways that few others in human history have achieved. And he has been amply vindicated.

February 16

From the World of Religion: TITUBA

Let us recall the sad story of Tituba (born: 16 February 1675) somewhere in South America, but whom the chaos of historical accidents brought all the way to Massachusetts, there to create a stir and to secure a place for herself in America's history. She was bought and brought to Boston by a certain Reverend Samuel Parris in whose household she served as a slave.

In 1688 Parris got a job offer from the village of Salem: he would preach in the local church. So the Parris family moved there. This included daughter Betty, a niece by the name of Abigail, and Tituba the slave girl. The following year, Tituba married John, an Amerindian youth.

In Salem poor Betty began to have occasional fits. She often ran around erratically. There were other young girls in the village who also displayed such unusual behavior. In the meanwhile a popular book talked about an Irish washerwoman in Boston as a real witch and source of much trouble. In those days this word had the ominous connotation as an instrument of the Devil. The Devil was not just an exclamatory sound, but a very real entity, moving in our midst and out to ruin everything good that God had made.

The general belief was that Betty and the like were possessed, instigated by one or more local witches. Tituba could very well be the culprit, some thought. Tituba's own tradition had taught her ways to get the evil spirit out of the system. This called for the concoction of a cake whose ingredients included a pint of Betty's urine. The cake was to be given to a dog which would then lead them to the culprits. When the Reverend heard about this, he got furious and thrashed troublesome Tituba.

The people of Salem were convinced there was a witch, perhaps a few witches, in their midst. Even a physician suggested, after careful examination of the patients, that witches could well have started the ailment. Upon harsh questioning, Tituba confessed to being one. She took the opportunity to point to a few others in town, like Sarah Good and Sarah Osborne: apparently, a whole lot of witches were inhabiting the cursed community.

Thus began the infamous Salem trials which lasted about four months in the summer of 1692, and have brought much embarrassment to future generations. The outcome of it all was that 19 individuals were declared witches and summarily hanged; a very senior citizen—an octogenarian—was stoned to death, and hundreds more were thrown in jail. Someone had paid a ransom and released Tituba from prison.

Slowly, good sense began to rise to the fore. A person by the name of Increase Mather wrote a tract entitled "Cases of Conscience" in which the now famous line appears: to the effect that it is far better that "ten suspected witches should escape than one innocent person should be condemned." Others like him began to speak out, and appealed to the governor to put an end to what was going on. The nightmare was over by May 1693.

It is important to remember that much more than the tools it provides to cure diseases, transport people, talk through cell-phones and blow up the world, science is the light which frees the mind of needless fears, exposes superstitions, and makes pseudo-sciences laughable. In so far as these sides of science haven't penetrated human societies, we are still languishing in the Dark Age. There still persist a variety of manifestations of the most obscene kinds of such beliefs, propagated with increasing success, ironically, by means of the internet. If the poetic images of religions add richness and meaning to life, their obscurantist vestiges keep the human spirit in chains under the spell of irrationality.

From the World of Science:
DISCOVERY OF TUTANKHAMEN

For a span of almost a thousand years (3400 BCE to 2475 BCE), Egypt flourished as a dynamic civilization, ruled in succession by dynasties whose kings were known as the Pharaohs (Great Houses). They were regarded as representatives of the gods. Under these ancient rulers a peaceful and productive people thrived, cultivating land, innovating tools, exploring the heavens, and dreaming up gods and post-terrestrial possibilities. Austere priests controlled the realm of knowledge, and the intellect occupied an important place in ancient Egypt. The society also had feudal lords and sweating slaves, for exploitation of humans by humans is not a recent phenomenon in history.

The scientific and technological achievements of ancient Egypt continue to impress us to this day. We must be grateful to archaeologists and historians whose efforts have brought those legacies to our understanding and appreciation.

Howard Carter was an Egyptologist whose relentless exploration of Pharaoh tombs led towards the close of the year 1922 to what has been described as "one of the most brilliant successes in the history of archeology." The slow penetration into the buried depths in the Valley of the Kings, hidden from human eyes for well over three millennia, reached a climax on 16 February. On that date Carter and his team entered the room where the bodily remains of Tutankhamen lay in peaceful solitude. It wasn't lying in a dismal dungeon, but in a magnificent chamber with glittering walls. As they entered the shrine which had been hallowed by the passage of time, the probing archeologists could "feel the tingle of excitement which thrilled the spectators behind the barrier…"

In that huge hall they discovered symbols of ancient rites, decorations and inscriptions, colorful paintings and funerary emblems. There were statues of gold and ebony. There were tiny models of ships to carry the pharaoh and his entourage to the world beyond. There were jewels and ornaments and more. They discovered gilt and gold beyond belief. Three huge coffins and a sarcophagus of glittering yellow quarzite were the central pieces. In this was found King Tut's mummy. A good deal is now known about this youthful king who died before he reached 20, about the switch of his name from Tut-ankh-aten (Image of Aten) to Tut-ankh-amen (Image of Amen).

Not everything they left behind has been preserved for posterity. Even in those days, petty pilferers and skillful grave-stealers took away much of the buried treasures. But King Tut's grave was hidden so deep that it escaped robbery for many centuries. And we are grateful for whatever has been left, for we cannot reconstruct the history of peoples who have left no relics behind.

The site is lavish in its grandeur, reminding one of Versailles, Granada, and such that we can visit as museums: places which remind the common people of the heights to which ancient splendor reached. Some have condemned such opulence, and regretted the sweating labors of human beings but for whom such ostentation would be impossible. But such creations also tell us of the material manifestations of civilization that add to its aesthetic glories. Who is to say that where there are no pyramids or great walls, no cathedrals or Taj Mahals, the workers weren't exploited by the oligarchs?

It was good that the ancient Egyptian kings believed in an after world to which they could carry gifts and riches, for it was that belief that inspired them to crowd their coffins with costly trinkets, with art work and vases. There were no museums in those ancient days, and it is thanks to their belief system that such precious relics lay hidden for posterity to see, admire, and interpret.

February 17

From the World of Religion: BURNING OF BRUNO

We don't know when he was born, but we know that he died under unhappy circumstances on 17 February 1600. His name was Filippo Bruno, and he changed it to Giordano when he joined the Dominican order in his teens. Like a good Dominican he read St. Thomas of Aquinas and Aristotle, but in the library of the monastery there were also books by Arab and Hebrew scholars, so he read Avicenna and ibn Garirol also. He was drawn to mysticism and magic, to Paracelsus and Agrippa. He began to question the basic tenets of his own faith, wondered about the possibility of transubstantiation and the logic of the Trinity. He was censured more than once for asking inconvenient questions. Intellectually speaking, he slowly moved away from the canonical teachings of his Church and his order. Spiritually, he was drawn to Hermes Trismegistus and to ancient Egyptian religion. He was persuaded that therein lay all religious truths. He left the monastic environment, casting off the robe and disappearing into the crowd. He was restless, often tossed between the quest for highest truth and carnal urges.

He went from town to town in his native Italy, then crossed the border into Switzerland where he got into trouble attacking a Calvinist scholar. He moved to France where King Henry III offered him a position at the prestigious College de France. While he was a professor, he wrote a play which was contemptuous of contemporary academics and theologians. Scholars did not applaud. Next he went to England, lectured at Oxford on the Copernican worldview which, he proclaimed, was far more profound than what its author had imagined. Copernicus was reviving, Bruno felt, the ancient Egyptian religion in which the Sun was God and also center of everything, and the earth and planets were like animals circumambulating the divine. Oxford had not yet embraced Copernicus, and some in the audience challenged the speaker with questions. Bruno was offended. Later he described one of the questioners as a pig, and expressed the view that Oxford University itself was a "constellation of pedantic and most obstinate ignorance and presumption...." He wrote a piece in the form of a dialogue (much as Galileo was to do later) presenting the heliocentric and the geocentric worldviews. He also published a book in England in which he suggested indirectly that the Triumphant Beast (of dogmatic theology) ought to be expelled from the civilized world.

Ironically, while we think of 16th and 17th century Copernicans as moderns, Bruno—perhaps the only Copernican who died for the cause—was very much an ancient, for he was pleading and propagating pre-Christian perceptions of the world rather than the modern. But his unfettered mind also spoke of an infinite world beyond what we can see, of life in distant planets yet unknown.

In 1591, though he had been declared an outlaw by the Roman Catholic Church, Bruno returned to Venice at the invitation of a certain Morcenigo who wanted to learn from him. Within two years, the host informed the Inquisition of the terrible things that Bruno was blurting out. He was extradited to Rome in 1593 and put in prison. Year after year he was questioned and rebuked and finally, after the Pope had declared him a heretic, he was handed to a secular court with the explicit instruction that his punishment should be "without effusion of blood." The court condemned him, and on 17 February 1600, the 52 year old Bruno's tongue was tied, he was stripped of his clothes, enchained to an iron stake at the Piazza de Fiori and set to fire in front of a watching crowd. 289 years later, they erected a statute of Bruno there at which tourists stop and take pictures.

From the World of Science:
HORACE BENEDICT SAUSSURE

In the 16th and 17th centuries some thinkers regarded mountains as grotesque protuberances on a smoothly rotund earth, somewhat like blisters on a non-smooth face. Little did they know about the role mountains play in rainfall and rivers.

When the mountain slopes are covered with snow, people ski down in exhilaration. Then there are those who during seasons not so cold find excitement in reaching mountain tops, to breathe the pure air at great heights and enjoy the panorama from the peaks.

But mountain sports and adventures are not very ancient in human history. True, there have been farmers and families in the higher levels of mountain ranges, and places like Tibet have been inhabited since antiquity.

But arduous mountain climbing as a self-imposed challenge did not begin until about the middle of the 18th century.

Consider, for example, the Alps in Europe, and the Alpine resort of Chamonix where thousands of tourists descend (ascend) each year, where the first Winter Olympic games were held. Well furnished and cozy these days, it was but a small and sparsely populated village once, quite isolated from the rest of the world. In

1741 some enterprising Englishmen spotted the Mer de Glace. A certain Marc Théodore Bourrit was also among the first to explore those regions.

But it was the Swiss geologist Horace Benedict Saussure (born: 17 February 1740) who instigated a scientific study of the Alps and of mountain formations more generally. His own expeditions to the Alpine slopes inspired him to shoot for the summit. No human being had until then set foot on Mont Blanc. De Saussure offered a prize to anyone who would make the effort and reach that peak. Two people won his prize in 1786, and the next year Saussure himself reached Europe's roof top.

During his many attempts Saussure explored valleys and passes, often being the first human to be in some places. He was the first to walk through the Theodule Pass at 10,899 feet. He climbed to Klein Matterhorn in 1792.

But he was more than a mountaineer. Even as he climbed the rugged slopes, he reflected on the rocks. He observed the strata and examined the minerals. He had instruments to measure air pressure. He took the temperature, in sunshine and in shade, at various heights. He even constructed an instrument, using dry human hair, with which to measure the moisture content in air. He devised ingenious ways for measuring the blueness of the sky, the clearness of the air, and electricity in the atmosphere.

He wrote voluminously on his trips in the Alps ("Voyages dans les Alpes"), and included a long essay on the natural history of the surroundings of Geneva. In his work he recorded his findings on rocks, plants, fossils, and on the forms of the Alpine mountains. From all this he began to speculate about how the great mountain chain could have been formed. He was thus among the pioneers who considered processes which give rise to rivers and valleys, to mountains and meadows: one of the first orologists.

De Saussure was also one of the first scientists to use the term geology in its modern connotation. Up until his time, the term geologia used to refer to earthly matters as distinct from heavenly ones, and the word geognosie meant a systematic study of the earth. How word-meanings change with time!

De Saussure had been a professor of philosophy for a couple of decades, a mountain climber for 25 years, and also a public official for some years. In this last capacity he brought about reforms in the governmental system as well as in Swiss education.

February 18

From the World of Religion:
BERNADITA SOUBIROUS

At the foot of the Pyrenees in south-western France there is a little town by the name of Lourdes through which flows a slender river called Gave de Pau. This is an ancient town, dating back to the Middle Ages. Ruins and relics still remain there. But the town became famous in the last decades of the 19th century, thanks to a simple peasant girl who had visions of Virgin Mary in that remote corner of the world.

Her name was Bernadita Soubirous, and she was living with her parents of modest means until 11 February in the year 1858. On that day, she went with two other girls to fetch some logs from the nearby woods close to the River Gave. While she was there, she was drawn to a field by a strange rustling sound. From where she stood, she saw a grotto, and at its entrance, lo and behold! there was the figure of a lady in white with a bright blue belt and a rosary of yellow hue. From the face of the figure exuded gentleness, love and compassion, and the grotto where the vision appeared was known to the local people as Massabielle. She rubbed her eyes, and she put her hands in the folds of her dress to take out her own rosary, but she had difficulty doing this. The lady at the distance made a sign of the cross, and now Bernadette (as she came to be known) could do this also. She began to pray. As soon as she stopped uttering the name of Mary, the figure vanished.

Her companions who saw nothing like that, wouldn't believe her. Bernadette went to the same place another Sunday, and had the same vision. It was only during the third encounter that the apparition spoke to her, instructing her to come there for fifteen consecutive days.

One day the Lady asked Bernadette to dig a hole into a muddy spot nearby, and from this arose a fount of clear water. On the last and 18th day, Bernadette was asked to wash her hands, instruct the priests to build a chapel, and convert the sinners to the right path. Finally, in the words of Bernadette, "with outstretched arms and eyes looking up to heaven, she told me she was the Immaculate Conception."

Young Bernadette was awe-struck by what she saw, and she could not let the vision go out of her mind. When she reported her experience to the local priest, he first suspected her of making up a story, and then he became quite angry.

Eventually the townspeople of Lourdes took Bernadette seriously, and they built a new chapel: the Church of the Rosary and the Grotto. It is built in the Byzantine style. The spring that Bernadette is said to have provoked is still there, with water that is deemed to have curative powers. On top of the grotto is a statue of Virgin Mary. News of the apparitions spread fast all through France and Europe and beyond. Over the years, millions of people from all over the world have been to Lourdes which has become a Catholic place of pilgrimage. Religious orders have been initiated in Bernadette's name: The Congregation of our Lady of Lourdes has its headquarters in Rochester, Minnesota. After her canonization, many Roman Catholic Churches were established in her name.

Skeptics may scoff and cynics may sneer, but how can one challenge the deepest experiential certitudes relating to the spiritual? Whether we believe or doubt, we can always respect the devout for whom there is something truly saintly in Bernadette, in her simplicity, piety, and devotion to the Christ principle, as when she said: "Nothing is anything more to me; everything is nothing to me, but Jesus: neither things nor persons, neither ideas nor emotions, neither honor nor sufferings. Jesus is for me honor, delight, heart and soul." French Catholics observe Fabruary 18 as St. Bernadette Day.

From the World of Science: ALESSANDRO VOLTA

We have used batteries, and we know that they are marked 1.5 volts, 6 volts, or whatever. And we have heard of 110 volt lines and 220 volt sources and the like. So where did this volt-measuring come from?

This measure of a property of electricity is named after an Italian Count with the penta-part name of Alessandro Giuseppe Antonio Anastasio Volta (born: 18 February 1745).

He was a good Catholic, educated in a Jesuit school. His intelligence and abilities could make him a good Jesuit priest, thought some of his teachers. It is said that with chocolates and other sweet things they persuaded him to the calling, but an uncle of his, a Dominican himself, snatched te nephew away from such possibilities.

Volta was very much interested in electricity which was in its infancy in the second half of the 18th century. He pictured that in every body there is normally a net neutral condition in which all electrical attractions are neutralized. This situation can be altered by some external means which would alter the relative configuration of the particles. In this electrically unstable state the body becomes electrically charged.

Even with this not quite correct concept of a single kind of electricity, Volta devised some very creative experiments to study electrical induction, thanks to his experimental ingenuity. He invented devices in which electric charge could be stored.

His reputation quickly spread and he received grants to travel to other countries from his native Como, during which he had the opportunity to meet many eminent scientists of the time. Finally he received a teaching position at the University of Pavia where for four decades he taught and did most of his fundamental research.

Inspired by the work of De Saussure's work (February 17)'s Volta got interested in atmospheric electricity. He improved the electrical instruments of the Swiss geologist, and made them more sensitive and more precise. He devised ways to measure what he called the electrical tension which was to be refined in later years as the volt.

Volta improved another instrument of the times: the eudiometer, used to measure the volume and composition of gases, With this, he estimated that ordinary air contains about 21% oxygen. His instrument also helped Lavoisier in the discovery of the composition of water (now known to everyone as H-2-O). Volta discovered the inflammable gas which bubbles out in marshes: methane, which is a major source of energy in our own times.

When Volta heard about Galvani's animal electricity (9 September) he first dismissed it as unbelievable. Then he tried to repeat the experiment himself, and found to his great surprise that the same effect (momentary electric current) that Galvani had found, could be obtained with just metals, without dead frogs. This cast some doubt on Galvani's theory of animal electricity, which made that eminent anatomist quite unhappy. Unwittingly, Volta had discovered that it is possible to generate electric currents by suitably connecting metals (wires). By 1800 Volta had constructed a simple arrangement with bowls of saline solutions in which a wire was placed. One end of the wire was of copper and the other of zinc. This resulted in a flow of electric current. Volta had made the first electric battery! Now it was a matter of improving the device and making it more sophisticated, using copper and zinc plates, and so was created the Voltaic cell (or pile as it used to be called).

The generation of steady electric currents is one of the greatest breakthroughs in the history of science. It has had dramatic impacts on the face of human civilization. It is appropriate that Volta's name has been immortalized in every battery ever made.

February 19

From the World of Religion: AANDAAL

When the saintly poet Periyaalvaar was plucking flowers in the garden for his worship of Vishnu he came upon a female child under a sacred tree. He brought the child home, and adopted her as his own. When the girl grew up she began to go regularly to the temple in Srirangam. She developed such great devotion to the deity Ranganatha there that she imagined she had fallen in love with Him.

She came to be called Aandaal. It is said that Aandaal made it a habit of wearing the flowers on her head before they were sent to the temple for her father's worship. By viewing herself in the mirror she would know if she was attractive enough for the Lord. This very objectionable practice wad discovered one day by the local priests when they discovered a strand of hair with the flowers. The father was very upset, and he reprimanded his daughter severely.

That night, God is said to have appeared to the father in a dream and told him that the flowers which had been tried on by the daughter were very much appreciated, for her unadulterated devotion added to the flower's fragrance. The father recognized that his daughter was saintly.

Aandaal's passion for God found profuse expression in poetry. From her heart and lips flowed magnificent words of supreme beauty, all as soothing music. Two of her works are regarded as masterpieces in Tamil literature. These are known as Tiruppaavai and Naichchiyaar Tirumozho. These are lyrical dedications to Krishna, exuberant outpourings of an aspirant longing for the love of her beloved. Tiruppaavai describes how on a festive morning after a night of fasting, a bevy of milkmaids marched merrily to the local river for a ritual dip, and their experiences thereafter. In the second work Aandaal recounts the exhilarating dream in which she is wed to Krishna. The verse narrates the colorful rituals of the wedding, after referring to Krishna's teasing naughtiness. One of the hymns in this poem is now part of the Tamil tradition in the Tamil (Vaishnavite) marriage ceremony. Here poetry blends with spiritual longing and has subtly enered the culture of a people.

The vigorous sensuality of Aandaal has been seen differently by different people. Most Tamil devotees sing the songs and enjoy its sheer melody. Some scholars and orthodox pundits have not been as appreciative of some of the thoughts in the poem whose sensuality borders on the erotic.

When Aandaal came of age, she refused to marry anybody except Lord Ranganatha of the Temple. She insisted moreover that a formal wedding ceremony be arranged between her and the icon of the deity, with all the traditional rites and rituals. The father and the priests understood that they were dealing with an extraordinary personage here. So they agreed to abide by her wishes. Aandaal was gorgeously dressed, decked with flowers and adorned with ornaments, and ceremoniously escorted to the sanctum sanctorum of the temple. There in the presence of a large gathering with joyous music in the background, the priests recited the sacramental wedding hymns. And then, so says the legend of Aandaal, all of a sudden and to the unaccountable surprise of everyone present, Aandaal gently merged with the hallowed icon of Lord Ranganatha.

Irrespective of the veracity of this time-honored story, this much is certain: Through her poetry and piety Aandaal has attained an immortality in the history and culture of the Tamil world. She will be remembered for as long as Tamil is spoken in the world. A day in February is dedicated to this ancient poetess of the Tamil tradition.

From the World of Science:
NICOLAUS COPERNICUS

A major factor in the transition from ancient science to modern science was the recognition that, with due respects to and admiration for the human species, our earth is simply not the center of the Universe. The person who formally and systematically presented this as a hypothesis was Nicolaus Copernicus (born: 19 February 1473). Copernicus (1473–1543) was born in Poland. He studied mathematics, canon law, astronomy, and medicine, at the universities of Cracow, Bologna, and Padua at various times. He served as canon of the cathedral of Frauenburg, worked on a currency reform for his country, and meticulously searched for a new view of the solar system. He published the fruits of his astronomical investigations in a book which he received when he was on his deathbed. He died without the faintest idea that his book would bring about a revolution of enormous significance.

His monumental work tried to establish that much of the data of observational astronomy could be explained even more simply than the Ptolemaic picture, by imagining the earth, as well as the other planets, to be moving around a fixed sun at the center. Copernicus wrote:

"As a matter of fact, when a ship floats over a tranquil sea, all the things outside seem to the voyagers to be moving in a movement which is in the image of their own, and they think on the contrary that they themselves and all the things with them are at rest. So it can easily happen in the case of the movement of the earth that the whole world should be believed to be moving in a circle."

It is difficult to evaluate the relative impact of books that have molded and affected human history. On all counts the Copernicus book was surely one of the most consequential. The Vedas, the Bible, the Qur'an, and other sacred works have no doubt formed the minds and sensitivities of millions all over the world. Most of these rested on the implicit assumption that Man and his habitat are central to all of Creation. The Copernican treatise was to wreak havoc on this intuitive conviction. This was not just a book, it was a jolting world-view that would create cultural and spiritual shocks.

Martin Luther, who rebelled against the authority of the Pope, did not applaud the rebellion of Copernicus against the authority of Ptolemy. He declared, upon hearing that Copernicus talked of a moving earth around a stationary sun: "This fool wishes to reverse the entire scheme of astronomy. But sacred Scripture tells us that Joshua commanded the sun to stand still, not the earth."

Fifty years after the publication of Copernicus's treatise, the Catholic mathematician Christophe Clavius pointed out that the heliocentric doctrine was verging on blasphemy. To be suddenly told that the earth is just another planet was the equivalent, on a much larger scale, of a political superpower being relegated to an ordinary membership in the comity of nations.

When one examines the life of Copernicus and the impact of his work, a number of interesting elements of the modern scientific enterprise emerge. [You may see a paper on this topic in the *American Journal of Physics* [41 (1973) pp. 1341-1349]

Insights rather than the details are more fundamental in scientific theories. Whether it was the concept of energy or the Bohr atom, new scientific visions are generally refined and modified in due course. This was so with the Copernican view also. In its details, the idea was wrong: planets do not move in circular orbits around the sun, and the sun is not the center of the universe. Yet, his basic insight of the solar system is correct.

February 20

From the World of Religion:
MR. NOYES' REVELATION

Over the eons, many biological species emerged and became extinct: only a few, like ants and roaches, have survived for billons of years. Likewise, there have been many more initiatives for religions than what have survived. It is interesting to remember some of these attempts that did not go too far, or last too long, or simply did not take off.

Consider the Oneida Community which was a 19th century creation of John Humphrey Noyes who had been told since childhood that he was born a sinner and needed to fear the Lord. Young Noyes was neither convinced nor frightened, and grew up to be a skeptical youth. But attending a four day revivalist meeting and listening to Charles Finney changed all this. It is said that when the young man was struck by a very bad cold which caused fever, he experienced the fear of early death. Upon recovery he joined the Yale Divinity School to become a minister. His theological reflections confirmed his feelings that he wasn't the sinner he was supposed to be, and the idea of Christian perfectionism took shape in his mind. In 1833, Noyes received a license to preach.

On 20 February 1834, Noyes informed his congregation that he had been saved from all sin. This was regarded as a heretical claim by many. But it did not prevent Noyes from propagating a new faith which claimed that upon joining it one became sin-less.

In 1837 Noyes began to feel that he had been designated by God to act on His behalf: a conviction or condition to which many other inspired souls have been subjected; not all of them have been successful in creating the critical mass of followers needed to spread the message of the master and its associated practices for long.

Through his writings and lectures Noyes managed to get a few who took him seriously. His religion called for communal living, sharing food and drink, and spousal partners too. This provoked angry reaction from the traditional folks around. Before he could be brought to court on charges of adultery, Noyes bought some land in Indian territory where he moved with his Christian Perfectionist converts. On 1 February 1848, the Oneida Community was formally inaugurated in "the Promised Land" near Syracuse and the Canadian border. Like all religions this one too had a set of doctrines and injunction which included complex marriage (every man in the community was married to every woman and vice versa), strict rules of continence in sexual encounters, public criticism of offenders, acceptance of Christ and the immediate release from sin and confession, acceptance of the Bible and of Revelation, equality of the sexes except in the context of the older men being allowed to choose young women as their first wives. The goal of the movement, like many other prophetic promises, was to bring Heaven on Earth.

Membership grew to more than 300, branches were established in other places also, but the movement did not survive for long. A professor at Hamilton College wrote unsympathetic articles about Noyes and his religion, creating stir and aversion.

For some time Noyes's son was in charge, and though he had no problems with the Complex Marriage system, when it came to Christ and the Bible he tended to be agnostic. The community thrived by hard work in agriculture They even built a nice central building (which is still open to tourists). But in a few decades the movement lost steam, and has become a footnote in the history of religions and cults. Had it not been for the printed word, archives in libraries, reports of burnt diaries detailing the sexual activities of the devout, and the building in Syracuse, none would be remembering Noyes any more.

From the World of Science:
LUDWIG BOLTZMANN

If a football is kicked with a well-defined speed and at a given angle, one can compute where it will hit the ground. If a billiard ball is hit with another billiard ball with a known speed, one can compute how the two would be scattered after impact. These can be done with the aid of what is called classical mechanics.

But what if we had a million or a billion billiard balls in three dimensional space, all bumping into one another and bouncing back and forth? The problem becomes considerably more complicated, but can still be handled by the use of sophisticated mathematics. What we need here is the theory of probability and statistics. When we apply statistical methods to the mechanics of systems consisting of an enormous number of constituents, we get statistical mechanics. Do such systems exist? Of course they do: A jar of gas is a good example. The molecules in it behave like minuscule billiard balls, moving around at random, colliding and moving way only for other collisions. In fact, the pressure exerted by a gas on its walls is simply the result of the frequent bouncing of the molecules from the walls of the container.

A major contributor to the founding of statistical mechanics was the Austrian physicist Ludwig Boltzmann (born: 20 February 1844) who developed methods of tracking down the overall features of the gas in terms of its molecular components by imagining a mathematical space (the so-called phase-space) in which the particles move. With these techniques he could derive the experimentally observed gas-laws from the more fundamental laws of conservation of energy and momentum.

Boltzmann's analysis revealed another fundamental aspect of the phenomenal world.: the arrow of time: The direction of time is simply related to processes in the world that are irreversible (i.e. result in an increase of the entropy of systems). Furthermore, even in the course of these changes, every system will at some future instant come back as closely as possible to where it started from. It is analogous to the following. If we keep shuffling a deck of cards indefinitely, any particular configuration (arrangement of cards) will repeat itself sooner or later. This has implications to time being cyclical.

Boltzmann's results also led to other fundamental results which turned out to necessary for the formulation of what we call the quantum theory of radiation.

Boltzmann's work helped put on a firm basis the so-called kinetic theory of gases which states that gases (and all matter) are made up of atoms and molecules. By the close of the 19th century, however, a handful of European physicists and chemists began to question the actual existence of atoms and molecules. They regarded these as useful mental constructs in terms of which one could explain certain macrocospic properties of matter, but which did not have any real existence. Strange as this view may seem now, in those years this view was embraced by a number of eminent scientists (like Ernst Mach, Wilhelm Ostwald, and Pierre Duhem). Boltzmann was alone in the defense of atomism, and he felt persecuted by his opponents. Whether due to this sense of being left alone and the potential undermining of all his work, or for other reasons, Boltzmann went into periodic depression. In 1904 he came to the United States and lectured in a few universities, wrote a book on his impression of Eldorado (as he described the country), and soon after his return to his native Vienna he committed suicide: not quite as a martyr for the atomic theory, but quite possibly because he felt that his vision of Truth was losing ground in the world. Ironically as the 20th century unraveled, atoms and molecules became more and more real, vindicating Boltzmann.

February 21

From the World of Religion: CHANDIDAS

Chandidas was an illustrious Bengali poet. He wrote devotional poetry that elevated the spirits of those who sang them. It was largely due to the impact of his lyrics on the saint Sri Chaitanya that he is remembered to this day. For Sri Chaitanya popularized by his singing the verses of the joyous poet.

Many of Chandidas's poems are love songs, frank and simple. "Love is nature, the riches of the arts, love is the air we breathe," he sang joyously. His verses became part of the most revered religious music of the Bengali people. These lyrics were often in the metaphor of Krishna's love for Radha. In this framework, amorous intimacy and even the thrills of illicit adultery were conveyed through a poetry which expresses the lofty love between the God and gopis.

Chandidas was born of Brahmin parents, but he is said to have been infatuated with a woman of "lowly" caste. Rami was her name, and she was a village washerwoman. Fearing the wrath of society, Chandidas and Rami used to meet secretly. In his torments for her he composed some beautiful poetry. Artists do not always realize their indebtedness to the sources of their fruitful frustrations: bigoted Brahmins in this case. He wrote odes to her, calling her the light of his eyes, proclaiming she was as proximate to his heart as the garland he was wearing, and declaring her the goddess of all gods. Soon the people came to know about the affair. This created a scandal, the caste-pure Brahmins were appalled by the depravity of Chandidas's caste-breaking sin. In an effort to appease them, to bring the matter into the open, and to seek permission from the establishment for his unorthodox alliance, the poet's brother or cousin (Nakul by name) arranged a hearty feast for the upper caste wielders of authority.

When the learned pundits were seated for the feast, in walked the low-born woman, creating consternation among the pure-of-caste. How dare a defiling washerwoman, temptress of a high-born youth, barge into the presence of the God-knowing Brahmins? It created a terrifying scene. Unfortunately, we don't know the details of what ensued, for the translator of Chandidas sadly informs us that "the manuscript from which these songs were copied, comes to an abrupt end here. The pages that followed the description of the feast were eaten by white ants..."

According to one tale, the Brahmins rose in fury, the woman rushed to her lover's arms. His arms increased in number, Vishnu-like, to four: two were used for serving food and two for embracing the damsel in distress. Thus, Chandidas revealed himself as the Supreme Principle, and Rami became Shakti. The wonder-struck pundits are said to have taken to their heels. We have no way of knowing how much of these stories are true. But they have become part of the folk legends of the land. Painstaking scholarship tends to explode beautiful myths.

Looking upon the man-woman relationship on the physical plane as a reflection of the soul-god merger on the spiritual is the essence of a poetic tradition in Bengali literature known as the *sahaja*. It is also part of the *tantric* framework. The works of Chandidas belong to the rich body of *sahaja* compositions which have been in vogue for many centuries in Bengal.

Religion finds expression in countless modes. Chandidas's work belongs to the poetic mode.

From the World of Science:
AUGUST VON WASSERMANN

The vital organs of our bodies function thanks to the life-giving oxygen that is furnished by the blood-stream. Blood itself consists of blood cells in a liquid called plasma which contains, among other things, proteins, hormones, and more. It also has ingredients which make it clot. When the clotting factors are removed from the blood, we get what is called blood serum. Many blood tests use blood serum because the anticoagulants can affect the results of the tests.

There was a time when young researchers would join institutions for the privilege of being associated with them, and receiving no remuneration for their work. August Paul von Wassermann (born: 21 February 1866) was one such. After receiving his medical degree from the University of Strassburg, he joined the Institute for Infectious Diseases in 1891. Two years later, he was given the responsibility to investigate the infectious disease cholera. Within five years he joined the Institute for Serum Research and Testing in Berlin of which he became the direction of the clinical division.

The dreaded sexually transmitted disease has been known to humankind for many centuries. Its gradual spreading both within a human body and in a society has been was a matter of pain and confusion for a long time. It was only in the 19th century that its bacterial origin was fully recognized. Then there was the question of detecting this bacterium in a patient. The bacterium does get into the blood stream before it does further havoc such as affecting the nervous system.

Wassermann discovered that it is possible to differentiate the blood of humans from that of other mammals by studying the antibodies in blood serum. In 1905 the bacterium *spirochaeta pallida* was spotted as the culprit bacterium which was responsible for syphilis. The following year, Wassermann developed a technique for evaluating the serums. Known as the Wassermann test, it was the first clinical test to uncover syphilis infection.

Soon his name became a household word in clinics all over the world. He received many honors and decorations from many countries, including Japan, Turkey, Romania, and Spain. He was nominated for the Nobel Prize.

Wassermann was one of the founders of the Free Association for Microbiology. belonged to the Judaic tradition, and was once president of the Academy for Knowledge of Judaism. But he also served in the German army as a brigadier-general during the first world war. He is said to have been an excellent speaker. Later he became Director of the Office of Hygiene and Bacteriology of the Prussian Ministry of War.

It proved to be so effective that it became a practice in the U.S., at one time, to have every bride and groom undergo a Wassermann test prior to formally exchanging rings. This practice is no longer required, although some prefer to check out for HIV infection these days. The Wassermann test has been replaced by other more sophisticated tests in our own times.

Men and women come and go in a long series of generations. Practically everyone leaves behind happy memories among family and friends. But a few do such things as affect the rest of humanities, whether in positive or negative ways. Wassermann was one such whose work had an impact on the world beyond his own circle. So he is remembered to this day as the scientist who first devised a test to detect a most notorious venereal disease. From is path-breaking work, others followed. That is how science grows, that is how its applications evolve.

February 22

From the World of Religion:
ARTHUR SCHOPENHAUER

Arthur Schopenhauer (born: 22 February 1788) was an avowed atheist. He was not a Christian in the technical sense. However, aside from God, the hereafter, and denominational affiliation, religion is also concerned with the human condition, its problems, and existential concerns. So he may be remembered in the context of religion.

Schopenhauer is counted among the great philosophers of the nineteenth century. But he was no ivory-tower thinker. His thoughts were not abstruse, nor his themes arcane. His ideas seeped into the world of the general reading public.

He was well-read in Hindu and Buddhist thoughts. These enabled him to develop spiritual perspectives. They injected in him a dark pessimism for which also he is remembered. He was still in his early thirties when he penned his most influential book: The World as Will and Representation (*Die Welt als Wille und Vorstellung*). Here he voices Upanishadic visions of subject and object, and formulates the notion that we can never know the Self, the knower, which is a transcendent principle. Indeed, he regarded the Upanishads as providing him with the greatest consolation in his life.

Schopenhauer was also influenced by ancient Greek philosophy, especially Plato. In his view, real objects have representations which are free from causal and spatio-temporal categories, that is to say, they are independent of the principle of sufficient reason (in technical jargon). These representations constitute the ideas of objects. Schopenhauer applied his ideas to an analysis of aesthetics: to art and music. Ideas are crucial in our appreciation of whatever we experience as beauty.

On the religious side Schopenhauer is fascinated by the notion of ascetic self-denial which he elevated to the level of holiness. He extolled chastity and fasting. He recognized its role in sophisticated religions, though, while paying tribute to it eloquently, he himself never practiced such virtues in his own life, revealing the difference between a philosopher and religious practitioner. He had an unfortunate contempt for the female sex, and described them in uncharitable ters, and as ill-fit for anything serious other than procreation. [DID HE MARRY?]

Unwittingly, in this he reflected the prejudice of most ancient religions. Though himself a non-practitioner of any religion he understood the importance of religion in societies and civilization.

Not surprisingly, he had few friends. Even his mother forsake him. Academics were indifferent or unfriendly to his writings, which turned him even more bitter and cynical.

He reflected more on the human condition than on the physical universe: a circumstance that led him to declare that the world is not rational. He claimed, not without a touch of metaphorical naiveté for an atheist, that the Cosmic is wicked, While his preference for human-centered reflections is acceptable, his intrusions into the world view of physics was unwarranted, indeed plain wrong, as he persisted in rejecting the wave theory of light long after Thomas Young had established it beyond any doubt to the understanding of all serious physicists.

Schopenhauer was surely an original thinker, certainly in the Western philosophical tradition, though much of it was a translation into a different framework of ancient Hindu-Buddhist thinking. In the twentieth century, if he had sported a saffron garb, and gone preaching instead of writing books, Swami Schopenhauer could well have gathered for himself a large follower-crowd. He did have a great impact on some eminent Germanic thinkers and writers.

From the World of Science: HEINRICH HERZ

If one is asked to name the most significant scientific achievement of the modern age, many items could come to mind. But few people would mention the artificial production of electromagnetic waves among them. And yet, the revolutionary impact of this achievement is incalculable. It is fair to say that no other scientific creation has had a great impact on the face of human civilization in the modern era.

Since the first Big Bang of Cosmic creation—or, in the terminology of the Judeo-Christian tradition—since God first pronounced Fiat lux!, the universe has been inundated by electromagnetic waves which are as omnipresent as the God of any religion. But it was not until the nineteenth century of the Common Era that these were consciously produced by human beings. The credit for this goes to Henrich Hertz (born: 22 February 1857).

Hertz was a brilliant student who completed his studies when still very young. He had an uncanny ability to manipulate and device gadgets. He enjoyed physics, and was familiar with the theory of J. C. Maxwell according to which there exist electromagnetic waves, of which visible light was an example. This was a revolutionary theory in many ways, but it was a few decades before such waves were actually produced and detected (by Hertz) in a laboratory.

This happened in a simple classtoom at the Polytechnic in Karlsruhe with the most meager instruments. The first electromagnetic waves were generated in 1888 by the discharge of a condenser through a loop with a spark gap, and were detected with a very similar device. Hertz had, in fact, produced and transmitted electromagnetic waves from one spot to another. This is at the very basis of all complex communication systems in today's world.

There is a story to the effect that Hertz's students were very impressed by what their professor had done, and wondered aloud what its applications would be. Hertz, perhaps out of modesty, made what may be regarded as the most serious blunder in predictions in all of history. "It is of no use whatever," he is said to have told his students. But he did rejoice over the fact that he had experimentally verified Maestro Maxwell's theory.

Indeed, a noteworthy aspect of Hertz's experiment is that is a historic example of an experiment verifying the existence of something that was predicted by a theory. A good theory in physics not only explains observed phenomena, but also predicts or reveals the existence of as yet unknown or unobserved phenomena.

But it took some more years before Guglielmo Marconi would succeed in using Hertz's discovery for sending telegraphic messages without wires. The rest is history: Wireless telegraphy led to radio communication, then television, and then to all kinds of other applications of artificially generated electromagnetic waves.

Sadly, Hertz died at the age of 37: of blood poisoning, it has been recorded. He did not live to see the enormous impact that his modest experiment on the course of human civilization. He is remembered as a very unassuming and amiable man, loved and respected by all who came to know him. His interests went beyond his field of specialization: He is said to have studied languages as varied as Arabic and Sanskrit.

Another remarkable effect of our capacity to generate electromagnetic waves is that we have sent signals from earth into outer space. Should there be other intelligent and technologically advanced civilizations elsewhere in the universe—not an improbability—they would become aware of our existence.

February 23

From the World of Religion: KARL JASPERS

Every thinking human has a worldview. How does this come about? Karl Theodor Jaspers (born 23 February 1883) explored this question in great detail from a psychological perspective in a book published in 1919. He made significant contributions to psychiatry, introducing the so-called biographical method in the treatment of patients in which the physician takes into account the entire life experiences of the person he is treating. He studied delusions, and stressed that they were of two kinds. One, which he described as primary, simply cannot be explained. It just comes out of nowhere. Secondary delusions are caused by known factors, such as one's background, experiences, etc. Primary delusions just cannot be tracked down to anything specific.

Jaspers started as a student of law, studied medicine, and then turned his interests to psychology. After this, when he was about forty, he was drawn to philosophy. It is mainly as a philosopher that he gained international reputation, and is remembered to this day. He held the view that the ultimate limits of human experience cannot be tracked down to rational thought: a idea that is recurrent in ancient Hindu thought. He used the term the *encompassing* (*das Umgreifende*) to describe the limits of being.

In this context he introduced the notion of Existenz (existence in a technical sense). It is an inner experience of being fully human, and cannot be defined in words. It includes the innermost core of being alive: suffering, conflict, guilt, and death itself. As we probe into the ultimate nature of reality we reach a limit beyond which we cannot go. This can throw us into despair or draw us into a deep faith in Transcendence. Transcendence was, for him, a state of no-thing, the sunyata of Buddhists.

It is in this context that one experiences unbounded freedom. This is what constitutes real Existenz. Again, we see here resounding echoes of the Upanishadic framework. This is not surprising, given that he studied Eastern philosophy with great interest. Jaspers sowed the seeds of existential philosophy which took different turns under different philosophers, and became very fashionable in Europe at one time.

Like many independent thinkers Jaspers did not accept any particular religious system, least of all a personal God. But he himself had been influenced by the lives and writings of Christian mystics.

Like other keen observers of the modern world, Jaspers was wary of science and technology, as also of modern economic systems and political institutions. He was convinced that these pose serious threat to civilization.

In his study of the history of philosophy he introduced the terms Axial Age: This was the first millennium of the Common Era which saw the emergence of great religious movements like Zoroastrianism, Confucianism, and Buddhism, as well as philosophical systems such as the Upanishads and of Greek thinkers in humanity's history.

Jaspers was born a German citizen, and he held a professorship at Heidelberg University until Nazi madness began to intrude into the German educational system. He not only refused to give in to the evil of that system, he was also married to a woman of the Jewish faith. And so, to the eternal shame of Nazi Germany, he, like other scientists and intellectuals, lost his teaching position at the university. He moved to Basel in Switzerland where he taught and wrote. After the end of the Second World War, the renowned philosopher wrote a book on politics in which he held the whole of Germany responsible for the Nazi atrocities that are a blot on human civilization.

From the World of Science: CASIMIR FUNK

Textbooks on organic chemistry will tell us that when one or more hydrogen atoms in ammonia (NH-3) are replaced by an organic group, we get an amine. Amines thus have a nitrogen atom in them.

Even without studying organic chemistry people have heard of vitamins as nutritionally important ingredients without which one may suffer all sorts of ailments. Historically, there is a connection between the terms vitamin and amine.

The Polish biochemist Kazimierz (Casimir) Funk (born: 23 February 1884) was working at the Lister Institute in London in an early decade of the twentieth century he came across a scientific paper by Christiaan Eijkman which reported that the disease beri-beri did not affect people who ate brown rice rather than white. He set out to isolate the chemical in the brown rice that gave this protection. It turned out to be an amine. So he called it a vital amine or *vitamine* for short. Today chemists know it to be the compound Thiamine. Other similar compounds which are essential for the prevention of other diseases like rickets, pellagra, and scurvy were discovered in due course. It was found that not all these compounds contain a nitrogen atom in them. Hence the letter *e* was dropped at the end, and so the term *vitamin* came to be.

Today the world of nutrition has a long list of vitamins, often with letters and numbers attached to them: Vitamin A, B1, B2, B3, B6, B12, C, D, K, etc. It is known that these do a variety of things for the body, from enabling us to perceive light and protecting us from certain types of cancer to serving as coenzymes in many physiological processes. Normally we get these vitamins from the common foods we eat, like carrots, apples, green leaves, and such. Occasionally, when we miss out on them, we need to take synthetically produced tablets of these.

It is remarkable how by the painstaking efforts of biochemists we have come to understand so much about our bodies and its connections with the world around. For millennia human beings have survived by eating the foods available: fruits, vegetables, and meat, without realizing the life-giving ingredients they all contain in varying measures. However, because of the lack of a clear knowledge of these, our ancestors were also often exposed to a variety of ailments from which they suffered and diseases which ended their lives prematurely. Now, armed with deeper knowledge, we are able to cope with and avert many diseases which used to be quite common in former times.

Funk also did research on a number of other biochemical and medical matters, such as hormones, diabetes, and cancer.

While the world is mired in its dirty politics and wars, in crimes and religious strife, scientists all over the world are advancing human knowledge, and many of them are also working for the common good.

Thanks to the internationalism that had emerged in the world of science Funk could move from country to country. From England he moved to the United States where he became a citizen. Thanks to the Rockefeller Foundation he went back to his native Warsaw to head the department of biochemistry in the State Institute of Hygiene. Politics made him an exile in France. And when the Nazis took over Paris, he fled from that country, and returned to the United States in 1939.

The following year he had resources enough to establish the Funk Foundation for Medical Research. By now his discoveries had given rise to the commercialization of the product. He became a consultant to the newly established U.S. Vitamin Corporation.

February 24

From the World of Religion:
THE GREGORIAN CALENDAR.

Every culture has its own ways of reckong weeks and months, seasons and years, and sometimes eras too. Thus we have various calendrical systems. Of these, the one that has managed to get the most universal recognition is the so-called Gregorian calendar. This calendar, which is named after Pope Gregory, was formally introduced on 24 February 1582: in accordance with a Papal Bull known as *Inter gravissimas...*(Among our most serious pastoral duties...) which the Pope had signed the previous year.

Until then, in all of Christendom, a system introduced in the time of Julius Caesar was in vogue. This system, based only on crude astronomy, took a solar year to be 365.25 days, so that every fourth year it made up for the defeciency if the 365 days calendar by adding a Leap Year in which February had 29 days.

But this was slightly in excess of what is actually the case: namely, a little less than 365.25 days per solar year. This resulted in a gradual shift in the vernal equinox, because the mean solar year is different from what is implicit in the Julian system. The Pope set up a committee to reform the calendar so as to avoid the awkwardness of a shifting vernal equinox. The committee took the services of a physician named Luigi Lilio (Latin: Aloysius Lilius) who did many of the relevant claculations for this, and died before his results were formally presented. Few remember him today, but the name of Gregory is for ever attached to the calendar.

The innovation in the calendar may seem slight, but it is significant. To make up for the excess that resulted from the Julian system which took the solar year as consisting of 365.25 days instead of the astronomically more precise 365.2422, thereby losing one day every 128 years, the new calendar began by skipping ten days: October 4, 1582 was followed by October 15, 1582. Then again, realizing that 365.2422 was slightly in excess too, though divisible by 4, centennial years are not to be regarded as leap years. This would be enroaching a little too much. To avoid this, ut was decreed that years which can be divided by 400 are to be taken as leap years. Thus, the years 1700, 1800, and 1900 were not leaps years, but 1600 and 2000 were. It is to be noted that even with such accuracies, the calendar is not perfect in that the earth's rotation is changing, ever so slightly, as a result of tidal friction.

The societal and cultural impacts of the calendar were interesting. Questions arose as to the interest on the loans during the period from October 5 to October 14 of the year when these dates were skipped. The interest was forgiven. What about wages? These too were not given. Next, the fact that the reform was initiated by the Roman Catholic Church, without consulting its rivals in Christendom, caused problems too. Protestant countries and those under the Eastern Orthodox Church refused to adopt the new system initially. For almost two centuries countries like Great Britain and its American colonies held on to the Old System. Eventually they discovered that, pope or no pope, there is no escaping astronomy.

On the other hand, religious calendars in the various traditions still have their own calendars—almost always lunar. With the result that whereas the days of (Catholic) saints are fixed by the same dates every year, the feasts and festivals of most religions (including Easter) occur on different dates.

If the calendar reform had been initiated by an international trans-religious body like the United Nations Organization, these problems would not have arisen.

From the World of Science:
JACQUES DE VAUCANSON

We live in an age in which robots and automata are commonplace, visibly or invisibly. Many science fiction stories talk about robots. Not many may know that the first robot was designed and made in the eighteenth century, prior to the French Revoluition. The man behind it was Jacques Vaucanson (24 February 1709). [The *de* was added as an honorific later in his life.]

Vaucanson is said to have come a family of very modest means. He was interested in religious matters, and wanted to make clocks as a profession.

When he was in his early twenties, he happened to meet a surgeon by the name of Claude Nicolas de Cat. He learned a lot about human anatomy from Le Cat. He was also one of early proponents of the mechanistic view of the human body, that the body is essentially a very complex machine with structures and functions. Inspired by this view, it occurred to Vaucanson that in principle it should be possible to construct a mechanical device that would imitate some the basic physiological functions. We recognize this as the underlying idea in today's robots.

Vaucanson spent much time in constructing a large size human-like entity that could play flute: le *joueur de flûte*, as it was called. It had a repertoire of tunes it could play. His flute-player was probably the first robot to have been created. Thus, he is often remembered as the inventor of the first robot. It is good to know that the function of the first robot ever constructed was to produce music. Vaucanson also made another robot which played the tambourine.

But the most spectacular robot he constructed was a duck which could flap its wings and drink water. This was not all: He had endowed his bird with a complex alimentary canal which enabled it to ingest grains, and eliminate waste products the way a live duck does in the biological world. Here was an engineer who had done what God or Nature does. Vaucanson did it with physics, rather than with chemistry. In this respect, he was not much different from modern day robotic engineers.

Soon Vaucanson's name spread far and wide. The famous Frederick II of Prussia who was in the habit of getting to his court celebrates, scholars and scientists, invited Vaucanson also. But the inventor refused the invitation. He said he would rather serve his own country, France.

In due course his expertise was sought by the government. When he was barely 32, he got involved with the silk industry in Lyons for which that city was quite famous in those days. Vaucanson helped the sagging French silk industry in some innovative ways. He introduced new techniques for weaving by inventing the first fully automated loom in the process. Here he began to use punched cards: the first ever and long before the invention of modern computers. At the age of 37, Vaucanson was elected life-member of the Académie des Sciences. Here he wrote many memoirs on his inventions for silk mills, describing their function. The first metal slide lathe was built by Vaucanson in 1751.

It has been said that Vaucanson was one of the first inventors who were consciously concerned with lessening the labors of workers which included women and children in those good old pre-Revolutionary days. For there was a time when workers in manufacturing centers were treated no better than beasts of burden. With all the ugly problems that have ensured from technology, we should not forget what a great relief it has been to members of the working class. And in this context we may remember the genius and commitment of men like Jacques de Vaucanson.

February 25

From the World of Religion: FEAST OF ESTHER (2002)

All through human history, it has been the misfortune of many groups to have suffered persecution on the basis of their race, religion, or beliefs. Perhaps no other group has had more episodes of such painful experiences than people of the Judaic faith. So there are periodic remembrances in the tradition of such events. Each generation needs to know its cultural history, as much to rejoice in its happy past as to grieve for the sufferings of its forebears.

Thus, on this day people of the Jewish people celebrate the Feast of Esther: a woman whose story forms an entire chapter in the Old Testament.

Ahasuerus was an ancient Persian potentate whose empire is said to have extended all the way to India, it says in the Authorized Vesion. [This is the only place in the Bible where India is mentioned explicitly. The Hebrew term "Hoddu" refers to the Indus valley region. Translating this as India is like rendering Vermont as the United States.]

Ahasuerus was upset by his wife Vashti who defied his orders to present herself at the end of a royal party to display her beauty to all the guests. So he decided to choose a new queen from among a bevy of beauties. His eyes caught the lovely

Jewish woman by the name of Esther. Esther became the new queen, but did nor reveal her ethnic identity, which was Jewish: for then, as in some places even now, there was virulent anti-Jewish sentiment.

One of the king's counselors, Haman by name, schemed to slaughter the Jews in the land because Esther's uncle Mordecai had not paid obeisance to him. He drew lots (*purim*) to decide on the date when he would carry out his nefarious project. Esther came to know about this and she invited King Ahasuerus and Haman to a feast which she would arrange.

Ahasuerus learned that, thanks to Mordecai, a palace plot to usurp the throne had been thwarted. He called Haman and asked what would be the best way of honoring someone whom the king would like to thank. Haman, not realizing it was Mordecai that the king had in mind, and imagining it was for himself, suggested an elaborate banquet. At the banquet, Esther revealed her Jewish identity and asked for Haman's life. This is the *Feast of Esther* commemorated on this day, and the term Purim (lots) is used for this.

Scholars doubt the historicity of this story. Closer examination reveals many anachronisms and inconsistencies. Thus, when one is out of the celebratory context, one is inclined to the more plausible interpretation of Purim as the relic of a Balybolian spring festival dedicated to Marduk (transformed into Merodach, then Mordecai) and Ishtar (Esther): two deities of Babylonian mythology. Perhaps the Jews in Babylon also celebrated that festival, and gradually created their own mythology through Esther's story. Theologians have given esoteric meanings to the story, even to some of the words in this chapter of the Bible, unique in being without the word G-d.

There is a reproduction of a painting by the Flemish artist Franc Francken II (17th century) entitled *The Feast of Esther* in which the banquet is depicted on the main part of the scene, and Haman is being executed at another end of the canvass. In the same century, the French playwright Jean Racine wrote a play based on the Book of Esther.

It matters not if Esther lived and saved the Jews of Persia more than 2400 years ago. We share in the collective remembrance of our Jewish friends of a story that symbolically refers to one of their mythic heroines who saved their people from one of the genocides with which they have been threatened more than once during their history.

From the World of Science: IDA NODDACK

In the world of science there are two ways in which one may be ignored: the report of an interesting observation (discovery) may not be taken seriously; or the enunciation of a new insight or idea may go unnoticed. One has to wait for a sufficient lapse of time, memories of fellow scientists, and probing by historians of science before the discoverer or the originator of the idea gets full credit. Even then one is not always recognized for what one accomplished.

Consider case of Ida Noddack (born: 25 February, 1896). She was a competent chemist who, with her husband Walter Noddack, discovered an element (atomic number 75) which she named in honor of Rhenany (Rheinland) Rhenany—Rheinland (her birth region in Germany) as rhenium in 1924. The discovery of a new element used to be a significant achievement. For this she received the prestigious Scheele Medal from the Swedish Chemical Society in 1934.

The Noddacks also thought they had discovered yet another element in naturally occurring rocks. It was believed to have the atomic number 43, and they even named it, calling it masurium. For quite a few years papers were written on this element. However, in the next few years, other physicists pointed out that this is not a naturally occurring element. It was named technetium now. In this sense, the Noddacks were among the first to discover an artificial element, though they were not aware of this when they made the discovery in the 1920s. Now not everyone is agreed that it was genuine discovery at all, because the isotopes of such an element are extremely unstable. Their half-lives are much less than the age of the earth.

In 1934, Enrico Fermi published a paper in which he reported that he and his coworkers had bombarded some nuclei with neutrons, causing transuranic elements to be formed. Upon reading this, Noddack wrote a paper entitled "On the Element 93" in which she doubted if Fermi was correct in his claim. In the course of her critical assessment she also noted: "It is conceivable that in the bombardment of heavy nuclei with neutrons, these nuclei break up into several large fragments which are actually isotopes of known elements, but are not neighbors of the irradiated elements." Unwittingly, she described here one of the most important types of nuclear reactions: nuclear fission. But Ida Noddack's paper was largely ignored. The phenomenon of nuclear fission was actually discovered some five years later by Otto Hahn. Some have criticized the fact that he made no mention of Noddack in his paper. It is not clear if he was unaware of her paper, or simply chose to ignore it. The eminent nuclear physicist Emilio Segrè recalled in his authobiography: "We (meaning he and Enrico Fermi) did not seriously entertain the possibility of nuclear fission, although it had been mentioned by Ida Noddack, who sent us a reprint of her work. The reason for our blindness, shared by Hahn and Meitner, the Joilot-Curies, and everybody else working on the subject, is not clear to me even today."

The Noddacks stayed in Germany during the dark years of Nazi rule. In 1942, they became professors at the University of Strasbourg (Alsace had been annexed by Germany once again, during World War II) where they may not have continued with their scientific research, because their publications suddenly stopped. It is not clear what they were doing during these years.

Ida Noddack was the first woman to address the Society of German Chemists. In 1925, this was an unusual honor. She was not yet thirty years of age. In her later years the Federal Republic of Germany awarded her the High Service Cross.

February 26

From the World of Religion:
THE COMMUNIST MANIFESTO

Communism has many features of any religion. It has its prophets in Karl Marx and Friedrich Engels. It is its promise of heaven—at least on earth. It has doctrines which one cannot repudiate with impunity. It certainly has its own world view. It has its days of celebrations which are different for different (Communist) countries. And it has its scripture: the original document from which the religion sprang.

That scripture is the Communist Manifesto (published on 26 February 1848.) Like the Vedas, the Bible, and the Koran, it has had a great impact on the course of history. It arose from the vision of history of two individuals. Unlike other scriptures which claimed revelation to be their source, here the claimed source was historical analysis. It rests on the doctrine that change and transformations are the hallmarks of human history, as also class struggles. Societies change from feudalism to mercantalism to capitalism to communism: the pinnacle of civilization. In this last ideal stage there would be perfect equality and social justice, no exploitation or oppression.

The industrial revolution created the city-dwelling middle-class (bourgeoisie) which is siding with the moneyed ruling class to exploit the laborers who are treated as simply another commodity, another cog in the wheel of industry. The sole interest of the capitalists—whose agents constitute the government of democratic countries—is to make as much profit as they can. To counteract this exploitative machinery the laborers will have to organize themselves into unions, and fight for their rights. Also, the capital which feeds industry and all means of economic production, must be taken away from the hands of a handful of greedy families, and taken over by the government whose administrators will be inspired by serving the common good, rather by greed. Moreover, the ruling classes have always numbed the minds of the masses into believing that the social order was as ordained by God, and that the poor will have to bear their burden because that was the will of God. The victims should wake up from the slumber caused by religion which is no More than "the opium of the masses."

But this leap from capitalism to communism will occur only through the violent process of a revolution. Like traditional religions the Communist Manifesto formulated its own ethical principles. It called on people of the faith to action specific ways. Convinced that every current political system is corrupt, Communism declares that its Utopian goal can be achieved only by "the forcible overthrow if all existing (1848) social condition." The manifesto warns that the ruling classes must tremble. It appeals to the proletarians to bring about the revolution, because they "have nothing to lose but their chains."

The Communist Manifesto had two impacts: one positive and one negative. On the positive side, it raised the consciousness of thoughtful leaders in government and industry, as also among intellectuals and working men and women. As result, emancipating laws and trade-unions emerged, and the plight of the working classes gradually changed for the better in most industrialized countries. On the negative side, in totalitarian countries where the exploitation was at its worst, the manifesto of Marx and Engels provoked bloody revolutions to overthrow the regimes. However, invariably, whether in Russia or China, in Vietnam, North Korea or Cuba, the same leaders who freed the oppressed from the tyranny of dictators, themselves became dictators, ruthless sometimes, stifling political freedom and basic human rights. In Stalinist Russia and Maoist China, Communists massacred millions in the name of liberation.

From the World of Science:
JOHN HARVEY KELLOGG

Perhaps the best-known brand of breakfast cereal is Kellogg. It owes it origin to a certain John Harvey Kellogg (born: 26 February 1852) who served as a physician for many decades at the Battle Creek Sanitarium. He was a competent surgeon and a vegetarian too. He was one of the earliest medical professionals to recognize the dangers of smoking, and warned about its potential for lung cancer.

But the man was also an eccentric. He had strong views on sexual indulgence, especially of the self-stimulating kind. In fact one inspiration for his concocting the cereal was the conviction that a bland breakfast would suppress in young boys any inclination to self-abuse (as masturbation used to be euphemistically called).

So he wrote and spoke about this sinful practice (as he viewed it), advising parents to keep watchful eyes on their growing adolescents, especially to see to it that they don't tinker with their private parts when they are in the seclusion of the bathroom. He even listed a number of behavioral patterns by which parents could detect if their lads were secretly masturbating or not. He went beyond such commendable behavior in his own personal life. It has been said that he abstained from any sexual titillations even with his own wedded wife. He belonged to the school which firmly believed that the sexual act should have the noble purpose of reproduction, of propagating the human race, especially of one's own religion, and not be instigated by such base incentives as deriving carnal pleasure. There is no record of his wife's views on the subject.

In addition, the man is also said have been obsessively bowel-focused. He was very particular about what he consumed—and that excluded meat of all kinds, and included fiber-foods and lots of water. Furthermore he was very keen on keeping his bowels always clean. For this, he subjected himself to periodic enemas. Obsessions can take on the most fantastic expressions.

Once he is said to have exclaimed: "Is God a man with two arms and legs like me? Does He have eyes, a head? Does He have bowels? Well I do, and that makes me more wonderful than He is!"

His brother William Kellogg who was the business-man. He established the Battle Creek Toasted Corn Flake Company in 1906 which became a huge business, making their family name practically a synonym for breakfast cereal.

One would have thought that such an eccentric person as John Harvery Kellogg would have had little effect on a culture or a civilization. Aside from initiating flakes, granola, rice crispies, and wheaties, it is due to the physician Kellogg that the practice of male circumcision for non Jewish male children was introduced in the United States. He argued, and obviously convinced many people, that by this means—which was to be done without anesthesia—the male child will for ever remember the pain associated with touching the organ which was reserved uniquely for reproduction, and thus refrain from what Dr. Harvey Kellogg regarded as a heinous sin, and against which he crusaded by making corn flakes.

His book entitled *Plain Facts for Old and Young: Embracing the Natural History and Hygiene of Organic Life* appeared in 1982. It is still worth reading if only because it reveals the thinking of this strange man who has had such an interesting impact of our breakfast to this day.

Human history and culture are shaped by great men and women, by heroes and thinkers, by philosophers and inventors and scientists, and sometimes by eccentrics too.

February 27

From the World of Religion: JALALUDDIN RUMI

There are religious traditions where poets inspire the faithful to spirituality. Not through dogmas and doctrines, but through poetic reflections life and death, on love and sorrow, and on the divine, poets from the Saiva Siddhanta of the Tamil world to the Lake poets have England have brought the human heart closer to the divine experience than many treatises on theology.

There is a mystical strain the Islamic tradition known as Sufism. One of its prime representative was Maulana Jallaluddin Rumi. He is reckoned among the great poets of the world. He was born in the first decade of the thirteenth century. He was a scholar at 24, and wrote knowledgeably on religion and the science of his day.

It is said that a wandering gad-man drew to mysticism. Rumi's poetic genius created much music and poetry when the dervish died. He began to write as one intoxicated with the divine. If, in the traditional mode, religious experiences are expected to guide one to a moral framework, it would seem that with Rumi it is the other way around: marality is not an end in itself, but a means to the spiritual path. For, like all Sufis, mystical experience was paramount for Rumi. Though Sufism is regarded as an integral part of Islam, being based on the Islamic vision of dogma *La ilaha illa 'llah*: There is No God but God, it has close parallels with the spiritual tradition of Hinduism. Some have even suggested that it took inspiration from the Hindu mode of spirituality. Others have argued that Sufism is closely allied to Christian mystics and to Gnosticism. In the view of yet others, it was a blossoming of the innate spiritual genius of Persia.

Indeed some have interpreted the Sufi movement as a symbolic re-affirmation of Persian spiritual and intellectual greatness in response to the imposition of Arabic Islam on its soil. As Cyprian Rice put it, "Persia's revenge for the imposition of Islam and of the Arabic Qur'an was her bid for the utter trans-formation of the religious outlook of all the Islamic peoples by the dissemina-tion of the Sufi creed and the creation of a body of mystical poetry which is almost as widely known as the Qur'an itself. The combination in Sufism of mystical love and passion with a daring challenge to all forms of rigid and hyp-ocritical formalism has had a bewitching and breath-taking effect on successive Moslem generations in all countries..."

Rumi was certainly the greatest of the Sufis. His *Mathnavivi Mahavi* is literally the Bible of the Sufis, a work that was rendered into English by R. A. Nicholson only in the twentieth century. It may be noted in passing that a major service ren-dered by post 18th century Western scholars—though seldom recognized as such—is the transportation of many local cultures and their wisdom on to the world stage. Rumi himself described a true Sufi as follows (Nicholson's transla-tion):

What makes the Sufi? Purity of heart;
Not the patched mantle and the lust perverse
Of those vile earth-bound men who steal his name.
He in all dregs discerns the essence pure:
In hardship ease, in tribulation joy.
The phantom sentries, who with batons drawn
Guard Beauty's place-gate and curtained bower,
Give way before him, unafraid he passes,
And showing the King's arrow, enters in.

From the World of Science: DAVID SARNOFF

The impact of science on society is on two different planes. First there is the plane of worldviews. Most people with only a modicum of scientific knowledge know, for example, that the earth is not really the center of the universe, and that dis-eases are not caused by evil spirits.

The other is the practical plane where scientific knowledge has found count-less applications: everything from airplanes to xerography and more. However, in this one tends to forget the role played by an important group of people: those who transform a powerful invention into a major industry or business enterprise without which no technology can reach millions of people.

In this context we may recall the name of David Sarnoff (Born: 27 February 1891). Sarnoff was born in Tzarist Russia, but the family migrated to the United States when the boy was 14 years of age. As a Jewish lad he studied the Talmud, and even sang in the synagogue choir.

Because his father Abraham Sarnoff died before young David could finish school, he got himself a job. He learnt the techniques of telegraphy to be hired by the Marconi Telegraph Company. He rose up in the company by his energy, enthusiasm, and innovative ideas. Those were the early days of radio, and Sarnoff proposed to the Radio Corporation of America that one should build (and sell) units which combined both a radio and a phonograph. It was a gem of an idea whose implementation brought large profits to RCA and a vice-president's post in the company for Sarnoff. He was the first to broadcast a running commentary.

We also remember him as a pioneer of the TV industry. He initiated the industry in the 1920s and established the National Broadcasting Company (NBC). Thus, he has the unique honor of bringing both radio and television in to homes of countless millions.

As with other great inventions of the twentieth century, TV has grown in sophistication, size, and variety in many different ways, and has become an industry which employees millions of people all over the world. It is also one of the few inventions whose utilization involve both complex technology and great artistry. Like other inventions, again, its potential for misuse was not foreseen by its early enthusiastic pushers who saw in it only entertainment and profit.

On the one hand, thanks to the TV industry, we have some fantastic entertainment programs, daily and instantaneous news, live broadcasts of major events from sports and royal weddings to the Olympics and national tragedies, and more. We also have educational programs, travelogues, special treats for kinds and such. Most of all, thanks to the associated video and DVD, classic movies and programs have come within reach of generations who had never seen them in the first place. We are grateful to David Sarnoff for having instigated all this.

On the other hand, in the name of freedom of expression, whether artistic or asinine, foul language, crime scenes, violence and all sorts of obscenities have become all too commonplace on TV screens, and within reach of all and sundry. It is as if in our attempts to harness energy from ocean waves, something happened, and destructive surges of water are lashing on the land, indiscriminately destroying people and property. Little can be done to stem the tide that has been let loose, and we must learn to live with it. For that is the very essence of technology: to bring in good thinks at one level, but also inflicting harm one way or another sooner or later.

February 28

From the World of Religion: SAINT VILLANA

There was a time when there used to be far more women and men drawn to a saintly life than in modern times. Even as youngsters in today's world are fascinated by the stars in the world of entertainment, and fantasize themselves to be one of those, in the middle ages, many young minds were drawn to the spiritual mode for that was very much in the air: church bells and sermons, psalms and choirs were very much part of daily life.

So it was with Villana of Florence who was born in 1332. She was so attracted to religious life that she left home and joined a convent when she was barely thirteen. But even parents who took their religion seriously don't like to see their young daughter run away from home and become a nun before she is a full grown adult.

One solution was to distract the mind to more worldly things. And what is more worldly for a young woman than a husband who can afford material things? So she was married off to a handsome young man who showered her with gifts. Signora Rosso di Piero suddenly found herself in the midst of fine jewelry, gorgeous costumes, and such. She began to indulge in these with great gusto. Her religious inclinations had been subdued, if not eradicated.

Then, in says in the tradition, something happened one day. She dressed up fabulously to ready herself for an soiree of feasting and dancing. And as any woman would do, she stood in front of the mirror to see how beautiful she looked for the occasion. It is said that what she saw was not a charming woman grandly attired, but a hideous figure, too ugly to behold. She saw herself as a repulsive female, drenched in sin. It is quite possible that her innate spiritual nature had been suppressed by the external forces of luxury and pleasure, and that they suddenly gave way as it happens when a powerful spring is compressed for long. She was so disgusted with what she saw that rid herself of the ostentatious attire right away, and slipped into very modest clothes.

Furthermore she began to sob, feeling very guilty for all the her pleasure-giving indulgences, and went to the local fathers of the Dominican Order for confession and redemption of what she regarded as grievous sins.

She was not only forgiven, but cheerfully accepted into the order. Now she was truly in the place where she belonged, in an atmosphere of prayer and worship. She dedicated all her time to thoughts of the Divine. She grew spiritually. She read often from the Scriptures, and did service to the poor.

People talked, for she was still married in principle, and what sort of a woman she, abandoning her husband for life in a convent, they would gossip. But Villana simply did not case. Her parents lived not far from the convent. They saw her during mass, as also everyone else in town. She was often in a state of total ecstasy for that is what true religious experience is at its best.

Then word went around that she had visions of Mary, and that Villana even talked with the Virgin. It was rumored that her room was sometimes lit by a strange bright light which could only have been of supernatural origin, and that she could foretell events. They began to treat her with reverence.

When time came die, she lay down on her bed and had the Passion of Christ read to her. They say that when the line "He bowed His head and gave up the spirit" was read, she too breathed her last. Some five hundred years after her life, a Villana cult was confirmed. And February 28 is taken as her feast day in the Catholic tradition.

From the World of Science: LINUS PAULING

It is common knowledge that every piece of matter in the world is made up of atoms. The ultimate unit of most of the substances we encounter are molecules: combinations of atoms of one or more elements. But how do these atoms stay together? Today we know that this is due to the chemical bonds between them. But what exactly are chemical bonds? What is their ultimate nature? How many kinds of chemical bonds are there? These and related questions are of great importance, and are studied in detail in a field known as quantum chemistry. A pioneer in this field was Linus Pauling (born: 28 February 1901.)

Pauling was a bright young man in his college days. His doctoral work at Caltech happened to be in the 1920s: the incipient years of quantum mechanics whose foundations were being laid and strengthened in Germany and Denmark. Pauling had an opportunity in this context to go all the way from California to Germany, there to study and interact with some of the giants of the quantum mechanics industry:, like Arnold Sommerfeld, Erwin Schrödinger, Werner Heisenberg, Niels Bohr.

Upon his return he became a professor at Caltech, the youngest faculty member. He continued with his research in theoretical chemistry, developing a highly original theory chemical bonds. He was barely thirty when he published in 1931 a classic on the subject: The Nature of the Chemical Bonds which was to have a tremendous impact on the course of theoretical chemistry. It was based on sophisticated mathematics, on intuitive imagery involving the orientations of electronic spins, as well as on a deep insight into the possible configurations of quantum mechanical (probability) waves.

In 1954 Linus Pauling was awarded the Nobel Prize for Chemistry for his path-breaking work. Pauling never lost interest in his scientific pursuits, but he was among the great scientists who were deeply affected by tragedy of the atomic bomb. He joined hands with other eminent pacifists like Albert Einstein. This did not sit well with the Communist-phobic forces that were gaining ground in the mid-fifties in the United States. So he was subjected to the harassment that many others like him suffered during that unfortunate phase in American history, sometimes called the McCarthy era. Pauling stuck to his American ideal of free thought and free expression, and would not be intimidated by anybody. During a questioning he is said to have stated famously, "Nobody tells me what to think, except Mrs. Pauling."

Rather than being silenced Pauling, in 1958 he and his wife drafted a petition to the United Nations, which was signed by some 11,000 scientists from nearily fifty countries.

The world was watching, and while the NIH and NSF did not grant him funding for his research for his alleged anti-American activities, The Nobel Committee decided he deserved to be honored and awarded him the Peace Prize for 1962. Thus Linus Pauling became unique in being the recipient of two unshared Nobel Prizes.

Pauling became famous in his later years for his research on diseases, and the role of vitamins in preventing cold and in maintaining good health.

Above all, he won the respect and admiration of millions of people all over the world. For, beyond his scientific genius and capacity for lucid lecturing, like other enlightened and compassionate thinkers, he longed to see a world where there would be no war. He was also prescient, like few others in the 1950s, that one did not arrest the madness of nuclear weapons production and testing, the madness would soon spread all over the world.

February 29

From the World of Religion: THE LEAP YEAR

Most of us go through our calendars, noting and marking dates. We also know that February 29 occurs only every fourth year.

Normally, it used to be a custom in the Western tradition—which still persists in some circles—it is the aspiring man who proposes to a woman for marriage. In those (old-fashioned?) days, on February 29 the woman had the prerogative to take the initiative and ask the man if he would marry her. This was not just a custom but one sanctioned by law. It is said that such a law, giving woman the right to propose was enacted in the Scottish Parliament in 1288, and later adopted by some other countries from where it spread to America as a custom rather than law. This may sound liberal, but actually the law was to restrict, and not grant freedom to women, because prior to that a woman could propose on any day in the month of February of a leap year. Apparently, if a man did not wish to accept the proposal, he was required to compensate the refusal in some way: it could be by a gentle kiss or with a a gown of pure silk.

According to *Brewer's Dictionary of Phrase and Fable*, the credit for this much female freedom goes to the Irish Saint Patrick. It is said that one day in February Saint Bridget reported to him that there was commotion in her nunnery because the ladies they were demanding the right for women to propose. The saint generously replied that she would give this right once every seven year. Whereupon Saint Bridget put her arms around the saint's neck. This so tickled him that he exclaimed, "Bridget, squeeze me that way again, an' I'll give ye leap-year, the longest of the lot." Bridget immediately proposed marriage to Patrick. Since this was a non-no for a saint, he simply gave her a kiss and a silk gown.

In 1980 a bunch of Frenchmen, calling themselves amateur journalists, launched a comical newspaper entitled *La Bougie du Sapeur*, which would appear every February 29. It was named after a character created by the cartoonist Georges Collomb. They printed 30,000 copies of first issue of this paper, but in 2000, the number grew to 100,000. The 24 page journal has humorous sections on a wide variety of topics, ranging from sports and puzzles to national and international news.

The Gregorian calendar repeats itself day and date every 400 years. Because of the pattern of days in 400 year periods, February 4 has a greater probability of falling on a Monday than on a Sunday. February 20 fell on a Sunday in 2004. Next time this will happen will be 28 years later, in 2032.

Questions have been raised about the birthdays, and therefore the ages, of individuals born on February 29. In Gilbert and Sullivan's *The Pirates of Penzance,* Frederic had sworn allegiance to the pirates until his 21st birthday. However, since he was born on February 29, he was told that he was obliged to stay with the gang until he was he was 84.

The town of Anthony in Texas/New Mexico calls itself the Leap Year Capital of the World, because it initiated a jubilatory festival there in 1988. Since then, it has attracted thousands of people there in the week of February 29 for a four-day festival to celebrate the birthdays of people born on that date. They have also formed a Worldwide Leap Year Birthday Club. All it takes is a $20 membership due which is payable every leap year. There are hundreds of thousands of 29-ers; perhaps quite a few of them have enrolled.

From the World of Science:
HERMAN HOLERITH

The collection and analysis of data are part of scientific methodology. But they are also useful and necessary in affairs of the state. Indeed the word *statistics* is cognate to the word *state* because initially it dealt with records of such matters as births and deaths for the government. Then there is the problem of estimating the number of inhabitants in a country. In the United States, for example, there were about 3.8 million people in1790. By 1860 the number jumped to more than 31 million. It took the Census bureau seven full years to come up with the final results of the 1880 census.

Something had to be done to accelerate the process of counting the fast increasing population. It was in this context that the engineering ingenuity of Hermann Hollerich (born: 29 February 1860) came in handy.

Hollerith had taught briefly at M.I.T. where he did some research on data storage. He experimented with paper tapes and pins before hitting on the idea of using the so-called Jacquard punched cards. Later he joined the US Patent Office where he developed and patented his inventions. Next, he joined the US Census Bureau as a statistician. Here he dedicated himself even more to the technical problem of collecting, storing, and analyzing the enormous bits of information that accumulate during a census.

Hollerith came up with a device which had an automatic tabulating machine with many clock-like counters. Run electrically these counters stored the results. Operators could control the machines which could read all kinds of data such as profession, marital status, number of children, etc. relating to a individual. It is said that initially he got the idea upon watching tram conductors punch the tickets.

It has been estimated that the US government saved some five million dollars in the 1890 census by using Hollerith's machine. This census revealed the total population of the United States to be 62,622,250. Canada adopted Hollerith's invention the very next year for its own census. Gradually it spread to some European countries as well.

Hollerith established his company in 1896 with the uninspiring name: *Tabulating Machine Company*. In due course his machines grew in sophistication. They came to be used not only in the context of taking census, but in taking and tracking other data as well, such as in banking, insurance, etc. Since his invention spread to many countries beyond his own, the company's name was changed in 1924 to International Business Machines Corporation, or IBM for short.

It is well known that during the second world war, many immigrants came to the United States from Germany. In a sense this was also true during the political turmoil in the 1840s. It was then that Herman Hollerith's family moved to the United States. It is said that though he was a very bright student, he had difficulty with spelling. The enthusiasm of one of his teachers in instilling accepted orthography on young Herman turned the kind off from school education. This prompted his parents to give the lad home schooling with the assistance of a Lutheran preacher.

In due course Hollerith received many honors. Columbia University awarded him a doctorate on the basis of his thesis on the mechanism of his invention. The Franklin Institute awarded him the Elliot Cresson Medal. He was also recipient of the Paris Exposition's Gold Medal and the Bronze Medal of the 1893 World's Fair in Chicago.

Herman Hollerith was a pioneer of age of computer in which we live where mounds of data are stored and transformed in milliseconds.

March 1

From the World of Religion: ON MARCH

The first of March is the beginning of yet another month. In the northern hemisphere, this is the month when Spring comes back.

The reckoning of dates and years has a long history, and although it all seems quite normal and natural in our own times (at least within particular cultures), it was not always so. The number of years was more tricky, and the beginning of a new year was by no means uniform. Even within Europe, during the Middle Ages, different countries and even subdivisions within countries, marked dates and years very differently. March, September, December: all were once taken as the beginning month of a new year.

It is generally accepted that in ancient Rome, this was the first month of the year: its vestige is seen in our own times in the names of the months from September to December, which are derived from the Latin words for seven, eight, nine, and ten respectively. There were perhaps two reasons for naming the first month thus. First, this used to be time of the year when the weather was good to re-start Romans expansionism, and it was deemed appropriate to invoke Martius, the God of War. Also, in Roman mythology, Romulus, the legendary founder of Rome, was the son of Martius. So it was that the whereas the names of other planets are invoked in the days of the week, Mars in the only planet whose name has entered a month.

It is said that in ancient times, Roman priests would get into a joyous frenzy on the streets, carrying shields and symbols of battle, starting on the March Kalends (first day of the month). This would continue for three and a half weeks. The Mardi Gras revelries of our own times has been traced to these festivities.

In Roman mythology, the mother of Mars was Juno, and she was taken as the patroness of this day. She was the wife of Jupiter, and was also the Goddess of matrimony and childbirth. She had all the great qualities of a good mother. So the first of Mars was also called Matronalia.

March has been called "the slayer of winter," and one writer observed that "out of sight, (thou, Mars) art nursing April's violets." Other poets have sung March's virtues too. Thus William Bryant wrote:

The stormy March has come at last,
With winds and clouds and changing skies;
I hear the rushing of the blast
That through the snowy valley flies.

Bayard Taylor's verse says:
With rushing winds and gloomy skies,
The dark and stubborn Winter dies;
Far off, unseen, Spring faintly cries,
Bidding her earliest child arise: March!

In other cultures also the advent of Spring (vernal equinox) was (is) taken as the beginning of the new year. In the Old Testament, the reference was to this month in Exodus 12: 1-2: And the Lord spake to Moses and Aaron in the land of Egypt, saying, "This month shall be unto you the beginning of months. It shall be the first month of the year to you."

In the Christian tradition, this date is dedicated to St. David of the 6th century, who was born of a king and of one who became a saint also, who fought the heresy that denied the doctrine of the original sin, an ascetic who became a priest and did much missionary work in Wales.

In Switzerland, they revel in Chalanda Marz on this day. In Scotland it is called Whuppity Scoorie Day and in Tasmania it is Labor Day. Thus every nation and culture has its own way of naming or mode of marking the first of March.

Ultimately, our values and World views are shaped in positive ways by awareness of what is good and what is right. That is what constitutes enlightenment, whether scientific or social, religious or racial. In this context, as February is Black History Month, the first of March inaugurates Women's History Month: the month is dedicated to remembering the role and accomplishments of women in the arts and sciences, in sports and politics, and more. During this month, there are numerous educational and informational activities to bring us greater awareness of the contributions of women, eminent and not so eminent, to society and culture. These include lectures, publications, discussions, essay competitions, etc.

From the World of Science:
FIRST HYDROGEN BOMB

The World first came to know about the hydrogen (H-) bomb on 1 March 1954 when the United States announced that it had exploded one in the Bikini Atoll which is part of the Marshall Islands. A previous attempt, one a year and a half earlier, had caused the Atoll of Elugaleb to vanish.

The destructive power of a H-bomb is unimaginably immense. The fireball from such a bomb can balloon to a diameter of a mile and a half. A one megaton bomb can release as much radioactivity as 300,000 tons of radium. Its fallout includes radioactive isotopes of cesium and strontium with half-lives of 33 and 28 years. The one that exploded in Bikini was a 14 to 16 megaton bomb. The radioactivity released from its activating fission bomb was deadly: in fact, unwitting fishermen miles away were afflicted by the radioactive contamination from it. The long-lasting nuclear fallout from the testing was quite dangerous also.

The principles of the H-bomb were known to physicists, most of all to its most ardent advocate, Edward Teller. But practical problems remained, and its detonation called for such high temperatures (or the order of a hundred million degrees) that one had to use a fission bomb to trigger it.

It appears that what prompted the rapid development of the H-bomb was the news that the U.S.S.R. had successfully tested its own fission bomb in September 1949. This was the beginning of the nuclear arms race which was a hallmark of the Cold War. That arms race resulted in tremendous wastage of the resources of nations, besides causing concern and perpetual fear in the hearts of countless people, for there was the potential for a nuclear holocaust. It has not completely died away.

Three aspects of science stand out in the context of the hydrogen bomb: First that, the deeper our scientific understanding of the physical World, the more awesome our power becomes, and there is no telling for what purposes that power may be used.

Secondly, since science is a human enterprise, sometimes the passions and rivalries and opinions of participating scientists come into play, overtly or subtly, even in the thick doing science. When this happens, there could be unexpected turns in the events. Thus, Robert Oppenheimer's lack of enthusiasm for developing the far more potent hydrogen bomb did not sit well with Edward Teller (often referred to as the father of the hydrogen bomb). As a result, serious disagreements arose between the two. Only a couple of months after the 1954 bomb exploded, Oppenheimer's clearance was taken away by the Atomic Energy Commission, his loyalty was questioned, and he was regarded as untrustworthy, though he had headed the project that built the first nuclear (fission) bomb. Teller too paid for his role in Oppenheimer's downfall during the McCarthy era, for he began to lose the respect of most of the scientific community, both national and international. At the same time, Oppenheimer's prestige grew tremendously in the international community. When he came to deliver a series of lectures on Elementary Particle Physics at the Sorbonne, the hall was packed with several hundred students and professors, and he was received a standing ovation on the first day. In 1963, four years before his death, he was given the Enrico Fermi Award by President Lyndon Johnson.

Leaving for a moment the political and the ominously destructive aspects of the thermonuclear explosion that blasted in the Pacific Atoll, let us reflect a little on the event from a purely scientific perspective. That detonation of the H-bomb in 1954 was a momentous event, not just in the history of human kind, or even of the planet earth, but of the universe at large.

From all that we know of the physical universe, it took eons after the initial Big Bang for vast amounts of hydrogen atoms to come together at various regions of space, largely by gravitational inducements, and then, after more eons they got compressed and made more dense and as a result of immense pressure, hydrogen atoms at the core were crushed to their bare nuclei, and because of the enormous temperatures that came about, nuclear fusion reactions began: in other words, stars were set aglow.

Indeed, from all that we know, the only spots in the vast cosmic stretches where fusion has occurred are in the depths of the myriad stars that we see in the skies. Nowhere in all the known regions of the universe has nuclear fusion occurred beyond the confines of a stellar globe. But here on earth, for the first time in Cosmic History as far as we know, such the star-instigating reaction did occur when a H-bomb exploded.

In the long run, therefore, beyond national distrusts and personal squabbles, beyond cold war politics and defense strategies, the hydrogen bomb would be remembered in terms of its physics. Viewed simply as an instance of human ingenuity, as a demonstration of the exopotency of the scientific World view, and of the power of the mathematics behind it all (the bomb would not have been possible without the sophisticated computations facilitated by the first computers ENIAC and MANIAC), the successful detonation of the hydrogen bomb was a matter of enormous significance and historical import, for, in effect, *homo sapiens* created a momentary star here on a tiny speck of the universe, showing what the human spirit can do.

March 2

From the World of Religion:
ST. AGNES OF BOHEMIA

In ancient times when much of Czechoslovakia and some neighboring regions constituted Bohemia, to King Premsyl and his wife Constance was born in the 13th century a lovable daughter. Regarding her birth, the queen is said to have had a dream in which she saw in a royal chamber, amidst all the rich and luxurious garments, an ordinary tunic of grayish hue, with a cord that was of the religious order of Saint Clare. As she stood in puzzlement, she heard a voice which declared: "Wonder not, because the child you are carrying will be wearing clothes like these, and she will bring light to all Bohemia. The new born child was often seen in her crib lying peacefully with her intertwined legs and outstretched arms very like the cross on which Christ died.

When she was barely three, the child who was called Agnes, was betrothed to Boleslaw, son of Henryk I, Duke of Silesia. At four or five she went to a monastery where she received blessings for religious practice. She worshipped and prayed more than any other person there, and urged others to follow her. Then little Agnes began to preach.

Before long her betrothed husband died, and Agnes returned to her father's palace. Seeing her pious tendencies, the father sent her to a cloister where she continued to live with great devotion, spending most of her time in prayer. She never interacted with girls her age in Worldly matters of any kind.

The lass was not yet eight years of age, at which time she came back to the palace again. Other royal families had heard about her, and Emperor Frederick sent word to her father that he would like her hand for his own son. Consent was given, and there was a grand celebration of the betrothal, but Agnes remained indifferent to it all.

When she went to Frederick's palace in Austria, she spent her time tending to the poor and praying and thinking of Christ and Mary. She was sparse in her food, lived barely on bread and wine. In the words of one her classical biographers, "putting on the mortification of Jesus Christ as a ring to surrounded her whole body, she used to torment (her) tender flesh, by constraining her concupiscences with a thong of parsimony, lest living among delights she be censured as dead before God."

She returned to her father's palace, and now, thinking perhaps that she had divorced the Austrian prince, the king of England wanted to marry her.

The princess of piety lived in the palace after her father died, and her brother Wenseslaus ascended to the throne. Devotional life, attending church and every mass, praying every day, repeating psalms of penitence, and serving the poor: all these continued. She wore only simple clothes, walked barefoot even in the cold and on rugged roads. In her own room in the palace he chose to use a hard board for sleeping, not the luxury of a comfortable bed. Her dedication to Christ and her extraordinarily simple life style were not secrets for long.

The emperor of Austria sent messengers to Wenseslaus to ask for his sister again, promising many precious gifts and comforts. But she refused again, making it clear that we was wedded to Christ and could take no mortal man as her spouse. This was announced to the reigning Pope Gregory IX who was immensely pleased and impressed with the maiden's unswerving devotion. When the Emperor heard her response, he is said to have declared, "If this injury had been brought upon Us by any man, We would not hesitate to vindicate the reproach of such a contempt. But because she chose a greater Lord before Us, we do not reckon this a contempt to our (person), since we believe this to have come to be by a divine inspiration."

Such is the story of St. Agnes of Bohemia whose Feast Day is March 2. She lived her long life of almost 82 years as a poor bride of Christ, humble, ascetic, and perennially devoted to Christ.

It is difficult for us, in this day and age, to picture a life of such religious intensity, and that too in a child born in royal luxury. But there have been many souls in the history of humankind, in every culture and country, who have been drawn, for one reason or another or even for no recognizable reason at all, to the God of the tradition, who have lived extraordinary lives of asceticism and unshakable faith. Agnes of Bohemia was one such, and we are reminded here of Meera of the Hindu tradition.

Agnes has been remembered fondly by the people of the region where her spiritual splendor shone at one time. But it was only after 707 years, in 1989, that she was made a saint by Pope John Paul II. It is not clear what factors and circumstances induce the Church to confer sainthood on an individual.

All that an outsider can say is that persons of spiritual eminence are periodically recognized for the purity and constancy of their faith and commitment to the divine, and are elevated to the saintly status. And often they are adopted by a community, city, or country as their own. As history moves on, changing the boundaries of nations now and then, the same person may be the Saint of Bohemia or of the Prague, as happened in the case of St. Agnes.

From the World of Science: PIONEER 10

In the current framework of science, the age of our earth is of the order of four billion years. During its long history it has been isolated in space, trapped in the Sun's gravitation. Over the eons it has been bombarded by countless protons and electrons from the Sun and beyond, struck incessantly by meteors, and irradiated interminably from all over. Except for molecules of hydrogen and helium which escape from the earth's hold, hardly anything left the earth, certainly nothing of a solid nature, until human ingenuity began to send to satellites and shoot out rockets and spacecraft in the second half of the twentieth century.

One of these, called Pioneer 10, has been most remarkable: Leaving our planet on 2 March 1972 from a spot in Florida, USA, it not only broke away from Earth's gravity, but zoomed in the direction of the outer planets: calculated to reach Jupiter in due course.

We were not so sure it would reach Jupiter's neighborhood in tact, for we know that between Mars and the big planet, countless asteroids of all sizes and shapes are hurtling around. Those who sent out Pioneer 10 felt like parents who had asked an offspring to swim to a ship in midocean, knowing full well that somewhere on the way there is a region abundant in sharks. All they could do was to keep their fingers crossed, however unscientific that gesture might be.

But it worked! For Pioneer 10 sailed its way merrily past the perilous asteroid belt, dodging fortuitously any violent encounter with one of those random rocks. And it did more: the spacecraft came as near as a 100,000 miles to Jupiter which, in astronomical terms is pretty close. It flashed back information after information about that gigantic planet which, during the long span of human history, has been worshipped, feared, and incorporated as a day in weekly calendars.

And Pioneer 10 did something even more spectacular. After taking and remitting meaningful photographs of the giant planet sped farther and farther, beyond Pluto and Neptune, and left the solar system in 1983! It had been speeding at 49,000 km (30,600 miles) an hour.

When it was a little over 5 billion miles away, space scientists noticed a perturbation in its path, caused perhaps by a one of the huge asteroids (a so-called Kuiper Belt Object) that circle the sun in very distant orbits.

Aside from its complex gadgets and instruments, the spaceship is also carrying an ingeniously etched plaque (designed by Carl Sagan) in symbols that, it is hoped, will give information on the earthlings who launched it all. The hope implies that some day, somewhere, Pioneer 10 and the plaque will come within reach of a very advanced technological civilization populated inevitably by physicists, mathematicians, and cryptographers who will be able to decipher the drawing. Perhaps this optimism displays a touch of naiveté in its assumption that the perceptual faculties and brain chemistry of creatures on that other civilization will be very much like ours. Even ignoring insurmountable differences between people of different faiths, it is not easy for humans to communicate with dolphins or whales, let alone ants and microbes. So who is to say how those super-physicists would have evolved elsewhere?

We do know that it will be a few million years before Pioneer has even a low probability of approaching the nearest stellar system, and it could well be a few billion years—perhaps after our own Sun has called it quits, before Pioneer 10 really lands on a safe and hospitable planet with Sagan-like creatures on it. But then, if our mythologies can weave beautiful and soothing poetry which make us feel good, why cannot science do the same? So we may picture that some day, smart little beings will unpack the spacecraft, understand the message, and be elated to discover that there are indeed, as their scientists had suspected, other intelligent creatures somewhere out here.

The Pioneer 10 saga is as eerily impressive as anything human beings have done thus far: making and hurling a sturdy little object beyond the solar system. If there was a Cosmic superintendent overseeing how its components function and behave, it would probably exclaim:

"You puny speck of a creature on a paltry little speck of matter bound to an average star in a galaxy of a few hundred billion stars, you have the nerve to concoct a little box and fling it beyond the boundaries of your central star! Who do you think you are?" To which we could give one or both of two answers:

"We are the creatures that discovered the framework and methodology of Science to understand the laws and principles governing the World."

"We are the creatures fashioned in the Image of God."

March 3

From the World of Religion: HINA MATSURI

Whether they arose from the artistic potential of *homo sapiens* or from an instinct to create an *imago hominis*, dolls, like God, are both ancient and universal in human culture. They were there in ancient Egypt and China and India, very popular throughout Africa, found in prehistoric Peruvian graves, indeed everywhere in the World. For some reason, there have been more dolls in female forms than in the male. Pupalogists (if one may so describe specialists in dolls) have suggested that love of dolls arise from the instinctive love of babies, and this fact may therefore explain why little girls like to play with dolls much more than little boys do.

Be that as it may, in the Japanese tradition, there is a festival dedicated to dolls, observed every year on 3 March. Known as Hina Matsuri (Festival of Little Dolls), it is generally a festival for girls. One of its goals is to ensure a happy and fruitful life for the daughters in the family. On this day, it is customary to drink some sweet sake and eat a special type of sushi, called chirashi. One also makes a special cake with rice in a geometrical form, called hinshi-mochi, for this occasion consisting of a few colored layers. Two of these are also placed with the dolls. Some like to have a special kind of clam soup (*ushiojiru*) as part of the celebrations.

Dolls are displayed in special arrangements, often in different tiers. Since this used to occur in the season of peach flowers, these are used for ornamentation. One also refers to this festival of Momo-no-Sekko (Peach blossom festival). In the Japanese tradition, peach blossoms represent auspiciousness. They are also regarded as representing the qualities of gentleness, peace, and equanimity.

As with all festivals, matters have become more sophisticated in modern times, when beautiful kimono costumes of classical times (of the Heian era) are made to dress up male as well as female dolls. These dolls are called Hina-Ningyo, and they represent the ancient emperor and empress of Japan. In many instances, these are old dolls which have come down from generations in a family. They have acquired a ceremonial solemnity by virtue of their age. Indeed, at the end of the season, they are packed back neatly like Christmas ornaments, to be taken out again only next year. Of course one may also buy new dolls when a girl is born in the family. Friends also give dolls as presents.

Often there are not just two, but a whole set of them, along with miniature things like furniture for the home. Aside from the emperor and the empress, there are dolls to represent ministers, court ladies, and musicians. The dolls are nicely left in place for all to appreciate for a whole month. [In passing I might mention that there is a very similar Tamil festival, called *kolu*, in which also dolls and figurines are displayed beautifully in several steps covered with colorful cloths.]

This is also the day when people's creativity comes to the fore, for they make lovely origami dolls.

This is not a very ancient Japanese festival, although some have traced its roots to Chinese civilization. It is said that the custom began only during the Meiji Era (1868–1912), as a festival for city folks, but it gradually spread all over the country. In our own times, the Kyoto National Museum holds a special exhibition of dolls between February and April to mark Hina Matsuri.

In more ancient times there used to be a festival called Nagashi-bina in which paper dolls were floated on rivers. The folk belief was that all the accumulated negative forces in the family, like bad luck and ill health and disappointments would be transferred to the dolls, and that the doll carried away all this down the river.

Many interpretations have been given to this custom. Some have said this is a mode of ancestor worship, others that it symbolizes the concern of parents for their daughters. In fact, this is an essentially a for-girls festival, and parents pray on this day that their daughters may be happily married. Many parents, irrespective of their financial resources, have been known to buy dolls for their daughters on this day.

As with some other festivals, there is a special song which all children sing today. It goes like this:

Akari o tsukemasyo bonbori ni
O hana o agemasyo momo no hana
Gonin-bayashi no fue daiko
Kyoo wa tanoshii hinamatsuri
Let's lamps be lit on the step-like stand.
Let peach flowers on them be!
Court musicians five play flutes and drums
For this joyful Hinamatsuri.

From the World of Science: GEORG CANTOR

March 3 is the birth date of Elmer Verner McCollum who discovered Vitamins A, B, and D; and also of Alexander Graham Bell, who invented the telephone. But I would like to reflect on someone else who too was born on this date. Though his name shines in the history of mathematics, and his work is fundamental to the subject, he is not as universally known. His name was Georg Cantor (born: 3 March 1845).

In the course of our everyday language and ideas we sometimes speak of infinity to mean something very, very large, something that seems to have no beginning or boundary. So we think of infinite space as space that stretches on and on without end, and of infinite time as eternity.

In the World of mathematics, we can think of simple integers (whole numbers like 1, 2, 3,...). How far can one go on counting? Until one is physically exhausted, but that wouldn't take us to the last number there is. In principle, counting can go on and on for ever, without ever reaching a last number. So we say that the number of integers is infinite.

Now let us skip even numbers and count only the odd ones: 1, 3, 5,...This sequence will also go on indefinitely. Thus there is also an infinite number of odd integers.

But then, by counting only the odd numbers, and excluding in the process all even numbers (2, 4, 6,...), we are counting only half of all the integers.

So, whereas there are 100 integers from 1 to 100, and only 50 odd integers from 1 to 100, when we consider all integers, there are as many (infinite) odd integers as there are both odd and even integers. At the very least, this should make us raise our eyebrows by this property of cardinal numbers.

The solution to this paradox is that this may be taken as a definitional property of infinity: Infinity is that whose fractions and multiples are also infinity: an idea which is implicit in an ancient Hindu reflection which says: Fullness remains fullness even when fullness is taken away from it.

Cantor tumbled upon a fascinating idea of infinity by proposing a rule for comparing sets (collections of things, numbers, etc.) If we find chairs and desks in a room, we can determine if there are more chairs or tables either by counting them directly or by pairing them up one to one. If, after the pairing up, a few extra chairs remain, we conclude there are more chairs than tables: i.e. that the number of chairs is greater. Likewise, if we pair up odd (or even) integers against all integers, we can go on and on, finding one odd integer for every integer. This is why the two are both infinity.

Now consider all numbers that can be written as a fraction of two integers (the so-called rational numbers): ½, 1/3, ¼,.. 2/3, 2/4,...178/189,...It would appear that there are far more of these than ordinary integers. Cantor showed that this is not really so. In fact, there are as many rational numbers as integers. One may say that this could have been expected since both are infinite. Fair enough.

But now Cantor went on to show that there are far more points on a bit of straight line than there are ordinary numbers! In other words, he established that some infinities are greater than others. In other words, he introduced the notion of orders of infinity. Indeed, he proved that whereas the number of integers is infinite, the number of points on a straight line is transfinite (a higher order infinity). He denoted these, remembering his Jewish heritage, as aleph-0 and aleph-1. [Cantor was Protestant, but his grandfather was Jewish.] He also showed by his method of one to one correspondence that there are as many points in a line an inch long as in one that stretches to a million miles long (i.e. they both have the same order of infinity), that there are as many points on the side of a square as within its boundaries, and that the number of transcendental numbers (numbers which don't satisfy algebraic equations) is infinitely greater still.

The notion of transfinite numbers was revolutionary. But reaction to it was not uniformly positive. Bertrand Russell was carried away to the point of describing the achievement as probably among "the greatest of which the age can boast." Theologians saw they found here yet another proof for the existence of God. Cantor himself took metaphysics as seriously as mathematics. On the other hand, Kronecker, another God-fearing mathematician and former professor of Cantor, was infuriated by the whole idea and wrote viciously against Cantor's notions of transfinite numbers. He saw to it that Cantor did not advance in his academic career at the University of Berlin.

Nevertheless, Cantor, by initiating the notion of sets in mathematics, opened a new chapter in the field. By his analysis of infinity and beyond, he took mathematical thought to newer realms. By his controversial probe into the nature of numbers and our concepts of it, he spurred heated debates among mathematicians on the foundations of the subject, leading to deeper under-standing and varying perspectives of the subject as the 20th century dawned. Unfortunately, consequent perhaps to the vehement rejection of his ideas, Cantor suffered serious mental depressions and spent years in an asylum.

March 4

From the World of Religion: ROYAL DEBT OF WILLIAM PENN

If it is sad when people die for their deepest religious beliefs, it is bad when peo-ple kill for the same reason. All through history both, both kinds of such terrible things have happened. Today we are happy about, and proud of, the religious freedom and tolerance we have in Western and other democracies, and are appalled by its lack and consequent ugliness we see in some other parts of the World which prohibit scriptures of alien faiths. But it is important to remember that things were not much better within the Western matrix just a few centuries ago. The history of persecution of religious minorities is a long and dismal narra-tive of atrocities and (from our perspective) stupidity.

In 17th century England, for example, the fear of the influence of the Roman Catholic Church (Popery, as it was called) manifested itself in many horrible ways. On the other hand, Puritans weren't spared either. It has been estimated that in the 1660s alone some sixty thousand people were arrested for their reli-gious non-conformity, of whom about five thousand died in prison.

But there were voices of reason and moderation. There were the more enlight-ened Latitudinarians, and thinkers like John Tillotson and Richard Baxter who were quite advanced for the age. Above all, there were the Quakers: members of the Society of Friends, who, notwithstanding their extreme fear of God and Satan, were basically progressive in their values. And they too were thrown into prisons in which "there was not room for all…to sit down."

William Penn, a fiery Quaker preacher, was one of the most illustrious of them. Thrown into prison again and again for his preaching, in 1671 he wrote *The Great Case of Liberty of Conscience* while he was in jail. This was one of the first persuasive pleas for religious tolerance: a somewhat new idea in those times. He argued against the persecution of Catholics. His *Address to Protestants of All Persuasions*, published in 1679, was another eloquent call for religious toleration.

In this matter, King Charles II of England was also of the more enlightened kind. There used to be a law in England when people were fined heavily for not attending the Anglican Church on Sundays. Charles refused to enforce it, saying he would not punish people for their conscience. He set 1200 Quakers free from prisons.

William Penn's father was the admiral who brought the island of Jamaica under England's sway. Charles was legally bound to pay a large sum to him, and then to the admiral's son. On 4 March 1681 this royal debt was erased in exchange for a Charter which gave a large territory in the Colonies to William Penn: the region between 40 and 43 degrees and extending 5 degrees west from the Delaware river. Because of the dense forests in the region, it was first proposed that it be called Sylvania (from the Latin word for woods), then Penn's name was prefixed to it.

It was here that the ideals of religious tolerance and freedom were first articulated explicitly in the New World. People of every shade of faith were allowed to settle down here. There was but one condition: They should believe in God, for Pennsylvania was to be "a Christian state on a Quaker model." This may seem restrictive to modern free-thinkers, but it was not as terrible in those times, and certainly a first step towards the complete religious freedom that citizens of the United States enjoy today.

Rather than claim that this model was something new which rejected tradition, Penn argued wisely in a work entitled "Primitive Christianity" (1695) that the Quakers were simply following the precepts of the early Church. He thus had the wisdom of religious reformers who, even as they condemn and reject the abominable dimensions of their religion, insist that what they are against was never part of their religion in its earliest and purest form. Whether true or not, this is always more effective in bringing about positive changes.

The first institution for treating in civilized ways the insane as sick people was established in Pennsylvania. In 1727, Quakers were the first to initiate a movement against the institution of slavery in America. Quite a few of them risked their lives in giving shelter to slaves. Many Quakers were also sympathetic to Native American Indians. The famous Quaker John Woolman was a pacifist who urged people not to pay taxes that went to wage wars. Like Buddhists and Jains, he cared for animals too, refusing to take coaches because they oppress horses. He insisted that all Christians are spiritually the same, no matter what their denominational affiliation might be. This was a first step towards more universal religious tolerance which humanity is still to achieve.

Enlightenment, like the physicist's Theory of Everything, is not something civilization achieves overnight. It is a long and slow march forward, with many ups and downs, detours and throwbacks. As long as there are even a handful of people to carry the torch, there is always for humanity. And in the context, institutions and proclamations are important too. As Bernard Shaw remarked, "Though all society is founded on intolerance, all improvement is founded on tolerance."

So it was that the Charter of Pennsylvania of 4 March 1681 gave a boost to the forces that served the cause religious tolerance, and it is good to remember it.

From the World of Science: GEORGE GAMOW

We have all heard of radioactivity, though not all of us may be aware of its technical aspects. In simple terms, the phenomenon of radioactivity involves the ejection from within the nuclei of certain atoms. Four different kinds of entities are involved. These are known as alpha particles, beta particles, gamma rays, and neutrinos.

Alpha particles are quite simply the nuclei of helium atoms: they consist of two (positively charged) protons and two (electrically neutral) neutrons. All the particles within atomic nuclei are held together very tightly by what is known as strong interaction which ensures the stability of the nuclei. It is as if these particles are held prisoners within an enclosure with tall and sturdy walls. They simply don't have enough energy to jump over the walls to escape to the outside World.

And yet, now and again, some of them do spurt out: this, in fact, is what radioactivity is all about. This was a great puzzle for physicists, some 75 years ago.

Now there came to the Theoretical Physics Institute of the University of Copenhagen a young post-doctoral fellow called George Gamow (born: 4 March 1904). He had studied the fast growing and recently emerged field of quantum mechanics which explores the laws and principles governing phenomena in the atomic and subatomic World. It had been discovered that in the microcosm the so-called fundamental particles (like protons and electrons and alpha particles) behaved like waves. An important difference between waves and particles is that particles normally bounce back from obstacles, whereas waves can bend around them. What this means is that, under appropriate conditions, microcosmic particles can in fact seep through the tall walls, as if a tunnel had been carved through the walls.

Gamow set out to analyze the phenomenon of alpha radioactive on the basis of the principles of quantum mechanics and the tunnel effect. Once the problem is formulated in these terms, its solution is straight forward: it calls for a good deal of mathematics, but it can be solved. Gamow presented a cogent and successful explanation of the phenomenon. A couple of other physicists arrived at more or less the same results at about the same time. This was one of the early triumphs of quantum physics: the explanation of the quantitative features of a well-studied microcosmic phenomenon.

Gamow's work was significant. It impressed Niels Bohr enough to offer him a fellowship at his institute. During his stay there Gamow came up with other fruitful ideas which turned out to be quite relevant in understanding nuclear fission and fusion.

When the Soviet Union began to restrict the movement of scientists to the Western World, Gamow took an opportunity while attending an international conference in the mid 1930s, to emigrate to the United States with his wife. Here he established himself at the George Washington University in Washington, DC. During his stay there, Edward Teller (the future Father of the H-bomb) joined him. The two worked on many problems together, and formulated an important principle governing the phenomenon of beta-radioactivity.

Gamow was also interested in astrophysics and cosmology. He was one of the active enthusiasts of the Big Bang theory. He theorized that there was some sort of pre-big-bang matter made up primarily of neutrons, protons, and electrons. He called this "ylem." From his theoretical analyses he was led to the conclusion that the big bang must have generated a radiation whose remnants should still be lingering everywhere in the universe—the so called isotropic background radiation, which was put into evidence by A. Penzias and R. Wilson in the mid-1960s.

George Gamow was a prolific writer. He authored some 140 articles. He had a tremendous love for physics, and the gift to convey this to non-physicists. He wrote a number of popular books for the general public, explaining the deep insights, abstruse formulas, and fascinating results of twentieth century physics. Thus, in his *Mr. Tomkins in Wonderland*, he explained Einstein's Relativity Theory in as intelligible a manner as one possibly could, and with a touch of humor too. His other popular books included One, *Two, Three, Infinity, The Birth and Death of Stars,* and *Fifty Years that Shook Physics.* These books are read by millions. They served to propagate appreciation for, and understanding of, physics for the intelligent reader much more than books which brought in misleading philosophical extrapolations and muddled metaphysics while presenting scientific theories. Equally, they probably also attracted many young minds to physics, for the books are within reach of most high school students. For these contributions he was given the Kalinga Prize: an award given to outstanding popularizers of science.

At one stage Gamow got interested in biology (the structure of the DNA molecule), and he made some contributions here also.

March 5

From the World of Religion: KYONCHIP

On 5 March, they celebrate Kyonchip in Korea: This is a day to mark a change of season, and the word connotes insects that have been aroused into action after a period of hibernation. It is customary on this day for farmers to sow seeds of crops. They also pay homage to their ancestors on this day. In the normal course of our daily lives, in the context of society and politics and economics, of conflicts and wars and religions, we are inclined most often to think of us humans as central to everything in the World. But we also know there are countless other species of creatures that come and go with the rhythms of Nature, have been doing so for ages before we ever came to be.

Of these, insects are the most numerous: little creatures with bodies segmented (whence the name), with a head, a thorax and an abdomen and generally with six legs and feelers called antennae. Many insects also have two pairs of wings. Entomologists have listed a million different insect species.

We think they live lives of their own, as we do ours. But now and again we know that some of them invade our World of garden and fields and become pests that exterminate with all the might of science. Unwittingly, some insects also help us in controlling these: wasps and lady bugs feed on them. We know too that yet others are either plain bothersome and worse: Insects bite and sting and causing sores. Flies are a downright nuisance, while other insects spread diseases. Mosquitoes carry malaria and fleas carry plague. That's why they are sometimes referred to contemptuously as vermin.

It was not until the late 1930s that we developed techniques for getting rid of the more harmful (to humans and to crops) insects. These used largely chemical toxins. Now we have also developed other (non-chemical) modes of insecticides. It is too early to predict the long range effects of these biological pest control methods.

But it is equally true that there are also insects that serve us in many ways. We would have no honey without them, for as Arthur Gutterman put it, "While honey lies in every flower, it takes a bee to get it out." Not just the butterflies in flower gardens, but other insects also pollinate our crop plants. Yet other insects recycle organic matter and serve to keep the soil fertile. Indeed, the fact of the matter is that whereas insects can sustain themselves without Homo sapiens on terra firma, we cannot last a generation if all insects were wiped out from the face of the earth. Such is our dependence are these minute creatures.

So, when Benjamin Disraeli referred disparagingly to ancient Egyptians worshipping insects, he was not well informed about the role and significance of insects in human survival. Insects are perhaps more omnipresent than any other land creature on earth. One species or another of them has been found in every region: from the very cold to the very hot zones, on mountain tops and valleys and on the plains. Insects are absent only in the oceans, for they don't seem to be able to survive a salt water environment. Human beings have been aware of the presence of insects all around them. Stories have been written about ants and bees, poems about the grasshopper and the butterfly. Insects have been studied by scientists, and eaten as gourmet food also.

Many cultures respect(ed) insects and remember(ed) them on special occasions. Perhaps the ancients recognized that the creatures have been there for a long, long time, and that they simply cannot be eliminated even if one wanted to. Instinctively they felt that by being nice to them, they would be less harmful to us: Is that not one of the psychological motivations for singing laudatory hymns to the mighty forces of Nature?

In China, one refers to March 5th as Ching Che. It is believed that the Dragon brings insects back to life on this day. In some parts of the country one places fetishes which are supposed to calm down the more excited insects. Blocks of ice are placed in the ground in the belief that this will cool them. One also prepares special dumplings to offer to the World of Nature, for in this way sleeping Nature comes back to the awakened state as spring arrives.

There is also a prohibition against sewing on this day, the reason being that one might inadvertently prick the dragon while it is doing its job on this important day.

The range and variety and contexts of religious celebrations and cultural customs are considerable. Not all cultures' religions dedicate a day for insects, nor do they all dedicate a day for somebody who is said to have performed a miracle in a distant century. But every celebration has a reason, each one the remembrance of something significant to the people, present or of a last generation.

From the World of Science: GERHARD KREMER

From the most remote times, human beings have been representing the concrete in abstract terms. Ancient cave paintings of bull or beast are instances. Even before the invention of the wheel, they probably devised ways to represent the terrain of where they lived and wandered, for whether nomad or localized hunter, one had to know how to return home from a distant excursion. That's why map-making became one of the oldest techniques to develop in any culture. Indeed, whether in Tahiti or Labrador, in ancient Egypt or Peru or wherever, they had maps of one kind or another.

From Ptolemy to Arab cartographers, and then among map-makers of the Middle Ages, a great many representations of lands and seas arose. These have left us with legacies of how people of different ages imagined and constructed the shapes and boundaries of land and sea. For one thing, all World maps prior to the 16th century had distorted projections of whatever they showed, and they showed only Europe, Asia, and Africa.

After the discovery of Ptolemy's maps in the early 15th century, many new maps were made, often with a background of degrees of latitude and longitude. Though there had been attempts to construct maps on a spherical surface earlier, globes became much more popular after Columbus.

Now the question arose as to how best one can make a faithful representation of the spherical surface of the earth on the plane surface of a paper.

This brings us to Gerhard Kremer (born: 5 March 1512), known generally by his Latinized name of Mercator. Though his academic training at the University of Louvain in Flanders was in philosophy and theology, Mercator was equally interested in mathematics and geography, and he took to calligraphy as well as map making. In 1554 he published in fifteen sheets the first accurate maps of Europe.

Mercator recognized that a plane map where straight lines along a direction intersect all meridians at the same angle would be very useful to mariners. Thus arose the Mercator projection which (with some modifications) are used in most maps to this day.

The idea is simple: Imagine the contours of countries and continents inscribed on a spherical transparent globe at whose center is a bright light. Now suppose we have a cylinder encircling and touching the globe at the equator. Let the images be drawn of the drawings on the globe that fall on sides of the cylinder. If we now remove the cylinder and unravel it, we will get a sheet with the map of the World in the Mercator projection. [Though it has come to be known by this name, he was not the originator of the idea. But he was the first one to apply it in the construction of many maps.] In such a map, there are vertical parallel lines, but these are not longitudes. Also the horizontal lines (latitudes) are not equally paced: those closer to the poles are separated more than those near the equator. As a result, areas in the higher latitudes appear much larger. In other words, the effect of the distortion in the Mercator projection is to make regions in the higher latitudes larger than they actually are. Greenland would seem to be larger than it is, and India smaller. Mercator's first World chart based on this idea was published in 1569. Here he specifically stated its usefulness for navigators. A decade later he brought out a critical edition of Ptolemy's maps which, like Ptolemy's astronomy, had been the guiding light for many centuries. Mercator's edition helped preserve the ancient work.

It may be mentioned that Mercator lived at a time when Catholic-Protestant animosities were quite acute in Europe. He was suspected of Protestant sympathies in Catholic Flanders, accused of heresy and arrested. Soon after that, he moved to Protestant Germany where he was received warmly and with the title of Cosmographer for the Duke of Juelich.

Mercator died in 1594. A collection of his maps was published by his son Rumold the following year, under the imposing title: "Atlas sive meditationes de fabrica mundi et fabricati figura: Atlas or Cosmological Meditations on the Structure of the World…." (1595). It contained 107 maps.

Recall that in Greek mythology the Titan called Atlas, when he was defeated in a battle against the Olympians, was condemned to hold the sky on his shoulders for ever. [This was the Greek mythological explanation for why the sky never falls down.] Ever since the publication of this book of Mercator's, any collection of maps has been generally called an atlas.

We have come a long way since Mesopotamian clay tablets etched regional contours, and people in other cultures and civilizations brought out crude, but often impressive, images of land masses in various parts of the globe. Today we have maps of countries and of terrain with astounding precision. We have at our fingertips via the computer key-board detailed maps of roads and rivers. But, like everything else, cartography too has a rich history, and in this Mercator will be remembered as one who made significant contributions.

March 6

From the World of Religion:
MICHEALANGELO BUONARROTI

Religion has many facets: doctrines and scriptures, festivals and fasting, prayers and penitence, and most importantly, perhaps, the spiritual experience. Those who choose to be beyond the orbit of traditional religions may or may not have this last item, indeed to some it may even mean nothing or be altogether expendable.

However, for those who are susceptible to spiritual ecstasy, the poetry and music, the paintings and sculptures of religious symbols can be a rich source of fulfillment. It is in this context that I like to remember this day: Michelangelo Buonarroti was born on March 6. The paintings on the ceiling of the Sistine Chapel are magnificent works of art which touch the heart of the beholder in very profound ways.

Grand mythopoesie is implicit in the Scriptures of all religions, but its impact has changed transformed over the centuries. The mythopoesie of the Judeo Christian Scripture finds expression in marvelous Technicolor, as it were, on the ceiling of the Capella Sistina. This hall was constructed during the papacy of Sixtus IV delle Rovere, and has therefore come to be known the Sistine Chapel.

It took eight years to build the chapel: from 1475 to 1483. Its dimensions were inspired by the wise King Solomon's Temple, as stated in the Old Testament (1 Kings 6: 1-2): namely, 40.93 meters by 13.41 meters, and 20.70 meters high, with side vaults. Twenty five years later, Pope Julius II felt it was time to re-do the ceiling, and Michelangelo was commissioned to undertake the task. It wasn't going to be an ordinary paint job, so it took some four years to finish the project. The completed work turned out to be one of the immortal works of religious art: grand and moving representations of some of the figures and episodes from the sacred history of the Bible.

We see here the Cosmology of the Book of Genesis, in which Light first separated from Darkness, followed by the creation of the Sun, the Moon, and the Stars. Then there is the creation of the essential substratum of Life, namely water. Next is the creation of Man. This is perhaps the most awe inspiring vision to contemplate. Here we see Divinity touching ever so slightly the finger of Man as if to remind us that there is always that touch of the Divine in each of us. This could be taken as the deeper meaning of Imago Dei (Man being created in the image of God). Yet, we also discern here a touch of sadness that comes with parting: a reluctant moving away of Adam from God, but with a hint that he will see Him again some day. One feels as if God is saying, "Fare well, My creature!" This glimpse of Michelangelo's Creation of Man will forever be etched in the mind of anyone who has had the opportunity to behold it. Then there is a depiction of the creation of Woman. Other episodes, like the Temptation and expulsion from Eden; the sacrifice of Noah are also there.

It is good that the frescoes are on the ceiling of the chapel, for as one views them one has to see upwards: after all, we are participating in heavenly themes here. Today, a great many of the visitors are curious onlookers, herded in groups by tourist guides who repeat by rote paragraphs from booklets. But when Michelangelo completed his masterpiece, the scenes and symbols were all real in the hearts of the onlookers. They were not artistic renderings of ancient tales, but faithful and powerful visions of historical truths. Goliath and Holofernes, Haman and the ancestors of Christ had greater immediacy and historical validity than they have to moderns who look upon these from artistic or touristic perspectives.

Another essence of religion is depth of feeling and empathy with the Divine that is in any true religious experience. This is amply present Michelangelo's Pieta: that marvelously sculpted marble which reveals the purest love of mother for son. The peaceful Mary seems to be accepting the inevitability of the end, for her face is serene rather than sad, sublime rather than in sorrow. It unites the pure of heart with that which is divine. This often happens in the context of love and sacrifice. The Pieta also reminds us of the miracle that brought forth God in flesh and blood through a personification of love and gentleness. Only those who recognize this as unfathomable mystery can know what the religious experience is.

When the sculpture was first exposed, some complained the mother looked younger than the son, that she was too heavily draped, etc. But such thoughts don't cross the minds of those who approach with piety. The perspective of the art critic, interesting as it may be, is different from the depth of feeling of the devout. The images and icons of religious art are not meant for art critics, but rather to convey and to assist in experiencing, the vision of profound religious truths.

So, on this birth date of Michelangelo who was of one of the greatest artists that ever lived, we reflect a little on just two of his many masterpieces that remind us of aspects of religion, because he also served the cause of religion in his own way.

From the World of Science:
THE ROYAL SOCIETY OF LONDON

One of the prime sources of power for science is its international character. Its efforts and tentative truths transcend, in principle, race and religion, national boundaries and language. These features are fostered through exchanges in meetings, and publications through journals in which people from practically all over the World participate. The seeds for this internationalism which has become the hallmark of science were sown in the scientific academies and societies which emerged at the same time as the first inklings of modern science were blossoming.

One such society was The Royal Society of London for Improving Natural Knowledge which came into full being in 1660, though it had less formal existence prior to that year. The founders of this institution formulated in unambiguous terms the philosophy that would guide them and the experimental framework in which they would work. They were convinced that "the forms and qualities of things can best be explained by the principles of mechanics, and that all effects of Nature are produced by motion, figure, texture, and the varying combinations of these." Furthermore they did not see any need for "inexplicable forms and occult qualities" as "a refuge from ignorance." As it describes itself today: "By virtue of its independent status and its body of some 1300 Fellows and Foreign Members covering all scientific disciplines, the Society is uniquely placed to represent the interests of top quality science and technology in its interactions with government, the public and the media. It adopts a high profile on issues which are vital to scientific progress and is taking an increasingly prominent position in furthering the role of science, engineering and technology in society by facilitating constructive dialogue between scientists and non-scientists."

Already in the early years quick-witted writers and skeptical thinkers made fun of the Royal Society. The Grand Academy of Lagado we read about in Gulliver's Travels is a satire on the Society. Swift wrote that the professors there "contrive new instruments and tools for all trades and manufactures, whereby, as they undertake one man shall do the work of ten, a palace may be built in a week, of materials so durable as to last for ever, without repairing..." He went on and on, imagining he was pooh-poohing science, when, in fact, he was unwittingly foreseeing some of the future achievements of science.

Samuel Butler poked fun at scientists who thought they had spotted an elephant on the moon when in fact it was only a mouse in their telescope. The framework and World views of science are yet to be universally accepted.

But the fact remains that those who took inspiration from this doctrine, and were guided by it, are the ones who have erected what we call modern science. With all its inadequacies and pitfalls, with all its undesirable side effects and the imperfection in its practice, the modern scientific enterprise has unraveled for humankind more knowledge and insights about the universe during the past 400 years than all previous generations had done during 4000 years.

On 6 March 1664 appeared the very first issue of a journal initiated by the Royal Society. It had the rather longish title, "Philosophical Transactions: giving some Account of the present undertakings, studies, and labours of the Ingenious in many considerable parts of the World." The journal began to publish the discoveries and theories of all who were engaged in science, no matter in which country. It gave reports of travels to different countries and distant lands, reporting on their findings and impressions. The members performed experiment at the premises of the Society, or sometimes in other places, as on the top of St. Paul's Cathedral to see how atmospheric pressure changes with height.

The Philosophical Transactions was also a medium for the propagation of the mechanistic philosophy. Indeed, its three most ardent members and active participants (Henry Oldenberg, Robert Boyle, and Robert Hooke) were committed to the view that the whole universe functioned like a giant machine. For example, in his description of the tiny feet of insects, Hooke wrote how Nature makes everything as simple and plain and efficient as possible.

The Society was called Royal because it was under the patronage of Charles II, but it did not mean that he financed it. The members paid not only their dues, but also bought the necessary instruments for their experiments from their own pockets. The publication expenses for the journal were covered by and large by subscriptions. Yet, now and again, the government assigned projects to the Society, especially in matters of navigation.

The internationalism of science was reflected right from the start. Oldenberg, the first secretary of the Royal Society, was from Germany. Leeuwenhoek, who published his findings of microbes with his microscope, was from the Netherlands. Malpighi, who published his discovery of the flow of blood through the lungs, was from Italy, and so the list goes on.

After two hundred years of continuous publication, the journal began to appear in two series: one for the mathematical and physical sciences, and another for the biological. Today, the scientific World publishes hundreds of journals in various languages which are devoted to different disciplines and sub-disciplines. With its continued existence, the Philosophical Transactions is easily the longest lasting journal of any kind in human civilization. And so we remember it on this date when it was first published.

March 7

From the World of Religion: VIBIA PERPETUA

Severus Septimus ruled Rome from 193 to 211. He was a conquering emperor who raided regions from Syria to Scotland, built new buildings in his capital, and would have nothing of Christianity. During his reign there lived a young woman by the name of Vibia Perpetua, educated and intelligent, who was drawn to the Christian faith. Her brother too, along with a few others, began to receive instructions on Christianity.

From the journals she left behind one has been able to gather a good deal of information about her. Her father was worried that she was thinking of becoming a Christian. She replied that she could not call herself anything else, any more than that a vase was anything but a vase. The father became furious and was about to hit her in anger, but left.

With many others, Perpetua who was nursing a baby, was thrown in a crowded prison along with her little child. It was almost suffocating there, and first she asked her mother to look after the child. But this turned out to be even more difficult for her. When she got back the child, she felt as if the prison had become a palace.

Upon the advice of her brother, Perpetua prayed for a vision that would tell her fate. And a vision she had: in which there was a narrow ladder of immense height, which reached all the way to Heaven. But it was flanked with sharp instruments like swords and spears, so it was not easy to climb. Indeed, if one tries to go up carelessly, the sharp metals would pierce through the body. She also saw a huge dragon at the foot of the ladder. Saturus, who had given the prisoners much courage, was seen up there in the upper rungs of the ladder, and he beckoned Perpetua to come, for he was waiting for her. But he warned her about the dragon, which could bite her.

She answered it wouldn't harm her, for she had Christ in her heart. Indeed, the dragon, looking meek, thrust its head from beneath the ladder, and served as a step for her to begin the climb. As she went up she saw a magnificent garden where a tall shepherd was milking sheep. He was surrounded by a vast number of people, all in white. Upon seeing Perpetua he said he was glad she had come there. He offered her some of the milk, which she received with her cupped hands and drank. She felt the sweetness in the mouth, and the vision vanished. She understood she was going to become a martyr.

The moment of her trial for wanting to become a Christian arrived. Her father begged of her to give up, saying how much they all would suffer if she were punished severely. She told him there was a higher power that would guide them all. All the adamant Christians were condemned to face the arena: The men had to fight wild beasts like boars and leopards, while Perpetua and her servant-companion Felicitas were thrown to wild bulls. The crowd cheered, but many were also shocked to see the women cast to animals this way. They all died horrible deaths, but it is said that Perpetua perished saying, "Stand fast in the faith and love of one another."

Eventually she became Saint Perpetua, and her name is always associated with Saint Felicitas. What is interesting about their story is that we have detailed accounts of the terrible experiences that many early Christians had to face in their unshakable adherence to their faith. There is no doubt that such stories inspired many others in future generations who risked their lives and braved the dangers, not only in their own embrace of Christianity, but also in their efforts to spread the Gospel among other people in other lands. March 7 is Saint Perpetua's Feast Day.

From the World of Science: STANLEY MILLER

It is a perplexing and never-ending question: How did life start? In the 19th century it was well established that there is no such thing as spontaneous generation: micro-organismic life forms suddenly appearing from inanimate matter. Yet, ironically, if we rule this out altogether, how can we account for the existence of life on earth, or anywhere else for that matter?

An answer to this paradox was given in the mid-1920s by Alexandr Oparin: in the early phases of the earth's history organic matter was synthesized in the primitive conditions of the time. The idea was explored further by J. B. S. Haldane and Harold Urey during the following decade. This is the theory of chemical evolution of life. It rests on the principle that the fundamental attributes of life may be tracked down to complex chemical structures, biochemical molecules, and on the fact that under appropriate conditions some of these molecules may be formed in nature or in the laboratory.

The two most important types of such basic molecules are proteins and nucleic acids: very large and complex at the atomic level, resulting from chain-like combinations of smaller molecules that more or less resemble one another. The question then is: How did the first proteins and nucleic acids come about?

In the remote past, more than three billion years ago, and barely a billion years after the formation of our planet, there were lands barren and waste, volcanoes steaming and puffing sulfuric fumes, and oceans of salt-free waters. The earth's atmosphere consisted then largely of hydrogen, ammonia, methane, and a few other gases. Gigantic clouds rose and torrential rains fell, seeping salts from land to pristine sea. In the mammoth laboratories of the earth's oceans and airs, kindled by heat and lightning, by radiations from the sun and other excitants, the turbulent chemistry of the early molecules churned out the first organic structures. Carbohydrates and amino acids were thus concocted. These increased in complexity as further reactions took place. The waters of the period constituted what has been described as a primordial soup in which mutual interactions of the components gave rise to molecules of ever increasing size and intricacy. Energy trapping mechanisms came into play. After myriad patterns and permutations, mysterious entities with the property of self-replication emerged. These again grew in numbers and variety, until at last nucleic acids and proteins were formed. The miracle of life had begun.

Once the spark of life was lit, the self-replicating systems began to multiply in number and variety. The nucleic acids embodying the subtle coding that preserve life patterns slipped now and then. These changes in structures were the mutations which may be looked upon either as responses to the unceasing turmoil in the earth's physico-chemical features, or as alterations resulting from changing conditions.

But no scientific theory is worth its salt if it does not have enough experimental backing. This was provided in 1953 by Stanley Miller (born: 7 March 1930) who designed a simple experiment in which he had a set up of glass containers: Pyrex flasks and tubes, tungsten electrodes and condensers, with water, methane, ammonia, and hydrogen (simulating the oceans and atmosphere of infant earth). The water boiled, the vapor mixed with the gases, electric sparks were induced. Lo and behold! In the course of a week he detected in the condensed liquids some of the basic amino acids that are part of protein. If this could happen in a small laboratory in Chicago, one can imagine the possibilities in the course of a billion years when the whole earth is a laboratory.

March 8

From the World of Religion:
INTERNATIONAL WOMEN'S DAY

The great religions of the World have contributed much to the psychological and spiritual well being of humanity. But they have also done—or at least many men have done in the name of religions—some shameful things. Since most historical religions were initiated by men, in the sacred writings of religions one can detect perceptions, statements, and injunctions that are self-serving to the male.

Religious apologists quote from Scriptures to show how their religion holds women in the highest regard, but one can also find in these sources some pretty awful attitudes towards women. In most traditional socio-religious laws, whether Hindu or Judaic, Christian or Islamic or Confucian, women were subservient to and dependent upon men. Even the great Buddha, in his quest for Enlightenment, quietly walked away from his sleeping wife at night. One wonders whether he thought of how she might feel about his departure.

Thus, when it comes to actual practice, one has to turn a blind eye to the records of social history to argue that women have been treated fairly or decently over the ages. True, there have been exceptions here and there: some poets and philosophers have recognized women's worth. Remarkably, several women have distinguished themselves in the arts and the sciences in spite of all such hurdles. But, by and large, the primary role of women has been to bear children, and many men used to be (as some still are) upset or embarrassed when their wives gave birth to a female child. Female infanticide was not uncommon. Often, women were confined to the home, or relegated to hard work outside and for menial jobs mostly, generally paid much less for the same job. Sometimes they were (are) forced to move in public only under a demeaning veil. Women were not allowed to go to school and they did not have the right to vote. They have been punished more harshly than male offenders for sexual transgressions, made the butt of obscene jokes and limericks. They have been exploited for power and pelf. They have been raped by soldiers. Wife abuse is still a scourge. Women have been denied membership in prestigious bodies. Even in cultures where mother is treated as goddess, the plight of widows has been woeful.

Women have not always been putting up with such atrocities silently. In every nation and culture there have been brave women who have tried to assert themselves. But it was only during the 20th century that humanity's collective conscience began to be aroused against such injustices. Along with movements that condemned racism, freed subjugated peoples, and demanded civil rights for one and all, there were also moves to rid the World of the injustice and ignominy implicit in the oppression of women.

In this context, in 1909 the Socialist Party of America declared 28 February as Women's Day. Towards the close of the First World War, and soon after the Czar of Russia was overthrown, the new Soviet government gave women the right to vote. This was on 23 February on the Julian calendar which corresponds to 8 March on the Gregorian. This day was proclaimed as International Women's Day. Since then, and more recently with the blessings of the United Nations Organization, this date is observed as Women's Day. Its goal is as much to remember the significant contributions of women to society and culture, as to re-commit oneself (whether man or woman) to the eradication of injustices against women. So on this day I join others in paying homage to humanity's mothers, wives, sisters, daughters, and all little girls of the World.

From the World of Science: HYPATIA

This being Women's Day, let us recall Hypatia (350–415), the first woman in the western World to have written and taught on the sciences of her day. She was a much respected mathematician in the Alexandria of the ancient World. Her father was the mathematician Theon, usually regarded as the last famous member of the Alexandrian school. She studied under her father and is reported to have contributed to his editions of Ptolemy and of Euclid, and to have herself written various mathematical works. She was the author of a commentary on Ptolemy's *Syntaxis*, whose edition of Euclid's *Elements* served as a standard for many centuries. An intellectual battle was going on in Alexandria between the Greek philosophical tradition and Christian World views. Hypatia was a pagan and was not looked upon with favor by the patriarch Cyril. According to one story, not universally accepted, Cyril once saw a crowd of admirers thronging near Hypatia's home to see and to listen to her. This filled Cyril with so much envy that he wanted to kill her. Instigated perhaps by him, she was brutally murdered by a mindless mob and her body was ripped to pieces right in front of her house, and then burnt. According to another version, this occurred in the very hall where she was teaching. No matter how the crime occurred, there is no doubt that Hypatia was murdered. This gruesome episode appropriately coincided with the setting of the sun in the glory days of Alexandria.

In the 19th century, Charles Kingsley wrote a historical romance entitled *Hypatia* on the life and death of this illustrious woman, somewhat like what T. S. Eliot did about the *Murder in the Cathedral* of Thomas à Becket. In this story, a Christian monk called Philommon is converted to her Pagan philosophy, and learns from her death about what religious intolerance can do.

Kingsley's fiction pales in comparison with that of St. Catherine of Alexandria. Many scholars now regard her as a fabrication based on Hypatia. She was much revered during the Middle Ages. Her statues were worshipped in many churches. She was listed among the fourteen most important saints who played a major role in Heaven. She was praised for her virginity. She was regarded as a scholarly woman who impressed an emperor by her learning and intelligence and eloquence, but imprisoned and tortured. Joan of Arc had a vision of St. Catherine. One effect of such stories was that St. Catherine was chosen as the patron saint of the Sorbonne in Paris. In 1969, the Catholic Church removed from the list of saints the name of St. Catherine of Alexandria.

Such is the impact of ancient legends on the minds of the people. The stories of historical figures, both real and imaginary, have more impact on the cultural feel-good state of a people than the cold facts and dates of history.

March 9

From the World of Religion: PYTHAGORAS

There have been countless cults in history. Some came and went like a comet, leaving no trace. Some survived and succeeded, creating major revolutions. Some left behind substantial impacts, though their founder and membership modes are but items in history.

Pythagoras (6th–5th century BCE) was the originator of a cult of this last kind. He had many disciples. Pythagoreans were primarily interested in four subjects: arithmetic, geometry, music, and astronomy. The Greek word *mathematike* simply meant learning.

Students in the Pythagorean school were divided into two groups: the outer students, called *exoterici* or *acusmatici*, who were given only summaries of the teachings of the master; and the inner students, called *esoterici* or *mathematici*, who were initiated into the details of his wisdom. Generally, the *acusmatici* were interested in the religious aspects of the teaching; the *mathematici* studied the mathematical physical aspects of the World.

Pythagoreans took portents seriously. They imagined that beans enclosed the souls of the dead. They believed in reincarnation. They were vegetarians for fear of eating a deceased relative who might have been born as an edible animal. Pythagoras preached that the goal of life should be to break away from the cycle of birth and death and rebirth.

Pythagoras taught that the essence of everything is in numbers. Pythagoreans assigned numbers to people, animals, events, and activities. The number corresponding to an animal, for example, would be the number of stones required to make an outline of its form. The pseudoscience of numerology has its roots in this number mysticism.

Pythagoras is credited with the discovery that the production of harmonious sounds is related to specific ratios of the lengths of the vibrating strings. He recognized that the ratios *1:3*, *3:2*, and *4:3* correspond to the basic intervals of (Greek) music. When the string lengths in a musical instrument are as *12:9:8:6*, harmonious sounds result. He also noted that the numbers 1, 2, 3, and 4, which are involved in harmony, add up to 10. He felt the order and beauty in all of this, and he called it *kosmos*. This is the origin of the scientific concept of cosmos, i.e. a universe governed by well defined mathematical laws.

The doctrine that everything can be reduced to integers ran into difficulty when Hippasus of Metapontum proved that the square root of 2 cannot be expressed as the ratio of two integers (or, as we would say today, the square root of two is an irrational number). This so infuriated the Pythagoreans that they are said to have drowned the poor man.

This number mysticism was next extended to heavenly bodies. Pythagoras thought that heavenly bodies move faster than anything on earth, and thus produced musical sounds. Then how is it that we do not hear them? Pythagoras' answer was that since we are all subjected to the same sounds right from the beginning of our existence, we have become numb to them. Sounds become audible only when they are contrasted with silence. The Pythagoreans believed that the master himself could hear this music of the spheres.

The Pythagoreans had an emotional reverence for knowledge. They considered wisdom (*sophia*) and the love of wisdom (*philosophia*) as the goals of life.

Eventually Pythagoras provoked much dislike as much for his person as for his ideas. Uprisings against him and his followers became common. Pythagoras was exiled, and the old sage went to a temple and starved himself to death when he was seventy-five.

The roots of the mystical penchant of even modern scientists, from Kepler to Eddington, have been traced by some scholars to Pythagorean World views.

From the World of Science: MESON CREATION

In the second decade of the 20th century, it was found that certain electrically charged instruments (electroscopes) discharged too quickly. It was also found that the effect increased with altitude. Electroscopes on top of the Eiffel tower and in balloons sent 15,500 meters high discharged even faster. V. F. Hess suggested that there was perhaps some Hoehenstrahlung (high-altitude radiation) that cause this. His research led to the discovery of what we now call cosmic rays: highly energetic charged particles which continuously come into the earth's atmosphere from the sun and other sources beyond.

Cosmic rays were seen to consist of new kinds of particles—the so-called mesons—which are very different from the more familiar protons and electrons. It was discovered that mesons actually result from the bombardment of the atomic nuclei (core of the atoms) in our atmosphere by highly energetic (very fast-moving) protons which come from outside. The study of the cosmic rays led to new insights into the physical World.

By mid-1930s it was understood that mesons play an important role in the stability of matter, serving as the glue that keeps the nuclear particles together.

More exactly, they are particle-aspects of what physicists call the strong interaction at the nuclear level.

To gain deeper understanding of mesons it would be useful to have them readily available from a source which is not as remote or balloon-demanding as cosmic rays. Knowing that mesons result from the collision of highly energetic protons on atomic nuclei (other protons and neutrons), physicists felt that they could accomplish the same thing by accelerating protons to extremely high speeds and making them impinge on nuclei.

A device whose goal is to accelerate charged atomic particles in order to make them collide with targets to produce nuclear reactions is known as a particle accelerator. In the 1930 such accelerators were already known. Now the problem was to accelerate the particles to significantly large speeds (energy). In simple terms, in the production of mesons, the energy of the incoming particles is transformed into matter as per Einstein's famous formula ($E = mc^2$) which gives the quantitative mass-energy equivalence. Thus, knowing roughly the mass of the mesons one can estimate the energy to which the particles must be accelerated to produce mesons. Making liberal estimates, the goal was to device an accelerator in which alpha particles would be accelerated to 150 million electron volts of energy. This was way too small. After more calculations and design work the synchrocyclotron was constructed which whirled alpha particles to almost half the speed of light (400 million electron-volts of energy), which struck the nuclei of carbon atoms and created a spurt of pions (pi-mesons). The great news was announced by the University of California in Berkeley on 9 March 1948: Human beings had produced by their ingenuity the most basic cementing particles that are found only within nuclei or in cosmic rays! Some physicists compared this accomplishment to the discovery of America. But this excitement was not enough for those who see science in terms of its potential for human need and greed. The *Time* magazine rejoiced by saying that this might "lead in the direction of a vastly better source of atomic energy than the fission of uranium." This of course did not happen. However, this first "meson factory" led to many other more accelerators of far greater energy range. These have brought to light the existence of a plethora of other subnuclear entities undergirding physical reality, including the quarks of which hadrons are made, and they have helped us better understand at a deeper level the ultimate nature of matter and forces.

March 10

From the World of Religion:
TRANSLATION OF "LA DIVINA COMMEDIA"

An important impact of religion is the World-view it creates in the minds of the faithful. This World-view includes beings and regions which have a reality of their own. Yahweh and Helel, Devas and Asuras, Lucifer and Gabriel, Houris and Iblis, are actual beings in minds conditioned by the magic of religions. There is a region in the universe called Heaven, and a counter-one called Hell. But, at least in evolving religions, the World-view also changes, slightly or significantly, with time: the first step in the transformation occurs when one makes a distinction between literal and poetic truths.

In medieval times, visions of heaven and hell, of paradise and purgatory were far more actual for the vast majority than now. We can form some idea of these through the arts and sculptures of the time, and also from philosophers and poets.

The Italian poetic genius Dante Aligheri (1265–1321) did a service for Christian history in his masterpiece, which has come down to us as *The Divine Comedy*, for it spells out the medieval World picture on these matters with great feeling and in considerable detail. It is sometimes stated that this work was first transcribed on 10 March 1307.

Dante is eloquent, articulate, and evocative as he narrates the labyrinths of Hell and the splendor of Heaven. The first lines of the immortal poem reminds us of our confusion as human beings in this vast universe which is like a dark forest where no path is clear until we have a more enlightened guide to show us the way.

The guide for Dante is the Latin poet Virgil who states that Hell is for those who have lived with indifference to good and evil. Dante was moved to pity when he saw the terrible punishment meted out to sinners: Those who had committed carnal sins were whirled around ceaselessly; gluttons were buried in mire, pelted by snow and hail; wasters and the greedy were punished in different ways, as were those given to anger and gloom At one point they were denied permission to enter until a friendly angel intervened. Then they saw tombs on fire wherein were heretics in torment. They went across a river of blood, to which were condemned those who had perpetrated acts of violence. Further on, they encountered seducers, flatterers, and more. In the ninth circle they saw, among cheats and alchemists, some eminent personages also. Here we have a terrible description of the pathetic plight of Prophet Mohammed. But then, an earlier Arab author, Abu-I-Ala al-Ma'arri, had written a work called Risalat al-Ghufran where he also gave the reader a guided tour of the nether World as imagined by the people of his time and culture, where we read about Christians being tortured in the Islamic Hell.

From the depths of Hell, Dante and Virgil go on to Purgatory where there is scope and hope for redemption. Here too there are steps and stages, pain and punishment. He meets Beatrice, who had captured his heart as a youth. She speaks to him of Love sublime that "moves the sun and all the stars." It alone is the key to heavenly bliss. She escorts him through the nine crystal spheres of Heaven. In each heavenly suburb is a planet along with brilliant stars, which are the departed saints. When he prays to the Virgin Mother, he gets a glimpse of the ineffable splendor: an "abyss of radiance, clear and lofty," such as Arjuna had seen in the *Bhagavad Gita*, a light brighter than a thousand suns.

Dante called his epic poem *Commedia*, for what else is Truth if not something that prompts our more joyous emotions? It has been said that Virgil stands for philosophy or natural religion, which enables us to see things clearly and dispassionately, whereas Beatrice symbolizes revealed religion, which is to be deeply felt and experienced.

From the World of Science:
MARCELLO MALPIGHI

It is common knowledge today that there are red blood corpuscles in the blood, that we taste food because of sensory receptors in the skin, and that blood passes from arteries to veins in the circulatory system. But when did we come to know about all this? They were among the discoveries made by Marcello Malpighi (born: 10 March 1628) in the second half of the 17th century.

As Galileo had turned the telescope skyward and reaped abundant astronomical information, Marpighi directed the newly invented microscope to biological entities, and uncovered many a secret of living organisms. He dissected bats and frogs and chicken embryos and examined various parts of their organs under the microscope. It was thus that he discovered the structure of lungs: its membranous alveoli, and also the hair-like connections between veins and arteries which are invisible to the naked eye. These are the capillaries (from the Latin capilla: little hair). This was a major discovery for at least two reasons: It established how the air (oxygen) we breathe enters the blood stream and serves the body. Secondly, this discovery gave a big boost to the idea of circulation of blood which, as yet, had not been universally accepted as true. Malpighi is also the one who first spotted red blood corpuscles, although this wasn't done right away. He uncovered the ducts by which glandular secretions enter the system, as also the mucous layer under the epidermis. Today anatomists speak of the Malpighian layer. He explored the kidney and the spleen also.

It took many years of careful and painstaking observations for these and more features of anatomy to be unraveled. Malpighi wrote about his results in the form of letters published in Bologna and Leiden. Some of his findings were challenged, but he defended his theses. The newly founded Royal Society published his results. In fact, before his death he made a long list of all his works, a kind of autobiographical resumé which the Royal Society also published.

There is an aspect of his work that many people nowadays do not appreciate: He used to cut open live animals in his studies, without any consideration of their pain. It must be pointed out that this was common for a long time, but we should note that humanity has also evolved on the moral plane, for today most anatomists do pay attention to the suffering of their research animals.

Malpighi's involvement with science had all the joys of a spiritual seeker. The excitement that Dante (in the Divine Comedy) had experienced centuries earlier upon seeing Heaven, Marpighi found in his discovery of the details of anatomy. Reporting on one of his discoveries he declared that he "experienced an internal pleasure that my pen could not describe," akin to the ecstasy of the mystics.

Malpighi's contributions were significant and trail-blazing. This is why he is regarded as the founder of modern anatomy. His life and work showed two important elements in the progress of science: tremendous breakthroughs can occur with the invention of suitable instruments, and the reliance on carefully acquired data of observation in the quest for understanding.

Bertrand Russell, speaking of the impact of Galileo's Inquisition on Italian science, said in his book *The Scientific Outlook* that Galileo was the last of the great Italians. When we consider Torricelli, Malpighi, Grimaldi, Morgagni and others, one is inclined to think that Russell's assessment was somewhat exaggerated.

March 11

From the World of Religion: MAHASHIVARATHI

This year, many in the Hindu World observe March 11 as Mahashivaratri: The great Night for the adoration of Shiva: the third of the Hindu triune of Creation,

Sustenance, and Dissolution of the Cosmos. The name Shiva literally means: auspicious.

The anthropomorphic representations of Shiva are invariably majestic, sometimes eerie: He has a blue neck around which is coiled a cobra. His body is whitish gray, and he is sometimes wearing a gruesome garland of skulls. His garment may be of deer or of tiger skin. He holds a terrifying trident. Then there is the esoteric third eye which opens when Shiva is provoked to anger, and it radiates deadly rays that pulverize the target. Often Shiva is seated with his consort Parvati on Mount Kailasha in the Himalayan range, the sacred Ganga trickling through his matted hair.

Every aspect of Shiva's image, sometimes simple and human, sometimes awesome and spine-chilling, has a mythopoetic story behind it. Thus the azure tinge of the neck came about when Shiva gulped, but did not swallow, a terrible poison. His body color was because he once smeared himself with ash from corpses in a crematorium. His form as Nataraja (the dancing Divine) conveys the ecstatic phase in Cosmic dissolution which will be followed by renewal. There is much symbolism and occult in all of this. The figure of Shiva fills the beholder with mystery and reverential submission.

Practical techniques for Shiva worship, and sophisticated metaphysical doctrines for contemplation on Shiva have evolved over the centuries in India. In the extreme north, there is the Kashmir school of Shaivism which rejects the Vedas and opens its doors to the lowliest castes. In the Tamil south there is the ancient tradition of *Shaiva Siddhanta* which spells out the doctrines in the poetic mode. Little known beyond the Tamil speaking World, this system embodies a large corpus of subtle reflections which are among the most sublime devotional expressions in the cultural history of humankind.

Beyond names and forms, transcending metaphysics and mythology, there is a principle that brings to naught all that has emerged. Not just the short-lived bloom of a flower and the steady heartbeat of healthy humans, but everything ultimately ends. From the frail whisper of the gentle breeze to the sturdiest rocks, from the mute interactions of hadrons and leptons to seemingly eternal galaxies, all is destined ultimately to be erased. The cause of this ultimate dissolution is the mystery of Shiva. Shiva is the dot that completes every sentence of existence, the last breath that lulls the lungs, the invisible rope that closes the curtain of the cosmic show, the ultimate sigh of the grand universe itself, the final puff of the physical World. On that principle we meditate on the night of Shivaratri.

From the World of Science: URBAIN LE VERRIER

For many centuries humankind had recognized only seven heavenly bodies moving somewhat differently than the stars: Sun, Moon, Mercury, Venus, Mars, Jupiter, and Saturn. These were called the planets. The Babylonian practice of consecrating on a periodic basis one day to each of these planets of ancient science gave rise to the seven-day-week we have to this day. The scientific revolution of the 16th century changed the age-old view that the earth is at the center of the universe, and placed the sun there. The moon was recognized as a satellite of the earth.

For the first time since the dawn of astronomy millennia ago, a new planet was discovered in the 1780s by William Herschel. He proposed to call it Georgium Sidus (George's Star) in honor of the British Monarch. Others proposed names like Minerva, Cybele, Herschel, and even Neptune. But finally the astronomer Bode's suggestion that it be called Uranus was adopted. Uranus is the god of the sky in Greek mythology, married to Gea (the earth). Saturn was his son and Jupiter his grandson.

Carefully combing through earlier data, it was found that Uranus had been spotted as a faint speck at least a dozen times before by other telescopic observers who had, however, failed to recognize it as another planet.

The motion of Uranus was studied with great care during the next 50 years, and certain discrepancies were discovered: Uranus did not seem to be following the regular smooth path that a self-respecting planet was expected to take under the Sun's gravitational pull.

By the 1840s, the peculiar behavior of Uranus was explained by two mathematical astronomers: John Couch Adams of Cambridge, England, and Urbain Le Verrier (born: 11 November 1811), a chemist-turned-astronomer in Paris. By applying sophisticated mathematics to the problem, both of them, independently of each other, came to the same conclusion: there must be another planet that it influencing the orbit of Uranus.

Le Verrier had already studied a slight deviation in Mercury's motion: the so-called shift in its perihelion, i.e. the closest point to the sun in its orbit. He suggested that there is perhaps another planet much closer to the sun. He even named it Vulcan. No such planet exists. The explanation for Mercury's perihelion was provided by Einstein in the 1910s.

On September 18, 1846, Le Verrier wrote in a letter to the observational astronomer Johann Galle: "It is impossible to satisfy the observations of Uranus without introducing the action of a new planet. "In about a week's time the planet was discovered, very close to the location that had been predicted by Le Verrier's calculations.

This point must be emphasized: A remote astronomical body's existence and position were discovered on paper on the basis of calculations, using the laws of physics and the knowledge of behavior of another planet! This was a truly impressive achievement of the human spirit, no less spectacular than any of our technological wonders.

Different names were suggested for the new planet, including Janus, Le Verrier, and Oceanus, but finally *Neptune* was adopted. This was the name of the Roman god of the sea, corresponding to the Greek Poseidon.

In less than a month, William Lassel discovered the large satellite of the newly discovered planet. This was appropriately named Triton, the son of Poseidon.

In 1989, the spaceship Voyager II sent us incredible amounts of fascinating information on distant Neptune and its moons. As we rejoice in the discoveries and achievements of our own times pertaining to Neptune and Triton, it is good to remember those whose efforts and talents laid the foundations for these.

March 12

From the World of Religion: GEORGE BERKELEY

The two most virulent enemies of religion have been atheism and materialism. Atheism arises from an unwillingness or inability to believe in any of the Gods of traditional religions. It is difficult to combat atheism because an atheist's belief is as strong as a religious conviction. Materialism is a philosophical conviction which results from a rational analysis of experiences. In other words, it is related to both observational data and a chain of reasoning based on these. Materialism can be attacked or argued against by keen philosophers, using likewise both logic and sensory data.

One of the most persuasive and influential philosophers to challenge the tenets of materialism was George Berkeley (born: 12 March 1684) who, like the youthful Sankaracarya in classical India, wrote cogently on the non-reality of the material World. Berkeley lived at a time when the power and success of the mechanical World-view was on the rise, when mathematics and experimental physics were not only drawing many brilliant minds, but were also nudging people away from matters of faith. He felt it absolutely necessary to demonstrate the shaky foundations on which materialism stood because he felt that "when this cornerstone is once removed, the whole fabric (of atheism and irreligion) cannot choose but to fall to the ground..."

So Berkeley wrote *An Essay towards a New Theory of Vision* (1709) in which he argued that the impressions of distance and shape and space are not more than that: impressions or illusions cause by sight. The following year, barely 25 years of age, he wrote *A Treatise concerning the Principles of Human Knowledge*. Here he reasoned very persuasively that since everything we know comes from our modes of perception, the existence of things is intimately tied to their being perceived. When perception disappears, everything disappears also. Or, as Vedantins would say, "Take away purusha (the experiencing priciple), and there is no prakrti (experienced principle)." Berkeley argued that it was impossible for matter to exist per se, that substantiality is a consequence of consciousness. What we regard as causality is, he maintained, actually a manifestation of the free spirit. All that we observe are signs and symbols of a Universal Mind, a Divine Intelligence.

Bishop Berkeley (as he later became) was versed in the sciences and mathematics of his day. He wrote an incisive analysis of the calculus which was growing and thriving in the first decades of the 18th century, sometimes without adequate regard to rigor. Berkeley wrote a book called *Analyst* (1734) which called into question some of the logical hanky-panky in which mathematicians were unwittingly engaging in their enthusiasm to develop the theory of fluxions (as calculus was called). Professional mathematicians benignly ignored him, but he wasn't really wrong in some of his criticisms.

The provocation for Berkeley's assault on analysis is interesting: There was a good Christian who lost his faith as a result of an alleged mathematical proof to the effect that there were serious logical flaws in ecclesiastical theology. The man refused to have his extreme unction when he was about to die. Berkeley was very unhappy, if not furious, and he wrote his learned treatise with the alternative title: "A discourse addressed to an infidel mathematician, Wherein it is examined whether the object, principles, and inferences of the modern analysis are more distinctly conceived, or more evidently deduced, than religious mysteries and points of faith." Whether he so implied or not, the title suggests that there are logical flaws in mathematics as also in theology.

From the World of Science:
GUSTAV ROBERT KIRCHHOFF

March 12th is the birth date of Gustav Robert Kirchhoff (born in 1824) who was a good scientist right from the start. Most students of physics have learned Kirchhoff's rules for electrical circuits. Not all may know that he formulated these when he was 21. He wrote many papers on the distribution of electricity in surfaces. He had a great capacity for giving problems in physics elegant mathematical formulations.

But Kirchhoff's greatest contribution to physics was in another experimental field. He worked in the laboratory of Robert Bunsen whose name is known to anyone who has worked in a chemistry lab through the burner that bears his name. Bunsen was studying the chemistry of substances at very high temperatures. His goal was to analyze salts by the light they emit at very high temperatures. Kirchhoff suggested that this could be done effectively by letting the resulting light pass through a slit and then a prism. Thus was born the spectroscope in 1859. He was not the first to experiment with light from hot sources, but he systematized it into an enormously fruitful science.

Kirchhoff's efforts in this matter led to three major discoveries: First, it was recognized that every element gives its characteristic spectrum (radiates specific wavelengths). This can lead to the presence of the element in a distant source, for by analyzing spectroscopically light from a star, one can detect which elements are present in any observed star. This most astounding possibility would have been considered little more than science fantasy until the first half of the 19th century. It gave the lie to the assertion of the positivist philosopher Auguste Comte (made in the 1840s) to the effect that human beings could never know the chemical composition of celestial bodies.

Furthermore, if a source gives spectra which don't correspond to any of the spectra from known elements, one may suspect the existence of a new element. A number of elements were discovered this way. Kirchhoff and Bunsen discovered two of these. One of them has two bright blue lines in its spectra. Hence they called it cesium (Latin, caesius: bluish great). The other was rubidium (Latin, rubidus: red), also because of its red spectral lines. These were the first elements to be identified from their spectroscopic characteristics.

We learn from the Kirchhoff story that the systematization of current knowledge into a clealr-cut discipline is as important as piecemeal discoveries. Also, there is no telling what science can accomplish in the future. Every generation has its eloquent commentators on the limits and limitations of science. For unfathomable reasons, some of them derive a peculiar delight in stressing that science can't do this and science can't do that. It is of course fair to say that science cannot do everything. But the history of science also reveals that it would be foolhardy on the part of anyone to be too specific on this matter. More than one intelligent thinker, even some scientists, has been shown to be embarrassingly wrong making such statements.

Kirchhoff also introduced the technical definition of a perfectly black body as one which emits and absorbs radiation of all wavelengths. This is a very important concept in physics. Later work showed that the distribution and intensity of the radiations are functions of the absolute temperature of the body. Careful and quantitative studies of these paved the way for the emergence of quantum theory of radiation which became the running theme of 20th century physics.

Kirchhoff received several honors for his scientific achievements. He is said to have been of a generally cheerful disposition.

March 13

From the World of Religion: GREGORIAN CHANTS

Sunday mornings we listen to the spiritual music of various traditions. They are invariably soothing. They draw us away from the troubles and turmoil of the world of politics and the hatred and hurt that are splashed in news headlines, away also from debates and discussions, points and counterpoints in arguments.

Gregorian chants are among these providers of serenity for us. Some people regard 13 March as Gregorian Chant Day. The CD we enjoy very much is by the Benedictine monks of Santo Domingo de Silos of Spain, a fine Romanesque cloister. Here the fraternity of monks sing the chants, not once, but seven times a day, seven days a week.

The chants date back to 1500 years. Though there was a time when Christians frowned upon singing in Church, fortunately the notion that music somehow detracts from worship lost ground in the Christian World. By the fifth century congregational singing was not uncommon. Monks and nuns were trained to sing the praises of God, even ask for mercy in musical terms. There was the belief that some of the singing that was occurring in church, lauding the glory of God, was very like what was occurring in high Heaven where angels were doing precisely that. Without such deep faith, the enjoyment of the songs could at best be at the aesthetic level, bereft of a deeper spiritual dimension.

In the late 6th century Pope Gregory I was instrumental in arranging collections of the songs that monks used to sing. Thus the collection of this devotional music came to be called Gregorian chants. Music historians have argued about whether should be attributed to Pope Gregory I deserves all the credit, but that shouldn't matter when we listen to the music.

As in all oral traditions the chants were handed down from generation to generation: The thought that we are listening to the reverberations of distant centuries generates a wonderful connection with the past. This monophonic music became a kind of chanted Bible which interlaced with the liturgy. It served as the official music of the Roman Catholic Church for well over half a millennium. It grew and transformed into many different musical modes and moods.

When Pope Pelagius II died unexpectedly, Gregory, who preferred a life of monastic simplicity, was made Pope much against his will. He is said to have lived on sparse food, wearing only very simple garments. He was kind to the poor even as a Pope. Indeed, he was known for his simplicity, compassion, and humility above all. He sent missionaries to many places, including England whose people he described as children of angels rather than Angles. He wrote several letters and books, including a biography of Benedict. These reveal the ease with which people believed in magic and miracles: moving of mountains and the curing of diseases by chants and relics, the effectiveness of the cross against poisons, the restoration to life of those who have been pronounced dead, and the like. Much of this may seem strange to those who have been touched by modern World views, but they still linger in the minds of countless millions all over the World.

But the same Gregory was also responsible for the grand anthology of Gregorian chants which fill our hearts with supreme peace. Herein lies the wonder of religion: its capacity to hold us in the abyss of darkness when it comes to understanding the World, but equally its capacity to raise the human spirit to wondrous heights of exhilaration through its symbols and poetry, and above all through the magnificence of devotional music. For this, the Christian tradition is grateful the Saint Gregory. And in today's World of multiculturalism, even non-Christians can derive some spiritual experience from them.

From the World of Science: JOSEPH PRIESTLEY

We live in an age when science has become so specialized, and divided into so many different sub-disciplines, that it is rare for someone trained in one field to talk intelligently about problems in another. It has also become simply impossible for one not trained in any of the sciences to make any contribution to science. But this wasn't always so, certainly not in the 18th century.

Consider Joseph Priestley (born: 12 March 1773). He wrote on philosophy, theology, and politics. He was sympathetic to the French Revolution, which, in those days was like an American being sympathetic to the Russian Revolution in the 1920s. He supported the American demand for independence, which in those days was like a Frenchman siding with the Algerians in the 1950s). He was a Unitarian Minister which was not unlike being a Buddhist in Taliban country.

But Priestley was also attracted to science. He started a school, emphasizing experimental science. He wrote *The History and Present State of Electricity* (1767) and a *History of Optics* (1772), and another work relating to the Human Mind in 1774. But he was not just a scholar. He was a theoretical physicist who derived the inverse-square law of electric charges from Newton's law of gravitation. He found out that caoutchouc—a sap from a South American tree—had the property of erasing pencil writing, and therefore called it rubber. He was also an experimentalist who probed into the phenomenon of fermentation. This led him to a recognition of what we now call carbon dioxide. He "impregnated" water with this, producing and tasting the first soda water (the first pop drink) in the World. Indeed, Priestley played with air under various conditions and discovered a number of gases, like ammonia, hydrogen chloride and some oxides of nitrogen. His most important discovery was made in 1775. He was one of the first to identify what is known today as oxygen. He called it dephlogistigated air in conformity with its properties in the context of the phlogiston theory of much of 17th century.

Priestley took a whiff of pure oxygen and reflected about the experience: "…I fancied that my breast felt particularly light for some time afterward. Who can tell but that in time, this pure air may become a fashionable article of luxury? Hitherto only two mice and I have had the privilege of breathing it." [The Swedish chemist Carl William Scheele (December 6) had discovered this also, a couple of years earlier, in fact; but his result wasn't known to the larger scientific community.]

He wrote a *History of the Corruption of Christianity* (1782) in which he summarily repudiated many of the fundamental doctrines of Christianity, and said there were no such things as miracles, but he did not deny the existence of God.

He was prescient when he wrote: "All knowledge will be subdivided and extended; and…human powers will in fact be increased; nature, including both its materials and its laws, will be more at our command; men will make their situation in this World abundantly more easy and comfortable; they will probably prolong their existence on it…"

Priestley's left-wing political views regarding the French Revolution, his pro-American stance in the context of American independence, and his Unitarianism: all these made him very much disliked in his native England. On 14 July 1791, while he was celebrating the second anniversary of the French Revolution, a mob became so furious that it set his house afire in Birmingham. Priestley got the hint, packed up his belongings and set sail to the newly born USA. Here he had friends in Benjamin Franklin and Thomas Jefferson. He was received warmly, and he settled down in Philadelphia.

March 14

From the World of Religion:
NISAN AND ROSH CHODESH

In our time reckoning, aside from days and weeks, we have the month. As the name suggests, and as the observance clearly shows, the origin of the month is related to the waxing and waning of the moon. Aside from its impact on the calendar, the moon has also influenced the religious observances of many peoples.

Thus, in the Judaic tradition, the beginning of a month is described as Rosh Chodesh: Head of the Month. Given that women's bodies also have a monthly cycle, this day is regarded as especially important for women. On the night after New Moon in March one can observe the crescent. It is therefore Rosh Chodesh. In 2002, 14 March was the first day in the Jewish month of Nisan.

Observances based on the moon's phases are very ancient. This particular one has been traced back to Babylonian civilization. It was a kind of shabath for women: a day of rest from the regular chores for the family. The custom of honoring women on this day in the Jewish tradition is also related to the story of the golden calf.

We read in Exodus (32-33) that when Moses did not return for long from the Mount of Yahweh where he had gone to receive the Covenant, his people were concerned and they wanted to plead to gods to bring Moses back soon. Aaron asked the men to bring their women's golden jewelry which would be molten and made into a calf for worship. This infuriated (the Jewish) God who explicitly commanded his people not to worship idols.

Elsewhere one also reads that many women absolutely refused to abide by the request, and they decried the idea of making an idol as an abomination. This firm stand on the part of the women was appreciated by the Lord, and it was as a reward that "they would observe the New Moons more than men, and in the next World...they would be renewed like New Moons."

The observance of Rosh Chodesh was an ancient practice, and like other traditions it was no longer taken seriously by modern women. However, now, as with other quests for roots and re-affirmation of ethnic identities, there is a resurgence of the practice among Jewish women. They gather at home or in dorms in universities, light candles, meditate, listen to music together, read and recite poems, say a blessing. In Israel, one follows the Talmudic custom before Rosh Chodesh Nisan at the Hulda Gates of the Temple Mount near the Western Wall. They blow the shofar and recite special prayers. Just before the new Moon is sighted, the arrival of the new month is announced to the public.

This a sign of beginning anew.

Blessed are You, as we start all over again.

New Moon, ancient light—

May my spirit rise to you, In Nisan's sky.

We may not know if Moses was indeed delayed on the mountain, if they tried to melt jewels to make a golden calf, and if God really was mad. But we do have a custom based on sacred history, a tradition which brings people together with soothing serenity, one in which poetry and music and reverence come into play. It carries the weight of centuries and has the beauty of a solemn ritual. It is not inappropriate to speak out to the unfathomable mystery: "You have granted your people New Moon festivals as a time of atonement throughout the generations."

So, on the first day of the month of Nisan one may offer to people of the Judaic faith their very simple greeting: *Chodesh tov!* Which simply means, A good month!

From the World of Science: ALBERT EINSTEIN

Every century has a scientist who towers over all others. For the 20th century, this was Albert Einstein (born: 14 March 1879). As with Galileo and Newton, not all may know about the technical details of his work, but everyone has heard his name. Once it was said, with a grain of truth, that just three people really understood Einstein's theory. And yet, indeed perhaps because of such publicity, his name became a household word.

Einstein was justly famous for many significant contributions to physics. He gave an elegant explanation for the zigzag (Brownian) motion of minute particles suspended in a liquid. He was the first to use effectively the then newly discovered quantum nature of light to account for the quantitative aspects of the photoelectric effect in which electrons are ejected from some metals when radiation of appropriate frequency falls on it. He unmasked the intrinsic intertwining of space and time, thereby demolishing the intuitive illusion of absolute space and absolute time which been entertained by human minds for millennia. He established the mathematical equivalence between energy and matter: E equals m c-squared. He did all of this in 1905 when he was barely a youth of 26.

As if this wasn't enough, Einstein probed into the structure of space and time, and discovered the effect of mass on space-time which is to distort it ever so slightly. This revolutionized our notion of matter, transforming it into a singularity (highly concentrated spot) of space-time, and it also reduced the great Newton's World-view of gravitation and force as just approximate metaphors useful in many calculations, but by no means reflecting the nature of reality. Einstein's gravitational theory demands an understanding of such sophisticated mathematics as Riemann tensors and Christoffel symbols, but it fits well with an expanding universe and big bang cosmology.

Einstein went on to seek bonds between gravitation and electromagnetism, instigated by a physicist's prejudice that multiplicity should always be reducible to simplicity. But his relentless search for a unified field theory turned out to be a wild-goose chase. Yet, physicists have not given up. All the esoterica of string and superstring theories are essentially lush high powered mathematics struggling to envisage observed particles and fields as different modes and states of a multidimensional abstract space.

Guiding light though he was for every physicist during the first half of the 20th century, revered and respected by one and all, Einstein was left alone with his quest for a unified field by the more youthful builders of quantum mechanics. He had difficulty subscribing to the altered views of Reality that the architects of quantum physics were formulating: irreducible indeterminacy, inseparability of subject and object, the centrality of consciousness in the measurement process, etc. He was unswervingly wedded to a classical deterministic world of which physicists of the 19th century were so sure. He argued in vain endlessly with no less a giant of 20th century physics: Niels Bohr.

Einstein was more than a brilliant physicist or absent-minded professor. He enjoyed playing and listening to music, he was a humanist who pleaded for peace, an unostentatious thinker who did not care for position or honors. He was driven out of his native Germany because he was born in the Judaic tradition. Though he did not subscribe to the details of religious doctrines, he had reverence for nature and for the Unknown, and recognized the relevance of religion: "Science without religion is lame, religion without science is blind." He once said that future generations would find it hard to believe that a man like Gandhi ever lived. In a sense this may be said of Einstein. He was *Time* magazine's Man of the Century, his work made Physics the Science of the Century.

March 15

From the World of Religion: ISLAMIC NEW YEAR

The ancient Romans used to call the 15th of March, May, July, and October, as well as the 13th of other months the Ides (Idus). In 2002, this date also happened to be is the first day of the first month of the year 1423 of the Islamic calendar. It was initiated in 638 C.E. Umar Ibn al-Khattab, a companion of Prophet Mohammed (saas: peace and blessings of Allah be upon him), consulted many scholars in systematizing it. Salla Allahu 'Alaihi Wa Sallam: may the blessing and the peace of Allah be upon him is a phrase that a Muslim is expected to use whenever he or she mentions the name of Prophet Muhammad.

Mohammed (saas) and his followers fled the city of Macca upon hearing of a plot to kill them. They hid in the cave of Thaur. After three days they moved on till they reached the town of Yathib whose inhabitants pleaded with him to stay there. It was thus that the city changed its name to Medinat al-Nabi: City of the Prophet. The Prophet's flight is known in Arabic as the Hijrah.

It was here that Mohammed did his worship which has been repeated by countless millions over the centuries. Here he uttered the words, *Allah ho akbar* (God is most great) which his followers repeated with zest. Here he bowed down and prostrated as they do to this day. What a powerful role model for worship he gave to his followers!

The originators of the Islamic calendar decided that the Hijrah should be taken as the beginning of a new era. That's why the Islamic new year is known as al-Hijrah, and the calendar is called the Hijri calendar. The abbreviation for the era is A. H. (*Anno Hijirae*). In the Gregorian calendar,1 Muharram 1 A, H. would correspond to 16 July 622 C.E.

Some commemorate the martyrdom of Husayn, a grandson of Prophet Mohammed, on this day. Therefore, for them, New Year day is not for joyous celebration. A traditional mode of observing the day, such as I recall seeing in India, is by marching in processions, wailing the death of Husayn, beating oneself on the chest, etc. But this is not universally approved. One scholar expresses his objection as follows: "The pages of Islamic History are filled with the blood of the martyrs. Should we begin to mourn the martyrdom of the Sahabah alone, every other day would be a day of mourning."

The Prophet is said to have declared that next to Ramadan, the month of Al-Muharram is best for observing a fast, especially from the ninth to the eleventh day. According to one canonical narrator (Hadith), when the Prophet (saas) arrived in Medina he noticed that the Jewish people were fasting on the tenth day of Muharram, called ashura. They said that this was to thank God for saving Moses and the Jewish people, and drowning their enemies. Upon hearing this, the Prophet (saas) said: "We are more worthy of Moses and nearer to him than you." He fasted on this day and instructed all to do the same. To be sure that a Muslim wasn't simply following a Jewish practice, he asked them to fast not only on the 10th day, but also on the 9th and the 11th or at least on one of these.

Islamic scholars have reminded us that their New Year does not start with a victory in war for them, and the death of a leader, but with the Hijra which actually represents a sacrifice for the preservation and spread of the Truth of Prophet Mohammed's (saas) Revelation. That Revelation was essentially to bring home to humankind that there is an eternal conflict between Good and Evil, between Right and Wrong, between Justice and Injustice. It is in this spirit that one should begin a new year, and make a resolution to be committed to whatever is good, right, and just.

So one may wish all Muslims a Happy New Year by saying, Blessed Muharram!, for, in principle, such observances bind a people to their cultural history, and should remind them of noble ideals.

From the World of Science: GEORGE P. MARSH

One is often inclined to believe that the smokestacks and automobiles of the 20th century, its pesticides and pollutions, radioactive wastes and rain-forest depletion are what made us first aware of our irresponsible behavior towards mother Nature, and that until the rampant technological assault on the environment of recent decades, no one really thought of the negative impacts of human activity on the environment.

But this is not entirely correct. Already in the 19th century, more than half a century before Alexis Carrel and almost a full century before a Rachel Carson, there was an American who was acutely aware of the ecological threats that mindless exploitation of Nature posed for the human condition. His name was George P. Marsh (born: 15 March 1801). He was a man of many talents: linguist, scholar, diplomat, writer, and one of the first environmentalists of modern times.

He grew up as a lad on a farm in Vermont, wandered in woods, was a student at Dartmouth, was fascinated by languages of which he learned quite a few, including Scandinavian and Icelandic, studied law, became an investor, owned a sheep farm, became a newspaper editor, and even a Congressman. He spoke out against slavery and the Mexican-American War. He was a diplomatic representative of the United States in Turkey where he preached religious freedom. In Italy where he wrote a remarkable book, he was the first U.S. ambassador.

It is this last item that brings his name to mind in the context of Science. The book which published in 1864 was entitled, *Man and Nature, or, Physical Geography as Modified by Human Action.* Here was a seer who could foresee disasters still in the mist of a distant future. The first part of the title sounds like a discussion of Adam in Eden, but the second part tells what the book was all about: the impact of technology on the World. Marsh was one of the first to realize that, unlike other creatures, we modify the earth's environment in substantial ways. An expanded version of the book appeared a decade later under the title: *The Earth as Modified by Human Action.*

This was the first work to point out that aside from the blind forces of nature that form mountains and rivers, the intentional forces generated by human actions also influence physical geography. This is a truism today, but it was an insightful observation in the 1860s. Marsh was not against the material benefits of applied science, but he warned that we should carefully consider the long range effects of our inventions and innovations.

Marsh was already concerned with human population growth. He noted, for example that "Man, who even now finds scarce breathing room on this vast globe, cannot retire from the Old World to some yet undiscovered continent, and wait for the slow action of such causes to replace, by a new creation, the Eden he has wasted."

As early as in 1849 he wrote: "I have had occasion both to observe and to feel the effects resulting from an injudicious system of managing woodlands and the products of the forest." It was Marsh's work that inspired the practice of having an Arbor Day. His work is what gave rise to the National Forest system.

George Marsh was not a technically trained scientist of any sort. But his love of nature, his first hand experience with Nature, and his deep sensitivity for the World around him made him aware of the interactions and mutual impact between human beings and the World around. As long as we don't tinker with what we study, there is no problem. But once we begin to intrude into natural processes in significant ways, we begin to upset the delicate balance that keeps life throbbing, and then we better watch out.

March 16

From the World of Religion: ST. UHRO'S DAY

Traditionally St. Nicholas (of Santa Claus fame) is regarded as a patron saint of Finland. But, like practically every other saint recorded in canonical hagiography, he was not a Finn by birth or nationality. We know that there have been English, German, French, Scandinavian, Spanish, Portuguese, and of course Italian and Greek saints in history, but really no one from Finland.

Though the people of Finland did not seem to mind this very much, in the 1950s, it occurred to Richard Mattson in Minnesota that it would be nice to have an authentic Finnish saint. One way to accomplish this would be to do some research and locate some truly pious Finn of the past who, besides being a Christian, had also done something that could be regarded as exceptionally devotional, if not a miracle, and report the matter to the Vatican. This would be a laborious ask without any promise of success.

So Mattson created a saint who was also really Finn, and gave him the same St. Uhro. Now he had to find a date to commemorate the saint's day, and attribute a miracle him. He chose 16 March as St. Uhro's Day: Just one day before St. Patrick's Day. As for the miracle, Mattson said that at one time Finland was invaded by a large swarm of grasshoppers. It was St. Uhro who got rid of them. He did this very simply by uttering to the green insects: "Heinäsirkka, heinäsirkka, mene täältä hiiteen!" The phrase has been roughly translated in a very unsaintly language as: ""Grasshopper, grasshopper, go to Hell!" This command must have been quite effective (and so deserving of sainthood for the personage who gave it) because grasshoppers have never again been a pest in Finland. Indeed, a side benefit of getting rid of the insects was that grapes and vineyard jobs were saved for fair Finland.

The next responsibility would be to specify modes of celebrating the day. It was recommended that the celebrants should wear something in royal purple and Nile green on that day.

The project of creating such an artificial saint was not unlike the introduction of Kwanza for African-Americans, and for all Africans more generally. Here, however, there is something more and something less. The *more* is in that there is also a saint for the theme. The *less* is that with a hymn like the following, there is little likelihood that his name will ever enter the Christian catalogue of saints, let alone a Psalm book.

Ooksie kooksie coolama vee—Santia Urho is ta poy for me!

He sase out ta hoppers as pig as birds—Neffer peefor haff I hurd dose words!

He reely told dose pugs of kreen—Braaffest finn I effer seen!

Some celebrate for St. Pat unt hiss nakes—Putt Urho poyka kot what it takes.

He got tall and trong from feelia sour—Unt ate culla moyakka effery hour.

Tat's why day guy could sase does peetles—What crew as thick as chack bine needles.

So let's give a cheer in hower pest vay—On this 16th of March, St. Urho's Tay!

In spite of the tongue-in-cheek dimension that is all too apparent here, we must not forget that there is much fantasy in the reports on the lives and deeds of many other customarily recognized saints as well. It is not surprising that the name of St. Uhro has spread far and wide among the Finnish Diaspora (and even in Finland), for the urge of cultural heritage is universal. There have been paintings and statues of this great saint who has the unique honor of being the only one who is explicitly recognized as purely imaginary. Celebrations include parties and parades and contests.

From the World of Science:
GEORG SIMON OHM

One of the features of modern technological civilization is the presence everywhere of wires: long and short, thick and thin, of copper or tungsten or whatever, hidden tiny gadgets or in huge enclosures or exposed on roadways, often protected by insulating materials, or sometimes exposed as in an incandescent lamp.

These wires are pathways for electric currents which serve us in myriad ways, and without which modern civilization would come to a standstill.

Of course, this has not been so always. Up until the beginning of the 19th century humankind managed without electric currents, though with considerably less comforts and conveniences. However, before electric currents could be used so widely, one needed to understand their properties: modes of generating them and the principles governing their passage through wires.

In this context we must recall the name of Georg Simon Ohm (born: 16 March 1789). He was a keen student who at an early age read the writings of the great scientific thinkers and of the eminent philosophers of that time, often guided and inspired by his father. Yet, when he was at the university he is said to have entertained himself at the billiard table and on the dancing floor to the point of upsetting his father. This prompted him to a self-exile from his native Erlangen. After spending a couple of years in Switzerland, he returned to the university and completed his doctoral work in physics.

Though equipped with competence and a good degree, he had difficulty in the job market. So he taught mathematics in sundry schools and wrote textbooks on elementary mathematics. He was very dissatisfied with his accomplishments, and felt he ought to do something worthwhile in life. So, he continued to do some research. Like some other physicists of that period, he became particularly interested with the effects of electric currents. In this context, he devised some ingenious experiments in which current was made to flow between the terminals of a battery through wires of varying lengths and thickness. These led him to the following significant results:

There is a property in wires which can be described as *Leitungswiederstand* (resistance to conduction). Today we simply call it the resistance (*Wiederstand*) of the current. We also know the origin of this: When electrons are impelled to flow (current) through the wire, the intervening atoms and molecules are like so many road blocks on the way. Ohm discovered that while the current through the wire is simply proportional to the tension (voltage) between the terminals of the battery, the resistance depends on the nature of the material. Furthermore, the longer the wire, the greater the resistance, and the broader the wire, the less it is.

The property of resistance is somewhat like friction on a surface on which a body is moving: As with friction, resistance generates heat. If we wish to get heat or light from the passage of current, we use very thin wires. If we wish to transport currents over long distances without such heat loss, we use thick cables.

Ohm's work won him recognition from the Royal Society with a fellowship and the Copely Medal. He came to be honored in his native country only after England hailed him as a scientific hero, although historians of science have argued about the correctness of this observation. In any event, future generations of physicists have immortalized Ohm's name by defining the unit of this property, called the resistance of a wire, as one ohm. The converse property of conductance (which is a measure of the ease with which a wire lets current flow) is measured in mhos (ohm spelled backwards).

March 17

From the World of Religion: ST. PATRICK

It is difficult for anyone in the Christian World not to remember St. Patrick on March 17 when so many people have a touch of green in their garment and there are joyous parades in cities with a significant Irish population. He is the patron saint for the people of Ireland and of Irish heritage. He is believed to have lived more than 1500 years ago. Though we remember his name and recall events from his life, much of what we know about the saint is shrouded in mystery. Over the centuries, fanciful legends, associating miraculous powers and magical phenomena, grew around his name: a price that many saints have had to pay. It used to be recalled that he brought life back to dead people, that he made the blind see, and that he authored as many books as there are days in a year. According to Edmund Quiggin, some scholars went "so far as to treat all the accounts of his labours as the fictitious creation of a later age." A biography by J. B. Bury, published in 1905, re-formulated, on the basis of well researched materials, the more reliable elements in the lore of the saint.

He is said to have been born in Western England to parents who were Roman citizens, and received the name of Patricius (which means an aristocrat). [In Irish—where P gets transformed into C—Patrick was transformed to Cothrige). An old British name for him was Sucat which used to mean warlike. He was raised as a Christian, read the Bible so frequently that he almost knew it by heart, but he wasn't particularly religious. When he was a youth of sixteen, he is reported to have been kidnapped by Irish adventurers and worked as a pig-herd in Ireland for six years. He escaped and went back to England.

One night he had a vision in a dream in which he was beckoned back to Ireland, he felt he heard the voice of the Irish telling him: "We pray thee, holy youth, and come and walk again amongst us as before." He went to Gaul to be trained as a missionary. Eventually he went back to Ireland in 432, ordained as a bishop.

St. Patrick left for posterity an autobiography entitled, "Confessions." Here he recounted the dozen times his life was in jeopardy, often captured by unfriendly forces. But he never forgot the call he heard in his vision, and never gave up his commitment to bring the Irish people in the embrace of the Christian Church, and this, many historians have noted, meant a transformation from the semi-barbaric to a much more civilized state.

That's why St. Patrick is remembered gratefully: He was responsible for many churches in the land, for monasteries and for training priests and countless people to piety. It was his efforts and persuasiveness that led to a more universal Christianization of Ireland. Not many saints have converted a whole nation such as St. Patrick did.

He was not a very learned man, no great scholar in Latin or philosophy, and he was well aware of this, as we see from his *Confessions*. But one doesn't need profound learning to be good and kind, caring and enlightened. For, aside from his missionary commitment and enthusiasm for church-services, St. Patrick is also known to have been an enlightened reformer who showed respect for women and spoke out against slavery.

So on March 17, in New York City and Boston and Chicago and in countless other cities, thousands of people march every year to celebratory music, clad with a touch of green. In some places they even dye the river with that color. In the hearts of many, whether Irish or not, St. Patrick is not a man who did impressive and incredible things in the 5th century, but rather a symbol of commitment to a noble cause, of service to others at the risk of one's own life, and of the cheerful Irish spirit.

From the World of Science: VANGUARD I

For eons our earth had but one satellite: the waxing and waning moon that had inspired calendars, poets, and festivals. But since the 1950s human ingenuity has been launching a series of satellites. They are minuscule in size and mass compared to the glorious moon, and though much closer, are hardly visible to the naked eye. But they are impressive because they emerged from human ingenuity, and they are useful to us too in a good many ways.

The year 1958 had been declared the International Geophysical Year, dedicated by the nations of the World to a thorough study of our home in the universe. At 7:15 a.m. on 17 March of that year, a three pound satellite was put into orbit from Cape Canaveral which began to circle the earth once every 107.9 minutes. It was called Vanguard I. It was a three-stage launch vehicle, using liquid propellant (liquid oxygen and kerosene) engines in the first and the second stages, and a solid propellant for the third stage. Its major goal was to evaluate the performance of the telemetry system and also to launch a system that could control flight altitude. We were still in the very early stages of rocketry and space exploration. The Soviet Union had taken the lead in the enterprise of satellite-launching: their Sputniks had been launched in 1956, and were far more massive. Sputnik II carried the dog Laika: the first animal to go up there.

A most impressive feature of Vanguard I was the extraordinary stability of its orbit. It charted the contours of land masses on the planet with such accuracy that some of the maps of islands in the Pacific had to be re-drawn. Furthermore, the data received from the orbit of Vanguard I revealed that the earth was much more bulging in the equatorial regions than had been suspected thus far. Also, the flattening at the poles is not quite symmetrical, which that means from a space perspective, the earth resembles a pear rather than a bulging orange. When, in the 18th century, the French Academy of Sciences sent expeditions to South America and to Lapland to figure out the shape of the earth by measuring the acceleration due to gravity in the different latitudes, they could never have imagined that a little over two hundred years later, the shape of the earth would be determined by artificial satellites.

In its highly elliptical orbit round the earth, Vanguard I comes as close as 650 km (perigee), and moves as far away as 1900 km (apogee) from the earth's center. Because of the atmospheric drag the orbit has been gently shrinking over the decades, and its period of revolution has also become less by a minute. We have come to know, by measuring the drag on the satellite, that the earth's atmosphere, in however tenuous a form, extends to higher elevations than had been assumed thus far. Vanguard I has been whirling around our planet for more than 45 years now. If all goes well (if it isn't hit by a meteor or affected by powerful solar winds) it can, in principle, remain in orbit for at least two more centuries. Already it has made more than two hundred thousand revolutions around the earth, covering almost 9 trillion million miles.

Vanguard I resulted from the persistence of space scientists (and continued public support for their efforts), because it was preceded by several repeated failures: aborted launches and explosions. This must be recalled because, as with efforts in theoretical physics when one tries to build reasonable theories, in experimental endeavors too a great many failures and frustrations often come before one can relish the sweetness of success. If one were to give up after the first few unsuccessful attempts, one can never hope to succeed.

March 18

From the World of Religion: EDGAR CAYCE

The thirst for the spiritual can manifest itself in two different ways: It may goad the thirsty one to an independent quest which may result in some deep insights or findings. When this happens there is often an urge to share the fruits with others, and through them, propagate the discoveries to the rest of humankind. The other is to accept the revealed truths as reported by one or another of the enlightened souls who have spoken.

A general rule is that one or more of the following should be associated with a person of the first category: He/she must have had a vision, he/she must have performed a miracle, he/she must have predicted significant events in the as yet unborn history, he/she must possess some psychic powers.

Edgar Cayce (born: 18 March 1877) was one such person. He was a family man who went to church and taught Sunday school. But he is said to have had some unique, not to say weird, experiences. Thus, he used to get into self-induced trance states from which he would hold conversations with unknown people all over the World. [Many do this in our own times in computer chat-rooms, but Cayce did this prior to 1945, lying on his stomach.] The conversations were actually question and answer sessions which would deal with such wide-ranging topics as personal health, interpersonal problems, and the ultimate secrets of the universe. In a radio talk-show format, he would give long distance answers and guidance to people. This went on for more than four decades. In 1931, Cayce founded an organization called Association for Research and Enlightenment (A.R.E.) in Virginia Beach, which has records of several thousand interviews of this kind. A.R.E. has a large membership from many countries even today.

Notions of the supernatural have been there since the most ancient times. Associated with them are concepts and technical terms, some old, some new, some borrowed from current science. They create a framework which has all the coherence of a scientific discipline. Terms like auras, holistic approach, akashic records, belong to the framework fostered by Cayce. The writings and popularization of Cayce have contributed, directly and indirectly, to making them current in the language. Cayce's followers and admirers remind us that already many decades ago he drew attention to "the importance of diet, attitudes, emotions, exercise, and the patient's role—physically, mentally, and spiritually—in the treatment of illness." They credit him with prescience about some of the problems our World is facing today. They have claimed that like Nostradamus of an earlier epoch, Cayce foresaw the demise of Communism, and even the September 11 tragedy. Some have gone so far as to say he even predicted the rise of some of the current theories of high energy physics. Impressive for someone who was deeply interested in astrology.

There is bound to be disagreement on the question of whether Edgar Cayce was helpful or hurtful in assisting humanity to understand the true nature of the phenomenal world. There have of course been scores of spiritual gurus like him in every generation who have subscribed to similar world views and acquired millions of devout followers. No matter what one's views on them, this much may be said: The impact and influence of charismatic leaders and writers who preach about the magical and the mysterious are enormously greater than those of impeccable logicians, keen rationalists, and incorrigible skeptics, because people experience greater thrill in listening to whispers from unknown sources in the dark than in the mathematical proof that pi is a transcendental number. Poetry is generally more appealing to than syllogism.

From the World of Science:
CHRISTIAN GOLDBACH

Proclamations of truths about physical reality may be shown to be correct or incorrect from observations. Proclamations of mathematical truths may in general be demonstrable through simple or complex mathematical reasoning. But this may not always be possible.

Sometimes, even simple statements in mathematics may remain unproved for a very long time. Thus, for example, the so-called Euclidean axiom to the effect that only one parallel may be drawn to a given straight line through a point external to the straight line, could never be proven. Now we know that this was no more than a postulate (consensually accepted as true) to define the geometry of one kind of space.

Likewise, in number theory, there is a famous proposition to the effect that every even number beyond 2 can be expressed as the sum of two prime numbers (i.e. two numbers neither of which is the product of two numbers). In the World of mathematics, this statement is known as Goldbach's conjecture, because it was first made by Christian Goldbach (born: 18 March 1690). For example, 22 = 17 + 5; 46 = 43 + 3.

What is remarkable about this is that it is a result that is intelligible to anyone: no more than secondary school arithmetic is needed for this. And with computers, its validity has been established, that is to say, no exception to it has been found for any number upto unimaginably large numbers. Yet, it has not been proved to be true on the basis of mathematical reasoning, though the brightest mathematicians have attempted to do this during the past 260 years.

A couple of years ago Apostolos Doxiadis published a novel entitled Uncle Petros and Goldbach's Conjecture in which the hero, who lives like a recluse in a suburb of Athens, gardening and playing chess, is actually a fist rate mathematician who was obsessed with finding a proof for Goldbach's Conjecture. The names of many 20th century mathematicians from Hardy and Ramanujan and Turing and Goedel are brought into the story. He fritters away his energies fruitlessly in trying to solve this very apparently insolvable problem. Even the non-mathematically trained reader can get a glimpse of the World of mathematicians from this story, where too there are rivalries and jealousies.

Goldbach, who was born in Prussia, became the first secretary of the Imperial Academy of Sciences in St. Petersburg in Russia. He was a man of great talents who commanded fluency in Russian, French, German and Latin. He studied to become a physician, published interesting papers in the mathematics, befriended and corresponded with many of the leading thinkers of the time. The Goldbach Conjecture itself was first stated in a letter he wrote to the most prolific and most prodigious mathematician of the 18th century, Leonhard Euler, in 1742. Euler was one of the first to try to prove it. When he couldn't there was little hope that anyone else would be able to.

Goldbach acquired familiarity with the mathematics of the period by random reading rather than by systematic study. Consequently, some of his results had already been published. Indeed, aside from his conjectures (there is another which says that every odd number can be written as the sum of three primes.) he is not remembered for any significant contribution to mathematics.

Incidentally, there is a million dollar prize available to anyone who can present an acceptable proof for Goldbach's conjecture.

There are puzzling truths that are intuitively obvious to those who can see. But even with a zillion illustrations of their truths they can never be logically established. Goldbach's Conjecture is one. God's existence may be another.

March 19

From the World of Religion: ST. JOSEPH'S DAY

This date (19 March) is celebrated by many Catholics as St. Joseph's Day. The name is an anglicized form of the Hebrew Yosseph which could mean a gatherer or a unifier. Practically everything we know about Joseph is from the New Testament. Unfortunately, not everything we read here is consistent. Matthew (i: 1-17), using the word "begat" a number of times, traces Joseph's genealogy all the way to Abraham in 42 generations. [There is a similar passage in Valmiki's Ramayana where all the ancestors of Lord Rama are listed likewise.] Luke (iii: 23–38), using the phrase "which was the son of" goes back in Joseph's genealogical tree all the way to Adam, "which was the son of God." Though Mathew's listing of names from David downwards are all of royal birth, Joseph himself is generally known as a simple carpenter in Nazareth.

Everybody knows that Joseph was married to Virgin Mary. It is clear from the Bible that Mary was betrothed to Joseph when she discovered she was with child. According to Mathew, Joseph had a dream in which an angel appeared and said, "Joseph, thou son of David, fear not to take unto thee Mary thy wife: for that which is conceived in her is of the Holy Spirit." But scholars and Christian religious sects have disagreed as to whether Joseph was the father of Jesus, or if the conception of Christ was immaculate.

Upon discovering Mary's pregnancy, and prior to his dream with the angel, Joseph had wanted to "put Mary away privily" rather than put her to public embarrassment.

According to some other sources (The Apocryphal Gospels) Joseph was a widower eighty years of age when he married Mary. In fact, he is said to have had four sons and two daughters by his first wife.

A careful reading of the Bible also suggests that Joseph passed away before Jesus began to preach. Therefore he was not there when Jesus was crucified. He did not do any miracles, he did not die a martyr, he did not spread the Gospel. This leads to the rather intriguing circumstance that, technically speaking, Joseph may be the only non-Christian who has been made a saint, and without doing any of the other things for which people have been canonized. Aside from his many good qualities as a human being, Joseph came to be regarded as saint only because he was (foster) father to Christ.

Thus, Joseph may be regarded as the ideal saint: a person with the finest humanistic qualities that one can possess. Joseph is remembered in the hearts of

Christians as a caring husband of Mary, a loving father to Jesus, a gentle and simple person, unassuming in spite of the royal blood in him. He followed the Judaic tradition. Luke says that when the child was born, Joseph circumcised him, as per the custom, and sacrificed two turtledoves. A lamb would have been more expensive. He made pilgrimages to Jerusalem for Passover. These are all commendable qualities, but may not be exceptional in that there are many simple, righteous, traditional, and caring people in the World.

The third Sunday after Easter is dedicated to St. Joseph. In 1642 the Roman Catholic Church adopted 19 March as the Feast Day of Saint Joseph. In 1870 St. Joseph was declared to be the Patron of the whole Roman Catholic Church. March 19 used to be celebrated with great joy in Italy where it is also Father's Day. In some parts of the country they have special feasts and art shows and processions. People enjoy making and eating a special pastry on this day. It used to be an Italian national holiday. After all, did the saint not serve as the father of Jesus? This is a good day to wish our Italian Catholic friends a happy *giorno di San Giuseppe* which is also *la festa del papà*.

From the World of Science: FREDERICK JOLIOT

In the phenomenon of radioactivity which was discovered in the last decade of the 19th century, the nuclei of certain naturally occurring heavy elements, such as uranium and radium, continuously emit certain types of particles and radiations. One reason for this phenomenon is that heavier nuclei contain considerably more neutrons than protons, causing instability. In ordinary uranium, for example, there are 146 neutrons and only 92 protons, whereas in the oxygen nucleus there are 8 protons and 8 neutrons.

In the 1930s experimental nuclear physicists were engaged in bombarding the nuclei of various elements with alpha particles that were ejected by naturally radioactive elements. One of those experimenters was Frederic Joliot (born: 19 March 1900) and his wife Irene Curie. In 1934, they announced a very important finding of theirs: Normally, when one bombards aluminum with alpha particles, one would expect the bouncing back of a proton or a neutron, and that would be all. However, here, careful examination showed that the target aluminum foil became radioactive. That is to say, even after the incoming alpha particles stopped, the foil continued to emit radioactive particles.

Joliot and Curie had created *artificial radioactivity*! Specifically, some of the aluminum nuclei in the foil had become phosphorus. This was the first clearly analyzed instance of *transmutation*: the change of one chemical element into another. Transmutation had been the fantasy of ancient alchemists who tried fruitlessly to convert copper into gold or lead to silver. After alchemy was discredited in the 17th century, no serious scientist imagined we could ever effect transmutation. Frederic and Irene accomplished transmutation, albeit not in alchemical mode. Unlike ordinary phosphorus, the one they created from aluminum was radioactive. They called it a radioisotope. Hundreds of other radioisotopes were made by radio-chemists in the next few decades. These are used extensively in medicine, agricultural research, and in many other contexts as well.

For this work Joliot and Curie shared the Nobel Prize for chemistry in 1935. Joliot added on his wife's name to his when he was married, becoming Joliot-Curie. Joliot-Curie was the first to observe the positron in radioactivity. His work also led to the discovery of the neutron. Furthermore, he was the first to point out that one possibility from nuclear fission was the production of more than one neutron which could be used to create a chain reaction: the foundation of the fission bomb and of nuclear reactors. Each of these could have won him a Nobel, but others published their results before him.

Joliot-Curie was remarkable as a scientist in that even while he was engaged in ivory tower research, describing a view of a bubble-chamber photograph as a most beautiful experience, he was deeply cared for the working class and for economic justice. Indeed, he was always a socialist at heart. During the Nazi occupation of France, he worked for the French Resistance. When a close friend of his was brutally murdered by the Nazis, he became a member of the Communist Party. At the close of the war, he urged General De Gaulle to create a French atomic energy commission. He was made its director. However, when, during the beginnings of the Cold War he made a Communist-inspired public statement to the effect that he would never be part of a war against the Soviet Union, he was relieved of this responsibility. [This was not unlike the Oppenheimer affair in the U.S. a decade later.] But he was still one of the greatest of French experts in the field of nuclear physics. He was an enlightened thinker who never ceased to speak out against exploitation, injustice and colonialism. In the World of science, however, he will be remembered for artificial radioactivity, transmutation and chain reactions.

March 20

From the World of Religion: ODUN

Most of the non-Abrahamic religions celebrate the Female as much as the Male. They have goddesses on a par with gods. One of these goddesses is Idun of the ancient Norse tradition. Also called Iduna, and known as the daughter of Svald and wife of Bragi. she used to be venerated as the goddess of youth. Unlike in Biblical narrative, in the Norse tradition the apple was an alchemically potent fruit which was responsible for the eternal youthfulness of the gods. It was Iduna who held the golden apples which the gods in heaven ate regularly, for in their World-view, an apple a day kept old-age away.

A difference between monotheism and polythesism is that in the latter, fascinating stories are associated with gods and goddesses. An episode associated with Iduna is the following: She was exploring the World with fellow deities Loki and Heonor. At one point they grew hungry. They saw an ox nearby which, they felt, would be good enough for a hearty meal. When they set up the oven and began to cook, the beef remained raw on fire. While wondering about this, they noticed an eagle up on a tree. The bird said it would help them if they allowed it to have few pecks on the ox's corpse first.

The trio agreed, and the eagle began eating. But it kept eating on and on. Loki got furious and tried to hit the bird with his long pole. But the bird grabbed the stick with his claws and soared high, carrying Loki at the other end. The terrified Loki begged to be released, but the bird said it would do so only if he would kidnap Iduna and her rejuvenating apples. Loki had no choice but to promise he would do it.

At last, when the three gods returned to Asgard, the realm of the gods beyond the Rainbow Bridge, Loki lived up to his word, and led Iduna to the eagle which was waiting outside. The bird was actually the giant Thiazi. He grabbed Iduna and carried her away to Thrymheim in the Jotunheim range of mountains.

Now the gods had no golden apples, and were beginning to age. They feared they would be immortal no more. So they sent Loki on an expedition to get Iduna back. He borrowed the falcon of Freya and reached Thrymheim where Iduna was left all alone. Loki transformed her into a nut, and carried her away. Thiazi noticed this, and he flapped his wings violently enough to cause a giant storm (pre-meditated chaos effect?) where the falcon was flying. But this time, the gods lit a giant bonfire whose flames reached as far as Thiazi, and burnt his wings to ashes. He fell down and died.

Scholars have debated about the origin and significance of this story. Some have even contended that this was a late addition to the more ancient Norse mythology.

The story may be no more than a fanciful tale. Or perhaps it symbolized the going away and the return of the bright days in northern latitudes, for spring time is rejuvenation. Or again, since myths also reflect human nature, one may give the following interpretation: The giant stealing the precious source of the gods' immortality even when they were willing to share part of their bounty with him may be taken to mean that the wealth and prosperity of the more successful people are always the envy of the less successful ones even when they received help, and they try, by hook or crook, to demolish that which is responsible for the well-being of the stronger ones. Such situations arise again and again between groups within a society as also among the nations of the World.

Whatever may have been the intent of those who came up with the notion of Odun and the rejuvenating apple, 20 March is marked on some calendars as the day to remember Odun, the Norse goddess of Youthfulness.

From the World of Science:
BURRHUS K. SKINNER

Why do people behave the way they do? Since time immemorial, there have been many theories to answer this question, ranging from karma in past births and God-had-ordained-it-so to education and how one has been brought up. The explanations have come from religion, genetics, psychology, neuroscience, and philosophy.

One of the scientific theories on this matter rests on the idea that the behavior of organisms (including humans) consists of reactions and responses to external stimuli. In other words, behavior refers to activities which have impact on the surroundings. Even as we operate (move around) in the World, we are exposed to various stimuli which reinforce our behavior. Every time we do something, there is a consequence to us too. Depending on if this is pleasant or unpleasant to us, we repeat or refrain from the action.

What this means is that if we know what stimulus will foster a desired mode of behavior, we can induce the organism to behave in particular ways by providing the appropriate stimulus. Likewise, by taking away the desirable (to the organism) consequences from certain types of behaviors, one can modify behavior.

These are not highly original ideas: they had been expressed by thinkers over the centuries. But during the 20th century, these ideas found ample corroboration in numerous experiments with rats, dogs, children, and even adults. All this is part of a school of thought known as behaviorism which has been explored, discussed, and debated vigorously for almost a century now. One of the most eloquent and effective proponents of behaviorism was Burrhus K. Skinner (born: 20 March 1904).

Skinner, respected professor at various universities, including Harvard, wrote a novel called *Walden II* which depicts his Utopia where behaviorism is the guiding principle.

Skinner has had sharp critics. At first blush, his theory sounds very interesting and acceptable, they said. However, upon reflection, we begin to realize that the implication of all this is that human beings are mere automata, robots which can be wound up in a variety of ways. Depending on which key is activated, we behave in a particular manner. There is no such thing as free-will or introspection or consciousness or values or independent thinking or anything of that sort. Skinner says, in effect, that we are no better that the dog that can be made to run by throwing a bone afar, or a monkey that grins every time we show him a banana. By introducing an array of technical jargon and rules like operant conditioning, schedules of reinforcement, extinction, continuous reinforcement, fixed ratio schedule, fixed interval schedule, etc, Skinner and his school were not only reducing Man to mindless machine, but also developing ways of *shaping* our behavior by those who have the technical know-how.

Skinner wrote *Beyond Freedom and Dignity*, explaining and insisting that these are unobservable constructs of the human mind, and have therefore no scientific validity, as is consciousness. Influenced by quantum physicists and positivist thinking, he noted that we can only observe behaviors and how they are modified by the environment. As far as science is concerned, this is all that makes sense. What we need to do to have a good society, he went on to suggest, is to recognize this, and do whatever we can and must to modify the behavior of the bad ones in healthy and wholesome ways by providing appropriate stimuli. Behaviorism has had significant impact on the treatment of the mentally ill, on education, in child-rearing and in animal-training. But its tenets continue to be debated by scholars, theologians, psychologists and others. It is not clear the complexity of human behavior and consciousness can be unraveled through neat theories.

March 21

From the World of Religion: VERNAL EQUINOX

The vernal equinox is the promise of spring. Poets have sung joyously about the return of the bright season. As a verse of Robert Burns says:

Now Nature hangs her mantle green
On every blooming tree,
And spreads her sheets o' daisies white
Out-owre the grassy lea

The ancient Assyrians used to honor their king on this day. The Zoroastrians of Iran took this as a day of celebration. In fact, it is the first day of the first month (Farvardin) on the Zoroastrian (Iranian) calendar. But it is celebrated by many people of the region: Tajkiks, Kurds, Afghans, Parsees, etc. The Persian word for it is Noe-Rooz: New Day.

We read in a work called *The Book of Kings* (Shah nama) King Jamshid of very ancient times is the one who started it all, to mark his victory over the forces of evil: demons called divs. He took control over their rich treasures, built himself a magnificent throne, and ordered the captured divs to carry him up in the skies.

On the day of this celebration, one places lentils in a dish to make them sprout, one colors eggs, decorates the table with fruits and other colorful edibles, places a mirror and a holy book and gathers as a family. In Iran there is also a custom by which one brings together seven things whose names start with the sound of s in the Persian language: words for hyacinth (*sonbol*) lentils (*sabzeh*), apples (*seeb*), and garlic (*seer*), for example, all start with that sound. Each is a symbol for something positive in life. On the 13th day of the month, there are picnics, and the sprouted lentils are thrown into the river.

When Islam entered Iran, some of the imams incorporated the Persian custom of celebrating the vernal equinox into Muslim practice. Islamic scholars went a step further by making it part of their sacred history. Many Muslims believe that this is the day when God made a covenant with humanity, when the sun first shone, when Noah's ark was grounded, and Gabriel first appeared to Mohammed, when Ali demolished the idols of Ka'bih. That is why the Shahs of Iran used to celebrate this Zoroastrian feast.

This is also New Year Day in the Baha'i tradition. Known as Naw-Ruz (or Navroz), this is the first day of the first month (named Baha in their calendar). It is referred to as the Day of God. Musical instruments are permitted on this day. On this night members of the faith are expected to repeat the following credo

361 times: "God bears witness that there is no God but Him, the Ineffable, the Self-Subsistent." There is another similar prayer for after sunrise. Baha'ullah asked his disciples to feast on this day. In fact, in the Baha'i tradition it is not permitted to fast during the first month of the new year. A Bahai prayer that is recited on this day is the following:

"Praised be Thou, O my God, that Thou hast ordained Naw-Rúz as a festival unto those who have observed the fast for love of Thee and abstained from all that is abhorrent unto thee. Grant, O my Lord, that the fire of Thy love and the heat produced by the fast enjoined by Thee may inflame them in Thy Cause, and make them to be occupied with Thy praise and with remembrance of Thee."

One may greet one's Zoroastrian and Bahai friends by saying, "Navroz Mubarak!"

And we rejoice in the vernal equinox because, in the words of Katherine Tynan,

This is the time when bit by bit
The days begin to lengthen sweet.

From the World of Science:
JEAN BAPTISTE FOURIER

The complex and often random World where things seem to move helter-skelter, a good many occurrences happen but once. But there are also many repetitive phenomena: the ceaseless return of day and night and the seasons; the waxing and waning of the moon; the ebb and flow of tides, for example. These are periodic phenomena. The swing of the pendulum is blatantly obvious, the vibration of guitar strings, but the oscillations of electromagnetic waves aren't that apparent. Mathematicians represent repetitive situations through *periodic functions*. The simplest of these are the so-called sine and cosine functions which many of us have seen drawn as rising and falling waves.

When a person sings a note, the sound produced may be represented as a periodic function. But this would not be as simple as the sine or the cosine curves.

It turns out that any arbitrary periodic function is actually the combined effect of many simple sine and cosine modes of different intensities. Or, as one would say in mathematics, any periodic function may be expressed, under certain conditions, as a combination of sine and cosine functions of different amplitudes. This is a very significant result, and is known as Fourier's theorem: established in 1807 by Jean Baptiste Fourier (born: 21 March 1768).

One may give an analogy: Suppose we have a certain amount of money in a box. Its total value may be that much, but it is actually made up of so many pennies, so many nickels, so many dimes, etc. Likewise, any given wave (periodic function) is made up of so much of each of the component periodic functions.

Thus a wave of light is made up of waves of various electromagnetic waves of different wavelengths, called the *Fourier components* of the given wave. Any arbitrary wave (be it of light or sound or economic cycles) may be Fourier-analyzed, i.e. split into its components periodicities of different intensities. This has found countless applications, and is also the basis of a sophisticated branch of mathematics.

Fourier had a very checkered career. He was born of modest parents whom he lost before he was ten. He went to a military school where he fell in love with mathematics. However, in the strange French caste system of his times, he was not allowed to join the army because of his low birth (son of a tailor), but he could become a teacher of mathematics. During the post-Revolution frenzy he spoke out against indiscriminate use of the guillotine, because of which he almost lost his life. When the grand episode was over, he was recommended to accompany Napoleon in the Egyptian expedition. He had diplomatic responsibilities in that country, but he also served as secretary to the *Institut d'Egypte*. [The colonizing country invariably had a scholarly/academic interest in the culture they dominated.] During his stay in Egypt he contracted a strange illness which confined him to well-heated rooms all through his life.

Upon returning to France, Fourier edited a descriptive account of Egypt, writing a historical introduction for it. He was made a nobleman and appointed prefect of a region. He no became interested in the transfer of heat from region to region: such as from inside a house to the outside via a window pane. His analysis of this problem led him to the Fourier theorem that has made him immortal. This classic work was published in 1822.

Later, he was elected to the French Academy of Sciences, of which he became the perpetual secretary, and also to the French Academy (of Letters). For some years he headed the prestigious Ecole Polytechnique. He was honored in many ways, and commemorated also. Unfortunately, a bronze bust made of him was melted by the Nazis and turned into an armament. All kinds of minds and values are found in human beings.

March 22

From the World of Religion:
WORLD DAY FOR WATER

We live on terra firma: It is but a small fraction of the earth's surface. It is estimated that there are some 1.33 million trillion cubic meters of water in the oceans and only some 231 trillion cubic meters in our rivers and lakes and ponds. There is also lots as ground water and in glaciers, but for the most part we depend on our rivers and lakes for our daily needs. Aside from serving as habitat for animals, plants, and microorganisms, rivers have also given rise to civilization: Herodotus described Egypt as the gift of the Nile. The Yellow River and the Ganges have done likewise. Lakes too have been nourishing and sustaining societies since time immemorial.

We have been interfering with river flows since ancient times, to avoid flooding and to ensure a water-supply throughout the year. We have straightened out meandering rivers, made them wider or deeper for our needs, built levees and dikes to contain floods, and re-channeled the course of rivers for irrigation. We build dams to prevent flooding, to store water, for maintaining a steady stream, and for generating electricity.

Such intrusions can have disastrous effects on the ecosystem. Creatures living on shore banks are displaced. By removing trees and plants soil erosion is facilitated. When rivers begin to run faster by course change, they can be destructive to aquatic creatures. Slowing them down is not helpful to larvae of some flies. Trout need gravel for laying eggs. When a river is widened or deepened, rain water tends to flush in pesticides, fertilizers, topsoil, and animal waste into the river. One can go on and on. But Nature is not always helpful to us either: As rivers flow into the oceans, they carry with them some material (land), causing steady erosion. This is a very complex process. It has been estimated that at the present rate, 2.5 inches of land surface is disappearing every 1000 years. In 12 million years, the entire North American continent will be washed away. We had better complete our projects before that.

Though water is a renewable source, its availability is not that easy for everyone. Many peoples face water shortage. For barely a century, and only for a small fraction of the World's population, tap water was safe for drinking. Now, it isn't so any more in many regions of the World. Buying bottles water for everyday use is an altogether new phenomenon in human civilization.

To make people in all countries more aware of the role and relevance of water for all of us, and educate us to conserve and refrain from polluting our water resources, a few years ago the United Nations General Assembly resolved that 22 March of every year will be observed as World Day for Water. The day was to be devoted "as appropriate in the national context, to concrete activities such as the promotion of public awareness through the publication and diffusion of documentaries and the organization of conferences, round tables, seminars and expositions related to the conservation and development of water resources and the implementation of the recommendations" of the U.N. In this context, the Director General of UNESCO reminded us: "The looming water crisis is one of the most critical challenges facing the World today. Global demand for this precious resource has increased more than six-fold over the past century compared with a threefold increase in World population. Without better management of water resources and related ecosystems, two-thirds of humanity will suffer from severe or moderate shortages by the year 2025." Injunctions for collective awareness and the common good are part of any religion. In our own times, the U.N. plays this role.

From the World of Science:
MUHAMMAD TARAGAY

The ancient city of Maracando in Central Asia which had been destroyed by Alexander in 329 B.C.E., was reborn as a great center of Arab civilization in the 8th century when it became Samarkand, named after a king of the Samanid dynasty. In 1221 it was plundered and subjugated by Jenghiz Khan. In 1369 it became the capital of the ruthless Mongol Timur (Tamerlane) who spread his brutal conquests far and wide, wreaking death and terror and destruction wherever he went.

Timur had a grandson by the name of Muhammad Taragay (born: 22 March 1394) who distinguished himself as a patron of the arts and the sciences. He established schools of learning and research. In 1420 he founded a *madrasah* devoted to astronomy. In the best sense of the word, a *madrasah* is an educational center, not the kind of mindless enclaves we see in some countries where young minds are fired up to fanaticism and hate for non-Muslims. The enlightened prince came to be called Ulugh Beg or Great Prince.

From the medieval manuscript records, scholars have been able to piece together some information about his work. Ulugh Beg built a three-storied astronomical observatory which was perhaps the largest and the most active in the whole World. Here were gathered numerous scholars, versed in mathematics and astronomy, all active in their commitment to the acquisition of knowledge. Work went on for some 17 years during which numerous careful observations were made, the precise positions of stars and planets were recorded, eclipse dates were predicted and confirmed, and a new star catalogue was prepared. Since the time of Ptolemy of Alexandria (2nd century C.E.) no catalogue of stars had been prepared until Ulugh Beg's. It included some 1020 stars.

Ulugh Beg's observatory was one of the best furnished of the time. It had a very large sextant, known as the Fakhri sextant, placed in a trench which had been dug up on a hill. The sextant had a radius of some 40 meters. With this, one could achieve very high resolution: about 600th part of a degree.

There one observed the maximum angular distance of stars from the horizon. By carefully noting the path of the sun, the obliquity of the ecliptic (i.e. the tilting of the earth's axis of rotation with respect to its orbital plane) was determined. The results differed from the actual value by only 32 seconds of arc. From observing the altitude of the Pole Star Ulugh Beg's observatory determined the latitude of Samarkand to be 30 degrees 30 minutes and 17 seconds.

From the extensive data gathered here, Ulugh Beg's *Zij* (astronomical table) was produced. It included calculations as well as a trigonometric table.

There used to be an atmosphere of free exchange and discussion among scholars. Ulugh Beg himself would participate in these, and he wanted to be treated as just another scholar, not as a king. In fact, he would reprimand those who sheepishly agreed with him on every matter, insisting that on scientific questions conclusions must be drawn only after a healthy debate and sharing of views.

Ulugh Beg was a Hafiz: he knew the Koran by heart. His desire to build an astronomical observatory was stirred when he visited the ruins of an observatory at Maragha, and learned about the work of Nasir al-Din al-Tusi who had worked there in the 13th century.

In 1447, Ulugh Beg ascended to the throne when his father died. In 1449, his son Abd al Latif had him killed. His tomb and the ruins of the observatory was excavated by archeologists in 1941. He had been buried fully clad, which in the Muslim tradition, is reserved only *for shakids* (martyrs).

March 23

From the World of Religion: TURIBIUS DAY

There was a youngster in Spain in the 16th century, who is said to have been unusually pious, ascetic even when at school, fasting and giving away his food to fellow students, and praying with uncommon frequency. His name was Turibius Alphonsus Mogrobejo (born in Majorca in 1536). He went beyond high school, and studied at the university, graduating with a degree in law from Salamanca. His unusual goodness was exemplary, and it even reached the ears of King Philip II who was then ruler of the realm.

The king appointed him to several high offices, made him a high-ranking judge of the Inquisition in Granada. But he was too gentle and pious to hold a secular position. At that time there was need for an archbishop in Peru where the Catholic Church, as elsewhere in Latin America, was converting an increasing number of the native population to the Catholic faith. Turibius had every. qualification for the position, as a committed Christian, but was not formally qualified in the Church. He was only a layman. They consecrated him without much ado, made him Archbishop of Peru in 1581.

He turned out to be very dedicated servant of the Church. The greed, selfishness, mutual rivalries of the adventuresome Spanish military men in the Peru and their cruel exploitation of the local people: all this was awful at the time. Aside from dissensions and mutual attacks, there was also much debauchery and godless behavior. At the same time the masses were in a sorry state. The sight of all this brought tears to Turibius, they say.

He determined to change the pathetic conditions that he saw in the new colony. He began work in right earnest. He appointed dependable and hardworking pastors in the dioceses, created new ones, enforced strict rules of conduct on one and all, spoke out strongly against unjust behavior towards the local people. At the same time, influenced the behavior of many of these transplanted 6migr6s more by his patience, simplicity, gentleness, and example, than by giving ecclesiastical injunctions: Ultimately that is how leaders work for the betterment of the led.

Turibius traveled widely in the new continent where the climate was very hot in some places, very cold in other, where the flora was thick and the fauna was wild. Often he would walk for miles on end, sometimes he rode on a mule, to visit hutments in remote places, preach to the local people, give them counsel and comfort and inspire them to Christian virtues. When a pestilence broke out, he fasted, shared in the pains of the afflicted, took part in prayerful processions, and wept with the suffering, is said to have brought a million new members into the Christian mold.

Turibius established the first seminary in the New World. News of his zeal for the cause of his religion reached Rome and Europe at large. It has been said that he worked in ways that became a model for behavior of the Christian priesthood and propagation: During one of his visits away from Lima, he breathed his last, bequeathing all his possessions to the poor. This happened on 23 March.

Such things have been said and written about this man who studied law and became a bishop, who grew up in Spain and died in Peru. He was credited with several miracles too. Turibius was canonized in 1726, and this date has become his Feast Day.

Whether everything we read about him (or any other saint of any religious tradition) really happened may be immaterial. What matters is that such biographies serve as inspirations for others, for in many ways they are meant to reflect whatever is good and glorious in the human spirit.

From the World of Science:
EMMY AMALIE NOETHER

This is a wonderful World we live in: with its variety and changes, with new things happening every day and an abundance of creativity all around. Yet, the World is also governed by immutable laws that don't change with time or place, for the laws that govern processes here today must have been here eons ago and must be there in the stars and in the farther-most galaxies too. Or, as physicists would put it, the laws of physics are invariant in space and time. When one probes into the fundamental features of the World with the microscope of mathematics, one uncovers quite a few other principles of invariance also. Invariance is intimately related to the symmetry aspects of the World. For example, if we move along a straight line in empty space, the World remains the same (translational symmetry). If we turn around in space from one direction to another, the World remains the same (rotational symmetry), etc.

Then too, processes in the World are constrained by rules of conservation. There is only so much matter-energy, so much momentum, so much electric charge, etc., and no matter what happens, the totality of these must remain the same. It is remarkable that much variety and complexity can arise under such meticulous constraints.

There are intrinsic connections between invariance, symmetry, and conservation. For instance, energy is conserved because the laws of physics don't change with time.

We now know that for every continuous symmetry there is a law of conservation, and vice versa. This is one of the most fundamental insights of 20th century physics. It was enunciated by Emmy Amalie Noether (born: 23 March 1882) in the year 1905.

We have all heard of Madame Curie who was an eminent experimental physicist/chemist. Emmy Noether was a prolific pure mathematician: much of her work is quite esoteric and little related to everyday experiences, which is why she is not as famous. When one writes a doctoral dissertation entitled *On Complete Systems of Invariants for Ternary Biquadratic Forms*, one cannot expect it to become a house-hold word. But among mathematicians she shines like a star of the first magnitude. In the appraisal of a mathematician-historian, "she was the most creative abstract algebraist in the World."

A hundred years ago (1900–1902) Noether was studying French and English because her goal was to become a teacher of these languages. In 1903 she began to audit courses in mathematics at the university. She could not register herself for a degree, because, after all, she was a woman. But then, some wisdom dawned somewhere, and she was allowed into a doctoral program which she completed in three years with the highest honors. From 1919 they let her teach in Goettingen at the insistence of the great mathematician David Hilbert, but only as a second class professor, and no remuneration!

But in the 1930s matters turned from the ridiculous to the ominous in Germany when the absurdity of not allowing a women to be professor was replaced by the outrage of not permitting Jews to hold any position. Like many others of her religious affiliation, Emmy Noether emigrated to the United States in 1933, and became affiliated with Bryn Mawr College in Pennsylvania. A good many future first rate mathematicians derived the benefit of her guidance and inspiration.

Fortunately we have come a long way from the ridiculous prejudices spelling out competence in mathematics or music on the basis of race or religion. But it was the likes of Emmie Noether who gave the lie to such mindless nonsense which fails to see that ultimately we are all human beings endowed with capacities and faculties that are independent of race, religion or gender.

March 24

From the World of Religion:
HILARIA AND MATRIS DEUM

In 2002, March 24 marked the beginning of the Holy Week (*hebdomada sancta*) in the Catholic tradition, since Easter came on the following next Sunday.

It is known as *Passionswoche* in German, because this is this is the week prior to the Crucifixion of Christ. That is why this day is also called Passion Sunday in English. In this context, the word *passion* is derived from the Latin (pati, passus) which refers to the pain and agony suffered by Christ after the Last Supper which is believed to have taken place on the Saturday before the Crucifixion. In fact, the suffering of all Christian martyrs is described as passion.

Unrelated perhaps to Passion Sunday, there used to be a Roman seasonal festival on 24 March which was a *hilaria*. The term was used for any day of observance. For example, one's own birthday would be one's *hilaria*. Sometimes *hilarias* were state-sponsored days of revelry. [Our word *hilarious* comes from this.]

The 24 March hilaria was dedicated to Cybele who, in the mythology was the mother of all gods. It was therefore called a celebration *Matris Deum* (of the mother of the god). On this day, as on other days of celebration, there used to be games and competitions, but also a procession in which an icon of the goddess was carried through the main streets, adorned and with many gifts from the rich.

The story of Cybele is interesting, whether or not there is an inner message in it: she was born as a hermophrodite, but transformed into a full-fledged female. Her severed masculine parts grew into an almond tree. A river nymph placed a blossom from the tree on her lap, as a result of which she conceived a boy: Thus was Attis born. Attis grew up, became a handsome young man, and fell in love with another nymph. This infuriated the jealous Cybele who thereupon cursed him to insanity. As a consequence Attis castrated himself and died. The *Hilaria Matris Deum* also commemorated the resurrection of Attis who was Cybele's son.

Religious observances are often based on mythologies and sacred histories. What must be noted that (certainly in olden times, and sometimes even in modern) they also involve some unpleasant features. One of these is the infliction of pain on oneself, often through self-flagellation in the name of some God. Thus on this day in ancient Rome, the militant priests of Mars (recall that Martius was the God of War) used to perform wild dances on the streets of the city, inflicting great wounds on themselves through self-flagellation, often in frenzy. The day itself was therefore called the Day of Blood.

The English word compassion literally means experiencing pain with. Thus there is an undercurrent of compassion in the act of self-flaggelation. In a sense we may regard this as the reverse of the notion of a Savior who takes upon himself the sin and potential suffering of others: In self-flegellation one imagines oneself to be taking the pain and suffering of someone whom one holds in reverence.

There are Hindu festivals like *Thai pusam* where one practices such self-torture. In the 11th century, Franciscan friars used to consider self-flagellation a commendable expression of religiosity. In Islam, self-flaggellation to lament for the martyrdom of Imam Husseyn was not uncommon on the day of Moharrum.

Fasting as a mode of self-sacrifice and giving of one's own comfort and pleasures for the benefit of others is one thing. But inflicting needless pain oneself when it does no good to a fellow human being may not be very sensible. We may be happy that in the course of our cultural evolution, most of us have moved away from such practices.

From the World of Science: ADOLF BUTENANDT

Since ancient times, people have wondered why some creatures are born as male and some as female. Furthermore, why are there some basic differences in body and function between the male and the female.

There have been all kinds of explanations for this at the speculative, religious, and mythological levels. Science too has traced the differences to many factors.

Early in the 20th century it was discovered there are chemical substances influencing the functioning of various organs in the body. In our own times it is part of general knowledge that the so-called sex hormones are responsible for the specific characteristics of males and females. The two types of sex hormones are estrogens and androgens. Both are present in all of us, but in disproportionate amounts, making some of us males and the other females. It is known that on an average adult men produce from six to eight milligrams of testosterone, which is an androgen, each day, and about half a milligram of estrogen also. The scientific World attaches normative meanings maleness and femaleness on the basis of hormones. Hormones have also come to play important roles in some physical disorders, and even in enhancing the sexual functions of people.

Testosterone and estrogen are among the many major scientific discoveries of the 20th century. The German chemist Adolf Butenandt (born: 24 March 1903) isolated estrone in 1929. Not all scientific research involves the investigation of pleasant matters: Butenandt's discovery resulted from a careful examination of a pregnant woman's urine. Small quantities of the substance, secreted by ovarian cells, are present in women's urine. Two years later, in 1931, Butenandt identified testosterone which is secreted by testicles. His work would not have been possible without the highly precise analytical techniques that had been developed by experimental chemists.

Before long, the chemical structures of these hormones were figured out which made their chemical synthesis possible by the Croatian chemist Leopold Ruzicka in 1934.

Scientific breakthroughs, especially when they are related to the human condition, have unexpected repercussions beyond their immediate relevance. Thus, the discovery of sex-hormones had a considerable impact on the popular mind. It led to a re-consideration of our traditional notions of sexuality. It also had effects on the psychological aspects of gender-identity. It even led to discussions on the eugenics movement which was a major theme at that time.

As it happened with advances in genetic engineering and the genome project, groups of biologists, medical people, and social scientists began to debate and explore the long range impacts of the discovery. In this context the Committee for the Research in Problems of Sex was formed. These cultural and historical consequences of the discovery of sex-hormones have been insightfully and interestingly analyzed by Julia Ellen Rechter in a 1997 doctoral dissertation for the University od California under the title *The Glands of Destiny*.

In 1939 Butenandt and Luzicka were selected for sharing the Nobel prize. One would think that countries are proud when one of their citizens is chosen for an international honor like this. However, the German government of the time did not give permission to Butenandt to go to Stockholm to receive the prize. [It must be recalled that this was at the dawn of the Second World War.] When ideologically poisoned governments are in power, and determine what is right and what is wrong for the people, the most atrocious and also the most ridiculous episodes can come to pass.

March 25

From the World of Religion: KUAN YIN

Every religion whose representation of the divine has multiple forms has goddesses as well as gods. In the Chinese Taoist-Buddhist tradition, there is a goddess by the name of Kuan Yin (Quan Yin), and she is celebrated every year sometime between late March and early April. We are told that her name means one who responds to the cries of the World. In Japan she is known as Kanzeon, and in Tibetan Buddhist tradition she is known as Avalokitesvara. Some have claimed that Kuan Yin was an incarnation of Mary as well as the goddess of Wisdom Sophia.

The personification of Mercy is more universal than in the lines of Robert Herrick:

Mercy the wise Athenians held to be
Not an affection, but a Deity.

For, this is equally true of the Buddhist tradition, and of the Christian tradition where, in the words of Shakespeare,

It (Mercy) droppeth as the gentle rain from heaven
Upon the place beneath
Because "it is an attribute of God himself."

The Koran uses the word *raheem* (mercy) as a quality of God numerous times.

Kuan Yin is said to be present in all of Nature in its gentler aspects. In the words of John Blofeld: "Rocks, willows, lotus pools or running water are often indications of her presence. In the chime of bronze or jade, the sigh of wind in the pines, the prattle and tinkle of streams, her voice is heard."

There are many ways in which her day is celebrated. In Taiwan there is a colorful procession in which participants jump and engage in mock battles with swords and shields and axes. They carry the gorgeously ornamented statue of the goddess in a dynamic way, swinging back and forth. The men who carry the deity are supposed to be under her spell, not unlike Kali Puja festivities in Bengal. Fire crackers create a din, and fireworks flash all around. The Sung Chiang militias are supposed to be protecting her today. They march into a pagoda. Watching this could bring to mind the celebration of Hilaria Matris Deum in ancient Rome. Indeed, when ancient traditions come alive in today's World, it is a resurrection of history.

All along the way there are eateries catering a variety of edibles—including such exotic items as bumble bee pupae and deep-fried crickets—which the onlookers enjoy as they watch and cheer.

There are legends associated with this goddess, miracles are attributed to her, and there is even a specific period on the Chinese calendar when she is said to have lived in the eleventh year of the Chin T'ien epoch (2590 B.C.E.). Kuan Yin is venerated for her infinite patience, gentleness, and mercy. In particular, she is said to protect women

John Blofeld has narrated movingly the legend of Kuan Yin in his book *Bodhisattva of Compassion: The Mystical Tradition of Kuan Yin.*

William Blake was very right when he said

Then every man, of every clime,
That prays in his distress,
Prays to the human form divine,
Love, Mercy, Pity, Peace.
Kuan Yin is such a human form of the Divine that shines in many hearts and minds.

From the World of Science: RAYMOND FIRTH

Usually when we hear the word science, physics, chemistry and biology come to mind. We think of laboratories, theories and explanations, of mathematics and calculations. But science is, above all, any systematic study of any aspect of the World of human experience, in an effort to understand and interpret it. In this sense, history too can be science. Ethnology and anthropology are also definitely sciences.

To be part of a culture, to participate in its customs and traditions can be personally enriching. But to carefully observe it, to try to understand and interpret it for others who are not familiar with its complexity is what the anthropologist often does.

When Europeans voyaged to distant lands and made far away places their own homes, by means sometimes legitimate and often illegitimate, some among them tried to empathize with the local population, and some also became serious students of the new cultures they encountered. These are the scholars who have brought within global reach the variety and richness of the human family.

Among such people was Raymond Firth (born: 25 March 1901). He was born in New Zealand, he studied at Auckland University as well as at the London School of Economics. He distinguished himself by his extensive work of the Maori people and of other cultures in the region. He studied their economic systems, cultural practices, social structure, and religious framework. He theorized on the origins of sacrifice as an institution, and connected it with economic forces.

Firth explored the practice of circumcision among the Maoris. Unlike custom in the Middle-East, circumcision is done to Maori boys, not when they are infants, but just when they are about to reach puberty. It is taken as a symbol of maturity. Indeed, an uncircumcised male was not regarded as fully grown man. The older procedure, using a sharp stone, may strike the modern as rather cruel, though mitigating measures, like singing soothing songs are part of the ritual.

Some indigenous thinkers have argued that the custom was imported. In any event, not all may agree that in our enthusiasm for preserving ancient cultures we should encourage or even ignore painful and inhuman customs (at least from our perspective). But the motivation for change should arise from the enlightened members of ancient cultures, rather than as impositions from alien ones.

His anthropological studies led Firth to a humanist interpretation of religion. He viewed religion as a mode of personal adjustment rather than as a societal activity. Though, like Marx, he stressed interconnections between religion and politics, he also saw much more in religion. He traced some of the sources in the World-view of Christianity to primitive World views. He analyzed the interplay between skepticism and faith in religious practice. Inevitably, as a scientific inquirer, he concluded that religion is essentially a human activity, its truths relate to the human condition rather than to divine transcendence.

During his long life Raymond Firth made numerous contributions to the World of anthropology, serving as the president of the Association of Social Anthropologists even at the age of one hundred. He was knighted for his many contributions.

It is thanks to the work of anthropologists like Sir Raymond Firth that we have all come to know a little more about the many cultures and races that constitute the human family. Their work also raises the question of whether and to what degree, others should transform, enlighten, or maintain cultures in their ancient states.

Raymond Firth was one of the new distinguished persons who lived through the full span of the 20th century. Thus, he was literally the Man of the Century.

March 26

From the World of Religion: JOSEPH CAMPBELL

There was a time when the people's attitudes to religion were formed mainly by what religious leaders proclaim in places of worship. In cultures where the majority is at a fairly unsophisticated stage in thinking about the questionable aspects of religions and mythologies, intellectuals play only a minor role in developing the sensitivities of people to religion. But as a population becomes literate and educated, minds are molded more by what one reads or hears from lay thinkers than from sermons and holy books.

In open societies, there are two kinds of religiously awakened thinkers: Those who have become well-informed, sensitive, and thoughtful within the framework of their own particular tradition; and those who are pan-religious. People like Vivekananda (Hindu), Gerald Schroeder (Judaic), and Cardinal Newman (Christian) belong to the first category. Huston Smith and Joseph Campbell belong to the second.

Joseph Campbell (born: 26 March 1904) was a reflective author who wrote and spoke profusely on the relevance and significance of myths. It is said that when, as a lad of eight, he saw Buffalo Bill's Wild West Show (portrayed in the musical *Annie Get Your Gun*), he was fascinated by American Indians. He read everything he could on Amerindian culture. At college he began as a biology student, but switched to English and comparative literature at Columbia University, studied medieval history at the Sorbonne and Sanskrit in Munich, and was drawn to Theosophy. He was associated with Sarah Lawrence College for almost four decades. He read voraciously on various mythologies and began to develop theories of his own on the subject. While editing Heinrich's Zimmer's works he came even closer to Hindu thought. Likewise he interacted with scholars from other traditions, and himself took trips to many holy places all over the World, equipped with both a refined sensitivity and profound scholarship. In 1949 his book *The Hero with a Thousand Faces* was published. Five years later the four volume work: *The Masks of God* appeared. After retirement at the age of 68, Campbell began to write even more: lecturing and publishing many volumes during the next fifteen years.

Many have argued that the essential ethical foundations of practically all the religions of humankind are the same. But Campbell reveals that which is common to the myths of the World.

He educated people on the importance of reading myths. In his writings, he urged people to read the myths of other cultures, for that is how one can get the deeper message. He reminded us that myths put us in touch with our deepest experiences. Indeed, when one participates in the rituals of a religion, one is transforming one's ordinary experience into a different plane of reality which belongs to the World of myths. Some psychologists have found his expositions of the meaning and relevance of myths to be helpful in therapy. He reflected more than half a century ago that "a transmutation of the whole social order is necessary, so that through every detail and act of secular life the vitalizing image of the universal god-man…may be somehow made known to consciousness."

Some may have watched his TV series called *The Power of Myth* which was aired in 1985–86. His idea of the Hero's Journey is said to have been one of the inspirations for the Star Wars movies.

Thanks to Joseph Campbell, the perception and appreciation of myths have been enhanced and enriched considerably for a great many people.

From the World of Science: PAUL ERDÖS

We have all heard of unusual geniuses in art and music, even in science sometimes. But there are extraordinary individuals in every creative field. It is not easy for everyone to understand, let alone appreciate, the work and value of their contributions to human thought and culture.

In the field of mathematics, for example, there have been quite a few exceptionally gifted people, and some of them lived rather unusual lives, bordering on the eccentric. As in music, some of the marvelous capacities of the human spirit are expressed through such geniuses.

Paul Erdös (born: 26 March 1913) was one of them. He born in Hungary and of Jewish parents, but he never felt strong affiliation to any region or religion, seeing himself only as a human being. He had no interest in politics or pettiness of any sort. He had equal contempt for communism and capitalism and their major spokes-nations of the 20th century. He derisively referred to the U.S. as Samland (Uncle Sam's country) and the Soviet Union as Joedom (the realm of Joseph Stalin).

His highly technical output is far too esoteric to be translated into everyday language. He received some of the highest awards and prizes conferred on the practitioners of the profession, like the Cole Prize and a letter of appreciation from the Fields Medal Committee. Because had passed the age of forty he was not eligible for the medal which he richl;y deserved otherwise.

Though some of these came with a hefty check, Erdös cared little for money. He gave it away of to poor students or as prize money. He himself lived a very sparse life. Like religious ascetics he never married.

But there is at least one major accomplishment of Erdös that must be intelligible to many people. All we need to know is that a prime number N is one which cannot be written as the product of different numbers (other than as $1 \times N$). Now consider the number 4 and its double 8. Between these two there are two primes 5 and 7. Or consider 15 and its double 30. Between them we have the primes 17, 19, 13, and 29. In the 19th century it was known conjectured (the Bertrand Postulate) that between any number x and its double 2x, there are is always at least one prime, as illustrated in above. In the 20th century some eminent mathematicians proved it, but the proof was complicated. At 19, Erdös gave an elegant proof for this result in number theory. He also proved (without invoking complex numbers) the so called *prime number theorem* which gives an estimate with an upper limit for the number of primes there are below a stipulated number.

Since he was interested in little else aside from mathematics, all of Erdös's intellectual energies were devoted to mathematics. His primary interest was in number theory. But he was also a major architect of what is called discrete mathematics which is of enormous import in computer science. He collaborated (wrote joint papers) with at least 462 mathematicians: more than anyone else had done. He authored more than 1500 papers during his lifetime. More were published posthumously.

Erdös had a pungent wit. As an atheist who had suffered under fascist regimes, he described God as a Supreme Fascist. He referred to children as epsilons (small entities in the mathematical jargon). He did not care for marriage, referring to women as bosses and to men as slaves in the context. He suggested the following for his epitaph: Végre nem butulok tovább (Finally I am becoming stupider no more).

Paul Hoffman's *The Man Who Loved Only Numbers* is an enjoyable biography of this genius. Epic poets, composers of magnificent music, great painters and mathematicians: They function in higher realms whence bring rich fruits and share them with the rest of us, if we are sophisticated enough to be able to relish them.

March 27

From the World of Religion:
DATE OF RESURRECTION?

It is not impossible to translate dates from one calendrical system into another. However, when an event has shaky historical validity, such transformations are really not very meaningful. But dates become very interesting in the matter of celebrating events of significance. That is why, even when one is fully aware that one is dealing only with sacred history, traditions are not shy of assigning dates to such events.

In the Christian tradition, for example, a great many serious scholars and historians don't take the Biblical accounts of the trial of Jesus literally. They have pointed out to ample inconsistencies in the accounts one reads in the Bible.

Others continue to ascribe dates and times to the trial, to the crucifixion and to the Resurrection. In this way, it is sometimes stated that the trial of Jesus occurred on March 27 of the year 31 or 33 C.E.

Five days before Passover, Jesus formally came into Jerusalem, and spoke out against the religious establishment. He declared that the Jewish Temple would fall. He even overturned the tables of the money-changers who gave silver coins. Some people were provoked, there was a disturbance, and Jesus was arrested in Gethsemane, and brought to Caiaphas, the high priest, and tried in the Sanhedrin: the supreme court of the Jewish nation in the presence of Pontius Pilate, the Roman governor of Judea. Jesus was also charged with subversion and opposing payment of taxes to Caesar, and claiming himself to be king. Some say that for Pilate, Jesus was just another Jew, arrested on the eve of a religious feast. So when he heard about a rebellion he acted swiftly. Jesus was sentenced to die.

We read in Psalm 69 how Jesus felt that day, for he said:
Save me, God, for the waters have reached my neck,
I have sunk into the mire of the deep, where there is no foothold.
I have gone down to the watery depths; the flood overwhelms me.
I am weary with crying out; my throat is parched.
My eyes have failed looking for my God.
More numerous than the hairs of my head
are those who hate me without cause
Too many for my strength are my treacherous enemies.

No outcome of a trial, in any land or at any time, has had greater and more far-reaching impact on history. From this distance in time, the charges against Jesus were minor: insulting the local religious establishment and refusing to pay taxes to an imperialist government. It is difficult to imagine how the story of civilization would have been written if Jesus had been let go that day with only a warning, and only a few who heard him had taken him seriously. Proclaiming himself as a Messiah was more serious. But again, many more have made similar claims, before and since, and not everyone has been crucified for it. In our own times, a number of such people even become rich with such announcements.

On the one hand, it matters very much if the reported incidents transpired or not, for that is at the very foundation Christianity. On the other hand, if one is a believer in the divinity of Christ and in the sanctity of the Bible, this cannot and should not matter. Faith transcends historical coherence, logical consistency, and empirical evidence. It is *endopotent*: its power transforms one internally. The divinity of Christ and his crucifixion are not matters for debate and proof, but rather experiential certitudes. Unshakable faith touches people in profound ways, for better or for worse.

From the World of Science: KARL PEARSON

This year the Hindu world celebrates March 28 as the festival of Holi. This very colorful festival is observed on the day after full moon in the month of Phalguni, and is related to the spring equinox. The mode of celebration of Holi varies from region to region, and the manner in which it is observed today is not quite the same as how it used to be in former times. At one time, the celebrations lasted for an entire week. But now there is only one Holi Day. Traditional activities during the festivities include the lighting of bonfires, the erecting of poles, the trans-planting of the castor tree, marching, singing, dancing and the like. In former times, as indeed now too in some parts of India, people used to throw dirt and dung at one another.

In the World of science, as in the World of scholarship, we sometimes encounter people who have an incredibly impressive range of interests and cre-ativity, polymaths who put to shame grumblers who complain they have to read two more authors for getting a degree. Karl Pearson (born: 27 March 1857) was one such versatile individual who studied mathematics in Cambridge under Cayley and Maxwell, attended lectures on biology in Berlin by Du Bois-Raymond, got a law degree at the age of 24, became taught mechanics before becoming a professor of eugenics at University College in London, read French, Italian, and German with ease, studied the history of religions, contributed to the curriculum for the teaching of Ancient and Middle German, wrote a literary piece entitled *The New Werther*, lectured on socialism, on Karl Marx, and on the suffragette movement in the UK. And did much more.

He published more than a hundred papers on statistics between 1893 and 1906. He coined the universally used term *standard deviation*. Though much of his work was to apply statistics in the context of studying heredity and evolution, his methods were used in epidemiology, anthropometry, social history, etc. His contributions to linear regression and correlation were path-breaking. He was one of the founders of the journal Biometrika which contains technical articles on sta-tistical theory and its applications. He also initiated a journal which became Annals of Human Genetics. The overall impact of his work was to transform sta-tistics as an important and separate mathematical discipline in its own right.

Pearson made some very insightful observations on "The Scope and Concepts of Modern Science." Known widely as *The Grammar of Science*, he spelled out in this book in emphatic terms the goal of science, and reminded us that this is only an ideal goal. As he put it: "The goal of science is clear—it is nothing short of the complete interpretation of the universe. But the goal is an ideal one. It marks the direction in which we move and strive, but never a stage we shall actually reach.

The universe grows ever larger as we learn to understand more of our own corner in it."

Pearson was among the scientific intellectuals of the close of the 19th century who believed that sound knowledge can protect us from the commission of ethical wrongs. He declared morality to be impossible for the ignorant. "Reason is the only lawgiver," he declared in *The Ethic of Freethought*, "by whom the intellectual forces of the nineteenth century can be ordered and disciplined." Of course he was thinking of the free thinker's ideal of morality. Recall that in the close of the 19th century, when the European military might, strengthened further with its scientific knowledge and technological know-how, was subjugating the rest of humankind in region after region of the World. It was natural for social scientists to apply Darwinism to account for this. They were convinced that 19th century Western scientific-technological civilization was the pinnacle of human endeavors. This framework gave rise to social biology and the eugenics movement. In this context, Pearson made the politically incorrect (by today's standards) statement to the effect that "the struggle of race with race, and the survival of the physically and mentally fitter race" is what gives rise to civilization.

Pearson received numerous honors and awards, such as the Fellowship of the Royal Society and the Darwin medal. But as a free-thinking socialist, he declined the Order of the British Empire (1920) and knighthood (1935) when these were offered to him by the British Government.

March 28

From the World of Religion: FESTIVAL OF HOLI

Every religious celebration has a mythology behind it. In the multi-mythic framework of the Hindu World, some festivals have varying regional interpretations. Some believe that it is to recall the triumph of prince Prahalada who was devoted to Lord Vishnu (the Supreme Being) that we celebrate Holi. Prahalada's father was a tyrant who thought so much of his greatness that he forbade the worship of even God almighty. The king had a sister by the name of Holika who could resist the heat of fire. She detested pious Prahalada, and took him into a blazing flame. But Prahalada emerged unharmed, and the evil aunt perished. Some say that Holi marks this event.

It is also said that the multihued mirth-making is 'meant to recall the jolly deeds of Lord Krishna in his boyhood days.' Others believe the festival celebrates the death of an evil giantess at the hands of colorful Krishna. When she was about to die, this monstrous mischief maker begged of the God that she be remembered at the close of a season. Krishna consented, and this is what Holi is all about. This is why the festival is celebrated with great joy in the cities of Vrindavan and Mathura where Lord Krishna is said to have lived and played.

According to yet another account, the shouts and howls generated during Holi are to bring back to memory the wailings of Rati, the mate of Kama—the Hindu Cupid—when the latter was burnt to ashes by Siva's third eye, and that the obscene expressions reflect mythic Siva's disgust for the female on that occasion.

The word Holika also refers to half-ripe corn, and the festivity probably originated as celebration of the fields in springtime. Indeed, the month of Phalguni is dedicated to the vernal season. The name Phalguna itself means, quality of fruit or fruit-maker.

Once in a while, people will have to let go. After all, civilization is the taming of instinctive behavior. It is important that our primordial desires be controlled, suppressed, re-directed or sublimated for societal safety. But by and large, such exuberance has been transformed these days. However, even now, in most places, it is impossible to step out into the streets without being drenched in waters of various colors and smeared with paints and powder that ordinary soap cannot erase with ease. There is hardly another festival in the World in which sheer color is splashed out in its wildest modes, on all and sundry, friend or stranger. This is also a day when one has license to suspend some of the usual inhibitions. Youths taunt and tease members of the opposite sex, with dances and gestures spiced with words and motions bordering on the erotic, not to say the obscene. Many smoke and drink substances which, on other occasions, would be considered taboo or even illegal. Revelry permits things that are not ordinarily allowed. It is also good to give them free play now and again.

Holi has parallels with the Roman celebrations of the advent of spring. Some have suggested that the festival probably began to take on certain aspects when conflicts arose between alien men and indigenous women.

That is what events like Saturnalia, Mardi Gras, and Holi try to do. So today, let's greet our Hindu friends with a Happy Holi Day!

From the World of Science:
THREE MILE ISLAND

Yesterday's hopes for something good can become today's happy reality. Thus in the 1950s we had hoped that the World's energy problems would be solved by the exploitation of nuclear energy. In December 1957 the first commercial nuclear power plant began to operate in Shippingsport, PA. by the 1970s we actually had more than 20 nuclear reactors functioning, and more were being built. But yesterday's dream can also turn into today's nightmare. There is no telling what the future holds: for an individual, for a community, for a nation, or for the whole World.

So it was that less than four decades after the successful generation of peaceful nuclear energy, after at least two decades of continuous electricity from nuclear reactors, suddenly on the morning of 28 March 1979, all hell seemed to be breaking loose at a nuclear reactor on Three Mile Island (TMI) in Pennsylvania, prompting puzzlement and panic to people all around. The State capital Harrisburg was barely ten miles away, and the nation's capital a hundred miles away. One considered evacuating more than half a million people from the vicinity, so ominous was the possibility of radioactive harm. It was surely the worst nuclear accident in the country. But it was not the worst that could have happened.

There was the fear of a melt-down: the nuclear fuel would seep out of the very protective casement of steel and cement. There could even have been the terrible explosion of a bubble of hydrogen at the core.

Later it was discovered that 90% of the core had been adversely affected, and that there was radioactive contamination of the containment building.

It took a whole decade to clean up the area, to collect the data, and to analyze what had happened, but still there does not seem to be any consensus on how bad the accident had been in terms of its lingering consequences. Remarkably there was no obvious radiation-related health problem on people in the area.

Though the accident was not terrible in terms of its consequences—the one in Bhopal in India a few years later was far more devastating—the potential disaster in a real blow up of a nuclear power plant is considerably greater. If we have not had any major or even minor mishap in the nuclear reactors, it speaks highly about the technological aspects of the safety precautions involved. More than a hundred nuclear power plants are still functioning in the U.S. alone, and more elsewhere in the World, providing clean electricity to millions of people. It may be recalled that in the course of more than four decades over three thousand highly radioactive spent fuel shipments have been carried out without any reported accident. This is not to say that human errors and (of late) intentional interference cannot bring about untold harm in the field of nuclear energy. Even with all that, the psychological and political impact of the TMI accident was so severe that many orders for new plants were cancelled, and only those that were in the books were completed.

Indeed, by the middle of the 20th century a new phenomenon was arising in the arena of scientific applications: A growing awareness of the negative sides of technological advances. Science was no longer regarded as an unadulterated source of boons and blessings for hungry humanity. Little by little it was becoming apparent that practically every material gift of science had some kind of a side effect or another: like the pills people pop into their mouths every day. The TMI accident was only one of many such scientific technology springing unpleasant surprises on us.

March 29

From the World of Religion: CRUCIFIXION

This is a day of mourning for Christians, for it marks a sorrowful event in their history: the Crucifixion of Christ. It was the darkest day for all who have been touched by him, inspired by his teachings, and transformed by his presence. It must have been heart wrenching for those who adored him, and particularly painful to Mother Mary.

Crucifixion was a barbaric Roman custom: the nailing of a human body that was first whipped mercilessly until the back was bleeding the flesh was out. This inhuman punishment was meted out to robbers and others convicted of crimes. In this instance, Roman soldiers are said to have derisively adorned the head of Jesus with a wreath of thorns. They inscribed in three languages, again in mockery, that Jesus of Nazareth was the king of the Jews. The torturing punishment was open to the public. They say the cross was raised at 9 in the morning, A Roman soldier, perceiving Jesus in thirst, is said to have held a sponge soaked with wine, brought it up close to Christ to moisten his parched mouth. There can be kindness and goodness even in the midst of harsh cruelty. According to Luke, Jesus said, "Father, unto thy hands I commend my spirit." By three in the afternoon that day, the mortal frame ceased functioning.

This was not just another instance of a custom by which the condemned were executed in those dark days. It was, rather, a milestone of great moment in the history of humanity. There was something deeply moving and meaningful in what transpired, for it was the climax of a life that exemplified sacrifice in the best connotation of the word. The figure of Christ on the cross with a crown of thorns, with his face turned to a side, his arms stretched out, the limbs nailed to the cross: this became the symbol for whatever is peaceful, gracious, caring, and all that is implicit in the teaching of one who came to be seen as the embodiment of qualities divine in flesh and blood.

When Christians say Jesus died for our sins, it means much more than the horrific drama of that day of lamentation. It means that in some mystical way, our many trespasses will be forgiven if and when we take refuge in a manifestation of the Divine.

I am not a Christian, but I have always felt that there is something profoundly serene in the sight of Christ on the cross: a reminder, perhaps, that even when many in the world are blessed with comfort and convenience, mirth and gaiety, there are also many in pain and suffering. The crucifixion of Christ reminds me that the little that many of us do as service or charity to the less fortunate is paltry nothing compared to the incredible torture that Christ in physical frame went through in his commitment to serve and save others: which means I should exert a little more.

The French call this day Vendredi Saint, and the Spanish Viernes Santo, meaning Holy Friday, and in German it is Kar-Freitag which has been interpreted as lamenting Friday. But in English it is Good Friday. Etymologists have had a tough time tracing the origin of the term. Some have suspected it is a modification of God's Friday, God becoming good as in Good-bye which (according to some) is a contraction of God be with ye! However, The OED refers to a 13th century document wherein one reads the Latin phrase: *die qui dicebatur bonus dies Veneris*: day which is called good Friday.

In any event, according to one official Catholic publication, "There is, perhaps, no office in the whole liturgy so peculiar, so interesting, so composite, so dramatic as the office and ceremonial of Good Friday." So on this holy day, to be followed by Easter, I convey my respectful thoughts for the day to all Christians.

From the World of Science:
EDWIN LAURENTINE DRAKE

If we are asked to name the factors that have had significant impact on modern civilization, we can come up with all sorts of things: electricity, communication, the air-plane, computers, and so on. But the list must include petroleum: oil from underground which has perhaps played a more dramatic role in changing the face of modern societies than anything else.

Unlike the other important factors, oil has also had a number of totally unexpected side-effects: It has become a major force in international politics, it has provoked wars, it has enormously enriched the economies of countries which have little else as resource. It has given rise to countless byproducts, such as lubricants, plastics, and other synthetic products which have come to play important roles in modern life. Its excessive use had caused pollutions of horrendous magnitude.

And when did it all start? Petroleum was not unknown to the ancients. Herodotus in the 5th century left descriptions of Babylonian oil pits. But in modern times, it all started in Pennsylvania. A man by the name of Edwin Laurentine Drake (born: 29 March 1819) drilled the first oil well in the World. It did not happen all of a sudden. There was a Seneca Oil Company which had been searching for oil. When Drake suggested that digging deep into the ground might be a way, no one took him seriously. But he persisted, and after 19 months of efforts, on 27 August 1859 the first underground oil gushed forth from 69 feet underground at Titusville, PA.

The oil thus extracted from the ground was used primarily for lighting and lubrication. Within a decade oil production shot up to 4 billion barrels a year. Within the next two decades this figure more than quadrupled. By the close of the 19th century, it reached 63 million barrels a year. By the close of the 20th century the World was consuming more than 3 billion tons of oil per year. By one estimate, in a hundred years we have used up half all the oil that had been there all these eons. By the most optimistic estimates, we have less than 400 billion tons of oil left to be taken out. At the current rate of increasing consumption, we will be lucky if we have oil left to be extracted fifty years from now.

What this implies is that by the time it is all over, oil-based civilization would barely have had a two hundred year history in all. There have been other ups and downs in human history, other entities have marked the features of periods: wind mill or horse buggy, cobble stone paths or type-writer. But never before has one been able to foresee the demise of a powerful factor such as the petroleum. We know for sure that, give or take a few decades, all this will have to come to a stop. Two centuries are but a glitch in the long stretch of human history, but the impact of this ephemeral factor would certainly linger for a very long time.

Many wonderful things have happened in the long history of our planet. One of these is that millions of years ago plants and organisms which lived in the waters several million years ago, were buried, then subjected to enormous pressure, and became what gushes out as petroleum today. Hundreds of billions of tons of oil have remained in the depths of the earth for millions of years until Drake and his people disturbed them with their drill.

Hitting oil is taken as a synonym for discovering a source of immense riches. Ironically, this did not apply to the first man who did this, for Edwin Drake is said to have died a rather poor man. He did not have the business acumen or the resources to mint millions from the fruit of his efforts. But he is remembered today through a museum with an attached library in Titusville, at the place where the first underground oil was found.

March 30

From the World of Religion: MAIMONEDES

In the Judaic tradition Maimonedes (born: 30 March 1135) towers above everyone else. His Hebrew name is Moses ben Maimun. He is often called the Second Moses: "From Moses to Moses there arose not one like Moses," is has been said.

Maimonedes was born in Córdoba at a time when its enlightened Arab rulers encouraged art, learning, philosophy, and science; and allowed Jews and Christians to live and work in peace. When the fanatical Almohades sect came to power, Christians and Jews were given the choice of conversion to Islam or death. The Maimon family moved to Fez. Here Maimonedes got to know Muslim scholars like Ibn Muisha. But when anti-Semiticism started here too, the family moved on to Cairo. Here Maimonedes became leader of the Jewish community. His family having suffered for their religion, he asked his co-religionists to pretend to accept a converter's faith if that would save them from persecution, torture and death. There is wisdom here, for it is in the heart that religion lives, not in public postures and confessions. When he lost his father, he studied medicine to earn a livelihood, and did so well that he became physician to King Saladin.

Maimonedes was a prolific writer. He is celebrated for his magnum opus: *Guide to the Perplexed*. Its original title was *Dalalat al-Ha'irîn*, for it was composed in

Arabic. In those glory days of Islam, Arabic was powerful and prolific in philosophy and science. It was not unusual for a Jewish scholar to write a major work in that rich language. This classic work was translated into modern European languages in the mid-19ᵗʰ century. Maimonedes' masterpiece was an early instance of the principle that at the hands of an able interpreter, any religion can be brought in consonance with the most recent or the most ancient science. Countless authors have emulated Maimonedes in this matter, or tried to, in every religious tradition. In his case, the concordance sought was between the philosophy of Aristotle (the science of the day) and the Talmud. In this, he was a great inspiration for the likes of Saint Thomas and Albertus Magnus. However, Maimonedes did not accept everything that Aristotle said. He rejected, for example, the idea that the universe had no beginning because it contradicts the Book of Genesis.

Maimonides wrote the *Mishneh Torah* which is a code of Jewish Law (like Manu's work did in the Hindu context). It contains simple ethical rules in accordance with the Torah which practicing Jews can follow without plowing through their scripture. He authored a credo for Judaism with 13 articles of faith. This is included now in prayer books used in synagogues. The first of these is belief in a perfect Creator who is the first cause of all that exists, and the last is belief in the resurrection of the dead.

But his rationalist modes, liberal theology, and non-literal did not sit well with Jewish orthodoxy. So he was attacked by fellow Jews. Some of them banned his works, others reported his blasphemous stances to the Christian Inquisition. This prompted Dominicans to burn the books of the master.

Such behavior persists in this so-called modern world of ours. It shocks the Enlightened sections of the world today, but it wasn't uncommon in Europe at one time, which is why we look upon book-burning, forced conversion, and intolerant theology as manifestations of a medieval mind-set.

Every tradition has its illustrious thinkers who were not universally honored during their lifetime, but who, in later centuries, gained such fame and prestige that they are touted as the greatest of the tradition. Maimonedes was one such.

From the World of Science:
MARY WHITON CALKINS

Mary Whiton Calkins (born: 30 March 1867) wrote a paper on Plato, entered Smith College as a sophmore at age 15, and graduated with a degree in the classics and in philosophy when she was 18. In 1890 she even taught Greek at

Wellesley College for a while. Then she decided to study psychology. She attended a course at Harvard Annex. Her professor, the eminent Josiah Royce, suggested she should attend Harvard where William James was lecturing. But this was impossible because, as Harvard president Charles Eliot explained, men and women could not possibly be in the same classes. When sufficient pressure was put on the president by high-ranking professors, he relented: Calkins was given permission attend seminars on campus, sitting in the same room as male students, but she could not register for any of the courses, let alone aspire to a Harvard degree. Rules may be bent, but not broken.

Even after she passed all the required exams, and formally presented a doctoral dissertation entitled, "An experimental research on the association of ideas," and five professors formally and unanimously voted to award her a degree in 1895, Harvard University wouldn't, indeed, couldn't give her a Ph.D. because she was a woman. In the matter of women's equality, Harvard in 1900 wasn't much different from Kabul in 2000. After Radcliff was established, they offered her a doctoral degree. But she declined it.

Calkins continued her work in psychology, and developed her theory of association of ideas further as an effective technique in memorization. She became a great educator, established the department of psychology at Wellesley, and in 1905, was elected the first woman president of the American Psychological Association. In 1909 Columbia University honored her with a D.Litt. and in the following year Smith bestowed upon her a Doctor of Laws degree. She was also elected the first woman president of the American Philosophical Association in 1918.

In the course of her long career Calkins wrote numerous scientific papers in professional journals, and four books, including *An Introduction to Psychology*, which was adopted as a text in many courses across the country.

That a bright and interested student wouldn't be allowed to attend classes at a university because of her gender strikes us as incomprehensible, not to say, outrageous today. This goes to show that, at least in some respects, our collective consciousness and conscience have been evolving ever so slowly. We are saddened to read about the struggles that women like Mary Calkins had to go through to gain fair recognition from a prestigious university, and we begin to wonder how many hundreds of women, perhaps less persistent but no less capable, have been snubbed and stifled in the long course of human history in various societies. At the same time, when we read about the pioneering persistence of women like Calkins, we are moved to heart-felt admiration for them. It is clear that even in this unfair and unjust World, it is very difficult, but not impossible to eventually succeed as long as there is commitment and tenacity of purpose. Those who only throw blame on the oppressive forces of society for every obstacle on their way may moan and cry and complain: but they are not likely to amount to much in the long run. The successful ones must plead the cause of the less advantaged in an unjust society, and also inspire the faint-hearted that it is necessary to dream the impossible dream, for then, through hard work and perseverance one can transform that dream into reality. It is good that we have role models like Mary Calkins for this. It is important to recall their stories to every new generation.

March 31

From the World of Religion: JEWISH PASSOVER

Religious traditions are sustained by sacred history: mix of fact and myth, with places still on the map, personages who probably lived, and events which couldn't have been. But the power of sacred history is such that the children of a tradition celebrate its memory with song and solemnity. Sometimes, they cause hate and slaughter too.

On this day of Easter when the Christian World celebrates the Resurrection of Christ, I will reflect on the Jewish Passover.

Millennia ago, in the days of the Pharaohs, the Israelites were held slaves by Ramses II. A Jewish shepherd beseeched the Egyptian ruler for his people's freedom, to no avail. It was then that God sent ten terrible plagues on the Egyptian people: blood, frogs and lice; flies, blight, and boils; hail, locusts, darkness, and death to the first-born. God also asked the Jewish people to mark their homes with lamb's blood so that when destruction came to the Egyptians, Jews could be passed-over and spared.

Finally, the Pharaoh in panic let the Jewish people go. As they fled through scorching desert their unbaked dough became *matzohs*: hard crackers. When they reached the Red Sea, the surging waves parted to enable the Israelites to cross over. And the Pharaoh's army which was pursuing them, was drowned by the closing walls of water.

All this is remembered during the week-long Passover period, starting with two nights of sumptuous dinners called Seders, served in rich and colourful utensils and dishes. At this time, the *Haggasah* (Book of the Exodus) is retold in Jewish homes. One eats *matzohs* and pungent horse-radish to remember the bitter days of the ancestors. They make a dish with nuts and chopped apples to be reminded of the hard bricks which the Jews were forced to work with for building the Pharaoh' palace. The ritual has salt water for the tears the people shed. And one sprinkles parsley as a symbol of new life. There are four glasses of wine which stand for freedom, deliverance, redemption, and release. Traditional rituals are living poetry replete with symbols.

Scholars have probed into the Exodus story. Here, as in other mythopoesy, there is not much that stands on factual bases. Traditional truths acquire an authenticity and a cultural sacredness which it would be inappropriate to question. Attempts to erase meaningful traditions that have survived for generations will be futile. Indeed, it is neither necessary nor wise to obliterate the collective consciousness of a people.

However, as one not of the Jewish tradition, rather than accept incidents of uncertain truth-content, and picture a punishing God who would inflict plague and pestilence on an entire population because of a heartless ruler, I interpret the Exodus story as the memory of a people who have been unduly, unfairly, and unfortunately persecuted over the ages in many regions of the World, but who, with their abiding faith in God, hard work, and perseverance, have not only survived the hardships, but have contributed immensely to art, music, science, and more. Is this not miracle enough in history?

Likewise, to me the Resurrection of Christ does not speak of the rising of the physical body of Christ after it had been cruelly crucified. Even if it had been so, it has little impact on me or on other non-Christians. However, the recall of the story brings to mind a profound insight: Great Truths and the Spirit of Goodness can never be stifled by brute force. In due course, they will rise again with even greater vigour, and they will never cease to touch the human heart. So my regards to both Jews and Christians today for the solemn symbolism in the Passover and in Resurrection.

From the World of Science: RENÉ DESCARTES

René Descartes (born: 31 March 1597) was one of the brightest stars in the 17th century scientific firmament: His method of representing a geometrical point through a pair of ordered numbers (coordinate geometry) was the starting point of modern mathematics, and his skepticism which doubted everything except his own conscious thought became the starting point of modern philosophy. He condensed the range and variety in the World by a pithy phrase: *matter in motion.* He wrote on optics, and explained the rainbows. He proclaimed there was no vacuum, but affirmed momentum conservation. He formulated the principle of inertia. He believed in the wave theory of light, and in a vortex theory for planets. He looked upon the universe and the human body as a giant machines.

Descartes' most important philosophical position related to the mind-body dichotomy. He said that mind was external to the physical body into which it entered through the pineal gland. For him, science is an effort by the observing mind (*res cogitans*) to comprehend an observed objective reality (*res extensa*). With only three words Descarted constructed the most famous phrase in Western philosophy: *cogito ergo sum*: I think, therefore I am.

For more than three centuries, working on this model, the positive sciences achieved success after success in their efforts to explore, explain, and exploit countless aspects of the physical World. By the close of the 19th century it seemed as if all our problems, material and moral, would be solved if only everyone followed the fruitful path of science. This unadulterated optimism had to be mollified before scientists became too cocky and contemptuous of other modes of human creativity.

Heisenberg's Uncertainty Principle in the 1920s has been interpreted as doing just that. It showed the interaction between measuring devices and measured entities in the microcosm. This imposes a limit on human knowledge, reveals the mind's role in our description of Reality, and affirms interconnections between subject and object: all these do damage to the dichotomy of Descartes.

The Heisenberg principle has been touted as a confession by scientists that they are not all that powerful. More seriously, one began to question the possibility of objective knowledge and external reality. Some philosophers pounced upon classical science's claims and methods to understand an external objective World, with a glee resembling that of a populace when an arrogant billionaire files for bankruptcy.

In all this clamor one tends to forget that thoughtful scientists whose hearts had been touched by the majesty of the starry heavens and the joy of love have always recognized that there is more to human experience than understanding gross matter and ordered laws, and that the Ultimate will always be a mystery.

Forgetting or re-interpreting the superstitions and abject fears of minds untouched by scientific awakening, some also began to belittle the Enlightenment, which had dared to consider possibilities of ethical behavior without expectation of Heaven or fear of Hell, and to initiate an examination of saints and sacred books in historical terms.

Scholars who disparage Descartes are like spacemen who look down upon earthlings because the new magnificent view is so much more thrilling than what appears from down below, but they forget they could never have reached their soaring heights and perspectives if the folks below hadn't done the needful.

Let us therefore remember Descartes *et al.* for launching us on the eye-opening and mind-freeing path of modern science from which still much more is yet to emerge.

April 1

From the World of Religion: APRIL FIRST

It is amazing how ancient and universal some customs can be.

Archaeologists have unearthed cuneiform tablets which show laughing figures with full moon beside them which have been interpreted as an ancient mode of observing the equivalent of a day when people made fun of one another.

In one of his *Monologues* Plato says that the people of Thales used to set aside a date for poking fun at one another. They called the day *Morosimera*. In the *Mityopanishad* of Sanskrit literature we read: *eka divas sakala varsha sarva loka pari haamana*: One day every year the whole world is a joke. The Latin poet Romulus Iocus wrote: *ridere secundum mensem sanus est*: To laugh in the second month (April) is healthy. According to Rabbi Ilan Nafta, in Hebrew Gematria (number mysticism) the letters the second month Iyar has the same number as the word for *teasing*. In the medieval Arab world, the philosopher Ibn Bei Ku'f declared that laughing at the folly of others is a sign of intelligence. In the 15th century, Saint Scurra is said to have noted that the angels in Heaven periodically laugh at the fools on earth. We read in the *Divino Tragedia*: *Danar si tolse e lasci-ollo di piano, e tutti divengono sciocci*: They took their gold and smoothly left them off, and they all became fools. The French poet Bois de Leaux wrote: *Nous sommes tous fous, un jour ou un autre*: We are all fools, one day or another. In a play by the Dutch writer Mathiaas Vendel we read: *Zelfs de verstandigen worden zot op een dag*: Even the wise become fools one day. Juan Picó said: *Cada uno es loco, un dia cada año*: One day each year everyone is fools. And who can forget the words of the jester in Shakespear's Richard III:

> In the stress and strain that flesh is heir to,
> Amidst the pain and pang that fleeing life doth impose,
> None that is spared,
> Neither lord nor serf, priest nor laity,
> Aye, not even the Rex of the Realm.
> Wherefore, with wisdom derived from keen council,
> The king of Merry England hath made
> This the first day of bright April
> When flowers bloom and birds coo,
> Yes, the gracious sovereign of us all,
> Hath declared this as the day
> When all and the brother of all

May, with words and acts and tricks,
Make mockery and conjure up events
To mislead, delude or fool friends and family,
and so treat even the wise of all the world,
If no harm be done or meant.

Schilling put it thus: *Heute mussen wir wachsam sein, nicht glauben was wir hören und lesen*: Today we must be watchful, not believe what we hear or read. And the Tamil philosopher says: *innikku yaaraiyum nambaathey*: Trust no one today.

Indeed, except for the last two lines, not one statement in all that I have written above is true.

Happy April Fool's Day!

From the World of Science: SOPHIE GERMAINE

She was way ahead of her times: In the closing decades of the 18th century this woman was daring enough to study mathematics. Her father dissuaded her from dabbling in numbers, kept her room dark and cold at night so she wouldn't be playing with factors and fractions, and resorted to other discouraging tactics, but to little avail.

She kept exploring the abstract realm of mathematics, taught herself differential equations, and even sent papers on the subject to such stars as Gauss, Legendre and Lagrange, and they were greatly impressed. Of course understood how scandalous it would be if the great thinkers knew it was a woman who was writing on technical mathematics, so she assumed the pen-name of Leblanc in her correspondence with the great.

She tackled some tough problems in number theory: including aspects of the famous Fermat's Last Theorem.

She was also bold enough to write to General Pernety of France during the Franco-German confrontation, asking for the safety of the great mathematician Gauss.

Her interest was not simply in pure mathematics. She was one of the first to explore the mathematical aspects of vibrating membranes. She was inspired to look into this topic by the experimental demonstrations of E. Chladni who put into evidence sand patterns on struck drum-heads. She in turn inspired Lagrange in his own formulation of the problem. In this context she defined the notion of mean curvature of a surface. She did work in the theory of elasticity.

She submitted her papers to the French Academy of Sciences anonymously, for one did not normally receive papers from members of the <weaker sex> in those days. Her name was Sophie Germaine (born: 1 April 1776).

The eminent mathematician Gauss was so taken by Ms Germaine's work that he stated in a letter: "But when a person of the sex which, according to our customs and prejudices, must encounter infinitely more difficulties than men to familiarize herself with these thorny researches, succeeds nevertheless in surmounting these obstacles and penetrating the most obscure parts of them, then without doubt she must have the noblest courage, quite extraordinary talents and a superior genius."

While playing with numbers she discovered that the following:

If we double the prime number 3 and add one (2x3 + 1) we get 7, which is also a prime.

But if we do this to the prime 13, we get 27 which is not a prime.

In other words, only some primes p have the property that $2p + 1$ is also a prime.

Primes numbers P with the property that $2p + 1$ is also a prime are called Sophie Germaine primes.

Some Sophie Germaine primes are even more interesting, like 191: This is a palindromic number (reads the same both ways), and 2x191 + 1 = 383 is also palindromic.

Another such palindromic Sophie Germaine pair is given by: 949393949 & 78987878987.

Mathematicians have detected 71 such pairs with 11 or less digits.

Like human beings, every number is unique in some way. Like human beings again, some display unusual characteristics. There is poetry and magic in the world of numbers. Some minds are able to read that poetry and elucidate that magic in ways that seem beyond the reach of ordinary mortals. Sophie Germaine had such a mind. A remarkable person she was, intelligent and gifted, but also bold and persevering. Her life and work brought credit to womanhood, but also revealed the capacity of the human spirit.

April 2

From the World of Religion:
THE LAST CRUSADE

The events in Palestine and Israel of the past few days have been heart-wrenching for all. Each side has its own legitimate reasons for wreaking havoc on the other. From the perspective of an uncommitted observer who looks upon Jews and Muslims as inheritors of great traditions, both claiming Abraham as a prophet, it is puzzling, and painful to see how religious difference and holy places, can give rise to such mutual hate and distrust.

Browsing through the history of the region, I came upon a statement to the effect that the seventh and last Crusade ended on 2 April 1291. This has little to do with the mindless madness and the ruthless response that tarnishes the region today. But it tells us that internecine religious clashes have a long history in the region.

From the time of Christ, up until the middle of the 7th century, the Holy Land had been visited by thousands of devout Christian pilgrims. Less than two decades after Prophet Mohammed's flight from Mecca, Jerusalem came under Muslim rule. After the Arab invaders established their control of the region, they were generous and tolerant, allowing Christians and Jews to practice their faiths in peace. In the year 800 the great Caliph Harun as-Rashid recognized Charlemagne as protector of Jerusalem. But in the first decade of the 11th century a fanatic by the name of Hakim became caliph, and he destroyed the Church of the Sepulchre. Towards the close of that century the Turks gained control, and they forbade Christians from coming to Jerusalem as pilgrims. It was in this setting that the Crusades began.

The story of these holy wars is replete with terrible tales of death and destruction, massacres of Muslims and of Jews and Christians, all in the name of religion. Peasants and knights, even children by the thousands, from France and Germany and England and other places were inspired to fight for a cause, to subdue the infidels, to regain the Holy Land. They all carried a cross to proclaim their commitment, which is what got these wars the name crusades, from the Latin *crux*, meaning cross. Countless people went through much pain and hardship, and inflicted much pain and hardship on others too. Many were imprisoned, sold as slaves, and won their freedom by paying heavy ransom.

The seventh crusade was launched by Louis IX of France. He is said to have taken fifteen thousand men with him, equipped with horses and other paraphernalia. His projected route was through Egypt, but he and his people had a terrible time. They were captured, taken prisoners, and quite a few were summarily executed.

In the end, after nearly two centuries of periodic attempts to regain Jerusalem, the Christian nations failed miserably. Aside from the fact that they had to go long ways to rescue the region, corruption, selfishness, mutual rivalries, greed, and other self-serving elements have been attributed as causes of the dismal failure of European nations. But, the experience brought many Europeans in contact with people of another religion, who were highly cultured, sophisticated, decent, and strong also, and from who, in fact, they learned a thing or two: of science and technology. It is difficult to see how five centuries later, the tables turned again, initiating European dominance. And now it seems as though one is at the dusk of a civilization that has seen its brightest days of glory.

One would hope that the future would be a pluralistic world, where all nations great and small, of all races and religions, will work together as fellow creatures on a planet, as friends rather than as foes, as comrades rather than in confrontation. But we may have to wait for a long time for that to become a reality.

From the World of Science:
FRANCESCO MARIA GRIMALDI

The nature of light has been speculated upon, argued about, and investigated into since very ancient times.

In the course of the 17th century, three of its principal properties were well established: That a ray of light travels in a straight line, that its is reflected from polished surfaces and refracted (slightly deviated in its path) as it passes from one transparent medium into another. As to its ultimate nature, this was still being investigated. One possibility was that light consisted of minute material corpuscles which, like a stream of bullets, shot forth in straight paths from a luminous source. In terms of this picture, one could explain well the property of reflection, for example, for it is not unlike balls bouncing back from a floor when thrown at an angle. The rectilinear (straight-line) path of light is also obvious when we hold an obstacle along the path of light: the source is hidden.

Now in the 17th century there was a man in Bologna, descended from a wealthy family, but devoted not to the silk trade of his father, but to pursuits more spiritual and intellectual. His name was Francesco Maria Grimaldi (born: 2 April 1618). He studied philosophy, astronomy, and mathematics, became a Jesuit, taught at the College of Santa Lucia, and made a discovery of capital importance in the field of optics: When a ray of light is made to pass through a narrow aperture made in the wall of a darkened room, and made to fall on the opposite wall, we see, not a single straight bright line, but a somewhat fuzzy patch. What this suggests is that the light ray did not go through like a tiny bullet, but rather spread out in some way. This implies that light is not made up of corpuscles after all, but perhaps has an undular nature, such as Da Vinci had suspected. This notion was further elaborated by Christiaan Huygens.

Grimaldi had discovered the phenomenon of *diffraction* by which light, like sound, can bend around obstacles. For this to be observable, however, the dimensions of the obstacle must be of the order of the wavelength of light. That is why the diffraction of light around a thick pole cannot be observed, but around a hair it can.

Grimaldi wrote a treatise expounding the nature of light. Generally known by the first few words, *Physico-mathesis de lumine,* the full title of the book is impressively long: *"A physicomathematical thesis on light, the rainbow and other related topics in two books, the first of which adduces new experiments and reasons deduced from them in favour of the substantiality of light. In the second, however, the arguments adduced in the first book are refuted and the Peripatetic teaching of the accidentality of light is upheld as probable."* Substantiality refers here to the corpuscular theory of light, and accidentality means some passing property of a substance, such as a wave in a medium.

Grimaldi also did some experiments to confirm Galileo's findings on free-fall. Like in the story of Galileo and the famous Leaning Tower of Pisa, he went to the top of the Asineli Tower and dropped different weights and studied their time of fall. Like Galileo again, he also studied the heavens with the aid of a telescope. He was one of the first to develop methods for measuring the heights of mountains on the moon, and also the heights of clouds.

Grimaldi was among the many Jesuits (and other religiously inclined thinkers) who have made significant contributions to science. Their lives and work show that, contrary to the contention of anti-religion scientists, one's theological convictions need not be a hindrance in the pursuit of physics or of any other science for that matter. Indeed, for many of them science is the unveiling of the glories of God's creation.

April 3

From the World of Religion: GEORGE HERBERT

Poets have played important roles in the growth and experience of religion. When hymns are sung and scriptures read, when epics are told and prayers recited, the words of poets come to life in the lips and hearts of the devout. But one rarely pauses to think about the authors of the words that breathe life in places of worship.

Some compose verses on themes divine. George Herbert (born: 3 April 1893) was one such. His poem "*Come, My Way, My Truth, My Life*" was set to music by Vaughn Williams. Herbert is remembered in the history of English literature more than in the context of religion. He studied at Cambridge and became a fellow at Trinity. He was elected to Parliament. At 33 he became a rector in the Anglican Church, at a place called Bemerton. Here he preached and tended to the parish people, wrote a manual for parsons, and composed many poems. He came to be called Holy Mr. Herbert.

It was Herbert's deep belief that a poet's responsibility was to adorn places of worship with poems on religious themes. This, he felt, would be an appropriate way to be thankful for the poetic gift. Herbert also loved music, himself sang his hymns and played on the lute, but it was words and rhymes that fascinated him. He played with words, sometimes to the point of punning even while being serious. For example, in a poem where he describes how God bestowed all gifts on Man except Rest, see how he puns on rest, though the poem doesn't rest on the pun:

When almost all was out, God made a stay,
Perceiving that alone of all his treasure,
Rest in the bottom lay.
"For if I should," said he,
"Bestow this jewel also on my creature,
He would adore my gifts instead of me,
And rest in Nature, not the God of Nature:
So both should losers be.
"Yet let him keep the rest,
But keep them with repining restlessness;
Let him be rich and weary, that at least,
If goodness lead him not, yet weariness
May toss him to my breast."

In a poem entitled *Virtue*, he noted that whereas all the beautiful things of the world perish sooner or later, virtue stays on for ever. In *The Quip* he recounts how the charms of the World, Beauty, Money, Glory, and Wit never attracted him. As to why this was so, he says: "But thou shalt answer, Lord, for me." He also published a collection of more than a thousand proverbs from various countries. In *Elixir*, he uses the language of alchemy in describing Christ as the (philosopher's) stone, "that turneth all to gold."

The lines in this poem:
In all things Thee to see,
And in what I do in anything,
To do it as for Thee
sounds almost like a translation of a verse in the *Bhagavad Gita*.

Poetry can draw us to piety and spirituality as effectively as good sermons and scriptures. One doesn't have to be a Christian to experience Herbert's poems.

From the World of Science: KATHETINE ESAU

Not many in the English-speaking world may know where Yekaterinoslav used to be, because its current name is Dnepropetrovsk. Even this may not be familiar to many. It is in Ukraine. I mention it here because that is where Kathetine Esau was born (3 April 1898). She studied German and Russian, did some college work in Moscow, and later on English. After the Bolshevik Revolution her family escaped to Germany.

She continued her studies in Agricultural Science, got the equivalent of a Master's degree, and when she was 24 her family migrated to the Unite States. They were among the thousands who used to land on Ellis Island, rejoice in the land of opportunities, and became truly thankful and loyal to the country that accepted them with open arms and offered them opportunities for self-fulfillment. Their goal was not just to make enough dollars and return to where they came from for their retirement years.

Here the family settled down in California where she used her knowledge of agriculture, especially in sugar beet farms and in a sugar company, until she got an opportunity to register for a doctoral degree program at UC Berkeley. She began to do research on the pathological anatomy of plants, examining the changes that occur in plants inflicted with diseases.

Some theoretical physicists think that their subject is the truly esoteric one and that a field like botany is no more than sophisticated gardening. The following paragraph from one of Esau's papers, entitled, "Ontogeny and Structure of Collenchyma and of Vascular Tissues in Celery Petioles," in a journal of agricultural science may make them reconsider that perception: "...celery petioles have crescent shapes in transverse sections, with prominent ribs on the abaxial side. A large collenchyma strand, is present in each rib under the epidermis...Two collenchyma strands occur on the adaxial side, but here two to three subepidermal layers of cells are collenchymatously thickened." All this is meant to explain why celery is crunchy.

Aside from teaching a variety of courses like Systematic Botany, Morphology of Crop Plants, and Microtechnique, Esau authored a classic in the science of Botany, entitled *Plant Anatomy* which had a great impact on the teaching and study of the subject. In the words of Ray Evert, "She took a dynamic, developmental approach designed to enhance one's understanding of plant structure. The book *Plant Anatomy* brought to life what previously had seemed to me to be a rather dull subject." Another book, entitled *The Anatomy of Seed Plants* has been described by Bill Lucas as "the Webster's of plant biology: it's encyclopedic." He also called her book *The Phloem* the bible on that subject.

Esau is said to have been a very dignified person, but not without a sense of humor. She once gave a lecture entitled, *The Saga of Vladimir-the-Virus and the Sad Fate of Norman-the-Nucleus.*

Esau was well recognized for her work. She received a Guggenheim fellowship, was elected to the National Academy of Science, and was awarded the National Medal of Science by President Bush in 1989.

She funded a Fellowship Program for junior faculty and post-doctoral fellows.

Scientists have impact on Science in various ways: through their discoveries, through their insights, through the inspiration they give to their students, through the knowledge they spread through writings, and so on. Katherine Esau was successful in all respects, and it is good to remember her on this day, especially at a time we don't hear too much about famous botanists.

April 4

From the World of Religion: DOROTHEA DIX

One of the unfortunate aspects of many traditional religious systems is related to their interpretation of ailments and diseases. Practically every major religion has maintained, at one time or another, that evil spirits, the devil, Satan, and the like are responsible for cough and cold, sneeze and stammer. And when it came to mental aberrations, the evil beings had literally entered the body of the insane: taken possession of it, as they used to say. It seemed natural to the upholders of such views that one should drive out the devil through spells and charms. There are, in the ancient lore of most traditions, powerful and harsh incantations for exorcising. Much of the romantic longing for the good-old days melt away when one examines the crass conditions under which the poor and the helpless lived, and the fears and superstitions that clouded many minds in those imagined times.

All this might seem pathetic at worst and amusing at best, from better-informed perspectives. But no, it was too terrible for that. Except for the pillage and plunder of innocent civilians by ruthless imperialists like Attila the Hun and Mohammed Gazni, the recall of the way the ancients treated the insane are among the more painful readings in history. The insane were chained, flogged, imprisoned, jeered, kicked, and spat upon.

In 1841 Dorothea Dix (born 4 April 1802) volunteered to teach women inmates in the East Cambridge (MA) jail. She was shocked to see the conditions there. The jail consisted of one big stinking hall wherein were confined die-hard criminals, prostitutes, drunks and the mentally ill. Rather than just feel sorry for their plight, Dorothea took it upon herself to bring about changes in this barbarity. She went to the courts, visited other prisons, collected gory details on how things were done, and presented a paper to the legislative body of the state. Then she moved on to Washington and managed to secure five million acres from the Federal Government to build hospitals for the mentally ill. Thanks to her efforts, 32 mental hospitals, a school for the blind, and other similar institutions came to be. Libraries in prisons are also due to Dorothea's campaigns.

As if all this wasn't enough Dorothea Dix crossed the Atlantic, traveled though a dozen countries in Europe, and instigated changes in the treatment of the insane there also.

When the American Civil War broke out, she served as the Union's Superintendent of Female Nurses, recruited and trained nurses, and thus continued her social service.

She worked relentlessly for many decades to humanize the treatment of the insane and civilize the living conditions of prisoners.

Perhaps it is worth recalling that Dorothea Dix had a difficult childhood. Her parents were constantly fighting, her father was addicted to alcohol, she was sent away to live with a grandmother who wasn't very sympathetic to her, then sent to another aunt, and so on. But she endured it all, and made her life worth living not just for herself, but for a great many others as well. At a time when young women could not go to public schools, Dorothea started her own *little dame school* in which she gave private lessons to girls.

This too needs to be told to young people because those who succeed when subjected to hardships, prejudices, or meager resources serve as effective role models for a great many people even in our times.

Dorothea Dix is among the well-kept secret successes. Scholars W. Viney and S. Zorich have pointed out that she hasn't received the recognition she deserves. It is important for us to remember the likes of her: who not only serve humanity in noble and selfless ways, but also inspire others to do likewise. When we ignore the likes of her, we are the losers.

From the World of Science: JOHN HUGHLINGS

Epilepsy is an ancient ailment. The Greeks named it after Hercules because he was believed to have been a victim of it. We know that Julius Caesar had it. The Romans called it by various names, such as *morbus caducus* (falling illness) and *morbus sacer* (sacred illness). In medieval Europe, as in many other pre-modern cultures, the disease was attributed to satanic influences. Attempted remedies included incantations and amulets. There was a belief in England for many centuries that it could be cured by the mere touch of the royal hand. For this reason it used to be known as king's evil. Even Henry VIII is said to have cured people of epilepsy by merely placing his kingly hands on the patients.

These are more than historical tidbits. We need to be reminded of them again and again to erase rosy misconceptions that many moderns have about the ancient past. At the same time, it is good to remember that there were also thinkers in the past who gave more physical interpretations to diseases, but they were in a minority in all cultures. They were either ignored or regarded as antireligious.

John Hughlings Jackson (born: 4 April 1835) was among the modern scientific investigators who helped us understand the true nature of the condition. He came to be regarded "as the greatest scientific clinician of the nineteenth century" in England. He was one of the first to trace the origins of epilepsy to malfunctions in specific parts of the brain.

After finishing his training in a London hospital Jackson served as a resident medical officer in a dispensary in York. Later he became a lecturer at a medical school. Jackson was, above all, a very keen observer, a careful thinker, and a thorough student of current work in the field. He recognized and understood the value of the microscope, but he himself seldom used it. However, he made extensive use of the recently invented ophthalmoscope, and saw significant relationships between diseases of the eye and ailments that affect the brain. He is said to have gained all his knowledge and experience from working in hospitals, and never to have done a formal scientific experiment.

Jacskon's wife died of what has been called septic cerebral emboli. She was barely forty years old then. Jackson devoted many years to the study of epileptic seizures.

Though by the 19th century, modern medical theories had overthrown the ancient views which connected seizures with demonic possession, the belief was that the source of the convulsions was located in the medulla oblongata. Jackson was one of the first to locate it at the cerebral cortex. He insisted that the seizures were a symptom rather than a disease, and proposed the theory that epilepsy resulted from discharges in the brain which started from a point and radiated outward. This idea was related to the notion of the brain as consisting of different parts, each of which controlled a different section of the body. Jackson gave detailed accounts of various stages of epilepsy. His description of epilepsy as "comprising occasional, excessive rapid and local discharges of gray matter" is still regarded as accurate.

Jackson contributed immensely to the organization and development of the fields of neurology and neurophysiology which were scattered, chaotic and unsystematic when he entered the field. His biographer describes him as a very decent person, but quite reserved. Those who knew him liked him as a person. He read a lot, but was not too fond of the arts or music. It has also been pointed out that, despite his significant contributions, he did not receive the high honors that many customarily do.

April 5

From the World of Religion: THOMAS HOBBES

We consider matters from very different perspectives than those who lived in the Middle Ages. Indeed, we can see this even in the current world, those who have not been exposed to the modern framework, function in ways that's hard for us to understand.

Shifts in the basic elements of world-views occur slowly and subtly, but they do occur. The notion of an earth-centered universe is gone for good. And the idea of looking upon society and ethics as human creations rather than as eternal elements in the world from the moment the earth and Man were created is not taken seriously by those who have had the benefit of basic science and data-based history.

One of the people who contributed to the paradigm shift was Thomas Hobbes (born: 5 April 1588). He was scholar and philosopher, imbued in the emerging science of the 17th century. He interacted with Galileo and Gassendi, with Bacon and Mersenne. He did not make contributions to physics or mathematics, but he was one of the first to recognize that science was more a mode of thinking than specific results. He understood that by analyzing situations logically, observationally, and reflectively, one can gain a better understanding, not only of the world of natural phenomena, but of human societies and systems like ethics and politics.

Hobbes worshipped reason and rationality. He was convinced that if only people thought out clearly, this would be a better world. So many wrong ideas are inculcated in the young: prejudices, sectarian religions, meaningless metaphysics, etc. He affirmed that ultimately all knowledge is derived through perception, through our sensory faculties. Even imagination and memory are connected to these. The world was, for him, essentially matter in motion (as Descartes was saying).

His most famous book was *The Leviathan*: a four-part classic which analyzes Man, the Commonwealth (State), a Christian Commonwealth, and the Kingdom of Darkness.

Hobbes was one of the first in the modern world to theorize on how organized societies might have come about. He suggested that human beings are basically self-centered, aggressive, and power-hungry. Left to themselves they'd probably kill one another out of greed and their innate tendency to grab what others have. Since this would spell the ruin of all, societies were created and people agreed to become subservient to a sovereign (constraint by law) in exchange for collective peace and security.

Long before Sigmund Freud, Hobbes traced all human actions and attitudes to what he called passion: feelings and emotions, real or imagined, like love and enjoyment, hate and pain. Everything may be traced to self-love which is related to the instinct of self-preservation. Long before Richard Dawkins, Hobbes explained even superficially commendable qualities or virtues in terms of egotistical motives. Pity for a suffering person springs from a deep fear that one might face a similar situation some day. When one is charitable one is deriving satisfaction through the exercise of one's power. In his view, all mankind was subject to "perpetual and restless desire of power after power, that ceaseth only in death." He described religion as "Fear of power invisible, feigned by the mind, or imagined from tales publicly allowed." Yet, he saw its relevance to societies.

Clearly, Hobbes was a materialist thinker who created a stir. His ideas slowly spread, and little by little, even Church-going Christians began to look upon rites and rituals in poetic rather than in devotional terms. People rarely proclaim themselves as materialist, but more often than not they conduct themselves and consider their myriad gadgets only thus.

From the World of Science:
HATTIE ELIZABETH ALEXANDER

Meningitis is among the deadly diseases that have killed countless human beings since time immemorial. The membranes of the brain or of the spinal cord are affected. One variation of the illness is influenzal meningitis. Children are often victims of this. When the 20th century began, there was neither understanding nor cure for meningitis.

One generally remembers 1939 as the year when madness in Europe initiated one of the worst wars in history. But it was also the year the first cure of infant victims of Meningitis was reported. The work of many people contributed to this. But, again as in the conquests of science, in each instance, some names stand out.

In this context we must recall Hattie Elizabeth Alexander (born: 5 April 1901). She was a 1923 graduate of Goucher College in Maryland, where she studied bacteriology. Soon after this she secured a position as health bacteriologist. Then she went on to get an M.D. from Johns Hopkins School of Medicine, and became Dr. Alexander.

She specialized in pediatric medicine, which had become a separate field with that name only in the last decades of the 19th century. She began to teach at an institution called Babies Hospital in New York. Here she also began doing research. She was affiliated with the Rockefeller Institute where one had already prepared an anti-pneumonia serum. Alexander became very interested in influenzal meningitis. She developed an antiserum for the microorganism that causes influenzal meningitis. Moreover, her work revealed the link between this and croup in which larynx and trachea are inflamed.

The serum became obsolete with the discovery of the wonder-drugs. Hittie Alexander used these antibiotics in the treatment of influenzal meningitis. In spite of significant successes, there were also many instances where the drugs did not work. Alexander did further work on this, and this led to the discovery that some bacteria develope resistance to the drugs. Further work was needed before she could combat these streptomycin-resistant bacteria. After all, in many instances, medicine is a warfare between humans and microbial terrorists in that medical researchers are trying to protect us from persistent pathogenic organisms which come and take the lives of innocent human beings when one least expects them. And when we develop techniques for destroying them, these organisms also devise ways of protecting themselves and continuing with their destructive assaults.

Probing into how the bacilli became resistant to antibiotics, she found that this resulted from genetic mutation. These investigations drew her to the emerging field of microbiological genetics.

Hittie Alexander was a very demanding professor, and would not brook slipshod work from her students. At the same time she is said to have been caring and compassionate, often pleading the cause of weaker students at times of granting degrees.

During her long and productive career, she was associated with the Columbia-Presbyterian Medical Center. Even after formal retirement she used to give lectures on pediatrics in that institution. She published scores of scientific papers in her field. She was recognized in many ways. Dr. Alexander was the first woman to be elected president of the American Pediatric Society.

While the world is often concerned with economic problems and engulfed in political turmoil there are also countless people engaged in research to better the human condition in various ways. Hittie Alexander was one such.

April 6

From the World of Religion: THAI FESTIVAL

Consider some of the epithets for God in traditional religions: magnanimous, glorious, majestic, powerful, merciful, caring. These were/are also the attributes of kings in traditional societies. So it is not surprising that God Himself (?) is often described as a King: Christ is called the new-born king in some carols. Kings have been regarded as deriving their power and authority from God. The pharaohs of ancient Egypt, the first kings of ancient China and Japan, Lord Rama in the Hindu tradition: all were divine. The Rex of ancient Rome had divinity too, or at least he was also a priest. In Christian tradition, investing a king with divine sanction began in Byzantium. Christian kings used to be formally anointed by the head of the Church, thereby investing sanctity to the crown.

After England severed connections with the Roman Catholic Church, arose the theory of the divine right of kings, whereby the kings claimed their right directly from God, rather than through the agency of the Pope. Even a rationalist thinker as Thomas Hobbes expounded and defended this principle. Arab potentates traced their lineage to Prophet Mohammed, thereby assuming intrinsic authority. That is why the birthdays of kings (also of queens) have been observed as a grand festival in many countries.

But in nations which have no monarchy, national days are celebrated as Bastille Day, Republic Day, Independence Day, etc.

Then there is a third mode. Even where a king still reigns over the land, one may celebrate the day when the nation was founded. So it is that in the kingdom of Thailand, however, they celebrate the founding date of the ruling Chakri dynasty, rather than the birthday of a particular king, as a holy day. This happens to be on 6 April. This is the equivalent of 4 July in the United States,14 July in France, or 15 August in India.

On this day, there is an elaborate religious ceremony at the Royal Pantheon, presided over by the king. Its main purpose is to pay homage to the Thai kings of past generations. The present king, Bhumibol the Great, government officials and common citizens, formally places a wreath at the statue of King Rama I, the 18th century founder of the dynasty who became the first king of modern Thailand on 6 April 1782. [Rama I was the assumed name of the valiant military leader Phra Buddha Yodfa Chulaloke who unified the country, defended it from the ruthless onslaughts of Burmese imperialism, and founded its present capital of Bangkok.]

If God is the symbol or personifications of the transcendental, then King (of government) becomes the focus of the temporal. If God is to be celebrated, so is the emblem of Government. And periodic celebrations are necessary not only because they add color and zest to the experience of life, but also because such traditions give meaning and cohesion to a people. Even nations that are founded upon explicitly atheistic doctrines need days to rejoice in: be it the birthday of a Lenin or a Mao. Other names, which used to be touted in the past have been pushed into the footnotes of history. Who is there to proclaim Caesar or Ramses any more?

But the mode of celebration is not gone, nor ever will it be gone. We are one thing as individuals, but as community or nation, we become a different kind of entity: a collective consciousness that feels in unison, one that also needs a common memory and some common experiences which transcends our individual needs and allegiances. That is why such days become important. Whether we are part of another group or not we may respect and recognize their collective expressions. Happy Chakri Day, my Thai friends!

From the World of SCIENCE:
PHILIP HENRY GOSSE

Many of us have been to aquariums where we have been amazed by the incredible variety of aquatic life forms. We have learned much from the explanations and pamphlets on such visits,. Aquariums house thousands of creatures: fish, crustaceans, amphibians, even some mammals. A reflective look at the multicolored marvels in an aquarium reminds us of our primordial ancestors, for if there be any truth to the current scientific picture, all life started in the oceans.

Since long ago, people have been struck by the beauty and richness of water creatures. They have built pools and ponds to cultivate, observe, and appreciate them. We see fish in Egyptian frescoes and also in ancient flags of ancient kings. But it was only in the second half of the 19th century that modern aquariums began to be constructed.

One of the pioneers in this endeavor was Philip Henry Gosse (born: 6 April 1810). It was Gosse's dedication that led to the opening of the first modern aquarium at the London zoo on 17 December 1853. The Smithsonian's National Museum of Natural History came about a couple of years later.

Gosse was an English naturalist who worked for a while at a whaler's office in Newfoundland, taught in Alabama, and collected natural history specimens from Jamaica. He was a naturalist at heart, with particular fascination for marine life. He had the keen eye of an observational scientist, and a deep appreciation for marine life forms. Stephen Jay Gould described Gosse as "the finest descriptive naturalist of his day." Aside from scientific articles on natural history, Gosse wrote a detailed account of marine life in a book called *Manual of Marine Zoology*. His other books included *Evenings at the Microscope*, and *A Year at the Shore*.

With all that, when it came to theorizing in science, he was somewhat out of place. This was because he was handicapped by an unswerving affiliation to a fundamentalist group which was committed to actions and attitudes governed by "their interpretation of the Scriptures." They just wouldn't accept anything in the Bible as symbolism or allegory, except for the parables.

So, the otherwise intelligent Gosse authored a book called *Omphalos* in which he argued with a straight face that fossils and other evidences for a much older earth were illusions, pure and simple, generated by God who is playing a big joke on fossil-mongers and evolutionists. So Adam had not just an apple in his throat, but a navel (*omphalos*, as they say in Greek) too, as did also Eve, even if they really didn't have a biological birth in which case alone a navel becomes relevant. Just as Adam's navel was a make-believe which make one suspect he had a mother, when in fact this was not the case, the fossils were there to just give us the impression that very ancient creatures once lived and died. Some theologians have been offended by such a proposition because it implies that God is a prankster at best and a deceiver at worst. Scientists scoff at this idea (which, incidentally, is presented seriously by some anti-evolutionists even today). But one must grant that it is logically irrefutable. Here lies the strength of unfalsifiable theories: they can't be shown to be wrong. On the principle that anything is possible, especially if it is God's work, scientists have to say, "Yes, of course," and resume more serious pursuits.

That such a good naturalist as Gosse could come up with the proposition that Adam and Eve were not only there as first Man and Woman, but also sported belly-buttons which were utterly uncalled for, shows to what extent reasonable people can rise or descend to defend what they regard as unshakable Truths in their holy books.

April 7

From the World of Religion:
WORLD HEALTH DAY

People are generally recompensed and rewarded for the things they do. So we get our salaries and compensations. Sometimes we receive gifts and presents too from those who care for us. But there are also things in each one's life that one has received without asking or working for it. Such, for example, are the parents one has.

Then there are things that are sometimes a combination of both: What we receive is beyond our control, but we can build upon it to make it better, or ruin it by our own negligence or reckless behavior. Such indeed are our health and inherited intelligence.

It is well known that there are serious health problems all over the world. In some countries, the health of millions is affected through poor living conditions: lack of sanitation, proper nourishment, needed medical care, non-availability of vaccines, etc. In other countries, cancer and cardiovascular diseases arise from environmental conditions, overeating, too much cholesterol in the food, etc.

Humanity as a whole periodically re-dedicates itself to improving the health of all its members. One way is by raising global awareness of health issues. And so, in 2001 the World Health Organization (WHO) decided to set aside one day (7 April) as the World Health Day (WHD). About 60% to 80% of the people don't do even the minimum for maintaining good health. The sedentary lifestyles of technological societies are extremely harmful. They increase considerably a variety of diseases like high blood pressure, osteoporosis and heart disease. On the other hand, crowded living, lack of parks and recreation, can all lead to crime and violence.

WHD hopes to emphasize the importance of physical activities, eating moderate amounts of food, doing regular exercises, abstaining from drugs, avoiding unsafe sex, etc. In schools and sports settings, through media and pamphlets, and other means one hopes to provoke better health-conscious behavior for millions of people all over the world.

Referring to *mens sana in corpore sane* (Sound mind in a sound body), George Bernard Shaw once quipped that it should be the other way around: A sound body is the product of a sound mind. What he meant was that if one has understanding and intelligence, one would do what is necessary and not engage in what is harmful, in order to maintain good health. It is that understanding that the WHD hopes to provide.

There must be both intake and output of energy: We need to consume energy to stay alive: That's what eating is all about: the complex molecules whose breaking up furnish the body the energy to keep up its vital functions. But equally, we need to spend energy in order to keep the body fit and usable. We consume almost a couple of thousand calories as food each day. It is recommended that we expend a minimum of 150 calories as physical exercise. This does not seem to be too much.

The WHO has been publicizing the most basic rules for exercise that must be within reach of the vast majority of humankind: About thirty minutes of walking a day. A vigorous basket ball game or bicycling would be even better.

None of this is really new knowledge of wisdom. Maxims and morals have been prescribing this for ages. Recall the lines of the poet Dryden:

Better to hunt in fields for health unbought,

Than fee the doctor for a nauseous draught.

The wise, for cure, on exercise depend,

God never made his work for man to mend.

From the World of Science: JACQUES LOEB

What in religion is known as Virgin Birth, biologists called *parthenogenesis* (which is simply Greek for the same phrase). More exactly, pathenogenesis refers to the development of a female gamete without being fertilized. Contrary to the generalization one might be tempted to make from the human experience, the phenomenon is not all that uncommon in other species.

Now it may be asked: can the ova of species which ordinarily require fertilization for bringing forth an offspring, be made to develop into full biological entities? The answer is yes. This was first established in 1901 by Jacques Loeb (born: 7 April 1859). He showed, in fact, that by placing the ova of certain sea urchins in appropriate saline solutions, these can be made to develop into full fledged creatures. This was as significant a scientific breakthrough as the production of artificial radioactivity. It opened up many possibilities, though also the fear of some to the effect that one day men would no longer be required in society for propagating the species.

Jacques Loeb had originally wanted to become a philosopher. He had read Schopenhauer and wanted to find out whether free will really existed. At one point he is said to have felt that philosophers, at least at the University of Berlin in the 1880s, were better at generating vast quantities of verbiage than in establishing concrete results. He had also read the writers of the French Enlightenment, and was therefore drawn to science.

The intrinsic penchant for philosophy combined with rigorous technical training in biology made him a biologist with a definite philosophical perspective. More exactly, he became a thorough-going materialist. He was convinced that there was no more to life than matter and energy transformations in accordance with the laws of physics and chemistry: the fundamental thesis which has been debated since the dawn of scientific reflection on the nature of life.

His interest in will, or rather in establishing that such a thing did not exist at all, was always in him. It was clear from his experiments on plant tropisms that plants respond to external stimuli, rather than make a decision to grow along a specific direction. Likewise, he said, all creatures respond to the world outside. Consider, for example, the behavior of certain caterpillars. They climb to feed to where the buds are. It used to be thought that this arose from the instinct to survive. Loeb showed from his experiments that the creatures were merely responding to light. By arranging the light elsewhere he made the creatures move along other directions, to a no-food place where they starved and died. It was heliotropism that instigated these photochemical creatures, not the will or instinct to survive, he argued. Shakespeare said:

By a divine instinct men's mind mistrust
Ensuing dangers.

For Loeb, instinct, in dog or man, is just response to external stimuli. To think that human beings act in accordance with a will is pure illusion, he felt. Whether by instinct or through freewill, or solely by external stimuli, he was unable to "live in a regime of oppression such as Bismarck had created." He left his native Germany and decided to settle down in the United States. Here he taught in various prestigious universities.

Needless to say, Loeb's godless philosophy won him many enemies. Besides being a devotee of pure mechanism in matters relating to life, he was also inclined to socialism. This did not make him popular either. But he was successful as a scientist, and controversial as a philosopher. This combination earned him name and fame.

April 8

From the World of Religion: HANA-MATSURI

Few founders of religion have their birthday celebrated on as many different dates as Gautama Buddha. Known by a variety of names, it is celebrated today (8 April) in Japan as Hana-matsuri which literally means Festival of Flowers. This is also the season of cherry blossoms in Japan.

On this day one takes a bouquet of flowers to a Buddhist place of worship. People dress in traditional costumes: a luxury which only non-Western people who have adopted suits and tie, have. The models in the feminine costumes usually have more patterns and colors. Men wear a white head band. Parades, with people young and old, sometimes with floats, are part of the celebration. There are images of the Buddha, sometimes seated on a white elephant: an animal that is not indigenous to the islands of Japan, but which is probably meant to remember the Buddha's place of birth which is in India. There are visits to Buddha's temples, and prayers to him with offerings of fruits and wine.

The origin of this festival is interesting. In historical terms, nobody was sure about even the year of Buddha's birth, let alone the month and date. However, as with Christ's birth, tradition ascribed dates for this momentous event, but not as per the Gregorian calendar. In the year 1901, a group of eighteen Japanese Buddhist students in Berlin decided to start observing Buddha's birthday on a certain date with flowers for the deity. So they called it a *Blumfest* (in the local language), which, when translated into Japanese became *Hana-matsuri*.

But for more than a decade after their return to Japan, the made-in-Germany festival had no impact in Japan. In 1917, the first Hana-Matsuri was celebrated in Japan at the Hibiya Park in Tokya under the leadership of Ando Ryogan and Watanabe Kaikyoku. Religious festivals sometimes travel in mysterious ways.

In many parts of the world one talks of different faiths living together in harmony. In Japan individuals have been doing this for generations. Many Japanese follow Shintoism, Confucianism, and Buddhism: One may be Christian and Confucian. It would be great if this becomes the model for humanity: that the same person can embrace whatever is beautiful in all the religious traditions he or she comes to learn about.

Religions have had considerable influence on the attitude and actions of people. By and large the message of Buddhism has been one of peace and compassion. At this very painful time in human history when so many regions of the world are ravaged by war destruction, when bombs tanks are rolling in towns, landmines are strewn in many places, when, in rage and frustration people blow themselves up to slaughter others, when the malodor of mutual hate and contempt pervades the air in so many places, when the worst passions of religion have been let loose, people of goodwill all over the world can only hope and pray for peace to return soon.

When we see a fellow being in pain, a bereaved mother or an orphaned child, how can we think in terms of race and religion and nationality? Should not compassion engulf us all? Indeed it does, but many are unable to forget the scars of the past which still give pain. And there are too many forces, overt and hidden, on every side that inflame our worst potential. There is no leader, in any group or nation, that has the wisdom or the wherewithal to awaken the best in every human being. Let us at least recall the precious few that once lived. Gautama Buddha was surely one of them. Remembering his name and message of compassion seems all the more appropriate at a time like this.

From the World of Science:
THE GREAT SUN SPOTS

The Sun has been experienced by human beings since the emergence of our species, but it has not been studied within the framework and with the instruments of science for very long. One of the first features of the sun that came to be recognized in the era of modern science is the fact that now and again one can detect dark patches on an otherwise unblemished surface. There is an ancient record of at least one sunspot observed in China in 28 B.C.E. Some scholars believe that in the 9th century passage of Mercury with the sun in the background could well have been a misinterpretation of sun spots. But it was only in the first decade of the 17th century that telescopic astronomy carefully noticed sun spots. One of the first to write a scientific work on the phenomenon was Johannes Fabricus. His book was entitled, *De Maculis in Sole Observatis*: On the spots observed in the Sun.

In the 19th century it was discovered that intense sunspots showed up periodically, roughly every 11 years. The largest patches thus far were observed on 8 April 1947: the Great Sun Spots. On the basis of the 11 year cycle, 2002 is a sun spot year.

We have come a long way since those patches were regarded as mysterious blots that revealed the rotation of the sun, for they all move on its surface in the same direction. Today we know that they are regions of enormous magnetic fields, appearing as pairs of north and south polarity. From our perspective, these are regions of stupendous surface area. The spots recorded in 1947 swept seven billion square miles. But that was only a 6000th part of the Sun's total surface.

The 1947 flare-up instigated great interest and further study of the sun by astronomers. Solar physics received a further boost. In the 1960s and 70s, interplanetary probes to Venus and mercury got pretty close to the sun. In the 1990s one of these revealed that, unlike the earth, the sun does not have any magnetic poles: If one gets lost on the solar surface, no magnetic needle would point the way.

Associated with sun spot activity are huge solar flares: ejection of enormous quantities of highly energetic electrically charged particles: essentially protons and electrons. Solar flares are huge hot ejections from the normal sun: like fireballs from a dragon's tongue. But during sun spot season they are thousands of times more intense. When they gush forth and arrive in our regions, they wreak havoc on earth's more stable magnetic fields. Their arrival in the geomagnetic polar regions at speeds of millions of miles per hour give rise to spectacular auroras, revealing that there can be magnificent aesthetic grandeur even in (what strikes us as) Nature's fury.

It used to be said that when America catches a cold, Europe sneezes. It is even more true that when there are sunspots in the sun, wild magnetic storms are created here on earth. They meant nothing up until we began an electro-technic civilization. To give but one example of how we can be affected, recall that when there was a geomagnetic storm in 1989, triggered by sun spots, there was a voltage collapse in the hydroelectric generators in Quebec causing a huge blackout.

There are also significant disruption of communication systems, including the transmission of TV signals.

While we earthlings live our fleeting years in all the gore and glory of our cultures and civilizations, pursuing our science and religion in great and grotesque ways, the sun and stars do their routines in accordance with the basic laws of physics, but on much, much grander scales. They have detectable impact on us: this much has been well established by science. As to subtler effects, we have no proofs as yet.

APRIL 9

From the World of Religion:
SAINT WALDERTRUDIS

The saints of the Christian world are like Hindu gods and goddesses in certain respects: there are so many of them, fascinating stories are associated with them, and they are remembered every year on special days. But the parallel ends here. For Christian saints were often martyrs: men and women who have given their lives for their faith. This was not so with Hindu saints.

Then again, not all saints are known as well, or remembered all over the world. Aside from the Biblical saints, St. Thomas and St. Bernadette are certainly better known than St. Waldertrudis whose Feast Day is on 9th April. Christians in Belgium remember her, certainly in the town of Mons whose patron saint she is. [I first heard of her when I visited Sainte-Waudu Collegiate Church in Mons many years ago.]

It is not often that many members of the same family receive the same honor or recognition. Here is a rare instance of this, perhaps the only case in its being so extraordinary: a saint whose parents and sister, husband and four children all have been canonized. I doubt if there is another saintly family-constellation with this many stars.

Waldertrudis was religiously inclined right from childhood. When she came of age, her parents chose for her a handsome groom of noble lineage. Count Madlegar was his name. It is said that other women in town were rather jealous that she was not only very beautiful but was also wedded to one so good. To make matters worse, Waldetrudis was kind to all and prayed more than others. So they gossiped about her. And they developed their own theory of what some moderns call the *selfish gene*: this woman was being kind only to impress people. She prayed only because she was sinning more than normal people. Anything good she did could be explained in terms of her own self-interests. Apparently, such bad-mouthing did not affect Waldetrudis. She continued to do her good acts and be pious, no matter what others said about her.

The couple lived in peace and harmony, serving the poor and devoted to God. They had four children. But after the birth of the fourth child her husband decided to renounce everything and become an ascetic. He left his family and joined a monastery. Waldetrudis stayed on at home with the children for two years, and then she too moved into a house of poverty. Her simplicity and wisdom drew many people to her who found consolation in her presence and wisdom in her words.

In due course, she founded a convent on a little hill in a village which eventually grew into the city of Mons of today. Here she lived a life of piety, so peaceful and helpful to all that soon people felt she was performing miracles. She died in the year 688.

Mons has commemorated the saint with a church dedicated to Sainte Waudu (as she is called in Belgian French). This Gothic structure date back to the 15th century. Its construction took two centuries. They say it houses some of the relics of the saint.

When one recalls such a story, one is struck by the power of symbols and legends. This woman is said to have died in 688. Almost 800 years later, the townspeople decided to erect a church in her name, and it is said to house the relics of her! During all the centuries, her name and life must have persisted through the oral tradition. Now all this narrative has acquired an authenticity that cannot be erased from the collective memory of the people by scholarly pronouncements or historical inquiry. So it is with many traditions all over the world. Monuments and sanctified legends perpetuate traditions. They are to be experienced, not inquired into. Only thus can we make the best of them.

From the World of Religion: HIPPOCRATES

As with Charaka of ancient India, certain extant medical works are attributed to Hippocrates of ancient Greece. These form the Hippocratic corpus. But little is known of the man. One modern historian went so far as to declare that such an individual never lived in flesh and blood. But there are references to Hippocrates in Plato's *Dialogues*, and interesting legends have grown around the name.

Hippocratic writings expound on the existing view of that time, with parallels in India and China, that ailments resulted from the imbalance of four bodily humors: blood, phlegm, black bile, and yellow bile. The idea may be traced to Empedocles' idea of the four *rhizomata* for the material world. Though such a framework was good in philosophizing, it was not always helpful in the actual curing of ailments.

Unlike many of his contemporaries, Hippocrates believed that imbalance in the humors resulted from external, natural causes, rather than from supernatural beings or upset deities. This is why, in the Western tradition, Hippocrates is regarded as the father of medical science. This is not to say that he denied a divine principle in the world as the cause of everything, but he traced physical ailments to specific physical causes. His theories were not always correct, as when he attributed impotence to interference with veins behind the ears, but they are naturalistic.

At least three works are attributed by some scholars to the individual called Hippocrates: *The Aphorisms*; *Airs, Waters, and Places*; and *On the Sacred Disease*. The last mentioned title refers to epilepsy which used to be attributed to unfriendly divine intervention. In this work, Hippocrates not only explains the ailment in terms of a malfunctioning of the brain, but is very critical of the upholders of supernatural explanations: "If these people claim to know how to draw down the moon, cause an eclipse of the sun, make storms and fine weather, rain and draught, to make the sea too rough for sailing or the land infertile, and all the rest of their nonsense, then, whether they claim to be able to do it by rites or by some other knowledge or practice, they seem to be impious rogues."

Two things may be noted in this context. First, it is clear that contrary to the general picture painted by a romantic view of ancient Greek science, not everyone offered naturalistic explanations there. Secondly, bold statements like this, with profound modernistic insight, have their parallels in other cultures too. But such views were often ignored or snubbed until the emergence of modern science. Even after that, there have been (and still are) people who call for a return to ancient scientific frameworks. The name of Hippocrates is associated with the oath that students of medicine take to this day before they become full-fledged physicians. In this oath which promises loyalty to the profession, and to do whatever is "for the good of the sick," one reads:

In whatever houses I enter, I will enter to help the sick, and I will abstain from all intentional wrongdoing and harm, especially from abusing the bodies of man or woman, bond or free. And whatsoever I shall see or hear in the course of my profession in my intercourse with men, if it be what should not be published abroad, I will never divulge, holding such things to be holy secrets.

Beyond the knowledge that science gives, we need a system of values for every practitioner whose work has an impact on fellow humans and creatures.

No one knows the date of birth of Hippocrates. So, even as one celebrates Buddha's birthday on 7 April, we may recall Hippocrates on 9 April.

April 10

From the World of Religion: HUGO GROTIUS

Tensions between races and religions characterize many conflicts in today's world. These are nothing new in human history. Yet, there have also been enlightened thinkers who have argued for mutual understanding, for freedom and peace for all. The efforts of such people have made this a better world than it was in the centuries when ideological intolerance and my-religion-alone-is-the-right-one mentality were far more rampant and powerful. It is important to remember that ominous forces are still active in our world to resuscitate such values. I fear during much of this new century there will be more confrontations between such forces and those that strive to move forward with newer visions for the problems of the world.

An illustrious representative of the tradition of enlightenment in judicial matters, both local and international, was Huig de Groot (born: 10 April 1583) or Hugo Grotius, as he is also known. We can't even imagine the kinds of religious bigotry, sectarian intolerance, and theological adamancy that characterized the Europe of his times. Precisians (orthodox Calvinists) were fighting Catholics; and wouldn't accept Protestants who tolerated Catholics. Free-will-supporters were quarreling with predestinarians (who insisted that everything is pre-ordained). In the political arena, maritime powers were laying claim to all the seas. Whenever a war broke out, it was a free for all: no rules of combat or respect for civilians. Machiavelli was the model for the warring kings of the period who regarded moral compunctions as detrimental to victory. That line of thinking has not died out altogether.

Grotius was a young man of 26 when he wrote a work on freedom of the seas in which he argued that the oceans belonged to all the people of the world, not just to the English and the Iberians who were then dominating the world. He was pained to see the Christian world warring in ways at which, he said, "even barbarous nations might blush. Wars were begun on trifling pretexts or none at all, and carried on without any reverence for law, Divine or human. A declaration of war seemed to let loose every crime." He wrote a book on The Rights of War and Peace (*De iure belli et pacis*) in which he proposed laws which would protect innocent citizens, respect the rights and properties of people, arrange for truces and treaties, etc. He was one of the first to explicitly argue for the protection of women, children, and older people from belligerent armies. He allowed that prisoners may be taken in a war, but was against killing them. Grotius condemned expansionist wars, but he did recognize the need to defend oneself. He pleaded for compromise and negotiation when possible, and even concession, if needed, rather than wage wars. It is good to know there are such thinkers.

Grotius wrote on universal laws transcending local religions, to which all would subscribe. He said there cannot be justification for any law based on religion, for belief and disbelief cannot be regarded as crimes. He expanded on the notion of natural law: a law that stands to reason, rather than to religious authority. God made the primary natural laws, and man wrote the secondary natural laws, based on reason.

Grotius was opposed by religious fanatics. He was even thrown into prison for his ideas, but he managed to escape with the assistance of his wife, and sneaked his way to Paris from where he continued his writings. His broad visions seemed either too blasphemous or too idealistic for his contemporaries. Slowly but surely the visions of Grotius' and others like him have come to be part of civilized humanity today.

From the World of Science:
SAMUEL HAHNEMANN

"Diamond cuts diamond" is an ancient expression. In the 1790s, while translating a medical treatise into German, Samuel Hahnemann (born: 10 April 1755) was struck by a curious fact: Cinchona bark (from the forests of Peru) from which quinine was derived had a toxic effect on patients similar to the malaria it cured. This led him to conduct many experiments, and eventually to formulate the principle in the cure of diseases: *similia similibus curentur.* Like is cured by like. [In the 16th century the quixotic physician Paracelsus had said something very much like this.] This formulation was meant to emphasize a truth which was to be understood as just the opposite of the principle on which the medical system in Europe has always rested: the other (*allos*), rather than the same (*homos*) is what removes the suffering (*pathos*). Thus Hahnemann advocated a new framework for treatment of diseases: *homoeopathy* (or homeopathy)which is radically different in principle from *allopathy*.

In 1810 his book entitled *Organon der rationellen Heilkunde* (System of rational therapy) appeared. Unlike other medical treatises, this was written as much for the patient as for the practitioner. It explained the principles of home-opathy in simple and straight forward terms. In other works, Hahnemann explained the effects of various drugs which he had tested. Another important tenet of his system is that there is a connection between the spiritual and the physical. As he put is, "It is only by means of the spiritual influence of a morbific agent that our spiritual vital power can be diseased, and in like manner only by the spiritual operation of medicine can health be restored."

Not unexpectedly, Hahnemann's doctrines produced considerable opposition, even anger, from the medical establishment. Some called it a sham and even dangerous. It was certainly a threat to the apothecaries. Hahnemann had to leave Leipzig, and eventually he settled down in Paris where he died at the ripe old age of 88, after years of successful practice. Furthermore, his system gradually spread far and wide, and today it has adherents in many countries all over the world.

One important difference between science and religion is this: In religions, many unwholesome and corrupt practices creep into the system in the course of time, and ruin the original purity. In science, changes and improvements occur which erase some of the no-longer acceptable features of the original framework. Thus, for example, Hahnemann's original thesis that every disease can be traced to one of three root causes: the itch, venereal disease, and fig-wart disease, is no longer taken seriously by many practitioners of homoeopathy. Nor is it universally believed that homeopathic medicines must be administered in extremely small doses.

There still are controversies as to the legitimacy of homeopathy as a valid system of medicine. (The same is true of acupuncture and the ayurvedic system). No matter what position one takes on these matters, this much is incontrovertible: Homeopathy (like ayurveda) prompted research into a great many drugs and herbal sources, and has thus contributed to allopathy. More importantly, countless people have benefited from the system(s). Like any other commodity sold to the public, such "unorthodox" systems could not have survived and been successful for his long if they were devoid of intrinsic merit. While one needs to be vigilant against the facile acceptance of nebulous poetry as authentic science, one should also recognize that the human body is way too complex to be constrained to just one framework in its interpretation. We need a variety of approaches in our efforts to cure disease and maintain health.

April 11

From the World of Religion: BHAKTA KABIR

An infant was abandoned by his widowed mother near a lotus tank in the sacred city of Varanasi and got picked up by a Muslim weaver who adopted it as his own. The weaver called the child Kabir (11 April 1398). The name means *The Great One* in Arabic. As he grew, the lad was attracted to godly matters. One day, he went to the sage Ramananda to become his disciple. Ramanda refused because the aspirant wasn't a Brahmin boy. Later, recognizing the deep devotion of the young man, Ramananda accepted him. Raised in a Moslem household and influenced by a Hindu saint, Kabir combined the essential simplicity of Islamic devotion with the intense mystical yearnings of the Hindu framework. He saw the absurdity implicit in casteism. He sang in a poems: *Jati pati puchai na koi; Hari ko bhaje so Hari ka hoi:* Let no one ask to what caste you belong. He who recites the Lord's name will be taken by Him."

He discarded abstract metaphysics and preached unquestioning devotion to a personal God. He wrote beautiful poetry and uplifting songs reflecting his love for God.

Legends grew about him in later times. Once, it is said, while he was weaving for a customer he lapsed into communion with the Divine, but the loom continued weaving a wonderful scarf. When Kabir came to himself he discovered what had happened. Some days later, two mendicants came to him, shivering with cold. Cutting the divinely created piece into two, he gave one to each. His mother was very upset by this, but she had a vision of God, and realized at once that Kabir was no ordinary human.

According to another story, when Kabir was first discovered as a baby, he spoke right away to the weaver's wife. The frightened woman left the infant on the road and began to run away with her husband, but the child ran after them without any difficulty at all!

Such stories won Kabir greater veneration than the simple beauty of his teachings and the wisdom in his poems. Essentially, he preached unadulterated love of God, and the rejection of the caste system. Like other spiritually inspired souls, Kabir was convinced he had been sent down here by God Almighty to spread the true word, and he warned, not unlike other prophets, "Those who will not listen to me, they will surely be drowned in the ocean of existence, in the midst of eighty-four lakh currents..."

Kabir was no scholar. He could barely read or write. Yet he has left behind many moving verses. Twenty one books of Kabir's poetry have been preserved. Words seem to have flowed from his lips like magic. He sang in simple Hindi (the *Bhasa*), the language of the common folk, never used Sanskrit or high flown Persian.

He was very clear about his own religious affiliation: "If you say that I am Hindu then it is not true, nor am I a Muslim. I am a body made of five elements where the Unknown plays. Mecca has verily become Varanasi, and Rama has become Rahim."

But such thoughts were not easily understood either by the masses, or their mini-minded religious leaders. When Kabir died, both Hindus and Moslems claimed him as their own. According to legend, he appeared in a disembodied form and asked the fighting fanatics to remove the shroud covering his corpse. When they did this, they saw only a heap of flowers. These were divided into two parts. One was burned and the other buried!

Kabir preached that all sects and creeds must unite into a single one and worship God. But he himself became the origin of another sect, called Kabir-panthis who established twelve principal branches in their order. Kabir-panthis respect all life forms, do not attach much significance to rituals, are against idol worship and do not believe in pilgrimages.

From the World of Science: JAMES PARKINSON

In the second half of the 18th century, pamphlets signed by a certain Old Hubert used to appear which were rather revolutionary in content. They called for many social reforms, demanded that the voice of the people be heard in the House of Commons. They pleaded for universal suffrage. The author was a member of the London Corresponding Society for Reform of Parliamentary Representation. In 1794 the society was implicated in an attempt to assassinate King George III by firing a pop-gun while the King was at a theater. [This reminds us of Abraham Lincoln's assassination.]

The real name of Old Hubert was James Parkinson (born: 11 April 1755). After the pop-gun episode, he began to do work in medicine. At the same time he developed great interest in geology and paleontology. In 1804 he published a work entitled *Organic Remains of the Former World*. His books on the subject are regarded as significant contributions to British paleontology. He also wrote a book called *Elements of Oryctology* which was meant to be an introduction to the study of fossils.

Yet, Parkinson was affiliated to the Bible. He accepted the Noah story, and believed that the hand of God was always at work in the creation and extinction of species. While he granted that life forms emerged after the formation of the rocks: vegetable, aquatic animals, bird, land animals, and finally human beings (remarkably close to a theory of evolution), he did not think one came from the other or in any theory of evolution. Rather he was interested in reconciling theology with science. He rejected the uniformitarianism of Hutton by which everything can be explained in terms of slow natural processes occurring over geological time. He was, with Humphry Davy, one of the founders of the Geological Society of London (1797).

Parkinson wrote a book called *Medical Admonitions* with the goal of improving the health of the public. He was always a socially-conscious individual, and worked for ameliorating conditions in the so-called lunatic asylums.

Parkinson's son was also a surgeon. Father and son were the first to describe, in 1812, what we call today appendicitis.

But Parkinson's name is most remembered now as a result of a piece he wrote in 1817, entitled *An Essay on the Shaking Palsy*. Here he described the disease which is now associated with his name, in these terms: "Involuntary tremulous motion, with lessened muscular power, in parts not in action and even when supported: with a propensity to bend the trunk forwards, and pass from a walking to a running pace: the senses and the intellect being injured."

It is interesting to recall how name and fame spread far and wide. The so-called Parkinson's disease acquired that epithet only in the 20th century when J. G. Rowntree (an American) published a paper on the subject in which he said of this man: "English born, English bred, forgotten by the English and the world at large, such was the fate of James Parkinson." The names of not only classical composers and artists, but also of scientific investigators are sometimes revived after years of oblivion.

Between 1952 and 1968, surgery was often a mode of treatment for Parkinson's, but it did not always cure the patient fully. After L-dopa became generally available in 1968, surgery became less frequent. In any event, this remains one of the great challenges of medical research to this day.

In this context you may like to read a recently published book: *James Parkinson: From Apothecary to General Practitioner* (1998) by Shirley Roberts.

April 12

From the World of Religion: CERELIA

The gods and goddesses of ancient Greece and Rome are not worshiped any more in church or temple, but many of them have entered our vocabulary in various ways. Thus when we talk of a jovial person or the martial arts, of a Herculean task or a phobia, of opulence or venereal disease, we are remembering one ancient God or another, no longer with a holy attitude.

We do this also when we order cereals for breakfast, for the word is derived from the Roman Ceres who was the goddess of crops. The creative genius of ancient Rome had plenty of deities who managed their agriculture: one for orchids, one for baking, even one for heaps of manure (Sterculus). There is wisdom in personifying the positive forces and helpful elements in Nature which are conducive to life and happiness, for in this way we have an opportunity to express gratitude for the countless bounties we human beings receive from nature, often without asking. But, as Cicero reminded us, perhaps this should not be taken too literally.

After Greek deities were brought into Rome, Ceres took on some of the attributes of the Greek Demeter. Most gods of mythology have a family made up of other gods. Thus, the parents of Ceres were Saturn and Ops. This made her sister to Jove and Pluto. She had a daughter Persephone who was abducted from her home in Sicily and taken to Hades. Mythology recounts how Ceres grieved and went to search for her daughter.

Ovid tells us about her: "Ceres was the first who invited man to better sustenance and exchanged acorns for more useful food. She forced bulls to yield their necks to the yoke; then for the first time the upturned soil beheld the sun."

Romans began to celebrate this deity every year in the month of April. On the 12th day of this month the games of Ceres (*ludi Ceresis*) or Cerealia began. They used to last for an entire week. During this time the people offered salt and grain to the goddess, and a female pig as sacrifice. As on some Semitic holy days, the Romans fasted until sunset.

On Cerealia, women would dress in white, and they went on a procession with torches to symbolize the quest of Ceres for her daughter. People walked three times around the fields with milk and honey and brought these to the temple of Ceres.

As on other festive days there were chariot races also. And cruelty to animals was as yet an unknown notion in much of the world, the Romans used to attach flaming bands to the tails of foxes, and then let them run. This was all part of celebrating a goddess. Like cock fights and game hunting in our own times, the sight of foxes running with their tails on fire used to amuse ancient Romans. In the matter of being more humane to creatures, and in not prescribing the slaughter of animals, some religions have evolved over the centuries, while others have long ways to go.

Ovid informs us that Cerealia (like the festival of Holi in Hindu India) was essentially for the plebians: lower classes.

Ultimately, all civilizations rest on agriculture. Most people take food for granted, but only as long as it is readily available. When it says in the Lord's prayer, "Give us this day our daily bread," it sounds as if one is only asking for satisfying physical hunger. But without that daily bread everything will come to a slow standstill. A week of starvation for a community or nation can wreak more havoc than tons of bombs. Take away grains from the fields, and in a short time there will be chaos and confusion. So a periodic salute to Ceres, by whatever name and in whatever mode, is quite appropriate.

From the World of Science:
CARL LOUIS LINDEMANN

Mathematics is a world in itself: it has it regions abstruse and abstract, it has its regions clear and simple. It has elements in it as obvious as one, two and three, and also some not-so-easily intelligible as special unitary groups and Banach spaces. Some steps in mathematics are as elementary as adding two numbers, others as involved as solving a higher degree partial differential equation. Some problems have been posed and solved the same day, others have been a challenge for hundreds of years, sometimes for more than a thousand.

A problem of the last kind is simple to state: How would one square a circle? It is not too difficult to understand: Given a circle (i.e. of a certain radius), how can one construct, using ruler and compass, and in a finite number of steps, a square which would have exactly the same area? The mathematicians of the ancient world, like Pythagoras and Anaxagoras, are known to have tackled this problem. Since then, over the centuries, a great many brilliant minds attempted it too. Many pseudo-solved the problem: They gave solutions which seemed right at first, but had a fallacy which was detected soon or later. The medieval philosopher Nicolas de Cusa was one of them, and the 17th century rationalist philosopher Thomas Hobbes was another.

But in the 19th century it was proved beyond any doubt that squaring the circle is, in principle, impossible. You might as well try to become a baby again.

Many of us have heard of the number called pi. [*pi* is a letter in the Greek alphabet, corresponding to our p. The number derived that name because it is equal to the perimeter of a circle whose diameter is one.]

Now, one of the important properties of the ordinary numbers we encounter, like 7, 3/4, .04, 23.9172, or even the cube root of 31, is that they are all roots of some algebraic equation or other. For example the cube root of 3 is a solution of the equation x-cubed equals 3.

There are, however, a great many numbers which don't have this property: That is, they are not roots of an algebraic equation. They are called *transcendental* numbers.

In 1882, Carl Louis Lindemann (born: 12 April 1852) proved that *pi* is a transcendental number. This was a significant milestone in the history of mathematics because its immediate consequence was that squaring a circle is an impossible problem, i.e. it simply cannot be done. Not that people innocuous of basic mathematics are still under the blissful delusion that this can be accomplished, but then some people still believe we can construct a perpetual motion machine or let the population grow at the current rate and still survive a thousand years from now.

Lindemann's proof of the transcendentality of *pi* followed rather simply from the fact that another number, (related to it through an equation), the so-called base of the natural logarithm, and represented by the letter *e*, is also transcendental. This had been proved some nine years earlier by another mathematician, Charles Hermite. Some have wondered why Hermite did not take the few more steps that Lindemann did.

In any event, Lindemann found a place in the history of mathematics because of his proof that *pi* is transcendental. Beyond this work, he wrote other papers in mathematics and mechanics, and contributed much to mathematics education in Germany.

It is difficult to know if *pi* and *e*, or even common integers, have objective existence or if they are simply creations of the human mind. They do play important roles in the quantitative aspects of physical laws, but they cannot located anywhere out there.

April 13

From the World of Religion: MAHA SONGRAN

In many traditions April ushers in a new year. In Thailand, Maha Songran, on 13 April, marks the end of the old year. On this day all offices are closed, and people who come to the cities for work, go back to their villages to spend time with all their kith and kin. According to folk astronomy, this is the day when the sun turns back its path from the southern towards the northern hemisphere. The word *songran* itself, they say, connotes movement. [It is probably a transformation of the Sanskrit *Sankranti*.] As per ancient Asian custom, one pays formal respect to one's parents, and symbolic homage to one's ancestors.

People clean houses for the day, gather as a family, and visit Buddhist temples. There is also a mutual sprinkling of water. One may use small cups, squirt guns, water pistols, even hoses to drench passers-by, mildly or considerably, but always in good spirits. It is all sanctioned by custom in the merry-making which is part of the celebratory mode. Like in the Hindu festival of Holi, the sprinkle may be a splash or a bucketful, except that in Thailand the water may have some fragrance, but no color. Everyone participates in this, and you don't have to be Buddhist or Thai to be targeted. Simple folk, teachers, shop-keepers, businessmen, the most exalted officials of the government, everybody is ready to participate in this revelry whether indoors or outdoors. Aside from serving as a coolant at the onset of tropical heat, water is said to be auspicious and purifying. Symbolically sprayed water is supposed to wash off the unpleasant remnants of the past year and bring in the freshness of the new one. But this washing is only symbolic since the water may not always be of the cleanest kind. In the very crowded sections of the city, near the Moat in Bangkok, people draw their aquatic ammunition from murky sources. In many traditions, the sprinkling of water is part of rituals. Perhaps this comes from the ancient recognition of the importance of water for life. But in few other festivals of the human family does water play such a central role as in the Thai Songran.

This is also the day when one makes special contributions to the monks. As in some ancient Roman and a few Hindu festivals, the celebrations include elaborately organized processions with icons of Buddha. The on-lookers respond with enthusiasm and the pouring of water too. A transformation that has occurred in modern times is the introduction of floral floats and the parade of Miss Songran. Buddha in any aspect is likely to be more puzzled than annoyed by this feature, but then the same may be said of Christ and the Christmas tree, or the special airline-fares to Makkah and Hadj. Modes of observance tend to change with time in all religious traditions.

People are asked to be a little reflective on this day: to think about how they spent the past year and how they can better spend the coming one. One is also grateful for all the blessings which one has received during the year that has elapsed. One of the functions of religions is to enable us to express gratitude for life's positive experiences. On this day one is also reminded of the basic virtues of caring and kindness, compassion and sharing. And, as elsewhere, spokespersons for the culture mention these as somehow unique to their people.

Years come and go, taking away the loads of experiences that they brought. The joyous celebration of the New Year implies: a rejoicing that in the return of the seasons which is as much of the past as we can get again.

So today we may say, *"Sawadee Pee Mai"* which in Thai means Happy New Year!

From the World of Science:
BRUNO BENEDETTO ROSSI

"There are more things in heaven and earth, Horatio, than are dreamt of in your philosophy," said Hamlet in Shakespeare. The word *philosophy* meant science in those days. A look into the history of science reveals this to be a perennial truth.

Who would have thought a century ago that aside from sunlight and other radiations the earth is also showered constantly with huge streams of electrically charged particles? These cosmic rays were studied by many physicists in the first decades of the 20th century, and among them was Bruno Benedetto Rossi (born: 13 April 1905).

It was found that cosmic rays consist largely of electrically charged particles. If so, their paths must be influenced by the earth's magnetic field. Rossi argued in 1930 from the laws of electromagnetism that if cosmic rays are positively charged particles, they must be deflected eastward. If they were negatively charged, they would be pushed westward, in the opposite direction. This would result in an east-west asymmetry in the intensity of cosmic rays. Experiments based on Rossi's conjecture showed that cosmic rays consist of positively charged particles.

Rossi studied the change in the intensity of cosmic ray showers as they passed through various thicknesses of lead plates. Plotting his results on a graph, he obtained what is now called a Rossi curve which shed more light on the properties of cosmic rays.

The cosmic ray particles, upon colliding with the nuclei of atoms in the earth's atmosphere, give rise to other high-energy particles. To study them before this happens, we need to catch them before they enter the atmosphere. After the development of rockets and their use in scientific explorationlate in the 1950s, Rossi initiated experiments to study cosmic rays above the earth's atmosphere. It was thus that we came to know them as mostly protons. From Rossi's work, we also became aware of the so-called solar wind: the endless rush of charged particles from the sun's fiery atmosphere. Rossi served as consultant to NASA in many scientific experiments.

It was also known that aside from visible light and ultraviolet radiation, X-rays too emerge from the sun. The so-called moonlight which we experience and enjoy is simply the reflection of sunlight from the surface of the moon. One may similarly expect moon-X-rays too: those that are reflected from solar X-rays. Rossi devised experiments to study this. One of the unexpected outcomes of those studies was the discovery that enormous bursts of X-rays reach us from distant sources. This opened up a whole new field: X-ray astronomy, which revealed X-ray stars and quasars. But Rossi was modest enough to say: "As for the role that I personally played in the development of X-ray astronomy, I must admit that it was more that of an interested spectator than an actor." Rossi received many honors for his contributions to physics. Among the contexts in which he is remembered is an instrument with the acronym RXTE: Rossi X-ray Timing Explorer.

One of the ironies of human history is that even its most vicious characters have unwittingly done some good. Thus, Hitler and Mussolini, by their persecution of Jews, provided the U.S. with enormous brain power during the 1930s and beyond. Bruno Rossi was among the many who fled their native country and enriched American science. In his reminiscences (*Moments in the life of a scientist*) Rossi recounts the scientific highlights in his life, spicing them with impressions of the people who came his way. His wife tells us that Bruno was as much a poet as a physicist.

As one of the active participants in the Manhattan project, Rossi experienced the ache of conscience when the first bomb exploded over Hiroshima.

April 14

From the World of Religion: INDIC NEW YEAR

In many parts of India, Hindus celebrate today as New Year Day. It is sometimes called Yugadi, which means the beginning of a *yuga*. A *yuga*, by Hindu reckoning is one of the four cyclical eons (each lasting several hundred thousand years) through which the universe goes. The traditional belief is that the so-called New Year Day recalls the Day of a phase of Cosmic Creation. This stands to reason in the mythological framework: The universe could not have started on some arbitrary date in the year. That should have been the first day of the first year that ever was.

The day has different names in different parts of India: *Noba Barsha* in Bengal, *Varushappirappu* in Tamil Nadu, *Rongali Bihu* in Assam, *Vishu* in Kerala, etc.

In the Sikh tradition, this day (usually 13th or 14th April) is called Baisakhi (pronounce: Baisaakhi), and it begins the year as per their history. In fact, 2002 is year 304 in their calendar.

Baisakhi has great historical significance in the Sikh framework. Briefly, it is as follows: Aurangzeb, the mean-spirited Mogul monarch who had ascended the throne in 1657 after murdering his kith and kin, started a frenzy of religious persecution whose goal was to Islamize the whole of India. His advisors told him that if he could convert the Brahmins, the rest would follow like sheep. He therefore levied exorbitant taxes on Brahmins and exerted other painful measures. The Brahmins of Kashmir, in virtual panic, approached the Sikh Guru Tegh Bahadur for assistance. When Guru Tegh Bahadur went to Delhi to talk to the emperor, he was promptly chained and thrown into prison. It has been said that the Sikh guru was then thrown into boiling oil, killed in this terrible manner, and his body was then thrown on the street. No one had the courage remove it to give it a proper funeral. Later two people came stealthily and removed the body and a proper cremation.

When Tegh Bahadur's son Gobind Rai heard about this, he was so ashamed of the cowardice of his people who had dared not go and claim his father's body that he decided to instill some martial spirit in the followers of the Sikh Guru. So it was that on Baisakhi day in the year 1699, the new Guru Gobind called for a meeting of all the Sikhs at Anandpur Sahib in Punjab. He spoke to the crowd passionately, and brandished his sword in a sign of valor and determination. He called upon volunteers to commit themselves to a life of bravery and sacrifice, initiated a ceremony called *pahul* (the equivalent of baptism), invested each of the five volunteers (from different classes an sects) with the five insignias of Sikhism, and asked them to baptize him in return. It was from that date that Sikh men stopped shaving and cutting their hair, started wearing a comb and an iron bracelet, and began carrying the dagger. From that day on, all Sikhs assumed the last name of Singh. This was the beginning of the *Panth Khasla* (order of the Pure). That is why Baisakhi is of great significance to Sikhs: It is more than just a new year celebration.

Today, much of the sordid details of the history are kept in the background. One pays a visit to the *gurudwara* (Sikh house of worship) where special devotional songs are sung. But there are also social dimensions to the celebration where one rejoices in festivities. People dance the dynamic *bhangra* which expresses the sheer joy of life. There are the rhythms of the *dholak* (drum) to add to the joy. There are musical enactments of plowing and sowing and *reaping*, for this is as much a welcoming of spring and harvest in that part of the world. Let us wish a Happy Baisakhi to all our Sikh brethren.

From the World of Science:
CHRISTIAAN HUYGENS

Alfred North Whitehead called the 17th century the century of genius. Among the geniuses who added luster to that age, though not as universally known, was Christiaan Huygens (born: 14 April 1629). A second *a* is not a typo; it is the right Dutch spelling) whose contributions to the advancement of science, both theoretical and practical, was no less significant than those of Galileo or Newton, Descartes or Pascal.

Huygens was one of the first to recognize and formulate the essence of the principles of conservation of momentum and of energy. [Not just mv, but mv-squared also was conserved when perfectly elastic masses collided.] He investigated the nature of the centrifugal force. He wrote the first formal book on the theory of probability.

Huygens was equally interested in the heavens. He constructed a telescope, more than twenty feet long, grinding lens with the assistance of the philosopher Spinoza. He attached a micrometer to the telescope, adding a quantitative dimension to qualitative observations. His observations revealed that the blur that Galileo and others had reported on Saturn was in fact what we now call Saturn's rings. Huygens stated his view on the matter in a Latin anagram as much to be anonymous to begin with as to ensure his priority. He discovered a satellite of

Saturn (Titan). He was also the first to spot the Orion nebula: an eerie and impressive patch in the heavens, more often photographed by now than any other nebula, and more easily detectable too with a decent pair of binoculars. He imagined it to be a gateway in the dark sky to more magnificent realms beyond. Huygens believed there were other planetary systems in the universe harboring plants and animals because the wisdom of God was most manifest in the creation of life.

Huygens' greatest contribution was the pendulum clock: a device that added immensely to precision in time measurements. He may be called the grandfather of the Grandfather Clock. The title of his classic: *Horologium oscillatorium* (1669) suggested (for the first time in history) that time could be measured by oscillations rather than by water clocks or descending objects. The book also included a mathematical analysis of pendular motion, in the course of which he established the tautochronism of the cycloid: if a pendulum bob followed the path of the curve called the cycloid, its period of oscillation would depend only on the length of the string.

Huygens was a firm proponent of the wave theory of light. He imagined a subtle ether whose constituents were set to oscillations in the propagation of light. He considered how such waves might propagate. In this he differed from his illustrious contemporary Isaac Newton who propounded a corpuscular theory of light.

Huygens was an able exponent of the mechanistic philosophy which was fast gaining ground. He felt that "the causes of all natural effects" are "by reasons of mechanics." Indeed, he confessed that he simply could not accept as explanation anything that did not put forth a mechanistic process to describe it. He argued that these causes can only be known by careful observation and experimentation. Thus he went beyond pure (Cartesian) rationalism into an empirical approach in science.

Huygens interacted with the major scientific thinkers of his time. He was elected a member of the newly established French *Académie des Sciences,* and became one of the outstanding members of that prestigious body. It is somewhat surprising that in spite of the range and merit of his works, Huygens is not as well known in the English-speaking world as Newton or Descartes. Reputation in the world community is not always determined only by the quality of one's work.

April 15

From the World of Religion:
TELLUS MATER FESTIVAL

There once was a religion whose followers worshiped Mother Earth as a goddess. They celebrated that goddess every year on the 15th of April. They were grateful to this divine Mother who gave them a place to live, who bore the crops that fed them, for all the beautiful fruits and flowers.

What would we say of such a religion? We would perhaps say that it was a wise, enlightened, and meaningful system. Its leaders were insightful in that they thought in the abstract about Earth as an entity and the role that it plays in the sustenance of life.

Now think of a religion which slaughtered 31 pregnant cows every year to pay homage to a deity. Its followers believed that by severing the heads of cattle they were showing their respect and gratitude to a divine being.

We would probably say that this was a primitive religion at a low level of civilization, whose leaders were too simple-minded to appreciate the cruelty they were inflicting on animals, and whose notion of what would please god was pathetically unsophisticated.

What is interesting is that the items I have mentioned above were part of one and the same religion: that of ancient Rome. The sacrifice I am referring to was called *Fordicidia* (the literally *killing of pregnant cows*), the festival in question was dedicated to *Tellus Mater* (Mother Earth). Tellus was the Roman Mother Earth to whom one paid periodic homage. She was the goddess of fertility, the one who tends to the seeds that are sown so that they might sprout some day. She was also invoked during weddings to bless the couple with offspring. Sometimes she was also regarded as the goddess of death for it is to her womb that we return when our days are done.

As I mentioned, the festival for Tellus Mater used to be observed on 15 April every year. It is being revived in our own times.

In the celebration of Tellus Mater we see the dual aspect of many religions of the human family. One of them reflects the profound insight of the founders of religions into the human condition in the context of the world in which we live: Religion is, above all, an affirmation of the human spirit as a presence in the physical world, the response and rejoicing of that spirit in the face of the mystery surrounding us. The other aspect of religion is the emotional and sometimes harsh behavior of human beings provoked as much by fear of the natural world as by naive efforts to appease the forces of Nature in hopes of being protected from its ravages.

Other cultures had their Mother Earth gods/goddesses too. There is Prithivi in the Hindu world, to whom hymns such as the following, are sung in the Atharvadeda:

O earth! All life on this earth emanates from you. All creatures live their lives on your surface. You sustain and support all life, man and beast. O earth! The human body is composed of your five elements. God infuses the light of knowledge in mortal man for his immortal soul.

The ancient Greeks had their Gaia who was Mother Earth, and she emerged with the whole universe. Not unlike in Vedic mythology, she was born of Chaos and Eros (Love).

In modern times, like the Earth-day movement in the West, there have been efforts to initiate a *Prithivi dharma* in the East. And we have our own Earth Day too.

In all of this we see the common elements in human culture, the same longings of the human spirit, the same urge to venerate unfathomable mysteries, the same wish to express gratitude. All of this find expressions in various religious celebrations.

From the World of Science: LEONHARD EULER

This is the birth date of one of the most extraordinary geniuses of the human family: Leonardo da Vinci. Since his name is so universally recognized, I will reflect on another genius who bore the same first name: Leonhard Euler [pronounced 'oiler'] (born: 15 April 1707). He was Swiss by birth, but he too belongs to the whole world. He learned his first mathematics from his father, a Calvinist minister, then began to study Latin, toyed with the idea of becoming a minister, but switched to mathematics after a Master of Arts degree at 16. He was interested in the theory of sound propagation. At 20, he won a prize in an international competition of the French Academy, and was invited by Empress Catherine to stay at the St. Petersburg Academy. Here he worked on every branch of mathematics, giving, like Midas, a golden touch to every field that he touched.

When he was not yet 35, Frederick the Great of Prussia invited him to adorn the Berlin Academy. Euler spent a few years here, writing memoirs on many topics, both mathematical and astronomical. He also took part in court discussions on philosophical and theological questions. It is said that he was relatively naive in some of these, compared to Voltaire who too was there, but Euler was himself amused by this sometimes. Any day he could stump his wordy opponents with a dose of higher mathematics wherein they were but children compared to him.

Euler wrote on mechanics, on lunar motion, on hydraulics, on geodesics, on cartography, on ship-building, on ballistics, and on optics. But above all, he published profusely on what mathematicians call *Analysis*, a wonderful play in the realm of pure concepts and proofs and mathematical symbols, sometimes reflecting aspects of the world, sometimes standing on their own like a work of abstract art. Analysis has always been there in the world of mathematics, but in the 18th century it burst forth like tulips or lilacs in season. And in this esoteric realm where none but the initiated can come and play, Euler created endlessly and magnificently, and came to be called Analysis Incarnate. He has left behind seventeen volumes of work on Analysis alone. Whether in algebra or in complex variables, in differential equations or number theory, in the calculus of variations or infinite series, Euler wrote and created like a gifted poet who churns out rhyme and verse, sonata and song at every inspiration: this, even after he lost his sight in later years.

If, as Galileo said, mathematics is the alphabet in which the laws of nature are spelled out, we need to have writing conventions for that alphabet. Here too Euler has left his mark. For when we write e for the exponential, $f(x)$ for a function of x, or i for the square root of minus one, we are following an Eulerian convention.

Euler engaged in correspondence with hundreds of people. Sometimes he also provoked controversies on priority. Though none of his contemporaries could surpass him, he did have some rivals in the attack on tough problems. One of these was D'Alembert.

Euler wrote on the current scientific world view in the format of *Letters to a Princess* (the niece of Frederick the Great). Though the book became very popular and was translated into half a dozen languages, it is not counted among his greatest works.

Early in the 20th century a project was initiated to collect and publish with annotations and brief essays Euler's *Opera Omnia*. The project lasted for several decades, and came out in sixty hefty volumes. People like Euler contribute immensely to human civilization, but their work is so esoteric that few beyond specialized circles even know their names.

April 16

From the World of Religion: BENEDICT JOSEPH

There lived in mid 18th century France, a man who had devoted his life to spiritual pursuits. His name was Benedict Joseph Labre. Already as a lad he showed such inclinations, displaying great self-restraint, piety, and, a great sense of moral rectitude. At 12 he was sent to an uncle who was a religious man himself. He was studious and read classical authors as well as history. But he felt all this was a mere waste of time, for to him service of God was the most important.

Benedict Joseph served the poor, taught the young their Catechism, and soon became well known in the community as the little religious man. At one time, when a plague struck the town, he went to help out the sick. Soon he joined a monastery where he could exercise his religious proclivities, unimpeded by secular commitments.

One day, Benedict decided to become a mendicant pilgrim. He lived on the barest minimum, and went on foot to as many sacred shrines as he could. They say he walked all through much of south-west Europe including Rome and Assisi, Ancona for the shrine of Loreto, Fabriano for the tomb of St. Romuald, and many other places. He would sing the Lord's name joyously as he walked from place to place, caring for the poor. It is said that he used to declare himself to be a tramp and not a pilgrim. He felt deeply that, no matter what he did or where he went, it was always God who directed him.

Benetich Joseph lived on charities, wearing the clothes and girdle of a Trappist monk. Whenever people gave him more alms than he needed, he would give it away to other poor people. He suffered much, he grew thin and lanky for want of enough food. At one place he was mistaken for a thief and put in prison. But he visited some towns so many times that he became quite a celebrity in various places where people would look forward to his return the next year.

In 1778 Benedict Joseph settled in Rome. In those days, Rome was like some cities in Asia today, with impressive monuments and palatial buildings, reflecting rich history, but also with lots of poverty, narrow streets, and shanty towns. There were mendicants everywhere. Benedict was perfectly at home among them. He served them, he preached to them, he prayed with them, he took them to church, and so this saintly man spent his years thinking of God and serving God's poor children. His biographer gives details of where he stayed, the churches he visited, the people he might have seen there, etc.

Benedict Joseph became quite famous for all of this. Then one day in the Holy Week of 1783, while he was attending Mass in the Church of Santa Maria in Monte, he became ill and died soon thereafter. It is said that his body was kept for a day at that church. Hundreds of people including cardinals and bishops, royalty and priests came to pay homage to this mendicant-saint. A book on him, published two years after his death, reported that he had performed as many as 136 miracles, mainly relating to the cure of the sick. Pope Pius VI later called him Venerable, which is an honorific title, not just an adjective. Pope Leo XIII formally canonized Benedict Joseph in 1881. His Feast Day was declared to be 16 April.

With all our technological advances and economic prosperity, there still are millions of people in penury, homeless and abandoned, in so many parts of the world. There are other Saint Benedict Joseph Labres too, who, individually or through organizations, do whatever they can for the poor. The lives of people like St. Benetict Joseph Labre serve as an inspiration to all of us, for the world badly needs many more like him.

From the World of Science: JOSEPH BLACK

One of the major threats to human survival today is the so-called *global warming*. A major factor causing this is excess of carbon dioxide in the atmosphere. All we feel is air around us, not its many constituents. It requires the probing of experimental science and the ingenuity of science to put into evidence the myriad aspects of the phenomenal world that our senses don't directly detect. Since when did we know that there is such a thing as carbon dioxide?

In the 18th century, Joseph Black (born: 16 April 1728) was experimenting with quicklime. He placed water under an air pump, and sucked the dissolved air from it. The extracted air was not absorbed by quicklime. Next he did the same with some lime water. In this case, quicklime easily absorbed the extracted air. Black concluded that air contains some gas which is not absorbed by quicklime. He called this part *fixed air*.

Now Black studied the properties of fixed air: Candles wouldn't burn in it. When dissolved in water, the latter became slightly acidic. Birds and other small creatures in an atmosphere of fixed air died very soon. Fixed air was obtained by heating limestone (calcium carbonate). Black also discovered that when we exhale, we give out fixed air. What Black called fixed air was, in fact, *carbon dioxide*.

So it is only for the past 250 years that humanity has been aware of such a thing as carbon dioxide, and today we know so much more about its properties and effects. We have come to know that the atmosphere of the planet Venus is made up largely of this gas. We also know that plants take in carbon dioxide during certain times, and that as the physical environment of the earth evolved, there arose a steady percentage of the gas in the atmosphere. Carbon dioxide absorbs infra-red radiation (heat waves). So, when sunlight which falls on earth, and bounces back as IR, part of it is absorbed by the carbon dioxide in the air. This serves as energy to fuel the weather systems and to maintain the right amount of heat for us all. If there is too little carbon dioxide, we will freeze to death very quickly. If there is an excess of it, there will be more heat than is healthy or helpful, for the polar ice caps will begin to melt, flooding much of the land on which we live.

Our factories and smoke-stacks are constantly spewing our carbon dioxide which is a byproduct of any burning. If too much of this is spilled in the air, we will be upsetting the balance, causing the global warming which some predict and which all dread.

Interestingly, and in quite unrelated ways, Joseph Black was also very much interested in the phenomenon of heat. He was one of the first to distinguish between the notion of temperature and that of heat. To this day, not many (who have not had a course in physics) know the difference between the two. The general notion is that temperature is a measure of how much heat a body contains. This is not the case. The cold lake in winter has far more heat energy than your body, yet it is at a much lower temperature.

Given the same amount of heat, different substances can be raised through different degrees of temperature. It takes less heat to raise the temperature of a gram of copper through a degree than it a gram of water. This leads to the idea of what physicists call the *specific heat* of a substance. This notion was also introduced by Joseph Black.

We know that as we give more and more heat to a body, its temperature keeps rising. But this is not always the case. If you place a can of water on the burner with a thermometer in it, the temperature will gradually rise, but it will stop rising when the water begins to boil, though we keep adding heat to the body of water. This is because of what is called *latent heat*: another idea due to Joseph Black.

April 17

From the World of Religion:
LUTHER BEFORE THE DIET

A fulfilling experience in affiliation to a religion is being part of a community. It is a frosting on the cake at the conclusion of religious gatherings. More importantly, it is a privilege to those services and to the sacraments of the tradition, from baptismal to obsequies. In the framework of most established religious institutions, the converse is also true. If a member breaks the prescribed rules in significant ways, he or she will lose the privileges. When one is thus formally excluded, one is said to be *excommunicated*.

The word brings to mind the Roman Catholic Church. But the practice is not unique to it, nor did it begin with it. In ancient Greece, culprits were denied holy water for some derelictions. The Druids did not permit participation in sacrifices by those who were polluted. In Judaism, one speaks of *herem*: which punitively prohibits some Jews from coming to the synagogue or associating with other members of the community. Spinoza was one of the recipients of this treatment.

A converse situation arises when a member of the fold voluntarily, even publicly, rejects some of the proclaimed tenets of the religion, and leaves it. This is an act of apostasy. Apostasy could include offering incense to a pagan deity and renouncing a religious vow in Christianity; blaspheming the name of the Prophet or rejecting the holiness of the Qur'an in Islam; not accepting the authority of the Vedas in traditional Hinduism. Depending on the religion and time in history, punishment for apostasy could range from rebuke and being ostracized to a price on the culprit's head.

Generally, the excommunicated individual suffers socially and religiously. He/she is said to be cursed by evil forces and one believes that the individual would eventually rot in a terrible place. Sometimes, even well-meaning Christians, devout to the faith, and eager to preserve it, have been excommunicated. Thus, in 140, Marcion was fired up to make Christianity a great religion without any trace of Judaism. He proclaimed that Hebrew Scriptures ought to be rejected. In his view, Christ appeared on earth in a spiritual body, already thirty years old. Marcion was rich and he gave large sums of money to the Roman church to propagate these ideas. Yet, the man was excommunicated.

Martin Luther waged his rebellion against the Roman Catholic Church when there were grumblings against excessive ritualism, unproductive idleness in monasteries, belief in trivial miracles, misuse of the Church's power to excommunicate, etc. The reaction to Luther was not sympathetic. A series of exchanges, pleas, and warnings culminated in Luther being brought before the Diet (six-monthly meeting of the estates of the Holy Roman Empire) on 17 April 1521 where there were many dignitaries, including a representative of the Pope. The protesting Luther was asked if he would retract the heresies uttered in his books. Luther did not give a firm Yes. The result was that Luther was excommunicated not long after that fateful day. And when the Protestant movement began, it was quickly adopted as a rule that anyone who contradicted what Luther had said would be excommunicated also. *Sic transit ineptiae mundi.*

In that the same year (1521) a book was published under the authorship of King Henry VIII of England in which it was asked rhetorically, "What serpent so venomous as he (Luther) who calls the pope's authority tyrannous?" For this book Henry was praised as *Defensor Fidei* (Defender of the faith). As the irony of history would have it, Henry VIII excommunicated himself long after this. Luther's excommunication led to Protestantism and Henry VIII's to the establishment of the Anglican Church.

From the World of Science:
GIAMBATTISTA RICCIOLI

Anyone (in the northern hemisphere) who has gazed at the stars as constellations must have noticed the Big Dipper: also known as Ursa Major or the Great Bear. But not everyone may know that of the constituents of this constellation of seven (visible) stars, Zeta Ursae Majoris, named Mizar by Arab astronomers, has a unique distinction in the history of astronomy: It is the first star recognized as a binary.

Binaries are systems consisting of two gravitationally-linked stars. In other words, they are stars which revolve around each other for eons. Sometimes one of them may burst forth, leading to spectacular episodes, like the appearance of a Nova. A catalogue of double stars, published in 1785, contained almost 700 of them.

I am mentioning Mizar at this time because its binary nature was discovered in 1650 by Giambattista Riccioli (born: 17 April 1598).

Riccioli was a Jesuit theologian who taught Italian literature for some time in Parma and Bologna. But he was also deeply interested in physics and astronomy. He did fruitful investigations on the pendulum for measuring time periods. He was an Aristotelian who was not particularly sympathetic to some of Galileo's attitudes vis-à-vis the church. So he did experiments on falling bodies to prove Galileo wrong. As it turned out, his work led to a confirmation, rather than a refutation, of what Galileo had found.

Riccioli wrote on the 1652 comet, and on the Gregorian calendar. As late as in 1668 he presented what he called physical-mathematical arguments against the daily motion of the earth. He studied sunspots, compiled star catalogues, made telescopic observations of Saturn and Jupiter, and was one of the first to note the colored bands on the surface of Jupiter. He made estimates of the radius of the earth, and of the distance of the sun from the earth which he found to be of the order of 24 million miles. Aside from becoming the discoverer of the first double-star system, Riccioli is also remembered as a thorough selenic cartographer: he mapped all the visible surface of the moon. He initiated a convention for naming the regions. Some of them were named after moods, like serenity and tranquility, and craters immortalized the names of eminent astronomers. That is how the names of Aristotle and Arago, of Cassini and Fabricus, of Roemer and Riccioli and many more came to be associated with addresses of lunar craters.

Riccioli was not a Copernican, though he was not averse to accepting Tycho's Brahe's compromise of the traditional planets moving around the sun, and everything moving around a fixed earth. He was also interested in the refraction of light from the stars as it enters the earth's atmosphere. He was very much interested in geography too, and he published tables of latitudes and longitudes for many places in various countries.

Riccioli was another of the many scientists of 17th century Italy who were also faithful Christians, loyal to the teachings of the Church. Some of them could not read the works of Galileo and Copernicus first hand, because the books were on the papal index, but they did come to know about the contents of those writings through indirect means, from references in other books, etc.

What is important to recognize in the life and accomplishments of such people is that, even when one is faithful to religious doctrines, and indeed even if one is mistaken in some aspects of science because of that, one can make (as many have made) useful and significant contributions to science.

April 18

From the World of Religion:
EARTHQUAKE IN SAN FRANCISCO

The earth had rocked a thousand times before, and will do so many more times. But the tremors that shook San Francisco and its environs on 18 April 1906 were among the most terrible. They provoked a fire that couldn't be quenched for four days, turning to naught countless homes and public buildings, causing the deaths of thousands of people. Most of these were due to the collapse of dwellings and the ensuing fire, but some died because they were shot by the police for looting and stealing when the disaster struck. Monetary losses have been estimated to be of the order of half a billion (1906) dollars.

Some people predicted more earthquakes soon, injecting fear in the hearts of the people. In spite of assurances that the worst was over, irresponsible statements persisted, prompting one official to say with a touch of anger, "Never mind foreboders of evil: they do not know what they are talking about. Seismometry is in its infancy and those therefore who venture out with predictions of future earthquakes when the main shock has taken place ought to be arrested as disturbers of the peace."

Earthquakes are natural disasters which provoke fundamental questions about God's relation or indifference to His creatures. The question was raised most emphatically by Voltaire after the terrible earthquake in Lisbon on All Saints Day in the year 1755. Thirty churches collapsed during a quake that lasted for six full minutes, killing fifteen thousand people, men women and children, most of them in praying postures. Then, as sometimes happens even now, some thoughtless spokesmen for God declared it was all a well-deserved punishment for all the sin and sensuality of the citizens of Lisbon, which hardly explained why children and monks were among the dead. Another theologian shamelessly proclaimed that the earthquake in Lisbon "displayed God's glory."

Voltaire reflected poetically in a masterpiece called *On the Lisbon Disaster*, inviting the silly sages who cry, "All is well" to contemplate on the horrible ruins. He asked them rhetorically if they would declare to the victims that God has been revenged, that their death has repaid their crimes.

He philosophized on the calamity, but did not solve the problem of theodicy. He could not, and nor has anyone else been able to. I rather doubt that anyone ever will. For among the mysteries that will for ever remain unsolved is the suffering of the innocent and the helpless, often in large numbers, for no apparent fault of theirs. In the face of such a disaster, I am reminded of another poem:

When lightning strikes a praying crowd, and the pious burn and die,
When earthquakes bury decent folk, and orphaned children cry,
When sick and old are abandoned too, and people lose their mind:
Try not for these and disasters such, answers clear to find.

There are times to argue if God is thought or real fact.
There are times at which we need to go and begin to act.
Let's search and see what we can do for those who are in need,
How we can console and heal, how we can clothe and feed.

It does not matter if we do not know why there's pain around.
What we need are helping hands, not learned views and sound.
With loss and pain and intense grief we don't have much to gain,
From arguments on heaven and hell, they'll all be just in vain.

From the World of Religion:
CLARENCE DARROW

We are still facing the debate provoked by Darwin's *Origin of the Species*: not just about its scientific validity, but as to whether it can be taught in schools without presenting competing models to explain the existence of *homo sapiens* on *terra firma*.

Already in the 19th century, there was a vigorous debate on the scientific aspect of Evolution, in Oxford, England. And in 1925, in Dayton, TN, there took place the famous trial of a school teacher who had dared to teach Evolution to his students in a biology course when a local law explicitly forbade teachers from doing that.

When science confronts religion on an issue like this, ideas clash and those who listen or read can make up their minds on the basis of the evidence presented. But when the confrontation occurs in a courtroom, whether of an Inquisition or of a state, the consequences for the accused can be serious. In a religious court those who are perceived as ungodly can expect harsh punishment, for the religious authorities control the outcome. In a secular court, a lot depends on how effective the lawyers are.

In the trial of John Scopes in Tennessee, it was Clarence Darrow (born: 18 April 1857) who defended the accused. Darrow was not just a defense lawyer. He had great interest in science, and had read Darwin deeply. He was also one of the awakened thinkers who would tolerate anything except intolerance. So, he volunteered to defend the school teacher at no cost at all, because for him, it was a social and civic responsibility to protect the freedom to teach.

It has been recorded that Darrow was "a sophisticated attorney with the mannerisms of a country lawyer." He was a scholarly type who enjoyed literature and poetry as much as philosophy and psychology. He had a passion for upsetting the apple-cart of conventional positions. That's why he had defended communists and anarchists as well. So it was no surprise that though he was approaching 70, he cheerfully accepted the responsibility.

It required much courage, especially in those days in that part of the country, to defend a position that was perceived as blatantly anti-religious. There were, as there still are, thousands of people who truly believe, irrespective of the scientific merits or demerits of Evolution, that any interpretation of human existence, or even of the existence of the universe, that does not take into account the role of an Almighty God, is sacrilegious, and that if, in addition, it also contradicts passages from their Holy Book, it is downright blasphemy. They believe that the upholders of such views must be dealt with severely for they are enemies of God. In the charged atmosphere, where placards proclaimed such statements as "You need God in your business" and "Where will you spend Eternity?" Clarence Darrow was called an infidel and worse, and some predicted lightning would strike and kill him.

Science began as a selfless inquiry into the nature and underpinnings of the phenomenal world. The intent of its practitioners never was, nor ever is likely to be, to be disrespectful to the God of any religion. Science is propelled by an eagerness to explain and understand on the basis of the data of observation, in a framework of reason and coherence. If that leads us to worldviews which seem to contradict the visions of some our ancestors, it is unfortunate.

But if one is taken to court for subscribing to or propagating scientific worldviews, however tentative these are, then we need able lawyers to defend science and its proponents. One such lawyer in one such context was Clarence Darrow. So, though he himself was not a scientist, I remember him today.

April 19

From the World of Religion:
DALAI LAMA'S REFUGE

The religious head of the Tibetan people, universally known as the Dalai Lama, had to flee his native land with a great many of his followers in 1959. On 19 April that year, he was given sanctuary in neighboring India. Eight years earlier, The People's Liberation Army of Communist China forced its way into unarmed Tibet, occupied it, and exerted every effort to cleanse the culture of Tibetans from their Buddhist roots. They have not been any more successful in this secularizing enterprise than in their attempts to rid the Chinese people of all vestiges of whatever religion they might be addicted to.

Born in 1935 in a simple rural family in the village of Takster, the current Dalai Lama is the 14th in a lineage which has its origins in the 13th century. He is regarded as the reincarnation of the last personage who held the title. This deity of compassion, or *Avalokiteshvara* as he is called, is believed to have come down to earth to serve humanity. He was given this title when barely five years old, and formally installed in Lhasa as Dalai Lama in February 1940, in the famed Potala Palace. The word *Dalai* is of Mongolian origin. It means *ocean. Lama* is a Tibetan word which refers to a religious guide or master, somewhat like the Sanskrit *guru.*

As a gentle spiritual guru he would have guided his people in a life of inner peace. But he was thrust into politics when still quite young. He had to travel to Beijing, meet the likes of Mao Tse Tung and Chou En Lai who tried their very best to make him recognize that Tibet was but a portion or province of the People's Republic of China. But the young Dalai Lama would never agree to this. He felt that the Tibetans were a unique people who had lived on the roof of the world for many long centuries, and he saw no need for them to become a Communist appendage. Needless to say, the obstinate stance of the Dalai Lama infuriated the Chinese who claimed to know what was good for Tibet. But the Chinese coerced the Tibetans into signing on 23 May 1951 a *Seventeen Point Agreement* for what they described as the Peaceful Liberation of Tibet. They did not quite say what they were liberating Tibet from.

After the Dalai Lama was ejected from Tibet, the Chinese propped their own (tenth) Panchen Lala (traditionally, the second in command) as the Buddhist leader in Tibet, but to little avail. The Panchen Lama remained loyal to the Dalai Lama, was imprisoned for a decade, and when released, he became even more vocal.

Quite unexpectedly, because of the Chinese intrusion, the Dalai Lama began to receive world attention. Every time the United Nations passed resolutions (1959, 1961, 1965, 1991) condemning China for violating the basic rights of the Tibetan people, it was a boost for the Dalai Lama and for Tibetan Buddhism which has gradually become a world religion.

Because of such publicity, the Dalai Lama has been invited to many countries, to speak to large audiences, to have private conversations with heads of state, including the Pope, to grant TV interviews, etc. It all culminated in his receiving the Nobel Prize for Peace. Scientists have had interviews with him to discuss science and Buddhism. Celebrities got interested in the plight of the Tibetan people, as did movie producers.

Religions spread in a variety of ways: with the sharpness of the sword, by inspiring evangelism, by opening up economic opportunities for converts, through propaganda at airports, etc. In the case of Tibetan Buddhism, the ruthlessness of an expansionist government unwittingly served its cause.

From the World of Science:
LYSERGIC ACID DIETHYLAMIDE

Many things happen in the laboratories, observatories, and research centers, which affect human history in direct and indirect ways. One such thing occurred on 19 April 1943 when Albert Hofmann of the Pharmaceutical-Chemical Research Laboratories, Sandoz, Switzerland, swallowed 0.5 cc of half promil aqueous solution of diethylamide tartrate which he had synthesized five years earlier. Hofmann began to feel dizzy and anxious, experienced visual distortions, and had symptoms of paralysis. He had a desire to laugh. From 6 to 8 p.m. that evening he had "a very severe crisis." He recorded all this meticulously. Later, he described the delirious effects: "Everything in the room spun around, and the familiar objects and pieces of furniture assumed grotesque, threatening forms.... The lady next door, whom I scarcely recognized, brought me milk...She was no longer Mrs. R., but rather a malevolent, insidious witch with a colored mask. Even worse than these demonic transformations of the outer world, were the alterations that I perceived in myself, in my inner being.... A demon had invaded me, had taken possession of my body, mind, and soul. I jumped up and screamed, trying to free myself from him, but then sank down again and lay helpless on the sofa. The substance...had vanquished me. It was the demon that scornfully triumphed over my will. I was seized by the dreadful fear of going insane. I was taken to another world, another place, another time."

Hofmann's tinkering with Lysergic acid diethylamide (LSD) had unexpected impacts on our attitudes to religion. First, it suggested a chemical basis for the mystical and spiritual experiences reported by countless individuals in all traditions and cultures over the ages. In doing this, it unwittingly trivialized what has generally been regarded as genuine and lofty incursions into dimensions of transcendental reality, reducing mysticism to hallucinations induced by alterations in brain chemistry. One began to re-think religious visions of the great saints and prophets as perhaps having been induced by the ingestion of unusual plants or herbs. Indeed, in some traditions, periodic sniffing of certain substances has been common for getting a religious high. The burning of incense in religious contexts is probably a vestige of this practice.

Just as the airplane made alchemical and yogic reports of teleportation within reach of all and sundry, and telephone and television did the same for clairaudience and clairvoyance, Hofmann's experience showed that by simply ingesting a drug, even sinners and students can get some of the effects (like seeing God) that used to be achieved only after years of spiritual discipline. As one writer put is elegantly: "This discovery has permitted the honest, earnest seeker to stand on the very pinnacle of human experience, the Unitive knowledge of the Godhead."

This led to more experiments with other chemicals, and to the rediscovery of plants and leaves that give people easy access to a world of psychedelic space. Thinkers like Timothy Leary and Aldous Huxley inspired millions to a drug-based culture with related music and gatherings, unleashing a pop-religion that has wasted the lives of countless people, young and old, and continues to have devastating side-effects. Except for these and the fact that such seekers of easy spirituality often look pathetic to those confined to normal Reality, can become lethal when they get behind the steering wheel of a car, and often need help from people in clinics and hospitals, there may be nothing immoral in such enterprises. Sadly, the drug culture has also given rise to violent crimes and murder, dedication of land to hallucinogenic botany rather than to nutritive vegetables, international problems, and countless other inconveniences to staid and proper life-styles.

April 20

From the World of Religion:
HANGING OF ELIZABETH BARTON

Episodes from alien cultures may strike one as rather strange, but this is equally true of episodes from one's own culture, if it was of a different period in history. Consider the story of Elizabeth Barton who lived briefly during the first decades on the 16th century. She was a simple woman, working as a menial servant at a home in Aldington, Kent. She also had frequent fits, perhaps of seizure, during which she would go into a trance. And in that state she would utter things that sounded quite odd even to people of those times, for she seemed to refer to events that occurred in far away places of which she could not have had any direct knowledge. In her trance she would speak harshly about people who engaged in immoral behavior. In one admiring narrative of her life, we are informed that her utterances were "of marvelous holiness in rebuke of sin and vice."

To continue with the traditional legend, news of her extraordinary prowess reached the ears of the Archbishop of Canterbury. That venerable personage dispatched a commission of dignitaries and holy men to investigate if she was genuine, deluded, or con-woman. The verdict was in her favor: Elizabeth Barton was certainly endowed with superior powers. This gave more credibility to her pronouncements. It is said that she predicted and cured herself of her ailment in the local chapel in the presence of a multitude. And she became a nun.

At this time, King Henry VIII of many-marriages fame was ruling England. It was common knowledge then that he was eager to divorce his queen Catherine and replace her by Anne Boleyn. But the king had difficulty getting papal permission to annul his marriage to Catherine. This led to the genesis of the Church of England.

In 1532, the king was passing through Canterbury when the Nun of Kent had the audacity to admonish him not to entertain thoughts of marrying Anne. This did not have much effect on the royal passions which had been unleashed in the direction of Anne.

In January 1533, while Catherine of Aragon was still the official queen but not in the palace, Henry married Anne Boleyn, if only because she was already carrying his child. Instead of celebrating the royal wedding, Barton blurted out that she not only disapproved for the king's behavior but had had a vision which revealing the exact location in hell where preparations were being made to install Henry in due course.

Some felt that Henry had behaved like a reckless royal rogue, and was therefore not altogether undeserving of such post-mortem discomfort. So his advisors wanted to check out if the nun's alleged vision was serious stuff, for there was the remote possibility that this could well be true. Along with six accomplices, Elizabeth Barton was brought to the (in)famous Star Chamber and tried. She is said to have confessed in the course of the trial (perhaps under duress) that her trances had in fact been a fake. For this offense Elizabeth Barton was hanged in public on 20 April 1533.

In our own times, in most civilized countries, no one is taken seriously for proclaiming that they have visions about a political leader of the country. Most of them are ignored, some undergo psychiatric treatment, and a few do get to write columns in newspapers and make tidy amounts by sharing their self-proclaimed knowledge of what stars and planets tell them. But there still are religious leaders who invoke God to spell the destruction of countries which they detest for valid and invalid reasons. All this is part of the magical tradition which is ingrained in the human psyche. But such individuals are no longer brought to court, tried, and hanged, as happened to poor Elizabeth Barton.

From the World of Science:
GERALD STANLEY HAWKINS

We see the sun rise and set, the moon change phases from New Moon to Full. We have sophisticated observatories and space stations also. But what about our distant ancestors? We know that in ancient China and India, in Babylonia and Greece, there were star gazers and interpreters of celestial bodies. We have come to know of their astronomical insights primarily from the writings they have left behind.

But there are also materials from past cultures and civilizations, most of them recovered by the efforts of archeologists which seem mere stones and structures at first sight, but which may, in fact, be relics of ancient instruments to study the skies. Scholarly attempts to reconstruct the astronomy of peoples and civilizations that are now buried in the irrevocable past constitute the field of *archaeoastronomy*.

Stonehenge is on Salisbury Plain in England. To the tourist this is no just a collection of huge stones in a large circular ditch, about 300 plus feet in diameter, to which one is led by what is called the Avenue where a massive upright stone called the Heel Stone stands. The stones are nicely organized. There is an external circular arrangement of sandstones which are linked by lintels. There is an inner circle of bluestones. Going further in, one sees a horseshoe arrangement, followed by an ovoid pattern. At the center of it all is an Alter Stone. Once it was thought that these are remains of a place of worship of Druids who arrived in Britain sometime in the 3rd century B.C.E. This theory had to be given up when the megaliths were dated to be much, much older. Today we know that the most ancient among them go back to much more ancient times.

In the early 1960s the astronomer Gerald Stanley Hawkins (born: 20 April 1928) put forward an altogether new theory to interpret Stonehenge. In his view, this was an elaborate construction meant for astronomical purposes. Using a computer, he charted the heavens such as they would have appeared in 1500 B.C.E., and argued that the megalithic arrangements were used by the sky-watchers of the time to determine with considerable accuracy the positions and movements of the sun and the moon, on the basis of which they also predict the periodic occurrences of eclipses.

The idea that four thousand years ago people (whether in Britain or elsewhere) could do observational astronomy using such precise instruments struck quite a few scholars as being a bit much. But Hawkins' book *Stonehenge Decoded* (1965) explains the matter persuasively. He located 165 points in the complex which have remarkable correlation with the rising and setting positions of the sun. The book inspired more people to explore the matter of archaeoastronomy in other places too.

Hawkins and his co-workers investigated the subject further in the temple of Michu Pichu in Peru, in Mayan ruins in Central America, and in Amerindian mounds in North America, in the Easter Islands, and in the Temples of Karnak in Egypt. In 1973 he published another books: *Beyond Stonehenge*.

Today archaeoastronomers are trying to reconstruct if prehistoric Polynesians were guided by constellations when they navigated in the Pacific, whether the puzzling patterns of Nazca in the *pampa* of Peru had anything to do with observational astronomy, the astronomical basis the Mayan calendar, and so on.

We recognize of course that modern science has brought to human understanding vast amounts of knowledge about the physical world. But it would be simplistic to imagine that the ancients had no scientific spirit or genius. We are grateful to investigators like Hawkins who bring to light the scientific dimensions of ancient peoples.

April 21

From the World of Religion:
BIRTHDAY OF SRI RAMA

As per Hindu sacred history, the birthday of the divine Ramachandra (popularly called Rama). fell on 21 April in the year 2002). The great Indian epic *Ramayana* narrates the saga of one of the major *avataras* (incarnations) of Lord Vishnu, the Sustaining Principle in the universe. Invariably associated with his consort Sita and brother Lakshmana, Rama is worshipped in temples and homes throughout the length and breadth of India and beyond.

The grandeur of the Ramayana lies, not in the history, geography, or science of ancient India (all of which may be seen here), but in the values and insights it inculcates on truth and justice, on monogamous love and filial duty. In serene Sanskrit or medieval Hindi, in Tamil or Bengali, or in any other language, in prose or in poetry form, as movie, dance drama, or as a TV serial, the Ramayana captures the heart and mind of people brought up in the Hindu tradition such as no other work of literature or history has done.

Traditionally, one reads the inspiring epic during the first nine days of Chaitra (March-April) in groups and in reverential modes. Sometimes, a scholar narrates the story with songs and sermons. This is a unique form of performing art in Hindu culture. It includes devotional music which stirs our spiritual yearnings. Humorous comments spice up the recounting. Anecdotes and references to current social mores make the presentation livelier. The narrator is usually a scholar who quotes profusely from other poets of the lore. Children and adults, men and women, the learned and the simple, all gather evening after evening to listen to the well known story. The skill and style of the narrator combine such a variety of ingredients that attending the *katha* (as this mode is called) becomes an experience that is inspiring, illuminating, entertaining, and spiritually uplifting.

Rama is God incarnate, but ideal human too. He represents the best of human virtues, standing for righteousness, word of honor, and obedience to parents. He respected elders, fought for fairness and justice, was gentle, compassionate, and merciful. Children brought up in the Hindu tradition derive their values by listening to the epic of Rama and anecdotes from it in various contexts. Ultimately, one purpose of religion is to inculcate a meaningful ethical framework that embodies the highest elements of the human potential. Rama's name has molded a dynamic civilization and given rise to magnificent art and music and poetry. The kingdom of Rama (*Ramraajya*) was ideal:

It has been said by Valmiki sage that when the great Rama ruled,
No disease was there, nor early death, nor persons there unschooled.
No man did die in a fruitful phase, leaving behind a wife.
Nor mothers wailed the loss of babes that died in early life.
No thieves there were, nor cheats, nor crooks; all did what they should.
People loved and cared for those who lived in their neighborhood.
Plants and trees did richly grow, yielding fruits and grains,
The earth itself enriched the land with breeze and regular rains.
No lightning, thunder, or blazing fire did bring to hearts alarm,
No gale or hale or quakes that would cause to people harm.
With valleys green and flowing streams all Nature smiled so well,
Men toiled hard and produced goods, traders' things did sell.
There was law and order and justice fair in this ancient realm:
That was the kingdom which had the great Rama at its helm.

From the World of Science:
PERCY WILLIAM BRIDGMAN

One of the reasons the world is the way it is, is because of external conditions. If these change to extreme heat or extreme cold, matter undergoes significant changes, its properties change. If matter is subjected to high pressure, its properties change too.

Physicists measure pressure in units of atmosphere. The pressure exerted by the earth's atmosphere at sea level is about 14.5 pounds per square inch. This means that we are walking around carrying a load of some 300 pounds on our head!

We can exert pressure on bodies by pushing hard or by placing heavy weights on them. It would be interesting to study how materials behave when they are subjected to high pressure. But what do we mean by high pressure? Would a pressure of ten atmospheres be high pressure or a hundred? Physicists have been experimenting the change in properties of materials when subjected to increasingly high pressures.

One who investigated the problem to incredibly high levels was Percy William Bridgman (born: 21 April 1882). He graduated from Harvard University in the first decade of the 20th century, became a faculty member in his alma mater soon thereafter, and spent the next forty years there. During these years he did considerable research on the compressibility, conductivity, viscosity, etc. of a hundred different materials, subjected to enormous pressures: sometimes reaching as high as a hundred thousand atmospheres. Bridgman developed techniques for growing crystals and making non-leak packages. He was dexterous and inventive as an experimenter, imaginative as a deviser of experiments, and philosophical in his appraisal of what science and physics are all about. His scientific work threw light on the nature of matter in the interior of the earth and of other planets. It also had practical applications: such as the possibility of making artificial diamonds from carbon. Bridgman's work in physics was recognized by many prestigious institutions by the awarding of medals and honorary doctorates, and crowned by a Nobel Prize in 1946.

Aside from scientific papers and many books, Bridgman is also remembered for his views on Operational analysis in the context of doing science. Two of his books on this theme have become classics in the philosophy of science. *The Logic of Modern Physics* (1927) and *The Nature of Physical Theory* (1936). In the first, he stressed that any concept in science has to be tied to well defined operations in the physical world. The concept must be linked in a clear-cut manner to effects of performable operations. As a superb experimentalist, Bridgman realized that no matter how refined and sophisticated theoretical and mathematical analyses might be, ultimately all of science hinges on well planned observational data. He stated categorically that meaning is associated with operations by which answers can be given. In the absence of any such operation, concepts have no meaning at all. This point of view has been challenged by others because in one stroke it makes all metaphysics meaningless.

Bridgman was a man of many interests beyond physics, such as music and skiing. He lived a full life, made significant contributions to science and to the enterprise of clear thinking. In his last years, when he was almost 80, he was struck by a disease that caused him unbearable pain from which there seemed to be no escape. He felt he should be given euthanasia so that he might die in dignity. He said: "...when the ultimate end is as inevitable as it now appears to be, the individual has a right to ask his doctor to end it for him." This plea has been reiterated by countless others in a similar condition. When this did not happen, he took his own life, leaving behind a note which said: "It isn't decent for Society to make a man do this thing by himself."

April 22

From the World of Religion: EDWARD DE VERE

To the extent that the scriptures, saints and sages of all religious traditions speak beautifully, effectively, and meaningfully about the human condition, the great writers and poets of the world may also be counted among them. There is only this difference: Poets and writers are more universal and less parochial in their insightful utterances.

In this sense, one of the greatest saints of the pan-Religious (humanistic) tradition is William Shakespeare, for, as Alexander Pope rightly noted: "He seems to have known the world by intuition, to have looked through nature at one glance."

But who was this Shakespeare, this bard of extraordinary understanding of every aspect of the human experience: the emotional, the psychological, the noble, the mean, the heroic, the cowardly, the admirable, the despicable; who had analyzed every passion and predicament: love, hate, frustration, excitement, despondence, mirth, and more? For generations he was believed to have been a man of modest origins, not schooled in Latin or Greek, who married Anne Hathaway while she was expecting their first daughter, who had been called *an upstart crow* by Robert Greene.

In the 1920s a school teacher in Durham (U.K.) by the name of John Thomas Looney gave a jolt to this applecart of traditional views by suggesting, in effect, that Shakespeare was not Shakespeare at all, indeed that no such person actually existed, and that a certain Edward de Vere (born: 22 April, 1550), a nobleman of Italian lineage, was the real genius who had authored all those wonderful plays and sonnets under the pseudonym of William Shakespeare. Needless to say, this was a bombshell in classical Shakespeareana.

The English literature establishment chose to ignore, rather then investigate, the Vere-ification of Shakespeare (as the thesis has been called). The American scholar Charlton Ogburn was an enthusiastic propagator of the De Vere-Shakespeare thesis. His slim volume, *The Man Who Was Shakespeare* is quite compelling.

Few doubt that De Vere, the English poet and the 17th Earl of Oxford, existed. His father was a patron of playwright John Bale. His uncle, Arthur Golding, had translated Ovid's *Metamorphoses* in English. Émile Legouis, in *A History of English Literature* (1926) noted (p. 288): "He (De Vere) exemplifies the taste for letters which reigned in the court circle and which might be found in a dissolute flop like himself as well as in a daring adventurer like Raleigh or in Sidney, the mirror of perfect chivalry."

The debate on the author of Shakespeare's plays hasn't died. De Vereists seem to be growing in number, in conferences, and in publications.

The parallel with traditional religion is striking. When, in a distant age, some thought of questioning the divinity of the Egyptian Osiris—if he was no more than a conquering general—Plutarch warned that such an inquiry "would open the door to atheism." The same may be said of Indra of Rig Vedic eminence, or of Moses of the Old Testament. Indeed, the De Vere thesis is not unlike similar perspectives in religions: that Moses was an imaginary character, that Jesus was a local cultist who lived and died like anyone else, that Rama and Krishna are more mythological than historical, that Mohammed was an eccentric who often had seizures, etc. When such theses are presented the reaction of the believers is seldom, "Ah, really? How interesting!"

Mark Twain said about Shakespeare and the Devil: "The two Great Unknowns, the two illustrious Conjecturabilities! They are the best known unknown persons that have ever drawn breath upon the planet." This is more applicable to Shakespeare and De Vere.

From the World of Science: EARTH DAY

22 April was Earth Day in 2002. Our earth is a speck in the vast stretches of the cosmos, infinitesimal in material substance compared to the mind-boggling mass of the universe. Our awesome abode hurtles around the sun at enormous speeds and is carried around the galactic center by our central star at a million miles an hour. During its few billion years existence, the earth has seen countless transformations: continents have shifted, rocks have been compressed and metamorphosed, hills and mountains have risen and fallen, streams and rivers have been forged and dried, ice ages have come and gone. Through processes not fully clear, the miracle of life has arisen here.

After our ancient ancestors emerged and became self aware and questioning, they learned to manipulate matter and energy. Other life forms came under their sway. In a couple of million years, humans became even more creative and clever. Land and water, birds and beasts, elements and compounds, the savannah and the tundra, the heat of deserts and the cold of poles, fruits and flowers and minerals deep down, coal and oil and gas, even the mighty forces that bind atoms and nuclei, all rapidly came under their control. In an orgy of exploitation of everything for creature comfort and monetary gain we unwittingly began to wreck the beauty of nature and the salubrity of our environment.

Less than two centuries since the ease-giving rampage of the Industrial Revolution began, we realize that much harm has been done to land, water and air: Toxic fumes are permeating the atmosphere, radioactive wastes are lurking around, rain forests are being depleted, species are made extinct, the ozone layer is cracked open, coral reefs are smashed by ships, acid is injected into rain-bearing clouds: Oh, the list goes on and on!

It is often said that we are destroying the earth. This is an arrogant appraisal of what we are doing, for *we* can never destroy the earth. A billion years from now, long after we are dead and gone, the earth will be dancing away merrily along its elliptical orbit to the tune of Keplerian laws. All we can do is to destroy ourselves, not the earth.

Why don't we stop this suicidal behavior? Our economic and international networks have evolved such that even with much goodwill and determination it is not easy to halt the harm we are wreaking. Every effort to control pollution adversely affects jobs and profits. Moreover, the danger and doom implicit in reckless technology will hit hard only generations yet unborn. This gives little incentive for today's self-centered hedonists.

We must act in sure but quick ways to dampen the damage and reverse the trends. For this we need consciousness-raising and global awareness. We must transcend our national and communal conditionings and think in planetary terms. For what is at stake is not the well being of this nation or that religious group, but the fate of the human family. The diseases of racial hatred, religious intolerance, and economic self-aggrandizement are the major threats to our harmony and existence. In our woeful inability to perceive the world as a habitat to be shared and nurtured by one and all, including other creatures of the planet, we pollute our minds and hearts too, and upset the ecological balance.

Enlightened industrialists and realistic ecologists must work hand in hand in a spirit of mutual respect to resolve the problems that *we all face together*. Through education, understanding, and enlightened values, through legislation and reasoning, and with the resources of science and technology, we must strive to increase our awareness of the assault on nature that humans have been perpetrating.

Each week we devote a day to a planet, but only once a year do we have an Earth Day. We need to treat every day as Earth Day.

April 23

From the World of Religion: SAINT GEORGE

Many nations have a patron saint, but some saints are patronized by more than one nation. St. George (Feast Day: 23 April) is celebrated by Estonians, Finns and Russians of Christian persuasion, as well as by Canadians and the English. He is the patron saint of England, even if many Englishmen don't take him all that seriously any more. But his symbol may be found in many contexts in England, including and especially, in the Union Jack which bears St. George's red cross. St. George is often pictured on a horse.

English poets have mentioned him. In Edmund Spencer's *Faerie Queene* there is a Red Cross Knight who is no other than St. George:

Thou St. George shalt callèd be

St. George of Merry England, the sign of victory.

Shakespeare's Henry V went so far as to say:

Follow your spirit, and upon this charge

Cry, "God for Harry! England and Saint George!

But who was this saint whose name is derived from a Greek word meaning a cultivator of land, who was famous for chivalry, generosity and valor, was protector of horses and cattle, whose Feast Day was once celebrated like Christmas, one after whom were named the Knights of the Garter and several English monarchs? What little we know of him is of questionable authenticity. This is what is generally said about him:

St. George lived in the third century C.E. when the anti-Christian Dioclesian was emperor of Rome. He was a tribune in the Roman army in Palestine, and a brave one at that. Once he was in Libya to confront a ferocious dragon that used to devour two sheep a day. Since meat was scarce, people sometimes offered a daughter to the dragon instead: so it is told in the tale. On one occasion, when a princess was to be so sacrificed, valiant George, by now a Christian, made a sign of the cross and, like Hercules, slew the dragon in one strong stroke. Then he is said to have given an eloquent sermon. All this so impressed the populace that they embraced Christianity en masse right away.

George cringed at some of the harsh measures of the emperor Dioclesian against Christians, and he vehemently protested the same. For this offense he was relieved of his post and thrown into prison. According a gory version of what happened, the conscientious objector was tortured and beheaded. Then his headless body was dragged on the streets of Lydda in Palestine.

It is hard to believe that such things happened. Worse atrocities may still be happening in our world, but never more in public. But then, those violent narratives were perhaps the equivalent of some of our movies where the most heinous acts of atrocities are displayed as entertainment. Could it be that the pious people derived thrill from listening to such revolting stories, as some do in our own times? And did the story-tellers perhaps intentionally spice up the episodes to make it all more interesting? Who can say?

Today we remember the Dragon episode more than the morbid martyrdom. That story spread far and wide, and centuries later, it became a recurrent theme in many works of art. In Raphael's painting, the youthful St. George, seated on a frightened horse, is piercing the dragon with his lance, while the princess who would have been sacrificed is praying nearby. In Ucello's (National Gallery, London), George is even more boyish, the horse is humped, and the dragon more ferocious. The princess is standing bravely by it. The finest relics of the saints may best be seen in paintings and music and poetry that.

From the World of Science: MAX PLANCK

The two most important theories of 20th century physics which had revolutionary impact on our worldviews are Relativity and Quantum Physics. The first was the work of Albert Einstein, and the second was initiated by Max Planck (born: 23 April 1858).

Towards the close of the 19th century, physicists could explain fairly well almost every phenomenon they had studied in detail, but there remained one tough problem. It was related to the radiation emitted from very hot bodies. We know that as we heat, say, a piece of iron, it begins to glow: as one increases the temperature of a body, higher frequency (light) radiations are given out. If we heat it more, it turns from red hot to blue hot. At higher temperatures there is more radiation of higher frequencies.

When the relative amounts of various radiations (of different frequencies) are carefully measured at various temperatures and plotted, one gets curves which could not be derived mathematically on the basis of the then accepted views of radiant energy. Planck solved the problem by proposing a fundamentally new view of radiation: Radiant energy is emitted and absorbed, not in a continuous manner (like water from a faucet), but in discrete units, like raindrops. The notion of radiation as being made up of minute and discrete little bundles was dramatically different from what physicists at that time imagined radiation to be.

Planck called these little droplets of radiation *quanta.* Hence his picture came to be called the *quantum theory* of radiation. Its implication is that at the core of matter whence radiant energy emanates, blobs of energy are spurted out (to give a much larger scale analogy) like bullets from a rifle rather than as water from a hose.

Planck's hypothesis explained the most puzzling paradox facing physicists of the 19th century, but it was also the seed from which the most fruitful and influential theories of physics germinated and blossomed in the 20th. One by one, a whole series of observational data on a variety of experiments were explained by the quantum hypothesis, and quantum physics became the foundation of all fundamental physics.

Planck's achievement has greater significance than just a solution to a specific problem. The two grand theories of 19th century physics were thermodynamics and electromagnetism. Planck's theory synthesized the two in one grand sweep. Beyond the revolutionary hypothesis which he propounded at the ripe age of 42, Planck reflected a good deal on the nature of physics and science, on philosophy and world views. Already in the first decade of the 20th century he spelled out that the goal of physics should be to unravel "a single grand connection among all the forces of nature." He worked on discovering natural units which would be culture-independent. He stressed the difference between the worldviews of philosophy and religion on the one hand, and scientific results and theories on the other. He recognized, as most scientists do, that science unites all humankind in its visions and framework. But he also understood, as most scientists do, science reaches its goal only asymptotically: that it will never solve all the problems there are. He emphasized that scientific propositions are never accepted on the basis of authorities or majority votes. He declared that there are ethical and spiritual dimensions to science. The scientific enterprise instills in the heart of the seeker a certain reverence for the world, for those who do science are getting a "glance at the divine secret." Max Planck was among the last of the great physicists who were also deeply religious, who felt that "the holiness of the unintelligible Godhead is conveyed by the holiness of the intelligible symbols." Not many physicists today dare speak thus, though they might make oblique references to religion and science.

April 24

From the World of Religion:
HAPPENSTANCE AND COINCIDENCE DAY

On April 23 I wrote: "…the conscientious objector (St. George) was tortured and beheaded. Then his headless body was dragged on the streets of Lydda in Palestine…Who knows, worse atrocities may still be happening in our world……" That same evening CBS News showed the corpse of a man who had been shot dead as a traitor, strung up dangling upside down, and then dragged on the street in Hebron in Palestine.

I was struck by the coincidence. Later at night, as I was doing some research for today's piece, I came upon a source which said that 24 April is observed by some as *Happenstance and Coincidence Day*. This leads me to a reflection on the matter of coincidences which many people have experienced in one mode or another.

We often tend to brush aside such experiences, but perhaps it would be rash to rule out physically intractable possibilities when it comes to human experiences. Thinkers since ancient times, in China, India and elsewhere, have pondered about this matter. Schopenhauer once said: "To ascribe an intention to chance is a thought which is either the height of absurdity or the depth of profundity…" Anatole France wrote: "Chance is perhaps a pseudonym of God when He does not want to sign."

It is said that during a conversation with Einstein in the 1920s the idea of what he called *synchronicity* came to Carl Jung. Normally we experience many things and behave in different ways. Most of our thoughts, words, and actions are at the conscious level. But underneath is the unconscious where there are continual activities of which we are, by definition, not aware. Jung put forth the thesis that when a coincidence is meaningful, it is actually a reflection of something that is going on in our unconscious. From this perspective—which has roots in ancient thought—there are two levels of reality: the external, palpable, phenomenological level which can be observed, analyzed, understood, and controlled through our rational and scientific modes; and an undergirding, holistic level with which the unconscious is connected. Once in a while, that interconnection is revealed. That is when (according to Jung) the *acausal connecting principle* or *synchronicity* manifests itself. In *The Roots of Coincidence*, Arthur Koestler proposed that one can understand ESP phenomena in terms of synchronicities.

It seems to me that remarkable coincidences are like the intersection of two parallel lines: impossible on a Euclidean plane, but not so on a Riemannian surface. So the consideration of a different level of reality is not at all that far-fetched.

Die-hard scientists would reject, all of this as needless mystical mumbo-jumbo. The ancient writer Plutarch already commented [*Lives: Sertorius*]: "It is no great wonder if, in the long course of time.... numerous coincidences should spontaneously occur." Indeed, for every thousand un-remarkable co-occurrences, perhaps one becomes an interesting coincidence. But the rarity of coincidences could be either due to their being just statistical probabilities, or because of other deeper factors. The fact that some radioactive nuclei disintegrate only once in several thousand years does not make radioactivity simply a rare statistically probable occurrence. In fact, we know that it is a very important feature of the physical universe, and we have a clear understanding of its probabilistic features. So it could be, some day, with synchronicity also. Ian Fleming's Auric Goldfinger quipped, "Once is happenstance. Twice is coincidence. Three times is enemy action." Perhaps he should have said, "three times is worth investigating." There may indeed be more things in heaven and earth than are dreamt of in our sciences.

From the World of Science:
HERACLITUS OF EPHEOS

Philosophers in ancient Miletus spoke of water (*udor*) and air (*pneuma*) as root elements whence arose the world. Heraclitus of Ephesos [born: 24 April (?) 554 B.C.E.] tried to answer the question of how it all came about: Not unlike the Yin-Yang duality of Chinese thinkers, he maintained that everything was characterized by the coexistence of *opposite tensions* which were normally in a state of balance. But the balance could be upset when one of the forces got the upper hand. The break in the equilibrium causes change. This is much like the three-*guna* theory of the Hindus. However, Heraclitus did not attach value judgments to the opposites, such as good or bad.

He went on to say that the opposite principles were intrinsically the same, as with up and down, right and left. Their existence resulted in fundamental symmetries. Here we are reminded of the current framework of particle physics.

That which permanently possesses change is Fire, said Heraclitus. It is possible that Heraclitus had something more in mind than burning fire. D. F. Furley suggested that Heraclitus may have been thinking of fire "as a paradigm for explaining (some or all) continuing natural processes: fire consumes things and changes them into itself, as smoke and hot vapor, and later there is condensation and re-formation of liquids and solids."

Heraclitus also declared that the world is "made neither by god nor by men, but it was, and is, and shall be, every living fire, in measures kindled and in measures extinguished." Atheism, like theism, is as old as reflective thought.

The most famous saying of Heraclitus is: "*panta rhei ouden menei*: everything flows, nothing abides." Another popular version of this is: "You cannot step into the same river twice." From the alternation of day and night, of summer and winter, Heraclitus formulated the principle that changes always occurred from opposite to opposite.

Tradition ascribes to Heraclitus a book entitled *Peri ta pantos*: On the whole. He is believed to have left this work in the temple of Artemis. The book has such statements as: "The eyes are more exact than the ears. The sun is new every day. Men do not know that what is at variance agrees with itself. To God all things are fair and good and right. Thought is common to all." Perhaps Heraclitus himself did not write these. Much of ancient history is based on oral traditions which are not always completely reliable.

To Heraclitus is also sometimes attributed an important concept that has lasted for ages: that of the *logos*: The term was coined to describe the principle that keeps order and law in the physical universe, keeps stars and planets in their paths, makes waves rise and fall, prompts winds to move and blow. It is the cause and reason behind all the harmony we see. Hindu, Chinese and the Persians thinkers had expressed similar ideas.

Diogenes Laertes described Heraclitus as an "arrogant misanthrope" who, in his old age, became a wanderer in the mountains, surviving on grass and plants. He grew sick and began to ask if one could cause drought after wet weather. No one could answer. Whereupon, we are told, he went into a shed and covered himself with the dung of oxen, in hopes of making wetness evaporate from him because of his body warmth. He died while doing this totally uncalled-for experiment, at the age of seventy.

Heraclitus has left behind the idea that Fire is an eternal dynamic entity in the universe, that there is never-ending change, and that every inkling of experience, even impressions of deja-vu, is new and fresh. He formulated impermanence as the fundamental feature of Reality. To recognize patterns in phenomena is one of the things scientists try to do. In this sense, Heraclitus was an ancient scientist.

April 25

From the World of Religion: MAHAVIRA DAY

Jainism is one of the very ancient religions of the human family. It is unique in having both mythical and historical founders. They are collectively referred to as *thirthankaras*. The 24th and last of these was Vardhamana Mahavira (6th century B.C.E.). In the year 2002, the Jaina world celebrated the memory of Mahavira on 25 April 2002.

Mahavira is deserving of our homage because he was among those who inspired humanity to lofty ideals. The two most important elements of his preaching were peace and *ahimsa*.

Peace is not simply an interlude between wars, not the silence of guns and the furlough of soldiers. Rather, peace is harmony and understanding among nations, the striving of peoples to assist and enrich one another for the betterment of one and all.

The ethical tenets of Jainism are eminently conducive to peace. They include non-possession of excessive material goods and elimination of greed. It is extended it to international relations. It is an injunction against one nation or group of people taking over what belongs to another group or nation. This Jain principle is simple in its statement, but profound in its consequences for the avoidance of wars.

However, the elimination of economic factors is not enough for peace. Even if one were satisfied with what one has, and has no desire to take over what belongs to someone else, other factors lead to unpleasant confrontations. For example, one group might maintain that a particular economic or political system is far better than another, or that one set of religious beliefs and values is the right one, and others are not.

Jain philosophers recognized this, and came up with an insight that has far-reaching implications. It could have enormous impact on humanity's quest for peace. The solution they offered was the *asti-nasti-vada*, by which a particular perception of truth is correct and yet is not so. What is meant by this paradoxical statement is that any contention of truth can only be from the point of view of a reference system. Whether you sympathize with the Israeli or the Palestinian cause, with the Irish Catholics or the Irish Protestants, with the Indian Hindu or the Pakistani Moslem position, will be largely conditioned by the group to which you belong and the particular experiences which circumstances in life have put you through. The question then is not so much who is right and who is wrong, as the position from which you are looking at a given problem. The recognition of this could lead to some understanding and compromise in very difficult confrontations.

A natural extension is that there is not just one ultimate truth, but a great many. Or, to use the classical phrase, *ekanta-vada*, the thesis that there is but one unshakable truth, is narrow and short-sighted. In fact, *anekanta-vada* (not-One doctrine) would be a better principle to hold. This is a key concept in Jain thought and is worth considering.

Then there is the principle of *ahimsa*: non-injury. It is a conscious refusal to cause harm to another human being under any circumstance. Jain thinkers extended this to all life forms: to animals and birds, even to insects. This led to vegetarianism as a life style in India. Practically all religions speak of love and kindness, of duty and responsibility. But Jainism is unique in recognizing the value, indeed the sanctity of all life forms. "If anything is sacred," said Walt Whitman, "the human body is sacred." "If anything is sacred," said Mahavira, "life is sacred.". It is natural to care for one's family, then for one's community and nation. To care for all of humanity is the next higher stage. But to care for all life forms takes to an even higher level. For this vision alone Mahavira merits our reverence.

From the World of Science: WOLFGANG PAULI

If we see the surface of our hand through a glass that magnifies it several trillion times, we will observe countless atomic nuclei and electrons separated by vast emptiness, for each atom is like the sun with its solar system. The surface of the hand would be like millions of solar systems. So will the surface of a table be. Now if we press the hand on the table, with all the emptiness around, one surface should pass right through the other. This, of course, does not happen, or else who can stand on the floor or sit on a chair? The reason is that there is a basic rule stipulating how many electrons can be in an atomic system. An atom will not allow another atom with electrons to penetrate into its territory. This is a crude description of a very sophisticated principle first formulated in 1924 by Wolfgang Pauli (born: 25 April 1900).

Pauli was a towering figure in the world of physics from the 1920s to the late 1950s when he died. In intellectual brilliance, keenness of grasping a problem in physics, and sharpness of wit (sometimes acerbic) he had no equal in the world of physicists where, for the most part, only the brightest interact, often in merciless mutual criticism.

At 20, Pauli wrote a classic exposition of Einstein's Relativity. At 24, he incorporated the idea of the electron spin into the mathematical formalism of quantum mechanics, and propounded the famous principle bearing his name, which stipulates the permissible configurations of electrons within atoms. This is the microcosmic equivalent of one occupant per seat (on our scale), for certain types of particles (the so-called fermions). But it has enormous significance and implications for cosmic construction.

In the early thirties, when physicists were puzzled by the apparent violation of energy conservation in what is called beta-decay, Pauli offered a solution: There was probably an as yet undetected extremely minute neutral (no electric charge) particle accompanying the electrons ejected from nuclei in radioactivity. The Italian physicist Fermi, noticing that this was like a bambino of a neutron, dubbed it *neutrino*. Almost 25 years later, neutrinos were detected with elaborate experimental set-ups. They are known to emerge in the core of stars, and they play fundamental roles in astrophysical processes. They pervade the universe. Their existence was first detected in Pauli's mind! This could be regarded as revelation in the realm of science. Pauli made important contributions to such esoteric fields as quantum electrodynamics, renormalization, and parity non-conservation.

Pauli was a formidable theoretical physicist, but not as good an experimentalist. Things broke down more than once when he was in a lab. This led physicists to joke about the so-called Pauli effect: Mishaps are bound to happen in a lab into which Pauli set foot. He was not a great lecturer. He would mumble and write illegibly on the black board.

Pauli was dreaded by many physicists because he would see through errors all too quickly and was all too eager to point them out in public. Once he disposed of a physicist with the terse comment, "Your theory is not even wrong!" On another occasion, a good physicist confronted him and asked, "Professor Pauli, how come your scientific papers are so good, but as a person you are so terrible?" Pauli replied: "How come in your case, it is just the opposite?" Other such legends have grown around this first-rate Pauli who was regarded as an *enfant terrible* among physicists.

He was, in the phrase of Victor Weisskopf, the conscience of theoretical physics, because for him the logic and coherence of science were of primary importance.

April 26

From the World of Religion:
MARCUS AURELEUS ANTONIUS

Words of wisdom are to be found not only in religious scriptures and the sacred words of saints, but in the writings of poets and philosophers too, sometimes even in the words of little children.

The author of a book of wisdom doesn't have to be an academic or an ascetic, nor a satirist or preacher in an established church. He could even be an emperor. Marcus Aurelius Antonius (born: 26 April 121) was an emperor of Rome who quelled rebellions, fought wars, and administered an empire. But he was also a stoic philosopher who authored a twelve-part work entitled *Meditations*, apparently to soothe his own soul, or perhaps to instruct his son. The book was translated into English some 1500 years later.

When I first read *Meditations* many long years ago, I thought parts of it were either translations of or taken verbatim from ancient Hindu writings. He talks of gods and sacrifices, lauds equanimity, refers to pleasure with scant regard. He asks us to observe "how ephemeral and worthless human things are," for much of yesterday will be "a mummy or ashes" tomorrow. Human life is filled with troubles, he says. He asks us to shield our minds from physical desires, passions, and anger. He addresses Nature as an Upanishadic seer would speak to Brahman: "From thee are all things, in thee are all things, to thee all things return." He reflects thus on himself: "Thou hast existed as a part; thou shalt disappear in that which produced thee." We are told we must adapt ourselves to the estate in which we are born: the *dharma* concept in the *Bhagavad Gita*.

Marcus Aurelius is said to have persecuted Christians more than his predecessors did. Yet, he hiumself spoke like Christ: "If any man has done thee harm, the harm is his own. It is thy duty to forgive him." "To act against one another is contrary to nature."

Some of his ideas are part of today's worldviews. He maintained, for example, that "All things are implicated with one another," and added that "the bond is holy."

He reflected on theodicy, and concluded that we cannot understand suffering here and evil there unless we can see the whole picture. From the global perspective, "everything that happens, happens justly."

Marcus Aurelius placed four qualities as the most important of all virtues: First is *wisdom* which to him was knowing what is good and what is evil. Next came the practice of *justice* by which he meant that every human being should receive what he or she is entitled to. The third is endurance: the capacity to bear pain and suffering and whatever life brings. Here we see his allegiance to Stoicism. Finally, like other great thinkers, he listed *temperance*, for it is moderation in everything that assures sound mind and sound body. Whether, as John Stuart Mill said, the *Meditations* of Marcus are at a par with the *Sermon on the Mount* may be debatable, but there can be little doubt that as in Tiruvalluvar and Confucius there is much wisdom in its propositions.

There was a time when Marcus Aurelius was worshipped in Roman households as a divine being. It was believed that he gave revelations to people in their dreams.

The undercurrent of resignation and pessimism, and the eagerness to end it all and to re-unite with God which we find in *Meditations* have their Stoic roots, and could be Buddhist or a strand of Hinduism. It arises from a recognition of the fleeting nature of life. If Marcus Aurelius had preached to throngs rather than written a book, he could well have become the founder of another religion. When it comes to founding religions, charismatic preaching, rather than the writing of books, is what does the job.

From the World of Science: CHARLES RICHTER

A few days ago many in the North East of the United States experienced an earthquake which was reported to have measured about 5.7 on the Richter scale. This brought to mind Charles Richter (born 26 April 1900) whose name is associated with the most widely used scale for the measurement of earthquake intensities.

Earthquakes have been known all through history. Even in the ancient world one had developed devices for recording, if not measuring, them. But it was only in the 18th century that the idea of relating earthquakes to seismic waves arose. In 1760, John Mitchell said that earthquakes were associated with wave-like disturbances in the earth. More a century later, in 1880 the modern seismograph was invented by John Milne. This instrument was fixed to a bedrock. It had a pen touching on a drum on which the slightest wavering of the rock would leave a mark. This was a more effective device than one with a horizontal tube with mercury invented by Luigi Palmieri a few decades earlier. Francois-Alphones Forel and Michele de Rossi had also introduced instruments for detecting earthquakes, but their efforts did not gain universal attention.

In the first decade of the 20th century, Giuseppe Mecalli introduced a twelve-point scale for measuring earthquake effects. It was based on their impact on buildings as well as on people's experiences of the event.

Richter began his work at the Seismological Laboratory at Caltech in 1927. In the 1930s he and co-worker Beno Gutenberg introduced a scale for measuring California earthquakes. Gutenberg had made significant contributions to seismology in his native Germany before coming to Caltech. The Gutenberg-Richter system came to be used worldwide largely because of Gutenberg's use of it in many regions of the world. It was a measure of the energy released in an earthquake at its epicenter. Even for mild earthquakes this energy could be considerable. Because the range of possibilities is vast, they introduced a logarithmic scale on which every unit increase corresponds to ten times the intensity. Thus, for example, an earthquake which registers 6 on the Richter scale is 10 times as intense as one whose reading is 5. Furthermore, the corresponding energy release is also much different. Thus, whereas an earthquake of magnitude 1 on the Richter scale releases as much energy as 6 ounces of TNT, one of magnitude 8 releases as much energy as 6 million tons of TNT.

The most intense earthquake known thus far would be about 8 or a little more on the Richter scale. This would be called a *great* earthquake. Earthquakes which are less than 2 on the Richter scale are said to be *very minor*. On an average, about a thousand very minor tremors occur every day of the year. Two to three *moderate* earthquakes, i.e. of magnitude 5 to 5.9, are recorded each day in the various seismological centers of the world. *Strong* earthquakes (6 to 6.9) number 120 per year.

Earthquakes result from the stress between rocky plates which press against each other in their slow motion. No matter what their cause, they have blindly wreaked immeasurable havoc. Perhaps the most terrible of them killed 830,000 people in China in 1556. Another, also in China, 420 years later, took the lives of 255,000 people.

Richter's name has been immortalized over that of his collaborating senior (Gutenberg was 11 years older) colleague. Just as some philosophers get greater renown and following than others who have spoken with no less wisdom, some scientists are mentioned more than others who might have done work of no less significance. That's why some would have preferred to call it the Gutenberg-Richter scale.

April 27

From the World of Religion: HANUMAN JAYANTI

In the Hindu tradition there is a unique sophistication in therolatry (worship of wild animals). The monkey has a special place in the scheme. Hanuman is the name of a specific simian personage who appears in the epics. He was chief of an army of monkeys, but was superhuman rather than subhuman. He was erudite and wise, heroic and virtuous, strong in physique, keen and clever in mind, Vedic scholar and grammarian. And he possessed magical powers. By all standards he was extraordinary.

Each year a day is dedicated in the Hindu world to a celebration of Hanuman. Called *Hanuman Jayanti*, it fell on 17 April in the year 2002. On this day hymns are sung in his praise, special worship services are held, and one reads sections of the epic where his deeds are recounted.

Hanuman is the focus in one of the books of the Ramayana: *Sundarkanda*. In the epic Ramayana, Hanuman rescues the kidnapped heroine Sita. When he hears about her abduction, he resolves to find her for Rama, and nothing would deflect him from this determination. The idea is that when one witnesses injustice, one should commit oneself to correcting it, and never flinch from the commitment. He sits on a hill and drowns it into the nether world, carries a mountain across continent and ocean, expands himself to a hundredfold and contracts likewise. Hanuman flies over to Sri Lanka, discovers Sita, razes the land whose king had done the crime, and comes back to Rama to report the matter. When one is determined to right the wrong, one acquires powers to accomplish it. Even his tail is magical: It could become frighteningly long if he chose to have it so, or it could become a tough long stretch that weighed a ton or more.

From the moment he saw Rama, Hanuman became his instant and intense devotee. Hanuman is revered in the Hindu world precisely because of his unswerving devotion to Lord Rama. He represents unsullied *bhakti* (love of God), yet in a framework of profound learning and wisdom, as if to remind us that these are not incompatible qualities. Even the scholar can be of faith, even the grammarian devotional. There is a saying to the effect that whenever and wherever Rama is worshipped, Hanuman will be found there in one form or another. The idea is, places of worship attract the pious.

The poet Tulsi Das wrote a hymn in forty quatrains addressed to Hanuman, called *Hanuman Chalisa*. Here he extols Hanuman's prowess, both physical and mental, mentions how the gods themselves sing his praise, describes his valiant deeds, and refers to his humility when he meets Sita. Above all, Hanuman is shown here to be an intermediary between the devotee and Rama himself. The Hanuman Chalisa is one of the powerful elements in (Hindi-speaking) Hindu culture. Few in that culture have not listened to or recited the Chalisa which hails Hanuman as the ocean of wisdom and virtue (*gyan-guna-sagar*). He is regarded as an incarnation of Lord Shiva.

To the outsider, Hanuman may just be a simiamorphic divinity. But to those who have been brought up in the tradition there is more to him than an ape-like visage. That is what cultural upbringing does: it infuses meaning and sensitivity to sounds and symbols that may seem weird to the outsider. To witness this, all one has to do us to visit the worship center of any religious tradition.

In the complex and increasingly pluralistic world in which we live, it is both necessary and enriching to learn and respect what touches the soul of others. For in every non-hurting manifestation of culture and tradition we may always be touched by its aesthetic dimension, even if the magic and the mystery elude us.

From the World of Science: HERBERT SPENCER

The second half of the 19th century was not exactly comfy for factory workers and orphanages in England (as reflected in the immortal classics of Charles Dickens), but those were the days when the Empire was expanding, monies were pouring in, and science was flourishing in the works of Maxwell and Kelvin and Darwin and the like. So it was a period of hope and promise, for, though the electric light, the automobile, and the telephone were still in the future, it seemed apparent to many that things were on the right track, that progress was not only there, but inevitable.

Herbert Spencer (born: 27 April 1820) was an eloquent spokesman for this point of view. He articulated clearly the notion that Darwinian evolution was not just for the birds and the bees, but for human societies as well. Societies too evolve from simple to complex, and they move along the making-everything-better direction.

Influenced by the science of the day, he was a matter-of-fact philosopher who did not enjoy wordy scholasticism. His dismissed metaphysical questions as unsolvable. All knowledge is the resultant of the interaction between an external world and our sensory faculties. He was willing to grant that there was some Power behind the phenomenal world, but quickly added that this was inscrutable, unknowable. He was speaking both of science and of religion. The so-called Absolute, whether scientific or religious, was for ever beyond reach. Spencer developed a synthetic philosophy in a number of volumes entitled: *First Principles, Principles of Biology, Principles of Psychology, Principles of Sociology, Principles of Ethics* which were well-thought out reflections.

Spencer contended that all positive knowledge arises from scientific inquiry. But scientists are unable to connect different domains of science and draw generalizations from them, such as philosophers do. However, if philosophers are concerned only with unverifiable metaphysics, that becomes a waste of time. Spencer was one of the first modern thinkers who called for a philosophy based on scientific results. He was an ardent evolutionist, and argued that Darwinian evolution should be the basis of all philosophizing.

Since he was not an active scientist, scientists didn't take him seriously And because he wasn't a trained philosopher, professional philosophers attacked him. His critics did not recognize that it was thanks to Spencer and others like him that the larger visions of science come within reach of the general public, that ethics was secularized, and that science became one of the major enterprises in society. Often, generalists tend to be looked down upon by specialists. But science has much more to say than what constitutes an animal cell, how light is refracted through a prism, or why planets move the way they do. The generalist paints a grand picture of science.

In the march of history, science is not just another activity like soccer or rock and roll, but a transformation of values and worldviews which prompt us to consider the phenomenal world in insightful ways. Unless a sizable fraction of society is imbued in this framework of reason, rationality, and empirical criteria, society will be swayed only by the raw passions that erupt from blind beliefs and the fears and fetishes of by-gone eras. When the powers of destructive technology comes within reach of a scientifically illiterate society, the consequences can be disastrous, both for itself and for the world. That is why thinkers and writers like Spencer who plead the cause of sane science serve the cause of civilization in important ways, even if in details and perspectives their assertions might be incomplete, imprecise, or be open to question.

April 28

From the World of Religion:
ORTHODOX EASTER

When we think of traditional religion, we usually have a certain view of it which is seldom complete or correct. Over the centuries all religions have changed, splintered and evolved in many ways. Thus the word Christianity brings to mind (for most Western peoples) Roman Catholicism or one of the many variants of Protestantism. This is only a partial vision. There are more than a hundred million Christians in Russia, Rumania, Greece, Serbia, and Bulgaria who don't belong to either of these two branches of Christianity.

The most ancient form of systematized Christianity is the Orthodox Eastern Church, also described as the Holy Orthodox Catholic Apostolic Eastern Church. This is the parent of Western Christianity. It was in Greek that the first Christian Scriptures were written. The split in Christianity between East and West resulted from a great many factors, many of them related to doctrinal interpretations. One might consider two important elements in the Christian framework: ethical behavior in accordance with God-given laws which, in association with the acceptance of Christ, will lead us unto salvation; and the transformation of corrupt humans into holy beings very Christ-like. Western Christianity emphasized the former. Eastern Orthodoxy, the latter. Thus, faith is fundamental in Western Christianity. In Eastern orthodoxy, *theosis* is what matters: the slow mode by which the devout acquire Christ-like qualities.

One result of the Roman take-over of Christianity was its spread to the barbarian West whose civilizations were profoundly affected by the Roman Christian framework. Unlike a single Pope in Western Christendom, the Eastern Church had four mutually independent patriarchs. Now there are some 13 autocephelous churches, all subscribing to the same interpretation of sacraments, liturgy, etc. For historical reasons, the patriarch of Constantinople has a special honorific position, but no special powers. This is like the Queen of England having a special position in the British Commonwealth without any extra power over other member nations.

Aside from deep doctrinal differences, most of the efforts at reunification of the Eastern and the Western Churches have failed primarily because of the question of whether the Pope in Rome would agree to being treated on a par with the other patriarchs.

Historical forces weren't as favorable for the Eastern Churches in Alexandria, Constantinople, and Antioch, for they became secondary streams in the more dynamic Islamic context to which they were relegated. But the roots that the Eastern Church took among the Slav people have survived well, in spite of efforts to eradicate them during the decades when Communism dominated those regions.

Over the centuries, the Eastern and Western Churches have not seen eye to eye on theological questions. Each one has also regarded the other as in error or downright unfaithful to the tradition. Being a heretic is like being a cousin: If you are one, you have one, because it is attitudinally reciprocal.

When, in the 16th century, Pope Gregory XIII appointed a commission to revise the calendar, he did not include a representative from the Eastern Church in the group. Because of this, the Eastern Church did not adopt the Gregorian calendar. They have continued with the one proclaimed by Julius Caesar. The Julian Calendar is now 13 days behind the Gregorian. By its reckoning, 28 April 2002 was Easter Sunday in the Orthodox tradition.

From the World of Science:
NEWTON'S PRINCIPIA

Newton's *Principiae naturalis principia mathematica* (Mathematical Principle of Natural Philosophy) is one of the milestones in the history of science. Often referred to as the *Principia*, the manuscript of the first book of this classic was formally presented to the Royal Society on 28 April 1686.

Three years of strenuous work and a tumultuous history involving controversies as to credits, priorities, and who will pay for publication, preceded the printing of the work. In its 500 pages, the book incorporated the findings of 17th century physical science and added much of originality. It presented a magnificent framework for the exploration of the physical world. It defined in precise terms concepts such as force and momentum. It propounded the law of universal gravitation which elucidated the laws of planetary motion. It enunciated the laws of motion that govern every aspect of the changing panorama of the world, in terms of which the entire range of matter in motion could be understood in all their simplicity and complexity, from the fall of an apple and the slide on an inclined plane to patterns in planetary swings. In brief, it inaugurated the field of investigation called *rational mechanics*.

Rational mechanics combines fundamental physical concepts with mathematical analysis to describe and predict the motion and evolution of systems from downhill skiers and simple pendulums to ballistic missiles and galactic rotations. All the analysis begins with a simple formula of incredible sweep, expressed by practitioners as $F = ma$. Here was an instance of human intellectual potential that is as magnificent as the creative prowess implicit in a major symphony, as insightful as the portrayal of love and pathos in a literary masterpiece, and as revealing in its meaning as a supreme work of art.

Isaac Newton was an extraordinary genius. His creativity spilled over in many fields. He delved into numbers and algebra, and created the calculus. He toyed with lenses and mirrors and contrived the first reflecting telescope. He recognized white light as a composite of colors. He tinkered with alchemy, firmly believing that copper could be transmuted to gold. He calculated Biblical chronologies, and thought he had proved the earth had been created in 3500 B.C.E. He was secretive, hypersensitive to criticism, not very generous in sharing credits, and absent-minded. He stayed a bachelor all his long life of fourscore years and five. He is said to have had good teeth and sight, good hearing and clarity of thought till the very end, notwithstanding a brief nervous breakdown.

The impact of the *Principia* extended beyond the ivory towers of physics and astronomy. The worldview it painted was on the canvas of law and reason. It looked upon nature, not as due to the whims of a God who may be pleased or angry, but as resulting from eternal principles, functioning immutably like clockwork. In this view, the purpose of life is not to keep asking God for favors or forgiveness from sins, but rather to understand His work in all its manifold details by the exercise of the mind.

Practically all the thinkers of the 18th century were influenced and inspired by this Newtonian world view which was essentially forward-looking and optimistic. Voltaire and Bentham, Hume and Adam Smith, and all the rest of the Enlightenment set brought in the notions of natural law, and extended it to the human condition at large. The Age of Reason had direct links to the *Principia*. Benjamin Franklin and Thomas Jefferson were intellectually Newtonians also. The Newtonian concepts of universality and order played their role in the enunciation of the enlightening principles of equality and freedom and justice for all.

April 29

From the World of Religion: SAINT CATHERINE

In the middle of the 14th century when Siena was a flourishing city, there appeared a divinely inspired maiden by the name of Catherine, as the 20th (some say 25th) child of her parents. She spoke but little, attended Mass regularly, prayed constantly, remained engrossed in the thought of God, and dedicated her life to Christ before she was 10. She became a sister in the Dominican order, and spent three years in silent meditation, reciting the scriptures even in the darkness of night. In 1367 she had a vision of Jesus and Mary and of saints too. During this experience, she felt that Virgin Mary handed to a her a golden ring, visible to her eyes alone, with a diamond at the center, around which were set four precious pearls. When she was canonized, April 29 became her feast day.

At 23, she heard a voice that instructed her to go out into the world and serve the needy. Before long she had a number of followers. She preached that part of the human condition was to live in self-knowledge. She was so inspiring and effective in reminding people of their erring ways that throngs of sinners used to overwhelm the confessionals in the local churches by their numbers, all to repent their wayward ways.

On another occasion, in the Church of Santa Christina in Pisa, she is said to have been struck by five piercing purple rays on her hands, feet, and heart: she experienced the *stigmata*, the visible wounds of crucified Christ. St. Francis had had exactly the same experience, and this generated a rivalry between Dominicans and Franciscans.

When a Frenchman from Gascony became pope Celement V in 1305, he moved the papal residence to Avignon. For many decades there was no pope in Rome. Catherine of Siena was one of the eminent individuals (Petrarch and Dante being others) who tried to transfer the Avignon papacy back to Rome. She was 29 when she went to Avignon as ambassadress to persuade Gregory XI to return to Rome and thus put an end to what used to be called the Babylonian captivity of the popes. She succeeded.

It is remarkable that this woman, still in her late twenties, carried such clout that popes listened to her. Barely four months after the election of Urban VI as pope in 1373, there was a rebellion of cardinals against him, largely because of his self-centered actions. They assembled in a place called Anagni, annulled Urban's election, and appointed Robert of Geneva to the post, who assumed the title of Clement VII. He was supported by the French monarch Charles V, and some others. Western Christendom now came to be controlled by two competing popes and their successors. The two heads had their respective followers among the various European kingdoms of the time. Thus began the Great Western Schism, during which the Western Church went through one of its low points in history: The one away from Rome came to be called the anti-pope. [This reminds one of the nomenclature of elementary particles in current physics.] Catherine spoke on behalf of the Roman pope, though in personal letters she spared no word in rebuking him for some of his policies. But she could not undo the schism that had begun during her lifetime.

Catherine authored books, often dictated them since she could not read or write, corresponded similarly with many people, and always served the poor and the sick. She risked her life in the religio-political turmoil of the times. It is difficult to believe that a woman of such humble origins and modest learning could have played such an important role in her time. In the 1970 the title of Doctor of the Church was bestowed upon her posthumously and rather belatedly. Catherine of Siena is represented in many famous paintings. The one by Beccafumi (in Siena) depicts her receiving the stigmata.

From the World of Science: HENRI POINCARÉ

Jules Henri Poincaré (born: 29 April 1854) was one of the most prolific mathematicians of all times, leaving behind more than five hundred technical papers on practically every branch of pure and applied mathematics, and some significant ones on celestial mechanics too. He was elected member of every one of the five sections of the *Académie des Sciences*: geometry, mechanics, physics, geography, and navigation.

People familiar with advanced mathematics know that Poincaré discovered automorphic functions, launched algebraic topology, etc. But more generally, in the first half of the 20th century, practically everyone who had some interest in mathematical thought and philosophy of science read his three masterpieces of popular expositions of these matters. All these books: *Science and Hypothesis* (1901), *The Value of Science* (1905), and *Science and Method* (1908), are within reach of people with some background in science. The writing is lucid and the reflections are insightful. In the original French, the language is elegant too.

Poincaré was brilliant in mathematics, and blessed with a prodigious memory. It is said that when he began his creative work, he was not familiar with many of the then current writings of great mathematicians: revealing that for creative processes in certain fields, knowledge of what others have done may not be quite necessary, at least for very bright minds. Poincaré must have thought about this a lot because he wrote insightfully on the mysterious element of creativity: the unusual faculty of some otherwise normal minds. He expressed the view that what strikes as a flash of sudden insight is often the climax of long periods of conscious and subconscious concentration on a problem.

As one who had such mathematical visions on a regular basis, it is natural for Poincaré to underscore intuition as a factor in mathematical thought. In the early decades of the 20th century, philosophers of mathematics (mostly high-powered creative mathematicians) were wrangling about what exactly constitutes mathematics. One influential school tried to make the case that mathematics was essentially logic pure and *par excellence* where clearly defined concepts and operations rather than objects and their properties constitute the elements to which the logic is applied. So arose the axiomatic school which attempted to reduce all of mathematics, including arithmetic, to logical structures built upon foundations which are accepted as postulates. Poincaré argued that there was more to mathematics than error-free thinking just as there is more to chess than making the moves according to the rules. Logic by itself is fruitless, unless it is fertilized by intuition. As he put it succinctly, "we prove by logic; we invent by intuition." Logic is necessary for reasoning out (establishing) what is revealed through intuition. One might add that even this may not be always easy or possible, as with Fermat's last theorem or Goldbach's conjecture.

Even as Kant erred in believing that Euclid's axiom was an example of synthetic a priori (that the mind can recognize aspects of the physical world without observing it) Poincaré was off the mark in saying that the descriptions of physical space in Euclidean and in Riemannian frameworks were equivalent (because of their topological equivalence). This, of course, is not true, as Einstein's General Theory clearly showed.

Though Poincaré did not leave behind his own students to carry on the torch, hundreds of students have been working at a major research center in Paris bearing in name (*Institut Henri Poincaré*). It was my privilege to have been one of them.

April 30

From the World of Religion:
NIGHT OF THE WITCHES

Practically every traditional religion takes for granted the existence of supernatural beings. Some of these are good and some are bad. Satan, the devil, asuras, Iblis, etc. are some of these evil spirits. In Western culture, a number of these evil ones are female beings with magical powers, especially when they take on semi-human forms, they are known as witches. There were there already in Roman times. In pictorial versions, witches are ugly, old-looking, often wearing a cap and a grin, using a broomstick as a flying vehicle.

Corresponding to Halloween on the last day of October, there comes another festival six months later,. In pre-Christian times, that day was to bid a send-off to winter, and to welcome sunny spring. Those were days when witches were worshipped rather than worried about. With the advent of Christianity the day was dedicated to cleansing the air of the vestiges of witches. In some Germanic countries they celebrate the close of winter and the advent of Spring on the last day of April. For reasons unknown, this last night of April is named in Germany after an 8th century English saint by the name of Walburga who came to that country as a missionary. It is also part of the tradition to believe that St. Walpurgis (as the name changed into) protected people from the magical arts.

The night of April 30 came to be called the night of the witches. As legends would have it, at the protruding peak of the Harz Mountain range on the spacious top of Brocken, all sorts of evil spirits congregate on this night, and have a party, so to speak. Fairies and elves come out from caverns and underground and dance merrily on the mountain top. These beings are said to be frightened of noise, so people generate all kinds of sounds to frighten them away. They toll church bells, recite loud prayers, beat on boards or just scream. Little girls are dressed up as witches, and little boys ride imaginary stick horses to drive away the witches.

Thanks to Goethe's Faust, the idea of *Walpurgisnacht* being a witches' night has taken deep hold in the minds of many people of the Germanic tradition.

When I read Faust many years ago, I was curious about this and looked into the matter. I found that in 1723 there was in fact a witch's trial in the Bavarian town of Eichstaett, not far from Heidenheim where St. Walburga is said to be buried. The 20 year old accused woman in this trial was Maria Walburga Rung whom the Episcopal church tried, tortured, and burned. This could have been a pure coincidence, but I began to wonder if this had anything to do with Goethe's calling the day *Walpurgisnacht*.

Walpurgisnacht is also known by other names, like Mayday, Galan Mai, Shenn da Boaldyn, and Beltaine. Perhaps not many take the existence of witches seriously these days. Youngsters in Bavaria enjoy the evening by playing pranks, as on Halloween night in some other places, causing minor inconveniences with toothpaste, toilet papers, and things like that. Such imitations of imaginary witches add fun to routine life. However, it is important to remember that while all the rich variety and complex history of witchcraft and witch-hunting may be interesting to read about, what is common to all of them is this: Every ancient belief in witches was associated with gross ignorance of the causes of many natural phenomena, every practice of witchcraft was associated with mischievous and hurtful behavior, and many elements in the framework of witchcraft arose from the male's (often deprecatory) image of the female in human societies.

From the World of Science:
CARL FRIEDRICH GAUSS

There are aspects of the human mind that it may never be possible for science to fathom: one such is creativity, be it in music or mathematics or poetry. The most we may be able to say is that there are peculiar or particular genes associated with the marvel of creativity, and leave it at that.

We may never know how Mozart came up with the most wondrous permutation of notes when still a playful lad, nor how Carl Friedrich Gauss (born: 30 April 1777) could correct his father's account when barely three years old. But these human beings did such things, and there have been such creative eccentrics now and again all through history.

Gauss was born of modest parents: an over-strict father who never understood the genius of his son, and a very loving mother who was always supportive of the same. He was unfortunate in the people which circumstances brought to his personal life: a sickly first wife, a second wife who died young too, five of his six children dying prematurely. It has been said that Gauss did not want any of his children to go into mathematics because he was afraid that if they did only second rate work the Gauss name would be associated with their work. The politics of the time took a heavy toll on him. His life was in danger when Napoleon's army invaded Germany. He was generally conservative in politics, a nationalist who refused to speak French. He had little respect for democracy, and preferred monarchy.

But amidst it all Gauss enriched mathematics, pure and applied, and physics, both theoretical and experimental, in the most amazing ways. Already in elementary school he discovered how to add up all the integers from one to hundred in less than a minute. He took the simplest field of mathematics, namely, arithmetic to a lofty height, added much to what has come to be called Number Theory, formulated the fundamental theorem of algebra, showed how one can construct a 17-sided regular polygon with ruler and compass, and explored non-Euclidean geometry also. He contributed to statistical analysis and developed the mathematics of the bell-curve that bears his name. From observations of the newly discovered asteroid (see 1 Jan) he worked out the method by which the orbits of planets can be computed. His method led to the discovery of Neptune. He also wrote papers on complex numbers.

Gauss was interested in geodesy and did surveying work under strenuous conditions. He invented an instrument which reflected the rays of the sun along specified directions: this turned out to be very useful in observational astronomy. He did significant work on terrestrial magnetism, a contribution for which his name has been immortalized as a unit for measuring the intensity of magnetic field. He was one of the early experimenters on telegraphy. He developed a consistent system of units for physical quantities.

Besides opening up new fields in mathematics, Gauss also gave a big boost to mathematical electromagnetism. Lots more original thoughts and results came from his work than were published in his lifetime. But whatever came from his pen, published or left for posterity, was of such quality and significance that he has been put on a par with Archimedes and Newton, and is often called *princeps*: *prince* of mathematicians.

Not many people have heard of Carl Friedrich Gauss. This is because practically all his works were published in Latin. He wrote mainly for specialists; much of his fundamental work had little to do with everyday physics and mathematics. After all, not everyone is interested in all the solutions of the hypergeometric equation or even in the proof that every algebraic equation has roots.

May 1

From the World of Religion: MONTH OF MAY

May is a welcome month in many countries of the world. Some have suggested that the name is probably derived from Maia, Mercury's mother whom the Romans venerated. From Roman writers to Chaucer, Shakespeare and De Musset, many have extolled the freshness and spirit of the fifth month in our current system. May has been called the month of gladness, dressed in the sweetest and fairest colors. In times past, one reveled with fruits and flowers, and in merry dances around the maypole. The month was hailed with the goddess of flowers in ancient Rome. In Germany and Switzerland young men secretly placed little trees on this day near the dwellings of their beloved. In England they set up maypoles on the first of May, early in the morning. The Puritans frowned at this because it was reminiscent of heathen practice. In Catholic France, little girls used go in processions, dressed up as Virgin Mary. In Hawaii they exchange lei flowers on this day.

But in the modern world, May Day has an altogether different connotation: It is celebrated to affirm the rights and dignity of the millions of people who work day after day and week after week in various industries and factories all over the world, thanks to whose labors so many more can work and live in greater comfort, receiving much more as remuneration for giving much less as arduous muscular effort.

There was a time in the industrialized countries (as it still is in many less advanced nations of the world) where men and women, even children, worked hard for ten to twelve hours a day under very harsh conditions.

In response to this unconscionable situation, the Federation of Organized Traders and Labor Unions in the United States passed a resolution in 1886 demanding that from May 1 onwards the law should allow only an eight-hour day for workers. A quarter of a million workers were behind this resolution. A huge rally was organized in Chicago for this purpose but rioting and chaos ensued, four people were killed, many were arrested, and big business painted the leaders of the movement as unpatriotic anarchists and radicals. The Commercial Club of Chicago bought large quantities of machine guns and presented them to the Illinois National Guard to handle the protesters.

In 1889 a Congress of Socialists which met in Paris backed the American labor movement and unanimously decided to declare 1 May 1890 as the first Labor Day. Since then, the tradition has spread to more than sixty nations. Ironically, in the U.S. where it all began, the support from socialist groups transformed the idea into something subversive, for Socialism was regarded (as it still is in the minds of many) as evil and inimical to capitalism, which needed to be kept away from the free air of the New World. So, while 1 May is the International Worker's Day in a great many nations, Labor Day was moved to the first Monday in September in the U.S. Leaving for a moment labor and conflict, protest and persecution, let us recall William Watson's jolly ode to May:

What is so sweet and dear,
As a prosperous morn in May,
The confident prime of the day,
And the dauntless youth of the year,
When nothing that asks for bliss,
Asking aright, is denied.
And half of the world a bridegroom is,
And half of the world's a bride?

From the World of Science:
SANTIAGO RAMÓN Y CAJAL

It had been known for long that nerves carry signals to and from the brain. By the last decades of the 19th century, scientists looked upon the brain as a network of fibers formed by the intertwining of the appendages of nerve cells (axons). This view of the brain was called the reticular theory. Camillo Golgi was among its eminent protagonists.

A major paradigm shift in this matter occurred as a result of the untiring work and persistence of the outstanding histologist Santiago Ramón y Cajal (born: 1 May 1852) who, using the chrome silver staining technique which had been introduced by Golgi, established that, contrary to the then current view, nerve cells do not actually touch one another, but terminate just before the one that is close to it.

Furthermore, he established that from nerve cells emanate growth cones from which arise extremely fine branches called dendrites. These make contact with other nerve cells. The dendrites are the parts that first collect the signals.

In Ramón y Cajal's picture, the nervous system is a chain of neurons (named thus by Heinrich Waldeyer), that barely touch one another. He laid the foundations of, and instigated important developments in, the field of neuroscience. He explored further what was known as the theory of dynamic polarization which stressed that nerve impulses were always transmitted from the dendrites and cell body to axon.

All these were revolutionary views. As such, they were not accepted by many histologists of the time. It did not help that he was working in Spain which, in the 1890s, was not one of the mainstream scientific countries of the world. His writings in Spanish were not read by other scientists of Europe or America. But, as generally happens in science, eventually his ideas came to be accepted as the correct picture.

Some of Ramón y Cajal's views were not unlike those of scientists in third world countries in our own times. He was frustrated with governmental bureaucracy and corruption, he resented the hegemony of English, French, and German in the scientific world. While he was proud of his country's great past, he was also embarrassed about its backwardness in science. He was unhappy that the English did not care to study Spanish.

Both Gogli and Ramón y Cajal were awarded the Nobel Prize for physiology in 1906. One Nobel committee member expressed this view: ""Cajal has not served science by singular corrections of observations by others, or by adding here and there an important observation to our stock of knowledge, but it is he who has built almost the whole framework of our structure of thinking, in which the less fortunately endowed forces have had to, and will still have to put in their contributions." It was also stated: "If the achievements by Golgi, on the one hand, and Cajal, on the other, in the research on the nervous system are considered, one can not, in justice, evade the final conclusion that Cajal is far superior to Golgi."

Normally, the recipient of the prize talks about the work which won him or her the honor. But Gogli chose to speak on "The Neuron Doctrine: Theory and Fact." He said: "While I admire the brilliancy of the doctrine which is a worthy product of the high intellect of my illustrious Spanish colleague, I cannot agree with him on some point of an anatomical nature which are, for the theory, of fundamental importance..." The next day Ramón y Cajal began his lecture on "The Structure and Connections of Neurons" with the statement: "In accordance with the tradition followed by the illustrious orators honored before me with the Nobel Prize I am going to talk to you about the principal results of my scientific work in the realm of histology and physiology of the nervous system."

May 2

From the World of Religion: THEODOR HERZL

The prophets of religions have had great impact on the course of history. Missionaries and monarchs have spread religions far and wide. But there are not many instances where a single practitioner, with zeal and commitment to his faith and people, affected their destiny, international politics, and history in dramatic ways. Such a one was Theodor (Binyamin Ze'ev) Herzl (born: 2 May 1860). Jewish by tradition, Hungarian by birth, and German in intellectual formation, Herzl was novelist and journalist. Above all, he was the activist who conceived of, promoted, and was deeply committed to the return of the Jews to Jerusalem. He was inspired to re-establish the realm of the Old Testament, where they would live no more as second class citizens or in ghettos, as they had done under Caliphs or in Christendom, ever since they were driven out their ancient land by Roman imperialism in 70 C.E.. When the shameful anti-Semitic Dreyfus Affair erupted in France in which, with forged documents, Dreyfus was convicted of treason, Herzl was fed up with the persecution that his people had been suffering in their Diaspora over the ages. He felt that assimilation into non-Jewish societies would simply be impossible.

In 1896 Herzl wrote a pamphlet entitled *Der Judenstaat* (*The Jewish State*) in which he said: "The plan (for a Jewish State) would seem mad enough if a single individual were to undertake it; but if many Jews simultaneously agree on it, it is entirely reasonable, and its achievement presents no difficulties worth mentioning." In 1897 he convened a World Zionist Congress at Basel which set the ball rolling for the eventual creation of the state of Israel. Some people had been toying with the idea of a homeland for Jews in Uganda, as suggested by the British, but this idea was summarily thrown out.

The region of Palestine was holy for Judaism because Eretz Israel (as it is called in Hebrew) had been promised to the Jews by God Himself. It was holy for Christianity because Jesus lived there. In 614 the Persians conquered Palestine and in 691 Islam erected the Dome of the Rock where the Temple of Solomon once stood. It was holy for Islam because Prophet Mohammed is said to have ascended to Heaven from Jerusalem. So all the three great monotheistic religions had claims for the region. The power of sacred history, like that of pseudoscience, can be tremendous, and sometimes terrible too.

There is a part of Jerusalem which is known as Zion. As one reads in the Old Testament (Samuel II 5:7): "...David took the strong hold of Zion: the same is the city of David." It has been an ancient conviction in the Jewish world that the Messiah would deliver Israel from the exile it had suffered. This had been the spirit of Zionism during many long centuries. When Herzl started the modern Zionist movement, Palestine was under the rule of the Sultan of Turkey who was not exactly sympathetic to the idea. The conflict between Britain and Turkey in 1917 was a blessing for Zionism, for it was in this context that the famous Balfour Declaration was made, which pledged that Great Britain would support the Zionist cause, on condition that non-Jewish people would not lose their rights in a Jewish national home in Palestine.

It took almost half a century and many complex and painful forces for the dream to be realized. Herzl had written in his book: "The world will be liberated by our freedom, enriched by our wealth, magnified by our greatness. And whatever we attempt there for our own benefit will rebound mightily and beneficially to the good of all mankind." It was an enlightened hope, expressed with profound sentiments by a member of Judaic culture. It has not yet been realized, but one may pray that one day it will come be.

From the World of Science:
D'ARCY WENTWORTH THOMPSON

Every object we see around us has a shape and a size. The sand particle is small, and so is the mosquito. Molecules and atoms are much, much smaller still. The elephant is huge and the mountain is even more so. The sun and the stars are much, much larger still.

But do forms and sizes arise at random? Are there patterns and proportions in them? Could Nature have chosen arbitrary sizes and sprinkled them everywhere. These are questions on which not many may have pondered.

D'Arcy Wentworth Thompson (born: 2 May 1860) did. He reflected on these matters insightfully in a book called *On Growth and Form* which first appeared in 1915. "Everywhere Nature works true to scale," he wrote. "Men and trees, birds and fishes, stars and star-systems, have their appropriate dimensions, and their more or less appropriate dimensions, and their more or less narrow range of absolute magnitudes."

As in the other sciences, biology too had its subdivisions: anatomy, evolution, histology, and so on. Thompson was interested in fisheries, taught physiology, translated Aristotle's *Historia Animalium* into English, and published *Fertilization of Flowers* from H. Mueller's German original. Most of all, he was drawn to morphology. His 1908 paper in *Nature* was entitled, "On the Shapes of Eggs and the Causes which Determine Them." He also wrote a paper on "Morphology and Mathematics."

Natural selection brings about changes in the biological world, but, said Thompson, physical forces and laws keep the changes within limits. In this sense he looked upon physical forces as rivals of natural selection.

Living organisms have form and function. The forms, Thomson explained, are determined by mathematics. The functioning, on the other hand, is constrained by physics.

Thompson's book is remarkable in many ways. For one thing, it is voluminous, filling a thousand pages. It is based on impressive scholarship and research, revealing that the author has read scores and scores of books, in different languages and from different periods, and on different topics too: There is not only botany and zoology here, but also astronomy, engineering, and mythology. The book talks of symmetry and of surface tension. It explains the shape of red blood corpuscles and the antlers of deer. And it shows us how, with a mathematical microscope, one can discern in the shell of the chambered nautilus a perfect equiangular spiral.

A mathematical equation is unaffected when both sides are multiplied by the same factor. This is not so in the living world. If the mass of an elephant were doubled, its legs must become four times as much in cross-sectional area for the body to be supported.

Thompson's book is unusual in that it is written in a most fascinating style, even though it is a technical scientific book. The author loved words, and was not shy of admitting that "to spin words and make pretty sentences" was his "one talent, and I must make the best of it." Consider how he asks the reader to reflect: "Among animals we see, without the help of mathematics or physics, how small birds and beasts are quick and agile, how slower and more sedate movements come with larger size, and how exaggerated bulk brings with it a certain clumsiness, a certain inefficiency, an element of risk and hazard, a preponderance of disadvantage."

The impact of Thompson's book has been considerable, not so much perhaps in biology, as in other disciplines like architecture, painting, and engineering. The human mind can reflect on the perceived world in a hundred different insightful ways.

May 3

From the World of Religion:
NICCOLÒ MACHIAVELLI

Religions have several dimensions. Broadly speaking, their concerns may be put under two categories: The world beyond and life on earth. To the first belong matters relating to God and heaven, prayers and post-mortem predicaments. To the latter belong ethics and community coherence, festivals and fasting.

In the newly awakening Europe of the 1400s there arose a thinker who was a government official for some time and became a political philosopher later. He had considerable impact on our understanding of the framework in which kings and nations function. His name was Niccolò Machiavelli (born: 3 May 1469). Of all his books, it is *Il Principe* (*The Prince*) which made him immortal. Scholars have generally appraised Machiavelli harshly. Even the language vilified his name. Macaulay said of him: "Out of his surname they have coined an epithet for a knave, and out of his Christian name a synonym for the Devil." Machiavelli's philosophy is usually summarized in a few words, like: unethical politics, political expediency, the end justifies the means, etc.

Perhaps the important difference between Machiavelli and traditional ethicists is that he *describes* the human condition whereas the latter *prescribe* rules for it. Machiavelli was of the opinion that human beings have always been the same in essence, so that the overall distribution of good and bad characteristics has not really been changing with time. Furthermore, he strongly suggested that the rules of conduct for those who are running a government need not, indeed should not, be the same as for individuals who act on their own. Caring and compassion may be commendable in personal interactions, but when it comes to holding on to political power or preserving the integrity of a nation, one should let go of scruples, and do whatever the situation requires. "Where it is an absolute question of the welfare of our country," he wrote, "we must admit no consideration of justice or injustice, of mercy or cruelty, of praise or ignominy, but putting all else aside we must adopt whatever course will save the nation's existence and liberty." There are political leaders in today's world who take Machiavelli quite seriously.

Machiavelli went so far as to say that one can lie and cheat in the interest of one's country. But he was also aware of the importance of appearance, of the impact that idealistic images have on the public mind. So he bluntly advised the prince to pretend to be "merciful, loyal, humane, religious, and sincere." The façade was very important.

No political leader will dare proclaim such things as a moral philosophy that they endorse whole-heartedly. Yet most political leaders practice such things, and most governments adopt such policies in their dealings with other governments.

Machiavelli also saw serious flaws in traditional Christian ethics. His thoughts on this matter are equally applicable to some other religious traditions. His point was that too much insistence on renunciation, submissiveness, meekness, turning the other cheek, etc. can only produce a body of weaklings who will be swayed and subdued by people inspired by more aggressive attitudes. The goody-goody approach was not conducive to turning out the tough guys we need to protect and defend the country from evil enemies.

Was Machiavelli helpful or hurtful to civilization? Perhaps neither, because with due respects to his insightful writings, he probably didn't say anything that most rulers were not aware of. He simply had the guts to spill it all out, stunning many readers. Like pornography, Machiavelli is shocking only because he put for public display and discussion what many (successful politicians) have known and been practicing all along.

From the World of Science: STEVEN WEINBERG

When Isaac Newton enunciated the law of gravitation, he accomplished three things: First, he explained why planets move as per Kelper's laws. Second, he discovered a force (interaction, as we say today) that pervades the whole universe. Third, he recognized that the force that keeps planets in orbits is the same as the one that makes the apple fall: He brought under one grand concept a variety of different phenomena.

In the 19th century, James Clerk Maxwell unified the phenomena of electricity and magnetism into a single mathematical electromagnetic theory. In the 20th century, Einstein tried, without success, to unify the gravitational and the electromagnetic forces.

In the meanwhile, two other fundamental forces, weak and strong interactions, were unraveled. The efforts of three physicists climaxed in the unification of electromagnetic and weak interactions. One of them was Steven Weinberg (born: 3 May 1933), who, with Sheldon Glashow and Abdus Salam, shared a Nobel Prize in Physics for the work.

The W.S.G. theory required the existence of three field particles: W plus, W minus, and Z zero. Their existence has been put into evidence in high energy accelerators.

Weinberg is a prolific writer. His lucid books have done much to popularize many results of modern physics. His *First Three Minutes* and *Dreams of a Final Theory* must be read for anyone who wishes to get some understanding of 20th century fundamental physics. Weinberg is one of the most eloquent and persuasive exponents of the reductionist perspective. Unfortunately, the non-initiates cannot quite fathom how physicists get a thrill from the revelation that "the Universe is an enormous direct product of representations of symmetry groups." The dream of a Theory of Everything (TOE) is yet to be realized. As Weinberg cautiously said: "There is a chance the work of unification will be completed by 2050, but about that we cannot be confident."

Weinberg has serious reservations about alternative pathways for unscrambling the mysteries of the universe. He is a no-nonsense scientist who is concerned about well-meaning but (as he sees it) misguided efforts to link science and religion. He fears, like other thoughtful scientists, that some of these efforts come from "the cultural adversaries of science." He is fed up with anti-evolutionists. He gets nervous when he hears physicists speak of God and physics in the same breath. Weinberg has been bold and forthright in expressing the view which many physicists share but few articulate, to the effect that the more we probe into the complexity of the world, the more it is clear that the world just happened. The Big Bang had no long range plans, least of all the fabrication of *homo sapiens* on earth. Weinberg's statement that the more comprehensible the universe is, the more pointless it becomes made him very unpopular in some circles. Unfortunately, it is often quoted without mentioning what he went on to say: that though science does not reveal meaning to human life, we humans can create meanings for ourselves through art and love and poetry. The fact is, science thus far has not been able to reveal any purpose to our 13 plus billion year old universe. But it is also true that in this pointless universe have arisen creatures whose brains yearn for meaning. Perhaps that mystery has to be acknowledged as a price for being reflecting humans. It is not resolved by saying that science shows no purpose to the universe. But unless scientists like Weinberg frequently bring out the framework and fruits of science to the public, and speak out strongly against pseudo-scientific extrapolations, society may slide back to the days of superstitions and magic-mongering.

May 4

From the World of Religion:
SPAIN, PORTUGAL, SOUTH AMERICA

We tend to think that religions are concerned only with God and prayer, festivals and morals. Aside from the power they have had on the minds of people and the laws of nations, some religions have also played a role in the destiny of nations. Proselytizing religions have caused cultural genocide, and the authority of religious heads has apportioned lands to conquering nations.

Consider the following episode: Christopher Columbus returned from his first voyage to what came to be called the New World. As soon as King John II of Portugal got the news, he declared that the lands Columbus had discovered belonged to Portugal, on the basis of a questionable treaty that had been signed in 1479. Columbus also sent the news of his return and discovery to King Ferdinand and Isabella of Spain who had sponsored the trip. The latter promptly informed Pope Alexander VI in Rome.

As Spain was securing its foothold in the New World, Portugal was rapidly pushing forward in its path of exploration. The outcome was rivalry between the two nations, and disputes about the rights and limits of discovery. Both crowns, Portuguese and Spanish, appealed to the pope, who accepted the task of arbitrator. Now Pope Alexander VI was Spanish by birth. Born as Rodrigo Borgia in 1431 he became a cardinal, thanks to the influence of Pope Callistus III who happened to be his uncle. Rodrigo had had an affair with a Roman lady, resulting in four children, of whom Cesare Borgia was the most corrupt. But this did not prevent the man from becoming the pope.

But he did not forget his native Spain. Upon hearing from the Spanish rulers, he promptly issued a couple of Bulls (formal documents to which a papal *bulla* or seal is affixed). The one which was issued on 4 May granted to Castile the lands which were discovered by her envoys, because that country had invested money and risked the adventure of Columbus. That historic Bull drew a demarcation line one hundred leagues west of the Azores, and declared that Spain had exclusive rights to any territory and to all trade west of that line, as long as by 1492 it was not ruled by a Christian king.

Alexander VI was exuberant in his praise of the Spanish king and queen, and spoke of the service to the spread of Christianity they were performing by acquiring the new lands and bringing its barbaric inhabitants within the Christian fold. Describing himself as "Alexander, bishop, servant of the servants of God, and addressing "the illustrious sovereigns, our very dear son in Christ, Ferdinand, king, and our very dear daughter in Christ, Isabella, queen of Castile, Leon, Aragon, Sicily, and Granada," he said that it was the Pope's duty to assist them in this laudable goal which was so pleasing to immortal God. Alexander VI felt that it was his duty to "give, grant, and assign to you and your heirs and successors, kings of Castile and Leon, forever, together with all their dominions, cities, camps, places, and villages, and all rights, jurisdictions, and appurtenances, all islands and main lands found and to be found, discovered and to be discovered towards the west and south, by drawing and establishing a line from the Arctic pole, namely the north, to the Antarctic pole, namely the south, no matter whether the said main lands and islands are found and to be found in the direction of India or towards any other quarter, the said line to be distant one hundred leagues towards the west and south from any of the islands commonly known as the Azores and Cape Verde."

When we recall such history, one is inclined to believe that after all, humanity has advanced in some ways.

From the World of Science:
THOMAS HENRY HUXLEY

Even as governments work to keep the home front in order, there are soldiers who are ready and combative to keep its borders safe. So too, while scientists work in their laboratories and academies to nurture and develop science, it has its spokespeople who proclaim its triumphs and defend it from outside threats. One such soldier of science, indeed a general in that army, was Thomas Henry Huxley (born: 4 May 1825). He did his share of science: studying marine animals and fossils, and publishing scientific papers on them. But it was as an expositor of science and its methods, its values and its framework that T. H. Huxley gained reputation and immortality in history.

Above all, Huxley was one of the most articulate spokesmen for Darwin's evolution. Scientist that he was, he took it as a scientific hypothesis: one that explains better than any other how life in all its variety and complexity came to be. Indeed he saw it as such a reasonable and convincing system that he is said to have exclaimed, "How exceedingly stupid not to have thought of that!" Yet, clear thinker that he was, he did not accept every bit of Darwinian evolution as the absolute truth. He recognized some difficulties in rejecting altogether the notion that there are no abrupt changes in nature. He was equally aware of the philosophical difficulties associated with Darwinism. For one thing, he was not very enthusiastic about reducing consciousness to molecular forces.

But Huxley defended Evolution from attacks that came from traditional religionists. His famous debate in June 1860 at Oxford was one of the high-points in the history of science. Here his intelligence sparkled and his merciless repartee to Bishop Wilberforce to the effect that he would rather be related to an ape than to an intelligent man who would pervert the truth has become an indelible episode in the annals of science. If Galileo had had the opportunity to debate the Copernican hypothesis with defenders of the faith rather than be subjected to the Inquisition, it would have been a fairer deal. Huxley also confronted the biologist Owen who (like Intelligent Design theorists of our own times) tried to show "scientifically" that Darwinian evolution was not scientifically conclusive.

As a keen student of the scientific enterprise Huxley recognized that science was based on certain unproven assumptions. Thus one assumes that there is a rational order in the universe. One may refuse to accept this and develop another belief-system, such as a world where magic and the whims of supernatural beings reign. Likewise, it is taken for granted in science that there are physical forces in the world, that these act all over the universe, and never change. Such assumptions are at the basis of science, and it would be false to claim that these are necessarily true.

In the context of ultimate questions, Huxley was wise enough to state that nobody can say anything on them with absolute certainty. He rather doubted that even science can ever resolve every puzzle regarding the why and the wherefore of origins and the eventual destiny. He preferred to claim ignorance on such matters, and coined the term *agnostic* in this context, in contrast to the *gnostics* who seemed to be so sure about heaven and hell and after-life and such matters.

Huxley rejected metaphysical materialism: the dogma by which everything is matter and molecule, including love and hope, caring and compassion. He had the highest regard for the Bible as a major work in human culture. He described it as the *Magna Carta* of the poor and the oppressed. But he was too sophisticated to take its lines as literally true. T. H. Huxley was more balanced and clear-headed than extremists on either side.

May 5

From the World of Religion:
SØREN KIEREGAARD

No matter what philosophers say, religions proclaim, and the sciences affirm, ultimately the only thing that is real at a profound and personal level is one's existence. All else is like covering on a kernel. Objectivity may give shared truths, but ultimately until it is transformed into the core of the subject, nothing is real or meaningful. It is at the existential level that truths are seen. This was the central theme of an unorthodox thinker of the 19th century. His name was Søren Kierkegaard (born: 5 May 1813)

Not all may resonate with his attacks on rationality or on the Hegelian adoration of objectivity. But with the onslaught of technology, the bloody World Wars, and the growing complexity of science, rationality was losing its appeal. Kierkegaard's ideas, initially little known beyond the borders of Denmark, began to influence thinkers and the public alike. Existentialism became the in-thing, radiating in modified versions from the Boulevard St. Germain in Paris and German philosophers to cafés and conferences all over the world. The drug culture, Beetles music, and alienation from society: all these of the second half of the 20th century have a dose of existentialist philosophy.

Existence becomes so important for Kierkegaard that for him only what is essentially subjective makes any sense at all. By definition, objectivity is independent of individual consciousness and is there for ever. Now Kierkegaard went on to say that therefore when one is objective one decimates one's own existence. This may be an interesting idea as a philosophical position, but we may be grateful that it wasn't taken seriously by investigators who explored the world as scientists.

In Kierkegaard's view, human beings evolve from the ethical to the aesthetic to the religious. In the fist stage, what matters is sensual experience, selfishness, and attempts to escape from being bored. By ethics he means much more than adherence to social or traditional norms. Finally comes the religious stage. However, by religion, Kierkegaard meant Christianity, and by Christianity he meant the kind which was practiced in the Denmark of his times. He himself had been affected by Lutheran pietism in which, as in Puritanism, guilt and individual responsibility dominated the religious experience. He saw in Copenhagen Christianity little of substance beyond well-clad god-men periodically pontificating from the pulpit and administering holy comunion. He complained passionately that the Church had grown too complacent. The true Christian, in Kierkegaard's vision, was one who is profoundly suffering from his separation from God. He saw no need for clergy in his communion with God.

Kierkegaard's direction of evolution is the reverse of what some might argue: The more sophisticated one is, the less religious one becomes in belief and practice, and the more ethical, while retaining the aesthetic dimensions of religion.

Kierkegaard was very serious about choice in human life. He felt strongly that everything we experience is a direct consequence of the choices we make. Christianity arose because people made a conscious choice to accept God's Word. More exactly, Christianity arises only for the individual who consciously makes this choice. It is a choice between temporality and eternity. To choose Christ is to be assured of eternal life in magnificence. To reject Christ would be condemnation to a black hole where nothing exists, not even space or time. No wonder the choice is preceded by a terrible angst. This is a beautiful idea, especially if, by Christ, one means recognition of a supreme divinity undergirding the world of experience.

From the World of Science: FERDINAND Von RICHTHOFEN

Ultimately the goal of science is to understand and explain every aspect of the phenomenal world. But before one can do that, one needs to carefully study every aspect of the world. That is why it is fair to say that there is much more to science than explanation. Indeed, a major part of the scientific enterprise consists in gathering data (systematic information) about the world.

Not everything one wishes to study may be within one's reach. This means that one will have to travel to places, near and far. A philosopher may be able to spend his entire life within the confines of Koenigsberg or wherever, but an observational scientist, especially if she is interested in lands and seas, cannot afford to do that.

Ferdinand von Richthofen (born: 5 May 1833) went with a team to explore the Alps and he presented a report on some of the geological aspects of the mountain range, suggesting causes for their formation. He was at that time a young man of 27.

The Prussian government was impressed with his work, and he was invited to be part of a mission to the Far East. During this trip he visited many places, including Siam, Sri Lanka, Java, and Japan, but all the notes he gathered on the way were somehow lost.

In 1862 he was off to California from where he wrote regularly on mines and minerals, as well as on the rocks in the Rocky Mountains and the snowy range (Sierra Nevada). Then, as a classic instance of the economic urge that has overtly or subtly propelled a good deal of scientific exploration, the Bank of California and the Shangai Chamber of Commerce sponsored Richthofen's several trips to Mainland China. By 1872 he had traveled to practically every province of that huge country, not as a tourist or to taste Chinese food, but to collect information on the rocks and the rivers, the land and the resources, the geography and the geology of the country. He studied the fossils of the region, he drew several maps of places from his surveys. He developed theories as to the land formation in China. Incidentally, and significantly for the economy of the country, he pointed out that the coalfields in Shantung held great promise.

Richthofen presented his findings in a multi-volume treatise entitled: *Ergebnisse eigener Reisen und darauf gegruendeter Studien* (Results of particular travels and studies based on them) which became a classic. Through this and other works he contributed significantly to the fields of geography and geology. He made a systematic classification of the different branches of and approaches to geography. Thus, collecting data on the broad features of the land was one thing. But the exploration of the forces and factors that give rise to these is a different matter. His work also spurred the field of geomorphology which studies the surface features of our planet in terms of the basic forces that cause them. The field of geomorphology has widened considerably since, for today we observe the earth from satellites, and we also study the impact of human activities on the planet.

It is interesting to note the intertwining of history, economic forces, and the development of science in various contexts. A good many results and breakthroughs in science that occurred in the 19th century, in fields like astronomy, biology, and geology, were the results of Western imperialism. Just as in a different age Islamic expansionism revived ancient scholarship and transported the quadratic equation and the decimal system from India into Europe, 19th century colonialism contributed to the charting of the southern skies, to the study of the geology of China, to the deciphering of the hieroglyphics, and to knowledge about the finches in the Galapagos which led to insights into evolution. It extended and enhanced human knowledge in a hundred different ways.

May 6

From the World of Religion:
RABINDRANATH TAGORE

Many poets in the Hindu tradition have echoed the insights of their ancient sages. Often they have transformed that wisdom into modern frameworks, and revealed the perennial nature of its philosophy. Rabindranath Tagore (born: 6 May 1860) was one such. His work in translation gained universal admiration and the Nobel Prize.

Tagore was a prolific writer, musical composer, artist, but above all, a Bengali poet par excellence. He was gifted through some mysterious genetic coding with rhyme and rhythm, with inner melody and exuberant creativity. His poetic vision struck resonant chords with the beauty in nature and the pangs of love through words and music. He would fly to romantic heights and words would burst forth from his heart to express robust passions and intense sensuousness. But Tagore was also a sensitive thinker who wondered about the meaning of life and the universe. The blood that coursed in his veins was of ancient vintage for he emerged in an ancient mystical tradition.

In his *Naibedya* (*Offerings*) Tagore he reflected on the inner essence of Reality, there first appeared his immortal lines:

Where the mind is without fear and the head is held high;
Where knowledge is free;
Where the world has not been broken up into fragments
by narrow domestic walls...
Into that Heaven wake this Indian land!

In Shantiniketan, he wrote *Gitanjali* during his seclusion from the political and social turmoil rocking his country, during a period when he was "very restless" and "anxious to know the world." He used to wander in the moonlit mango groves, sleeping very little. *Gitanjali* turned out to be the most famous book of the poet.

We see him here as one who is intimate with nature. He is touched by the color and beauty, the rhythms and sounds of the wondrous world around. Nature is a heart-throb of love for the bliss of the sensitive soul. There is God in the glorious sense, immanent and revealing, the light that illumines the human experience. In all the poetic chiseling of nature's beauty, there is also a deep mystical recognition, for, the word of a poet gives utterance to the divine rhythmic movement in the world. If Tagore was profoundly moved by the glorious insights of

Upanishadic seers, he was no less appalled and pained by the inhumanity of casteism and the mindless mutterings of heartless orthodoxy.

Leave this chanting and signing and telling of beads!...
He is there where the tiller is tilling the hard ground,
where the path-maker is breaking stones."

But ultimately, the longings of the ancient *rishis* are given utterance:

"Let all the strains of joy mingle in my last song: the joy that makes the earth flow over in the riotous excess of the grass, the joy that sets the twin brothers, life and death, dancing over the wide world, the joy that sweeps in with the tempest, shaking and waking all life with laughter, the joy that sits still with its tears on the open red lotus of pain, and the joy that throws everything it has upon the dust, and knows not a word."

The perennial prayer of ancient India, the vibrant theme that has echoed all through Indian history, is also given due place in Gitanjali, for the poet pleads: "Oh grant me my prayer that I may never lose the bliss of the touch of the One in the play of the many."

It is in the words of poets that the deepest religious feelings of humankind survive.

From the World of Science: SIGMUND FREUD

Of all the puzzles in the world of experience the human mind is the most mysterious. So our philosophy and literature, religion and metaphysics have been enriched by ideas and speculations on the human mind. Some of these are interesting, some insightful, and some, like Patanjali's treatise, have even been helpful to our well-being.

But no theory, in the guise of science or speculation, has served to remedy ailments of the mind, nor effected a revolution in how we consider human behavior and attitudes, as the ideas of Sigmund Freud (born: 6 May 1856) did. There are still debates as to whether what Freud unleashed was science or speculation, theory or theology, serious or silly. But no one can deny that countless thousands of mentally affected people at various levels of disturbance have undergone treatment by being analyzed in the Freudian framework. Millions more have been transformed by his visions of the mysterious underworld of the unconscious to which he traced every thought and word, deed and dream.

Every aspect of the human being is seen in his system as fueled by what he termed the *libido* and the *id* which have subtle links to our sexual dimension.

Then there is the *ego* which is a kind of crude conscience, as it were, guiding the manifestations of id, whereas the *superego*, molded by culture and upbringing, constrains us to do only what is good and proper. If and when the id, the ego and the superego cease to work in unison, elements of the id are pushed back into the unconscious, then some, if not all, hell breaks out: there emerge fears and phobias, fretting and fuming, nightmares and neurosis. For in that unwitting process of repression, the psyche is deeply wounded. By recognizing the cause and source of the wound, the hurt can be removed. This is a simplistic formulation of Freud's elaborate theories which grew over the decades, corrected, criticized, and improved upon by himself and his students, by fellow psychologists and philosophers.

Many practitioners of therapy have rejected Freud, but the language has not been able to free itself of the concepts and terms that ensued from his work: so we still speak of repression and sexuality, complexes, sublimation, and long-range impacts of childhood experiences. If Marx said that the root cause of human behavior is greed, Freud insisted it was desire of the sexual kind: silent, subtle, and secretive most of the time.

The Rig Veda said that it was from Desire that the cosmos arose. Freud gave it a sexual touch. One effect was to transform everything to the base and the banal. Traditional respect for parents is regarded as sublimated incestual instincts, and interpreted as the disguised misbehavior of Oedipus or Electra, God is reduced to a fantasy for a Father-figure, and an unwitting omission is seen as an aspect of the libido trying to stealthily get out. Everything from an infant sucking its thumb to a musician composing a grand symphony is traced to some aspect or another of the sex instinct.

Novels have been written, movies made and caricatures concocted, based on Sigmund Freud's theories. Not just patients in asylums, but great personages and literary characters have been psychoanalyzed, including Freud himself and Hamlet. Someone once wrote a satirical play in which a young man was happily married to his mother, and upon discovering that his wife was not really his mother, he committed suicide.

The human brain is the most complex system to have evolved in the universe, the mind is its most mysterious aspect of it. To fathom its roots is no easy task. Freud was one of the few who have attempted this. In Freud's view we are like boats tossed by waves, but we see and experience only the surges of the boat. Unless we know the forces that stir the waters, we can never calculate the how and the why of the boat's movements.

May 7

From the World of Religion:
CHORAL FINALE OF BEETHOVEN'S NINTH

Religions have a variety of impacts on the human experience and on culture. One of these is the joyous component. Every religion is conducive to creating in us at some time or other feelings of sheer exhilaration. It is a joy that comes from being outside (ex) of one's normal place (stasis), i.e. being one with the universe as a whole. In that state of ecstasy, we also feel an oneness with the all fellow creatures, we recognize in a profound way, in the words of Schiller, that

Alle Menschen werden Brüder (All humans are siblings)

Schiller described joy as a beautiful flash from God and as the daughter of Elysium. Fired up by the state of divinity, one enters the holy shrine of that heavenly joy, Schiller went on to say. The immanence of ecstatic divinity in the living world was expressed by the power in these lines (I give my own translation):

Freude trinken alle Wesen Anden Brüstender Natur;
Alle Guten, alle Bösen, Folgen ihrer Rosenspur.

Ev'ry being drinks the joy that from Nature's heart does flow
All that's good and all that's evil, do her rosy path follow.

The poet calls upon us to embrace one another and remember that the kiss is for the whole world. We are reminded of the Vedic prayer: *Lokaa samastaa sukhino bhavantu*: May happiness be for all humankind. When Schiller affirms that a beloved Father must live over the starry firmament, he articulates the deepest conviction of all religions that there must be something with love and understanding in this otherwise cold cosmos.

Beethoven set to music parts of Schiller's *Ode to Joy*, as the choral finale for his immortal Ninth Symphony, as if to assist us in experiencing that ecstasy. This was first performed in Vienna on 7 May 1824, conducted by Beethoven himself. We have heard the story of how the master was still waving the baton when the audience was applauding the music, because Beethoven, grown deaf, was hearing nothing at all.

Since that date, the Ninth has been performed thousands of times, and it has stirred the souls of millions all over the world. It begins with subdued mystery and closes in rapturous joy as indeed all religious pursuits should. The alternations between the slow and the tumultuously joyous also reflect the range of religious experience from the serenely meditative to the jubilance of festivals.

If poets express profound religious truths, composers translate them into a medium which enables us to experience those truths even more directly. In the process, two things could happen: Given that few poets are traditionally recognized prophets like the Vedic *rishis* of ancient India, poetic utterances tend to secularize the sacred and the religious.

Secularization could take away the spirit of religions, and prompt narrow chauvinists to claim a great creative work as their national treasure. Thus, forgetting the spirit of the Chorus, the Third Reich promoted the Ninth Symphony as an expression of German spirituality to infuse Nazi soldiers with "strength for battle." This was as much a perversion as killing fellow humans while screaming "God is great!"

On the other hand, one positive result of secularizing the spiritual yearning is that the more universal elements of religion are elevated from the local to the human level. Religious truths and experiences take on trans-cultural, rather than parochial, significance because terms and concepts in poetic visions are humanistic rather than ethnic or local-prophetic. More of this is needed in the global village in which we live.

From the World of Science: ALEXIS CLAIRAULT

Is the earth a perfect sphere, ignoring its mountainous dimples, or is it somewhat flattened at the equator or maybe at the poles? We know the answer today, but what about the state of human knowledge in the first half of the 17th century?

One of the people who contributed to the resolution of this question was a bright young man by the name of Alexis Clairault (born: 7 May 1713).

Clairault was a child prodigy. When he was 10 years old, he was exploring conic sections and infinitesimal calculus. At 12, he read a paper at the *Academie des Sciences*. At 13, with a handful of other youngsters he founded an intellectual discussion group. At eighteen, he published a monograph in mathematics based on his own researches which was deemed so good that they elected him a member of the Academy. Really...

At 23, he was part of an expedition sent by the French *Academie des Sciences* to Lapland to measure the distance corresponding to a meridian degree of arc in the arctic circle. Comparison with a similar measurement in the equatorial region established the correctness of Newton's conjecture (and Clairault's own suspicion) that the earth is flattened at the poles rather than at the equator. This is an example to illustrate the fruitfulness of scientific methodology. No amount of ethical behavior, compassion, prayer, or meditation, and no inspired book of revelation, can unravel the flattened rotundity of our planet. Only careful observations, measurements, and reasoning can.

Clairault analyzed the shape of the earth from mathematical, physical, and dynamical perspectives, and arrived at results which are relevant to this day. In a treatise on the subject he derived a formula for the acceleration due to gravity as a function of latitude.

He also did much work in celestial mechanics. He compared the gravitational forces on the earth due to the moon and due to Venus. He estimated the sizes of these bodies. He studied lunar motion, using the principles of mechanics. This was an instance of the famous three-body problem in which one calculates the effects of the mutual gravitational pulls of three different bodies: like the sun, the moon, and the earth.

He also investigated the effect of the gravitational pulls of Jupiter and Saturn on the comet whose return years had been worked out by Edmund Halley. Halley had predicted, after the 1682 sighting, that the comet would be back in 1758 or 1759. Clairault got interested in the problem and, armed with his mathematics and celestial mechanics, he computed that it would come closest to the sun on 15 April 1759. With further approximations, he could get as close as 31 March. The observed date was 13 March. An error of less than three weeks is impressively small in estimating the path of a body whose orbital period is about 75 years.

Clairault assisted the Marquise de Châtelet in the translation of Newton's *Principia*, and in the process he made his own annotations and additions to the French version. Clairault wrote many papers on mathematics also. A differential equation is named after him, though it had been studied independently by another mathematician before him. Bright and sociable, often charming and sometimes confrontational, Clairault is said to have been quite a success in the salons of 17th century Paris. But he remained matrimonially unattached all through his life.

It is only when one understands the mathematical details and methodological complexity involved in the practice of science that one can fully appreciate the difference between speculative reveries about the nature of the phenomenal world and the relatively weightier validity of the scientific assertions on a matter.

May 8

From the World of Religion:
HENRI DUNANT & THE RED CROSS DAY

Henri Dunant (born: 8 May 1828) was born in a fairly well-to-do Swiss family in Geneva. He was inclined to piety and to serving others. He was active at YMCU (Young Men's Christian Union) in his youthful years. After his travels in North Africa, he wrote a book comparing slavery in the United States with that in the Islamic world.

He initiated a land venture for which he needed water rights which could be given only by the French Emperor Napoleon III. But the monarch was minding a war in Italy, trying to evict the Austrian army. Dunant made his way to see Napoleon in Solferino, and happened to be, unexpectedly, in a theater of war.

These days we see the terrible scenes of wars on TV screens at home. Like vile words and violence, frequent visual exposure to maiming and killing on the battlefield has made these common place. Nowadays, if transported to a war zone, some might even take pictures to show their friends at home.

But for Dunant this was a terrible personal experience. He had never seen nor imagined such pain and torture, such bloodshed and anguish on such a grand scale. He saw how some of the wounded men were simply left behind, to suffer and perhaps to die. He saw the despair in the eyes of the soldiers, the agony caused by their wounds. He took careful mental notes of everything he witnessed, and in 1862 wrote a book entitled: *Un Souvenir de Solférino*. In it he powerfully described the gory scenes on the battleground. He also painted the aftermath of a bloody confrontation Most importantly, in this book he proposed the formation of relief organizations for the victims of Wars. The book created a stir.

Dunant called upon the nations of the world to establish relief organizations which would coordinate their efforts in attending to the wounded in any war. He appealed to people to become volunteers in such service. He suggested that such volunteers be given professional training in the discharge of their commitment.

As a result of his book, a committee was assembled to explore these possibilities. Dunant himself traveled widely, soliciting funds for such an organization, contributing much from his own resources. Thus emerged the Geneva Convention and the Red Cross in 1863–64. The emblem of the Red Cross is a tribute to Dunant's Swiss nationality, the flag of that nation has the same colors, reversed: white cross in a red background.

Over the decades, chapters of the Red Cross were established in practically every country of the world. The organization has been doing valuable relief work everywhere, not just in times of war, but in the context of all human disasters, be it natural and human-activated.

As if this was not enough, Dunant tried to form a society for the "Revival of the Orient," and thought of a project for the publication of a sort of world library (somewhat like the Harvard Classics) which would publish all the masterpieces of world literature. He was engaged in other international movements too.

But Dunant's own life suddenly took on unexpected turns. His company failed, he lost all his money and property, he was reduced to a state of mendicancy, and he vanished from public view for almost two decades. He was spotted in 1890 in a small Swiss village, but he continued to live in a modest room, ignored by everyone. But in 1895 he was taken note of again, given many awards, including the first Nobel Peace Prize. In 1948, his birth date of 8 May was proclaimed as the Red Cross Day.

From the World of Science:
EMIL CHRISTIAN HANSEN

Cultural anthropologists and historians have revealed that brewing and beer are ancient elements in human culture. And the associated process of fermentation has also been known for ages. However, it was only in the 19th century that the chemistry behind these was elucidated, after a good deal of controversial exchanges among eminent chemists. In particular, the nature and role of the yeast was clarified in the process. Yeast had been spotted under the first microscope already in the 17th century, but was mistaken for an inorganic globule. In the first decade of the 19th century, the role of yeast in fermentation was recognized, but there were controversies as to whether it was a plant or an animal. It was Pasteur who established that fermentation resulted from physiological processes in the organism called yeast.

Yeast came to be known as a sugar fungus (*Saccharomyces*), and soon it was known that there is a whole variety of them. Scientists work in all kinds of places, at all sorts of hours and with all types of materials. Some look at distant stars, others at minute molecules. Some study lakes and mountains, others plants and animals. Some are also interested in knowing about fungi in mammal dung. One such scientist was Emil Christian Hansen (born: 8 May 1842). His scientific curiosity led to these organisms that have silently plays a major role in human culture (no pun intended).

Initially, Hansen was interested in botany, but not in common leaves and flowers. He probed into all kinds of places to uncover unusual things. Thus he was thrilled when he brought to light beech leaves in the peat stratum of a moor. This showed, contrary to the accepted belief, that beech trees had been in Denmark since prehistoric times.

Hansen studied various fungi and their variations, developed methods of culturing them, and also discovered new varieties of them.

Then he was drawn to a study of fermentation, and he received a doctoral degree for his dissertation on this subject. This got him a position in the laboratories of the most famous brewery in Denmark: Carlsberg.

It was believed at the time that if there was only yeast in fermented beverages, the latter would never be adversely affected, because it was bacteria that spoiled the stuff. But Hansen showed that this was not necessarily so. Emerson reminded us that "God made yeast, as well as dough, and loves fermentation as dearly as he loves vegetation." Hansen went on to see what kinds of yeasts God made. He discovered that there are good ones and bad ones. The bad yeast (i.e. those that spoil wine and beer) carried no bacteria, but they did their dirty job anyway. He studied different kinds of yeasts, showed how each species could alter the flavor of the beer, and that the yeast in the body of the beer is different from the one in the froth on top. He found that mutations occurred in them, leading to different beer varieties. He also developed techniques for preparing pure yeast cultures. His work had great impact on the beer industry.

Hansen came from a modest family. His father used to paint houses for a living. Hansen is said to have written novels and sold them: From this income he financed his studies. But he amassed a sizable wealth. He was himself not a very cheerful person, but he bequeathed lots of money for scientific research and awards.

The long-range impact of a scientific investigation can never be predicted. Thus no one could have foreseen that Hansen's initial interest in fungi would some day lead to his thorough investigation of what different types of yeast do in fermentation which, in turn, would to influence the kind of beer people consume today.

May 9

From the World of Religion:
CHRIST'S ASCENSION TO HEAVEN

We all know about astronauts being blasted into space in rockets. But in ancient times, as per mythology and sacred history, other human beings have been bodily transported beyond the earth's atmosphere. Icarus flew almost near the Sun. Trishanku in Hindu lore tried to reach heaven in flesh and blood, but was arrested half-way. The Old Testament says that Elijah was taken to heaven in a golden chariot, propelled by in a whirlwind.

It is stated in Mark (16:19) that "...after the Lord had spoken to them, he was received up into heaven, and sat on the right hand of God." In Luke (24.51) we read that Jesus "was parted from them, and carried up into heaven." Jesus himself is reported to have said: "Do not touch Me, for I am not ascended to My Father..."

From such passages arose in the Christian world a celebration of Christ's Ascension to heaven forty days after the Resurrection, which is 9 May this year. The celebration is believed to have started a couple centuries after Christ, as authenticated by St. Augustine.

Scholars have pin-pointed the location where this momentous event in Christian sacred history occurred: It was on Mount Olivet (*Mons Olivertus* in Latin), a hill on the east-aide of Jerusalem, where, at one time, there must have been many olive trees. St. Helena is said to have built a basilica there to commemorate the event.

So on this day there are time-honored rituals: like the procession showing a banner with a lion and a dragon at the bottom to represent the triumph of Christ and the downgrading of Evil. In some churches they make an opening in the roof to permit (symbolically) the passage of Christ heavenwards. On this day, they also snuff the paschal candle as if to say, Christ is now bodily leaving us.

Inspired as he was by Moses and Christ, the Prophet Mohammed also had a dream in which the archangel Gabriel escorted him on a white horse to that same Mount Olivet whence he too took off for heaven in flesh and blood. Its impact on history has been greater than any other dream, and it persists to this day. This story made such an impression on Mohammed's ardent followers that not long after he passed away, they invaded Jerusalem, renamed the hill Haram esh Sharif (Noble Sanctuary), and built a magnificent mosque (El Aqsa) there. This is commendable as a gesture of honor for the founder of the religion. But the Persians also destroyed the basilica which had been built by St. Helena. When it was rebuilt, they destroyed it again and again. It is not clear if the Prophet, who respected Jesus and Moses, would have applauded this type of enthusiasm, but then, over the centuries worse atrocities have been perpetrated in his fair name.

Known as *analepsis* in the Orthodox tradition and as *Christi Himmelsfahrt* in the Germanic, the ascent of Christ to heaven forty days after the Resurrection is observed by many Christians with solemnity today. Those not of the faith may regard it as a symbolic remembrance of the leaving if a divine being who was once with us in flesh and blood.

Science and rationality may make it difficult even for some devout Christians to take the episode literally. So the Catholic writer John Wynne noted: "To say that He (Christ) was taken up or that He ascended, does not necessarily imply that they locate <u>heaven</u> directly above the earth; no more than the words 'sitteth on the right hand of <u>God</u>' mean that this is His actual posture. In disappearing from their view 'He was raised up and a cloud received Him out of their sight' (Acts 1:9), and entering into <u>glory</u> He dwells with the Father in the <u>honour</u> and power denoted by the <u>scripture</u> phrase."

From the World of Science: GASPARD MONGE

We can draw on a sheet of paper a triangle or a circle. But how about a cube or a sphere? This too can be done by those who have some acquaintance with mathematics or draftsmanship. The depiction of a three dimensional body on a two dimensional plane with geometrical precision started from the creative genius of a mathematician who is not too well known among those who have not plodded through courses in technical mathematics. His name was Gaspard Monge (born: 9 May 1746).

Monge was enrolled in a small provincial military school in pre-revolutionary France when the notions of *égalité* and *fraternité* were as unknown as in some societies today. This son of a modest merchant was not of the upper caste, and was relegated to menial tasks. During his stay there, a theoretical problem arose relating to the design of a fortress no part of which would be exposed to bombardment from an enemy. The traditional method involved lots of numerical calculations. Monge solved the problem in very little time by his own geometrical method. The officer in charge refused to look into the solution because it was presented in an unduly short time. Recalling this and similar incidents, Monge said: "I was tempted a thousand times to tear up my drawings in disgust at the esteem in which they were held, as if I had been good for nothing better."

It was there that descriptive geometry had its rebirth in the modern world: rebirth, because the great artist Albrecht Duerer, born in the 15th century, had already tackled the problem of representing three dimensional bodies on a two-dimensional plane.

Monge's ingenious method also had military applications. He was asked to keep his technique a secret. It was fifteen years before it became public. Monge was now a professor at a prestigious school in Paris where most of the big-wigs worked. The leading mathematicians of the time hit their heads and exclaimed, "Why didn't *I* think of that!" or, "I have been doing this unknowingly in some of my work!" Descriptive geometry played an indispensable role in the design of machines in the industrial revolution.

Eventually, Monge was elected to the *Académie des Sciences*. He worked on the theory of surfaces and on partial differential equations, and saw the relationship between the two. He was one of the first to recognize that such equations have whole classes of functions as solutions, rather than specific ones. He introduced the notion of characteristic curves. He also did work in chemistry and metallurgy.

Monge held high positions in the aftermath of the French Revolution during which he enjoyed the favor of the revolutionaries because he came from the lower classes. He was given responsibility in the Ministry of the Navy. He retired for a while. When Bonaparte, an admirer of scientists and mathematicians, came to power, Monge moved into the inner circle. He wined and dined with Napoleon and traveled to Egypt with the conqueror.

Monge gained the esteem of Napoleon by his knowledge and intelligence, and was appointed to several high positions again, besides his professorship at the *École Polytechnique*. At one point he even became president of the French senate. He received numerous awards, including the *Legion d'Honneur*, and was made a count. The price he paid for being Napoleon's protégé was that when Napoleon was dethroned, Monge was also thrown out of the *Institut de France*, and there were demonstrations against him.

Politics is seldom clean, and it never wins universal acclaim such as mathematics, poetry or music does. When one is drawn into it, no matter what one's intrinsic merit, anything can happen to one's reputation and treatment. So it was with Monge. But in the long run, he is remembered for his mathematics much more than for his politics.

May 10

From the World of Religion: KARL BARTH

Every religion has its theologians. Theologians serve many purposes: one of these is to give their own interpretations of the doctrines, scriptures, and traditions of their religion. In the process, they are sometimes obliged to comment upon and criticize what they regard as erroneous interpretations of God and godhead given by fellow-theologians of their own persuasion and by rival theologians of other religions.

Karl Barth (born: 10 May 1886) is among the very influential Protestant theologians of the 20th century. He is remembered for his many writings, and most of all, as a critic of what is sometimes called *liberal theology* which, as he saw it, mistakenly identified theology with anthropology. In other words, instead of making an effort to know God, liberal theology tries to understand why and how human beings try to know God. Well, said Barth, God is totally different from anything we humans can conceptualize. We are no part of Him. He is totally, wholly, entirely, altogether, a hundred percent, "the other." His interpretation of the Fall from Eden was that Man lost not only his capacity to see right from wrong, but also his ability to see God through logic and reason.

Being a true Christian, he also affirmed that the only inkling we ever had of God was with the death and resurrection of Jesus. This is not a matter for discussion, but for interiorization. Barth proclaimed that ultimate truth about God could be seen in the Bible: a contention that is echoed in the writings of theologians of other traditions too, and with equal conviction. This may sound like parochial prejudice, but in a deeper sense he was a true Christian: In the dark days of Germany, unlike many Church-goers who had no problem saying the Lord's prayer and also *Heil Hitler*, Barth rejected the Nazi craze, lost his position in a German university for this, and went back to his native Switzerland. He cared for the human condition, he was a socialist at heart, and he simply wouldn't stand injustice. In his later years, he even began to talk about the humanity of God.

Furthermore, unlike Augustine who believed that all non-Christians are damned for good because that's what God wanted, Barth felt that others also had a chance: sooner or later they too, here or elsewhere, will accept Christ and will be saved. Some theologians criticized him for this universalism because, in principle, it rules out freedom, for it is not by one's choice (of Christ) that one is saved; not whether one so chooses or not.

In his voluminous writings over the decades Barth sometimes changed his position, but he was always firm in his views, and he provoked polemics.

In broad terms, Barth belongs to the group of religious thinkers who have held that God is, and will ever be, elusive to the human mind. Only those whom God has chosen to be revealed to, will ever know what God is all about. God is not a theorem to be proved. As I once put it, trying to apprehend God through reason is like trying to catch a fish-egg using a net that has very large openings.

Except for the fact that he was erudite and professorial, an academic and an author, Barth was writing in learned ways what inspired evangelists often speak out with stirring eloquence. Barth elaborated his visions of God in thousands of foot-noted pages. So his words will live for ever, and scholars will be talking about him rather than about others with similar views who had neither his vast knowledge nor a publisher.

The Reverend Martin Luther King and a fellow scholar once wrote a commentary on Barth in which they said: "one wonders how he came to know so much of the Unknown God." The same may be said of all of us.

From the World of Science:
AUGUSTIN JEAN FRESNEL

The nature of light has been an enigma since time immemorial. But, as in many other fields of inquiry, one began to learn a good deal about the laws and properties of light as a phenomenon since the emergence of modern science in the 17th century. But it was not easy to figure out the ultimate nature of this aspect of perceived reality. All through the 18th century, scientific investigators were arguing about whether light consisted of particles (*corpuscular* theory) or waves (*undulatory* theory).

A crucial experiment in 1801 established clearly that ultimately there is something wave-like associated with light. Now a wave is a periodic disturbance that carries energy. The question was: a disturbance of what? In water waves, water is disturbed, in air waves it is air, and in the wave on a guitar string, it is the string that is vibrating.

So physicists imagined a subtle medium permeating all of interstellar space which is set into vibration when light travels through it. And they called it the *ether*. No one had ever seen or felt this super-subtle medium whose existence is a requirement in the mechanical theory of light as a wave.

Two things characterize a wave: a line of oscillation (or vibration) of the medium; and a line of propagation of the wave. In a wave in a slinky, the oscillation occurs along the line of propagation. In a string, one is perpendicular to the other. The first type of wave is called *longitudinal*; the second, *transverse*.

Now came Augustin Jean Fresnel (born: 10 May 1788). He was not a child prodigy: he was almost eight when he learned to read. Yet he entered the prestigious *École Polytechnique* in Paris at the age of 16, became a civil engineer, and got a job with the government, working on projects for laying roads and highways. In his spare time, he read some philosophy and science. He got interested in the wave-corpuscle controversy about light. At this time Napoleon returned from his exile in Elba. Like other inspired radicals who blurt out extremist statements about politicians they don't like, the 26 year old Fresnel considered Napoleon's return as "an attack on civilization." As a result, he was promptly relieved of his governmental job.

Fresnel returned to his home town, and plunged into research on optics. He did experiments on diffraction and confirmed the wave nature of light. During the following decade he gave a mathematical formulation to the wave theory which are taught to this day in standard courses. In the meanwhile, Napoleon was no longer in power, and Fresnel was offered engineering positions in Paris. By now, he established that light consists of *transverse* waves and explained the phenomenon of double refraction on this basis. Fresnel's theory led to the prediction of what is called conical refraction. He was acclaimed by the *Académie des Sciences* and by the Royal Society of London.

Unfortunately, Fresnel did not enjoy good health. But his deep faith in God and hope of an afterlife stood him in good stead. He led a rather self-disciplined life, with few distractions, devoting himself entirely to serious work.

Fresnel was philosophically inclined to the belief that there is an underlying unity in nature. Somewhat like modern searchers for a Theory of Everything, he fantasized that there was a fundamental fluid whose diverse manifestations were heat, light, and electricity. He became such an expert on light that he was asked to work on lighthouses. In this context, he designed the Fresnel lens which is still in vogue in lighthouses and stage lights, and even in spacecraft on solar panels. One wonders how physics might have developed if Fresnel had not died before reaching the age of 40.

May 11

From the World of Religion:
JIDDU KRISHNAMURTHI

Many factors contribute to the recognition and propagation of a person's ideas. One of these is charisma. Some people have an uncommon power in their personality by which they are able to win the hearts, minds, and attention of countless followers and admirers.

One such personage was Jiddu Krishnamurthi (born: 11 May 1895). When he was 14, he was discovered by the theosophist Annie Besant who declared him to be the Maitreya: the final Bodhisattva. The Bodhisattvas are periodic incarnations of Buddha, as per Mahayana Buddhism.

Thus selected, J. Krishnamurthi founded a World Order of the Star. He was taken on a lecture tour to England and America between 1929 and 1931 where he was acclaimed by many. But at the end of it, he called it quits, and declared he was no incarnation of Buddha, and did not want any disciples. In fact, like most secular intelligent thinkers, he was against the follow-the-leader mentality in matters religious, and went so far as to declare that "to follow another is evil, and it does not matter who it is." This had such an impact on so many people that they became his followers. He said no one had the right interpret his work, so some of his warm admirers began to do just that. But he did allow his talks and dialogues to be widely circulated after his death, and this is being done now.

J. Krishnamurthi maintained that our sense of individuality is a result of our ignorance of our true nature. Every conflict and confusion is cleared as soon as we dispel this ignorance. Ultimate Truth and God are within us, he said. Our life's course is like that of rivers and we ultimately merge with the ocean of infinity. There is a process by which we become more and more acutely aware of our individual consciousness until ultimately it explodes into the totality, and one merges with the Whole: Not very original thoughts perhaps, but effectively articulated.

J. Krishnamurti was a very good speaker. He was invited to many countries, and he spoke to audiences on spiritual and metaphysical themes. He discussed the social, political, and environmental ills. He expressed the concerns that all of us feel, and called for a change of heart and mind to arrest the violence and chaos that torment the world.

He asked rhetorically: "Can the mind be free of this egocentric activity?...Which means, can the mind stand alone, uninfluenced?...Being alone does not mean isolation...When one rejects completely all the absurdities of

nationality, the absurdities of propaganda, of religious propaganda, rejects conclusions of any kind, actually, not theoretically, completely put aside, has understood very deeply the question of pleasure and fear, and division—the 'me' and
'not me'—is there any form of the self at all?"

Such reflections impressed countless people, including the eminent and brilliant quantum physicist David Bohm who began an intellectual collaboration
with J. Krishnamurti in 1959. They explored the nature of thought in metaphysical rather than in scientific terms. They came to the conclusion that the root
cause of all the political and social chaos of the time was our ignorance of how
our thought processes occur.

Bohm wrote: "…we do not see what is actually happening, when we are
engaged in the activity of thinking. Through close attention to and observation of
this activity of thought, Krishnamurti feels that he directly perceives that thought
is a material process, which is going on inside of the human being in the brain
and nervous system as a whole."

Every age has its philosophers who discover the cause of our ills. Surprisingly,
even with such an abundance of wisdom, humanity continues to totter in
pathetic modes.

From the World of Science: RICHARD FEYNMAN

Poets describe nature in soothing and inspiring language. Philosophers reflect on
the human condition in insightful and meaningful ways. Theoretical physicists
formulate the microcosm in mathematical and fruitful equations. Of those who
caught the magic of the microcosm with profound and new ways was Richard
Feynman (born: 11 May 1918).

When in his mid-twenties Feynman was involved with the Manhattan project.
At Cornell he worked out his path-breaking techniques in quantum electrodynamics. When he presented his (second renormalization) theory to the major
players in theoretical physics at an exclusive conference in 1948, Niels Bohr is
said to have commented that this young man hadn't grasped the basics of quantum mechanics. More than once, Feynman was ignored because others did not
understand his revolutionary ideas. But he always persisted, and always won. He
took the physics establishment by storm with his ingenious diagrams and their
implications, with his path integrals with their powerful computational consequences.

He worked on superfluidity (motion without friction of liquid helium at temperatures very near zero K), insightfully elucidated the results of deep inelastic scattering, and helped unravel the mystery of weak interactions. He played with flexagons (geometrical figures of several sides and faces constructed by folding a sheet of paper in multiple ways). He recognized what was later re-discovered as intragenic suppression.

Feynman's name is indelibly linked with certain diagrams in microphysics which are transparently illustrative of the processes they describe and also valuable in doing the associated sophisticated calculations, and strike those who revel in such matters as sublime modes of penetrating into the deep-down mysteries of the micro-world.

Some brains function in extraordinary ways. Geniuses create great art and music, science and mathematics, open up new pathways for thought and perception, and make revolutionary breakthroughs in our understanding and utilization of the world around us. Such indeed was Feynman. His first love was physics, but he had other interests too: like playing bongo drums and teaching himself Chinese.

Intelligence shines in accepted modes, but genius strays from the trodden track. Feynman was unorthodox in his attitudes and approaches. He was blessed with a razor-sharp mind and an uncanny ability to recognize the core of a problem. He was also a practical joker, delightful speaker, and author of some excellent physics texts. He influenced the course of physics, and also physics courses, contributed substantially to its conceptual framework, and touched the professional and intellectual life of many fellow physicists. He provoked laughter and reflection, the jealousy of some, the wrath of a few, and the admiration of all.

Next to Einstein, and maybe Oppenheimer, Richard Feynman was probably the most widely known physicist of the 20th century. Thanks to his prodigious intellect and eccentricity, his name became a household word among physicists. Since the 1986 Challenger disaster for which he discovered the O-rings as the cause, and the Nova program about him, his fame became even more universal. Whenever he entered a hall with physicists or students, an eerie silence or hushed whispers would ensue. Looks of admiration would result as if a famous movie star had arrived. There was great affection for this unusual man who was honest to the point of being blunt, serious yet jovial, a master of complex calculations, yet also a prankster. Some wondered, half-seriously, if Feynman was a human being.

May 12

From the World of Religion: MOTHER'S DAY

When we try to recall the distant past phase of our existence, we hardly remember the days of our infancy when for food, warmth, and bodily hygiene we depended entirely on Mom's milk, love, and attention. But this has always been so. There is a Jewish saying to the effect that God could not be everywhere and therefore he made mothers.

Human beings must have recognized this since the dawn of conscious thought, for Mother enjoys a special place of honor and affection in every culture of the human family. Indeed, Mother was often transformed into divinity. Thus the Mayans had a mother goddess named Ilamatecuhtli though there were associated cruelties when they tried to appease this divine lady. In Japan they had Izanami, a mother goddess too, as was Isis in Egypt, Mader-Akka in Finland, Mzambi in the Congo. Ishtar and Demeter, as also Ceres and Shakti were all Mother Goddesses of one kind or another. A Tamil maxim, taught to children at a tender age, declares Mother and Father as the first gods we know. Samuel Coleridge described mother as "the holiest thing alive." We read in the Book of Genesis that "Adam called his wife's name Eve because she was the mother of all living. [In Hebrew, *hawwah* means life.] In Sanskrit a word for mother is *Janani*: One who engenders life. In the Christian tradition, the notion of *Theotokos* or Mother of God venerates Mother in a different way, like Rhea of Greek lore.

One might ask, why create poetic names and look for unreachable personages when she is right in our midst, omnipresent, as it were, in every home? In the Hindu tradition one seeks mother's blessings before undertaking a project, or embarking on a journey. Invariably, in the face of a delicate dilemma, it is the mother who is expected to clarify. If a hasty or erroneous decision is made, it is mother who is generally more understanding. If unpleasant situations arise, it is mother who is more sympathetic. With due respects to exceptions, mother is love without conditions. Given that she is so real and concrete, why not recognize this mother in flesh and blood instead of worshipping mythic beings?

The recognition of the physical mother is a matter of daily observance. Because her services are routine and expected, one tends to take them for granted. The sheer familiarity and unerring repetition of mother's love blurs its supreme significance.

On Mother's Day (12 May in 2002), children are reminded of the love and sacrifices of mother. If mother is no longer with us, we may still pause to reflect in silent gratitude on mother's dedication without which we might not have become sane and salubrious. Near, far, or beyond life, every mother deserves to be remembered at least once a year.

They had a *Mothering Day* in England in the 17th century. In the 19th, Anna Jarvis of West Virginia campaigned for a day for the remembrance of mothers: her mother had died a couple of years earlier. In 1914, President Wilson declared the second Sunday in May to be Mother's Day. Several dozen countries have followed suit since then.

After her proposal was realized, Jarvis saw that, like Christmas and planetary alignment and everything under robust capitalism, Mother's Day also became an excuse for selling cards, candies, carnations, chocolates, and more. She found this offensive and depressing, and once said she wished she had never started it all.

Who knows, many prophets, if they were to see how many absurdities and atrocities have flown from their lofty leadership, would probably be thinking in the same way about the religions they launched. It looks as if good, helpful, or commendable ideas also often lead to negative and hurtful effects.

From the World of Science: JUSTUS Von LIEBIG

Perhaps the most essential of all human activities that contribute to the survival and sustenance of human civilization is agriculture. It is also the most ancient of all human enterprises, and thrived for thousands of years on the basis of knowledge and experience gathered from trial and error.

However, the practices of agriculture such as they were prior to the second half of the 19th century simply cannot produce enough food for all of humanity today. The basic revolution that made this possible arose from the use of what we call chemical fertilizers.

Since ancient times, manure from cattle and other mammals has been used to enrich the soil. [The word manure is derived from the Latin word for *hand*: manure simply referred to materials on which one worked with hands for making the soil better.]

In the 19th century, spurred primarily by the work of Justus von Liebig (born: 12 May 1803), the revolution began: the discovery that chemical manures, as they used to be called, can be used to enrich the soil.

Liebig went from organic chemistry to biochemistry and became the founder of agricultural chemistry: a science which has given rise to more industries, solutions and problems than most other scientific disciplines.

The chemical principles involved seem quite simple today. The development of organic chemistry revealed that plants need carbon dioxide, ammonia, and nitrogen for their growth and development. But they also need elements like phosphorus and potassium. Whereas carbon dioxide and nitrogen can be replenished, the elements and minerals cannot. Once they are used up, we need to replenish the soil with them. Animal manures used to serve this purpose. Liebig was the first to realize that this can also be done through raw chemicals. He thought initially (and mistakenly) that plants absorb nitrogen and ammonia also directly from the atmosphere.

Our modern chemical fertilizer industry had its origins in Liebig's experiments in the ten acres of sandy soil in Giessen in Germany in 1845. The town became a center to which students and teachers came from many parts of the world to learn agricultural chemistry. Liebig's was the first student-oriented laboratory of its kind in the world. It was the prototype of the chem labs in the schools and colleges of today where students do their experiments in qualitative and quantitative analyses. The many editions and translations of his *Chemistry in its Applications to Agriculture and Physiology* (1840) has had a far greater impact on the human condition than Darwin's classic.

In many ways, Liebig symbolized both the strengths and weaknesses of the scientific enterprise. He was a thorough and careful investigator, keen in his observations and meticulous in his measurements. In this he reflected the strength of science. He was wrong in some of his surmises, but seldom recognized them as such, indeed adamant in clinging on to them, often harsh and impatient with those who thought differently. This is sometimes a weakness of the scientific establishment too. In the practical impact of his work he was very much like science: positive and enriching the quality of life for the most part; but with great potential for disaster if thoughtlessly overused. Initially, chemical fertilizers were used only as a supplement to composts and manures. But later on, the rash application of chemical fertilizers and associated pesticides have led to some disastrous consequences. As with science more generally, Liebig's greatest contribution was to furthering the cause and application of a fruitful methodology, rather than the correctness of the specific results he derived.

May 13

From the World of Religion: FATIMA

In 1917, when Europe was in the midst of a terrible war, the Tsar of Russia had abdicated and the Soviet Union was about to emerge, the Blessed Virgin Mary is said to have presented herself (13 May 1917) to three simple Portuguese girls at a place called Fatima. She appeared again and again for the next five months, and promised to reveal herself on the last appearance when she would also perform a miracle.

The vision is said to have told the girls to sacrifice themselves for sinners, and urged them to say: "O Jesus, it is for love of You, for the conversion of sinners, and in reparation for the sins committed against the Immaculate Heart of Mary."

The message of these visions was that the war in Europe was punishment for sinning humanity. Unless humanity changed its atheistic and materialistic ways, "Russia will spread its errors throughout the world, raising up wars and persecutions against the Church." The Pope and bishops were asked to consecrate Russia to Virgin Mary.

There was an injunction to pray every day with the rosary, but also a revelation of Hell. The children said they saw demons and humans floating in a sea of fire. They could hear their shrieks and groans. The children even recognized some faces in the multitude. And a hope was given to the effect that the war would come to a quick end if the entire world accepted the immaculate heart of Mary. But there was also a warning: Unless this was done, worse things would happen during the pontificate of Pius XI.

The peasant children may not have understood all this. But by 1925 when one of them had become a postulant in Spain as Sister Lucy dos Santos, she had another vision in which Mary appeared with Jesus as a child. She showed her a heart with thorns, urged her to begin a fifteen-minute worship to Mary during five consecutive Saturdays, and promised to assist all who would do this "at the hour of death with all the graces necessary for the salvation of their souls."

Recall that there are five blasphemies against Mary: doubting the Immaculate Conception, doubting Mary's virginity, doubting her divine motherhood, doubting her spiritual motherhood to all humankind, and teaching children to disrespect and hate her. It is for redemption from these that the five Saturday worships were to be consecrated.

Yet another secret was revealed by the Vision of Fatima that became public only in 2000. It was predicted that the Catholic Church would be facing dire difficulties. Earlier, it was believed that this had been a reference to problems the Church encountered in the 1970s. Now, perhaps, interprets that prediction in terms of the more recent problems confronting the Catholic Church.

The Lady of Fatima spoke not just about European politics and the Christian religion. She also predicted an astronomical event: the Miracle of the Sun. It is said that thousands of people watched some peculiar solar phenomenon in Fatima on the day predicted (14 October 1917). Miracles, even at astronomical levels, usually have only a local impact.

When I visited the shrine of Fatima, I was struck by the simplicity and serenity of the place. The beautiful icon of Mary, with a long flowing robe from head to visible toes with a huge crown on the head and with hands in a prayerful posture evoked a feeling of piety. It says in six languages that it is a holy place, and asks all to come as pilgrims. Indeed, that's how we need to remember and visit sanctified places, even if we carry cameras. They are part of the spiritual memory of the human family: to be experienced and cherished if it is part of one's own tradition, and respected if it belongs to others.

From the World of Science: RONALD ROSS

One of the goals of the World Health Assembly (which opened its annual meeting in Geneva on May 13, 2002) is to eradicate malaria from the face of the earth by the close of this decade. According to another group of scientists who are studying global warming, tropical diseases like malaria will be coming into northern Europe and North America in due course. But when and how did we come to know about what causes malaria?

He was born in India of English parents in the year when Indian patriots rose up in arms against British occupation. And he worked to rid India and the world of the deadly disease of malaria which used to kill a million people a year in India alone. His name was Ronald Ross (born: 13 May 1857). As a youth, he wrote poems, composed music, and did some painting. But, on the advice of his father, he took a degree in medicine, became an army surgeon, traveled back and forth between India and England, had an attack of malaria, and got interested in the new field of bacteriology. He was an idealist. He reflected: "...what had I attempted towards bettering mankind by trying to discover the causes of those diseases which are perhaps mankind's chief enemies?"

In those days it used to be thought (as the name betrays) that malaria was caused by bad (Italian *male*) air (Italian *aria*). But Ross was persuaded by a hypothesis put forth by Patrick Manson in 1894 to the effect that mosquitoes had something to do with the disease. He dissected mosquitoes to see if they had disease-carrying germs, but he did not find any.

He did not give up, and soon discovered that there were different types of mosquitoes. One of them, when dissected, revealed something unusual in its stomach. He paid less than a tenth of a cent (by today's reckoning) per mosquito-bite to a malarial patient, he examined scores of the creatures until, on 20 August 1897, he discovered that *anopheles* mosquitoes were the real culprits. These carry the malaria parasites, called *sporozoites*. The parasite develops in the mosquito. When the creature sucks blood from a human, the parasites are transmitted through its saliva into the victim's bloodstream. It took another 50 years for scientists to uncover the various stages of the life cycle of the anopheles.

This was a major discovery for two reasons. First, it pointed out the cause and mode of transmission of a disease which had been taking the lives of millions all over the world. This knowledge helped in the prevention of the disease: get rid of and keep away from mosquitoes and their breeding regions. Secondly, it revealed how diseases may be transmitted through complex and unsuspecting modes. The idea of a disease-vector (agent) arose from Ross's work. Ross was knighted for his achievement, and he was also one of the early recipients of the Nobel Prize for Medicine (1902).

Roland Ross met with many (bureaucratic) hurdles on his way, as reflected in the following verse in which he reveals his mature humility and religious inclination:

Before Thy feet I fall, Lord who made high my fate;
For in the mighty small, Thou showed'st the mighty great.
Henceforth I will resound but praises unto Thee;
Though I was beat and bound, Thou gavest me victory.

So it has been with wars against diseases. Preachers and traditions say with smugness that diseases, like earthquakes, are expressions of divine disgust with misbehaving mankind. But scientists have a different vision of divinity, and they work hard in ideal god-like fashion to mitigate the pain, to relieve the suffering, and to uncover the cause rather than curse the victims to more agony and death as naive God-pictures suggest.

May 14

From the World of Religion:
WINFRID, THE DO-GOODER

Scientists reject religion because many aspects of its worldviews contradict facts of observation. Atheists reject it because they have no need for God. Those who study history, and witness some of the current atrocities in the name of religion, are against religions because they seem to engender acrimony and hateful deeds. But it is also true that religions have raised human consciousness to loftier levels, introduced civilizing ethical frameworks, and tamed instinctively irresponsible behavior.

It is hard to imagine what would be the current status of Holland or Germany, say, if ardent evangelists had not Christianized those countries in the 7th and 8th centuries. One such evangelist came from a noble English family, but was so inspired by Christ that he became a Benedictine monk when in his teens. His name was Winfrid (650–784).

His own country was still half-wallowing in pagan promiscuity. Monogamy was more the exception than the rule. In fact, Winfrid complained that the English were "refusing to have legitimate wives, and continuing to live in lechery and adultery after the manner of neighing horses and braying asses." He wrote a stern letter to King Ethelbald condemning his life style, calling the debaucheries of king and nobles which included liaisons with nuns, disgraceful and damnable.

Winfrid's ancestors had come from Friesland (Holland), so he had an urge to go there and convert the pagans. Other missionaries like Willibrord and Wolfhard were already struggling there with this project. Winfrid's successes were appreciated by Pope Gregory II who, on 14 May 719, dubbed him *Do-gooder*. This sounds better in Latin as Boniface (from *bonum facere:* to do good). The pope entrusted Boniface to bring all of Germany into the Christian fold. He thus came to be called the Apostle of Germany.

By now, the Arabs were on their own mission to Islamize Europe. They had come as far as Tours in France. Charles Martel of Gaul felt rightly or wrongly that Europe would fare better under Christian worldviews. So he not only saved Gaul from Islamic intrusion, but also encouraged Boniface in his German mission. It takes only a couple of generations to transform an entire people to a different religious framework.

At Geismar the heathens used to worship the thunder-god Thor through an oak tree: From environmental perspectives, this is wise. But this sort of thing was what the Abrahamic faith wanted to snuff out. So Boniface cut down the ancient tree and built a church with the logs. The pagans were amazed that Thor could not strike him down. They took this as a sign of the superiority of Christianity. So everyone was baptized on the spot. Some have said that this event symbolized the triumph of the faith in Germany.

Unfortunately, though Christianity did have salutary effects on the mores of the common people—perhaps because of threats of lasting existence under extremely hot conditions—the clergy was still engaging in activities that would, to use a modern expression, make a sailor blush. In fact, Boniface complained to pope Zacharias that greedy people with concubines were becoming bishops. He also reported that loose women were making pilgrimages, selling their bodies as they went from town to town.

It would seem that in many religious contexts, preachers have helped the masses behave better without they themselves practicing what they preach, especially in matters sexual. That this behavior shocked Boniface speaks very highly of the saint.

Eventually, during his missionary work in Friesland, he was murdered with several of his companions, and thus became a martyr.

From the World of Science:
DANIEL GABRIEL FAHRENHEIT

People in many parts of the English-speaking world know that when their body temperature is 100 or more they have a high fever. They know that when the weatherman says it will be 30 degrees tomorrow it's going to be freezing outside.

Where did these numbers come from? Then again, referring to a thermometer we sometimes say that the mercury is rising. When did mercury come in the picture?

Way back in the first decade of the 17th century, Galileo made one of the first thermometers ever. During that century many other thermometers were constructed, often with colored water, alcohol, spirits, etc. But there was as yet no standard calibration of fixed points. The Danish astronomer Olaus Roemer was one of the first to introduce 60 degrees as the boiling point of water.

But the man who standardized thermometric calibration and also first used mercury as the liquid component in a thermometer was Daniel Gabriel Fahrenheit (born: 14 May 1686). His parents died unexpectedly when he was barely 17, and he was sent from his native Gdansk in Poland to Amsterdam to learn a trade. Here he became very much interested in the making of scientific instruments. He traveled widely to learn more, but finally settled down to manufacture his own precise temperature-measuring instruments. He toyed with many reference points, making the normal body temperature 90 degrees and the freezing point of water 30 degrees. [The Babylonian relic of sixty was still there very much in the mind of many investigators. After all, there are 60 seconds in a minute, 60 minutes in an hour, 60 degrees in an equilateral triangle, etc.] After much experimentation and reflection, he decided to mark the melting point of ice as 32 degrees and the normal temperature of a healthy human to be 96 degrees.

Because he used mercury, Fahrenheit's thermometer could read temperatures much lower than the freezing point of water and also greater than the boiling point of water: mercury continues to remain a liquid beyond these standard points. This was a significant advance in the technique of temperature measurement.

Aside from introducing a convention in thermometry through his scale and fixed points on the graduated instrument, and his invention of a new type of thermometer, using mercury rather than alcohol, Fahrenheit also made a fundamental discovery in physics: He found out that the boiling point of a liquid depends on the external pressure. Most people simply say that water boils at 100 degrees celsius or 212 degrees Fahrenheit. This is not an entirely correct statement. One must add: under the pressure of one atmosphere. If the pressure is increased or decreased by a certain amount, the boiling point would also be correspondingly increased or decreased. Under enormous pressure water would boil only at a very high temperature.

Given that the atmospheric pressure is steadily decreasing as we go higher and higher above the sea-level, this property could be used to measure the elevation of a mountain, for example. This is the idea behind the *hypsometer* which too Fahrenheit invented: a calibrated gadget with water and glass tubes from which, by noting at what temperature the water boils, one can also read the elevation of the place. This fundamental discovery led to another idea in physics: that of the vapor pressure which is useful to meteorology.

So Fahrenheit, the instrument maker, with no great formal degree in the sciences, made significant contributions to theoretical and applied physics. For this he was recognized, elected to the Royal Society, and remembered at least in those countries of the world which have not switched to the Celsius scale.

May 15

From the World of Religion: PARASURAMA RISHI

In the Hindu world the notion of saint is quite different from what it is in Christianity. Here, a saint is often a spiritual individual who is revered and respected for his or her unstinting devotion to God. The honorific is given by the person's followers. A saint could also be a mythological hero who gained his hallowed status by virtue of noble and remarkable deeds in the sacred history of the tradition.

To the latter category belongs Parasurama (Rama with the Ax) *rishi* (sage) who was commemorated on May 15, 2002 by many people of the Hindu tradition. Sometimes he is regarded as one of the *avataras*: incarnations of the Divine.

Parasurama appears in many episodes in the Hindu epics. He was one of five sons, born of the sage Jamadagni and his lovely wife Renuka. It is said that on one occasion, Renuka engaged in some improper erotic fantasies, unbecoming of a woman of virtue. Her knowing husband became so incensed by this that he commanded his sons to decapitate her for this ethical transgression. Four of the five refused to obey the father, but Parasurama did. Sage Jamadagni condemned the four disobeying sons to a state of imbecility and promised Parasurama any boon he would ask. "Pray restore my mother to a life of chastity and my brothers to one of normal intelligence," he requested, and Jamadagni had no choice but to keep up his word. The episode reflects Parasurama's filial piety, as well as his intelligence. The moral of the story: As long as one does one's duty, nothing terrible will happen in the long run.

On another occasion, a king named Kartavirya paid a visit to Jamadagni's hermitage when he was away. Renuka received him with hospitality. The king ungratefully did havoc to the hermitage, and ravished a magical cow. When Jamadagni and his sons returned and heard what had happened, Parasurama was incensed. He went into Kartavirya's kingdom, grabbed the king, and severed his arms. In furious vengeance, the king's sons set Parasurama's hermitage ablaze. This angered Parasurama even more, and he vowed to rid the world of the entire race of kings, which he did.

This story is probably a faint echo of feuds and furies among groups and castes of distant times. Perhaps the ruling Kshatriya caste asserted its power over the priestly Brahmins who rose in revolt, and reasserted their preeminence. More importantly, the story is to remind us that anger begets anger, hurtful action leads to more hurtful ones, unless somebody decides to stop the unending tit-for-tats and talks peace. This is an ancient message, but rarely followed at times when they need to be, nor by individuals who have to. Indeed, it is a lesson that is urgent in our own times.

Parasurama is said to have been a great devotee of Shiva, one of the triple principles of the Divine in the Hindu tradition. It is said that he received great supernatural powers because of his devotion. This is what enabled him to accomplish all the wonderful things.

To one not brought up in the tradition, it might be difficult to understand how a mythopoetic personage comes to be celebrated in this way. But then, when one probes into the historicity of the revered personages in any tradition with a scholarly microscope, the clear pictures evoked by narratives of their lives get blurred into hazy contours. History serves as much to inspire a people as to inform.

Likewise, the purpose of hagiography is not so much to tell it like it was, but to portray men and women of supreme spiritual stature who are worthy of remembrance and respect in the celebratory contexts of tradition.

From the World of Science: PIERRE CURIE

It is well known that we can generate electricity from chemical reactions, as in a battery, and from changing magnetic fields, as in a generator. Conversely, electricity can produce chemical reactions and affect magnetic fields.

But it is not as universally known that it is possible to produce electricity in some crystals by applying pressure on them. Conversely, electricity applied to crystals can generate pressure in them, and by changing the applied electricity, the crystals can be made to vibrate. These were among the important discoveries of a 19th century physicist by the name of Pierre Curie (born: 15 May 1859).

As a youngster, he did not give any indication that he would achieve anything extraordinary. He was a somewhat reserved individual. His early schooling was at home where he was inspired by his physician-father. Pierre's older brother Jacques was also a scientist. The two often worked together in the laboratory. The electrical effect on crystals like quartz, tourmaline, topaz, sugar and more was discovered when Pierre Curie was only 18 years old. The brothers named the phenomenon *piezoelectricity*, from the Greek word *piezein* which means to press. When this was announced, it was pointed out by another physicist that the converse must also occur: that the crystals must experience a pressure when subjected to electricity. Little did anyone suspect that some day this would be used in acoustical systems.

Pierre Curie became a chemist. In 1882 he was appointed director of a newly established municipal school of physics and chemistry. His experimental research included the magnetic properties of materials, and their variation with temperature. He discovered that the *ferromagnetic* properties of materials diminish with rise in temperature. At a certain temperature, depending on the material, the substance is no longer ferromagnetic. This temperature is known as the Curie point. Now a different property, called *paramagnetism*, comes into play. Curie's findings are fundamental in modern (quantum mechanical) theories of magnetism.

A year before he presented his doctoral dissertation, Pierre Curie met a young Polish woman by the name of Maria Sklodowska who had come to study physics at the Sorbonne. A friendship developed between the two, and they were married in the following year. Pierre had once quipped that a wife would be a distraction for a scientist. It turned out to be very different in his case.

In 1894 Henri Becquerel had discovered a new phenomenon: he reported that certain peculiar radiations were given out by some substances. Marie and Pierre Curie began a thorough investigation of this new frontier of basic research which was to open the field of nuclear physics with the dawn of the 20th century. Marie Curie gave the name *radioactivity* to the newly discovered phenomenon.

Pierre and Marie Curie worked day and night, separating out radium and uranium from minerals and uncovering other radioactive elements. Pierre Curie measured the heat generated from a given quantity of radium in a given time. This was the first recorded case of a measure of nuclear energy, and it revealed tremendous possibilities for nuclear energy generation. Pierre expressed the possibility that "in criminal hands radium might become very dangerous." The Curies risked their lives in studying the biological effects of radioactivity. Their combined work won them a Nobel Prize in 1903. Their life is narrated with sensitivity in a biography of Madame Curie by their daughter Eve Curie.

Pierre Curie died in a tragic accident in 1906, run over by a horse carriage.

May 16

From the World of Religion: JOAN OF ARC

Skeptics may scoff and unbelievers may not understand, but it is a fact of history that the voices and visions experienced by a teenage girl brought victory to her country in a war that had raged for a hundred years, and changed the course of history. This happened early in the 15th century. For this she was declared to be a saint on 16 May 1920.

Her name was Jeanne, and she has come to be known (in English) as Joan of Arc. Her life story is simple, as she herself was: She was born in the village of Domrémy where, as elsewhere, everybody knew about the devilish English who were claiming France as their own. A rumor went around to the effect that heaven would send a maid to rescue France. Growing up in that atmosphere, Joan began to hear voices when she was 13, which, she was persuaded, were those of saints of remote antiquity. They seemed to be very much in touch with current French politics, and convinced her that she was there to save France from the British. She kept hearing this for four years and more. When she announced this to her father, he laughed and tried to get her married. But she could not be subdued. When the English were on the verge of taking over Orleans, she rode all the way to Chinon, a good 450 miles away. There she spotted the king disguised in the court, and thereby won his confidence. The ruins of that court still stand as a tourist attraction.

Theologians were convinced about the celestial origin of her inspiration, and teenage Joan led the French army, seated on horseback in armor, and brought victory. As a result, the Dauphin was crowned King Charles VII of France at Reims. But when she continued her campaigns against the English, some of the French sold her to the enemy. The British handed her over to a religious body which tried her in Rouen on two counts: The first charge was that she was sporting masculine costume. The second was heresy, pure and simple: presuming to communicate with God directly, instead of going through proper channels, i.e. the Church of Rome. The august body forced her to confess, and condemned the young woman (in her twenties) to life imprisonment. But she continued wearing the male dress which was deemed so offensive that they brought her to a secular court which condemned her to be burned alive in the public square at Rouen. There she is still fondly remembered by tourist guides who describe how she was set ablaze on 30 May 1431, exactly as Ingrid Bergman portrayed the scene.

Joan was vilified in English books for many centuries. Even Shakespeare presented her in Henry VI as the agent of the devil. But so did Voltaire who portrayed her as a mindless country girl. Interestingly enough, it was Robert Southey's epic poem on Joan of Arc by the close of the 18th century that changed the British attitude towards Joan. Through the 19th century, Joan's reputation recovered, and by and large she was looked upon positively by the public. Just as TV does today, poets and writers used to do in former times: change the reputation of figures from positive to negative or vice versa.

Aside from provoking volumes of scholarly work, Joan inspired plays and poetry, painting and sculpture, not just from her own countrymen. Schiller and Shaw wrote plays on her life. She has been celebrated by essayist Mark Twain, playwright Maxwell Anderson, and sculptress Anna Huntington.

Whether it was St. Michael who spoke to Joan or whether it was her imagination, the net effect was to affect French history as well as Joan's own personal life: Instead of becoming a good housewife and mother in Domrémy, she was consumed by fire in Rouen, became a saint and was immortalized. Those ethereal voices were powerful.

From the World of Science:
MARIA GAETENA AGNESI

The 18th century was one of the most creative and productive periods in the history of mathematics. Sometime in the middle of that century there appeared a two volume treatise in Italian which expounded the whole gamut of the mathematics of the time: from algebra and coordinate geometry to differential and integral calculus, as well as a measure of differential equations. Though, as per its title, it was addressed to Italian youths, the work was promptly translated into French and English. Writing about the second volume of this work, a committee of the French Academy of Sciences said the following: "This work is characterized by its careful organization, its clarity, and its precision. There is no other book, in any language, which would enable a reader to penetrate as deeply, or as rapidly, into the fundamental concepts of analysis. We consider this treatise the most complete and best written work of its kind."

The title of the book was *Istituzioni analitiche ad uso della gioventu italiana* (Analytical Institutions for the use of Italian youths). Its author was a thirty year old Italian woman by the name of Maria Gaetana Agnesi (born: 16 May, 1718). In this book she also discussed at some length the curve represented by a cubic algebraic equation [$y(x^2 + a^2) = a^3$]. The shape of this curve is somewhat like a beaten down Gaussian (bell) curve. It gained much reputation in the 18th century, and came to be called the *witch of Agnesi*.

The curve was studied by Guido Grandi (1672–1742) who named it 'versoria', which is Latin for a rope that guides a sail. Maria Agnesi called it *versiera*: devil's grandma or female goblin.]

Agnesi is said to have authored a lengthy commentary on a classic mathematical work by L'Hopital, but this was not published. Maria Agnesi has been described by Edna Kramer as "the first woman in the Western world who can accurately be called a mathematician..."

Agnesi was also a polyglot wonder. By the time she was a teen she had mastered French, Spanish, German, and Hebrew. Aside from her native Italian she studied Latin to the point of writing a work in that language at the age of 9, in which she elaborated on the idea that general education wasnot unsuitable for women. By 11, she also spoke Greek fluently.

As with Mozart, the unusual abilities of the little girl became a matter of curiosity for neighbors and others, and she was often turned into a spectacle. Her father used to have a discussion group where grown-up thinkers would gather to discuss philosophical matters. Here young Maria used to be asked to make serious presentations also. Young Maria did not enjoy this very much. At the age of 20, she decided to become a nun. Her father dissuaded her from this, but she became a recluse all the same. During the next decade she worked on her mathematical treatise.

Though endowed with a mind for mathematics, her heart was for service to others. When her father died, she was 34. But the father had left behind some 20 children through his three marriages. She was appointed professor of mathematics in Bologna, but she did not find time to discharge her responsibilities in this capacity.

Maria became the ward and guide for all her siblings. Later in life, she gave all her time to social work, becoming a sister in a religious organization.

Who knows how many women of such caliber have lived and gone, whose talents and genius did not find full expression, or were only partially recognized, who worked under strenuous conditions, with maternal responsibilities on their shoulders, with familial constraints and social hurdles to boot with? We may be glad that in our own times, at least in some societies, one makes conscious efforts to mitigate and eliminate such circumstances for women.

May 17

From the World of Religion:
SHANKARACHARYA JAYANTI

17 May 2002 was Shankaracharya-jayanti in the Hindu world. This is to commemorate the illustrious Shankara (born: 788) who was saint and scholar,

spiritual leader and intellectual giant, religious reformer and founder of a sect. He was one of the keenest minds in the history of Hindu philosophy, a mighty force in the restitution of many thoughts, beliefs, Hindu scriptural writings and metaphysical subtleties.

Shankara was born in the small village of Kaladi in Kerala. He mastered Sanskrit at an early age and studied the scriptures thoroughly. He knew all the competing doctrinal trends and Buddhist notions that were then very popular. He became a monk much against his mother's will. Shankara wrote on the principal Upanishads, on the Bhagavad Gita and on the Brahma Sutra, elucidating their basic messages.

He was a brilliant debater. He traveled widely, taught and preached, established major centers in four cities in the four cardinal directions for the study of spiritual wisdom.

In Shankara's theology, there is but one God, and He alone is Real. All else is *Maya* (illusion) arising from our ignorance. In essence, there is no difference between individual souls and the Supreme One. Prayers to personal gods are fine as long as we live in a world of *Maya*. When one reaches the state of higher consciousness, all distinctions dissolve, all is One in the cosmic sea. This thesis of the identity of the Brahman and its manifestations is referred to as *advaita* (non-dualism).

But this realization cannot be had through reasoning, declared Sankara. Like other religious metaphysicians he belittled the relevance of the intellect in matters spiritual. He must have realized that incisive logic could rupture the foundations of faith.

Many legends grew around Shankara's name. According to one, Shankara once got into a debate with a reputed scholar and defeated him. The opponent's wife was the judge. Before she would crown him winner she challenged him on his knowledge of erotica. Shankara, the celibate, asked for a week's study of the subject. He left his mortal frame, and entered that of a deceased king. Through this he explored the range of delights that the monarch's many wives and playmates had to offer. This study became his only interest, and he forgot about his own body. Seeing this distraction from a saintly course, his disciples went around singing devotional melodies. When he heard these, the saint-in-a-king's-body woke up from his stupor, and transmigrated back into his own body. He went to the debating forum and taught his questioners a thing or two on the theme of lust.

Even this spiritual giant who regarded all humans as sparks of the great Brahman, was very conscious of his own Brahminhood, and is said to have insisted that a Shudra had no right to the scriptures. He declared, "He who has learned to look on phenomena in the monistic light is my Guru, whether he is of very low caste or a Brahmin."

Shankara was as much a systematizer and exponent of ancient wisdom as a proponent of a philosophy. He was an insightful commentator on classical aphorisms as well as composer of the beautiful poetic melody called *Ananda Lahiri* (Waves of Bliss).

Shankara became the Aquinas of the Hindu world: an erudite scholar and interpreter of ancient wisdom, a reviver of the metaphysical foundations of the tradition, a must-be-read author for anyone who wishes to understand the canonical framework, a keen intellect with more than a spark of spirituality in his core, one with countless admirers and scholarly commentators, and also a few critics. His spiritual lineage continues. So we pay homage to the memory of this sparkling jewel in the Hindu tradition.

From the World of Science: EDWARD JENNER

One of the wonders in earth's biological history is the survival of *homo sapiens* for a few million years in the midst of a thousand unfriendly microbes and viruses that have been causing plague and pestilence over the ages. Of these deadly adversaries to human health and life nothing has perhaps caused more ravage than the small pox virus. It is known to have afflicted humanity for at least three thousand years, and has been explored and combated for many centuries. It has been estimated that some 100 million people have been killed by small pox, and perhaps twice as many have been blind by this highly contagious disease. The horse and the cow are also victims of the disease.

In ancient China they had a technique for preventing the disease, and in later times, a similar practice was in Turkey also: one infected a healthy person with puss from a patient; and this often had a preventive effect.

In the 1770s some physicians in England began using fluid from other patients for inoculation. In this context, a more systematic assault on small pox began with the work of Edward Jenner (born: 17 May 1749). After more than a decade of investigating and pondering about the disease, he made a daring experiment in 1896 on a lad named James Phipps. In his own words: "I selected a healthy boy, about eight years old, for the purpose of inoculation for the cow pox. The matter was taken from a sore on the hand of a dairymaid who was infected by her master's cows, and it was inserted...in the arm of the boy..." He introduced the word *virus* to describe the matter from the cow pox.

After some light fever the boy recovered and became healthy again. Jenner published a pamphlet on his findings. Since the material for the inoculation was derived from the cow, he called his method *vaccination*, from the Latin word *vacca* for cow. Jenner's brochure was read by many, but the effect on the medical establishment ranged from skeptical and cautious to downright opposition. Some untrained people began inoculating others for small pox. But there were also people who criticized him for what they regarded as vivisection which was considered a grievous crime. He felt so guilty about this that he agreed to build a little house for one of his subjects, rose garden and all.

Jenner's success spilled over to the Continent, and across the Atlantic. Kings and queens were vaccinated. Preachers recommended it from the pulpit. In some cities they held religious processions prior to vaccination. In Russia the first child to be vaccinated was named Vaccinov, in Germany Jenner's birthday was a holiday. This was the first large scale protection from an ancient disease. This was also the first case of an alternative medicine: a move away from cures based on an accepted system, to try what the ancients had done, and to find out if the so-called folk medicine had intrinsic worth.

In England, Jenner won some recognition. He was granted a substantial sum by Parliament, and awarded an honorary M.D. by the University of Oxford. But the Royal College of Physicians would not admit him unless he passed an exam in the classics: Hippocrates, Galen, Greek, etc. Jenner refused, calling this "irksome beyond measure."

Jenner is regarded as the founder of modern immunology. It was announced in 1977 that small pox has been completely eliminated from the face of the earth. By the 1980s vaccination was stopped altogether. But it was also revealed that the Soviet Union was preparing large amounts of the virus for possible use as a biological weapon. Such are the extremes of the human potential: we eradicate a deadly disease, and also propagate it with greater efficiency than Nature. What we do is often what we choose to do.

May 18

From the World of Religion & Science:
UMAR AL-KHAYYAMI

He was one of the most brilliant mathematicians of his time in the 11th–12th century. He studied cubic equations, classified them, and is said to have declared their solution impossible. He examined Euclid's fifth postulate as seriously as

18th and 19th century mathematicians. He wrote on astronomy too. He helped formulate a new calendrical system. He computed the number of days in a year as 365.24219858156. He had, like Paracelsus of later times, an impressively long name: Ghiyathuddin Abu'l-Fath Umar bin Ibrahim al-Nisaburi al-Khayyami (born: 18 May 1123).

We know him as Omar Khayyam, one of the greatest Persian thinkers. The world remembers him as the author of some 1200 quatrains (*rubaiahs*). Scholars are not sure if all of these can be attributed to him. Less than ten per cent of them were translated into English by Edward FitzGerald in the 1850s. Since then, Omar Khyayyam's name has come to be known all over the world. J. R. Lowell commented:

These pearls of thought in Persian gulfs were bred,

Each softly lucent as a rounded moon.

The diver Omar plucked them from their bed,

FitzGerald strung them on an English thread.

The Rubiyat's rhyming sceme (AABA) is slightly altered here (ABAA)

Omar Khayyam was blessed with a keen and critical mind. He was a no-non-sense philosopher who would not take the religious mumble-jumble of his (Islamic) tradition seriously. He had little respect for the *ulema*, even less for the mystery-mongering Sufis. He was a philosopher: pessimistic here, cynical there, but always reflective. He declared that it's good to refrain from everything, save wine, and to be inebriate, squalid and vagrant. He has been compared to Voltaire, but, as Karl Ethe reminded us, the French wit never wrote "fascinating rhapsodies in praise of wine, love and all earthly joys" as did the Persian philosopher who sounds like a *bon vivant* when he says:

A Book of Verses underneath the Bough,

A Jug of Wine, a Loaf of Bread—and Thou

Beside me singing in the Wilderness-

Oh, Wilderness were Paradise now.

It is not surprising that he came to be decried as a freethinker, materialist, atheist. He expressed in poetic terms what physicists call irreversible processes:

The Moving Finger writes, and, having writ,

Moves on: nor all thy Piety nor Wit

Shall lure it back to cancel half a Line,

Nor all thy Tears wash out a Word of it.

Indeed, he was always aware of the ticking away of irrevocable time. He wrote:

Whether at Naishapur or Babylon,

Whether the Cup with sweet or bitter run,

The Wine of Life keeps oozing drop by drop,

The Leaves of Life keep falling one by one.

For the poet, truths always relate to the human condition. Thus, it is not simply Laplacian determinism that reigns, but fate, destiny, and Judgment Day. So Omar wrote:

The First Dawn of Creation wrote
What the Last Day of Reckoning shall read.

From the World of Religion & Science: BERTRAND RUSSELL

Today is the birth date of another mathematician and free thinker, also with a long full name: Earl Bertrand Arthur William Russell (born: 18 May 1872).

Russell was excited when he discovered Euclid at eleven because every proposition had to be proved, but he was disappointed that geometry rested on unproven propositions. He was an incisive critic of the world around him, and revealed in his reminiscences that he "derived no benefits" by attending the lectures of his professors at Cambridge. As a graduate student he dug into the foundations of geometry, and later wrote on the foundations of mathematics. He labored on the thesis that mathematics is a special and sophisticated system of pure logical thought. The magnum opus that he and A. N. Whitehead produced together (1910–1913) was entitled *Principia Mathematica*. It is a *chef d'oeuvre* of the human capacity to reason in symbolic terms. Even those unfamiliar with Peano's symbolism and Boolean algebra would be induced to make appreciative *wow!* sounds when they glance into the pages of the three-tomed classic. The monumental effort delves into the plush richness of mathematical thought and uncovers its skeleton of logical framework.

When the First World War broke out, Russell was drawn to issues beyond the ivory tower. He became an ardent pacifist, protested the war, and was thrown into prison for sedition. When out of prison, he was treated as an outcaste, dismissed from his professorship. The notion of academic freedom was yet to evolve. Russell lectured and wrote on education, on Western philosophy, on Leibniz, on the meaning of truth, on the scientific outlook, on mysticism and logic, and much more. He was a social critic who reflected on the folly of human actions which are spurred by selfishness and greed. He had little respect for the brutal Bolsheviks and less for the close-minded Catholic Church.

He wrote provocatively on sexual morals, did not consider adultery a terrible offense, recommended experimental marriage, and spoke out in such un-Victorian terms that he was frowned upon as an advocate for promiscuity. His ideas seem mild by today's standards, but it was thinkers like Russell who, for better or for worse, brought about the transformation in sexual mores. In 1950, he was awarded the Nobel Prize for literature.

Russell was also a passionate spokesman for disarmament and world peace. With Einstein he issued a manifesto on this. He sounded like an unpatriotic maverick fifty years ago, but today, if not out of wisdom, at least out of fear of mutual annihilation, governments are trying to follow Russell's prescriptions.

Bertrand Russell was a no-nonsense modernist who had little regard for institutionalized religions, a moral atheist who had no need for God, a liberated intellectual who did not have to proclaim himself a Communist to plead for the oppressed and the exploited. He was an apostle for science and rationality. He was a humanist, pacifist, and skeptic. He was inspired by "the longing for love, the search for happiness, and unbearable pity for the suffering of mankind."

I once proposed to Russell to form a *Bertrand Russell Society*. He said that I hadn't understood his message. He referred to Buddhism, Christianity, and Mohammedanism, and said that any institution named after a historical personage is doomed to become a mindless body of people who forget the message and worship the messenger. I thought he was right. In 1974, a *Bertrand Russell Society* was formed, and his fears have not come to pass. Unless the framework of science and enlightened compassion are preached and propagated as religions are, they will never become an intrinsic part of human societies.

May 19

From the World of Religion:
MALLEUS MALEFICARUM

The power of books, both for good and for evil, can be considerable. What is interesting is that not all influential books present highly original ideas. Consider, for example, a notorious volume, authored by two dark-age Dominicans named Heinrich Kramer and Jacob Sprenger. They published a treatise on Witchcraft in 1586. It is said to have been given an official stamp of approval by the Theology Faculty of Cologne University on 19 May of that year. Sprenger was a Dean in that university. In 1584, Pope Innocent III had already given an injunction to prohibit any objections to witch-hunt.

The book was call *Malleus Maleficarum* (Hammer of Witches), and it soon became a guidebook for those who wished to recognize and bring to justice what was regarded as a plague in the medieval world: the subtle presence of witches in Christendom.

In fairness, belief in witches did not originate with Christianity. It is stated in no uncertain terms in the Old Testament (Exodus: xxii-18): "Thou shalt not suffer a witch to live." *Hexenhammer* (as the book came to be called in German) consisted of three parts: The first discussed what witchcraft is all about, and what its symptoms are. The authors made it clear that anyone afflicted with the witch-ailment repudiated Catholicism. This makes witches of practically all Protestants. Yet, the book became very popular in some Protestant countries. Witches were carnally involved with incubi and succubi (demonic beings who had intercourse with humans while the latter were asleep). If one did not believe in witchcraft, then one was a heretic. This was a valid position to hold inasmuch as the Bible affirms the existence of witches. Unfortunately, this could bring the charge of heresy against the vast majority of educated Christians to day.

The second part of the book classified witches and described the most absurd powers and practices of witches. These may strike the modern reader as grotesque and gruesome, but when the mind is ill-lit with sparse and perverted knowledge, and clouded by fear and superstition, every tale seems a news-report, and every fantasy becomes a fact.

In the third part, rules and techniques were prescribed by which witches can be charged, arrested, tried, and condemned effectively. Detailed recipes are given for breaking the silence of reticent or dumb-founded witches, as also for sustained and systematic torture. The book also presented some twisted etymologies, like: the word *femina* (Latin for woman) is derived from *fe:* faith, and *minus:* less; thus *famina* means one who is without faith. Were it not for the enormous hurtful impact of the book for almost two centuries, this work could be a source of entertainment for the casual reader. There were more than 16 German editions, 11 French editions, 2 Italian editions, and several English editions of the book. One source says that between 1584 and 1669, the book was translated into 29 languages.

It would be naive to imagine that only in a distant dark age such an evil book could have been composed. It is true that few sane people in our own times will not be appalled by the nonsense spewed all through its pages. But, in fairness, the book was only a systematized presentation of the Zeitgeist rather than the creation of the authors. It is good to remember that Hitler's *Mein Kampf* was the *Malleus Maleficarum* of another era, for the only goal of such books is to instill hate and horror towards a whole class of people. It is frightening that the world of the internet has opened up possibilities for the free circulation of mindless venom of this genre. We must be aware of this because hate and unreason tend to spread with greater ease than messages of love and rational thought.

From the World of Science: TITUS LUCRETIUS

Scientifically inclined thinkers have existed in all cultures at all times. Consider, for example, Titus Lucretius (Born: 19 May? 95 B.C.E.): poet and philosopher who spoke out against the superstitions of his age. Even without knowing about caste-untouchability, the crusades, Islamic conquests by the sword, the Inquisition, and the countless religious warfare which have continued to our own times, Lucretius wrote: *Tantem religio potuit suadere malorem*: To so many evils religion has persuaded (people).

Lucretius' most important work was a didactic poem in six books. It was entitled, *De rerum natura*: On the Nature of Things. In this work, Lucretius spoke of atoms and the void, of our modes of perception and our will. He wrote on the origin of the world and of earthquakes, on life and virtues, on good and evil and suffering, and he reflected on language, art, and religion.

Lucretius was one of the first to state that everything, including planets and stars, decay. Long before the formulation of the second law of thermodynamics in the 19th century, he stated poetically that one day "the walls of the sky will be stormed on every side, and will collapse into a crumbling ruin." He stated that "nothing exists but atoms and the void." Atoms alone were eternal and immutable. Their mutual penetration leads to the variety in the physical world. [He took inspiration from Democritus and Epicurus.] For him, consciousness ceased with death, there was no after-life. The body, made up of atoms, was governed by the laws of nature, and there was no need to fear the gods or death, he declared. It must be recalled that the Roman world, like much of the ancient world, was replete with magic and superstition. Even among the small minority of thinkers, there were many who argued that it was useful and important to feed the minds of the ignorant masses with fantastic beliefs so as to keep them well-behaved. Thus, Varro explicitly stated that one function of religion was for the state to deceive the people. Recall Karl Marx's comment that religion is the opium of the masses.

Lucretius did not deny the existence of gods, but asserted that they were for ever beyond our reach, "beyond the flaming ramparts of the world." However, he maintained that the gods did not create the world, nor were they the causes of things.

Rome may not have produced great scientists, but it had Lucretius who was clearly one of the greatest of ancient thinkers. He eloquently expressed what, to a large extent, continues to be the scientific world view, as illustrated in the following lines:

In the beginning the earth gave forth all kinds of herbage and verdant sheen about the hills and over the plains; the flowery meadows glittered with the bright green hue, and next in order to the different trees was given a strong and emulous desire of growing up into the air with full unbridled powers. All feathers and hairs and bristles are first born on the limbs of four-footed beasts and the body of the strong wing, thus the new earth then first put forth grass and bushes, and next gave birth to the races of mortal creatures springing up many in number in many ways after divers fashion.... And many races of living things must then have died out and been unable to beget and continue their breed.

Lucretius is said to have lost his mind periodically, and probably committed suicide. His book was condemned, and was not taught in schools for many long centuries.

Every generation has its own debates on the topics on which Lucretius wrote. As it says in Ecclesiastes, "there is no new thing under the sun." Or, as Mademoiselle Bertin put it, "There is nothing new except what has been forgotten."

May 20

From the World of Religion: NICENE COUNCIL

In the 4th century, a priest in Egypt propounded a theological thesis which shook the foundations of Christian doctrines. His name was Arius. He said that Christ was neither coeternal, nor consubstantial with (having the same substance as) God. Christ was the highest of God's created beings. [This was like attacking capitalism and democracy in the USA.] Bluntly put, the historical Jesus wasn't intrinsically divine, though he reflected God's glory. The enunciation of this idea was vehemently attacked by Bishop Alexander, but it quickly spread everywhere, causing conflict and chaos among believers.

When Emperor Constantine heard about this, he convened a conference of theologians to bring about some peaceful resolution to the controversy, though he himself felt that these were "problems that idleness alone raises, and whose only use is to sharpen men's wits." Thus began the first ecumenical council—the

Nicene Council—in Bithynian Nicaea, an ancient town in Asia Minor, on 20 May 325. It ended on 25 July. More than 300 bishops, mostly from Eastern Churches, attended what was perhaps the first international meeting of its kind in history. The Roman Pope was too sick to be there, but he sent a representative.

There were heated debates and discussions, arguments and counterarguments, forceful declarations and angry exchanges. These included the determination of a date for Easter celebrations, and whether celibacy should be enforced on all priests. But the most important of all related to the Arian proposition. The principals in this debate were Arius who would not budge on his thesis of the essentially human aspect of Christ, and Athanasius who warned that if the identity of Christ and the Holy Spirit was questioned or denied, it would bring down the entire Christian worldview, and encourage paganism.

The Council finally proclaimed a creed which began thus: "We believe in one God, the Father Almighty, maker of all things visible and invisible; and in one Lord Jesus Christ, the Son of God, begotten of the Father, only begotten, that is of the substance of the Father, God of God, Light of Light, very God of very God, begotten not made, of one substance with the Father, by whom all things were made, both those in heaven and those on earth…" Athanasius won. Arius and two bishops defied the document. They was made anathema (cursed and excommunicated). Arius' books were ordered to be burned. If anybody was caught hiding a book by Arius, the punishment would be death. The Council ended with a royal banquet, not unlike conferences in our own times.

The pagan world, hearing about all the bickering on coeternity and consubstantiality, is said to have had a hearty laugh, wrote satirical commentaries, even as much of the world does today upon watching Democrats and Republicans wrangling about how to win the war on terrorism. It is said that Arius, who had been exiled in Gaul, eventually came back to Constantine and accepted the Nicene Creed, but that Constantine himself had second thoughts about it. In any event, according to one version, on the eve of a visit to Church, Arius suffered a most gruesome experience in which his bowels were ejected from his body, and he died in pain.

Creed is essential for organized religions, more so for those which proselytize. For if one does not swear allegiance to the prescribed doctrine, how can one be regarded as a member of the group? The creeds of traditional religions are tied up with this savior or that prophet, with this holy book or that divinely inspired ethical system. Perhaps we need to formulate creeds that transcend local morals and parochial beliefs, and expand our visions to the well being of humanity as a whole.

From the World of Science:
BUREAU INTERNATIONAL DES POIDS ET DES MÉSURES

The Latin poet Horace wrote: *Est modus in rebus,* there is a measure in all things. Measurement, as we all know, is the lifeblood of science. Indeed, this is one important difference between religion and science: you can do serious religion without making any measurement; but serious science, you cannot. The most basic measured quantity is length. Lengths have been measured since the most ancient times in all cultures, using fingers, feet, or elbow-to-finger-tip.

In the seventeenth century, Jean Picard proposed to take the length of a pendulum which swings once every second at sea level as a standard for measuring lengths. This would be scientific: culture-independent and unrelated to body parts.

After the French Revolution, other suggestions were made and a committee appointed by the French National Assembly defined the *meter* as a ten-millionth part of the distance from the equator to the North Pole via Paris. [It is not surprising that the word *chauvinism* had its origin in France.] Later, a platinum-iridium bar at 0°C on which are etched two thin scratches a meter apart was installed in the International Bureau of Standards at Sèvres, near Paris. Copies of this have been distributed to all nations that became signatories of the international standard.

But what is this *Bureau International des Poids et des Mésures* (BIPM)? It arose from an international agreement which was signed on 20 May 1875 by seventeen nations. The French government gave a parcel of land and a building to an International Committee on Weights and Measures. There is the Pavillion Breteuil. A laboratory was formally inaugurated there in 1884. In 1889, the first General Conference on weights and measures took place here. This was a momentous occasion in that for the first time in human history, many nations of the world discussed and accepted precise standards in the physical evaluation of things.

Since then, the laboratory in Sèvres has been considerably expanded, and the unit of length has been defined in more sophisticated terms. The meter was defined in the 11th General Conference of Weights and Measures in 1960 as follows:

The meter is the length of 1,650,763.73 wavelengths in vacuum of the radiation corresponding to the transition between the levels 2 p^{10} and 5 d^5 of the krypton-80 atom. Since 1983, it is taken as to length of the path travelled by light in a vacuum during the time interval of 1/299,794,458-th of a second. quoted from mary blocksma, reading the numbers, a survival guide to measurements, numbers and sizes encountered in everyday life,

Precision, measurement and consensus are essential for the scientific enterprise. Science is not one person's views about how the world functions, nor hand-waving speculations and speculative generalities. Science is based on sustained observations and meticulous measurements by countless people scattered in many regions of the world. That is what gives science its credibility, reliability and power. That is where its contentions overshadow assertions about the world inspired from other modes. It is not enough to say that another system of thought hit upon the same insight. What matters is how it came upon the idea, and to what extent the idea was made quantitatively precise and measurable.

The international agreement signed on 20 May 1875 has this symbolic significance: It proclaimed that humanity would agree to take as true that which is empirically verifiable, quantitatively calculable, and precisely measurable by all who are committed to the scientific quest, no matter what their race or religion, nationality or political persuasion. Like the Nicene Creed, this too is a pledge of allegiance, by all who are part of a group. It is a pledge, not to a doctrine, but to a methodology: the methodology of science. Even those who decry science or reject it as the construct of a culture, are its beneficiaries.

May 21

From the World of Religion: ELIZABETH FRY

There are prisons in most civilized societies. Their original purpose was to keep criminals enclosed until they would be tried, but in due course they also came to be used for incarcerating people who displeased a king or a tyrant, and to restrain trouble-makers. Law breakers from petty thieves to murderers were imprisoned too, but until the 19th century, conditions were unbelievably woeful: prisons were over-crowded dungeons with little water, infested with vermin and with few facilities. Men and women were sometimes dumped together and there was little control over their behavior which tended to be violent. Prisoners were at the mercy of wardens for food and water. They begged and stole and fought for their basic needs. They were treated like animals in cages.

If such is no longer the case in many parts of the world, it is because of the selfless and tireless commitment of some people to strive to make things better for the less fortunate members of the human family. Elizabeth Fry (born: 21 May 1780) one such.

Elizabeth was born in a Quaker family, and was greatly influenced in her tender years by a very caring and enlightened mother who believed women should be educated and also play a role in society. So, aside from listening to Bible stories and singing Psalms, little Betsy also studied, read books on history, learnt French and Latin. Equally importantly, she accompanied her mother on trips to help the poor and tend to the sick.

Elizabeth took the Quaker practices of simplicity and service very seriously. She prayed, but felt that serving others was a necessary aspect of being religious. She began a Sunday school for children in which, aside from teaching morals from the Bible, she taught the children to read and write. At 19, she married a well-to-do gentleman by the name of Joseph Fry, and began having a child practically every year. When she was feeling that her life was spent to no useful purpose for society, she happened to hear about conditions in Newgate prison, and decided to look at the place herself. She was appalled by the squalor, by the screaming and yelling of women in tattered clothes, by the sight of prisoners lying on stone floors, of babies born in prison which lived stark naked, etc. In 1817, Elizabeth Fry started a program which magically transformed the pathetic state of the prisoners into something more decent and orderly in a very short time.

Her work jolted law makers. However, in public debates on the issue of prison reform, conservatives poked fun at her bleeding heart liberalism: this weakness used to be called *ultra-humanitarianism* in those days. The mindset of condemning and caricaturing any compassion for the less fortunate is as pathetic a psychological ailment as racism and religious bigotry. It continues to plague even modern societies. In 1817, an *Association for the Improvement of the Female Prisoners in Newgate* was founded. Elizabeth Fry traveled to study and improve prison conditions in Scotland and in other European countries like Belgium, Holland, Germany, and Denmark. She also expanded her efforts to improve living conditions in hospitals and in what used to be called insane asylums. Today there are a number of Elizabeth Fry Societies in the world, as also other organizations dedicated to ameliorating the plight of prisoners in many countries.

Every religion has its saints and sages. Most of them have sung the glory of God, given their lives for their faith, or are credited with miracles. But it is good to reckon that men and women who feel the pain and sorrow of fellow humans, who dedicate their lives to caring for the sick, to helping the poor and for the cause of the downtrodden are also saints: not of this religious tradition or that, but of the human family.

From the World of Science: ANDREI SAKHAROV

Andrei Sakharov (born: 21 May 1921) was a physicist of high caliber. He had heard about nuclear fission as a physical phenomenon in the late thirties. But when he read about the nuclear bomb dropped on Hiroshima, he shuddered at the thought of what the future might hold. Now it was time for his government to emulate, and it recruited the best physicists to build a Soviet bomb. Sakharov got involved in the design and completion of the first Soviet hydrogen bomb. He received the dubious honor of being dubbed "father of the Soviet hydrogen bomb." The honor was dubious because, unlike his American counterpart Edward Teller, Andrei Sakharov became disillusioned with the bomb-approach to solve the world's political confrontations. Like most people with a conscience, he was shocked to see the impact of its successful explosion. He wrote later: "When you see all of this yourself, something in you changes. When you see the burned birds who are withering on the scorched steppe, when you see how the shock wave blows away buildings like houses of cards, when you feel the reek of splintered bricks, when you sense melted glass, you immediately think of times of war...All of this triggers an irrational yet very strong emotional impact. How not to start thinking of one's responsibility at this point?" This is what differentiates an enlightened thinker from a robot: The capacity to feel horror at whatever is terrible and unjust, painful and hateful.

Sakharov reflected on the question for days and months, even when he was engaged in military research. He was very concerned about the potential for enormous pain and destruction that was implicit in the nuclear arsenals of the world. Eventually, he wrote an article on *Peaceful Coexistence and Intellectual Freedom* in which he called for a "democratic, pluralistic society free of intolerance and dogmatism, a humanitarian society which would care for the Earth and its future." It was bad enough to express such outrageous ideas in Russian. But when the article somehow appeared in the *New York Times* in 1969, he became an international celebrity overnight, and, in the framework of Soviet values, there was sufficient reason to brand him an enemy of the people. Like Oppenheimer in the United States, he lost his position in government. But he managed to make irritating noises, calling for human rights and condemning Soviet behavior in Afghanistan. He was promptly dispatched to Gorkii where he remained unknown and unheard-from for six long years.

His bold commitment to a non-war approach under a system which equated pacifism with siding with the enemy, won him the Nobel Peace Prize in 1975, as also the epithet of *conscience of mankind*. But the Soviet Union, which was making speaking aloud in the international arena about the freedom of peoples all over the world, would not allow its own citizen Sakharov to go to Norway to receive the honor. Such was the sham and shame of that system, perhaps of any system that preaches to the world when its own citizens are facing serious problems. But the human spirit cannot be snuffed by brute force. So Sakharov persisted.

But, the calendar moves on, the face of history changes. Yesterday's foes become today's allies, and yesterday's rebel is today's hero. Sakharov's name and dignity were restored. A Sakharov Foundation was established in 1989 soon after his death. In 1995 a two-storey building was dedicated to the Sakharov Foundation by the city of Moscow.

Being a humanist-physicist, and living at a time and place where there was no freedom of religion, Sakharov expressed the conviction that in due course a rapprochement between science and religion would come about.

May 22

From the World of Religion: DANIEL DEFOE'S ARREST

Today, at least in some parts of the world, it is easy to voice one's opinions, to speak out one's mind, and to openly refuse to kneel before an altar or salute a flag. Human rights, ultimately, is unfettered opportunity to make whatever noise, or do whatever one wants, as long as one is not treading on someone else's toe or territory.

This wasn't always so, as it still is not in countries where Holy books, rather than the human spirit, dictate thought and behavior. At one time, the so-called Non-conformists were persecuted in awful ways in England. These Dissenters were not even Hindus or Buddhists, but Christians, bearing such epithets as Presbyterians, Baptists, Quakers, etc. The one thing they all had in common was that they were averse to taking communion from the Anglican Church. According to the then current law, however, everyone had to do this and accept the Book of Common Prayer. If a minister disobeyed, he was relieved of his post, and wasn't permitted to come anywhere within five miles of his former church (the *Five Mile Act*). The situation changed when Puritans came to power in Cromwell's time. They, in turn, banned Anglicans and the Book of Common Prayer.

The *Toleration Act* of 1689 was a civil rights bill of sorts: It gave Dissenters license to practice their faith in specially reserved places. There were numerous Dissenters in England at this time. One of them was a wholesale hosier who was also an essayist by the name of Daniel Defoe, known to the world as the author of *Robinson Crusoe*. He wrote on subjects like banking, road management, insurance, idiot asylums, and on education of women as well.

In 1703 Defoe published a pamphlet entitled, *The Shortest Way with the Dissenters*. This was a satirical work on the absurdity of intolerance. He wrote: "This is the time to pull up this heretical Weed of Sedition, that has so long disturbed the Peace of the Church, and poisoned the good corn!...It is cruelty to kill a snake or a toad in cold blood, but the poison of their nature makes it a charity to our neighbors, to destroy those creatures! Not for any personal injury received, but for prevention; not for the evil they have done, but the evil they may do! Serpents, toads, vipers, &c., are noxious to the body, and poison the sensitive life: these poison the soul! (They) corrupt our posterity, ensnare our children, destroy the vitals of our happiness, our future felicity, and contaminate the whole mass! Shall any Law be given to such wild creatures!..."

Some Anglican Churchmen took this seriously and endorsed its proposals to kill all Dissenters. But when it was discovered that it was all a joke, the authorities were furious. They called for his arrest. Defoe went into hiding, but eventually he gave himself up to the authorities (22 May 1702). He was tried, fined, and jailed. He was also pilloried: that is, his wrists were tied, as was his neck, and he was exposed to public ridicule, though his ears weren't cut. Pillorying was a common mode of punishment in those days. Later, Defoe wrote an ode to the pillory.

When we are appalled by the stoning of adulteresses in some places today, it is good to recall that such practices have not been the monopoly of some cultures. Societies evolve, and hopefully some day dissent would be allowed all over the world, rather than be forcibly suppressed. We may learn this from history: Any country which is under the authority of a religion or sect, or a monomorphic political ideology, is unsafe, even dangerous, for people who don't subscribe to that faith. There are still many countries like that in our world: all respectable members of the United Nations Organizations.

From the World of Science:
WILLEM EINTHOVEN

We have all felt our heartbeat, and with a stethoscope we may even listen to the heartbeat of others. The thumping sound is like the rhythmic beating of a drum. But it was only during the 19th century that the electrical aspects of the heart—as indeed of other organs and processes in the living body—came to be recognized more fully.

As in every field of scientific investigation, many people were involved in these studies and discoveries. One of the pioneers here was Willem Einthoven (born: 22 May 1860) who devised and improved upon a delicate instrument to observe and measure the electricity in the heart.

It is said that when horse carriages rolled on the cobblestone street of Leiden where he worked, his whole lab would shake, jerking the delicate instruments. He dug deep holes in the ground, installed rock walls, and firmer floors, but nevertheless, the capillary tube with mercury rose and fell with the traffic on the road.

He gave up, not his research, but the crude instrument then in vogue. He took a galvanometer (current-measuring device) and made a new version of it in which he replaced the heavy coil with a string made up with silver-coated quartz. This was Einthoven's string galvanometer. He kept modifying this device, and started to get good data. The first EKG recordings were published by Einthoven in 1902. The next step was to produce the instrument on a large scale and market them.

In 1905, Einthoven connected his machine to the local hospital, more than a kilometer away, via a telephone wire, so as to transmit the data. On March 22 of that year, his 45th birthday, he recorded the first tele-cardiogram of a robust man, and interpreted the tall R waves as arising from the bicycling that the man did from home to hospital. In his paper *Het Telecardiogram* he wrote: "We should first endeavor to better understand the working of the heart in all its details, and the cause of a large variety of abnormalities. This will enable us, in a possibly still-distant future and based upon a clear insight and improved knowledge, to give relief to the suffering of our patients."

Einthoven studied the hearts of many patients in that hospital. He found that sometimes electrical currents in the heart were blocked. He could also notice premature heartbeats in some cases. With his device he could detect if the chambers were dilated, and know the effect of drugs on the heart. Furthermore, Einthoven standardized the measure and nomenclature of the readings of EKG readings. Incidentally, Einthoven's galvanometer was also used in other contexts, besides cardiology.

Einthoven's researches were the starting point of what has come to be called electrocardiography. The Einthoven device has been considerably modified as a result of technological changes, but in principle the new versions still serve the same goal: systematic observation and measurement of voltages in heat beats, and deducing therefrom the heart's pathology. Willem Einthoven received many honors for his work. Thomas Lewis' classic text, *The Mechanism of the Heart*, was dedicated to Einthoven. The Nobel Prize (1924) was awarded to him for his contributions to elctrocardiography.

Today we use EKG to test the heart's normal condition as well as when it is under stress. It has been found that certain heart ailments reveal themselves on the EKG when one is under stress. Poets gave rhymed a thousand thoughts on the heart, spoken of its spark and fire, but no one ever considered electricity in it. For this, we need the probing eye of science. Science sheds light on aspects of the world that reflective wisdom and revealed knowledge seldom unveil.

May 23

From the World of Religion: HERMAN GUNKEL

Religions may be approached from at least three different perspectives: the perspective of the practitioner, the scholar, and the outsider. The first is most meaningful, the second is most insightful, and the third could be interesting if undertaken with sensitivity and sympathy.

The scholarly study of scriptures may focus on doctrines and dogmas, the language and grammar, or on the history and influences.

Historical probes into Christianity, into the personage of Jesus and the periods when the Bible was composed, are by no means recent. However, a scholar who contributed immensely to the modern elucidation of the doctrinal foundations and historical roots of Judeo-Christianity was Herman Gunkel (born: 23 May 1862). His penetrating analyses of the Old Testament and the psalms have had a lasting impact on theology.

Gunkel investigated both the written and the oral traditions of the Bible. He believed that it is important to take the Bible literally in order to fully understand and correctly interpret its contents. He emphasized that the Israelites were very careful and calculating of the potential consequences of whatever they did.

He explored the psalms, interpreted their contents, and offered explanations as to their origins and motivations. He showed that some of the psalms, though they seem to be praising God, may also be praising other things. By comparing the commonly spoken language with the way in which the psalms are composed, and the everyday life of the people of the time, he explained the forms of the psalms. By this technique, Gunkel shed further light on their meaning and method. His approach came to be known technically as *form-analysis*. It enables the student, even the practitioner, to get deeper into the spirit of the original psalmists. Gunkel combed through the texts and sorted out the cults, the legal aspects, the prophetic pronouncements, the tribal narratives, the experiences of everyday life, etc. In other words, all the richness and complexity of the Hebrew scriptures were analyzed in great detail by the erudite tools that Gunkel developed. His original work led to a classification of psalm types (*genres*). It must be remembered that the hymn tradition is much more ancient than the Old Testament whose roots may be traced, among others, to Egytian and Canaanite models. The ancient Hindus too had their Vedic hymns which date back to very ancient times.

Gunkel's analyses of the psalms were insightful, but they also provoked some controversies. For example, while Gunkel believed that certain psalms arose from the psalmist's conviction that the enemies really had no magical powers, others believe that they were written precisely because it was believed that the enemies had magical powers.

Gunkel saw in some of the psalms prophetic proclamations about the arrival of the Messiah and the final reign of God, and in others an assurance that everything would be fine again. Some have disagreed with this assessment, saying that it was Gunkel who was projecting Christian ideas into the Old Testament. His critics maintained that the original authors did not think in those terms. In any event, the notion that all the psalms refer to Christ in one way are another is one that gained great strength from Gunkel's work.

It is not clear that people who sing *Hineh Mah Tov* or *The Heaven declare the glory of God* feel more elated after reading Gunkel's commentaries, but they will be intellectually enriched by his work. And those who wish to get a degree in theology simply cannot afford to skip his writings.

From the World of Science:
FRANZ ANTON MESMER

It is a fine line between science and pseudoscience. Those who blurt out unscientific nonsense are less dangerous than those who speak the language of science, spicing gibberish with jargon. The latter succeed, as alchemist, astrologer, numerologist and necromancer. One such personage who thrived well was Franz Anton Mesmer (born: 23 May 1734). He has sneaked his way as a verb into the English dictionary.

Mesmer started with theological studies, then switched to law, and finally got a physician's degree which won him a teaching position at the University of Vienna. He received a doctoral degree for a dissertation on the physico-medical flows of planets. It was not as outrageous as it might sound today, because ideas of invisible fluids were floating all around. Thus, some people imagined gravitation was pulling on water in human bodies. A Viennese astronomer was trying to treat people with magnets. Mesmer was fascinated by this, and he began to use magnets in the cure of some of his patients. He discovered that the same soothing effects could be brought about by simply moving his hands, without any magnets. He developed a theory to the effect that living creatures also had magnetic properties. The interaction between animal magnetism and ferromagnets repaired the imbalance causing the disease. In the apartment which he acquired from his wealthy wife, Mesmer practiced magneto-therapy lucratively. But as he became more and more successful and ostentatious, he provoked the displeasure of traditional Viennese physicians. Mesmer had amassed enough money to move to Paris.

In Paris, he had greater success and became a celebrity. He would ask groups gathered in his chamber, to sit down and hold hands. Dressed up in austere modes, he would gently place his hands close to them, and by his penetrating eyes, he would transfer his animal magnetism, sending his patients into states of trance or screaming. Some have commented uncharitably that his not-very handsome features helped to get people into confused states. Upper-class patients of pre-Revolutionary years came to him, vowed they were cured, and became his most effective propagandists. Conventional medicine, which depended on bloodletting, purging and such, was overshadowed by this version of nature-cure based on tantalizing occult powers and subtle fluids. The French Academy of Sciences appointed a committee to investigate. The committee's report granted that some of his claims of cure seemed valid. But it also bluntly declared 'there ain't no such thing as *mesmerism*.' Mesmer did not care. He was like some of the modern day M.D.s with credentials from reputed universities who have an exotic charm, who speak and write well, and use the terminology of quantum physics and field theories to pander mystical medicaments. People came to him too by the droves, and felt relieved of their tensions, and of some cash. This must be said of Mesmer as of many modern-day magicians: he was sincere in whatever he said and did. He wasn't trying to pull a fast one. Nothing of what he claimed corresponded to anything known to science. But he made people feel better: what more can you ask of a physician?

Mesmer is remembered today only through the word derived from his name. But he had his followers in his days. Hayden was impressed by him. So was Louis XVI of France. Animal magnetism is brought in a scene in Mozart's *Cosi fan tutte*.

Mesmer made a bundle in Paris, traveled to England and other countries, lecturing and winning more believers, and finally went to Switzerland where he spent his last days.

His secret was just that he really cared for his patients, softly touching them with heart-felt sympathy. In many contexts, genuine caring can be more effective than drugs.

May 24

From the World of Religion: ABRAHAM GEIGER

Religions have a static (traditional) component, but they also have a dynamic (modernizing) aspect. Thinkers and philosophers tend to explore new paths and practices. When a religion is affected by the worldviews and visions of modern science, it tends to look upon its roots in different ways: from the reverential to the scholarly. When religious leaders are bold enough to question the belief systems of their ancestors, while respecting scriptures as meaningful and inspiring insights rather than as absolute truths, the religion is saved from stagnation and mindless existence.

When this happens in a religious tradition, positive transformations begin to occur. Consider, for example, Judaism. For many centuries, the guardians of the religion preserved their practices and beliefs in communal seclusion. There was nothing wrong in this, except that Jews in Western Europe found themselves in a constrained state compared to Christians whose thinkers boldly deviated from ancient practices, and rejected or re-interpreted passages from their holy book which contradicted the findings of science. So, during the 17th and 18th centuries, practically all scientists, inventors, bold thinkers and unorthodox theologians were Western-European Christians.

One of the pioneers who instigated a reform movement in the Judaic tradition was Abraham Geiger (born: 24 May 1810). [He had a not-as-successful predecessor in Moses Mendelssohn.] Geiger was a rabbi who realized that if his people were to find a respectable place in the evolving German society, they had to re-think their theology and ancient modes. So he rejected the idea that Jews were a chosen people and saw nothing wrong in bringing musical instruments into synagogues. He said it was okay to read the Torah in German. He abridged the Jewish prayer book. He questioned the divine origin of the *mesorah*. He declared that the Bible was a collection of "beautiful and exalted books."

Geiger shocked the orthodoxy who felt he was harming an ancient tradition which had been entrusted by God to be the spiritual teacher for all humankind with its message of monotheism and ethical covenant. What traditionalists did not realize was that many young Jews who went to school in Germany and were exposed to new thought currents of mainstream Europe did not take the claims and practices of their sheltered parents seriously. They were in effect closet non-Jews. Geiger's movement was to keep new generations within the system in an awakened framework. Initially, those who switched to Reform Judaism went to the extreme of rejecting every practice, from circumcision and Bar-Mitzvah to Hebrew and Sabbath. But gradually the pendulum swung to a moderate level, and established enlightened respect for the beautiful aspects of the tradition. Jews began to contribute significantly to the art, music, science, technology and philosophy of Western culture. Geiger's movement spread to New York, Pittsburg and beyond where Rabbi Isaac Myer Wise and others took the lead. Thanks to Geiger, Jewish people began to realize, as did the Japanese in the 19th century, that you either take modernity seriously, even if it means having to stare straight into your tradition's face and call a poem a poem, or decry science and modernity as the White (Christian) Male's creation, and shun it. It is no surprise that the first crop of Jewish scientists were from Germany.

These were the choices, at least until the rise of post-modernism. Now things have changed: Some scholars try to show that quantum mechanics says nothing that was not in ancient aphorisms, that those who used medicinal herbs as medication knew all about bacteria, etc. Such naiveté generally results in self-congratulating sterility.

From the World of Science: WILLIAM WHEWELL

As important as research and discoveries are for the advancement of science, science's framework and methodology need to be periodically analyzed and explained to the general public for the propagation and appreciation of science. Also, it is important to have some understanding of the historical evolution of science over the centuries. Among the people who contributed to these extra-scientific dimensions of science was William Whewell (born: 24 May 1794) who was scholar and educator. He was the scientist who coined the word *scientist*. Before he introduced the word, there were only natural philosophers and men/women of science in the vocabulary.

Whewell was versatile in his interests and prolific in his writings: He taught mineralogy, studied theology, authored a treatise on mechanics, and wrote articles on virtually every science: architecture, astronomy, geology and moral sciences. He wrote on liberal education and Platonic Dialogues. He published technical papers on tides. There are more than 150 items in a listing of his publications, from books and scientific papers to articles and reports.

But Whewell is remembered most of all for his *History of the Inductive Sciences, from the earliest to the present time* (1837), and his *Philosophy of the Inductive Sciences* (1840). The former was written when scholars in Europe generally believed, in the absence of much data on other cultures, that everything in science began with Thales of Miletus and his speculation that the whole universe emerged from water. Whewell was very impressed with this early attempt at a naturalistic explanation, and went into rhapsodies about ancient Greeks:

The sages of early Greece form the heroic age of science. Like the first navigators in their own mythology, they boldly ventured their untried bark in a distant and arduous voyage, urged by the hopes of a supernatural success; and though they missed the imaginary golden prize which they sought, they unlocked the gates of distant regions, and opened the seas to the keels of the thousands of adventurers who, in succeeding times, sailed to and fro, to the infinite increase of the mental treasures of mankind.

He disagreed with Kant's idealism and Locke's sensationalism, but his own view was very close to accepting *synthetic a priori*: That is to say, that the human mind can become aware of some aspects of physical reality without actually experiencing it. Indeed he regarded the mind, not as a basket into which information is dumped, but rather as an active participant in the acquisition of knowledge, equipped with certain *fundamental ideas*. He was much criticized by John Stuart Mill for this.

Whewell was one of the founders and an early president of the *British Association for the Advancement of Science*. He advised working scientists on the coining of new terms. He is responsible for technical words like ion, cathode, paramagnetic, and diamagnetic.

Whewell had strong conservative leanings on many matters. For example, he was very much opposed to admitting Dissenters into Cambridge University. He believed in a final cause for biological entities, and deduced from this that there is an intelligent and purposeful God who created the universe.

Among the neologisms that Whewell introduced is *consilience*: a jumping together of inductively derived generalization and theoretically deduced knowledge which creates in us an inner conviction about the truth of a proposition. This word became the title of E. O. Wilson's best-seller, published in 1998.

May 25

From the World of Religion: RALPH WALDO EMERSON

Religions arise and evolve from the experiences and utterances of unusual individuals. Such individuals reveal to the common people their visions and feelings of deeper levels of the human experience, perhaps of Reality, and they articulate powerfully and effectively profound insights into the nature of the human condition, its strengths and weaknesses, its possibility and potential. Some of them beckon us to new insights, forge new paths, or just verbalize what most of us feel deep in our core.

Ralph Waldo Emerson (born: 25 May 1803) was among those who have thus enriched humanity's heritage. He came from a lineage of preachers. His father was a minister at the First Church of Boston. Emerson is also said to have been inspired by a remarkable aunt who was sometimes referred to as an *eccentric saint*. When still young, Emerson already wrote beautifully, reflected with intelligence, and composed poems. He went through Harvard Divinity School, and became a preacher in Boston at 26. But his doubts about the sacramental nature of Christ's *Last Supper* disturbed a good many in his congregation. Emerson, poet and essayist as much as sermonizer, went on a trip to Italy, France, England and Scotland, where he was excited to meet the great poets and writers of the time, like Samuel Coleridge, William Wordsworth, and Thomas Carlyle. He was fascinated as much by Swedenborg (29 January) as by the *Bhagavad Gita*. When one is touched by such variety, it is hard to be affiliated to a single system of thought.

Back in Boston, Emerson became part of a group of sensitive intellectuals who were too independent in thought to accept traditional religious authority, but who yearned for something spiritual. They were convinced there must be some subtle thing beyond brute matter, and they explored the (Immanuel) Kantian notion the *transcendental*: entities beyond perceived reality. They felt God's immanence in Nature, the divinity within everyone. In his essay on Nature,

Emerson argued that beyond the unreal world of appearances and sensations there is the transcendental realm of the spirit and the over-soul. Hegel and Schelling influenced him, but let us remember that he also read the *Gita* and wrote a poem on Brahma. Anyone familiar with Hindu thought will see in Emerson's worldviews graceful echoes of *tat tvam asi* (Thou are That = a bit of God), of *jivatman* (spirit) and *paramatman* (over soul).

Emerson's writings are replete with pearls of wisdom. He had a vision of humanity that transcended national and religious differences. "I see that sensible men and conscientious men all over the world," he wrote, "are of one religion—the religion of well-doing and daring." He understood the true spirit of science when he said, "Men love to wonder, and that is the seed of our science." He defined philosophy as "the account which the mind gives to itself of the constitution of the world." In another essay he noted that "truth is the summit of being; justice is the application of it to affairs." He reminded us that "We have a great deal more kindness than is ever spoken."

J. R. Lowell referred to Emerson in these terse and rhyming lines:
'Tis refreshing to old-fashioned people like me
To meet such a primitive Pagan as he,
In whose mind all creation is duly respected
And parts of himself—just a little projected;
And who's willing to worship the stars and the sun,
A convert to—nothing but Emerson.

From the World of Science: PIETER ZEEMAN

Many have heard of sunspots, and the magnetic fields associated with them. We may even have heard of the magnetic fields of planets and stars. One may wonder how, without taking a compass to the celestial bodies, scientists have been able to detect the existence of magnetic effects in such distant regions. The answer, as might guess, is that we gather such information from the light from those bodies.

In this instance, it all arose from a simple experiment carried out by Pieter Zeeman (born 15 May 1865) in 1896. The experiment consisted in observing through a spectroscope light from a sodium flame. Normally, one observes a couple of yellow lines. Zeeman placed the flame in a strong magnetic field (i.e. kept the flame between poles of magnets), and found that the lines appeared a little smeared (broadened). Soon after he reported his finding to the *Amsterdam Academy of Sciences*, it came to be called the Zeeman effect. In due course, the phenomenon was investigated in greater detail, and extended features of it were also discovered. It was also found that no such thing happened when a magnetic field is placed in the path of the light ray, rather than at the source.

As often happens in science, others before Zeeman had attempted, both experimentally and theoretically, to unravel relationships such as he had done, but they had not been successful. Again, as often also happens, Zeeman's discovery seemed at the time to be only interesting. Little did one suspect that it would lead to a deeper understanding of the structural components of the atom, or indeed of the stupendous magnetic storms and fields that rage in the heavens above.

An explanation for the Zeeman effect was offered by an eminent compatriot-colleague of Zeeman: H. A. Lorentz. The phenomenon was also a strong confirmation of the notion that was brewing in those days: that atoms contain electrically charged particles. In 1902, Zeeman and Lorentz shared the Nobel Prize in physics.

A couple of decades later, when it was well established that electrons whirl around nuclei within atoms, yet another property of the electron, namely its spin, was also discovered, thanks to some observed anomalies in the Zeeman effect. Science always builds on the discoveries of yester-years.

What is interesting is that a simple and carefully conducted experiment revealed messages in light about the source of the light. It is no less remarkable that from results obtained in a small laboratory on earth, we are able to unravel aspects of the sun and stars that would otherwise remain obscured for ever from human knowledge.

Zeeman was a superb experimentalist, but he was also versed in the abstract theories of physics. He conducted extremely sensitive and precise experiments on crystals and radioactive materials to establish the equivalence of gravitational and inertial masses: a matter of enormous theoretical import in physics.

Practically everything we have come to know in scientific terms about the sun and the stars lies implicit in the light that comes from them, directly or indirectly. And yet, though we are inundated with light in the course of our everyday experience, we don't normally learn about such matters. This is because, no serious knowledge about the physical world can be obtained without sustained and systematic experimental investigation of a phenomenon. This is the lesson we learn as we recall the discoveries that have been made in our laboratories, with microscopes and telescopes and countless other instruments, in the conceptual framework erected by scientific theories.

May 26

From the World of Religion: VAISHAKH

There is something perfect in the silvery splendor of a full moon. Some traditions attach to it. The full moon in the month of Vaishakh (26 May 2002) marks the birthday of the great sage from Sakya, universally known as Gautama Buddha.

Tradition tells us that Mahamaya, the mother of the great one, was traveling to her parents' home when the wondrous child was born under the spread of shady trees. Scholars have reckoned the year as 544 B.C.E., but there is not unanimity on this. Legend also says, among other things, that an astrologer predicted that the new-born child had come to redeem the world of pain and suffering. We don't know when this story began to be told. But it adds to the poetry which are to religions what flags and festoons, flowers and fanfare are to traditions: they add much color, a sense of joy, and aesthetic thrill.

He was the prince exposed only to pleasure who became pensive, and set out on a quest for the cause of suffering in the world. After his years of contemplation the kindly Sujata who brought some milk-porridge to the emaciated ascetic, and the first light that dawned on the Enlightened one: that wisdom does not come to a starving body.

Not just in the Indian subcontinent where the Buddha emerged, but in South Korea and Indonesia, as in other regions of the world, this day is celebrated as the day of the founder of what has become a world religion: Buddhism. In the tradition, the Buddha was the supreme principle that brought new light and direction to the world. But some Hindus claim him too, even though there was a time when he was not regarded with favor in some parts of the Hindu world, when his ideas and creed were sweeping the land, often diverting the allegiance of Vedic Hindus to the sect or cult that made the Buddha the God. Today those historical confrontations are gone, and Gautama Buddha is described as the ninth *avatara* (descent in human form) of Vishnu: the sustainer of the universe.

For devout Buddhists, this is a day of special prayers to the Buddha principle. Monks in monasteries serenely read from Buddhist scriptures, and they do this continuously for hours on end. The *pipal* tree takes on special significance too, for tradition tells us that the great Gautama attained enlightenment when he was meditating under such a tree.

This is the day for listening to pious discourses on the Buddha by erudite scholars. And on this day one reaffirms one's commitment to the pentalogue of the tradition, called *Panchsheel*, which are injunctions against killing, stealing, lying, getting intoxicated, and committing adultery. In carnivorous lands where Buddhism has spread, the followers refrain from meat on this day, as a symbolic affirmation of the first commandment. When one cannot live up to every thou-shalt-nots every day of the year, the least one can do is to periodically confess and abstain.

Scholars have written learnedly on Buddha's findings as to the source of pain and of his teachings to overcome it. The root cause of every suffering, the Buddha revealed, is craving (*tinha*) for pleasure and sensual satisfaction. Eradicate this, and you will attain an inner peace that cannot be described in words: more easily preached than practiced.

As I see it, the central message of the Buddha is not so much with how to rid oneself of one's own pain, but compassion for others. The Buddha did not undertake his quest to relieve himself of a pain afflicting him, but because he was moved by the pain of others. The path to world peace does not lie in how we lessen our own problems, but in how deeply we feel for the pain of others, and how we strive to help our fellow creatures cope with their suffering. Caring and compassion are the central teachings the Enlightened One(s).

From the World of Science:
ABRAHAM DE MOIVRE

We remember the revocation of rights from people of the Judaic tradition in Germany during the 1930s, and the consequent immigration of German Jews to England, America and other places. Reprehensible as this was, it was not the first such situation in history. In France, for example, the Edict of Nantes which had given equal rights to French Protestants, was revoked in 1685, and this led to terrible persecutions of the French followers of Calvin. Many of them left in a hurry to other places, including England.

One of the families which thus moved to England bore the name of De Moivre. One of its members was Abraham de Moivre (born: 26 May 1667). He was gifted in mathematics, but did not study it formally in his earlier years. He used to read the classics in mathematics on his own. Some have said that De Moivre was imprisoned during the turmoil that followed the royal sanctioning of intolerance towards the Huguenots (as the French Protestants were called).

After the family emigrated to England, De Moivre got a chance to teach mathematics at a school. He happened to see a copy of Newton's *Principia* (then recently published), and began to devour it with enthusiasm. It is said that he used to tear off a few pages from his volume each day, and carry it along to school where he would read it during spare hours. The book was bulky and they did not have nice brief-cases in those days.

De Moivre got interested in the mathematical theory of chance which had been initiated by Blaise Pascal and Pierre Fermat, and investigated further by Pierre Montmort: all his former countrymen. In 1718 De Moivre published a major work on the subject, entitled in English as *The Doctrine of Chances* (*De mensura sortis* in Latin). This was a classic for a long time. In this book, a fundamental result of the theory of probability, namely the relation between the binomial and the normal distributions, as well as the so-called Stirling's approximation for the factorial of a large number, were first derived.

Abraham de Moivre is remembered even more for a beautiful formula that connects trigonometric functions and the realm of complex numbers. It is the kind of result—and there are countless others like that—that is the equivalent of magnificent sculpture in the realm of art or a grand symphony in the realm of music: a source of immense aesthetic, even spiritual, joy for those who are fortunate to experience their inner beauty.

When, in the 18th century, a public feud arose between Newton and Leibniz as to how much credit each one deserves (and how much discredit for the stealing of ideas) in the formulation of the calculus, an impartial commission was established to investigate the validity of mutual national recriminations. Abraham De Moivre served in that prestigious body which declared more or less that the two giants had hit upon the calculus quite independently of each other.

There is an interesting, if incredible, story associated with De Moivre's death. He is said to have predicted the day of its occurrence on the basis of a calculation. He said he would be sleeping for fifteen minutes more each night. On the night when, by such incremental measure, he was to sleep for twenty-fours hours at a stretch, he did exactly that and never got up again! True or not, like other legends in humanity's traditions, it is a nice one to remember and re-tell.

Countless investigators have contributed to major breakthroughs and minor results in the never-ending quest of science and mathematics. Some of them are oft remembered, and a good many are only occasionally mentioned. Abraham de Moivre belongs to the second group.

May 27

From the World of Religion: MEMORIAL DAY

From the time one group of humans attacked another for grabbing the carcass of a hunted animal or a piece of land conflicts between countries and nations have exploded into wars of one kind or another. No matter what the provocation, no matter if the war was just or unjust, no matter who won and who lost, what is common to all wars is that in the end, human beings die and many families grieve who otherwise would not have.

To a pacifist, war is a deadly manifestation of the human proclivity for cruelty and violence, a scheme for the rich to get richer, and the powerful to oppress more people. So C. W. Eliot made the simplistic, though heart-felt, generalization: "War gratifies, or used to gratify, the combative instinct of mankind, but it gratifies also the love to plunder, destruction, cruel discipline, and arbitrary power." But to those who are in war, not to start but to respond to attack and aggression, war is the call of duty, a sacred responsibility, a commitment to nation. As Nietzsche's Zarathustra spoke: "War and courage have done more great things than charity." He should have said: *some wars.*

There is no question that some wars in history have resulted in more good for more people, indeed even for humanity at large, than if they had been shirked. But that does not diminish the sadness in the death of the young men and women who die in the war that their country waged.

Whether a war is right or wrong, every soldier who loses his life has served the cause of his country. Bravely or in fear, voluntarily or by compulsion, those who die in war perish for no selfish reason. Whether the fallen on the battlefield goes to heaven or whether it is the end of another conscious entity, the people of a nation remember with gratitude the sacrifice of individuals who lost their lives in a distant field, their hopes of returning home sadly smashed for good. And every nation has learned to remember its sons and daughters who died because of the war. It is to celebrate their memory that we have a Memorial Day (27 May 2002 in the U.S.)

In ancient times, kings and emperors arranged to have their bodies preserved and marked, building pyramids and impressive tombs. Queen Artemisia constructed a magnificent monument in memory of her husband Mausolus, unwittingly giving us the word *mausoleum.* But for simpler folk, at least in some traditions, it is only the families that remember the departed in annual ceremonies. The idea of remembering common people in a collective way is of modern origin when ordinary citizens became no less important than royalty or dignitaries in power.

Soon after the end of the American Civil War, it occurred to Henry Wells of Waterloo (N.Y.) that a people should remember with respect the men and women who had lost their lives in that war. So, on 5 May 1866 they had their first *Decoration Day* when they placed flowers and bouquets at the graves of the soldiers, organized processions to the cemeteries, displayed flags at half-mast and played martial music. The idea caught on to other towns and states. The government began to recognize unknown soldiers, and the name of the day became *Memorial Day*. Other nations adopted similar practices. France has a Tomb of the Unknown Soldier at the *Arc de Triomphe* in Paris, England has one in Westminster Abbey. Every nation has its fallen heroes. No matter what one's views on war, on Memorial Day one feels like Robert Nichols when he said:

O loved, living, dying heroic soldier,
All, all my joy, my grief, my love, are thine.

From the World of Science: RACHEL CARSON

Paradigm shifts in science occur when new and successful theories capture the conviction of the scientific establishment. Paradigm shifts in society's overall views on history or politics occur when new insights and perspectives are brought out by thoughtful writers. A major paradigm shift in the public's view of science and technology occurred as a result of a very powerful book which was published in 1962. It was entitled *Silent Spring*, and its author was Rachel Carson (born: 27 May 1910).

In the 1950s, the grand successes of science and technology were most impressive: aside from automobiles and an endless range of gadgets that were adding to creature comforts, nuclear energy had been tapped for peaceful purpose, malaria was being conquered by DDT, and agriculture was becoming more abundant by the liberal use of fertilizers and pesticides. The hope and dream was that in due course these would be multiplied a hundred-fold and every material need of humankind would be met, and we would have happier and richer nations all over the world. But something happened.

In 1957, when a airplane dusted Olga Huckins' wooded land with DDT, quite a few songbirds dropped dead. She wrote to her friend Rachel Carson if she knew anyone in Washington to stop the insecticide-spraying service on her land the next year. Carson was a marine biologist who was working for the U.S. Fish and Wildlife Service. This request prompted her to inquiries and further research into the impact of pesticides. She discovered case after case of dismal effects of pesticides in many parts of the country. It was important to present all this information so that the public might know.

So the *Silent Spring* came to be written. It began with an explanation of the book's title through an imaginary town where the folks nonchalantly sprayed pesticides in abundance, imagining it was like swatting flies in the kitchen or stepping over an intruding bug in the foyer. Most of the pests were no doubt decimated, but stronger strains began to develop which were resistant to the poison. More seriously, the DDT itself stayed in the soil and water for much longer periods, and slowly got into the food chain of birds and bees, of algae and fish, until, little by little, all the birds died. Then, when the cold of the winter gave way to the sunshine of spring, it was silent: no crow or cuckoo, no swan or sparrow. It was an eerie silent spring indeed.

The book went on to report specific cases: the Clear Lake in California where dichloro-diphenyl-dichloroethane (DDD) entered plankton and fish, attempts to eradicate the gypsy moth in New England which killed birds in the region, etc. The book was a shocker. The public got angry. The pesticide industry was furious. It financed its own negative propaganda, calling Carson extremist and hysterical. But Carson's critics had a disadvantage: They were in an open society. It was difficult to arrest the calls for facts, and the appraisal of reckless industries which were polluting air, water, and land.

So began the environmental movement, spurred by a book that was informative and powerful. Congressional hearings began, and soon the National Environmental Policy Act and the EPA came to be. Rachel Carson died of cancer before the end of the decade.

Sadly, many of her warnings have materialized. More seems to be in store. The paradigm shift from regarding science and technology as the panacea for all problems to looking upon them with the gravest concern and fear has already occurred. It remains to be seen how, in the context of so much knowledge, but also under economic pressures, humanity handles this most serious threat to its very survival: the continuation of indiscriminate industrialization.

May 28

From the World of Religion and Science

Religions enrich our lives by providing a framework for thought and action. We may take to a religion as a traveler who chooses a vehicle to reach a destination. We may also choose a car or horse carriage, mule or camel back, ship or plane, and sometimes walk from place to place on our own. There is variety in experience and enjoyment, and when one does a little bit of each, one realizes that, depending on the context, one mode may be better than another.

The practice of deriving enrichment from different religions, yet shunning each when it becomes uncomfortable, was adopted by one who was born and brought up in the Hindu tradition. He learned to recite Vedic hymns in Sanskrit and *Pater Noster* in Latin. He read the Koran and the Torah too, but was nauseated when Hindus and Muslims killed one another in communal hatred. He had witnessed his pious father help the poor and the destitute. So he was moved, not by *mantras* and *swamis*, but by the caring and compassion that his father exemplified. Helping people in need and bringing cheer to them is all that counts, he told himself, all the rest of religion is soothing and insightful poetry, or amusing, or absurd noise. But he had been so deeply touched by the aesthetic and cultural aspects of religions he felt that religions should (or could) never be thrown out of civilized societies. They must be tamed: for underneath all the wildness of religions there is a sublime core. Each of us is a spark of the consciousness that pervades the cosmos, every one a lamp that shines dimly or brightly, all equally precious.

As a youth, he was drawn to poetry and philosophy, to mathematics and music, to languages and literature also; but most of all to physics. He was fascinated by the depth and scope of meaningful knowledge that science has brought to humanity, and impressed by the power and coherence of scientific methodology.

He proceeded to Paris to work for a doctoral degree from the Sorbonne, but his thirst for cultural enrichment spurred him beyond the pages of *Physical Review*.

He read and reflected on humanity's heritage. Even with strong links to his own tradition, he came to regard himself as a human being most of all, with respect and sympathy for all that is enriching, ennobling, and enlightening in human culture. He wondered why there was so much conflict and confrontation when there are so many beautiful things in nature and culture, and so much capacity for love in the human heart.

He tried to understand why people of goodwill often hold opposing views on important issues. It occurred to him that perhaps we need to distinguish between facts and truths. Facts are registered in all normal human brains through the doors of perception. Truths are interpretations of facts. Interpretations are functions of the previous state of the brain. That state is determined by the inputs the brain has received. Some of these inputs are culture-dependent and some, culture-independent. The latter have little to do with feelings and emotions; the former have much to do with feelings and emotions.

Interpretations of facts which are heavily influenced by cultural factors give the truths of religion, politics, and history. Interpretations triggered by the other kind lead to scientific truths. Truths arising from the first kind are *endopotent*: they have considerable impact on how one feels within oneself. The so-called scientific truths as *exopotent*: they enable us to manipulate the external world.

What has been said above is about the author of these reflections (born: 28 May 1932).

From the World of Science:
JEAN LOUIS AGASSIZ

We are concerned with global warming these days, but we have also read that the planet once went through an Ice Age when much of the land from the North Pole to the latitudes of the Mediterranean was submerged under stupendous sheets of ice. Some fifty years ago there was fear that the world would suffer yet another Ice Age in the near future. We don't know whether human life will be drastically affected, perhaps erased, from the planet by freezing cold or by burning heat, but the notion of a past Ice-Age was first popularized only in the 1830s. Jean Louis Agassiz (born: 28 May 1807) who studied glaciers in the Alps, refined and propagated the idea which had been considered by some others also.

Agassiz had started out as an ichthiologist: one devoted to a scientific study of fish, specializing in Brazilian specimens, and went on to study long-dead remains of the creatures. He devoted ten years of his life to the systematic study of fish fossils and wrote an impressive treatise on the subject in which not a few scores but seventeen hundred fossil fish were listed, described, and classified. This was no mean work of paleontology. Yet, he always held on to the view that each species maintained its identity: an idea that is contrary to the evolutionary model.

This keen student of science and indefatigable researcher of fossils was never persuaded by Darwin's theory of evolution. He refused to accept the tenets of that view of life-origins. At one point, he proposed the dangerous view that different human beings emerged from different ancestral branches, which provided scientific buttress to racial prejudices. Some slave-mongers justified their feelings of superiority on the basis of this so-called "plural origins of mankind." At one point Agassiz also asserted that much of South America was once under ice-sheets. This left many scientists cold.

By now Agassiz was in the United States as a prestigious Harvard professor. We read in *Science at Harvard University: Historical Perspectives*: "Charismatic teaching was a rare and treasured activity…brought to Harvard by Louis Agassiz, possibly its first spellbinder in science…" He initiated many projects here, including the establishment of a museum of natural history, and the publication of a ten volume work on the natural history of the United States. Only two volumes were completed. Agassiz was also involved in the founding of the National Academy of Science.

Long before popularizing biologists of our own times, Agassiz felt that Darwin ought to be challenged in the popular press rather than in scientific journals to stop the spread of his ideas. He traveled on well-paid lecture tours, and became a scientific celebrity. But not every aspect of his reputation was positive, for the gossips murmured about his authoritarianism and rash treatment of assistants, even of a marital mess, confirming that scientists are as human as politicians and other specimens of *homo sapiens*.

Agassiz summarized his scientific work thus: "I have devoted my whole life to the study of Nature, and yet a single sentence may express all that I have done. I have shown that there is a correspondence between the succession of Fishes in geological times and the different stages of their growth in the egg,—that is all. It chanced to be a result that was found to apply to other groups and has led to other conclusions of a like nature."

Agassiz has been described by some as one of the founders of the scientific tradition in America, but also as a scientist of modest attainments who constantly strove to emulate the great ones of his time, like Cuvier and Humboldt. He brought to us the chilling thought of a phase in our planet's history when all was a stiff and silent sheet of ice.

May 29

From the World of Religion:
PASSING AWAY OF BAHA'ULLAH

The birthday of religious prophets are remembered by the devout. In some traditions the day of their passing away is also commemorated. For people of the Bahai faith, the day the founder of their religion died is an important date. Baha'ullah passed away peacefully on 29 May 1892. Compared to other religious founders, he died quietly.

An intriguing feature of religions affiliated to the Abrahamic tradition is the violence and strife in which its founders were involved. This was true of the overall struggles of the Israelites, of Jesus of Nazareth and of Mohammed. Baha'ullah too was subjected to much persecution. The reason for this is perhaps the following: Middle-eastern monotheism proclaims there is only one God, and adds that this is the God Whom its own followers worship. It insists further that the gods of others are false and intolerable. Thus, religious intolerance is a built-in feature here.

So, when Mirza Hussayn Ali Nuri of Iran, who came from the same tradition, joined a religious group led by a certain Bab, he was arrested on charges of attempted assassination, and thrown into a prison known infamously as the Black Pit. He was also tortured: a not uncommon practice in societies adhering to medieval standards. In prison, he is said to have had his revelation from Bab that he is to be the leader of a new movement. When released, the authorities relieved him of all his material possessions—he was from a wealthy family—and they kicked him out of the country. Such were (still are) the laws in some nations whose spokesmen never tire of telling the world they are guided by a religion whose name means Peace.

Ali Nuri went into involuntary exile, and assumed the name of Baha'ullah when he was in his mid-forties. He traveled through Iraq and Turkey which were not places where one held interfaith dialogues. He declared himself to be a manifestation of Bab. Finally, he landed in the Holy land, where his own brother tried to poison him. He was put under house arrest in a place just outside of Akka in Palestine. His all-embracing message of universal tolerance, so alien to Middle-Eastern mind-set, spread far and wide, and gained followers. It is said that in 1852 the first persecutions started, when the 20,000 followers of Bab were killed by the Persian government. No international inquiries in those days.

Baha'ullah died peacefully at the age of 75. One of his disciples by the name of Jináb-i-Mírzá Ismá'íl, who was present at the scene, has left behind the following reminiscence of the event: "Tears flowed from my eyes and I was overcome with feelings of grief and sorrow after hearing these words. At this moment the Blessed Perfection bade me come close to Him, and I obeyed. Using a handkerchief which was in His hand, Bahá'u'lláh wiped the tears from my cheeks. As He did so, the words of Isaiah [25:8], 'and the Lord God will wipe away tears from off all faces...' involuntarily came to my mind."

To those not of the Bahai faith, the passing away of yet another charismatic figure may not mean much. But to those who are part of that tradition, Baha'ullah's death was a milestone in their history, the equivalent of Good Friday. So they remember the day with reverential memory of one who is regarded a material manifestation of divinity. That's why Baha'ullah's devout followers sometimes refer to the demise of their master as ascension: a term used by Christians and Muslims to bodily transfer to heaven. For they hold that that he was "the latest in God's manifestations, of which Zarathustra, Buddha, Krishna Jesus and Muhammad are other prominent ones."

From the World of Science: PAUL EHRLICH

The 21st century may well be the *ultimate century*: ultimate in being the climactic one in which the major problems and challenges of science and technology, disease and health, education and enlightenment, peace and harmony, that face humanity will be fully solved; or, ultimate in the sense of being the very last one when *homo sapiens* will be crawling and swimming and soaring on the earth's land, water and air.

Every age in human history has had doomsday-sayers. The threat of global catastrophe and planetary conflagration are as old as mythologies and charismatic prophets. But humanity has survived, not simply like ants and roaches, but improving its lot, increasing longevity, and growing in numbers too. And this very success, as if in a moralistic tale of ancient wisdom, has come to haunt it. Contrary to Malthusian prediction that when populations grow exorbitantly, Nature will solve the threat to survival through famine and flood, human population has been growing at an ominous rate during the past century, with potential for disasters of incalculable magnitude.

The public at large was made acutely aware of this lurking time-bomb by a powerful book by Paul Ehrlich (born: 29 May 1929): *The Population Bomb*

(1968). It brought to the attention of an indifferent world some shocking numbers: Five hundred years after Christ, the population of the world was a quarter of a billion. A thousand years later it had doubled to half a billion. Less than three centuries later (1825), it became one billion. In 75 more years, by the dawn of the 20th century, the number shot up to 1.5 billion. By mid-century, it was 3 billion. By the end of the last century, the world had to support almost 6 billion people. By current estimates we will have more than ten billion people in another sixty years. Such rapid population growth has resulted from science and the consequent revolutions in technology, medicine, and food production.

It does not require complex mathematics to realize that such doubling mode cannot continue indefinitely. If it does, in a thousand years every square foot of the earth's surface will have a human standing on it: an unworkable absurdity. We are experiencing population pressures all over the world: in health, human welfare, literacy, malnutrition, energy needs and international rivalry, hatred and envy, and most of all, in the assault on the environment: an inevitable consequence of increasing energy consumption.

In their 1996 book, *Population Explosion*, Paul Ehrlich and Ann Ehrlich explored further the carrying capacity of the land: the sustainable resources of a community and nation, and brought home the idea that no nation is really independent when it comes to its resource-needs. In this economically interconnected world, the industrially advanced nations draw vast amounts of material and energy from other regions to maintain their high standard of living. Sadly, if science and technology ever bring the standard of living of all the peoples of the world to the level of its most successful ones, the planet with its current population would collapse, environmentally speaking.

In spite of such repeated warnings, much of the world is still ignorant of, or indifferent to the horrendous effects that are bound to occur when the population time bomb explodes at the global level. Or, it simply does not know how to cope with the very real threat. The partial explosions of the population bomb here and there and the inability or the incapacity of governments to feed their citizens and find work for them all are what are causing immense pressures and frustrations among many people all over the world, prompting immigration into the more economically and industrially developed nations of the world. It is too early to know how it will all work out.

May 30

From the World of Religion: MIKHAIL BUKANIN

One of the goals of religion is to present guidelines by which human beings can live and act in peace and harmony in the context of a spiritual framework. Though there can be little disagreement among people of goodwill as to the goodness of the goal, problems arise when different paths are recommended to attain the goal.

Except for the spiritual framework part, laws and governments also have the same goal. However, laws have a constraining character, and governments have an authoritarian one. Most ordinary people are content to live under law and authority for the benefits of security and orderliness. But for some free spirits, especially if they also happen to be reflective by nature, any kind of imposition is terribly uncomfortable. Unless they are themselves enforcing the law or exercising authority over others, they seek ways of liberating themselves and others from all external constraints.

Since the time of Zeno in ancient Greece and perhaps even earlier, there have been philosophers who have fantasized societies without government and laws. They have spoken and written on such utopias, and even been activists in bringing humanity to such a state of (what they regard) as supreme freedom. One thinker in the list of anarchists was Mikhail Bukanin (born: 30 May 1814) who came from Russian aristocracy. He served in the army, but was so disgusted by a ruthless Polish campaign that he quit. He went to Berlin and Paris and was converted to the anarchist movement. He was summoned to Russia, but he refused. His property was confiscated, and he published a scathing pamphlet against his country. He was involved in an insurrection in Dresden, was caught and sentenced to death. But the punishment was changed to life imprisonment and he was handed over to the Russian authorities who packed him off to Siberia: the terrestrial hell for Russian trouble-makers. Bakunin escaped, managed to sneak into the United States, and then went to England in 1861. There were no passport and visa requirements those days. Bakunin resumed his activism, became an active member of the international socialist movement, and soon became an eloquent spokesman for anarchism.

Bakunin's view was that ultimately all states must be abolished. He was convinced that the idea of states has its roots in religion, and belongs to a primitive phase of civilization in that it is intrinsically a shackle. Ultimately, he insisted, all states will have to be dissolved, and the world should have only autonomous and mutually unhurting communes. There could be federations of such communes, and these would form nations. He said that in order "to make men moral it is necessary to make their social environment moral. And that can be done in only one way; by assuring the triumph of justice, that is, the complete liberty of every-one in the most perfect equality for all. Inequality of conditions and rights, and the resulting lack of liberty for all, is the great collective iniquity begetting all individual iniquities."

Anarchism is by no means a thing of the past. In modified versions, it is still present today in various countries of the world where ideas can be freely expressed. As with all religions, its motivating principles are commendable and civilizing. As with all ideals, especially of an extremist nature, its practice may be far more difficult and far less long-lived than its enunciation in inspiring books and documents.

I reflect on Bakunin, as on other thinkers here, not to criticize or to justify his stance, but to remember yet another member of the human family whose life and writings have had significant impact on the course of events, at least in some places at some time.

From the World of Science:
HANNES OLOF ALFVEN

When it comes to ultimate questions, the primary differences between science and religion are that in science the picture is based on current data, in religion, on revelation of one kind or another; in science dissenters are ignored rather than persecuted; in science, in due course, the model will be changed. But it is difficult to be sure that any final answer as to the ultimate, of the past or the future, is the really, truly the correct one.

For example, consider the ideas of the eminent astrophysicist Hannes Olof Alfven (born: 30 May, 1908) who was awarded the Nobel prize (1970) for his significant contributions to the field of *magnetohydrodynamics*. To get a feel for what this is all about, let us recall that when substances are heated to enormously high temperatures: of the order of a few million degrees, their atoms are shorn of orbiting electrons. The sea of nuclei or of other pure fundamental electric charges constitutes what physicists call plasma. Plasma may be regarded as a state of matter far beyond solid, liquid and gas. In highly dense concentrations, it is at the core of stars. As tenuously spread out pure charge, free of atomic and molecular binding, plasma pervades the whole universe.

The mathematics governing the properties and flow of plasma under the influence of magnetic fields is a part of magnetohydrodynamics. The topic becomes relevant not only for our understanding of stellar interiors, but also in the context of nuclear reactor design and of deriving energy from fusion: which may some day become our primary non-polluting source of energy.

In 1937, Alfven put forward the idea that a magnetic field must be spread all over the universe. *Cosmic magnetism* is now an important field of research. Alfven's theories of magnetospheres have been confirmed by space probes. He was also one of the first physicists to suggest that when free electrons and protons in space enter regions of intense cosmic magnetism, they emit what is called *synchrotron radiation*: a fact of considerable relevance in astrophysics as well as in particle accelerators.

Alfven was an early proponent of what is known as plasma cosmology at a time when the scientific establishment fully endorsed and was widely propagating the Big Bang model for cosmogenesis: the universe came into being at a given moment and has been growing ever since with ever-expanding fury. Alfven proposed the theory that the universe never had a beginning, nor will ever come to an end, that it has always been there with the most fundamental of all features: the electromagnetic field, thanks to which we have organized matter of atoms and molecules.

Aside from his technical contributions, Alfven was among the physicists of conscience who spoke out against continued nuclear arms build-up, and pleaded for eventual nuclear disarmament.

Though Alfven received many honors during his lifetime, he was generally regarded as a maverick by many mainstream scientists working in his field. Perhaps this was because of his persistent refusal to accept the Big Bang model. He is said to have had difficulty getting some of his ideas published in mainstream journals.

We learn from Alfven's career that heretics are not treated well in the scientific world either, for when those who know, or think they know, are in power, they have little tolerance for the ones who challenge established frameworks and knowledge. Though the goal of science is to achieve correct understanding, the enterprise is made up of humans who have their personal pride and vested interests. So it is not surprising that such things also happen in the world of science.

May 31

From the World of Religion: FIRST CATACOMB

There have been many great personages of the distant past who have founded religions and changed the course of human history. We have come to know about them through writings and references. But given that photography was invented only in the 19th century, we have no way of knowing how exactly they looked.

Consider, for example Jesus Christ. The artists of later periods, like Da Vinci in the *Last Supper*, have presented us with images of how Christ might have looked, but these are not any more authentic than Charleston Heston posing as Moses. In this context, it is interesting to recall how the most ancient known portrait of Jesus was discovered.

In our own times, one of the spots to which tourists are guided in Rome are the catacombs about which we can hear an earful from multilingual guides. As per one etymology, because it was a huge hollow (*kumbi*) which was down (*kata*) below the normal level of the ground, the Greeks referred to it as *katakumba*. There are a number of them. Catacombs served as places for the internment of corpses, an underground mass graveyard, one might say. But they were also the enclaves where early Christians etched their beliefs in stone, and engraved figures of Christ and scenes from the Bible.

With the passage of time and the accumulation of ruins, like many vestiges of ancient times they too were forgotten, buried as if for ever. And for centuries, generations of Romans and Christians did not even know that such things existed. Scholars have pointed out that contrary to popular history the catacombs were not places where persecuted Christians used to hide. Aside from the presence of so many corpses which might frighten the faint-hearted, there was a certain coolness in the damp underground that probably served as a natural air-conditioner in days gone by.

In the 16th century, Antonio Bosio, a scholar turned archeologist, began to explore subterranean Rome. His quest led him on 31 May 1576 to the first catacomb unearthed in modern times. He came to be called the Columbus of Catacombs and the initiator of Christian archeology. One of the unexpected treasures from the re-discovery of the catacomb was that on the ceiling of Orpheus cubiculum, Bosio found a drawing of a Christ-like figure. It is remarkable that he noticed it in that darkness.

Almost 300 years later, an English artist by the name of Thomas Heaphy, with the meager candle light at his disposal, discovered the portrait of what was surely of Jesus Christ, drawn on the ceiling of the subterranean labyrinth. Given that the catacomb itself dated back to the early centuries of Christianity, this was probably the most ancient drawing of Christ's face humanity has. It seemed to be a profile when it was discovered, but later study seems to suggest that it was a peculiar effect of the dirt that had accumulated over the centuries that gave the image that impression, when in fact it was simply a portrait of Christ.

I remember visiting the place near the basilica of San Sebastiano, herded into the somber chambers by a very knowledgeable exponent of things past. He talked about the bones and other remains of the Christians in Rome, and of the relics they had left behind. There was something eerie in the thought that those mute remains resting there for centuries once served the bodies of live people who thought and prayed, laughed and loved as we do now. When the guide told us it was the place where Peter and Paul had once been buried, I was tempted to ask, "But where is Mary?" Since I wasn't sure if he was familiar with the modern singing trio, I resisted this temptation for levity.

From the World of Science:
DISCOVERY OF KRYPTON

One of the characteristics of most chemical elements is their propensity to combine with other elements to form chemical compounds. This is what produces millions of different substances from the 92 or so naturally occurring elements. But there are some elements whose atoms simply don't grab hold of other atoms to create molecules. These are the so called inert elements, of which helium is perhaps the most widely known. Of course, we have also heard of neon and argon. All these are present in minuscule amounts in our atmosphere. How and when did we come to this knowledge?

In earlier times, careful analysis of substances in chemical laboratories led to the discovery of new elements. In the 19th century, two new factors were introduced: The first was the tabulation of all known chemical elements in terms of their chemical properties. It was found that this orderly *Periodic Table* had quite a few gaps, suggesting that not all elements in nature had been recognized. Secondly, the science of spectroscopy identified characteristic light-prints (spectral lines) for every element.

This was the context when William Ramsay made a statement in 1897 in Toronto to the effect that it was highly probable that there existed an element with properties between those of helium and argon.

The following year, starting with a liter of liquid air, Ramsay and his assistant Travers recognized on 31 May 1898 a residue of the liquid after the oxygen and nitrogen in it were allowed to boil off. The residue gave spectroscopic green and orange lines which corresponded to none of the known elements. A week later they announced their discovery to the world. Since it had been hidden all along from our general perception, Ramsay named it krypton (from the Greek word for *hidden*). In 1960, the orange-red line of krypton was used to define the internationally agreed upon unit of length: a meter was taken to be 1,650,763.73 wavelengths (in vacuo) of the orange-red line of Kr-33.

Krypton, like other inert gases, is colorless. It is also odorless. It is used in some fluorescent lamps as well as in flashlights in photography. It is present in air to the extent of one part per million, and thus qualifies to being called a *rare gas*. With our sophisticated methods of analysis, we have been able to determine that the atmosphere of Mars contains still smaller amounts of this gas.

In the biological world we sometimes encounter strange and exotic creatures whose role in the biosphere is not all that clear. In other words, it is difficult to see their relevance in the larger interconnected web of life. Likewise, we don't know what role krypton plays in any aspect of the earth's visible features and properties. But this much can be stated as a fact: Without the empirical methods of science, the precision of measurements, the interlinking of concepts, and the hypothetico-deductive method, krypton, like a million other hidden features of the physical world, would never have come to light. In that sense, krypton, through its name and by the way in which its existence was uncovered, symbolizes the power and pattern of science which lie in its capacity to unveil the hidden aspects of the physical world through careful experimentation, analysis and reasoning, all done in a theoretical framework.

When one is unaware of the tortuous routes and complex groping by which things and processes are discovered by serious and systematic science, one tends to declare that scriptural utterances reveal a knowledge of science, and that any mode of gaining knowledge is as valid as the scientific.

Most of the inert gases were discovered during the last five years of the19th century.

From the World of Religion:
MONTH OF JUNE AND MARY DYER

This is the first day of June. There are many views on the origin of this name. According to one version, it is connected to May which was dedicated to older people (*majores*), and is itself dedicated to younger ones (*juniores*). On the other hand, the name also reminds us of the Roman goddess Juno who, in the incestuous mythology of the ancients, was both wife and sister to Jupiter. Then again, June may have been a contraction of *Jovino*: one who answers to Jove or Jupiter. Juno, the goddess for women, plays an important role during child-birth. She is also associated with marriage and sexuality: a reason for the celebration of June brides.

In the words of the poet N. P. Willis:
It is the month of June,
The month of leaves and roses
When pleasant eyes salute the eyes
And pleasant scents the noses.

As we probe into events that occurred on this day in a world filled with events joyous and lamentable, we come upon the name of Mary Dyer of New England in mid-seventeenth century, who was a devout Puritan. But she also believed, like some others, that the Holy Spirit was within every individual, and that one really did not need the intermediary of Church, priest, or minister to get into communion with God.

To the orthodox Puritans who then wielded power in Massachusetts, this was heresy. So Mary Dryer and her husband William were ostracized, and they moved to Rhode Island. They sailed back to England where they came under the influence of the newly emerging Quaker movement. They became Quakers themselves. When Mary visited Boston some years later to see friends who had been thrown into prison for their religious views, she was herself arrested in jailed. According to a law which was passed in Boston in 1658, Quakers were regarded as more dangerous than Communists in the 1940s: They had to leave the territory or die. It is hard to believe that Puritans had come to the New World to escape religious persecution themselves.

Mary Dyer's friends were executed, she was released and let go to Rhode Island. But she came back to Boston, determined to fight for the repeal of what she called the wicked law. "Was ever the like laws heard of among a people that profess Christ come in the flesh?" she asked rhetorically, and also said, "Search with the light of Christ in you, and it will show you of whom, as it hath done with me and many more..." Fights for justice may eventually be won, but not all fighters come out unscathed. Every victory for the righteous cause is paid for by the lives of many dedicated people.

Mary Dyer was sentenced to death for refusing to recant her heretical views. On 1 June 1660 this fifty and odd year old woman was hanged in cold blood by a system which truly believed it was protecting the word and commandment of God. It is small consolation to remember that she was not the only Christian martyr killed by Christians.

We recall such episodes, not to condemn those whose dark-age worldviews perpetrated such acts of inhumanity, but to pay homage to the bold people who gave their lives for an enlightened cause. We need to remember them because we live in an age when, as reaction to the negative impacts of science and modernity, some are calling for a return to the good-old days. Not every aspect of the old days were good: In fact, much of it was far more terrible than we tend to imagine in our more romantic moods.

From the World of Science:
NICOLAS SADI CARNOT

In the context of the energy crisis, one often talks about fuel-efficient cars. What one has in mind are fuel-efficient engines. When and how did this notion of efficiency enter our thinking?

The first heat engines were invented in the 18th century (*vide* 19 January). While they served some practical needs, there was as yet no systematic framework to describe and analyze their functioning. In the first quarter of the 19th century, one tried to conceptualize the notion of steam engines to better understand how they worked and to make even better engines. The most successful such effort was by Nocolas Sadi Carnot (born: 1 June 1796). In 1824, he published a slender volume entitled *Reflexions dur la puissance motrice du feu*: Reflections on the motive power of fire (1824).

To get some understanding of this classic in the history of science, let us recall certain key ideas and terms. We know that when coal or wood or anything burns, heat is generated. Also, when something moves, it possesses mechanical energy. A *heat engine* is a device that converts heat energy into mechanical energy.

Not all the heat energy that is supplied to the engine is converted into mechanical energy. The percentage of heat that is becomes mechanical energy is a measure of the engine's *efficiency*. The heat that does not become mechanical energy is released into a sink: exhaust pipes in cars and smokestacks in factories. When the car burns fuel, heat energy is released. Only part of this is used to move the car (mechanical energy). This measures of car's efficiency. The other part is released into the air (sink).

Carnot's analysis showed that every heat engine functions in cycles: It starts from one state and after a series of processes comes back to the same state. His work showed further that the efficiency of the engine depends only on the temperatures of the source from which heat is derived and the sink into which the unused heat is deposited.

Indeed, it is fair to say that through his first systematic analysis of the relationship between heat (*thermos*) and mechanical work (*dynamis*: power), Sadi Carnot founded one of the most important branches of physics: *thermodynamics*.

The most significant result of Carnot's analysis was that even in a theoretically perfect engine, we can never convert all the heat-intake into mechanical energy. In other words, it is impossible to construct, even in principle, a 100 % heat engine. This result is generally known as the *Second Law of Thermodynamics*. Carnot's valuable results and fundamental discovery were arrived at on the basis of a very incorrect understanding of the nature of heat. He was still working on the caloric fluid theory of heat.

It is also a matter of some puzzlement that though Carnot's work was presented to the French Academy of Sciences, copies of his monograph were hardly sold, and in due course the work was forgotten. It was only after more than two decades of negligence that its importance was recognized, thanks to Lord Kelvin's chance encounter with the book.

Science progresses in two quite different modes. In one, theoretical concepts and the ensuing analyses give us a better understanding of the phenomenal world. This understanding is often used for practical purposes. In the other mode, useful devices, like the windmill or the lever, are constructed on the basis of trial and error; then these are carefully studied to draw from them the basic principles and laws which enable their functioning. Thus the very practical heat engine led to the formulation of thermodynamics which is at the basis of our understanding of a great many features of the phenomenal world: from aging and the arrow of time to the final fate of the universe.

June 2

From the World of Religion: HARRIET TUBMAN

Religions sometimes speak of spiritual liberation: the Buddhist *nirvana*, the Hindu *moksha*, and the Christian *redemption*, for instance. But just as there can be no spiritual fulfillment without food and physical nourishment, there can be no spiritual liberation without physical freedom to move and do what one chooses. So the first step that is to be taken by people who are in shackles is to break the chains. And if they are of the more special type, they would also help others in obtaining such a release. That is why Moses was a great leader: He helped his people attain full freedom.

One such person in modern times was Harriet Tubman of the 19th century. She was born in Maryland, and owned by the slave-monger Edward Bordas. She labored in his plantation when she was barely five years old. As she grew up, she became more and more defiant, for which she was punished. Once she was hit so hard on the head that she fell down and went into a coma. Even after recovery, she used to have spells of dizziness.

She was married to a freed slave when about 24 years of age. When her slave-master died, she was going to be sold and shipped off to a southern plantation. She decided to escape. And escape she did. Trudging day and night, alone and half starving, through rough roads and marshy lands, she managed to reach Philadelphia where she got a menial job. Once settled, she visited Maryland periodically and rescued her sister's family.

Even in the midst of the darkness of inhumanity, the positive in the human spirit shines here and there. So in the somber days of slavery, there were secret schemes and modes of assistance to help some at least to escape. One of these schemes was called the Underground Railroad, by which, it is estimated, a hundred thousand slaves stealthily found their way to freedom in the north in the period prior to the Civil War. The leaders in this movement included Salmon Chase, Levi Coffin, and Frederick Douglass.

Harriet Tubman was also an active member of this Underground Railroad. The freeing of hundreds of slaves is credited to Harriet Tubman's efforts, and she came to be called the Moses of her people. She is said to have proudly proclaimed once, "I nebber run my train off de track and I nebber lost a passenger."

She became a wanted woman: Authorities put a price of several thousand dollars on her head, but she was too clever. She disguised herself and moved in and out of the environs of people who knew her, without being identified. She continued to fight to free the slaves. It is said that she would sneak into plantations and urge the slaves to escape at night, and if anyone hesitated, she would point a gun and say, "You will be free or die!"

When the Civil War erupted, she served the Union Army, slipping into the opposite camp as a spy, with no long-range recognition for her services. In the words of General Saxon, Harriet Tubman "made many a raid inside the enemy lines, displaying remarkable courage, zeal, and fidelity." On 2 June 1862, along with the abolitionist James Montgomery and with some 300 African American troops of the Union's Volunteers she raided and set fire to a plantation in South Carolina and freed 750 slaves.

In her simple and heart-felt way she expressed the feeling of *nirvana* that comes from emancipation: "I looked at my hands to see if I was the same person now I was free. Dere was such a glory trou de trees and ober de fields, and I felt like I was in heaven."

It is a feeling that every human being deserves to have. The days of slavery haven't ended for millions of human beings in many parts of the world. We may hope that some day no one will ever know freedom as a new and strange experience.

From the World of Science: DONATI'S COMET

Humanity has witnessed hundreds of comets, but the first one to be captured on a photograph was seen in the night sky of Florence on 2 June 1858. It was discovered by the astronomer Giovan Battista Donati who developed spectroscopic studies of stars, and wrote many papers on comets more generally. That was a year of many comets, Donati's comet being the fifth one to be noticed that year. It was estimated to be about 87 million miles away when first observed, rushing in the neighborhood of the sun at the unimaginable speed of 150,000 miles an hour. Astronomers estimated its tail to be about 6 million miles long. Comets are the only known heavenly bodies in our vicinity that stretch to such size. There are red giant stars which are swollen to millions of miles also, but they do not belong to our system.

From observations again, it was deduced that the Donati comet has a period of recurrence of some 292 years. Flipping back through the pages of history, it was recalled that this same comet had appeared in 1556 too. It one came to be called the comet of Charles V (of France) because that poor monarch was so terrified upon seeing it that he gave up his throne and retreated into a monastery. He was convinced he had done the right thing because though the comet came and went he did not die after the comet left. If astrological science had been true (as he assumed it was), a comet in the sky meant a king in a coffin. Charles V wasn't impressed by the fact that other kings survived the bad omen; but then, he thought perhaps that the others weren't as important as himself.

The 292 year period should have brought the Donati comet back to our skies in 1848. The reason for the ten year delay, astronomers suspected, was that its path had been perturbed by the gravitational pull of one of the larger planets, and not, as one commentator of the times seriously suggested, because it wanted "to witness the completion of the Atlantic Telegraph."

Indeed, it would be rash to think that in the 1800s the scientific view on astronomical appearances had enlightened public consciousness. Actually some people maintained that Donati's comet presaged, if not provoked, the outbreak of the American Civil War.

A writer of the times, who did not subscribe to such views, wrote: "If its (the Donati comet's) present visit should have the same effect upon some of the cruel despots and wicked rulers of our day, leading them to repent of their sins, and behave well for the future, its mission would be a blessed one."

On the other hand, an English poet wrote a verse connecting Donati's comet and the painter William Turner's work, of which the following is a stanza:

William Turner of Oxford is on his horse,
Riding between fields and old barn doors.
Fields that should be blacker than a widow's dress
But tonight there's a comet burning in the west.
The frost is building on the thatched walls as
William Turner picks up his pen and draws.

The history of science is replete with great discoveries and breakthroughs, and not a day goes by when something or other of interest or significance comes within the field of investigation of one scientist or another. Donati's comet of 2 June 1848 was one such. Like other unusual astronomical events, it did create a stir, and made its name in history by being the first comet ever to be photographed, and the first one whose composition had been analyzed by the newly developing field of celestial spectroscopy.

June 3

From the World of Religion:
UGANDAN MARTYRS

Christianity and Islam have been spreading their wings all over the world. In the process, which continues to this day, they have both brought in much good, but they have also caused the decimation of local religions which, at the core, were not much different from most ancient belief systems. Here and there, Christianity and Islam have come into confrontations, because their goal is not simply to introduce aliens to the grand notions of Creator, ethical systems, and after-life. Rather, it is to make them accept these and related beliefs as a function of this Savior or that Prophet: the only ones who are supposed to be licensed to bring religion to a sinning and ignorant humanity.

This pattern has been universal in the propagation of Christianity and Islam. Let us recall it, in particular, in the Uganda of the last quarter of the 19th century. There, people had a variety of local religions which accepted the existence of a Creator whom they called Ntu (or Muntu). They believed in the spirits of the dead to whom they paid homage, not unlike ancient Romans, Confucians, Shintos, and Hindus. They also believed, as did 19th century European spiritualists who held séances, that some of the spirits communicated with the living. Again, as elsewhere, only men could see the spirits, though women could receive information on social ills. It was accepted that the members of the priestly class had the power to curse bad people, similar to Atharva Vedic chanters, and cure diseases by appropriate utterances, like some faith-healers in Christian world.

But the Ugandans had not heard of Allah or Mohammed, Christ or the Holy Spirit. This, in the view of Muslim and Christian missionaries, was a problem that had to be rectified. So, in the latter half of the 19th century, Arab traders from Zanzibar tried to engulf Bugandans and Ugandans into the Islamic fold, and replace their spears with swords. They were followed by British, German, and French traders, who brought guns and Christian preachers. Whereas only one Islamic sect brought the Word, two brands of Christianity showed up: Anglicans and Catholics. And these had their mutual rivalries.

In 1884, a king by the name of Mwanga came to power in Uganda. Neither Muslim nor Christian, he wanted to keep his people from the influence of all alien religions. Unfortunately, he was also an chronic pedophile. He is said to have had 200 pages for his lustful needs. He was ruthless in his treatment of European evangelists as well as of Ugandan converts to Christianity. He had some of them murdered, and many were also tortured. But, in the spirit of the ancient Christians under Roman dictators, his victims suffered it all with great courage and deep faith, and calm acceptance.

After Mwanga killed a young Catholic leader named Mkasa for protesting the murder of Christians, an even more ardent Christian took up the lead. His name was Lwanga. Lwanga was charged with obstructing the king's ways by converting his pages to Christianity. In May 1886, the king became furious and he ordered a whole caravan of Christians to walk a 37 mile trek to a place called Namugongo where they were incarcerated. On 3 June, all the Christians were burned to death. One was the unrelenting son of one of the executioners. It is said that, with customary confidence, the martyrs declared: "You may burn our bodies, but you cannot harm our souls!" Lwanga was canonized later as St. Charles Lwanga. June 3 is the Day of Ugandan Martyrs.

A hundred years later, two thirds of the population of Uganda had become Christian, and barely a fifth was affiliated to their ancient religion. How the world had changed in that country! Such is the power of evangelism.

From the World of Science: JAMES HUTTON

We walk on land and sail on water, but how often do we reflect on how land or water came to be. We see soft soil and feel hard rock, but how many of us wonder about their origins? Yet such wonderment is what leads to science. One person who probed into such matters was James Hutton (born: 3 June 1726) who studied law, switched to medicine, did some farming, and then got interested in the nature and formation of rocks. Others before him had considered these topics too. For example, there was the eminent Abraham Werner at the time, who investigated the action of water in the formation of layered strata of rocks. His ideas were based more on interesting speculation than on field observations. Because of their stress on the role of water, Werner and his followers came to be called Neptunists.

But Hutton did a good deal more. He carefully observed the form and structure of rocky protrusions, whether in his native Scottish highlands or in the Alps. He recognized that the science of the earth must be studied as a slow process over long periods of time rather than as a sudden event. In other words, what Darwin was to do for life forms, Hutton did for the physical earth. He was led to believe that the rocks we see today are the results of gradual sedimentation, or melting from the fire of the earth deep below, or rocks which have changed forms, or the product of enormous pressure, etc. They are certainly not as they were eons ago. He also held the view that when rocks from the earth's interior come to the upper regions and are exposed to air and sunlight they tend to slowly degenerate and become transformed. The worn out rocks get submerged again, and are subjected to other kinds of changes, and so on.

In 1788, Hutton presented these ideas and more to the newly formed Royal Society of Edinburgh in a learned paper entitled *Theory of the Earth*, or *An Investigation of the Laws Observable in the Composition, Dissolution and Restoration of Land upon the Globe.* This classic work inaugurated, it is generally agreed, the science of modern geology. (The name was popularized by De Saussure.) Hutton was also one of the first to analyze the phenomenon of rain in terms of humidity in the atmosphere. Because of his reference to heat in the earth's interior, Hutton and his followers came to be called Plutonists.

Inevitably, controversies arose between Neptunists and Plutonists, not just among scientists, but in the popular press as well. The former, because of the closeness of their ideas to Biblical Deluge, were regarded as being more faithful to religion. Goethe, whose literary genius spilled into scientific matters sometimes, devoted a dialogue in his Faust (Act IV) to the two schools of thought, making Mephistopheles the spokesman for Plutonism, revealing his own preference for the Neptunist school. Elsewhere, he spoke in harsh terms against the Plutonists. As the historian of geology Frank Adams stated: "...Goethe found in the Neptunian theory a magnificent picture of slow and stately progress in the development of the earth, while his indignant opposition to the Plutonic conception was due to the fact that it destroyed this fair picture, by introducing violent and sporadic upheavals and eruptions due to igneous forces, which marred the beauty and symmetry of the whole."

Indeed this tends to happen all too often in literary and philosophical interpretations of the world: One chooses that which is more pleasing, motivated by a desire to see the world such as it should be rather than such as it is. On the other hand Hutton wrote: "In interpreting nature, no powers are to be employed that are not natural to the globe, no action to be admired except those of which we know the principle..."

June 4

From the World of Religion: NELSON GLUECK

Two important questions of reliability arise in the context of any religion. The first relates to the reliability of the assertions of its originators: To what extent, or on what basis, can one accept the revelations or injunctions of the initiators of the religion.? A quick answer to this would be: If you are among the faithful, you accept the words of the Rishi or the Enlightened One or the Prophet or the Savior. If not, don't even bother.

The second is about the authenticity of the stories and books on which the religion is based. In order to answer this question satisfactorily, one needs to do historical research. In the case of very ancient religions, this includes archeological work too. Most members of a faith accept whatever is said in the holy books out of reverence for them and/or because of the scholarly and field work that others have done.

One such person was Dr. Nelson Glueck (born: 4 June 1900) who was rabbi, Hebrew scholar, and archeologist. He began his visits to the Holy Land when he was in his early twenties. At that time, most of the people in the region were living as they had been for centuries. For at least twenty five years, Gluek could go into Jordan and Palestine and Israel without fear of a terrorist ambush or of being kidnapped. He rode on camelback, traveled miles in the sweltering heat, and got involved in digging into desert sands to uncover the relics and remains of distant days. He found it a fascinating enterprise because, as he put it, Biblical "archaeology is like burning the mist off the Bible."

By his tireless work, he unearthed countless buried sites in Jordan and Negev. He pin-pointed the famous copper mines of King Solomon and the port on the Red Sea where, as per the Bible, Solomon received the Queen of Sheba. His excavations dated the Exodus and rendered more than plausible a number of other episodes narrated in the Old Testament. In a way, this is not surprising, given that, except for occasional exaggerations and blurred distortions that are inevitable in oral traditions, much of what is written in the Old Tstament is a narration of ancestral history.

Glueck's deep affection for the region is reflected in a statement he made about the place: "These are more than conglomerations of rocks and soil," he said. "These are the haunts of the Children of God, and His spirit is imprinted on the very atmosphere." Being himself of the Judaic tradition, he empathized with those who longed to have a Jewish state there. He said: "I have never wandered up and down the banks of the Jordan without seeing the people of Israel cross over into the Promised Land and wondering what the spiritual equivalent of the Promised Land might be in our time."

One effect of such scientific corroborations of Scriptural assertions of any tradition is that the more enthusiastic among the average educated readers jump to the conclusion that science has proved one's religion to be true. Indeed, in our own times, people from many traditions are trying to use archeology to establish the historicity of their epics and mythologies, symbolic stories and claims of miracles. Whereas simple folk are quite content with faith, the so-called educated ones crave for confirmation of their faith in scientific terms, and sometimes they get carried away. Though a rabbi himself, in this context Glueck was an archeologist first. So, when he appeared on the cover of *Time* Magazine in 1963, he made it clear in public statements that his work had nothing to do with giving incontrovertible proof for the existence of God. This was a wise alert since many still believe that such proofs are possible. He urged people not to "confuse fact with faith, history with holiness, science with religion."

From the World of Science:
JEAN ANTOINE CHAPRAL

Chemists have contributed a great deal to the economic prosperity of nations. It has been said, for example, that the amount of sulfuric acid produced in a given period in a country is a good index of its industrial success. In pre-revolutionary France, when Antoine Lavoisier was laying the foundations of modern chemistry, there was another Antoine who, trained to become a physician, studied the developing science of chemistry. His full name was Jean Antoine Chaptal (born: 5 June 1756). He secured a position as professor of chemistry in Montpellier.

Chaptal acquired a tidy dowry from his marriage, and a rich uncle left him a generous inheritance. He invested these monies in a chemical factory for the manufacture chemicals, including sulfuric acid. This acid had been known at least since the 16th century, and various methods had been developed in England and Germany for producing this vitriolic substance. Soon it would be used in the manufacture of sodium carbonate, and of synthetic organic dyes: other widely used chemicals.

Chemicals of various kinds have been used at local levels in various cultures, but now began the large-scale production of substances in factories. Chaptal's factory produced chemicals of considerable economic value to the country. This brought him much income and renown. He became famous in many parts of Europe and beyond. For all of this he was rewarded with honors and titles by the king of France. It is difficult to imagine that in our own times, the founder of a successful chemical factory would be thus recognized.

Chaptal was also interested in theoretical chemistry. He proposed the name of *nitrogene* (niter-producing) to the gas that Lavoisier had named *azote*. The French did not adopt it, but the English did. When we speak of nitrogen, we are using a word that Chaptal coined. This is a rare instance in which a word coined by a scientist in one language was taken over by a different linguistic stream, rather than the original one.

Chaptal was invited to work in some other countries. He is said to have received an offer from George Washington to work in the United States. Had he accepted the offer, he would have been the first European scientist to have emigrated to the new country. But he declined the invitation, preferring to stay and work in his own native France.

When the Revolution broke out in 1789, Chaptal published a controversial book of a political nature. He was promptly arrested. But fortunately he happened to have some connections with the upper strata of the revolutionaries. Also, though they had said that the new republic had no need for a Lavoisier who was therefore beheaded, Chaptal was regarded as being more useful. So he was put in charge of a factory to produce saltpeter, an explosive ingredient of gunpowder. He had worked on other useful materials like beet sugar, and in matters of interest to chemists, like fermentation.

After Napoleon came to power, Chaptal was appointed to high positions in the government. In his capacity as minister of the interior he initiated a number of factories and institutions of great value to the country. Towards the end of his life, however, he is said to have died in poverty because his son had squandered all his accumulated fortunes.

Chemists like Chaptal were the mainsprings for one of the greatest cultural revolutions in human history: the chemical-industrial revolution which has enriched human life in a thousand ways for much more than two centuries now, but which also has the potential for arresting human life altogether on planet earth. Both science and religion are double-edged.

June 5

From the World of Religion: RUTH BENEDICT

There are many languages, many religions, and many cultures in the world. One is generally attached to one's own language, religion, and culture in special ways. When we encounter a different language, we may find it interesting or strange, but we seldom say it is inferior to our own. With religion, most people tend to think that their own religion is the doctrinally right one. With cultures, the matter is even more difficult. Here again, most ancient cultures generally regard(ed) their own as in some way special. Quite a few did (do) not hesitate to call their own culture superior to others.

Cultural anthropologists try to study cultures in an effort to understand, rather than evaluate. Unlike tourists who, on the basis of their comfort level, are persuaded that their own culture is much better than the one they get to know, cultural anthropologists bring to bear their scientific objectivity in the appraisal of cultures.

One such cultural anthropologist who gained eminence in the first half of the twentieth century was Ruth Benedict (born: 5 June 1887). She studied Amerindian cultures, compared and contrasted them, especially their obsequies. She concluded that some cultures were placid and harmonious, while others were excessive and sensuous. Her book *Patterns of Culture* (1934) became a classic, and she gained the high esteem of anthropologists. She looked upon culture as "personality writ at large." She recognized the tremendous influence that custom and learning have on individuals: these diminish in the influence of natural tendencies. She also stressed the boundless capacity of individuals to change. Indeed, her studies revealed that only a small percentage of the behavior of individuals constituting a society is reflected in the personality of the culture at large. In other words, no matter how strong the influence of one's surrounding culture, the individual has the capacity not to succumb to it. Indeed, without such individuals cultures will stagnate. She also did some controversial psychoanalysis of cultures.

From the sympathetic studies of different cultures, Ruth Benedict concluded that it is scientifically untenable to declare one culture to be better than (superior to) another: a view that should, in principle, be appealing to most enlightened people.

But then, when Nazism emerged in Germany, and Fascism in Italy and Japan, she had to reconsider the notion of cultural relativism. Now she talked about cultural evaluation. In her words, "any society that is compatible with human advancements is a good one, but a society that works against basic human goals is anti-human and evil…"

This, no doubt, sounds reasonable, but only if one is clear about the terms "human advancements," "basic human goals," and "evil." In the current state of the world, as during the now defunct Cold War, different groups have (had) different interpretations of these terms. Thus it is not clear that her criterion has any scientific significance.

Ruth Benedict's switch from relativism in the evaluation of cultures to the need for some absolutist criteria resulted from putting together in a single bag various elements of culture. I would modify this by saying that every culture has its aesthetic, moral, and explanatory components: The first of these includes art, music, festival and poetry. On these there can be no absolutist judgments. On the moral components there could be absolutist criteria that each culture may adopt for itself, without imposing them on others. On the explanatory dimension of a culture, which is part of its scientific worldview, there are only two broad classes: the modern scientific and the ancient scientific, and both these may be found within any present-day culture.

From the World of Science:
JOHN COUCH ADAMS

There once was a young man who was gifted as much in mathematics as in classical languages. He mastered many branches of mathematics, studying by himself from textbooks. When he was a student at Cambridge, he received several first prizes in mathematics as well as in Greek. His name was John Couch Adams (born: 5 June 1819).

In 1841, it was reported that Uranus, the planet which had been discovered in the 1770s, was not moving in the expected elliptical orbit. Its mass had been calculated from its period of revolution. Some thought that the discrepancy was due to the non-universality or the inexactitude of the law of gravitation. Another suspicion was that there was perhaps another planet out there which was exerting its pull on Uranus, in addition to the gravitational force of the sun.

If the latter was the case, then in principle it should be possible to locate such a perturbing planet. This called for the solution of a set of ten equations with as many unknown parameters in them. It was a good challenge for anyone who was really good in computational mathematics.

Adams managed to solve the system of equations, which meant that he could roughly locate where that hitherto unrecognized planet would be in the scheme of the sun's system of planets. He was a young man of 25 at that time. After a few unsuccessful attempts, he finally presented his results to the astronomer royal Sir George Airy on 21 October 1845,. For some reason, Sir George had only some criticisms of the work, and he decided to ignore Adams' theoretical discovery of a so-called new planet, and did not undertake any telescopic search.

The French astronomer Leverrier (*vide* 11 March), had arrived at the same result, quite independently and almost simultaneously. He managed to have his results published and this happened on 23 September 1846. The new planet, which came to be called Neptune, was spotted through a telescope soon after this. The world of astronomy rejoiced. The public was excited. Leverrier, some 8 years senior to Adams, was appropriately recognized and honored. Adams wished very much that Airy had shown greater interest in his calculations.

Fortunately for Adams, the eminent astronomer Sir John Herschel spoke out and wrote about Adams' earlier contributions. Advocacy from people in power can be very helpful even in science. As a result, Adams too began getting more and more recognition. Nevertheless, Adams was so bitter about what had happened that when Queen Victoria offered him knighthood, he politely declined the honor. But he did accept the prestigious Copley medal which was presented to him by the Royal society.

One consequence of this simultaneous discovery was that there arose controversies between the French and the British as to who should get credit for the paper-prediction of Neptune. When it comes to credits in science, the universalistic scientific spirit tends to shrink to petty nationalist vainglory. Adams did not stoop to make his claims, perhaps because he was aware that as per accepted convention, credit goes to the one who publishes first.

The episode illustrates the fact that many people experience a sense of importance for themselves in the achievements of their compatriots, especially to the world at large. This is the national equivalent of parental pride about the successes of their children. This seldom happens in religion: not only because specific revelations are well-defined in place and personage, and no simultaneous revelations occur, but also because all who are affiliated with a religion accept the founder, and don't worry about his or her nationality.

June 6

From the World of Religion: YMCA

Many people in the modern world are beneficiaries of industry and technology, not only by their products, but also by the gainful employments they pro*vide*. Much more needs to be done for the safeguard and protection of people working in the lower rungs of industries. But if we look into the history of the industrial revolution in its early stages, we are appalled by living conditions of the workers in the 18th and 19th centuries. A number of novels of the period portray their pathetic plight.

Very young men were drawn away from their homes to work in factories or for laying railroad lines. They lived in shacks under very unhygienic conditions. After working hard for six days of the week, ten to twelve hours a day, a great many of the workers were drawn to alcohol, prostitutes, gambling, and the like. Some were tempted to increase their cash flow by thievery or beggary. The upper classes used the muscles of the lower classes to keep the factories functioning, and felt no moral obligation towards them.

But, as in all contexts of difficult human experiences, there always arise some who care for the suffering of others and see what they might do to make matters a little more bearable. So it was that 26 year old George Williams, a sales assistant in a draper's store, assembled a group of like-minded people at 112 Great Russell Street in London. The group explored ways to make life a little more meaningful to the laboring class. Given that for most normal people, meaninglessness in life results from spiritual vacuum, he initial goal of the group was to unite and direct "the efforts of Christian young men for the spiritual welfare of their fellow in the various departments of commercial life." With this in view, they formed a Christian association of young men on 6 June 1844, and appropriately called it Young Men's Christian Association, abbreviated as YMCA, or simply Y.

There are any number of instances in which science and technology have moved people away from religion and spirituality. But in this case, the sheer emptiness of mechanical existence prompted a search for meaningful religion. The YMCA was more than an association: It was a movement inspired by and based on the Christian faith. The goal was to study the Bible and to spread the word of God even among Christians who had moved away from their religion. It was also to bring together the diverse sects and factions of Christianity under one unifying spirit.

The idea spread fast, first within England where, in less than a decade, there arose some 25 branches and 30,000 members. Then it went to France, the United States, Australia, India, Canada and to other countries also. By 1854 there were almost 400 branches all over the world, with a total membership exceeding 30,000. In the U.S., in keeping with the standards of the time, there were separate YMCAs for African Americans: The founder, Anthony Bowen, was a freed slave. Needless to say, things have evolved considerably since those days. In 1866, the New York YMCA stated as its goal: "The improvement of the spiritual, mental, social and physical condition of young men." Today even non-Christians are members of the Y, and there is also a YWCA for women. As the organization grew, so did its activities: reading rooms, swimming pools, games, social service, assisting veterans. A not very widely known fact is that both volley-ball and basket-ball were invented by sports-leaders in YMCA in 1891 and 1895 respectively.

On the occasion of the 50th anniversary of the Y, its founder George Williams was made Sir George by Queen Victoria: the secular equivalent of canonization.

From the World of Science: REGIOMONTANUS

Paradigm shifts occur, whether in science or in religion, in slow and subtle ways. Sometimes one even loses track of the first seeds that eventually lead to the change.

Consider the Copernican Revolution: a shift from the geocentric to the heliocentric model of the universe. No doubt, the treatise of Copernicus [*vide* 19 February] is what instigated the new picture. But what were the influences on Copernicus himself that prompted him to reconsider a view that had held well for more than a thousand years?

This question takes us to outstanding astronomers of the 15th century: Johann Regiomontanus (born: 6 June 1436). His last name is the Latinized version of the place of his birth which, in German, means King's Mountain (Koeinigsberg). Regiomontanus was as much a Greek scholar as an astronomer: This was essential because the classic on the subject of astronomy was Ptolemy's work, entitled *Syntaxis*, whose Arab translations described the work as *The Greatest* (*Almagest*). Regiomontanus' close friend Peuerbach began a Latin translation, but died before he could finish it. Regiomontanus completed the work which was published under the title: *Epitome in Cl. Ptolemaei magnum compositionem* (1496). This was the first work on astronomy to be published in Europe.

This was more than a translation: It included commentaries, and it presented some of the more recent astronomical data. In other words, it was not simply a work of historical interest, but could be used for current astronomical research as well.

For example, Regiomontanus pointed out that as per the Ptolemaic system the Moon's apparent diameter must vary by a certain amount, whereas in actuality it does so to a much lesser degree. This was taken as an interesting, perhaps even ignorable, observation by most readers. But when the young Copernicus read this, it occurred to him that perhaps there was something very wrong with the Ptolemaic system.

Edward Rosen drew attention to a passing comment by Regiomantanus in a letter. This "portentious statement," as Rosen describes it, is the following: "The motion of the stars must vary a tiny bit on account of the motion of the earth." This was a revolutionary thought, not only in its implication of a moving earth, but in its suggestion that there would be detectable phenomena pertaining to stars as a result of the earth's own motion: an idea that was utilized by Friedrich Bessel in the 19th century in his estimate of stellar distances. Ironically, Regiomontanus didn't believe that the earth was spinning on its axis.

In this context, Rosen also reminded us that the letter may have been sent to Novara who regarded Regiomontanus as his teacher, and that Copernicus himself had studied under Novara. This seems highly probable, and indeed if it were so, the roots of the Copernican Revolution may be traced to some of the thoughts and writings of Regiomontanus. Equally, we also see again the role that scholars and historians play in elucidating and correcting normally accepted accounts of the past.

Regiomontanus was meticulous in avoiding typographical errors, and in being faithful to the original. Nor would he tolerate others who dared to engage in translations without a thorough grasp of the original language. Thus, he hurled a severe criticism of another author who published a Latin translation of Ptolemy's *Geography* on the grounds that the man lacked "an inadequate knowledge of Greek and of mathematics." Regiomontanus' works contributed to the introduction of Arab algebra and trigonometry into Europe, and his revised edition of the Alfonsine tables exposed the need for a calendar reform. Columbus had a copy of Regiomontanus' work when he set out on his voyage of discovery.

June 7

From the World of Religion: VESTALIA

In the centuries before Christianity had the effect of a paradigm shift on the Roman views of God and religion, there were many deities, male and female, doing many things to keep the world such as it is. Exciting tales were associated with these. The Romans had their festivities too when they regaled, often giving sacrifices, human at one time, but only animals later, to praise and propitiate the gods. Most of the gods were of Greek import. Like other religions, the Roman religion was also tarnished by superstition and magic. Most of all, the Romans had a highly systematized omen-mongering: the experts would predict what was going to happen from the direction of the flight of birds, for example.

Fire has been recognized since ancient times as an important element in living. Thus, many ancient cultures worshiped it in different ways. As the Hindus have Agni, the ancient Greeks had Hestia as goddess of fire in the hearth, and this became Vesta for the Romans. Vesta was worshiped as the one who protected home and hearth. Perhaps because it was not always easy to light a fire, a little flame was kept burning all the time, in the home and even in some public places. The Romans used to have a grand temple on the Palantine Hill where, as at the tomb of the Unknown Soldier in some countries, a perennial flame was kept alive. This sacred fire was maintained by a group of young girls who were known as the Vestal Virgins. Aside from having to be between six and ten years of age when they started, to be selected as a Vestal virgin, the girl had to be without any physical or mental blemish, both her parents had to be alive, and she should not be of slave birth. The Vestal Virgins often served for thirty years. Their responsibilities included bringing fresh water each day from a spring nearby to clean the floors of the place of worship. Thus vestals were the priestesses of Vesta.

In later times, the term came to mean any chaste woman with a pure heart. It is in this sense that Shakespeare wrote in *Venus and Adonis*:

Love-lacking vestals and self-loving nuns,
That on the earth would breed a scarcity
And barren dearth of daughters and of sons.

In ancient Rome, at the beginning of each year (*vide* 1 March) the fire at the altar used to be re-lit in the *Aedes Vastae*: House of Vesta, which was more sacred than any ordinary *templum*. It is a magnificent structure, standing proudly near the temple dedicated to the twin-stars of the constellation Geminii. It is believed that the fire in this temple was kept alive for almost four centuries after Christ.

On 7 June each year there was a whole week of festivities dedicated to this goddess. Called Vestalia, the celebrations concluded by mid-June. In Roman homes there were special dishes made with fish, and families sat around the household hearth for the formal dinner. The inner sanctum of the Vesta shrine was kept closed during the year. But on this day it was opened. Only women would come in, and as in Hindu temples, they would leave their sandals outside and walk in bare-footed. They brought offerings to Vesta.

Those days are gone for ever, for in these days which Roman lass will dedicate herself for thirty years of chastity and service to an ancient goddess, cleansing the place where no one worships any more! In less than four centuries the place and the practice of Vesta became obsolete, ancient, and meaningless. In a sense it is sad that all the magic and poetry of ancient beliefs wither away, or are promptly cleared up by another religious vision: the Christian. The least we can do is to preserve their memory in the recall.

From the World of Science: JAMES SIMPSON

Since ancient times, medical practitioners have been experimenting with drugs that render some part of the human body insensitive so that a surgical intervention could be made. In the 17th and 18th centuries it was found that the inhalation of certain gases or vapors, especially nitrous oxide and ether, made one temporarily lose consciousness altogether, and this was taken advantage of by dentists in extracting the teeth of their patients. This practice began in the United States in the first half of the 19th century and spread to England and elsewhere also.

At this time a surgeon in Scotland by the name of James Simpson (born: 7 June 1811) got very interested in the matter. He began a search for other substances which could be as effective as sulfuric ether or nitrous oxide. He discovered that chloroform was one such.

Simpson was also an obstetrician. And he had witnessed the groans and shrieks that are associated with childbirth. It occurred to him that chloroform could perhaps help women avoid the excruciating experience. But this raised some "ethical" questions: With dentistry or amputation, the situation was to correct an unnatural situation, to prevent a pain that was not part of being human. But childbirth, argued some highly ethical people, was a different matter. Since time immemorial, women had been delivering babies. There was some pain in the process, they granted. But was this not part of the larger scheme of things?

Had not the Creator ordained it that way? Was this not a punishment for the sin that Eve had prompted Adam to commit in the painless garden of Eden? Needless to say, these weighty arguments were presented by men who did not have the faintest notion of the experience of childbirth. None of them could have said what Margaret Sanger said so pithily: "She goes through the vale of death alone, each time a babe is born."

Simpson reminded the Bible-quoting clergy of Genesis (2:21-23): "And the Lord God caused a deep sleep to fall upon Adam, and he slept: and h took one of his ribs, and closed up the flesh instead thereof; and the rib, which the Lord had taken from man, made he a woman, and brought her unto the man." God may not have used chloroform in this first human birth, but the effect was the same, and Adam suffered no pain. So Simpson said that if anything chloroform should be called St. Anesthesia.

Then there was a physician in Liverpool who was outraged that Dr. Simpson would encourage such cowardly behavior, for what else was any effort to avoid pain! There was a matter of principle, he added: The doctor should not succumb to every demand of the patient. So he asked rhetorically, "Are we going to allow the patient to tell us what to do?" Other doctors, perhaps a little more rationally or to clothe their narrowness in enlightened garbs, expressed the fear that chloroform might be injurious to the mothers, with potential for paralysis and permanent brain damage.

At that time Britain was ruled by the great Victoria who, unlike the great Elizabeth, was not a Virgin Queen. And when she was about to have a baby, she called upon Dr. Simpson to attend to her, chloroform and all. This shocked, but also silenced the loud critics of anesthetics in childbirth. After all, if the Queen approved of something, it must have some intrinsic merit, or at least, it should not be attacked too vehemently. Every British mother was grateful to the Queen Mother.

With all that, the exclamation of Isodora Duncan is still valid: "It is simply absurd that (even) with (all) our modern science painless childbirth does not exist as a matter of course..."

June 8

From the World of Religion:
ANGLICAN CHURCH

All religious traditions have undergone schisms and sectarian divisions. These have resulted from a variety of causes: diverging doctrinal interpretations, assertion of power by different religious institutions, rival claims of who is the rightful inheritor of a tradition, etc. Each is a fascinating case study of its own.

Consider the Anglican Church, which in many ways subscribes to the fundamental doctrines of Catholicism. But, as its name suggests, it is an English Church, the other Catholic churches being Roman. Its origins go back to the 16th century, not long after the Reformation begun by Martin Luther. Here, the severance from papal authority was made by a very strong willed Henry VIII of England, known in history for his frequent divorces, multi-marriages, and the prompt beheading of those who displeased him.

According to one official version, the king had been challenging the authority of the pope of Rome over matters of state for a very long time, and his split from Rome wasn't much different from a similar independence that Byzantine had declared a few centuries earlier.

But it is also true that the pope had conferred upon Henry VIII the title of Defender of the Faith because of his attack on Luther whom he described as a venomous serpent for calling "the pope's authority tyrannous."

As years rolled by, the king's amorous inclinations moved away from his first wife Catherine, a few years older than himself, to whom he had been wedded forcibly by his father for political reasons. Catherine had lost all the charms she might have had in her spring-years. Henry was drawn to dark-eyed Anne Boleyn with whose sister he had also played. To get married to Ann Boleyn who was by now his constant companion, his marriage to Catherine had to be annulled, and this could be done only by a papal dispensation. This, Henry could not get, in spite of all his previous allegiance to the pope. Henry VIII had no choice but to ask the parliament to proclaim him the supreme ruler of England, with authority over the church. This would be an *Ecclesia Anglicana* (Anglican Church). According to some sources, the Anglican Church was born on 8 June 1534.

Think of the factors which led to the establishment of the Anglican Church: premature deaths of Catherine's male children and the attractiveness of Anne Boleyn in the eyes of Henry VIII: a remarkable instance of chaos theory in the human domain.

Out of that rebellious reaction to the pope's uncompromising attitude in granting permission to an impatient monarch to legalize his liaison with a woman of his fancy arose one of the most powerful branches of the Christianity: the Anglican Church. Like the Roman Catholic, it too had a geographically limiting name, and like the Roman Church again, it too spread far and wide: to the New World, to India, to Australia, and to Africa. It also became, again like the Roman Church, one of the wealthiest institutions in the world.

From it emerged the Book of Common prayer: authored by Cranmer, approved by parliament, simple in its formulation, beautiful in composition, pious in sentiment, fairly faithful to Catholic doctrines. But in its enforcement, the Anglican Church displayed the zeal that characterizes all true-believing defenders of the Faith: If you don't accept my version, you are fit for prison or worse. And more than a few succumbed to the punishment. The gradual shedding of monolithic theocracy in England, though it called for many struggles and sacrifices, gives one hope that similar enlightenment would come some day to societies and traditions which are still ailing under such bigotry.

From the World of Science:
GIAN DOMENICO CASSINI

Of the many astronomical discoveries of Galileo with his telescope, perhaps the most startling was that the planet Jupiter has its own satellites. Till then the earth was believed to be the only body with a moon. So the recognition of a Jovian satellite was somewhat like discovering life in another stellar system in our own times, since, as far as we know, life exists only here on earth.

The next step was to see if some further information could be drawn by careful observations of the satellites of Jupiter. This was done by Gian Domenico Cassini (born: 8 June 1625) who had been drawn to astronomy from a revulsion for astrology which never ceases to capture the imagination of people in every generation. From his patient observations of the shadow of the satellites on the planet, he could recognize the rotation of Jupiter: a remarkable achievement in itself. But he also calculated from his data that Jupiter spun around its axis once in about ten hours: a very high rate for such a large planet. Cassini constructed detailed tables of the motion of the satellites, and these proved to be very valuable for Olaf Roemer in estimating the speed of light. Ironically, Cassini did not believe that light traveled with a finite velocity. Cassini also estimated the period of rotation of Mars: here again he got a figure very close to the currently accepted value.

His fame spread to all scientific circles. So, when the Academy of Sciences was established in Paris, he was among the foreign scientists who were invited to become part of it. He left his native Italy to work in Paris for a limited period, but like people in our own times who come to the United States with similar intentions, he settled down in the country and took up citizenship there.

Cassini became an active and influential member of the French academy. From the observatory there, which he helped develop, he discovered in quick succession four satellites of Saturn. He studied Saturn's ring very closely and discovered that it is actually made up of two separate sections. He also suggested that they were perhaps made up of a very large number of discrete grains: an idea which was resuscitated in the 19th century and inspired other developments in physics.

Cassini was also involved in setting up an expedition from the Paris Academy to South America (1672–73) to make geodesic and astronomical observations. By noting the position of Mars from French Guyana and from Paris, he estimated the distance of Mars from the earth. This was the first instance of a scientific determination of the distance of a planet. Knowing this value, Cassini calculated the distance of the sun to be some 87 million miles from the earth: an impressive distance in those days; earlier guesses seldom exceeded 20 million miles. Cassini was not too much off the mark. Today we know that distance to be about 93 million miles.

With all that, Cassini was at best a reluctant Copernican. He even doubted Kepler's laws and tried to see if planetary orbits could be fitted into some curve other than the ellipse. He did not support the idea that the earth may be slightly flattened at the poles, believing staunchly that the earth was perfectly spherical. He was also a vigorous opponent of Newton's theory of gravitation.

We see from the life and accomplishments of Jean-Dominique Cassini (as he came to be called in France) that even scientists who make significant discoveries could be dead wrong on some matters. The general misperception still persists that when one is trained in science, one automatically becomes a clear thinker on very issue. Not necessarily.

June 9

From the World of Religion: EPHRAIM SYRUS

There was this impressionable youngster growing up in the home of a pagan priest in Nisibis when Constantine was king in the early part of the 4th century. He came under the influence of the bishop of the town, and moved away from the god Abnil whose idol the young man's father was worshipping ritualistically. At the age of 18 he took baptism and became a Christian. He wrote later in his life "I was born in the way of truth:Though my childhood was unaware of the greatness of the benefit, I knew it when trial came."

His name was Epharaem, and since he came from Syria he came to be known as Ephraem Syrus. He died on 9 June 373.

Long before the Arabs went on their conquering spree, the Persians did a similar thing, as did the Greek. When the city of Nisibis was besieged and taken by the Persians in 363, all the Christians were chased out. This was not an unusual practice in the Persian framework. Ephraem was among the many who had to move away, and he settled down in Edessa (Iraq).

By now his commitment to Christianity had become very intense. He spent his years as a hermit, living on very little, surviving on measly amounts of barley bread and some water to quench his thirst. One of his biographers described him as skinny and bald and sullen in face, seldom given to laughter. But then, it is difficult to be eating sparsely and indulge in a belly laugh.

Ephraem Syrus had an in-born gift for poetry and song, which he put to good use in composing some beautiful verses for the Lord in heptasyllabic and pentasyllabic meters. Many of these, all probably written in his native Syriac, were quickly translated into other regional languages like Coptic, Greek, and Ethiopian: which probably gave rise to the rumor that he learned some of these languages overnight.

The topics of Ephraem's poems ranged from the nativity of Christ to descriptions of heaven. But most religious writings also have something harsh and antagonistic about other groups. So Ephraem too had many harsh things to say against heretics, skeptics, and Jews. Aside from the fact that condemnation of opponents seems to add a measure of righteousness to one's own cause, Ephraem was living at a time when there were many heresies and skeptics and unbelievers who were propagating their unchristian and antichristian views everywhere. Indeed, Ephraem felt that some of the blasphemous ideas were superficially good. So he wrote:

I have chanced upon weeds, my brothers,
That wear the color of wheat,
To choke the good seed.

In the Carmina Nisibina he called upon "everyone everywhere to become one with God." In the same work we also read that the apostle Thomas died in India, and that his remains were brought to Edessa.

It has been said that it was because of Ephraem that the practice of singing hymns in worship services began in the Christian tradition. He was the one who made it part of it. Those who have been to church on a Sunday know that hymns add to the aesthetic dimension of the service, contribute to the meaningfulness of experience.

From the World of Science: GEORGE STEPHENSON

Railroad tracks crisscross the world in a good many countries in the world. Their comfort and quality range from modest and rickety carriages moving people and things over short distances to luxurious trains with sleeping cars and restaurants and baths and TV monitors. But when and how did all start?

There once was a lad who, as he grew up, did several things: He herded cows, labored in a coal mine, and became a manual laborer assisting a man running a steam engine. His father was a fireman whom he would help sometimes. He had attained the age of seventeen without entering school. So he could neither read nor write. His name was George Stephenson (born: 9 June 1781).

But he got interested in the steam engine and much wanted to read about it. So he started taking lessons in the evening, mastered the alphabet, and began to read. Now he got some good jobs, like clock cleaning and managing engines. He invented a safety lamp for mine-workers, independently of Humphrey Davy who had invented a very similar device at about the same time and was substantially rewarded for this.

Stephenson heard about Trevithick's locomotive (1804) which pulled 20 ton loads. But the cast-iron rails often broke under the weight. Stephenson worked on this, and made the first steam engine with wagons attached in which passengers could ride. The first Stockton-Darlington railroad was a 12 mile stretch. The wagons were like horse-buggies, some passengers were inside and some outside. This was in keeping with the caste-system of the times which kept the lower classes at a distance from the higher. When several wagons were introduced, and all could ride inside, first and second class compartments came into vogue. It continues to this day even in airlines.

Human beings have been moving from place to place since time immemorial, mainly on foot or on large mammals like horse, elephant, or camel. The elephant and the camel are slow, the horse fairly fast. In this context, what is interesting to recall is that in 1825 George Stephenson accomplished a first in humanity's history. His thirty-eight wagons transported people at a speed, sometimes reaching 16 miles an hour: unheard of till then. And goods were also put in a wagon. The potential was obviously enormous, both for human interactions and for trade. A major revolution had been initiated. Before the century was over, there would be railroads and trains in every continent of the globe.

However, while the railway was gradually becoming a new mode of transportation in the 1820s, it was also perceived as a cultural and economic threat. Until then, people moved between towns and villages in mostly by horse-drawn carriages, halting at inns on the way. This life-style had survived for many centuries. It pro*vide*d steady income for thousands of horse-breeders, inn-keepers, and coach-drivers. Private lands were encroached upon to build railroad tracks. The sound of the locomotives frightened birds, and their massive movements could hurt cows and sheep that wandered on the tracks. But, as with other innovations in human history, once it was unleashed it was difficult to arrest its growth. The reason was not just the sheer economic power of the people who were pushing it. It was rather the conveniences it gave and the job opportunities it pro*vide*d for an increasing number of people. And, of course, there was the wonder of it all. Even poets sang about it. Emily Dickinson wrote "I like to see it lap the miles", and Walt Whitman wrote an ode "To a Locomotive in Winter". So the old order changed, yielding place to new.

June 10

From the World of Religion: IMMANUEL VELIKOVSKY

Every traditional religion and culture has its myths and legends, sacred history and (what strike many as) highly improbable events. We, in the modern world, generally tend to interpret them in symbolic or metaphorical terms, and rarely see connections between the hallowed tales of different traditions.

The scientific, historical, archaeological researches from 18th century on have molded the modern mind in ways that simply cannot accommodate fantastic occurrences as part of natural phenomena. Claims by theologians, cultural patriots, and myth-mongers to the effect that the stories in the epics and scriptures do have factual bases are usually ignored, if not openly attacked, by the scientific establishment: often for good reason.

Now and again, some creative writer with scientific background publishes a book that speaks of *a physics of immortality* or *a new kind of science* to overthrow four hundred years of the enterprise. One such book was on the best-seller list in the 1950s. Its author was Immanuel Velikovsky (born: 10 June 1895). He wrote many books, but the one that launched him to international fame and notoriety was entitled *Worlds in Collision* (1950). Velikovsky described it as "a book of wars in the celestial sphere that took place in historical times." But it was not like a planetary collision or the bursting of a supernova that astronomers witnessed and wondered about. Rather, earthlings also participated in it. The learned author quoted from a variety of ancient sources ranging from sacred books to inscriptions, archaeological finds, paleontological material and more.

From the perspective of standard science, the book's thesis was so outrageous that when news of its impending publication circulated, some prestigious academics threatened the publisher with a boycott if he dared to bring it out. The publisher quietly passed the project on to one of his subsidiaries. Later, the book was even banned from some university libraries. Velikovsky quickly became a pariah in the scientific world, the equivalent of a heretic in the medieval ecclesiastical framework. No self-respecting scientist would nod agreement with him in public. Whether all this reflected the unflinching commitment of academics to freedom of expression and their profound convictions about the truth of it all, or whether it arose from their concern that pseudoscience, when nicely clothed, could pass for the genuine stuff among the unsophisticated masses, you may decide for yourself.

Velikovsky was undeterred. In 1956, he published another work: *Earth in Upheaval* in which he re-presented his idea on catastrophic events on a planetary scale. This time, he made no reference to myths and presented "stones and bones as the only *evi*dence." He held on to the view that a catastrophic event of mammoth proportion in which both Venus and Earth were involved brought about cultural and physical changes which altered human history and perception of events in major ways.

In the 1970s, Velikovsky's fortunes changed. He began receiving invitations from universities like Brown, Yale, Columbia, and Harvard. Now there is a journal named after him. For someone who was born in Vitebsk in Tsarist Russia, got medical degrees from Moscow and Montpellier, and wondered about parallels among ancient stories, it was no mean achievement to have authored a book that hit the top of the top ten, publishing without the pitfalls and perils of peer-reviews. But then most of his revelations are essentially *endopotent*: They make us feel something inside, without furnishing us with any tool to handle the external world.

From the World of Science: E. O. WILSON

Not many scientists write lucidly, sensitively, and beautifully for the general public. Among the thousands of people who devote their lives to science, there are a few who do that. An illustrious instance of this is Edward P. Wilson (born: 10 June 1929): a biologist of eminence who devoted many years to unraveling minute details about ants: of which almost a thousand species have been recognized. We worry about the growing human population, but seldom reflect on the fact there are a thousand trillion ants silently surviving on our planet along with us. Though fellow biologists recognized his finding that ants exchange chemical messages as a major discovery, E. O. Wilson's reputation shot up with the publication of his highly controversial *Sociobiology: The New Synthesis* (1975). Darwinian biology speaks of the evolution of the physiology and morphology of creatures by natural selection. Wilson argued that this is true of behavior also. What this means is that genes also affect behavior, and will be preferred if they are better fitted for the social environment. The generalization from ant to anthropos was not favorably received. The book provoked many uncomplimentary epithets because of its political and racial implications when applied to human beings. Racism and misogyny were imputed to the ant-watcher. Scientific generalizations about human nature and culture are not simply incomplete: they can be emotionally disturbing. Wilson's Marxist colleagues Richard Lewontin and Stephen Gould were among those who engaged in intellectual pugilism with Wilson. They did not pour water on his head like protesting students did at a meeting, but they were harsh. This was religion as much as science.

Wilson tried to clarify some of the misconceptions about his ideas in his book *On Human Nature* (1978), but this was not a revision of his thesis. Here he noted that "the intellect was not constructed to understand atoms or even to understand itself but to promote the survival of human genes." This is a profound observation, and explains why science is not the primary concern of the vast majority of *homo sapiens*. But it does not explain why religion is so, for at its core religion is the mind's struggle to understand itself. In his *Genes, Minds, and Cultures* (1981), which he wrote with his assistant, Wilson cast his ideas in a mathematical framework, and here he stated explicitly that for humankind "behavior is not explicit in the genes, and mind cannot be treated as a mere replica of behavioral traits." He also recognized the stupendous power of culture. Materialist-scientist that he was, he maintained that the genes held culture on a leash. In his imagery, if man represents the totality of genes and the dog represents culture, it is a very strong dog that can drag the man here and there, but still, it is man who controls the dog's meandering.

Consilience (1998) was another masterpiece in science writing: Here the role and relevance of the scientific method is presented. Gene culture, and coevolution are also discussed in the context of a penetrating synthesis of many disciplines.

Wilson's most recent book, *The Future of Life* (2002) is a timely warning about our future survival. There are countless life forms from bees and butterflies to fish and fowl that have been helpful to our own existence and nourishment. Our destruction of precious species, whether from greed, or ignorance, will boomerang. It is reassuring to hear him say that there is still hope, that an intelligent and informed perspective will make economics and ecology cooperate rather than be confrontational, and that the best in all religious ethics is in consonance with care for all creatures. This book must stir the thinking and action of people, ordinary citizens or leaders in various spheres.

June 11

From the World of Religion: JOHN BALL

It was part of the grand scheme of things in much of the ancient world: An upper class which owned land and labor, for which a working class toiled: building houses, cleaning homes, and serving lords and ladies with subservience. They tilled the soil, planted the seeds, and reaped the harvests for the rich. They rarely complained because they had been taught to believe this was how the great God had intended humans to live.

But rebellious spirits always find courage and power of expression to challenge social injustice. Such a one appeared in England in the 14th century when the aristocracy of Church and State lived in peace and plenty from the tithes and taxes of peasants in poverty. The name of this trouble-maker was John Ball (died 11 June 1381). He preached in ways worthy of a true religious leader who deeply cared for the common folk. His language was prescient of Marxist rabble-rousers of much-later centuries, and even of many voices that are rising in our present world of precarious economic imbalance.

"My good friends," he is said to have once exclaimed, "things cannot go on well in England, nor ever will until every thing shall be in common; when there shall be neither vassal nor lord, and all distinctions leveled; when the lords shall be no more masters than ourselves. How ill have they used us! And for what reason do they hold us in bondage?"

He went on to ask, and not just rhetorically, how there could be lords and serfs, masters and servants if all human beings were descended from Adam and Eve, as it says in the Bible. And he reminded the peasants of the ermine and fur that the privileged class enjoyed while the poor wore simple and tattered clothes. "They have wines, spices, and fine bread," he went on to complain, "when we have only rye and the refuse of the straw; and if we drink, it must be water."

John Ball used to preach to peasants at the market place after they came out of church on Sundays. With such words and reasoning he made the peasants aware of social injustice, causing legitimate worry to the establishment. The archbishop of Canterbury had John Ball thrown in prison at least three times, but each time he was released, he would resume with even great vigor, sometimes putting his thoughts into rhyming couplets like:
When Adam delved and Eve span
Who was then the gentleman?
Instigated by John Ball and others, the peasants of Kent went to King Richard II to redress their grievances. The king wasn't helpful. The mob marched to the Tower as Parisians were to go to Versailles 1400 years later, became unruly, and created much disturbance. They killed a lord or two, but the king and his forces quelled the rebellion. John Ball was brought to the angry King Richard and beheaded right in his presence.

Christ too preached fairness and compassion for the poor, and for this his followers venerate him. But when John Ball said pretty much the same thing, people who claimed to revere Christ called John a mad preacher, put him in prison and finally finished him off. One of the great puzzles in human history is the incompatibility between preaching and practice in the framework of any religion. Is it any surprise that many men and women of conscience have been turned away from traditional religion when they come to know about this fact?

The guardians of traditional religions have but two choices: Either transform the associated practice in more humane and enlightened ways, or keep the masses in a state of illiteracy and ignorance through the droning of holy verses.

From the World of Science: CHARLES FABRY

Even school children have heard of the ozone layer and of the holes that are being caused in by fluorochlorocarbons, etc. But the average educated person on the street—accountants, history professors, ministers, ophthalmologists, stock-brokers, and the like—may not know what exactly ozone is, and how from earth a layer of it was discovered in the upper realms of the sky, and if it has any relationship at all to life on earth.

To review these, we first recall that a molecule of oxygen consists of two atoms of oxygen. When oxygen is subjected to an electric current, the molecules split up into independent atoms, and new molecules with three atoms of oxygen are formed. Molecules with three atoms of oxygen have a bluish tinge and a sweet sort of smell. This is what ozone is: a triatomic *other form* (*allotropy*) of oxygen.

Ozone has many properties, but the following are relevant today: First, it can be converted into oxygen in the presence of chlorine atoms. Chlorine serves as a catalyst in the conversion: i.e. a chlorine atom can keep instigating the formation of three oxygen molecules from two ozone molecules. Secondly, ozone absorbs ultra-violet radiation.

There was a physicist by the name of Charles Fabry (born: 11 June 1867) who, along with a colleague neamed Perot, developed a very sophisticated optical instrument: an interferometer. The Fabry-Perot interferometer has two plane half-silvered glasses held parallel to each other, between which a series of multiple reflections occur before two rays undergoing different numbers of multiple reflections are made to interfere. Such interference produces clearly observable patterns. One can calculate many things from these patterns. With this instrument, they measured the velocity of light and verified the Doppler effect in a laboratory. These were impressive experimental accomplishments.

With his interferometer Fabry also made spectral analyses of light from the sun and the stars. In the course of his studies he discovered two important facts of enormous relevance to earth's environment: The first is that there is a layer of ozone enveloping the whole atmosphere of the earth. The second is that this ozone layer absorbs much of the ultraviolet radiation from the sun that falls on the earth.

In the later 1920s the world of technology introduced the so-called chlorofluorocarbons: a perfectly harmless (non-toxic) and chemically inactive substance in refrigeration. What was not realized is that this gas eventually rises up to the upper layers of the atmosphere where the ultraviolet radiation breaks it up, releasing free chlorine atoms. These chlorine atoms serve as catalysts for converting the ozone into oxygen. The end result is that the ozone in the upper atmosphere is being gradually depleted. A consequence of this is that less of the ultraviolet from the sun is absorbed, and more reaches the ground. This has negative impacts on our skin and eyes. It is believed that in some complex ways the ozone and the ultraviolet radiation were both involved in the genesis of terrestrial life.

When we look into the complex paths by which scientific discoveries are made we are able to see more clearly how the knowledge basis of science is fundamentally different from other modes by which one affirms how the phenomenal world comes about. Without fruitful conceptual frameworks, instruments, and measurements we could never have known about oxygen and ozone and chlorine and ultraviolet radiation. No "new kind of science", using only simple rules in computer programs, can put into *evide*nce all this. We also see in this episode the utter unpredictability of the long-range consequences of technological innovations. Chlorofluorocrbons served us well in our air-conditioning units and refrigeration. But they were also slowly sowing seeds of disaster.

June 12

From the World of Religion:
BUDDHA'S ASCENSION IN BHUTAN

Browsing through an old calendar I saw a marking to the effect that June 12 was Buddha's ascension in Bhutan. I doubt that this date is fixed, and I recall also that Bhutan used to be a pristine country, untouched for long by technology and TV, cozily ensconced in Himalayan seclusion, and blessed by the inner peace that comes from Buddha's teachings, yet joyous in its festivities, and colorful in its pagodas.

But what struck me was this notion of ascension: The Mahabharata speaks of the ascension of the Pandavas after the Battle of Kurukshetra. Moses is said to have made a prophesy of ascension of the whole of Israel. Christ and Mary are believed to have ascended to heaven. And the Prophet Mohammed had a dream to that effect also. Now Buddhists celebrating the ascension of Buddha. The idea of a superior personage being transported to the celestial world is consistent with capabilities of spiritual giants.

But there is also another version of Buddha's last days which can be read in the Buddhist *Suttas*. Here there is no mention of such a supernatural ascension. According to the account one finds here, when the great Buddha was an octogenarian, he started out on a journey to Kusinara. On the way, he rested in an orchard where he was received and fed by a goldsmith named Chunda. Soon, Buddha was back on his feet again. Next he halted for a dip in a river. But now the Enlightened One began to feel that the end was fast approaching. He summoned his disciple Ananda and asked him to assure Chunda that the two most precious things he remembered were the food he had received from Sujata after which he obtained his Enlightenment under the Bo tree, and the food he had just gotten from Chunda. What the Buddha meant was that there could be no enlightenment in the physical frame when the body is unnourished. Then he talked to Ananda about his own imminent demise, which brought tears to the disciple's eyes. Unable to bear the painful circumstance, Ananda moved away, but Buddha called him back and reminded him that sooner or later everyone must die. The physical body just can't last forever. All composite things must eventually dissolve. [This was one of the earliest formulations of the second law of thermodynamics.] We remember and revere the Buddha, not for his alleged miracles, but for such wisdom about the human condition, about the fleeting nature of life, and about how one needs to act in the face of the phenomenon of perishable existence.

By midnight, a visitor came to learn more from the teacher. Ananda told him that this was not a time for talking. The Buddha, frail and fainting, overheard this, asked the visitor to come in, answered some questions, and even counseled him. The event reminds us that the great ones serve others till the very last breath, for a life not dedicated to service is a wasteful existence. The service given by the greatest among us includes the sharing of knowledge, insight, meaning and positive values, as the Buddha did.

It is said that the Buddha then made this statement to his disciples: "When I have passed away and am no longer with you, do not think that the Buddha has left you, and is not still in your midst.... The Buddha has not left you." So the world was told that the Buddha was not the flesh and bones that made up that body, but the truth and spirit that were enshrined in it. It is this Buddha that has stayed with humanity all these centuries. So it has been with Krishna and Christ, with Moses and Mohammed. And when we speak of their ascension, we should mean, not the physical flight to a distant realm, but their elevation to universality and their accessibility to the entire world.

From the World of Science:
OLIVER JOSEPH LODGE

A matter of great interest and controversy in the world of physics by the close of the 19th century related to existence of a super-subtle medium pervading every stretch and nook and corner of it. It was the cosmic insubstantial analogue of the ocean where water pervades its whole. Physicists called it the *ether*. Just as giant fish and flimsy creatures move here and there through the vast waters of the sea, so stars and planets float through this ethereal ocean. One had to postulate the existence of such a medium to account for the propagation of light-waves across empty space, for waves were known to be disturbances, and something had to be disturbed.

Now, just as the water in the vicinity of a swimming salamander is disturbed, so the ether near moving planets must also be perturbed. Among the physicists who set out to detect such an ether-wind was Oliver Joseph Lodge (born: 12 June 1851). From his ingenious experiments with light interference, he established in 1893 that there was no such effect generated by the earth's motion. This more or less settled the question: there is no such thing as ether. Physics now took on a different turn.

Prior to this, Lodge had also experimented with electrical oscillations which generate electromagnetic waves: a necessary consequence of Maxwell's theory of electromagnetism. But, like J. C. Bose in India who did similar experiments, Lodge lost out the credit to Heinrich Hertz. As important as the generation of electromagnetic waves is their detection, and here Lodge made a substantial original contribution: He developed what he called the coherer. It was based on the observation that loose bits of metals tend to stick to one another when exposed to electromagnetic waves. Crude as it may seem from today's sophisticated devices, Lodge had created the first radio receiver. In 1894, in a public lecture at the Royal Institution, Lodge demonstrated how radio waves could be transmitted over a distance of almost 200 feet. His book on the subject, entitled *The Work of Heinrich Hertz and His Successors* (1894) contributed considerably to the development of the radio as a universal entity in human civilization.

There was another side to Oliver Lodge. He belonged to the group of physicists of the second half of the 19th century who were drawn to psychic phenomena. The group included the likes of Michael Faraday and William Crookes in England, Marie Curie and Charles Richer in France. These people took telepathy and communication with departed ones quite seriously. They participated in séances in dim light, using planchettes. The Ouija board owes its origin to these reputable scientists. Physicists that they were, they investigated the alleged spook-sponsored phenomena by means of experiments and data. They established the *Society for Psychical Research*, of which Oliver Lodge served as president at one time. They developed a theoretical framework to explain telepathic phenomena: that brains emitted waves of extremely short wavelengths, etc. Interest in these have never abated. Post-modernist calls for equal weight to every idea and world-view, loud proclamations of the limitations of modern science, and frequent reminders of the mess in which Cartesian-Galilean worldviews have landed us: all this promotes greater commitment to extra-scientific modes.

In the case of Oliver Lodge, a personal tragedy aggravated the matter. When he lost his son during the First World War, he was convinced he could communicate with the departed son through psychic means. This enabled him to cope with the bereavement, and to continue to live meaningfully for two more decades. The importance of belief systems lies as much in how they assist or hinder us in life as in their truth-content.

June 13

From the World of Religion: SAINT ANTHONY

In the first quarter of the 13th century, a group of Franciscan friars from Portugal went to Morocco to save the souls of Muslim heathens. The Moroccans were not onlynot persuaded, but they severed the heads of the evangelists: among these was St. Bernard. News of this brutality reached Coimbra in Portugal, along with their mutilated bodies. This touched the heart of an ardent Christian youth who had known the men at one time. He decided to join the Franciscan order himself so that he too could become a martyr in Morocco. His name was Fernando.

Now Fernando took on the name of Anthony, and determined to consecrate his life for Christ. As he insisted, Anthony was sent to North Africa. Soon after his arrival he became very sick, and was forced to take a boat back to Portugal. The boat was caught in a storm, and shipwrecked in Sicily. From there Anthony moved to a small monastery in Italy. On one occasion there was a solemn ceremony of hermits at which the main speaker did not show up because of illness. The person in charge asked for a volunteer to serve as a substitute, and when no one volunteered, he commanded Anthony to address the gathering. After some hesitation Anthony started to speak. As if by magic he broke into a most remarkable eloquence which kept the audience in awe and admiration.

News of the event quickly spread, and it reached the ears of St. Francis who immediately assigned Anthony the job of preaching the Gospel in every part of Italy. Anthony discharged this assignment exceedingly well. He was electrifying in his words, and people listened to him in rapt attention. He attacked unbelievers and heretics with the force of incisive words. He was ruthless in his criticism of the rich and the selfish who cared not for others. He was so popular there wasn't enough room in the churches for the crowds who came to hear him. They had to move into the open. They say that stores were closed and all activities stopped when Anthony came to sermonize. One of his biographers says, perhaps with some exaggeration, that tens of thousands of people used to come to listen to him. It is difficult to imagine "twenty to thirty thousand" people in an open ground listening, without any sound system, to a preacher on a Sunday afternoon, even from a raised platform. According to a legend, when he came to Padua to give (what was to be) his last sermon, there was great commotion in the very large crowds. But when he began his oration, everyone calmed down. The people were literally transformed and became good and caring and friendly and mutually helpful. Oh, the power of the spoken word! But for great speakers, the course of history would be different.

There are other interesting legends relating to the extraordinary preaching abilities of St. Anthony. One says, for example, that he even made fish listen to his sermon. Likewise, upon listening to him preach, a very hungry mule is said to have bowed in reverence to an altar. He is said to have had a vision of the Christ child.

Anthony lived a short, but fulfilling life, but it was not full. For he died on 13 June 1231 when was barely 35. He had an ecstatic smile on his face on that last day of his, and said he was seeing the Lord as he passed away. Thousands poured into the streets to mourn his death. The word spread that even after his body had decayed, his tongue stayed clear and alive, prompting St Bonaventure to say: "O blessed tongue, you have always praised the Lord and led others to praise him!" The following year, Anthony was canonized. Such was the life of St. Anthony of Padua: one of the most eloquent preachers in the Christian world.

From the World of Science: THOMAS YOUNG

It happens sometimes in science that two competing hypotheses explain a given set of observations equally well. The question then is: Which of the two is the correct one? This was taken up by the scientific investigators of the 17th century who said that there must be an *experimentum crucis* (crucial experiment) in such instances which would give victory to one or another of the rival hypotheses. This idea has been refined in the 20th century by philosophers of science like Pierre Duhem, Karl Potter, and Imre Lakatos.

Back in the 18th century every known phenomenon of light could be satisfactorily explained in terms of two diametrically different views as to the ultimate nature of light: One held that light consists of very small particles (corpuscles) whereas the other considered light to be made up of waves. Each view had its strengths, and each was open to some criticism also, but both were reasonably satisfactory in explaining the laws of reflection and refraction.

The question was resolved by the crucial experiments of Thomas Young (born: 13 June 1773). He was a child prodigy who began to read at the age of two, learned a dozen languages—including Syriac, Samaritan, Arabic, and Ethiopic—before fifteen, studied Newton and Lavoisier in Latin and French, did significant research on the eye by the time he was 20, and got a medical doctor's degree at 23 from Goettingen where he investigated the nature of sound and the human voice. In London he was not very successful as a physician, so he began to attend meetings of the Royal Society. He got interested in pure science, and began to see parallels in sound and light: the octaves and colors, and resuscitated the debate between the corpuscular and the wave theories of light. He discovered an important phenomenon that is known today as interference of light: a property that is exhibited by waves and only by waves. In other words, Young performed a crucial experiment by which it was firmly established that the corpuscular theory of light would have to be discarded, and that the wave theory was the only one that is satisfactory in accounting for the phenomenon of interference. By his experiments Young could also measure the incredibly small wavelengths of various colors of light. To this day, the experiment that Young performed in 1801 is a required exercise for all students of physics all over the world.

Young did other interesting work in physics: with the pendulum and with elasticity. But by the time he was forty, his early fascination for languages came back. He was drawn now to Egyptian hieroglyphics. He devoted himself to the decipherment of the Rosetta stone. He discovered that proper names were represented by ovals, and he succeeded in assigning phonetic values to the drawings on the stone. Young revealed the meaning behind directions of the bird flights, as also in the directions along which the animals were looking. This ancient slab of basalt on whose surface we find the scribbles of those distant days (196 B.C.E.) bears mute testimony to the thoughts and things that inspired the people of that civilization. It also served as a first bridge between them and us of the modern age. The Rosetta stone had been picked up by a French soldier when he came upon it accidentally in a town called Rosetta during Napoleon's Egyptian expedition in 1799. Today it is carefully preserved in the British Museum.

Creative people are seldom constrained by the boundaries of fields: And we see in Thomas Young an unusual mind that switched from exotic languages to sophisticated science, from abstract mathematics to precise experiments. Young clearly established the wave nature of light, and the phonetic nature of hieroglyphic patterns.

June 14

From the World of Religion:
INDEX AUCTORUM ET LIBRORUM PROHIBITORUM

We are all aware that the internet has opened the doors for the dissemination of knowledge and information. We know equally well that it has also opened up the possibility for spreading hate, misinformation, irrationality, non-science, and much more. A somewhat similar possibility arose when the printing press came into being. True, the Bible was the first that Gutenberg brought forth. But very quickly all kinds of other books were also emerging from the presses. Some of these were simply immoral, and others, more dangerously, were heretical. Something had to be done.

There were two ways of preventing the unleashing of books with potential for moral and spiritual corruption. The first was to require that all books, prior to being published, get the formal approval of the Church. So was instituted a decree called *De Impressione Librorum* by which an appropriate Church authority had to look into and give permission before it could be published. This would have served the purpose except that there were publishers in Protestant countries who brought out books without consulting Catholic authorities. So, in the spirit of *If-it-can't-be-suppressed-avoid-it*, Pope Paul IV issued an *Index auctorum et librorum prohibitorum*: Index of prohibited authors and books. The document included the names of 62 publishers of heretical books. The list of prohibited authors included quite a few obscure names. Even the Pope regarded the first Index to be too severe, and hence issued a milder version of it on 14 June 1559.

The practice of issuing an Index continued, so that revised list of prohibited books kept appearing periodically. The 1948 Index had as many as 4000 titles.

When a book was included in the Papal Index, in principle, a Roman Catholic (unless he belonged to the censoring committee) was simply not allowed to read or possess it. It is some consolation that, unlike in some other traditions, the pope did not issue a death warrant on the author of the book: no, not even in the 16th century.

It is sad and surprising to see the list of authors whose names entered the Papal Index. It included Rabelais, Montaigne, Descartes, La Fontaine, Pascal, Montesquieu, and Voltaire from France; Milton, Locke, Bishop Berkeley, Hume, Swift, and Defoe from England, etc. Incidentally, not only all the works of Luther and other Protestants, but also all translations of the Bible were put on the index.

From the perspective of many people in the 20th century, all this seems not only unnecessary and exaggerated, but also morally unacceptable. And yet, from the perspective of the upholders and defenders of a certain worldview it was natural to take such steps for protecting their fold from the horrible consequences which, deep in their hearts, they felt would ensue on those whose minds were poisoned by contrary views. Thus, what is important when we recall this matter is to see to it that we and our children never fall prey to an absoluteness that is blindly intolerant. To believe in a cause we deem right and moral, and even to accept a vision of God that is meaningful and appropriate to our needs and tradition, doesn't have to push us to a corner from where contrary perspectives become automatically evil and dangerous.

The Vatican woke up to this realization in 1966 (14 June) when it announced that the *Index librorum prohibitorum* was eliminated forthwith. Barring the victory of darker forces that are still lurking in many regions of the world, one could hope that similar awakening would dawn in the hearts and minds of leaders in all religious traditions. It would take a long time for this, but it is not an impossibility.

From the World of Science: ALOIS ALZEIMER

We think of ourselves in terms of our name and possessions, our body parts and intelligence, our achievements and capacities, but we define ourselves through memory. We are what we are only because we remember what we were. Every moment of experience is etched in the complexity of the brain. Memory is more than a book from our library or data from our computer which can be retrieved at will. It is more than our ability to recall an incident of yester year or a past encounter with this person or with that place. Memory is a subtle continuity in experience—periodically interrupted during sleep—that underlies our existence. Memory identifies us by illumining what we thought and said and did. History is the memory of a nation, culture springs from the collective memory of a people. As Cicero said, memory is the treasury and guardian of everything.

We may be robbed of many decades of self-identity if through accident or age, our brain is bereft of this, its most important function. Many people have suffered from partial or total memory loss. But it was only in 1907 that this was recognized as due to a specific degenerative disease of the brain. The physician was a clinical assistant at the *Irrenanstalt* (asylum) in Frankfurt. He was exploring the cortex of the human brain. One of his patients was a woman who reported frequent memory loss and a number of associated problems. He described the condition in the following words:

"The Disease begins insidiously with mild weakness, headaches, dizziness, and sleeplessness. Later, severe irritability and loss of memory develop. Patients complain bitterly of their symptoms. At times the Disease is associated with a sudden apoplectic attack followed by hemiplegia. Increasing loss of memory and progressive clouding of mind appear later, with sudden mood changes, fluctuating between mild euphoria and exaggerated hypchondriasis; terminally the Disease leads to stupor and child-like behavior. The features differ from patients with general paralysis by apparent calmness, by an organized behavior pattern, and by general ability of reasoning..."

The name of this investigator was Alois Alzheimer (born: 14 June 1864). He was a psychologist who had worked in neurology too. He had conducted research under Emil Kraepelin who gave due credit to his assistant by proposing to call the condition *Alzeimer's disease*. It is a condition to which seniors are more likely to fall victim. It is recognized as a degenerative and irreversible deterioration of the brain's remembering modes, caused by the death of brain cells, often resulting from age. With the neurologist Franz Nisl, Alzheimer published a six-volume treatise on the cerebral cortex.

Science pursues the causes and possible cures for this serious ailment. Alzheimer's is one of the few diseases which causes more suffering to those around than to the patient who ceases to recognize or respond to the words and gestures of affection from the tearful loving ones. Seeing a victim of Alzheimer's, we begin to realize that there is much more to each of us than flesh and bones, than body, limbs and face.

Those who work in the field simply tell us that keeping the brain regularly engaged and eating good portions of vegetables are among the preventive precautions against the onset of Alzeimer's, and they are also working on drugs to preserve and restore memory. It is sad when memory is taken away right at the stage in life when it can serve us best. Sadly, it is not always as it says in the old song:

When Time, who steals our years away shall steal our pleasure too,
The mem'ry of the past will stay, and half our joys renew.

June 15

From the World of Religion: MAGNA CARTA

Society and civilization rest on significant stories and symbols. Not everything we read in history books is true. Less perhaps by intention and more by repetition over the ages, many events and episodes have undergone transformations from their original version. These also occur to make later generations feel better and more cohesive.

So it was with the Great Charter which, as per the sacred history of tradition, was forced out of a cruel king and became the first document ever to affirm the rights of the common people. It was the beacon of democracy, we sometimes read, that shone with its British brilliance to lands far and near, and it declared the rights of the citizen. It was the foundation for the Mother of Parliaments. Maybe a trifle exaggerated, yet important.

King John was a ruthless tyrant who starved to death the families of rebellious barons, hanged young boys because their fathers had not been loyal, raided Ireland and Wales to bring them under his sway, and did other such horrible things. When the French king was preparing to invade England, John abjectly surrendered to the pope. He made himself a vassal of the Roman Church to which he promised to pay tributes. He won protection from Rome. For a fee, the king of France was barred from attacking England.

But now, John planned to invade France himself, to reclaim parts of it. His barons refused to participate in this, and his subjects resented the tax he wanted to levy for his war. Eventually, the barons assembled and decided to march together to demand the restitution of their rights and privileges, as per the pledges of Henry I, the previous king. In the document they prepared, they also wanted assurances to the effect that no one would be arrested and sent to prison without trial, no one would be tried for the same offense twice, trial should be by a jury of peers, etc. The statement "No freeman shall be captured or imprisoned...except by lawful judgment of his peers or by the law of the land" was a momentous declaration, as were some others in the document. These concessions were among the articles of the *Magna Carta* which King John signed at Runneymede on 15 June 1215.

Almost 750 years after this momentous event, they built a modest memorial at the spot where the signing ceremony is said to have taken place.

What is significant about the *Magna Carta* is the symbolic stature it attained. Its concessions were soon forgotten, and some of them, pertaining to individuals, became irrelevant with the passing of time, But more than three centuries later it was brought back to life, and slowly it came to symbolize liberty and democratic ideals. Not unlike the Ten Commandments or the Sermon on the Mount, it came to inspire people not so much by its contents, but by what it stood for. The *Magna Carta* became a reference point for a worldview, a symbolic affirmation of the rights of the people vis-à-vis the government, rule of law rather than rule by a king.

Many elements in history and scripture are there not so much to inform us of what happened as to inspire people as to our potential. They remind us of how our ancestors grappled with the problems and frustrations of life, how they sought ways to free themselves from external constraints. Every sacred book has incidents that recall conflict and struggle, and they are meant to convey the message that eventually it is the good who win, not the strong and the mighty. This has often been so in history too. Irrespective of the details of John's misdeeds and oppression, and the eagerness of the feudal lords to regain their privileges, it is the spirit of that *Magna Carta* that commands respect and reverence when we see its ancient illegible scribbles in a glass case at the museum.

From the World of Science:
LEONARDO FIBONACCI

We are all familiar with basic numbers. From the dial of some clocks we also know that numbers can be represented with the letters of the alphabet, as the Romans did. But no one in today's world would use V for 5 or IX for 9 in any computation. Yet that is exactly what they used to do in Europe until about the 13th century.

The change from the Roman to the Hindu (decimal) system of numerals was brought about by a slow and complex process in which Leonardo Fibonacci of Pisa (born: 15 [?] June 1175) played an important role.

Fibonacci is reckoned as the greatest mathematician of the period, indeed the first great mathematician in modern Western civilization. His father was an official in the Moorish (now Algerian) town of Bugia (Bougie). In those days, like other centers in the Arab world, Bugia was thriving in trade and scholarship.

[Later, the French got their candles from there which is why the French word for *candle* is *bougie*.]

Fibonacci thus had his first schooling in Arabic, his teachers were Moors, and he was so fascinated by their knowledge and the many manuscripts in their language that he traveled widely in that culturally rich and scientifically dynamic world, going to Syria and Egypt, and then on to Greece. In the course of these travels, he saw many different number systems, and also came upon the Arab translation of Hindu mathematics in which he encountered for the first time the decimal system. He was fascinated by it and declared it to be far better than any other he had seen. He also absorbed a lot more of value in the cultures he saw, and returned home to spread the knowledge and information that he had gathered in his travels

Thus it was that Fibonacci gained the credit for introducing the decimal system into Europe. His book entitled *Liber Abaci* (Book on the Abacus) was published in 1202, some 800 years ago. Here he correctly described the number system he was introducing as *nove figure indorum*: new figures from India. This was not just an equivalent mode of representation. Rather, this was one of the seeds from which modern mathematics was to blossom in Europe in the centuries to come. It was not unlike the introduction of some European languages in the non-Western world during the 19th century which revolutionized people's perspectives in major ways. In his book, Fibonacci discussed the fundamental operations of arithmetic, practical problems in business and mensuration, as well as, for the first time in Europe, the basic principles of algebra. He wrote other works on mathematics. Like many major breakthroughs in thought and vision, there was considerable opposition to its adoption. Not many professors even in the best universities could fully understand the contents of his books. As one historian of mathematics put it, "Leonardo's works were like a voice crying in the wilderness."

Fibonacci is known today for a sequence of numbers in which we start with two arbitrary numbers and construct others by adding the two preceding ones. Thus, for example, *2, 5, 7, 12, 19, 31, 50,....* is a Fibonacci sequence. A more commonly mentioned one is *1, 1, 2, 3, 5, 8, 13, 21, 34, 55, 89,...*, also known as the rabbit sequence. The sunflower arrangement of pods follows this.

It is said that he was led to this while studying the breeding habits of rabbits. What makes the Fibonacci sequence interesting is that it occurs in various contexts in the natural world. For example, in the arrangements of pods in the sunflower, the seeds are patterned in spiral curves. The number of clockwise spirals are successive terms in a Fibonacci sequence. The sequence also shows up in contexts in archeology, economics, etc. An entire technical journal is devoted to the subject today.

June 16

From the World of Religion: FATHER'S DAY

One of the basic differences between Abrahamic religions and some others, like the Hindu and the ancient Greek, is the relative importance given to father and mother in the two traditions. In the Hindu worldview mother comes first, and there is a mother-goddess too. But in the Abrahamic framework, God is Father, Father is the first of the trinity, and the Creator Allah has no female counterpart. Yet, in the Hindu tradition it is departed fathers (*pitr*) that one remembers, and in the Western tradition, it is Mother's Day that was first introduced as a day of remembrance.

Biologically, father is originator, and mother is nourishment-giver. This is why one looks upon God as Father. As Wordsworth exclaimed: "Father! To God himself we cannot give a holier name." And one speaks of Founding Fathers, and the Father of a Nation. Juvenal tells us that "Free Rome spoke of Cicero as the father of the country: *Roma patrem patriae Ciceronem libera dixit.* The word patriotism is related to the (Latin) word for father. Hindus refer to Brahma the Creator as *pitaamaha*: the Great Father.

Culturally, father has been the protector and provider, and mother has been care-taker and comforter. It is in this context (protector) that one prays that the kingdom of the Father who is in Heaven may come. It is in this sense (pro*vide*r) that one asks the Lord to "give us this day our daily bread." It is in this sense that Vishnu is worshipped as the sustainer and protector God in the Hindu tradition.

In most cultures, in the growing phase, father pro*vide*d guidance, and mother pro*vide*d values. In the Catholic tradition, one speaks of Church Fathers and refers to the pope as the Holy Father. Hindus invoke the Creator Brahma as *guru*: spiritual guide.

So, there are these roles that fathers play: the procreation of their children, but equally their protection from external dangers, and guiding them in their tender years that they may grow to be well-adjusted adults who can meet the challenges that they may confront in life. Not all paternal advice may be taken seriously, for, as one wit quipped, "The worst waste of breath, next to playing a saxophone, is advising a son." Yet, every father deems it his duty, at some time or other, to tell his offspring what exactly must be done and when.

The father-offspring relationship changes during the years between birth and youth, through the carefree days of childhood and the awkwardness of adolescence. Then there comes a time when it becomes stable and serene. It is then that most people begin to recognize any good they might have received from the man they have been calling dad: For this may range from very little to immense strength and enrichment.

Sonara Smart had been raised by her father, since she lost her mother at an early age. So, when she listened to a Mother's Day sermon at her church in Spokane, WA, back in 1909, it occurred to her that a Father's Day would also be in order. The very next year the first Father's Day was observed in Spokane. In 1924 the third Sunday in June was designated as Father's Day for the whole nation with presidential approval. Now it has spread to several other countries as well.

Father's Day fell on 16 June in 2002. There is much truth in Alexander Pope's lines:

We think our fathers fools, so wise we grow;

Our wiser sons, no doubt, will think us so.

But on this day at least, it has become customary for most children to think fondly of their fathers. Therein perhaps lies the value of such celebrations.

From the World of Science:
BARBARA McCLINTOCK

Poets and philosophers have reflected on aging, and we have come to accept that sooner or later we all must go. But we would still like to know what exactly is causing this gradual move to the geriatric phase. Sure we can wear toupees and rub off the wrinkles with plastic surgery, but these don't arrest whatever is going on inside.

This whatever-is-going-on-inside is what some geneticists investigate, and they have arrived at a reasonable understanding of the source of senescence: as the *olding* process is called in Latinized jargon. Very simply, many of the chromosomes in our cells are gradually being nipped away with the march of time. In technical terms, our *telomeres* keep getting shorter and shorter. Telomeres are specialized DNA-protein complexes at the tip of the chromosomes. Fortunately, though there is a drastic reduction in the telomere, we can afford to carry on without them, but the cells stop dividing. Eventually, things get very bad, the cells can't do even their minimum, and it's all over for good.

One of the scientists who worked on these gruesome details pertaining to our march towards physical termination, indeed one who made fundamental discoveries about telomeres, was Barbara McClintock (born: 16 June 1902).

Normally, we consider seeds and grains in terms of their appearance, taste, and nutritive value. But biologists also look into other aspects, not so directly perceptible. For example, what happens when corn is irradiated with X-rays? This was investigated by Lewis Stadler at the University of Missouri. He sent McClintock samples of maize exposed to X-rays. She examined these under a microscope and discovered that some of the chromosomes had formed loop-like structures. She called them *ring-chromosomes*. She found out that the effect of the X-rays was to break up the chromosomes, and that the broken ends re-connect to form the rings. From these observations she pursued the idea of the *telomere* at the tip of the chromosome which ordinarily assure its stability. She was the first to suggest that genes can be transposed on and between chromosomes. The idea was contrary to the then current paradigm. More than two decades later, using molecular techniques, the hypothesis was confirmed to be correct. Today, gene transposition has become a key idea in understanding evolution, It is one of the methods by which mutations occur in natural selection. About 30% of the human genome is transposable.

One may wonder why chromosomes let their tips degenerate and expose themselves to cancer, aging, etc. Some geneticists try to explain this suicidal behavior of chromosomes as resulting from a perennial struggle that exists between individual cells on the one hand and the whole body on the other.

McClintock also studied plants from Central and South America and became a pioneer in ethnobotany.

Barbara McClintock was recognized for her work with many prestigious honors, including election to the National Academy of Sciences (third woman to be so elected), the MacArthur Foundation Award and the Nobel Prize in 1983. She was 81 when she received it. She was elected president of the Genetics Society of America. She was respected for her professionalism, versatility, sense of humor, and high standards when it came to student work. She was described as a premier cytogeneticist.

It has been said that McClintock was initially more interested in meteorology than in maize. But when this 1927 Cornell Ph.D. got into the field of plant genetics, she explored it with thoroughness and intelligence. She succeeded very well in her discipline, but she was the kind who would have done equally well in any other field or profession also.

June 17

From the World of Religion: JOHN WESLEY

There was a young preacher in Oxford in the 1720s who felt that there was more to religion than attending Sunday services. His name was John Wesley (born: 17 June 1703) He formed with some students a spiritual fellowship. They prayed and studied the Bible in a methodical manner. This seemed a strange practice to some observers who therefore referred to the members of this group as *methodists*. This did not offend Wesley. He accepted and adopted the appellation for his group. So began the Methodist movement which has spread to many regions of the world, near and very far from Oxford, England.

Wesley was a sincere Christian who felt the holiness of his religion deep in his core. He began as a preacher in the Church of England at a time when not many were taking religion seriously. He was convinced that there is a profound difference between claiming to be godly and the experience of true godliness within. He emphasized the direct interaction between the individual and the Holy Spirit. This was interpreted by some to undervalue the role of the (intermediary) church. He was very much a puritan at heart, believed in miracles and witchcraft. He rejected reason in the religious context. Wesley and his supporters were made to feel unwelcome by the Anglical establishment. So they took to preaching in the open, and this became a fairly common practice among Methodists. Wesley also served the poor and the needy.

In 1735, he crossed the Atlantic to Georgia to spread his version of the Gospel among Amerindians. He was turned off by the Indians. He translated beautiful hymns from German and Spanish, but his introduction of hymns which were not officially sanctioned by the Church into worship services was not appreciated by many people.

He returned to England, and continued preaching. He was a supreme example of a man of deep faith. It is said that he had an intense experience once at a meeting where he heard a passage from Martin Luther. There, in his own words, "I felt I did trust in Christ, Christ alone, for salvation; and an assurance was given me that he had taken away my sins, even mine, and saved me from the law of sin and death."

On an average, he gave at least two sermons a day. Some of these would incite the listeners to hysterical response. Even in those days, many years before cars and planes, he traveled some 5000 miles a year, propagating the Methodist vision of Christianity.

Wesley was born in the first decade of the 18th century, and he died in its last decade. On the day of his death, he wrote to Wilberforce to continue the fight against slave-trade. He was enormously successful in spreading his message in the New World as in the old, indeed in the revival of heart-felt Christianity throughout the English-speaking world.

All major religions have split into divisions and subdivisions with the passing of time. Methodism started as a break from the Anglican Church, and as it spread, it too splintered into subdivisions: there are more than a dozen Methodist denominations within the United States alone, bearing such names as Wesleyan Methodists, Primitive Methodists, United Methodists, and Congregational Methodists.

The reason for a split may or may not be doctrinal. In the Methodist Conference of 1844, a southern bishop happened to own slaves: a serious impediment to being a bishop. He was asked to give up his office by some, but this was objected to by people from southern states because such a move would make it difficult for them to maintain the Methodist movement in the South. They decided to split the Methodist Episcopal Church into two wings: in one, slaveholders could be bishops.

From the World of Science: WILLIAM CROOKES

Two essential features of the scientific enterprise are careful observation and efforts to explain in terms of principles and entities that may not be as directly observable. Every bit of knowledge that science has brought to humanity is the result of taking these two steps with respect the countless aspects of the phenomenal world. Whereas the first step is straightforward—which is not to say it is always easy—the second requires imagination and speculation, and may not always lead to correct views of the unseen. Among those who contributed to both modes of scientific investigation was William Crookes (born: 17 June 1832), very successful in the first, not quite so in the second.

Crookes will be remembered, among other things, as the discoverer of the element thallium whose existence he suspected from a spectroscopic analysis of a substance left in the manufacture of sulfuric acid. He observed a bright green line which had not been tabulated in the spectra of any of the known elements. Since this came as an offshoot of something else he gave it the name from the Greek word *thallos* (green shoot). The element has found all sorts of practical applications, including as an ingredient in rat-poisoning. It recent years it has been detected in some stars.

Meticulous measurer that he was, Crookes weighed a substance in vacuum, and at various temperatures, getting different values. He was convinced that this was due to some force exerted by radiation. To investigate this further, he invented the radiometer in which four vanes are attached to a vertical rod in an evacuated glass bulb. One side of the vanes is coated black and the other is silvery bright. The vanes turn like a windmill when placed in sunlight. This device has become a toy sold in science museums. A number of conflicting and mistaken theories were presented to explain its functioning, such a radiation pressure, molecular bombardment, etc. Actually, the observed effect is due to tangential forces at the edges of the vanes where warmer gases from one side tend to move towards the cooler gases on the other (*thermal creep*).

Crookes' most significant contribution came from his study of electrical effects on gas in glass tubes in a near-vacuum state. He thought these were electrically charged molecules. "In studying the Fourth state of Matter," he wrote, "we seem at length to have within our grasp and obedient to our control the little indivisible particles which with good warrant are supposed to constitute the physical basis of the Universe." His work with high vacuum tubes in which electrical potential was maintained made possible the discovery of two foundational elements of 20th century physics: X-rays and the electron. From a systematic exploration of near-nothingness in a glass tube arose our knowledge of some of the subtler aspects of the physical world.

Crookes was interested in the impacts of science on society. He feared that while human population was increasing, food production was not keeping up with the pace. He warned that unless new agricultural methods were introduced the world would be face starvation. He strongly recommended the use of disinfectants and fertilizers.

Crookes lived in the heyday of spiritualism. Initially skeptical about mediums and conversations with the departed, he was soon persuaded that such matters were for real. He spent at least thirty years of his life participating in spooky séances, and he spoke and wrote about them openly. In one instance he went so far as to give full credence to a claim by someone that a phantom by the name of Katie King had been materialized. Crookes proved that one can be a physicist and still believe in ghosts. This is embarrassing only if one ignores the complexity of the human psyche.

June 18

From the World of Religion: IBN SINA

There is no culture or civilization where there have not been men and women who have indulged in abstract thought, in speculation about the unknown, and in pronouncing on the nature of reality. While the vast majority of people are engaged in the production of food and attending to other matters related to survival needs, the abstract thinkers and metaphysicians produce ideas which are often of little relevance to our day-to-day needs but which, somehow, add to the experience and stature of civilization as a whole.

Many metaphysicians were both theologians and scientists in the ancient world. They were interpreters of ancient and current wisdom, scriptural and secular.

Ibn Sina (born: 18 June?) was an eminent personage who enriched classical Arab civilization. Known in the English-speaking world as Avicenna, he was among the foremost interpreters of Aristotle. He is said to have displayed extraordinary mental powers even as a lad. When he was barely 10, he could recite by rote the entire Holy Qu'ran. They say he was a physician at 16, and by the time he was 21, he authored a treatise on medicine. The work was known as *Qanun*: the Canon which was a virtual encyclopedia of medicine. It served as a standard text for a very long time, both in the Islamic world and in Europe which was awakening under Arab intellectual stimulus

Avicenna classified philosophy into a lower class which consisted of knowledge about the material world (basically physics), a middle class which dealt with numbers and geometry (mathematics), and a superior class which concentrated on metaphysics, theology, and God. [Similar categorizations of knowledge were done in ancient India also.] Indeed these were the three factors at the root of the world: matter, form and existence. Like other metaphysicians, he talked about the existence of God, about God as the origin of the world as also of all ideas. God, he maintained, was pure existence, devoid of form and matter. [Hindu thinkers had a very similar notion of God as *satt*.] God's existence was necessary for the emergence of the world. Then she spoke of practical philosophy which is concerned with the day-to-day aspects of living. Such, for instance, are ethics, economics, and politics. Avicenna also examined why ideas are universal, that is, what makes all human minds perceive the world in the same ways.

He expounded on Aristotle and his commentators. He wrote on logic. To a large extent, he echoed the ideas of Aristotle. He maintained that motion is never permanent here on earth. He stated that unlike material substances, motion is something that is increasing or decreasing all the time. Hence, he argued perceptively, motion may be quantified. A state of rest, he said, does not imply there is no motion at all, but simply that motion is potential. He also talked about voluntary and involuntary motion.

This towering figure in Islamic philosophy was among those who argued for compatibility between science and religion. He saw them as parallel visions of Truth. For him, religion was a dramatization of higher truths, a symbolic way of communicating the higher truths to the masses. He gave an interpretation of revelation in terms of the unusual capacity of certain individuals to go beyond the normal modes of understanding and arrive at a total vision of Reality.

Avicenna may not have propounded new things, but he systematized a great many ideas with intelligence, clarity, and wisdom. This was not looked upon very kindly by Islamic orthodoxy which considered him dangerous. He was therefore vehemently attacked for his views. But Roger Bacon regarded him as one of the greatest thinkers of all time.

From the World of Science: WILLIAM LASSEL

Astronomy is one of the few fields of science where one can still work in isolation, although, when it comes to sophisticated observations, it is much better to be associated with an established observatory. But, even in the 19th century, some people who were attracted to the stars, built their own telescopes, even carried them here and there, for nocturnal investigations.

One such person was William Lassel (born: 18 June 1799). Strange as it may sound, he was initially interested in brewery, and made lots of money in the business. However, at one point, his interest turned astronomy. He decided to build a couple of large reflecting telescopes for his studies, and was the first to use speculum metal (highly polished metal which serves as a mirror) for this. His equatorial mounting was one of the first of its kind, and it served as a model for many others.

Equipped thus, Lassel began to explore the heavens. A hot news in astronomy in those days was the discovery of Neptune. So Lassel turned his telescope towards this brand "new" planet. And 10 October 1846, he spotted the first of Neptune's 8 moons. It was named Triton, after the son of Poseidon (Neptune) of Greek mythology. Today we know that Triton is air-freezing cold, with nitrogen crystals on its surface where a thermometer would read—235 degrees celsius. It is spinning in a direction opposite that of Neptune. This is an exceptional mode for any satellite in the solar system.

Saturn is always nice to watch, with its ring and all. And as he looked at it systematically from his private observatory not far from Liverpool, he discovered yet another satellite of that planet: the 16th at the time. Another astronomer across the Atlantic had also discovered it at about the same time in 1848. This tiny chunk of rough rock has been named Hyperion, after one of the Titans in Greek mythology.

Lassel could never have imagined that a space-probe (Voyager 2) from earth would take pictures of Hyperion and Triton in the 1980s, and transmit them back to earthlings. Who can predict what our descendents will be doing a hundred years from now!

In 1851 Lassel discovered a small satellite of Uranus, pock-marked like the moon. It has been named Umbriel. Mordern pictures show a peculiar glow near its pole. Astronomers call it the fluorescent cheerio.

In the same year he also spotted another small satellite of Uranus. It has been named Ariel. Its surface, as shown in photographs, reveals many craters like the surface of the moon. Astronomers suspect ammonia and methane on it.

These names were taken from Alexander Pope's *Rape of the Lock* where we read:

For, that sad moment, when the Sylphs withdrew,
And Ariel weeping from Belind aflew,
Umbriel, a dusky, melancholy sprite,
As ever sullied the fair face of light,
Down to the central earth, his proper scene,
Repair'd to search the gloomy cave of Spleen.

Lassel became quite famous as a result of these discoveries. When Queen Victoria visited Liverpool in 1851 Lassell was the only local notable whom she wanted to meet.

In the 1850s Lassel took a trip to Malta, hoping to find clearer skies in the southern regions. He hoped to discover more satellites. In this he wasn't successful, but he managed to identify some 600 new nebulas, which was more than a modest achievement. Countless workers plod through every facet of perceived reality to create science.

June 19

From the World of Religion: BLAISE PASCAL

In history there are a few illustrious names which shine is science as also in religious thought. Blaise Pascal (born: 19 June 1623) is one of them.

He was precocious in his grasp of mathematics. He experimented with atmospheric pressure and contributed to hydrostatics. Between the ages of 25 and 30, he indulged in some passing pleasures, which included a young woman who inspired him to a discourse on the passions of love. Pascal's sister admonished him to keep away from excesses. And he did.

When he was 31, Pascal had a near-death experience. He barely missed being plunged into the Seine river when the horses pulling his carriage went berserk. During a brief state of unconsciousness, Pascal had a mystical experience which drew him closer to God, and he prayed that he would "never be separated from Him." Pascal was not the first to have discovered God during or immediately after a frightening experience.

Then he got involved with a religious group (the Jansenists), one of whose leaders managed to win him over to their theology. Pascal preferred the God-had-ordained-it-so vision to the freewill-doctrine of the Jesuits. When a public debate arose as to whether Jansenist thinkers should be booted out of the Sorbonne, Pascal decided to write a series of anonymous letters to a friend down south about the controversy. The letters were persuasively pro-Jansenist, and anti-Jesuit. They even challenged the infallibility of the pope. Scholars of French literature have extolled the literary quality of this work as among the best in the language.

The Jansenists also convinced Pascal that science was really superficial knowledge, constrained by the limitations of our faculties of perception, and that true knowledge could be had only through faith, by which one meant unquestioning adherence to the Jansenist version of Christianity. The great Pascal, keen and mathematically inclined thinker though he was, fell for this science-cannot-answer-the-ultimate-questions mind-set which has driven many creative minds away from the only enterprise that gives non-absolute, but coherent answers to a thousand questions that are not related to the ultimate.

Pascal also suffered from chronic ill-health, but instead of sulking or becoming downright unpleasant to people around, he began to philosophize. Thus emerged his great thoughts, the *Pensées* (Thoughts) for which he will always be remembered. During Pascal's time, modern science was in its youthful vigor, harvesting success after success in astronomy, physics, mathematics, and more.

As a consequence, religious faith was dwindling, and the number of materialists and freethinkers was growing. Part of Pascal's goal was to bring out the reasonableness of Christianity. Instead of doing this in a systematic way in a treatise, he merely scribbled his thoughts at random. Pascal considered two types of skeptics: Those who recognized their skepticism as a kind of mental ailment, of which they needed to be cured, for whom he had some sympathy; and the doubters who don't even feel sorry for their state of mind and don't seek ways to be redeemed. Pascal had no sympathy for this second group. He brought all his gift for writing and clarity of thought his Pensées.

Pascal's *Pensées* contains disconnected gems of pithy thoughts such as:

Man is but a reed, the most feeble thing in nature, but he is a thinking reed.

The heart has its reasons that reason doesn't know.

The eternal silence of infinite space frightens me.

Pascal was precocious in mathematics. At the age of fourteen he participated in weekly gatherings of French mathematicians from which the French Academy of Science arose in 1666. His essay on conic sections, written when he was sixteen, was shown to Descartes who could not believe that it was the work of a boy and thought it must be that of his father. Pascal invented the first calculating machine when he was eighteen. He was one of the mathematicians of the period who laid the foundations of probability.

From the World of Science:
FRIEDRICH SERTUERNER

There can be no life without the pain and pleasure. Normally they pass, and their intensity is bearable. But sometimes the pain persists, and its intensity becomes intolerable. Under such circumstances we take recourse to pain-killing drugs. We should be grateful for such drugs, for after a limit, life with pain becomes unworthy of continuation. An extremely potent drug that has been useful in this context is morphine.

Like the three monotheistic religions, opium had their origin in the Middle East. The delirious effects of this drug were relished by the people, and the drug spread all over the world. The Greeks got it, Alexander introduced it into India, the Portuguese and the Dutch spread it in China. Gradually inducing drug addiction among a whole people is a terrible thing to do, but nations have done that, often consciously. Much of the misery we experience today in this context is a slow historical repercussion of past behavior.

It had been known for a long time that opium is, among other things, a soporific. Linnaeus called it *Papaver somniferum*.

In the first decade of the 19th century, there was a chemist who wanted to find out what component of opium caused one to sleep. His name was Friedrich Sertuerner (born: 19 June 1783). In the process, in 1806 he isolated what he called *morpheus*, after the Greek god of dreams. He recognized that this was not an acid. The general view then was that only acids were active in plant materials. Sertuerner had thus isolated the first vegetable alkali. This was the starting point of the very rich field of alkaloid chemistry.

But Sertuerner's work was ignored for at least a decade, largely because he was not in the mainstream of science. He persisted and re-published his results.

When news got out, writers and poets generously imbibed opium, and began to extoll its virtues just as the gurus of LSD were to do in the next century. So we read De Quincy exclaim: "I took it, and in an hour, Oh Heavens! What a revulsion! What an upheaving, from its lowest depths, of the inner spirit! What an apocalypse of the world within me. What had opened before me—an abyss of divine enjoyment suddenly revealed. Here was a panacea for all human woes. Here was the secret of happiness, about which philosophers had disputed for so many ages, at once discovered." And Keats wrote an *Ode on Indolence* in which he said,

The blissful cloud of summer-indolence
Benumb'd my eyes; my pulse grew less and less;
Pain had no string, and pleasure's wreath no flower:
O, why did ye not melt, and leave my sense
Unhaunted quite of all but-nothingness?

The pain-relieving property of morphine was quickly recognized, as also its sleep-inducing nature. For a long time morphine was one of the most potent anodynes in the physician's arsenal. It used to be administered for a variety of physical conditions: severe bronchitis, asthma, pain associated with kidney stones, etc.

On the one hand, Sertuerner was a good experimental pharmaceutical chemist. On the other hand, he was also given to free speculation on many matters, and coined words which did not always have an empirical counterpart. Thus he spoke of fire oxide, and of an element that was responsible for life which he called *zoon*.

Sertuener's imaginative notions were not always fruitless. He was one of the first to suspect and declare that cholera could well be caused by a micro-organism. This was before the germ theory of diseases emerged.

June 20

From the World of Religion:
DAY OF CARRIDWEN

There is an ancient Celtic legend which says there once was a land beneath the waves where the dark Morfan was born. They also called him Afagddu, for he was ugly to look at. According to one version of the story, his mother was the mysterious Cerridwen who possessed magical resources. She became worried that her son who was so ugly would have difficulty coping with life in the world. So she decided to bestow upon him unusual powers with which he could confront all difficulties.

With this in her mind, Cerridwen concocted a magical brew in a cauldron. After all, Cerridwen had wisdom and prophetic powers. She was the goddess of fertility, and she could also change the shapes of things. She observed the sun and the moon and the stars to time the preparation of the potion, for astral and planetary influences were needed for it to work. She put the appropriate ingredients in the brew. She had a blind man attend to the fire and a lad called Gwion to stir the liquid. Then there were nine women with occult powers who breathed periodically into it while it boiled day in and day out, and this added to its strange powers.

It took more than a year for the potion to be ready. By then Cerridwen was very tired, and she fell briefly asleep.

When she had gone to rest, the lad Gwion, who was stirring the liquid shoved Morfan to a side, and imbibed three drops of the magical brew himself. Thereupon the brew became wild, it ripped the cauldron with a thundering noise, and poured out on the ground. The noise woke up mother Cerridwen. She discovered what had happened and rushed to catch the offending Gwion.

But by now Gwion had acquired the power to metamorphose. So he became a hare and ran away swiftly. Cerridwen transformed herself into a greyhound and went on hot pursuit. Close to a river, Gwion became a fish and slipped away, but Cerridwen became an otter. Then he became a bird, and she, another bird.

Gwion saw a wheat field below, and he plunged there and became a grain of wheat. She became a black hen and managed to spot the particular grain which she picked up and swallowed. She said she would destroy Gwion when he would be born to her.

In nine months, Gwion was born of her as a beautiful child, but now Cerridwen did not have the heart to kill him. She encased him comfortably and left him in the sea to the care of the gods.

Some people affiliated with the Celtic Pagan tradition observe 20 June as the Day of Cerridwen. They burn a herb, which is said to have a favorite of that goddess, in little cauldrons to remember her. They tie green ribbons to tress and light green candles in front of the altar of Cerridwen.

Not many beyond the small group of Pagans may have even heard of this or other gods and goddesses that the group takes as seriously as the better known mythic figures of other traditions. The Cerridwen legend might strike a Christian as a weird tale, just as the story of archangel Gabriel delivering messages from Allah might sound to a Celtic Pagan, or as the story of Krishna might sound to one from the Judaic tradition, and so on. All we know is that the cultures of the human family have created an endless variety of myths which they have found to be contextually meaningful. Some of these have gained greater numbers of adherents and have lasted for greater spans of time than others. But it is perhaps naïve to declare that ours is history and theirs is mythology.

From the World of Science: ROGER BACON

Among the many medieval thinkers who were influenced by Arab writers was Roger Bacon (?20 June 1220). Indeed, he was deeply learned in the works of Arab scholars. He was generous in recognizing his indebtedness to them. He regarded Avicenna as one the greatest thinkers of all times. In astronomy, he discussed ibn al-Haytham's solid-sphere model of Ptolemic astronomy. In optics, he was inspired by Alhazan. Bacon's writings helped propagate the theories of this Arab scholar. Even though he declared that "all truth is rooted" in the Holy Scripture, he tried to persuade the Church that there was much to be learned from those heathens, and that the new learning would be helpful in establishing the cause of Christianity. Bacon was also inspired by another medieval thinker of eminence, Grosseteste, whose ideas he further developed.

Bacon recognized the value of mathematics more than many of his contemporaries, though sometimes for the wrong reason. He believed, for example, that mathematics would be helpful "in ascertaining the position of paradise and hell." He stated that one can conclude by looking at an equilateral triangle that there must be a Trinity. But he also asserted that for science to achieve its fullness it must incorporate mathematics into it, and this was a prescient thought in the 13th century. In his *Opus Maius* he makes this most insightful comment: "He who wishes to rejoice without doubt with regards to the truths underlying phenomena must know how to devote himself to experiment."

This does not mean that Bacon himself followed this prescription, for he was subject to all the prejudices and superstitions of his age.

He also saw the potential of science for the future, for he spoke of flying machines, or for moving in vehicles without animals with incomparable speed, and of navigating without oarsmen more swiftly than would be thought possible through the hands of men…. Flying machines can be made, and a man sitting in the middle of the machine may revolve some ingenious device by which artificial wings may beat the air in the manner of a flying bird. He was one of the first to look upon the eye as an optical instrument.

Roger Bacon displayed some of the characteristics of the scientific expert of later times: highly original in his thoughts, utterly convinced that his own theories were the correct ones, attacking fellow experts, and pointing to their shortcomings and errors, often justifiably. In one regard he was quite right and way ahead of his times: He was one of the first in medieval Europe to recognize the shortcoming in the then current calendar which he described as "intolerable to all wisdom, the horror of astronomy, and the laughing-stock from the mathematician's point of view." In 1267, he wrote a long letter to Pope Clement IV, appealing to him to mandate a reform of the calendar. Unfortunately, Clement IV (who himself was interested in the matter) died the very next year, and Roger Bacon's proposal did not come to pass until the latter half of the 16th century. Roger Bacon was condemned, his works were banned, and he was put in prison. Going against established authority did not go unpunished in the ancient world.

As we read the works and lives of people like Roger Bacon it becomes clear that while the emergence of original thinkers is a necessary condition for the rise and development of science, it is by no means sufficient. Unless there is freedom of thought and expression science can never take deep roots in society. As long as original thinkers are subdued and snuffed, and the guardians of ancient wisdom think there is little more to be learned, and they persecute and punish the new thinkers, science can only falter, and in extreme cases, it may even die away.

June 21

From the World of Religion: REINHOLD NIEBUR

No matter how rationally we present arguments for the existence of God, no matter how clear we are in our thinking and coherent in our reasoning, we can never establish to everyone's satisfaction anything of logical impeccability about God and the ultimate mystery. This fact has been stated over the ages by many mystics and wise theologians.

One of the eminent thinkers who formulated such ideas effectively was Reinhold Niebuhr (born: 21 June 1892) whose writings had, and still have, great influence on (Christian) theological thought.

Niebuhr recognized that one of the most important functions of religion is to give meaning and purpose to human existence. Such meaning may be found in a connection with an entity that is beyond human history, and is in fact a love that is timeless. This is what we call God: not a supernatural being getting ready to judge us for our acts, but rather a source of never failing love. In order to be enriched by that meaning, we need to go beyond our sensory world and strive to get connected with a transcendent reality which alone can enable us to truly experience that love. To Niebuhr, transcendence is intimately related to this timeless love.

For this to happen, that is to say, for experiencing that transcendence, what is needed is faith, pure and simple, or more exactly Christian faith. For, said Niebuhr, Christian faith pro*vide*s a meaningful purpose.

How do we become aware of God? We become aware of God's presence when we become aware of such a thing as sin, said Niebuhr. For sin is a morally impermissible act. And who is it that permits or does not permit it? God? Just as fear of driving through red-light is tantamount to an awareness of police, so too recognizing sin implies a consciousness of God. The converse is true too. As Dostoevsky put it, "Take away God, and everything is permitted."

But Niebuhr was too modern a theologian to take literally the story of Adam as the originator of sin for all humankind. To him, there are sin-laden societal structures which all of us inherit. These include injustice and oppression.

Niebuhr stressed the importance of recognizing human finitude. When we imagine that we, who are but finite, can grasp all the mysteries of the world, we are committing a sin. As he put it, "Evil arises when the fragment seeks by its own wisdom to comprehend the whole or attempts by its own power to realize it." In other words, it is self-love and undue claims of one's own capabilities that constitutes sin.

Niebuhr was an unusual blend of socialist inclinations in politics and Christian orthodoxy in religion. He did not have much respect for marketing and consumerism which he aptly described as "unlimited devotion to limited values". Niebuhr gave a scathing criticism of modern civilization in his Moral Man in Immoral Society (1932). In his Faith and History (1949) he reminded us of the irony of history by which every technical advance eventually results in "a new dimension of ancient perplexities."

He was among the modern Christian theologians who formulated classical teachings of St. Augustine and of the Reformation thinkers in the modern context. His core ideas were presented in several works, the most important of which was entitled *The Nature and Destiny of Man* (1941–43). Here he stated that rationality instigates egoism and leads to materialism. Though our spirit is free we are chained by our material necessities. This is the cause of anxiety: One almost hears the words of the Buddha.

From the World of Science: SIMÉON-DENIS POISSON

Not every creative scientist who has made significant contributions to human knowledge attains universal recognition. Even within one's domain of expertise, reputation often suffers from politics and political rivalries. However, if a scientist's work is substantial, then the legacy continues in the pages and pursuits of later generations. So it has been with Siméon-Denis Poisson (born: 21 June 1781).

Only those who have been initiated into the technical details of mathematics and physics can fully appreciate the contributions of Poisson: the Poisson equation in potential theory, the Poisson distribution in probability theory, and the Poisson bracket in quantum mechanics, are fairly esoteric stuff, but unavoidable if one is studying physics or mathematics at a serious level. So his name is not unfamiliar to many, even if it is not always pronounced as it ought to be in French. But few beyond the ivory tower have heard of this man.

Poisson got into the prestigious *École Polytechnique* by doing well in the competitive entrance exam. Here he studied under Lagrange and Laplace who recognized his mathematical abilities. They held him in high esteem for his substantial work. He was elected to the Academy when he was still in his early thirties. Some have said that the approval for this came quickly because of his sympathetic attitudes towards some government policies. Soon he was drawn into the affairs of the government, especially with regards to science education. He served the cause of science well when some forces in the government were trying to undercut science education.

But Poisson incurred the displeasure of a great many people, including some fellow mathematicians like Evariste Galois who made some scathing criticisms of his role in French mathematics. Such judgments by his contemporaries colored the comments of others of later generations too. Some said he had no original ideas, that he adopted and worked on what others had done, and that he quite often even lacked judgment. But then, there is no such thing as the judgment of history: only the judgment of historians. Thus, Edmund Whittaker, in his classic *History of the Theories of Aether and Electricity* stated that "even after allowance has been made for what is due to his predecessors, Poisson's investigation (mathematical aspects of electricity) must be accounted a splendid memorial of his genius." And Pierre Costabel made this balanced appraisal: "Poisson was certainly not a genius. Yet, just as surely, he was one of those without whom progress in French science in the early nineteenth century would not have occurred."

In any event, Poisson discovered a new distribution in probability and on the theory of definite integrals, coined the phrase *law of large numbers*, investigated elasticity, calculated the path of projectiles taking into consideration the rotation of the earth, generalized Laplace's equation, wrote some excellent texts, and was intensely absorbed in doing scientific work.

Yet, in the larger canvas of science, his contributions were not of the same order as of Lagrange or Fourier. So he is not remembered as often in popular writings on science. But it is impossible to go through technical science courses, in mathematics, physics, or probability theory, without encountering his name in one context or another, though not all may know his first name. Books meant to inspire the young also mention him. Thus, Richard Gregory wrote: "Many of the intellectual giants to which the human race will do homage came from the most unexpected places...Poisson, one of a brilliant array of mathematicians whom France produced a century ago, spend his early life in a hovel."

June 22

From the World of Religion:
COUNCIL OF EPHESUS

If religion enriches the spiritual life of the person of faith, theology may clarify or confuse the minds of those who spend much time on the significance and tenability of the doctrines of a religion. So, whereas the simple practitioners of religions pray and sing and derive whatever peace of mind or ecstasy they might derive from these, the analytical theologians are keen on defending a dogma or propounding a new interpretation of a long-held doctrine. If in the process he or she diverges from the canonical views, the consequences may not be very palatable.

Consider what happened to Nestorius, a devout Christian from Antioch who had been appointed patriarch of Constantinople by Emperor Theodosius II in 428. He expressed the view that Mary should not be called Mother of God, because she was only the mother of the human manifestation of God. Thus the divine Jesus was the son of God, and the human Jesus was the son of Mary.

To some moderns, especially if they are not Christians, this might sound like an interesting alternative way of looking upon Jesus, but to orthodox upholders of church doctrines, this was heresy. Cyril, bishop of Alexandria, became so furious that he complained to the pope of Rome, who instructed Cyril to give Nestorius ten days for recanting the heretical thesis, failing which he would face excommunication.

Nestorius managed to evade the ultimatum by persuading his protégé, the emperor, to convene a general forum where the matter could be discussed openly by all parties. So was convened the Council of Ephesus (in western Asia Minor) which began on 22 June 431. The politics and intrigues behind the scenes prior to this council are fascinating to anyone who enjoys history-thrillers. Thanks to correspondence among the participants and the labors of historians, these have been reconstructed. It is impressive, if sometimes amusing, to see how seriously these matters were taken by the participants, and with what outrage the defenders of long-held views reacted in those days. Similar reactions are not impossible in our own times: All one needs is a medieval mind-set. The net effect was that it became even more official that the truly divine and human natures were inextricably bound in Jesus Christ of divine substance. Also, Nestorius was declared anathema, and sent back to Antioch and beyond.

Nestorius traveled to Egypt and Iraq where he found many followers, eventually leading to the establishment of the Nestorian Church. Over the centuries they succeeded in spreading to the Malabar coast of India which is among the few pockets in the world where the church has survived down to our own times. During the 19th century there were some terrible genocides of Nestorians by the Kurds and the Turks. Like the massacre of Christians in Sudan in our own times, one seldom mentions the atrocities perpetrated in the name of religions that wail as victims in current political contexts.

So it will go on and on, the excommunications and the persecutions and the massacres in the name of religion as long as the leaders of the tradition mindlessly hang on to ancient texts and worldviews, unable or unwilling to see into the deeper messages and meanings that are implicit in the religious and spiritual visions of the great prophets and sages of the human family. But one may hope that a day will come in the cultural history of humankind when the religious gold is cleansed of its dirty dross which has all too often corrupted the minds of religious leaders who alone wield the power to mold the thoughts and direct the behavior of the flock they shepherd.

From the World of Science:
HERMANN MINKOWSKI

In the 17th and 18th centuries the genius of Newton was universally recognized. This was good and well deserved. However, the effulgence of his fame sometimes cast into darkness others who had also made important contributions to the fields which Newton enriched. Likewise, in the 20th century everyone had heard of Einstein and Relativity, but not many beyond the specialists' circle had even heard of lesser lights who had nevertheless enriched the field in different ways.

Those familiar with Einstein's special relativity theory, even through popular books, know of space and time being merged into a single four-dimensional structure. The first pronouncement to this effect was made in a lecture delivered in 1908:

"The views of space and time which I wish to lay before you have sprung from the soil of experimental physics, and therein lies their strength. They are radical. Henceforth space by itself, and time by itself, are doomed to fade away into mere shadows, and only a kind of union of the two will preserve an independent reality."

This statement was made by Hermann Minkowski (born: 22 June 1864), a mathematician who had done considerable work on pure mathematics, exploring generalized version of the biquadratic forms whose study had been initiated by Gauss (*vide* 30 April). Already at the age of 17, Minkowski took up a challenge of the French Academy of sciences relating to the question of how a number may be expressed as the sum of the squares of five numbers. Though the entry had to be in French, Minkowski submitted his work in German, with a French abstract. This caused some difficulty, but he did get the prize anyway. It was shared with a highly regarded veteran British mathematician Henry Smith. Some Britishers thought it was an affront to their nation when one of their senior mathematicnas had to share a prestigious prize with a mere teenager.

What Minkowski did was to formulate the key formulas in Einstein theory in the framework of a geometry in four dimensions of which three are of space and one is of time. For the formalism to take on a mathematically elegant aspect, one needs to attach the so-called imaginary number i to the fourth dimension t (the variable for time). With this strategy, the so-called equations of Maxwell for electromagnetism also take on neat aspects. In turns out that the electric and magnetic fields are all components of what mathematicians call a tensor.

Two things must be emphasized here: First, Minkowski's formulation made the mathematical aspect of Einstein's theory very elegant and powerful in its manipulation. In this context it became natural to use terms like space-like and time-like vectors, light cone, and world line. However, these served mainly as compact terminology, clear and unambiguous for those trained in the field. When such terms are transposed in everyday language and in qualitative terms, they take on meanings that just don't have any semblance with their contextual significance in technical physics. Thus Minkowski's use of the imaginary number in the time-coordinate gave rise to metaphysical interpretations of time which have absolutely nothing to do with relativity or the Minkowski formalism of what he called the *Raumzeitskontinuum* (Space-Time Continuum). The absurdities that often ensue from extrapolations—whether poetic or pseudoscientific—pervade many regions of 20th century philosophy, psychology, and metaphysics are often the butt of jokes among practicing physicists. In recent years this topic has been expounded by Sokal and in their book on what they call *Sophisticated Nonsense*.

Unfortunately Minkowski died prematurely in 1909 because of a ruptured appendix.

June 23

From the World of Religion: SAINT RAMANUJA

Ramanuja (?23 June 1017) was one of the keenest thinkers of classical India. He was inspired by the Tamil hymnal poets known as the *Aalvaars*.

Ramanuja's metaphysical thesis concerned the relationship between the individual soul (*jeevâtman*) and the supreme soul (*brahman*). Shankara had proclaimed that they were one and the same, seeming different only because of our state of ignorance. Ramanuja maintained that the two were not identical, that even after the ultimate cosmic merger, the soul preserves its dentity. To give an analogy, it was not like a cup of water poured back into the ocean which becomes indistinguishable from the Whole, but like a sand grain that retains its identity even in the ocean depths.

Ramanuja questioned the concept of *Maya*. He affirmed that the world was not an illusion, as Shankara had said, but all too real. The individual soul emerged from brahman, but is now an independent entity. Its glories will be recognized by recognizing its Creator and dwelling in His vicinity, not by losing itself into a quality-less substratum.

What this means is that God Himself is One, a non-dual (*advaita*) entity; but He is possessed of, or is qualified by different (*vishista*) parts. Ramanuja's thesis is known as *vishistadvaita*. There are three fundamental realities: God (*ishvara*), conscious soul (*cit*), and unconscious matter (*acit*); the last two being dependent on the first. The Upanishadic phrase, *tat tvam asi* (That Thou art) simply means that atman and Brahman are very much alike, the former being dependent on the latter.

Ramanuja's philosophy is essentially religious. In his system *brahman* is a personal God, the universe is His body. Spiritual knowledge calls for intense devotion and for love of God through *bhakti*. Reason has a role, but faith no less. The two should merge in religion. His system is a guide to worship as much as for intellectual understanding.

Ramanuja wrote commentaries on the *Brahma Sutra* (aphorisms on Vedic philosophy) and the *Bhagavad Gita*; a *Compendium of the Sense of the Veda*, and a work entitled *Essense of Vedanta*.

Vishistadvaita philosophy is a complex system of thought, with detailed discussions on epistemology, metaphysics and practical paths to follow for salvation. It too grew into different sub-schools and contending variations. But invariably Ramanuja was regarded as supreme. Indeed he came to be seen as no less than an incarnation of Vishnu, one of the three aspects of the Divine in the Hindu framework.

This medieval Tamil scholastic first studied at Conjeevaram under expert exponents of Shaivite philosophy, but later abandoned it in preference to Vaishnavism. He traveled as far as Kashmir with his message. Upon returning to Srirangam, he began converting Shaivites to his school. The local Shaivite ruler tried to suppress Ramanuja. Religious persecution is not the monopoly of any one tradition. Ramanuja escaped to another kingdom where he is said to have performed some miracles. Tradition says that he lived to the ripe age of 120.

Ramanuja was more generous towards members of the lower castes, and was even in favor of women's education. Like Shankara, he too founded religious centers. However, the heads here were not celibate monks but devout householders.

Ramanuja and his successors propagated Vaishnavism very effectively. They worship Rama and Krishna with great devotion, and are against animal sacrifices. They are generous with fruits and flowers to the deities, sing and meditate peacefully. Their worship also includes giving the idols periodic baths and perfumes.

From the World of Science: ALAN TURING

It is common knowledge that we live in an age of computers. We know too that computers resemble the human brain in many ways: they store, retrieve, and process data. They behave like intelligent entities. They are sometimes called thinking machines. And one still asks: Can a machine really think? Actually the question was asked and answered as long ago as in 1936 by a brilliant young mathematician/thinker by the name of Alan Turing (born: 23 June 1912).

In the 19th century, thanks to the work of George Boole (*vide* December 8), mathematicians had developed a technique for determining the truth or falsity of propositions by expressing them as symbols.

In the beginning of the 20th century, David Hilbert had raised the question of whether all mathematical systems are (can be proved to be) *consistent* (no inner contradictions), *complete* (every proposition in a system can be proved within it), and decidable (it can be shown if a proposition is definitely true or false). These questions have profound consequences for the human ability to comprehend the world. The decidability criterion is equivalent to asking: Is it possible to determine if a proposition is true by the mechanical manipulation of symbols in a finite number of steps? Taking off from the works of Hilbert, John von Neumann and Kurt Goedel, Turing rigorously established that certain types of logical and mathematical problems simply cannot be formulated in the algorithmic mode. The implication of this is that there are logical and mathematical problems that cannot be solved by any computing machine.

When Turing analyzed this question, there were no such things as computers. Indeed, he was the first to envisage such a universal machine using a limitless tape. Indeed, the roots of modern computer programming may be traced to this so-called Turing machine. In principle, the Turing machine was not unlike a typewriter. It could print out strings of symbols. But it also had the ability to read and get rid of the symbols. Turing imagined the machine to be using, not a sheet, but a strip or tape. The tape had the capacity to read only one symbol at a time. This machine had a memory bank with a finite number of states, and was governed by rules which determined various aspects of the tape-data.

Turing proved that it was possible to build a programmable machine capable of reading and assimilating the rules of other Turing machines from tapes fed into it. The net effect of Turing's analysis was to answer Hilbert's decidability question in the negative. The so-called Church-Turing thesis is "that no consistent formal system of arithmetic or even first-order predicate logic is decidable." At the same time Turing also showed that the mathematical processes of the human mind (not merely computations) could be replicated in a machine. This led to the revolutionary conclusion that it was possible to construct machines that can think. Such machines would display Artificial Intelligence, a term that was coined only two decades later.

During the war years (1939–45) Turing served the British government in decoding thousands of enemy messages. That in itself is a fascinating chapter in the history of the war. Some have suggested that Turing's work shortened the duration of the war by at least two years.

After the war he served in various capacities in Britain's national laboratories. Unfortunately, his homosexuality was regarded as a serious crime in those days, which prompted Turing to take his life at an early age. In any case, Turing will be remembered as a pioneer in the field of cognitive science and Artificial Intelligence.

June 24

From the World of Religion:
ENCYCLICAL OF POPE PAUL IV

At the root of most religious visions is the notion that human existence has two aspects: the physical and the spiritual, associated with the physical body and the subtle spirit. The body derives satisfaction from worldly pleasures. The spirit is beckoned by the divine. The allures of the body blind us to the call of the spirit. If one wants to evolve spiritually, one needs to learn to resist the joys of the flesh. This is the reason why asceticism has been a feature of most religious traditions. This is why in the religious framework there is the idea that for spiritual fulfill-ment one needs to undergo sacrifices which range from the giving up of pleasures to the voluntary experiencing of pain.

Of the many physical satisfactions one derives in life the most important are from food and the gratification of the sexual desire. Therefore, in many religious contexts one recommends periodic fasting, and also abstention from carnal pleas-ures. In some traditions, even music is prohibited because it too gives physical enjoyment to the listener.

Sometimes, complete abstention from sexual activity is recommended at cer-tain stages in life: prior to marriage and after the completion of responsibilities as a householder (i.e. as spouse and parent). It is also required of people who choose monastic life, as monk or nun, in their quest for spiritual fulfillment.

In the Roman Catholic Church, this has been an absolute requirement for the pope and the clergy. In this context, it is interesting to recall that the injunction against marriage of the higher clergy was initiated only in the 4th century in the synod of Elvira (305) in Spain, and later as part of the Nicene creed (325). It is not clear that this was strictly adhered to in many parts of Christendom even after these. Indeed, by the 10th century, ecclesiastics indulging in open marriages and living with concubines was so rampant that some observers openly criticized the lechery of bishops. It was Pope Gregory VII who reinstated with firmer terms the celibacy of the Catholic clergy as rules to be strictly followed. He gave permission to the laity to bring the offenders to justice. The common people were forbidden to attend any service that was conducted by a priest who was known to have a concubine. Pope Leo II and Pope Urban II were among the church leaders who recommended severe punishment to the concubines also.

The Eastern Church, the Protestant Churches, the Judaic and Islamic traditions, the Hindu world: these don't demand priestly celibacy. The question has been periodically raised in the Catholic Church as to the advisability of repressing the sexual instinct. The discussions came to a close with an encyclical from Pope Paul IV on 24 June 1967. It was addressed to bishops, priests and all the faithful of the Catholic World. It began with the statement: "Priestly celibacy has been guarded by the Church for centuries as a brilliant jewel, and retains its value undiminished even in our time when the outlook of men and the state of the world have undergone such profound changes." It noted that "Amid the modern stirrings of opinion, a tendency has also been manifested, and even a desire expressed, to ask the Church to re-examine this characteristic institution." It concluded that the celibacy of the clergy was to be an important element of the Catholic Church.

The leadership of the Church had only the noblest thoughts in mind when it insisted on maintaining celibacy among those who had dedicated themselves to spiritual life. But one wonders if due weight was given to the social, psychological, and biological forces to which most humans—including the clergy—are subject. When the will succumbs to the urgings of the body, it may not be so much a moral transgression as a physical collapse.

From the World of Science: FRED HOYLE

From technical science, there arise words and phrases which eventually seep into everyday language. Sometimes these words may not have been coined in earnestness, but their power in explaining or evoking an idea are such that they are adopted by practitioners as well as by outsiders.

Consider, for example, the term "big-bang." It has entered our vocabulary and encyclopedias too. It refers to the first explosion several billion years ago by which, according to a currently accepted theory, the universe of space, time, matter, energy and laws emerged. Now, the interesting thing is that the epithet was coined by a 33 year old astronomer and astrophysicist in a sarcastic tone. He himself did not subscribe to that theory of cosmogenesis. His name was Fred Hoyle (born: 24 June 1915).

From astronomical observations of distant galaxies and their mutual recession, and from a careful study of Einstein's equations of General Relativity, it was speculated in 1927 that perhaps the universe arose from the hatching of a cosmic egg, reminiscent of the Hindu *hiranyagarbha:* golden egg. Two decades later, this idea was given formal structure by George Gamow (*vide* March 4). Gamow and Ralph Alpher calculated how at the extreme temperatures, hydrogen atoms would have been formed, and even some helium and lithium. But one could not account for the existence of heavy elements in the universe.

Hoyle was not convinced by the Gamow-Alpher theory, and he referred to it sarcastically as the big-bang theory. Like the names *Jesuit* and *Methodist* hurled by non-sympathizers, the big-bang was also embraced by the targets.

Hoyle developed his own theory of cosmology in 1948 which ruled out any Genesis. In his model, the universe had neither a beginning nor an end: it always maintained the same steady state. For almost two decades the two theories, big-bang and steady-state, were in competition. One implication of the steady state theory was that in order to account for the steady state in an expanding universe, matter had to be created in a continuous manner. This was deemed impossible. The problem could have been resolved perhaps by assuming that some of the fundamental constants changed. Thus, if the value of the speed of light decreased at a slow but steady pace, for the total energy in the universe to remain constant, the mass *m* should increase in the formula $E = mc$-*squared.*

It is not only for his steady-state universe idea that Hoyle will be remembered. In the context of developing his cosmological theory, Hoyle became one of the pioneers in astrophysical theories of nucleosynthesis which trace the heavy elements in our universe to the core of unimaginably hot supernovas where simpler nuclei fuse to form the heavier nuclei of elements. In other words, the interior of supernovas is where the heavy-elements-producing factories are located. This cleared up the mystery of how these elements came to be. Hoyle's work served to combine two separate branches of physics: astrophysics and nuclear physics.

Hoyle worked on the idea of *panspermia* which traces epidemics on earth, perhaps even life, to spores from outer space which happened to land on our planet.

In this matter he was assisted by Chandra Wickramasinghe. The two authored some important papers together. Hoyle also wrote some science fiction of which *The Black Cloud* was the most famous. In this, extraterrestrial clouds have consciousness, and one of them attacks our world.

Ironically, on many issues, this eminent astronomer and astrophysicist who influenced science in important ways did not belong to the main stream. And he did not care.

June 25

From the World of Religion: FORMILARIO CONCORDIAE

In our modern world there are not any Christian countries where if you don't belong to one sect of Christianity, you will be executed or expelled from there. Unfortunately, this practice still persists in watered-down versions in some other countries.

In 16th century Christendom this was not uncommon in some Germanic countries. As a result of the rise of Protestantism, regions were predominantly Catholic or predominantly Protestant, and the rule used to be that if one did not belong to the wing to which the ruler subscribed, one had to change faith or leave. This, in effect, was the decree of the Diet of Augsburg (1555).

After the death of Martin Luther, schisms arose within the Protestant movement: Lutherans, Calvinists, and others. Their mutual differences were sometimes as serious as their individual differences with the Roman Catholics. Doctrinal differences led to hurtful behavior: indeed this is the root cause of all the religious wars and persecutions which have given, as the expression goes, a bad name to religion. It is small consolation that this has been a common feature of practically all the major religions of humankind. Sadly, the potential for this still persists in the world.

In the 1560s and 1570s, some religious leaders and scholars recognized that it was not in the best interest of anyone to allow such animosities to persist and grow. So they met and tried to come up with a formula that would bring some harmony among the differing factions.

The Formula of Concord (*Formilario concordiae*) was issued on 25 June 1580 which was the silver jubilee of the Augsburg Confession. It is the final part of what is known as the *Book of Concord*. The goal of this Book was to bring together in a single volume the most basic beliefs of all Christians from about the 4th to the 16th century. These beliefs were based on the Holy Scriptures as well as the creeds enunciated by authorized bodies at various times. The Book also included a number of Protestant writings such as Melanchthon's *Augsburg Confession* and its apology.

The *Book of Concord* has been described as a work that embodies the essential Protestant *Confessions*. In this context, the term Confessions simply means a statement of profound conviction. The very high regard in which this work is held by the Protestant community is reflected in the following comment by William Arndt, "The Confessions are the brightest jewel in the crown of the Lutheran Church. In speaking of our Confessions we dwell on facts that should make the heart of every Lutheran swell with joy and thanksgiving. We look here on one of the brightest pages of our history as a church."

There is more to religion than faith and prayer. The doctrines of the tradition are important too, though not many of the church-going flock will be able to spell them out with unambiguous clarity. Of equal importance is the source of the doctrines: Who said what and when. Here again, the names of the persons are far more important than what they said. Then again, in some traditions the history of the documents is remembered with reverence. So the Book of Concord has been celebrated during its various memorable anniversaries. In all of this we see how religion is not just a spiritual quest, nor a clear-cut guide to an ethical and religious life. It is an institution, a vast body of knowledge and writings, and above all, an interpretation of the holy books by learned scholars and keen theologians. The main difference between science and religion in this matter is that the former is transcultural, the latter is very much group-circumscribed and culture-dependent.

From the World of Science: WALTHER NERNST

Human beings generally want to reach the highest there is: to climb the tallest mountain, to jump the highest hurdle, to attain the noblest goal. But there is a context when human beings have tried to reach the ultimate at the lower extreme: to reach the lowest possible temperature. Experimentalists have been striving to make things colder and colder so as to record lower and lower temperatures. At one time it was thought that some day we would hit rock bottom: the zero on the absolute scale.

It is good that theory and experiments go hand in hand in science, each guiding the other. For it was recognized through theoretical analysis that this would be a wild-goose chase. In principle, absolute zero is as unreachable as absolute rest. This was the discovery of Walther Nernst (born: 25 June 1864). It follows from Nernst's analysis of entropy changes as one tends towards absolute zero. The physical impossibility of attaining absolute zero temperature is known to physicists as the *third law of thermodynamics.*

Human ingenuity may lead us very close to that ultimate state of extreme coldness, but it cannot reach it. [This is strictly true for crystalline substances.] We have managed to get temperatures of the order of a millionth part of a degree above absolute zero.

We know that the atoms and molecules of a solid are in constant vibration. As the temperature is lowered, they vibrate less energetically. At extremely low temperatures they grow more and more sluggish. One implication of Nernst's discovery is that there will always be a remnant of molecular vibration, however low the temperature may become. This zero-point energy (as it is called) reveals that in some ultimate sense the universe is immortal, never to be reduced to a motionless freeze. The heart-beat of the cosmos will never cease.

Thus, absolute zero is like an ideal for which we may yearn but which can never be reached. However, unlike the last tick of time which we cannot even conceive, absolute zero temperature is a perfectly valid concept. It is very much there, but simply beyond the grasp of nature. It is like the point that begins a line, surely present, but unidentifiable as a separate entity when we approach it step by slow step on the line. Conceptually, space and time extend to infinity both ways. Temperature extends to infinity only at one end.

It has been said that a recurring theme in 20th century physics is the impossibility of accomplishing certain things: of finding absolute rest, of measuring with 100% precision, of reaching the absolute zero. On the logical plane it sounds ironic that with the gathering of more knowledge and understanding, we are discovering more of what cannot be done. On the plane of wisdom, however, this is a revelation: the more we learn, the more we realize our finiteness and limitations. This is not an indictment of the scientific enterprise. Rather, it reflects science's potency not only to unravel the roots of perceived reality, but also the scope and constraints of human intellect and ingenuity.

Nernst was a physical chemist who gave the first satisfactory chemical explanation of how a voltaic cell works. An equation that is named after him is still useful in solving many problems in physical chemistry, though it has been much improved upon. He also recognized how light can sometimes initiate a chemical chain reaction. Nernst was one of the non-Jewish German scientists who were furious about the Nazi treatment of Jewish scientists. He is counted among the last of the great German scientists of a period which saw its low point in the dark days of Nazi madness. His remains are alongside those of Max Planck and Max von Laue in Goettingen: a city whose fair name had been tarnished during the Third Reich.

June 26

From the World of Religion:
UNITED NATIONS CHARTER

Most religions prescribe ethical codes whose goal is twofold: First, it is to guide people to behave in such a way that one does not hurt others (which is usually assumed to be other members of the faith), such as not stealing, not killing, not lying, etc. The second is to adhere to principles that may or may not have any impact on others, such as praying to God periodically, going to places of pilgrimage, etc.

Traditional religions seldom talk about how one group should behave towards another. If anything, there are recommendations, not always friendly, in some scriptures on how to treat out-castes, infidels, pagans, etc. One religious leader even allowed that one not of his faith could be enslaved. Episodes of how religious and racial minorities have been treated in societies professing noble religions are among the unhappy pages of human history.

Over the ages, warring nations have signed truces and peace treaties, often promising not to attack one another. But for many centuries there was no ethical document that all the peoples of the world would agree upon, at least in principle. One sees the need for such agreements especially after the end of bloody wars.

So it was that on 26 June 1945, many nations got together and freely signed the *Charter of the United Nations Organization*, the very first of its kind in all of human history. The goals of the U. N. Charter were fairly simple, and theoretically non-controversial. They were:

"1. To maintain international peace and security, and to that end: to take effective collective measures for the prevention and removal of threats to the peace, and for the suppression of acts of aggression or other breaches of the peace, and to bring about by peaceful means, and in conformity with the principles of justice and international law, adjustment or settlement of international disputes or situations which might lead to a breach of the peace;

2. To develop friendly relations among nations based on respect for the principle of equal rights and self-determination of peoples, and to take other appropriate measures to strengthen universal peace;

3. To achieve international cooperation in solving international problems of an economic, social, cultural, or humanitarian character, and in promoting and encouraging respect for human rights and for fundamental freedoms for all without distinction as to race, sex, language, or religion; and

4. To be a center for harmonizing the actions of nations in the attainment of these common ends."

Like the Ten Commandments, the Sermon on the Mount, and similar civilizing injunctions in other traditions, who can object to these beautiful goals? Which nation will openly declare it is against peace and security, or will not work for the prevention or removal of threats to peace? As with personal behavior, it is not in the preaching but in the practice that the challenge lies. We know that many signatories of the U. N. Charter have openly and secretly broken the promise, offering reasons for the transgressions.

It does not follow from this that the U.N. Charter is irrelevant. Like the rule about driving past red light, though a few sneak through it now and then, the Charter keeps many nations in check, both in what they do and in how blatantly they break the rule. Civilization survives by ideals and imperfect efforts to live up to them, and not by abandoning them altogether as being impracticable.

From the World of Science: CHARLES MESSIER

Of the countless celestial bodies that shine in the night sky, the moon alone looks different to the naked eye. But once in a while we see a faint body with a long trail behind it, looking very much like the long hair of a person running in the wind. This, as we know, is a comet. Comets have been observed since time immemorial, but because they are so different and appear only occasionally, it was thought for a long time that they were atmospheric phenomena.

Star gazers identify comets, but there has perhaps been none as committed to comet-spotting as Charles Messier (born: 26 June 1730). He is credited with the discovery of a dozen comets. He had meticulously observed at least 41 of them. Messier was drawn to astronomy in his early teens when the world was treated to a six-tailed comet. When he came to Paris at the age of 21 he found employment in a observatory where his responsibility was to keep careful records of everything he observed. In this role, he observed with great precision the transit of Mercury that occurred in May 1753.

Scanning the sky systematically, Messier came upon a faint patch in the background of the constellation Cancer. Such patches had been observed before. Their cloudy appearance earned them the name of nebulae. Messier started preparing a catalogue of all the nebulae; these have come to be called Messier Objects. The first Messier Object of this kind that he recorded, denoted as M1 by astronomers, happens to be a very important one. Known also as the Crab Nebula because of its location, we now know this to be the vestige of the spectacular supernova of 1054 of which Chinese astronomers had made a special record. Today we know that it is at the unimaginably large distance of 6000 light years from us, and that at its center is a tiny neutron star, as massive perhaps as our sun, but no more than a few kilometers in diameter, and spinning at the maddening rate of 30 revolutions a second! Messier's catalogue is a landmark in astronomy. It includes the description of 45 important celestial islands, ranging from star clusters to dust clouds and galaxies.

The object listed as M31 in Messier's catalogue is an example of what we call a galaxy. Known as the Andromeda galaxy, its nature and distance were not recognized for more than a century. Today we know it to be at a distance of some 2,000,000 light years from us. It is faintly visible to the very careful observer on a really dark night. The unaided human eye has not seen an object that is at such a great distance

Messier was eager to distinguish nebulae from comets. He became one of the first to locate the famous Halley's Comet whose re-appearance had been predicted in the previous century as a first vindication of Newton's laws applied to a comet. Because of a calculational error resulting from underestimating the effect of Jupiter on the comet, Messier had been looking in a wrong region, which is why he lost the credit for locating it to another astronomer. Even after he spotted it, Josephe Delisle, the director of the observatory, asked him not to announce it yet. Delisle did not know that a German astronomer had already observed it a month before.

It is easy to conceptualize eternity: time that never had a beginning, nor ever will have an end. But with occupied space, it is different. Mere speculation cannot tell us how far stars are strewn. For this we need astronomers and telescopes. Charles Messier was one those whose observations led us to entities which lie in realms whose distances no mortal had ever imagined before. Aside from the Messier objects, his name is associated with a lunar crater and an asteroid.

June 27

From the World of Religion:
DAY 17 OF TAMMUZ

Many religious observances are based on remembrances of events past: some happy and joyous, others sad and tragic, some historical, others mythopoetic.

The 17th day of the month of Tammuz is a memorable day in the Judaic tradition. In the year 2002 it fell on 27 June.

According to the tradition, this was the day when Moses came down from Mount Sinai. Upon doing so, he saw his people worshiping the idol of a golden calf that had been sculpted by Aaron as a substitute for God. This infuriated Moses who, in his anger, broke the first tables that had been given to him by God.

It is said that on this day in other years, the Jewish people were made to suffer and their tradition was insulted in many ways. Thus, the Jewish King Menashe is said to have desecrated the sanctuary of a Temple with an idol on this day. Also, the Roman Apostomos set the Torah on fire on this day. In the year 1239, on this day again, Pope Gregory IX had all the manuscripts of the Torah confiscated.

In 1391, 4000 Jews were massacred in Toledo, Spain; in 1559 the homes of Jews were set afire in Prague, in 1944 the ghetto in Kovno was completely demolished: all on day 17 of Tammuz. So the date is regarded as one full of calamities for Jews, and is remembered with great sadness. So on this day, many people of the faith observe a fast from sunrise to sunset. Those under difficult circumstances are allowed some simple food. Children too may have a little to eat, but should be told that this is for remembering their ancestors who have suffered through the ages. One also recites special prayers for this day.

In the *Book of our Heritage*, Rabbi Eliyahu Kitov says that the fasting that is done on this day is "to awaken hearts towards repentance through recalling our forefathers' misdeeds; misdeeds which led to calamities…" This is a very insightful statement, for sometimes the people of a generation suffer because of what their parents, grandparents or ancestors did. This is what I have called *collective karma:* the positive or negative experience that a people go through because what their ancestors did. Some may say that the boons or penalties are given by God. Others may see more clearly defined historical forces connecting the past with the present.

Those who are of an inquiring mind might wonder how it came to be that every pain and persecution of the Jews happened to have occurred on the same

17th day of Tammuz. One explanation could be the following: As a group, the Jewish people have suffered mistreatment and persecution many, many times from a wide variety of quarters. Therefore, it is quite likely that during the more than two thousand years of Jewish history, such events occurred half a dozen or more times on that particular day.

However, such a matter-of-fact explanation, whether right or not, tends to rob the event of its poetry. For what must be remembered in religious observances is not the historical authenticity of what it is supposed to be commemorating, but rather the symbolism behind the event. It is important for people of the Judaic tradition, especially those in the European and Middle Eastern context, to remember that they have been maltreated all too often by the majority. They must remember this, not only to pay silent homage to those who have been victims of the persecutions, but also be sure that such events are never again repeated. For this, the younger generation should be told the history. That is what this day is expected to accomplish. So today, people who don't belong to the tradition may also convey their sympathies to their Jewish friends.

From the World of Science: EUCLID

Science is an effort to comprehend the world in rational terms. Rationality refers to the structured process in the brain which accepts or rejects conclusions on the basis of certain rules that seem to resonate in the normal conscious brain. The purest form of this process is reflected in mathematics, of which geometrical reasoning is a supreme example.

Just as the Vedic rishis of ancient India made hymnal invocation to the forces of nature a canonical form of poetry, Euclid (born: 27 June? 295 BCE) presented a formalized format of geometrical reasoning in such a systematic manner that for many centuries his name came to mean a branch of mathematics known especially for rigorous proofs and standard theorems.

Geometry, in Euclid's work, is not what the word literally means: measurement of the earth. Rather, it is a logical realm in which numerous properties of lines and triangles and circles arise like buildings from the foundations in the ground of self-*evid*ent truths. These self-*evid*ent truths constitute the axioms of Euclidean geometry.

That every geometrical form which can be drawn with ruler and compass has some interesting properties should be clear to anyone who draws figures. But to recognize what these are by carefully climbing step by step on the logical ladder is more than a game of the mind: It is a spectacular harnessing of the powers of the human mind to walk on the tightrope of reasoning without faltering and falling. Engaging in geometrical reasoning is as fulfilling for the awakened mind, and perhaps as useless for our everyday needs, as listening to good music. The following anecdote is appropriate. One day, when Euclid the teacher was expounding to his disciples in Alexandria the proof of an interesting theorem, a student raised his hand and asked how, if at all, it would come to any practical use. Whereupon Euclid threw a paltry coin at the student, and asked him to leave the class, saying the coin would fetch him something useful. Those who are interested only in useful things have no business opening a book of pure mathematics or astronomy.

Euclid's classic work was *The Elements*. Its significance lies in its methodology: clear statement of definitions, assumptions, goals, illustrations, proofs, conclusions, etc.. These pro*vide* a systematic framework in mathematics. The *Elements* consists of thirteen Books. Book I, which defines a point as "that which has no parts," contains the famous five postulates on which Euclidean geometry is based. The first three assume the possibility of geometrically (a) drawing a straight line through any two points; (b) producing a finite straight line continuously in a straight line; (c) drawing a circle with a given center and an arbitrary radius. The fourth postulate states that all right angles are equal; the fifth that if a straight line intersects two other straight lines and makes interior angles whose sum is less than two right angles, then those two other straight lines will meet.

This fifth postulate is equivalent to saying that through a point external to a straight line only one parallel can be drawn. Over the centuries, many tried to prove this, until it was discovered that this is not necessarily true. This recognition led to the formulation of non-Euclidean geometries in the 19th century.

Euclid is said to have been modest and kind, and an inspiring individual. He gained immortal fame, not by discovering anything himself, but by doing for geometry what Ptolemy did for astronomy: collecting, systematizing, and presenting the accumulated knowledge of his predecessors. There was a time when the study of Euclidean geometry was a requirement for being declared a high-school graduate. Times have changed. Now some young people graduate without being able to read a book from cover to cover.

June 28

From the World of Religion:
JEAN JACQUES ROUSSEAU

Religions, from a historical perspective, are the inspired visions of a few individuals that gathered sufficient admiration and following to influence the world views and life styles of large numbers of people. In this sense, there have been originators of more religions than we count in standard listings which include only those that have acquired names and days of feasting and fasting and sacred books to refer to on special occasions.

Jean Jacques Rousseau (born: 28 June 1712) did not exactly found a religion, but through his writings he influenced many thinkers and movements. He is counted among the instigators of the Romantic movement. Born a Protestant, he became a Catholic when he went to Italy, then reverted to Protestantism to get back citizenship in his native Geneva. Like marriage, there can also be religions of convenience.

As to whether science and art have had any positive impact on morals, he replied with an emphatic No, adding that advancement in knowledge has only made us less happy. He was unabashedly anti-intellectual. Like some moderns who decry science and technology while typing away on computer key-boards and city-hopping in planes to promote their writings, Rousseau said how much he detested books and civilized society in many volumes which were written in the comfort of homes in the suburbs of Paris or in Geneva.

He theorized on the origin of inequality humans, was convinced that we are innately good and that civilization corrupts our nature. His complaint was that "man is born free, but is found in chains everywhere". This happens because of a social contract we all make: we give ourselves to what he called the *general will*. He venerated the noble savage, convinced that in the care-free joys of Nature and nakedness the pristine human is in the best state, reminiscent of Adam and Eve in the glory days of the grand Garden and apple tree. The original sin, for Rousseau, was civilization, the root of all injustice and evil. Even as diatribes against science fascinate modern readers saturated with technology, 18th century readers were charmed by such romantic reveries. He was so obsessed with the evils of civilization that he declared: "everything degenerates in the hands of man."

In his novel *Emile*, Rousseau gave his theory of education in which he recommends that no disciplinary action should be taken against a child, no restriction of any sort. [Dr. Spock was not the first one to come up with this idea.] The child is intrinsically good and should be allowed to develop its moral goodness without interference from corrupt civilized elders. The goal of education ought to be, he said, to draw out of the child whatever morally good things are already there. The religious implications of his theory were appreciated by neither Catholics nor Protestants, so his book was burnt by ecclesiastics both in Paris and in Geneva.

Rousseau knew the irreversibility of cultural evolution. "We never return to the times of innocence and equality, when we have once departed from them," he ruefully declared.

He propagated the view that it is the people who must be sovereign in a nation, not the king. This was among the key ideas that led to the French Revolution.

Ideas, when persuasively articulated and widely circulated, have enormous potential. They can stir the hearts of people, direct them to new ways of envisioning the world, and prompt them to actions, good or otherwise. That is why books and other media of communication are very powerful. Just through his books Rousseau had immense impact on literature and the arts, on political theory and education, and on history too. We can never tell the long range impact of the internet and easily accessible TV.

From the World of Science: ALEXIS CARREL

Thousands of surgeries are performed these days by trained and skillful professionals in countless hospitals all over the world. But every new procedure was first tried out by some particular individual. Thus, for example, a new technique in vascular surgery was introduced in 1902 by Alexis Carrel (born: 28 June 1844) who also showed some years later that it is possible to keep blood vessels in cold storage for a long time before they are used in surgical transplants. In collaboration with the aviator Charles Lindbergh, Carrel invented a machine that acted like a respiratory system for organs which had been separated from their original bodies.

Because conditions for his work were not very comfortable in his native France, Carrel moved to the United States. He worked in Chicago and in New York. In an experiment that he did during his stay at the Rockefeller Institute for Medical Research, Carrel placed tissues from a chicken embryo in a nutrient solution which was renewed every day. In this way the tissue continued to be alive for a full 29 years. As Carrel expressed it, "The cell is immortal. It is merely the fluid in which it floats and which degenerates. Renew this fluid at regular intervals, give the cell something on which to feed and, so far as we know, the pulsation of life may go on forever…" This has important implications for human longevity in that it revealed the persistence of cells over very long periods under appropriate conditions.

Alexis Carrel was a Catholic who was also deeply concerned about effects of science and technology on the human condition. At a time (the mid-1930s) when most people were singing the praise of the triumphs of technology, he published a book entitled, *L'homme, cet inconnu* (*Man the Unknown*) which opened the eyes of the reader to the not-so bright side of modern technological civilization. It painted the most terrible picture of the modern life-style on the people of New York and, more generally, of the United States. While recognizing the positive contributions of medicine and hygiene to the physical well being of people, the book exposed the awful psychological mess into which American society seemed to be slipping. The book had at least fifty reprints and numerous translations. Carrel wrote:

"The triumphs of hygiene and education are perhaps not as beneficial as they seem to be at first blush…. In certain States (of the U.S.) the number of insane people confined to lunatic asylums is greater than that of all other hospital patients. Aside from insanity, nervous breakdown is also increasing in frequency."

Sadly, many of the things mentioned there relating to the dehumanizing and psychological havoc of industrial civilization seem to be as valid today as when they were first written, if not more. Some of the social, spiritual, and ethical crises that are rampant in our own times in industrial societies have a long history, and if anything, they are growing and spreading all over the world.

Carrel's book also analyzed the nature of rational and other modes of awareness, such as intuition and mysticism. He said: "Science, which has transformed the material world, gives man the power of transforming himself. To progress again, man must remake himself."

When the Second World War broke out, Alexis Carrel returned to France to head the *Carrel Foundation for the Study of Human Problems*. Unfortunately, this was under the aegis of the pro-Nazi Vichy Government. Carrel died before the free government was formed, which might have tried his collaboration with the Vichy government.

June 29

From the World of Religion: SAINT PETER

It would be inappropriate to compare saints of a tradition, but most Christians would grant that St. Peter is to be reckoned amongst the foremost of Christ's apostles. Both Catholics and Lutherans observe his feast day on 29 June.

Peter's name appears in various forms in the Bible. He is also referred to by other names also: Simon and Cephas. Simon (Symeon) was his original name in Aramaic. Christ gave him the other name, Cephas which is Aramaic for *rock*. This became Petros in Greek, Peter in English, Pierre in French, and so on.

Peter was a fisherman by trade. We read in Luke that Jesus miraculously healed Peter's mother-in-law, and so when he was summoned by Jesus, he readily accepted. According to Mark, the healing occurred after Peter had been called. Scholars have argued on which version is right, but it is of little relevance to the fact that Peter played a major role in spreading the Gospel.

Peter was the one who declared: "Thou are the Christ, the son of the living God." To this, Jesus said: "And I say unto three, That thou art Cephas, and upon this rock I will build my church; and the gates of hell shall not prevail against it." Jesus said he would give Peter the keys of the kingdom of heaven. This is the source of the popular belief that Peter is standing guard at the portals of heaven. Peter was also one of the three apostles who witnessed the Transfiguration as well as the Agony of Jesus.

At first, Peter's vision of Christianity was that of transformed Judaism. He propagated the new faith among fellow Jews, in Jewish Temples, and followed many of the rituals of the Jewish tradition. For several decades after the crucifixion of Christ, Christianity was preached to, and practiced only by, Jewish people. In his letters (Epistles) Peter urged the Jewish people to lead an upright life so that the Gentiles might come to praise God from observing them. At one point, he is said to have hesitated when one spoke of preaching to non-Jews. But, says the Book of Acts, he once had a vision to the effect that pagans too could be included in the Christian fold. This was a revolutionary idea in religious history: that a message from God could be fit for people who don't belong to one's group.

Peter and his wife went to Syria to spread the word. Like Christ, he too is said to have performed some miracles. Peter was among the early Christians who were convinced that the world would soon come to an end, after which Christ would return to establish the kingdom of heaven on earth. The prayer "Thy Kingdom Come!" was taken literally.

In about 42 C.E., Peter went to Rome, there to tell the people about Christ and his message. Paul was already there, perhaps imprisoned by the infamous Nero who was then the emperor. Paul and Peter in Rome were like the Hare Krishnas in the 1970s in some American cities: curious vendors of a new brand of religion, quite alien to the locals. Unlike the Hare Krishnas in Europe and America, however, they were not tolerated. They and their followers were persecuted and incarcerated.

Then there came a day when Peter was condemned to be crucified, along with his wife. They say he was crucified with his head downward, apparently at his own request, perhaps because he did not wish to be treated the way Christ was.

At the very place where this horrific crime was committed, now stands the magnificent Cathedral of St. Peter. Nero's name has shrunk into a painful and pathetic episode in history. In contrast, Peter's name shines to this day as a powerful fount from where the message of Christ spread far and wide.

From the World of Science:
GEORGE ELLERY HALE

The sun has been seen observed since time immemorial. It has been the theme of magnificent mythologies, and regarded for long as the center of our universe. Its broad features and superficial aspects began to be studied with the rise of telescopic astronomy.

The person who began a thorough and modern study of the sun inside out, was George Ellery Hale (born: 29 June 1868). His dedication and discoveries were such that he came to be called "the father of modern solar observational astronomy."

Hale had been fascinated by astronomy since his boyhood. He was barely 21 when he thought of his spectroheliograph by which solar prominences are photographed in broad daylight. By using a prism and a grating, the instrument can photograph the sun in a single wavelength emanating from one of the elements on the surface. This instrument enabled astronomers to study the changing magnetic fields on the sun. Hale's love of astronomy was so deep that he took his bride to the Lick Observatory during their honeymoon.

Hale was also a designer and builder of telescopes of ever increasing power. He was unique in having founded three of the most prestigious observatories in the United States, indeed in the world: Yerkes (1897), Mt. Wilson (1904), and Mt. Palomar (1948).

He was as interested in the physics of the sun and the stars as in their telescopically observed features and locations. So, while at Yerkes, he co-founded the *Astrophysical Journal* which continues to this day to be a leading periodical in the field.

The 60-inch telescope at Mount Wilson was used by Harold Shapley to estimate for the first time the dimensions of the Milky Way and locate the sun in our galaxy. Hale went on to construct a 100-inch telescope, thanks to which Edwin Hubble could detect not only the mind-boggling distances of some galaxies, but also their velocities of recession. This discovery revealed the expansion of the universe, and served as the observational impetus for big-bang cosmology.

With a substantial grant from the Rockefeller Foundation, Hale next set to work on the construction of his famous 200-inch reflecting telescope for the observatory in Mount Palomar. This was a mammoth undertaking, involving the finest glass-works in the country, and the collaboration of countless designers, engineers, and builders. The formal dedication of this observatory took place in 1948, ten years after the demise of George Hale. This telescope probed far deeper into observable space than any in the world. Thanks to Hale's untiring dedication, we have come to know about galaxies of all shapes and sizes millions of light years away, zooming away from one another, in a mad rush, as it were, making the universe like a balloon that is being blown up.

When Hale first got excited about the sun—his favorite star in the firmament—little could he have suspected that some day his passion for the telescope would be revealing the farthermost edges of the physical universe. People who speculate in metaphysical and theological terms about cosmology don't always realize the tremendous hard work, based on observation, and using sophisticated instruments, from which scientists arrive at their conclusions on this subject.

Hale was an astronomer, an astrophysicist, and also an organizer and fundraiser. He was involved in the establishment of many research facilities, and felt that in those days there was greater emphasis on engineering than on pure science. When he was a trustee of Throop Polytechnic Institute in Pasadena he decided to overhaul its mission and goals. Bringing in outstanding scientists, he transformed the modest polytechnic into the prestigious California Institute of Technology.

June 30

From the World of Religion:
THE TUNGUSKA EVENT

In the writings of the ancients, some of which are part of the scriptures of the great religions we often read about spectacular or catastrophic events, like a great fire or a global deluge. It is difficult to believe that events of such proportions could have occurred, especially when supernatural elements are added to the stories.

However, very recently in historical times, less than a hundred years ago, on 30 June 1908, to be exact, at 7:17 early in the morning, a most unexpected natural disaster of mammoth proportions is definitely known to have occurred in the wilderness of Siberia, at a place called Tunguska. Later analyses of whatever remained after the event showed that it was a stupendous blast, a horrendous fireball perhaps, an enormous explosion, the equivalent in energy release, some have said, of a thousand Hiroshima bombs.

Countless people were panic stricken, and many died. The number of fatalities would have been considerable more if it had occurred at a more densely populated area. Some reported seeing a fiery object come down from the skies. The effect of the catastrophe was felt at great distances. And there was no efficient communication system in that part of the world in those days. Unbelievably, the matter was either unknown or ignored for over a decade. In 1921, the Soviet Academy of Sciences sent investigators to find out what had happened, by asking the local inhabitants, based on their memory. They said that a shining body came crashing on the ground, and that a "huge cloud of black smoke was formed and a loud crash, not like a thunder, but as if from the fall of large stones, or from gunfire, was heard. And the buildings shook and at the same time, a forked tongue of flame broke through the cloud.... Everyone thought that the end of the world was approaching."

From such reports grew the theory that the place was perhaps struck by a huge meteorite—a mini-asteroid perhaps, for nothing else could have caused devastation on such a grand scale. Then some suggested that it must have been a comet. So, even in the 1930s, one was not quite sure of what exactly had caused this grand mishap, though the meteorite theory had gained much popularity. Then, in the 1990s, a new theory was put forward to account for the disaster. According to that, it was a purely geological phenomenon. Described as a Non-local Natural

Explosion (NNE), the phenomenon was described as "an explosion of a high-speed ball-lightning tectonic origin."

The Tunguska event may be seen from two different perspectives: The scientific, and the human-religious. From the first, it is a matter of explaining how the event happened at all, what prompted it, whether it could happen again, etc. From the second perspective, we get a chill, just to recognize that a whole community, perhaps a nation, or even the anthroposphere could be wiped out by one major catastrophic event. Astronomers do keep track of the mindless asteroids that are hurtling by the thousands in interplanetary wilderness. With a perverse enticement from gravitation, one of these mammoth rocks may be deflected earthwards. In principle, there is always the possibility that within the next few centuries, a rogue asteroid would impinge on our planet, and bring to naught in short notice our millennia of civilization, along with our regional squabbles and religious acrimony. Each day that nations interact and negotiate, they would do well to recall the Tunguska tragedy, for, all our self-interests and vengeful feelings towards others can be turned to dust and smoke by the rude intrusion of a celestial stone gone astray. Like the dog that destroyed Newton's manuscripts, it knows not what havoc it wreaks. At the very least, this perspective could inspire us to more compassion towards fellow beings.

From the World of Science:
ADOLF FURTWÄNGLER

Often one tends to look upon science uniquely as a study of the phenomenal world. But it is much more. Science is characterized more by its methodology: by its criteria for accepting or rejecting propositions about the observed features of the world, and by the tools and concepts it uses for these, than by the subject matter of its investigation or even the results.

In this sense, explorations into ancient history are as much science as astronomy. The routes and reasons by which one comes to the conclusion that that there was or there was not a Noah's Ark will be different from the scientific perspective than from some other.

Consider, for example, the famous golden Tiara which had been reportedly discovered in the last decade of the 19th century at an excavation site in a region in Russia. It had an inscription which suggested that it had been presented as a gift to a certain prince Saltaphernes. It was not uncommon in the 19th century for precious relics from the past from many parts of the world to find their way to the British Museum, the Louvre, and to a handful of other centers like these. In this case, the tiara had been acquired by the Louvre for a tidy sum. The *Académie des Inscriptions* was so pleased and proud of the new acquisition that it was planning for a publication in which the Tiara of Saltaphernes was to be featured.

At that time, Adolph Furtwängler (born: 30 June 1853), a highly regarded archaeologists, announced that the tiara was, in fact, spurious, that it was more recent in its construction than the French scholars were led to believe. This infuriated the Gallic pundits who attributed Furtwängler's skepticism to petty jealousy and anti-French sentiments. While the French, ignoring Furtwängler, were making preparations for their publication, a goldsmith from Russia made it known that he was the one who had fashioned the beautiful tiara and sold it for more than its actual worth because of its professed antiquity.

Furtwängler had participated in the major excavations in Olympia in 1878, where games had been held in the distant past. This discovery led to the reinstatement of the Olympics. He did work in Aegina and wrote a work on the masterpieces of Greek sculpture. His work demonstrated the important differences between the kinds of pottery from different regions of ancient Greece. In fact, he developed a system by which one could classify prehistoric artwork into categories on the basis of stylistic qualities. Thanks to such classification, archaeology assisted scholars in the reconstruction of ancient history.

Furtwängler, who was once described as "probably the greatest classical archaeologist of all time," exemplifies the relevance of the scientific methodology in fields beyond physics, chemistry, and biology. This is a major transformation that has occurred in our appraisal of the past: not the mere acceptance of verbal testimony from ancient authorities, but the careful investigation of their authenticity; not the mere admiration of ancient relics, but the careful dating and interpretation of them.

Such a perspective has two important consequences: On the one hand, it throws light on the past and thus gives us more reliable information on the ancients. It enriches our understanding of the past. On the other hand, it may also demolish the myths and soothing fantasies which give substance and meaning to traditions. Like the unweaving of the rainbow for which physics was condemned by some of the poets of Romanticism, the interpretation of scriptural miracles as misinterpreted natural events by scholars and archaeologists is not always appreciated by the religiously inclined.

Index of Topics

A HORRIFIC RELIGIOUS PERSECUTION	18-Jan	50
AANDAAL	19-Feb	144
ABDUS SALAM	29-Jan	83
ABRAHAM DE MOIVRE	26-May	436
ABRAHAM GEIGER	24-May	429
ADOLF BUTENANDT	24-Mar	249
ADOLF FURTWÄNGLER	30-Jun	539
AJINATH DAY	25-Jan	70
ALAN TURING	23-Jun	519
ALBERT EINSTEIN	14-Mar	219
ALESSANDRO VOLTA	18-Feb	142
ALEXIS CARREL	28-Jun	533
ALEXIS CLAIRAULT	7-May	380
ALFRED RUSSELL WALLACE	8-Jan	22
ALOIS ALZEIMER	14-Jun	492
ANDRÉ MARIE AMPÈRE	22-Jan	63
ANDREI SAKHAROV	21-May	422
ANGLICAN CHURCH	8-Jun	474
APRIL FIRST	1-Apr	272
ARTHUR SCHOPENHAUER	22-Feb	152
ASH WEDNESDAY	13-Feb	126
ASSASSINATION OF MAHATMA GANDHI	30-Jan	85
AUGUST VON WASSERMANN	21-Feb	151
AUGUSTE PICCARD	28-Jan	80

AUGUSTIN JEAN FRESNEL 10-May 389

BARBARA McCLINTOCK 16-Jun...............................498

BÉGUYER DE 20-Jan 57
CHANCOURTOIS

BENEDICT JOSEPH 16-Apr 316

BENJAMIN FRANKLIN 17-Jan 48

BERNADITA SOUBIROUS 18-Feb 141

BERNARD DE FONTENELLE 11-Feb 121

BERTRAND RUSSELL 18-May...............................413

BHAKTA KABIR 11-Apr 301

BHASKARA 3-Jan 8

BIRTHDAY OF SRI RAMA 21-Apr 331

BLAISE PASCAL 19-Jun...............................506

BRUNO BENEDETTO ROSSI 13-Apr 308

BUDDHA'S ASCENSION 12-Jun...............................485
IN BHUTAN

BUREAU INTERNATIONAL 20-May...............................419
DES POIDS ET DES MÉSURES

BURNING OF BRUNO 17-Feb 138

BURRHUS K. SKINNER 20-Mar 237

CARL FRIEDRICH GAUSS 30-Apr 359

CARL LOUIS LINDEMANN 12-Apr 305

CASIMIR FUNK 23-Feb 157

CASPAR FRIEDRICH WOLFF 18-Jan 51

CERELIA 12-Apr 304

CHANDIDAS 21-Feb 150

CHARLES DARWIN 12-Feb 124

CHARLES FABRY 11-Jun...............................484

CHARLES MESSIER 26-Jun...............................527

CHARLES RICHTER 26-Apr 347

CHINESE NEW YEAR 12-Feb 123

CHORAL FINALE OF BEETHOVEN'S NINTH 7-May.................379

CHRIST'S ASCENSION TO HEAVEN 9-May.................385

CHRISTIAAN HUYGENS 14-Apr.................311

CHRISTIAN GOLDBACH 18-Mar.................231

CLARENCE DARROW 18-Apr.................323

CLYDE TAMBAUGH 4-Feb.................101

CONFUCIUS 23-Jan.................64

COUNCIL OF EPHESUS 22-Jun.................514

CRUCIFIXION 29-Mar.................262

D'ARCY WENTWORTH THOMPSON 2-May.................365

DALAI LAMA'S REFUGE 19-Apr.................325

DANIEL BERNOULLI 8-Feb.................113

DANIEL DEFOE'S ARREST 22-May.................423

DANIEL GABRIEL FAHRENHEIT 14-May.................401

DATE OF RESURRECTION? 27-Mar.................256

DAVID SARNOFF 27-Feb.................168

DAY 17 OF TAMMUZ 27-Jun.................529

DAY OF CARRIDWEN 20-Jun.................509

DIAN FOSSEY 16-Jan.................46

DISCOVERY OF TUTANKHAMEN 16-Feb.................136

DISCOVERY OF KRYPTON 31-May.................451

DOGEN KIGEN 19-Jan.................53

DONATI'S COMET 2-Jun.................457

DOROTHEA DIX 4-Apr.................280

E. O. WILSON 10-Jun.................481

EARTH DAY 22-Apr.................335

EARTHQUAKE IN SAN FRANCISCO 18-Apr 322

EDGAR CAYCE 18-Mar 230

EDWARD DE VERE 22-Apr 334

EDWARD JENNER 17-May 410

EDWIN LAURENTINE DRAKE 29-Mar 264

ELIZABETH BLACKWELL 3-Feb 98

ELIZABETH FRY 21-May 420

EMANUEL SWEDENBORG 29-Jan 82

EMIL CHRISTIAN HANSEN 8-May 383

EMILIO SEGRÈ 1-Feb 92

EMMY AMALIE NOETHER 23-Mar 246

ENCYCLICAL OF POPE PAUL IV 24-Jun 520

EPHRAIM SYRUS 9-Jun 477

EPIPHANY 6-Jan 15

EUCLID 27-Jun 530

EVE OF CANDLEMAS 1-Feb 91

FATHER'S DAY 16-Jun 497

FATIMA 13-May 397

FEAST DAY OF APOLLO 9-Feb 114

FEAST OF ESTHER (2002) 25-Feb 161

FERDINAND J. COHN 24-Jan 69

FERDINAND Von RICHTHOFEN 5-May 374

FESTIVAL OF HOLI 28-Mar 259

FIRST CATACOMB 31-May 450

FIRST HYDROGEN BOMB 1-Mar 177

FORMILARIO CONCORDIAE 25-Jun 523

FRANCESCO MARIA GRIMALDI 2-Apr 276

FRANZ ANTON MESMER 23-May 427

FRED HOYLE	24-Jun	521
FREDERICK DOUGLASS	7-Feb	108
FREDERICK JOLIOT	19-Mar	234
FREYJA AND ST. GUDULA	8-Jan	21
FRIEDRICH SERTUERNER	19-Jun	507
FRITZ ZWICKY	14-Feb	130
GALILEO GALILEI	15-Feb	133
GASPARD MONGE	9-May	386
GEORG CANTOR	3-Mar	185
GEORG SIMON OHM	16-Mar	225
GEORGE BERKELEY	12-Mar	212
GEORGE ELLERY HALE	29-Jun	536
GEORGE GAMOW	4-Mar	189
GEORGE HERBERT	3-Apr	278
GEORGE P. MARSH	15-Mar	222
GEORGE STEPHENSON	9-Jun	478
GEORGE WASHINGTON CARVER	10-Jan	28
GERALD STANLEY HAWKINS	20-Apr	329
GERHARD KREMER	5-Mar	192
GIAMBATTISTA RICCIOLI	17-Apr	320
GIAN DOMENICO CASSINI	8-Jun	475
GIUSEPPE PIAZZI	1-Jan	2
GREGORIAN CHANTS	13-Mar	215
GROUNDHOG DAY	2-Feb	94
GURU GOBIND	5-Jan	12
GUSTAV ROBERT KIRCHHOFF	12-Mar	214
HAM'S SUBORBITAL FLIGHT	31-Jan	89
HANA-MATSURI	8-Apr	292
HANGING OF ELIZABETH BARTON	20-Apr	328
HANNES OLOF ALFVEN	30-May	448

HANUMAN JAYANTI	27-Apr	349
HAPPENSTANCE AND COINCIDENCE DAY	24-Apr	340
HARRIET TUBMAN	2-Jun	456
HATTIE ELIZABETH ALEXANDER	5-Apr	285
HEINRICH HERZ	22-Feb	154
HENRI DUNANT & THE RED CROSS DAY	8-May	382
HENRI POINCARÉ	29-Apr	356
HERACLITUS OF EPHEOS	24-Apr	341
HERBERT SPENCER	27-Apr	350
HERMAN GUNKEL	23-May	426
HERMAN HOLERITH	Feb-29	174
HERMANN MINKOWSKI	22-Jun	516
HIDEKI YUKAWA	23-Jan	66
HILARIA AND MATRIS DEUM	24-Mar	248
HINA MATSURI	3-Mar	183
HIPPOCRATES	9-Apr	296
HORACE BENEDICT SAUSSURE	17-Feb	139
HUGO GROTIUS	10-Apr	298
HYPATIA	8-Mar	203
IBN SINA	18-Jun	503
IDA NODDACK	25-Feb	163
IMMANUEL VELIKOVSKY	10-Jun	479
INDEX AUCTORUM ET LIBRORUM PROHIBITORUM	14-Jun	491
INDIC NEW YEAR	14-Apr	310
INTELLECTUAL FERMENT IN ISLAMIC WORLD	6-Feb	105
INTERNATIONAL WOMEN'S DAY	8-Mar	201

ISIDORE OF PELUSIUM	4-Feb	99
ISLAMIC NEW YEAR	15-Mar	221
JACQUES DE VAUCANSON	24-Feb	160
JACQUES LOEB	7-Apr	291
JACQUES MONOD	9-Feb	115
JALALUDDIN RUMI	27-Feb	167
JAMES HUTTON	3-Jun	460
JAMES PARKINSON	11-Apr	302
JAMES SIMPSON	7-Jun	472
JAMES WATT	19-Jan	54
JANUARY	1-Jan	1
JAPANESE MARTYR'S DAY	5-Feb	102
JEAN ANTOINE CHAPRAL	4-Jun	463
JEAN BAPTISTE BOUSSINGAULT	2-Feb	95
JEAN BAPTISTE FOURIER	21-Mar	240
JEAN JACQUES ROUSSEAU	28-Jun	532
JEAN LOUIS AGASSIZ	28-May	442
JEWISH PASSOVER	31-Mar	268
JIDDU KRISHNAMURTHI	11-May	391
JOAN OF ARC	16-May	405
JOHN BALL	11-Jun	482
JOHN C. ECCLES	27-Jan	77
JOHN COUCH ADAMS	5-Jun	466
JOHN HARVEY KELLOGG	26-Feb	165
JOHN HUGHLINGS	4-Apr	282
JOHN WESLEY	17-Jun	500
JOSEPH BLACK	16-Apr	317
JOSEPH CAMPBELL	26-Mar	253
JOSEPH PRIESTLEY	13-Mar	217
JUSTUS Von LIEBIG	12-May	395

KAGAMI-BIRAKI	11-Jan	30
KARL BARTH	10-May	388
KARL JASPERS	23-Feb	155
KARL PEARSON	27-Mar	258
KATHETINE ESAU	3-Apr	279
KENKOKU KINEN NO HI	11-Feb	120
KING JAMES' BIBLE	16-Jan	44
KUAN YIN	25-Mar	250
KYONCHIP	5-Mar	191
LAO TZU	11-Jan	31
LAZARRO SPALLANZANI	12-Jan	34
LEONARDO FIBONACCI	15-Jun	495
LEONHARD EULER	15-Apr	314
LEWIS M. TERMAN	15-Jan	43
LINUS PAULING	28-Feb	171
LUDWIG BOLTZMANN	20-Feb	148
LUTHER BEFORE THE DIET	17-Apr	319
LYSERGIC ACID DIETHYLAMIDE	19-Apr	326
MAGNA CARTA	15-Jun	494
MAHA SONGRAN	13-Apr	307
MAHASHIVARATHI	11-Mar	209
MAHAVIRA DAY	25-Apr	343
MAIMONEDES	30-Mar	265
MALLEUS MALEFICARUM	19-May	414
MARCELLO MALPIGHI	10-Mar	208
MARCUS AURELEUS ANTONIUS	26-Apr	346
MARIA GAETENA AGNESI	16-May	407
MARY DOUGLAS NICOL	6-Feb	107
MARY WHITON CALKINS	30-Mar	266
MATTHEW F. MAURY	14-Jan	40

MAX PLANCK	23-Apr	338
MAX THEILER	30-Jan	86
MEERA BAI	3-Feb	96
MEMORIAL DAY	27-May	438
MESON CREATION	9-Mar	205
MICHEALANGELO BUONARROTI	6-Mar	194
MIKHAIL BUKANIN	30-May	447
MONTH OF JUNE AND MARY DYER	1-Jun	453
MONTH OF MAY	1-May	361
MOTHER'S DAY	12-May	394
MR. NOYES' REVELATION	20-Feb	147
MUHAMMAD TARAGAY	22-Mar	243
MUHAMMED IBN 'ALI IBN 'ARABI	10-Jan	27
NELSON GLUECK	4-Jun	462
NEWTON'S PRINCIPIA	28-Apr	353
NICCOLÒ MACHIAVELLI	3-May	367
NICENE COUNCIL	20-May	417
NICOLAS SADI CARNOT	1-Jun	454
NICOLAUS COPERNICUS	19-Feb	145
NIGHT OF THE WITCHES	30-Apr	358
NISAN AND ROSH CHODESH	14-Mar	218
ODUN	20-Mar	236
OLIVER JOSEPH LODGE	12-Jun	487
ON MARCH	1-Mar	176
ORTHODOX EASTER	28-Apr	352
OSCAR MINKOWSKI	13-Jan	37
PARASURAMA RISHI	15-May	403
PARINIRVANA DAY	8-Feb	111

PASSING AWAY OF BAHA'ULLAH	29-May	444
PAUL EHRLICH	29-May	445
PAUL ERDÖS	26-Mar	255
PERCY WILLIAM BRIDGMAN	21-Apr	332
PHILIP HENRY GOSSE	6-Apr	288
PIERRE CURIE	15-May	404
PIETER ZEEMAN	25-May	433
PIONEER 10	2-Mar	181
PLANETARY CONJUNCTION IN 1962	5-Feb	104
PONGAL FESTIVAL	14-Jan	39
PYTHAGORAS	9-Mar	204
RABINDRANATH TAGORE	6-May	376
RACHEL CARSON	27-May	439
RALPH WALDO EMERSON	25-May	432
RAYMOND FIRTH	25-Mar	252
REGIOMONTANUS	6-Jun	469
REINHOLD NIEBUR	21-Jun	511
Religion and Science	28-May	441
RENÉ DESCARTES	31-Mar	269
RICHARD FEYNMAN	11-May	392
ROBERT BOYLE	25-Jan	71
ROGER BACON	20-Jun	510
RONALD ROSS	13-May	398
ROYAL DEBT OF WILLIAM PENN	4-Mar	187
RUDOLF CLAUSIUS	2-Jan	5
RUTH BENEDICT	5-Jun	465
SAINT AGNES	21-Jan	58
SAINT ANTHONY	17-Jan	47
SAINT ANTHONY	13-Jun	488

SAINT BASIL 2-Jan 3

SAINT CANUTE 13-Jan 36

SAINT CATHERINE 29-Apr 355

SAINT GENEVIÈVE 3-Jan 6

SAINT GEORGE 23-Apr 337

SAINT PAUL IN MALTA 10-Feb 117

SAINT PETER 29-Jun 535

SAINT RAMANANDA 9-Jan 24

SAINT RAMANUJA 23-Jun 517

SAINT SAMBANDHAR 24-Jan 67

SAINT VILLANA 28-Feb 170

SAINT WALDERTRUDIS 9-Apr 295

SAMUEL HAHNEMANN 10-Apr 299

SAMUEL MORSE 6-Jan 16

SANTIAGO RAMÓN Y CAJAL 1-May 362

SATELLITES OF JUPITER 7-Jan 19

SEKHMET 7-Jan 18

SHANKARACHARYA JAYANTI 17-May 408

SIGMUND FREUD 6-May 377

SIMÉON-DENIS POISSON 21-Jun 513

SOCRATES 15-Feb 132

SOPHIA LOUISA JEX-BLAKE 21-Jan 60

SOPHIE GERMAINE 1-Apr 273

SØREN KIEREGAARD 5-May 373

SPAIN, PORTUGAL, 4-May 370
SOUTH AMERICA

ST. AGNES OF BOHEMIA 2-Mar 179

ST. JOSEPH'S DAY 19-Mar 233

ST. PATRICK 17-Mar 227

ST. UHRO'S DAY 16-Mar 224

ST. VALENTILE'S DAY 14-Feb 129

STANLEY MILLER 7-Mar 200

STEVEN WEINBERG 3-May 368

SUNYATA AND ZERO 10-Feb 118

SWAMI VIVEKANANDA 12-Jan 33

TELLUS MATER FESTIVAL 15-Apr 313

THAI FESTIVAL 6-Apr 286

THE ÂZHVÂRS 4-Jan 9

THE COMMUNIST 26-Feb 164
MANIFESTO

THE CYCLOTRON 26-Jan 74

THE GOLDEN GATE BRIDGE 9-Jan 25

THE GREAT SUN SPOTS 8-Apr 293

THE GREGORIAN CALENDAR. 24-Feb 158

THE LAST CRUSADE 2-Apr 275

THE LEAP YEAR Feb-29 172

THE ROYAL SOCIETY 6-Mar 196
OF LONDON

THE TUNGUSKA EVENT 30-Jun..538

THEODOR HERZL 2-May 364

THOMAS HENRY HUXLEY 4-May..371

THOMAS HOBBES 5-Apr 283

THOMAS YOUNG 13-Jun..489

THREE MILE ISLAND 28-Mar 261

TIMOTHY 22-Jan..61

TITUBA 16-Feb 135

TITUS LUCRETIUS 19-May..416

TRANSLATION OF 10-Mar 207
"LA DIVINA COMMEDIA"

TU B'SHEVAT 28-Jan..79

TURIBIUS DAY 23-Mar 245

UGANDAN MARTYRS 3-Jun..459

UMAR AL-KHAYYAMI 18-May..411

UNITED NATIONS CHARTER	26-Jun	526
URBAIN LE VERRIER	11-Mar	211
VAISHAKH	26-May	435
VANGUARD I	17-Mar	228
VERNAL EQUINOX	21-Mar	239
VESTALIA	7-Jun	471
VIBIA PERPETUA	7-Mar	198
WALTHER NERNST	25-Jun	524
WILHELM BEER	4-Jan	10
WILLEM EINTHOVEN	22-May	425
WILLIAM CROOKES	17-Jun	501
WILLIAM HUGGINS	7-Feb	110
WILLIAM LASSEL	18-Jun	504
WILLIAM WHEWELL	24-May	430
WILLIASM SCHOCKLY	13-Feb	127
WINFRID, THE DO-GOODER	14-May	400
WOLFGANG AMADEUS MOZART	27-Jan	76
WOLFGANG PAULI	25-Apr	344
WORLD DAY FOR WATER	22-Mar	242
WORLD HEALTH DAY	7-Apr	289
WORLD RELIGION DAY	20-Jan	56
XENOPHON	26-Jan	73
X-RAYS	5-Jan	13
YMCA	6-Jun	468
ZAOWANG	31-Jan	88
ZOROASTRIAN BEHMAN	15-Jan	41

978-0-595-35840-3
0-595-35840-3

Printed in the United States
39204LVS00003B/44

9 780595 358403